LOCATION
AND
PUBLIC PROBLEMS

LOCATION
AND
PUBLIC PROBLEMS

A POLITICAL GEOGRAPHY
OF THE CONTEMPORARY WORLD

Kevin R. Cox
The Ohio State University

MAAROUFA PRESS, INC.
CHICAGO

Maaroufa Press Geography Series
Eric Moore, Advisory Editor

© 1979 by Maaroufa Press, Inc.
All rights reserved
Library of Congress Catalog Card Number: 78-71125
ISBN: 0-88425-015-6
Manufactured in the United States of America

Designed by Holly Heim

Contents

Preface

A preface provides an author with the opportunity to set forth the concerns which informed his project. In this instance the concerns are especially clear: a dissatisfaction with the state of political geography realized over a decade of attempts to develop a course in the topic for undergraduates. Four problems have seemed central: internal coherence; external coherence; scale; and relevance. On each of these criteria considerable shortcomings have been evident.

With respect to internal coherence, political geography has traditionally consisted of an assortment of ill-related topics: federalism, local government boundaries, and capital cities, for example. Typically a course in political geography does not leave the student with the feeling of having confronted a tightly organized body of knowledge that he or she can master simply by virtue of its internal integration.

The problem so far as external coherence is concerned is to find in what way and to what extent political geography can relate to studies in human geography as a whole. For me, starting to teach geography in the first flush of enthusiasm for locational analysis, this reduced to a question of how political geography could complement studies conducted from that theoretical perspective. This problem has become increasingly more urgent as locational analysis has come to recognize its limitations with regard to questions of planning and policy.

Third, there is the question of scale. In political geography the whole urban area has been conspicuous for its neglect. I wanted, therefore, to develop a set of concepts that would be applicable in a scale-independent manner, concepts that would be as helpful in illuminating problems of regional policy, for example, as in clarifying urban conflicts.

And, finally, I wanted a political geography that would be relevant: one that would help the student to relate, for example, to contemporary global resource problems, conflicts over central city-suburban fiscal disparities, and the environment-jobs trade-off in resource development controversies. It has seemed self-evident that a political geography clinging to issues of locating capital cities, gerrymandering, and irredentism was quite limited in its ability to address today's problems.

Obviously, developing a framework for political geography that would answer these problems was no easy task. Certainly it was much harder than I ever imagined and I consequently had to discard two separate and completed manuscripts along the way. Whether I have succeeded—or indeed whether I threw away the correct manuscripts—is still uncertain.

In retrospect I regard the book as a stepping stone, but only a stepping stone, to a deeper understanding of the issues and relationships involved. For while I believe the book adequately describes the surface features of the world of politics as it relates to location, further work may be needed in order to probe the deeper structural forces. Final judgment on these issues must clearly remain with the reader.

Many contributed in various ways to the development of the book. There are three people, however, whom I would like to single out. Tim Nyerges of the Department of Geography at The Ohio State University gave unstintingly of his time and patience in developing the artwork. In addition, the project was blessed by two reviewers who provided excellent critical review of the manuscript in various stages of its preparation: John Mercer and David Reynolds. While in no way responsible for any defects in the book, their advice and suggestions were always timely, to the point, thought provoking, and as helpful as any writer could wish. To them I will always be grateful.

Finally, I dedicate this book to my children, Nicole and Gerard. Their willing self-exclusion from my study during the writing of the volume demonstrated a nice anticipation of the principles of political geography.

Worthington, Ohio
March 1979

PART ONE

Basic Concepts

This first section explores, exemplifies, and amplifies the concepts introduced in chapter 1. Chapters 2 and 3 discuss major dimensions of welfare geography: residential desirability and private income. Each component is characterized in terms of its distinctive geography and explained in terms of locational choice, public policy, and the institutional framework. Chapter 4, on the other hand, attempts a more rigorous examination of the political process linking up the locally impacted to the policies by which they hope to secure a more conducive set of welfare outcomes.

Chapter One

Introduction

The principal intent of this introductory chapter is to provide some context of ideas within which the remainder of the book can be placed. Since we are concerned with the relationships of location and the state, it is logical that these should provide the focus of this chapter.

Four concepts, or integrating ideas, are basic to this mission. They are discussed here in sufficient detail to provide a background for what follows in the remainder of the book:

1. the concept of a welfare geography;
2. the role of individual location processes;
3. the role of governments as locators;
4. the role of the juridical context.

Each of the four concepts will be discussed in turn. The end of the chapter then describes, in outline, the rest of the book, showing how it relates to these basic ideas.

A Welfare Geography

Central to politics is the question, Who gets what? People become involved in politics in an attempt to secure policies that will be enhancing to their well-being and increase their share of society's pie. Still others become involved to defend the status quo and to protect *their* share of the pie. Politics, therefore, is fundamentally concerned with the issue of individual well-being and how well off some will be compared with others.

Well-being, or welfare, however, has a geographical expression. Well-being varies with location. While "who gets what?" is a central issue in politics, a central issue for the political geographer is "who gets what where?" It is for this reason that the concept of a *welfare geography* occupies a central place in the approach to political geography developed in this book.

Consider this idea in detail. We can demonstrate the existence of a welfare geography by mapping various indicators of well-being (Coates, Johnston & Knox 1977; Smith 1973). We have become more

3

and more aware, for example, that clean air is vital to our health; there is, as a consequence, a geography of exposure to air pollution. In the same way one can conceive of geographies of personal income, per capita incomes varying from one region of the country to another. Geographies of congestion, crime, public spending on education, access to public parks, and the like would provide further dimensions to the welfare geography of a particular area.

Obviously, well-being is not a simple concept. There is a tremendous variety of forces whose immediate impact varies geographically and affects our welfare according to where we happen to be. In this book, however, a distinction is drawn between two basic components of welfare: *personal, or private, income,* which includes wages, rents, interest payments, etc; and *residential quality,* which can be very broadly thought of as *environmental quality.* We can therefore break down welfare geography into (1) a *geography of private income* that has to do with the business of earning a living and (2) a *geography of residential quality* that has to do with the business of living, itself. Like all classifications this is an artificial one, separating aspects of life which, in the world of experience, are wholly bound up with one another. For exposition purposes, however, the distinction is useful.

Geographically, welfare differences exhibit considerable order. In the welfare map there is often some locational regularity that excites our curiosity. Exposure to air pollution decreases with increasing distance from the central business district (CBD); suburban jurisdictions tend to have lower property tax rates than central city jurisdictions; a common contrast referred to by economic geographers (Conkling & Yeates 1976, p. 282; O'Sullivan 1968) is that between a nation's "center," where personal incomes are higher and public provision is on a more opulent scale, and its "periphery," where incomes are less, the housing standards are lower, and less money is spent on education, for example.

In particular, welfare geographies exhibit *scale variations.* Welfare varies among neighborhoods within a city, but it also varies among regions. In a descriptive sense, therefore, one might break down the total geographic variation into components at different geographic scales: some of the variation in welfare across the globe is clearly related to the nation state one happens to live in; within nation states, however, there is a further set of variations that have to do with regional location; while within regions, the state, city, and neighborhood inject variations at still smaller geographical scales.

At an international level major dimensions of welfare attach to the distinction between less-developed and more developed countries. There are not only differences in levels of personal income; more developed countries tend to spend more on public health and education, for example. Within nation states, on the other hand, additional components of welfare geography are related to city size: larger cities—whether in less-developed or more developed countries—tend to have higher wages but to be more congested and more polluted, with more serious problems of crime than smaller cities.

Of special interest to political geographers are variations among jurisdictions and variations in welfare within jurisdictions. In metropolitan areas, there are *interjurisdictional variations* that have to do with property tax rates and educational spending; while within municipalities there are *intrajurisdictional variations* for example in crime, air pollution, and traffic hazard that differentiate neighborhoods. These scale relationships, of course, suggest something about the forces creating welfare geographies: some forces originate at the national level; some at the regional level; some at the state level; some at the municipal level; and some at the neighborhood level.

Individual Location Processes

The locational choices of individuals—households, firms, property developers—are important to political geographers for several reasons. First they provide insights into the generation of welfare geographies; at the same time, as a result of the way they impact on the welfare of local groups in specific neighborhoods, regions, or nations, they help us to understand why people get involved in politics. And finally such processes help us appreciate why, when people do get involved, their policies represent an attempt to regulate locational choices to the advantage of the local turf. We have seen that individual well-being has critical locational dimensions; where one lives and works has important implications for one's income, health, safety, and the like. The closer we live to the airport, the more noise we have to endure; the further we live away from the central city, the less air pollution we suffer. Living in a jurisdiction with a large business tax base means that our property taxes will be lower than if we live in a jurisdiction with a smaller business tax base.

All these examples suggest an important conclusion: the locational choices of others have substantial impacts on our welfare. The sort of neighborhood we live in—publicly safe with pleasant neighbors and good friends for the children—depends on the sort of people who move into the neighborhood and the sort of people who move out. Whether there will be jobs in the city where we live depends on the locational choices of businessmen, not simply at an intercity scale but also on an internation level. Likewise whether our tax rates will be high or low depends on the locational choices of those who make small or large contributions to the tax base and small or large demands on the services provided by local government. In brief, our individual welfare is critically dependent on the locational choices of others such as residents, investors, workers, industrialists, retailers, and travelers. In order to understand an individual household's welfare we need to understand the nature of the locational context in which that household finds itself; and then we need to explain that locational context.

Recently in geography the major contribution to explaining location has come from location theory (Lloyd & Dicken 1972; Conkling & Yeates 1976). This has provided explanations of industrial location, retail location, migration, and residential location. The critical assumption of location theory from the viewpoint of this book is that locational choices are market choices. Locators confront a geography of locational advantage and disadvantage. Some locations are advantageous from a market viewpoint in the sense that, for example, they allow either the industrialist to minimize his transportation costs; the worker to maximize his wage; or the home buyer to maximize his utility subject to a budget constraint. Hence, at any one time we can explain the locations of those others impacting on our welfare in terms of a market process in which locational choices are made so as to maximize market advantage.

The resultant welfare geography, however, is subject to transformation—often quite dramatic—as market calculations and, consequently, locations change. Disinvestment may take place in some regions, producing depressed areas. Investment may take place in other cities or towns regarded as advantageous from a market standpoint, creating higher rents for landlords but congestion for existing residents as migrants, lured by new jobs, move into the area. Similar relations are apparent at smaller geographic scales. As middle-class buyers come to see a neighborhood as less residentially attractive, home prices there will fall. This will permit lower income residents to move into the area, bringing with them—to the distress of the existing middle-class residents—problems of public safety, falling property values, and difficulties in the local schools. On the suburban fringe, on the other hand, new residential development will impose on existing residents problems of highway congestion, traffic safety, and destruction of landscape esthetics.

Culture and social variables also seem to exercise a certain influence of their own on location (Wagner 1972; Sopher 1972). While some aspects of residential segregation can be explained in terms of a market process, others just as surely cannot. The ethnic ghetto, for example, may represent the desire of those sharing a certain language and cultural background to live close to each other. Social and cultural factors also seem important at larger geographical scales: French-speaking Algerians go to live and work in France, for instance, while English-speaking Jamaicans emigrate to Britain. Both sets of migrations, of course, have impacts on the respective labor markets of the two countries.

Location, therefore, has clear welfare implications. Where those welfare implications are of a negative character, existing locational processes can be regarded, for the impacted at least, as *publicly problematic.* Migration from small towns to large ones, for instance, results in a number of public problems for those left behind and for those among whom the migrants come to live. In the small town landowners and retailers suffer from diminished rents and retail turnovers, respectively. In the large town, on the other hand, the migrant is associated with congestion of public facilities and increasing housing prices. In other cases the publicly problematic locational relations may involve commodity flows or labor flows; American imports of Asian textile goods are problematic for the textile workers of the Piedmont, just as movements of Mexican labor into the United States are problematic for American labor as a whole.

To the extent that public problems are seen as stemming from existing locational relationships, however, we can anticipate some attempt to restructure them to local advantage. At the neighborhood level, for example, suburban groups will oppose rezonings in an attempt to preserve the esthetic attractions and the peace and quiet of the area they live in. At the national level labor unions may press for a measure of labor market protection by the imposition of quotas on foreign immigrants; and industrial firms may press for an element of tariff protection against foreign goods. The medium for this protectionist activity is politics.

Governments as Locators

Most textbooks on location theory have a section dealing with the impact of public policy on location (Lloyd & Dicken 1972, ch. 11; Hoover 1948, pt. 4). This is not surprising. Governments, at both national and local levels, exercise significant influence over the locational decisions of firms, migrants, property developers, and the like.

A variety of public policies have effects, for example, on location *within* jurisdictions. In Britain a consistent aim of successive governments has been to direct industry into so-called "depressed" areas characterized by relatively high rates of unemployment (McCrone 1969). Policies have involved both subsidies to firms agreeing to locate in depressed areas and also constraints on the expansion of firms located outside depressed areas. Other national-level policies have locational effects that are more inadvertent than intentional. It is doubtful, for example, that the impact of interstate highways on suburbanization and selective metropolitan growth was foreseen at the time their construction was first considered.

Similar relations are observable at more local levels. Within urban municipalities the location of public facilities—public parks, new schools, one-way streets—may do much to affect the residential desirability of particular neighborhoods. Individual rezoning decisions can have similar effects, precipitating in some cases massive neighborhood deterioration as an area loses its residential attractiveness. At the edge of the city, on the other hand, sewer line and waterline extension may stimulate suburban development.

Within their respective jurisdictions, therefore, the public policies of governments contribute towards the creation of a geography of locational advantage. At the same time controls on movement—zoning decisions, restrictions on the expansion of firms in specific locations—may limit strategies of adaptation with respect to that geography.

Similar relations are observable *among* jurisdictions: the different policies of governments help to create an interjurisdictional geography of locational advantage. In metropolitan areas rates of property tax vary from one municipality to another; levels of per pupil school expenditure also vary. To some degree suburban municipalities tend to spend more on schools and levy a lower tax rate to do so; this is one source of the general residential desirability of the suburbs. At an international scale, on the other hand, the locational decisions of multinational corporations are structured according to variations in tax policy from one country to another, variations in depreciation allowances, or the security different governments offer the private investor.

At the same time other policies serve to channel locational decisions with respect to that interjurisdictional geography of locational advantage. In metropolitan areas suburban municipalities limit, by so-called "exclusionary zoning," the residential influxes seeking to take advantage of their lower tax rates and more opulently endowed public schools. At the international level, national governments channel movements by resort to tariffs, immigration quotas, and currency controls.

At both intra- and interjurisdictional levels, therefore, one can pinpoint a variety of policies latent with locational effects. In some cases these implications are inadvertent, while at other times their intentionality is clear. Some policies contribute towards the geography of locational advantage. Others regulate movements and so restrict the ways in which locators can adjust to that geography. At the same time these controls feed back to affect the geography of locational advantage. Doubtless much of the continuing desirability of the suburbs, in terms of tax base and public spending, stems from the success they have enjoyed in excluding the fiscally undesirable; i.e., those adding little to tax base but imposing burdens on local public spending.

Clearly, governments have substantial powers over individual location. These same locational processes moreover have important welfare implications for local groups at neighborhood, regional, and national levels. This suggests an important function for government policy. *It can be used by impacted groups to structure locational processes to their advantage;* i.e., to solve those public problems stemming from existing locational relations. A general rule, therefore, is that local pressure groups, more-or-less parochial in their goals, will attempt to implement public policies so as to attract to the local turf the utility enhancing and to deflect or exclude the utility detracting.

Indeed many of the policies of national and local governments are exclusionary in character; furthermore, they are patently directed towards the solution of existing public problems or towards forestalling their emergence. Many local governments use land use planning regulations to keep out polluting industries, airports, and other "obnoxious" activities. Quite recently, for instance, in an attempt to prevent further development and increased congestion, the state of Colorado decided that it would not host the Winter Olympics.

Other policies are less exclusionary in character but still designed to regulate locational choices to local advantage. A variety of locational incentives may be offered. At the state level in the United States a number of western and southern states have attempted to attract industry by outlawing the union shop. At more local levels cities may attempt to attract new office employment by offering urban renewal land at federally subsidized prices.

What is being described here are the attempts of groups sharing some common location—a nation state, a city, or a neighborhood—to regulate the locational choices to the advantage of the local turf. The overall goal, in brief, is to attract those activities—businesses, residents, land uses—that will enhance utility and to keep out those detracting from utility. In many cases these processes are competitive, pitting one country against another or one neighborhood group against another. Each suburban community in a metropolitan area is engaged in an attempt to push new residential development off on other suburban communities. Neighborhood groups will support different traffic and highway improvement plans according to how they will affect the groups' particular turf; but what will leave their turf in peace and quiet may bring traffic, fumes, and congestion to the turfs of neighboring groups.

Likewise, at the international level, governments compete for capital investment. The immediate reason for this competition is plain: at a given geographic scale different localized groups—national, regional, or neighborhood—want the same thing. All nation states want to grow economically; all cities want to grow in population; all neighborhood groups have the same conception of what is residentially desirable. As a consequence one turf's gain is very often another's loss. In this respect, therefore, the welfare geographies we observe are an outcome of competition among governments to regulate individual locational choices to local advantage. This, however, would be to overlook the institutional framework within which these competitive relations occur.

Juridical Context

The juridical context regulates the activities of both individual locators and governments. As a consequence, it too will receive an expression in observable welfare geographies. At the same time, and to the extent that on some it imposes welfare impacts of a serious and negative character, it will become publicly problematic and the object of politics as the impacted attempt to change it to their advantage and the favored protect their vested interests.

The juridical context is defined by constitutional and statutory law. It is significant for us because it specifies the bounds of action for individuals and governments; it details what they can and cannot do with respect to location and therefore has great importance for understanding observable welfare geographies. More specifically it sets forth, in the form of constitutional and statutory law, the rights, obligations, powers, and responsibilities of citizen and government.

On the side of the citizen, it specifies the law of private property detailing the privileges of property ownership such as the right of transfer or of exclusive use. Additionally it specifies both the rights of compensation should property be condemned by government and also the very large body of contract law without which the modern market economy would be incapable of functioning. Laws govern the rights of workers to form unions and the rights and obligations of large firms occupying a monopolistic position in the economy. Laws govern wages and much price setting, particularly of public utilities. And, of course, the juridical context prescribes the voting rights of the individual citizen, registration procedures, petition procedures necessary for obtaining a referendum, and so forth.

On the other hand, the juridical context defines the powers and responsibilities of governments both central and local, federal and state. More than likely, for example, it will reserve the right of trade regulation and currency coinage to the central government while delegating to local governments responsibilities for the provision of education, land use control, and the regulation of housing. The powers and responsibilities of the government with respect to redrawing electoral boundaries will be specified; for example, how often it must be done and whether it must be carried out by a nonpartisan committee. Exercise of these powers requires revenue, so the juridical context must also lay down the revenue-raising powers of government. Local government may be limited to the use of the property tax, the sale of bonds, and the sale of public services such as water and public transport. The income tax and sales tax may be reserved for the use of the central government. Fund-raising powers, however, will be limited. Raising tax rates above a certain amount may be made subject to public referendum, while the sale of bonds by local governments may be restricted by limits on bonded indebtedness.

In a federal constitution, of course, the powers and responsibilities are allocated to federal and state governments, respectively. Certain functions such as currency coinage or defense will be allocated to the federal government. Others such as highways, schools, or housing may be the prerogative of the states, functions they may then choose, if they wish, to delegate to local governments. Still other functions will be shared: with respect to trade, for instance, regulation of intrastate commerce in the United States is the responsibility of the state government, while regulation of *inter*state commerce is a matter for the federal government.

The juridical context has crucial implications for the observable welfare geography. Earlier in this chapter we drew attention to the role of the market in regulating locational choice. This determines the sort of locational contexts people live in and, consequently, influences their well-being in no uncertain manner. The individual's rights and responsibilities as defined by constitutional and statutory law, however, are critical for the emergence of that market process constraining locational choices.

Most importantly, without private property rights—defined and protected by the state—there would be no markets at all. Private property rights require that owners have exclusive rights of use to their property and be able to sell it to whomever they please. Given this, markets can be formed. Suppliers will be persuaded to come forward and purchasers will buy what suppliers offer, secure in the knowledge that the transfer is perfectly legal and that they will be entitled to exclusive use of their purchase. As markets are formed in this way prices come to be determined by the aggregated decisions of others.

In a locational context these decisions are locational in content. Markets tie people together over geographical space and within that space—city, region, nation, or the world—suppliers and buyers attempt to obtain market advantages by locational choice. What is one locator's market advantage, however, may be, as we have seen, someone else's market disadvantage. Labor, attracted by higher wages, moves into a region. The presence of these immigrants tends to depress the wage level to the disadvantage of those already there. Likewise, as people move in search of higher wages in larger towns, landowners and retailers in the small towns they leave behind will tend to suffer, the former from diminished rents and the latter from reduced retail turnovers.

Market choices also impact on residential quality. In a private-property-rights regime locators are responsible only to themselves and their financial accounts and not to society at large. This is not to say that individual market decisions do not necessarily redound to the benefit of society as a whole. Indeed according to the doctrine of the "hidden hand" (Heilbroner 1967, ch. 3) decisions taken in accord with narrow market interest will tend to maximize the size of the pie available to society as a whole. The private accounts of individuals nevertheless do tend to ignore some social costs, and these adversely affect the welfare of those happening to get in the way. Although a businessman pays for the labor he hires and the raw materials he uses, for example, he does not pay compensation to those who suffer, in the form of higher cleaning bills and physical disease, from the smoke his factory emits. Nor do people pay for the noise, traffic, diminished neighborhood esthetics, and other irritants they create as a result of their market decisions (Mishan 1967, pt. 2).

The definition and implementation of a private-property-rights regime by the state, therefore, necessarily implies the creation of private markets. Private market behavior, in its turn, involves a wide variety of impacts on the welfare of local populations. Capital movements place employment at risk; movements of households within cities, all attempting to maximize utility subject to their respective budget constraints, impact in a variety of ways—some of them negative—on the residents of particular neighborhoods.

To some degree these welfare impacts are exacerbated by the responsibilities and obligations placed on governments by the juridical context. Consider, for example, the implications of local government home rule. In many states in the United States local governments must raise the larger part of the revenue they spend; at the same time they are enjoined by the state to maintain certain minimum standards in the provision of services such as education, highway repair, and public health. Under these circumstances locators may be the bearers of good or ill. If the newcomer brings with him a large amount of property in the form of a shopping center, office building, or even a large house, then he will make commensurately large property tax payments and will be looked on more favorably than, say, the small-property owner. If, in addition, the newcomer brings with him a minimal demand for locally provided public services, then again his welfare impact on the local population will be favorable.

Under local government home rule, land uses consuming large amounts of property without consuming large quantities of locally provided public services are courted, since they facilitate a reduction in the local property tax rate for existing residents. Those new arrivals adding more to demand for services than they contribute in revenue, however, are regarded as a fiscal burden: their presence will increase the property tax rate to the detriment of existing residents. This type of juridical context moreover should be contrasted with one where the central government provides the larger part of local revenue. Under these circumstances the fiscal impacts of comings and goings will be muffled. Where governments are totally dependent on locally generated revenue, as are national governments, then fiscal impacts will be magnified.

Under certain assignments of obligations and responsibilities to governments, therefore, the welfare impacts of locational choices will tend to be intensified. Some local populations will gain and some will lose. As a consequence the incentives to government to regulate location to local advantage will be enhanced.

The degree to which regulation is feasible, however, will depend on the rights allocated to governments by the juridical context. Within the United States the states have limited powers to control locational choice simply because the federal constitution guarantees freedom of movement among them. It is not possible, therefore, for a state to protect its industries by erecting tariff barriers; nor is it feasible for a state to regulate labor competition by imposing quotas on migrants from other states. On the other hand, the states do have rights to levy taxes, and these can be manipulated so as to enhance their attractiveness to investors (Alyea 1969).

In metropolitan areas of the United States local governments hold significant discretionary powers for regulating locations. The most important of these powers is that of zoning. We have already seen that in many instances this has been used in an exclusionary manner (Danielson 1976).

As a consequence of these considerations it is not difficult to see that a given juridical context can provide substantial advantages to some local populations and substantial disadvantages to others. In U.S. metropolitan areas, for example, a combination of local government home rule and exclusionary zoning (Danielson 1972) has resulted in a marked differentiation between, on the one hand, more middle-class jurisdictions with low tax rates and well-funded schools and, on the other hand, lower class jurisdictions with higher tax rates and less well-endowed schools. This distinction is especially apparent in the contrast between the prototypical U.S. central city and its surrounding suburbs (Cox 1973, ch. 3).

Given these unequal consequences for, in this case, residential quality, it is not surprising that the juridical context should itself become a political issue. On both local government home rule and the regulation of zoning, therefore, lower income populations and the local governments that represent them have found themselves on the same side. With respect to zoning, it has been a matter of testing the constitutionality of exclusionary zoning (Danielson 1976, ch. 7). With respect to local government home rule they have been on the side of a coalition pressing for a statewide financing of education (Meltsner 1972, p. 863). If education could be financed by a statewide income tax or property tax and distributed to local school districts on an equal per pupil basis, then the fiscal pressures on lower income, low tax base jurisdictions would be greatly reduced. At the same time this would permit a decrease in the variation of locally levied tax rates across all municipalities and make it easier for the weak tax base municipality to attract the fiscally desirable.

Structure of This Book

The remainder of this book can be understood in terms of the context provided by the present chapter. The volume is divided into four major sections. In the first section the intent is to explore and amplify the set of concepts set forth in this chapter. Chapters 2 and 3, therefore, examine respectively the relationships between, on the one hand, the two major sources of well-being—residential quality and private income—identified in this chapter and, on the other hand, locational processes, governments as locators, and the juridical context. Chapter 2 considers residential quality, while chapter 3 looks at private income. In both cases the approach is the same: an exploration of the source of well-being; a characterization of its geographic expression; and an explanation of that geography in terms of interactions among locational choice, public policy, and the juridical context.

Chapter 4 assumes a more dynamic posture. The juridical relationships and public policies constraining individual locations are not immutable. As locational behaviors alter, for whatever reason, and impact on welfare, public problems emerge and more-or-less localized groups express demands for some change. Chapter 4 addresses itself to (1) the circumstances under which localized groups are likely to express such demands and (2) the likelihood of their obtaining some alteration in the juridical context or in ongoing policies so as to mitigate the public problems encountered.

In the three remaining sections of the book this conceptual schema is applied to an understanding of public problems at successively smaller scales: international, intranational, and metropolitan or intraurban. In each section the approach is the same: an initial chapter descriptively outlines the nature of the public problems—of residential desirability or private income—apparent at that particular scale. At the international scale, which is the focus of the second section, problems include those associated with income disparities from one nation to another. At the intranational scale presented in section three, however, there are two descriptive chapters.

In each section the next chapter then outlines the government policies to which these problems can be connected; it also relates these policies to a set of circumstances to which they can be regarded as an adjustment. A final chapter in each section then links policies to the welfare outcomes of which the public problems examined are particular manifestations.

So far as additional reading is concerned each chapter is followed by a select bibliography intended to provide a basis for supplementary reading. A serious attempt has been made, therefore, to tailor the selections to the level of comprehension typical of undergraduates. As a result of the readability criterion, however, the number of selections it was possible to devise varies from one chapter to another. Parts 2, 3, and 4 are also provided with their own bibliographies (further readings); the readability criterion again applies, and this explains the absence of a bibliography for part 1. Finally, a master bibliography can be found at the end of the book; this includes all the references made in the body of the text as well as the materials appearing in the select bibliographies and further readings.

Chapter Two

Location and Residential Quality

As was seen in the last chapter, a major component of individual well-being derives from the residential environment: quietness, levels of noise and air pollution, public health, public safety, school quality. Residential environments, therefore, can be ranked as more-or-less desirable or as having higher or lower degrees of residential quality.

This raises the descriptive issues of exactly what constitutes residential quality and its geography. It also raises an analytic issue. How are we to explain that geography? In chapter 1 we suggested that welfare geographies can be explained in terms of individual locational processes constrained (1) by the public policies of governments and (2) by a juridical context that also regulates public policy. This is the logic to be pursued here.

This chapter, then, has three objectives: first to elucidate the concept of residential quality; second to examine and characterize the distinctive geographical expression of residential quality; and finally to consider the question of explanation and the processes by which individuals acquire their residential environments.

Residential Quality

Residential quality refers to the desirability of residential environments. Desirability depends on individual preferences. The actual nature of the residential environments confronted by a population with a given set of preferences derives from quite different forces altogether. In explicating the concept of residential quality, therefore, we need to consider both preferences and residential environments.

PREFERENCES

The desirability of a residential environment clearly depends on what the individual in question wants. Even though, for example, some schools in a school district may have higher pupil-teacher ratios and less-opulent physical facilities, one cannot conclude that households with children in the less well-endowed schools are worse off: quite possibly their demand for education may be considerably below that of households with children in the better endowed schools. There is in fact some reason to believe that households in poor neighborhoods have lower evaluations of education (Robson 1969). Consequently, the well-documented neglect of public schools in poor neighborhoods may not signify any reduction of residential quality when compared with that of wealthier neighborhoods.

The heterogeneity of preferences is not a random phenomenon: rather, preferences are clearly related to individual characteristics such as income, occupation, age, life cycle status, and relative location. Older, childless couples, for example, may have a minimal preference for good neighborhood schools; families with children in school, on the other hand, may have intense preferences in that direction.

Household income appears to be a particularly critical correlate of preferences for residential environments. It is often argued, for instance, that wealthier individuals have more intense preferences for quiet and clean air than do the less affluent. This is often articulated in terms of a trade-off between these aspects of residential environments and private income. Conflicts over industrial development or the location of airports, therefore, often polarize groups according to income: upper income groups anxious to keep out investment that they regard as leading to a deterioration in residential quality; lower income groups anxious to attract such investment, which they regard less in terms of the environmental problems generated and more in terms of the jobs and increased income possibilities created (Winham 1972).

Of course what people prefer is partly a function of what they have. Those who live in smoky, noisy, but prosperous areas are likely to be more concerned about residential quality than about jobs. Those who live in industrial backwaters characterized by lower incomes and relatively more attractive residential environments are likely to be more concerned about jobs than about air pollution. Figure 2.1 suggests that this is the case in France. The figure draws on opinion polls conducted in major French cities and suggests that in the industrial cities of the east and northeast, concern about air pollution was higher than elsewhere in France. Smoke, however, is a by-product of industrial development, which also generates jobs and prosperity. As a consequence little concern for jobs was evinced in those cities. In the more depressed areas of western and southwestern France, however, the reverse situation applied: jobs were the major priority and pollution levels aroused relatively little concern.

RESIDENTIAL ENVIRONMENTS

In evaluating the residential quality experienced by an individual, preferences constitute only one of two concepts that we have to consider. There is also the residential environment itself, which more or

Figure 2.1   The Environmental Quality-Jobs Trade-off in French Cities

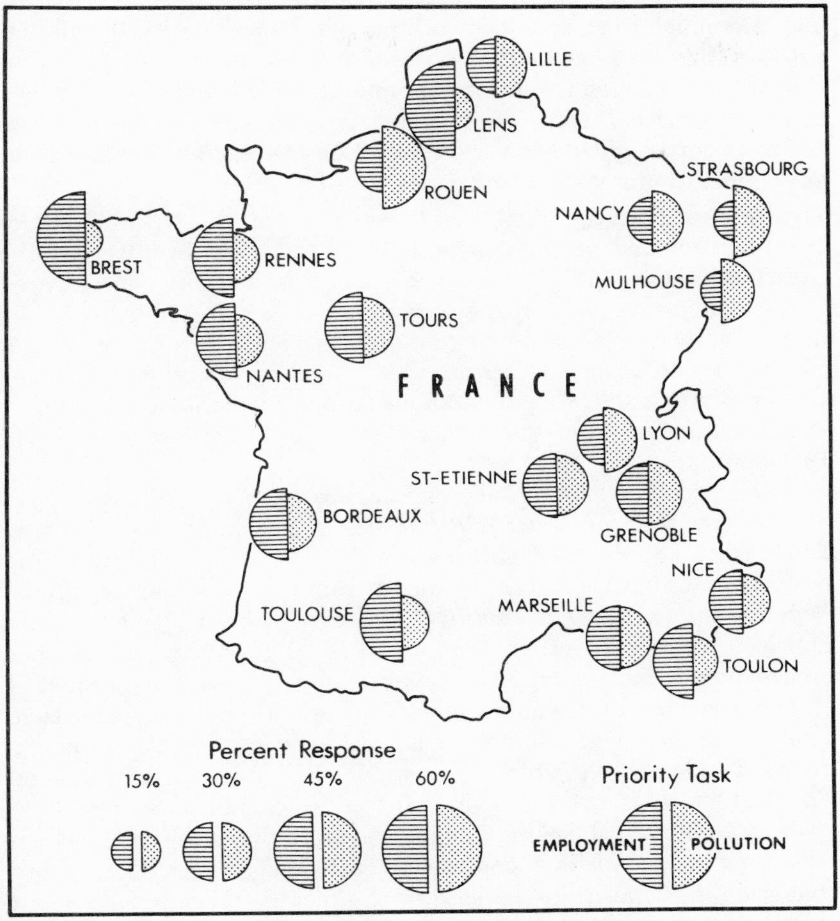

NOTE: The map is based on responses to a questionnaire that asked, Among the different problems with which a municipality must concern itself, what do you consider the three priority tasks at present in your city? Semicircles on the left indicate the percentages, including employment, as a priority task; while semicircles on the right indicate the percentages, including air pollution, as a priority task.
SOURCE: After *L'Express*, no. 1210, 16–22 September 1974, p. 65.

less satisfies those preferences. This residential environment is constituted by two major forces: public provision and externality effects (Wingo 1973).

Public Provision   Goods and services provided by governments include, among others, education, law and order, land use planning, clean air, labor conditions, and highways, and they clearly affect the residential environment as we experience it. The cleanliness of the air may owe much to antipollution ordinances. The education of children will certainly be dependent on the quality of local schools. The security of homes depends on, for example, the efficiency of local police and fire services, while the possible deterioration of the building fabric of our neighborhood will depend on the degree to which local government enforces housing codes.

Externality Effects   Externality effects are the by-products of consumption and production activities that have an effect on the utility of others. They tend to be more-or-less spatially concentrated in their impact on residential environments. There is, for example, the airport, imposing noise on surrounding residents as a by-product of its production of airport services. Alternatively a resident's attractive garden and smartly painted house provide benefits for neighbors, even though these were not so intended and can therefore be regarded as by-products.

More specifically externality effects are *unpriced effects on others of the activities of households, firms, governments, etc.* (Turvey 1966). Useful distinctions here involve those between (1) negative and positive externalities and (2) asymmetric and reciprocal externalities.

Negative and Positive Externalities   Negative externality effects are unpriced costs; in other words, there are certain costs that households, firms, governments impose on others as a by-product of their activity and for which they do not provide any compensation. The factory, for instance, may pollute the air in a residential neighborhood and impose cleaning costs and health care costs on residents. The factory does not, however, offer any compensation for those costs. Literally, in the case of negative externalities the producer *externalizes costs*. This is in contrast to costs that are not diffused but that are *internalized*: in the case of the factory these include labor costs and raw material costs.

Positive externality effects, on the other hand, are unpriced benefits; i.e., there are certain benefits that people provide for others as a by-product of their activity and for which they do not receive any monetary compensation from those beneficiaries. A residential developer who for example refrains from constructing blocks of apartments at their maximally efficient height in order that adjacent residents can continue to enjoy a scenic vista is providing certain utilities for those residents without collecting any fee for his service. There is, literally, a diffusion, or *externalization of benefits*, to neighboring residents as a result of the developer's actions. This is in contrast to the benefits internalized by the developer: the price he or she receives from investors in apartments, for instance.

Governments are also producers of positive and negative external effects. While charged with the responsibility of providing sewage services in exchange for taxes, for example, governments provide uninternalized benefits for some landowners by locating sewer lines close to their raw, developable land; they provide uninternalized costs for others, however, by locating the municipal sewage treatment plant close by. To the extent that consequent changes in land values result in equivalent increases or decreases in taxes paid, then the government will internalize all the costs and benefits of its activities. Generally, however, this will not be the case.

Governments also impose external benefits and costs on populations that are *not* under their jurisdiction: consider, for example, the positive externalities involved in brain drains (Thomas 1967) or the negative externalities involved in pollution across international boundaries (Russell & Landsberg 1971).

Asymmetrical and Reciprocal Externalities   One can also differentiate between asymmetrical and reciprocal cases. In asymmetrical externality relationships one can distinguish between a producer of the external effect and a consumer of the external effect on whom the producer imposes utility or disutility as a by-product of satisfying his or her own utility. Common asymmetric externality relationships include: smoking factory chimneys, noisy airports, public housing projects, and public parks, on the one hand, and surrounding residents on the other hand. Where the externality at issue is a positive one we can regard it as a transfer from producer to consumer: the consumer gains at the producer's expense. Where the externality at issue is negative in character, however, we can regard it as a transfer in the other direction.

In reciprocal externality relationships, however, the producers and consumers of external effects—positive or negative—are one and the same. In the case of positive reciprocal externalities individuals are both producers of benefits for others and consumers of the benefits these others produce. In the case of reciprocal negative externalities individuals both produce costs for others and experience the costs imposed by others.

Traffic congestion is typical of negative reciprocal externality relationships: drivers impose disutility on one another when trying to get somewhere. A closer look at pollution due to auto emission also reveals a reciprocal nature: widespread auto use results in auto drivers imposing foul air on each other.

Alternatively, reciprocal externality relationships may be positive in nature. Members of an ethnic community in the city provide positive externalities for one another by adding to the demand for ethnic-specific services—food, recreation, religion—and facilitating

Figure 2.2   Per Pupil Public School Expenditures by State, 1974

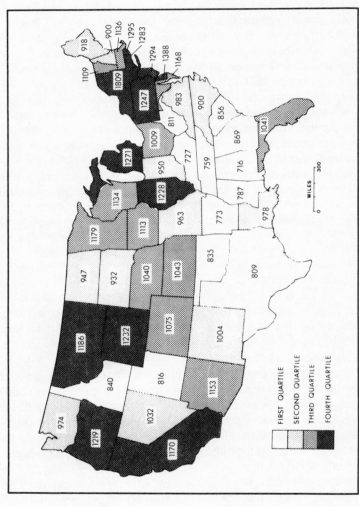

SOURCE: U.S. Bureau of the Census, *Statistical Abstract of the United States, 1974* (Washington, D.C.: Government Printing Office, 1974), p. 130.

the achievement of market thresholds for those services. Residents in a neighborhood provide benefits for each other in the form of mutually working for a residents' association lobbying local government for neighborhood improvement. The states of the United States exchange benefits in the form of educated manpower. In all these cases individual decision-making entities are mutually providing utility.

In reality, of course, most externality relationships involve both asymmetrical and reciprocal elements. Pollution results from widespread auto use: to some degree, therefore, the air pollution problem is a reciprocal one. To the extent that some—industrial firms, for example—pollute more than others, however, the externality relationship assumes a more asymmetric character.

Public provision and externalities, therefore, provide the major sources of residential utility for individuals. Each, however, has some distribution over space. We now turn to consider the geographical expression of residential quality.

Geography of Residential Quality

Very briefly we can envisage geographic regularities in residential quality at two levels: (1) there are variations among jurisdictions according to levels of public provision and (2) there are variations among different localities or regions within jurisdictions according to the variable incidence of externality effects.

INTERJURISDICTIONAL VARIATIONS

Variation in public provision tends to be interjurisdictional. Accordingly, by choosing a particular jurisdiction in which to reside, households are also selecting a particular bundle of publicly provided goods and services. Variations in public provision create the basis for a variety of environments conceptualized by households and forming that set of environments from which one will be chosen. A common image in U.S. metropolitan areas, for instance, distinguishes between unsafe central cities with poor educational provision and safe, independent suburbs that, for example, allocate large sums of money to education and have good college admission records for their students (Cox 1973, ch. 3; 4).

At more intermediate levels of the jurisdictional hierarchy similar differences can be perceived. The states of the United States, for example, vary tremendously in their educational provision (figure 2.2). A sharp dichotomy in this respect exists between southern and non-southern states, the southern ones spending appreciably less than the northern. In a context of migration from the South this has posed

Figure 2.3   Noise Exposure and Distance, Chicago's O'Hare International Airport, 1970

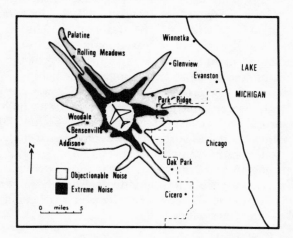

SOURCE: After Brian J. L. Berry et al., *Land Use, Urban Form and Environmental Quality*, University of Chicago Department of Geography Research Paper no. 155 (1974), p. 358.

Figure 2.4   Utility and Distance from Freeway: Schematic Relationships

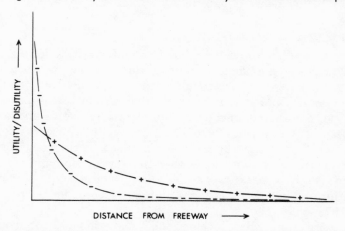

NOTE: Negative externality relationships are indicated by minus signs; positive externality relationships are indicated by plus signs.

public problems of a critical magnitude for a number of northern cities (Kain & Persky 1968).

INTRAJURISDICTIONAL VARIATIONS

Within jurisdictions, on the other hand, there are smaller scale variations in residential quality tending to coincide with characteristically localized externality effects, which vary in their intensity with locational relations. In particular the intensity of external effects frequently exhibits some *distance decay*: the intensity of the utility or disutility resulting from consumption or production by some other household or firm declines with increasing distance from the act of consumption or production in question. For example, consider: distance from a freeway or airport and the magnitude of noise (figure 2.3); distance from the source of pollution and the costs of cleaning and of health care; distance from a highway and the probability of an auto accident involving one's child. The positive externalities that residents can provide for each other via, for example, preferred public behaviors also vary with intervening distance.

Schematically, these relationships can often be represented by distance decay functions, the intensity of the externality effect declining with distance from the point or line of origin. It seems, however, that such functions are likely to be complex rather than simple. Many activities have a variety of externality effects that are conceptually distinct and that have variable relationships to relative location. The case of the freeway is illustrative (figure 2.4). It seems plausible that the freeway imposes negative externality effects associated with noise and air pollution, which decline in intensity quite rapidly with distance from the freeway. In addition, however, the freeway also provides the positive externality of improved access; conceivably this effect decays at a slower rate with distance from the freeway.

A corollary of distance effects concerns the effect of *density*. Where the by-products of the activities of individuals impose costs on others, then, and given a relationship between distance and the intensity of the negative externality, increased density is likely to be associated with increased negative externality effects. This is obvious in the impact of auto density on the negative externalities of air pollution and noise. Air pollution within cities, therefore, increases with nearness to the CBD; this can be related to the fact that as a result of (1) increasing population density with closeness to the CBD and (2) the centripetal focus of highways, traffic density increases the closer one gets to the downtown area.

Density effects are also quite apparent in the negative externalities associated with private sewage and water arrangements. In unincorporated areas on the edge of American cities it is common for

Figure 2.5   International Externality Effects: Acid Rain in Scandinavia

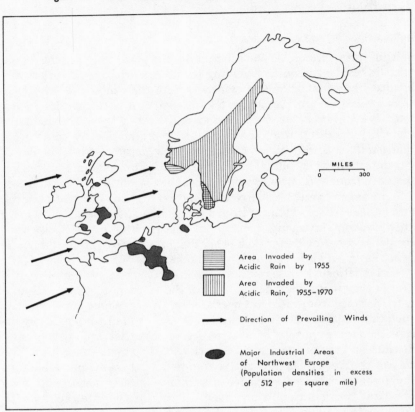

Area Invaded by
Acidic Rain by 1955

Area Invaded by
Acidic Rain, 1955–1970

Direction of Prevailing Winds

Major Industrial Areas
of Northwest Europe
(Population densities in excess
of 512 per square mile)

NOTE: Combustion of coal and oil in the industrial areas of northwestern Europe produces sulphur dioxide, much of which is released into the air. Combined with water vapor, this eventually falls to the ground as a dilute form of sulphuric acid. Since prevailing winds carry the water vapor to the east, it is Scandinavia that has received the most serious negative impacts of this pollution. In particular increasingly acidic soils in Scandinavia threaten forest productivity, and acidic runoff is reducing freshwater fish yields.

residential households to rely on wells for water and on septic tanks for sewage. As these areas fill in residentially, however, water tables are lowered by the inceasing number of wells and, consequently, wells run dry in periods of drought; groundwater sources are also often contaminated by the increased burden of raw sewage escaping from generally inefficient septic tanks. The increasing inadequacy of private water and sewage systems as residential density grows is a major reason for annexation and incorporation efforts in the unincorporated suburban fringes.

Alternatively, where the externalities in question are positive, then increasing density may be associated with increasing positive externalities. Consider in this light the residential site selection behavior of ethnic or religious minorities. To some degree they tend to cluster residentially as a result of the positive externalities that they provide for each other; for example, acceptable dating partners for children or a market for common facilities such as synagogues, temples, and ethnic restaurants and delicatessens (Lieberson 1963).

These remarks on the impact of density concern reciprocal externalities where individuals are exercising on one another effects of the same type. Another distance-related concept that has more relevance for the case of asymmetrical externalities concerns the degree of *segregation* of two distributions with respect to each other. Where the externality at issue is negative, its consumers clearly benefit by occupying a segregated pattern with respect to its producers. This presumably is the basis of land use zoning that separates industrial land uses from residential. It also has relevance for arguments regarding the location of public housing: should it be dispersed throughout a private residential area according to the scattered site concept (i.e., residential *integration*) or should it be concentrated at a limited number of sites (i.e., residential *segregation*)?

In addition to distance relationships, however, externality effects may also exhibit directional bias. This may increase the localized character of external effects. Movements communicating externality effects therefore tend to have a *trajectory over space*. Prevailing wind directions bias the direction in which noise and air pollutants are carried. It is suspected that sulfur dioxide from power stations and factory chimneys in Northern England is carried by the prevailing westerlies to Scandinavia where it falls to earth as acid rain (figure 2.5). As a result, trout fishing in southern Norway has deteriorated; and it is thought that the growth of trees has been retarded.

Explanation

There is, then, substantial variation in residential quality from one place to another. The geographies of public provision and externalities moreover are not random in their locational properties: they reveal considerable predictability of a spatial character. There are, for example, externality effects with their characteristic distance decays; variations in public provision likewise bear a strong relationship to the underlying tax base geography.

How might we explain these geographies? Recall that in chapter 1 we identified three critical forces: the locational choices of individuals

(e.g., firms, households); the public policies through which governments, on behalf of their citizens, attempt to exercise some control
over location; and the juridical context that constrains both individual locational choice and the public policies that are so often an attempt to structure those choices to local advantage. We consider in
turn the relevance of each of these forces for the geography of residential quality.

INDIVIDUAL LOCATION PROCESSES

It is an easily verifiable proposition that people, as a result of their
various locational behaviors, create each others' environments. The
character of the different neighborhoods of a city as places in which
to live, for instance, is clearly dependent on their respective balances
of inmigration and outmigration. A common conception of house-
holders is that the safety of the neighborhood and the quality of local
schools are highly dependent on who happens to live close by: controlling the social composition of the neighborhood, therefore, emerges as
a critical consideration in the attempts of residents' organizations to
maintain residential attractiveness (Molotch 1972; Wolf & Lebeaux
1969, pt. 1). These attempts may take the form of opposition to rezonings and to the construction of public housing, for example.

Likewise at the interjurisdictional scale, what the local government is able to provide and the means at its disposal for such provision depend critically on the various comings and goings. In the
United States, for instance, local government tax bases depend to a
great extent on the amount of real estate residential households consume: the more housing and land consumed per capita, the higher the
value of the property taxes paid per household member. New arrivals
not only contribute to revenue, however, they also impose demands:
local governments, for example, may attempt to exclude low-income
families on the grounds that they generate a need for public safety expenditures that makes the satisfaction of needs for educational
spending more difficult (Cox 1973, ch. 3). The migrations of households with respect to municipal boundaries in urban areas are, therefore, important determinants of public provision and, hence, of
residential quality.

Over and beyond the environment-creating effects of human
movement, however, are those that stem from the location of human
artifacts: consider, for instance, the impact of airports, factories, and
mining operations, on the residential environments of those unfortunately living in their vicinity. By the same token, at the interjurisdictional scale these uses may have salutary fiscal effects: the
shopping center not only congests, but it also pays sales taxes and

property taxes to local government, thus creating the idea that it is a net contributor to the residential desirability of the local government's jurisdiction.

GOVERNMENTS AS LOCATORS

We have described a situation in which the map of residential quality is dependent on locational shifts both within and among jurisdictions. Within jurisdictions residential quality depends very much on the sort of neighbors one has; and this, of course, is contingent on residential mobility processes. Likewise at the jurisdictional level we have remarked on the significance of comings and goings—of businesses as well as of residents—for tax base and, consequently, for levels of public provision.

These movements, however, take place within, and are constrained by, a context created by government policies: a context moreover that, by channeling and deflecting movements, either intentionally or inadvertently, helps to determine the geography of residential quality. Within jurisdictions, governments have policies that tend to establish variations in residential desirability: certain neighborhoods may benefit from traffic diversion schemes or the construction of public parks; others may benefit from housing code enforcement schemes or from the establishment of smoke control areas. These variations in residential desirability moreover tend to set up flows that reinforce the residential advantages of those favored in other respects. In a real estate market context, for example, competitive bidding for residential properties will result in the rich displacing the poor in the better neighborhoods. Given that even the poor would prefer to live among middle-class households, this adds to the attractiveness of the rich neighborhoods and detracts still more from the residential quality of those congested, polluted neighborhoods to which the real estate market consigns those of lower income.

Among jurisdictions there are similar effects. Some local governments spend more per pupil on education than others; some spend more on street lighting; while still others may, as a result of particularly healthy tax bases, have rather low tax rates. The result of policies that, for whatever reasons, vary in this way is a setting up of differentials in residential environments among jurisdictions, promoting movement from those regarded as less attractive to those seen as more attractive.

If such movement were allowed to continue, the conditions that permit some local governments to have low tax rates and spend large amounts per pupil on education would of course erode. Since the poor generally occupy housing of lower assessed value, they tend to contribute relatively little per capita to local revenue. On the other hand, they tend to generate rather large expenditures for public safety. In a world of self-interested citizens, therefore, there is a need for the local governments of the residentially attractive jurisdictions to keep out those who would destroy that attractiveness. Land use control policies or, more specifically, exclusionary zoning policies provide one answer to this problem: by zoning land for large lots or for single-family housing a local government may be able to exclude those who would be able to afford only small lots or apartments; i.e., the poor (Downs 1973, ch. 6).

JURIDICAL CONTEXT

At one level of explanation, therefore, we might conclude that the map of residential quality is simply a function of individual locational behaviors constrained by the public policies of different governments attempting to structure locations to the advantage of their citizens. This, however, would be a shortsighted view. The degree to which individuals are able locationally to adjust to these differentials is a function of the juridical context. Likewise, what governments are empowered or required to do in the way of policy is a function of that same body of law as set forth in constitutional documents and in subsequent statutes.

Public policy, for example, may have only limited impact on the geography of residential quality unless households are able to react to the differentials of attractiveness so created. In particular there must be a real estate market that allows persons to move out of less-attractive into more desirable neighborhoods and, hence, to improve their welfare levels. We noted above, for example, how publicly created differentials in residential quality were exaggerated by the tendency of the wealthier residentially to displace the poorer. In like manner the ability of a local government to enhance its tax base by implementing policies attractive to the rich depends on the ability of the rich to move into its jurisdiction. Yet these mobility processes are contingent on a residential property market; and a residential property market, of course, is contingent on a regime of private property rights that facilitates and provides incentives for the transfer of real property from one party to another.

In addition there are those aspects of the juridical context regulating the types of policies governments can implement. In U.S. metropolitan areas delegation of powers by state government imposes certain obligations on local governments to which these are able to respond in varying degrees. The requirement that local governments be responsible for education, for example, and for raising the revenue to fund education means that certain local govern-

Location and Residential Quality 31

ments—those with more opulent tax bases—are able to spend either more per pupil at the same tax rate or the same at a lower tax rate. If, however, the funding of education was a responsibility of central government, local variations in tax base would be less apparent in educational spending and local tax rates; i.e., the geography of residential quality would be considerably more uniform than it is.

Concluding Comments

This chapter has had three objectives: to clarify the concept of residential quality; to characterize the distinctive geographies of residential quality; and to explain these geographies.

As to residential quality we saw that the degree to which it is experienced by individuals is contingent on their preferences and the nature of the residential environments brought into contact with those preferences. The utility of an environment, therefore, clearly depends on what an individual wants. Where preferences are heterogeneous we can anticipate conflict between, for example, those who would rather see some landscape preserved and protected from human alteration and those who would like to see it "developed" for commercial purposes.

Two major variables constituting residential environments were defined: public provision and externality effects. Externalities are the uncompensated costs and benefits resulting from the production and consumption activities of others: uncompensated benefits are known as positive externalities, while uncompensated costs are referred to as negative externalities.

The geography of residential quality is the outcome of the intersection of two geographies: that of public provision, which tends to vary largely at an *inter*jurisdictional scale, and that of externality effects, varying largely at *intra*jurisdictional scales. Particularly prominent in the geography of externality effects is the tendency for their intensity to attenuate with increasing distance from the source.

Explanation of these geographies is in terms of a triad of interrelated forces: individual location processes; the public policies governments institute in an attempt to control those processes to local advantage; and the juridical context, which constrains both locational processes and public policies. Individuals, by their locational choices, create each other's externality environments; as a result of the externalities of a fiscal character that locational choices impose, they may also have important effects on the geography of public provision.

The implications of locational behaviors for residential quality, however, cannot be understood outside their interaction with public policies implemented in order to control them. Policies set up differences in residential quality to which individuals respond in their residential choices. The range of policy variation, however, can be traced to the juridical context. That same juridical context is what enables individuals to respond locationally to variations in residential quality: the formation of a real estate market is fundamental to such responses, and private property rights are basic to the formation of a real estate market.

Residential quality, however, is only one aspect of utility for which individuals turn to the political process for some regulatory activity. Private income represents a second aspect, one to which we turn in the next chapter.

Select Bibliography

Aronson, J. Richard. "Voting with Your Feet." *New Society* 29, no. 621 (August 29, 1974): 545–47.

Lave, Lester B., and Seskin, Eugene P. "Air Pollution and Human Health." *Annual Report, 1973*, pp. 15–26. Washington, D.C.: Resources for the Future, 1973.

Page, Talbot; Harris, Robert H.; and Epstein, Samuel S. "Drinking Water and Cancer Mortality in Louisiana." *Science* 193, no. 4247 (July 1976): 55–57.

Turvey, Ralph. "Side Effects of Resource Use." In Henry Jarrett, ed. *Environmental Quality in a Growing Economy*, pp. 47–60. Washington, D.C.: Resources for the Future, 1966.

Chapter Three

The Geography of Private Income

Welfare is not dependent on the quality of the residential environment alone; perhaps even more fundamentally it is a function of private income. The geography of private income moreover can be considered from a viewpoint similar to that for the geography of residential quality: the explanatory forces of locational choice within the constraints of the political process are, for example, highly apropos.

This chapter, therefore, begins by evaluating the concept of private income and then turns to the forms assumed by geographies of private income. It goes on to consider the role of the generating forces and, finally, the interrelationships of residential quality and private income.

Private Income

Generally in advanced industrial countries such as those of North America and Western Europe, income is defined in terms of the sum total of factor payments received by the individual. This includes wages in exchange for the provision of labor; rent on buildings and land; and interest on loans made by the individual. In any given year these factor payments may be supplemented by revenue from the liquidation of stocks of wealth. Large landowners may sell off some of their land; home owners may sell their houses; and landlords may divest themselves of their stock of apartments.

This, however, is an ethnocentric definition of income. Reflection suggests its inadequacies (Carter 1971). Are we to deduce, for instance, that those who receive no cash income receive no income at all? Surely not. Income can be received both in the form of cash payments or as payments in kind; in less-developed countries, most income falls into the latter category. Much individual income in India or Africa consists of goods and services produced by the consumer; i.e., there is a very strong subsistence element in the economy. Any exchange of goods that takes place is moreover likely to be bartered, thus reinforcing the insulation of individual income from the cash economy.

Even in developed countries it would be rash to overlook a significant "in-kind" element supplementing cash incomes. Viewing house-

33

Figure 3.1   The Shape of Data-collecting Units and Income Geography

1. Assume that the area is divided into counties of equal population size and with per capita incomes as follows:

3000	7000	3000	7000
3000	7000	3000	7000
3000	7000	3000	7000
3000	7000	3000	7000

2. Then assume a division of the area into four regions for economic planning purposes. Clearly, the sense that economic planners obtain of inequality in income geography will depend on whether they adopt partition 1 or partition 2.

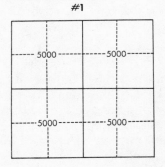

#1

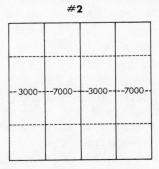

#2

holds as the income-receiving units, for instance, the various services contributed by housewives—food preparation, child rearing, laundering—provide significant elements of income in kind. Anyone doubting this should reflect on the life of a working housewife. She may not only have to send wash to the local laundry and pay for child care services, but she may also find herself eating in restaurants more frequently simply because she is too tired or harassed to prepare food herself.

An additional problem with the concept of private income as cash income is that it may, in fact, tell us little about the material welfare for which it will exchange. It is, for example, not so much private income that is important as *private income after tax*. Some forms of income are more desirable simply because they are tax free or taxed at reduced rates. In the United States income from capital gains is taxed at half the normal rate: a person whose annual income consists of $10,000 from capital gains, therefore, will be considerably better off than a person whose annual income consists of $10,000 from wages.

Tax considerations also serve to underline the significance of income in kind: it is untaxed. The landlord who collects rents from his tenants must pay tax on them. The individual home owner, on the other hand, who, in effect, lets his house to himself, pays no tax on the imputed rent. The individual who grows his or her own vegetables pays no tax on those vegetables; the individual who works for a wage to purchase those vegetables, however, must pay a tax on it, leaving less money to purchase vegetables.

What a private income after tax will purchase in terms of real goods and services furthermore depends on a variety of other circumstances. Particularly critical is the cost of living. What a $10,000 income after tax will purchase in New York City is nowhere near what a $10,000 after-tax income will purchase in Peoria, Illinois: differences in housing and transportation costs alone are striking (Hoch 1972, pp. 315–16).

Despite all these qualifications, however, the implications of private income for material welfare are obviously overwhelming. Over and above simple purchase of the mundane, day-to-day necessities it is clear that income also facilitates access to other self-evident sources of utility. Disparities in the purchase of health care services and vacations are enormous and must account for the substantial life span differences between the poor and the rich (Hauser & Kitagawa 1973).

Private income also has implications for the environmental quality experienced by different individuals. The rich, for example, are able to outbid the poor for housing in more desirable neighborhoods. This may also have implications for differential life span. Who can doubt that living on the South Side of Chicago close to the steel mills and their smoke has different implications for health than living on the less-polluted North Shore?

The rich furthermore are more able to substitute private alternatives for the goods normally provided by governments. As neighborhoods change in their social composition the rich may withdraw their children from public schools and send them to private ones. Such strategies along with residence in an apartment building with a private security guard may make even the most threatening environment tolerable. It is perhaps for reasons such as these that the rich are able to remain in Manhattan, surrounded by a lower class sea, while the less-affluent middle class flees to the safer suburbs.

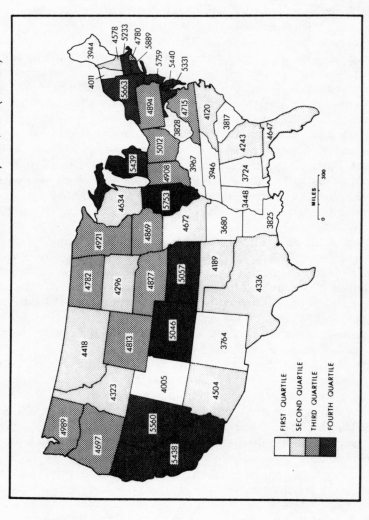

Figure 3.2   Per Capita Personal Income in the United States, by State, 1973 (in dollars)

FIRST QUARTILE
SECOND QUARTILE
THIRD QUARTILE
FOURTH QUARTILE

MILES
0   300

SOURCE: U.S. Bureau of the Census, *Statistical Abstract of the United States, 1974* (Washington, D.C.: Government Printing Office, 1974), p. 130.

Geographies of Private Income

Assuming that we have arrived at an adequate operationalization of the concept of private income, we are still confronted with problems of geographic evaluation. In particular, precisely what we see when we look at a mapping of private incomes will depend on certain assumptions made when mapping.

An initial problem concerns whether private income should be mapped by geographic source of income or by the residential location of the recipient. A mapping of income sources would probably differ substantially from a mapping by place of receipt. Suburban ownership of ghetto properties, for example, results in a substantial translation of rents over space. Foreign investment may produce similar flows from the country where most of the share capital is owned. Generally, of course, private income is mapped by residential location of the recipient. Determining income sources is not only difficult; in addition it raises awkward political questions.

A second problem is posed by the choice of a set of areas for mapping purposes. The geometry of the data-collecting units employed has important implications for our sense of spatial inequalities in private income (Reiner 1963). As figure 3.1 indicates this is partly a result of the shape of data-collecting units. Geographical scale, however, is also significant. Generally, private incomes vary much more over the small scale than over the large scale: there is much more variation in per capita income across the counties of the United States than there is over the states. One's sense of inequality will consequently be seriously affected by the choice of county or state as the basic data-collecting unit. These issues, therefore, pose serious problems for a consideration of the geography of income at intranational and international levels and limit us as to the types of conclusions at which we can arrive.

INTRANATIONAL INCOME GEOGRAPHIES

Figures 3.2 and 3.3 present geographies of per capita income for the United States and United Kingdom. In both cases there is clearly substantial variation. In the United States, the South stands out as an area of relatively low per capita incomes, though the Dakotas and the upper New England states of Maine, New Hampshire, and Vermont are not far behind. The states of the industrial Midwest and Northeast and the Pacific Coast states are clearly the wealthiest.

In Britain the general pattern is one in which per capita incomes are generally higher in the southeast and decline in all directions from there. The London area is obviously the wealthiest in terms of cash incomes, while peripheral regions such as Scotland, Wales, and Northern Ireland are substantially poorer.

Figure 3.3   Per Capita Personal Income in the United Kingdom, 1964–1965

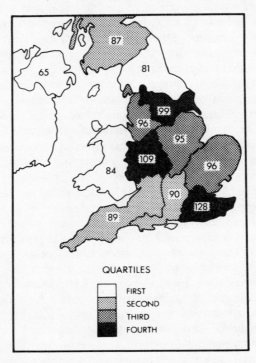

NOTE: Figures are indices of per capita personal income (U.K. = 100).
SOURCE: After V. H. Woodward, *Regional Social Accounts for the United Kingdom* (Cambridge: At the University Press, 1970), p. 163.

The image of interregional variation conveyed by these mappings of course needs to be qualified considerably. Given a progressive income tax in both countries, national tax payments per capita in richer regions are far in excess of those in poorer ones. Income in kind should also be taken into account. In the United States, for instance, southern agriculture still has an important subsistence element, just as does that of Northern Ireland in the British case. Cost of living differences serve to reduce variation still further. There is no doubt that the cost of living tends to be higher in the wealthier areas: in the British case housing costs in the London and southeastern regions are generally regarded as twice what they are elsewhere in the country.

Even when all these qualifications are taken into account, it seems nevertheless unlikely that all variation in private income would be eliminated. Disaggregation of our data, however, provides some further clarification. Consider the case of wages. Let us assume that instead of plotting wages per capita for the population as a whole we plotted wages per capita by occupational group. This would give us maps for, say, dentists, fire fighters, auto assembly workers, coal miners, and school teachers. These maps would reveal little or no variation in wages per capita between one region and another. Table 3.1 presents data consistent with this idea for British regions. This produces a startling conclusion: Most of the variation in wages per capita (undifferentiated by occupation) from one area of the country to another must be due to occupational mix. The poverty of Northeastern England, therefore, is due largely to an occupational mix emphasizing low-paying jobs such as those in coal mining and shipbuilding, as opposed to the high-paying jobs in service industries in the London area. The poverty of the U.S. South can be explained in similar terms.

We can extend this form of analysis to other components of cash income. Profit rates in a given industry, for example, tend to vary little from one area of the country to another: the return to an investment in copper mining in Montana is pretty much what it is in New Jersey. The exception to the idea of interregional homogeneity in factor payments is provided by the case of land.

Consider, for example, some classification of land by properties such as drainage, fertility, flatness, or stoniness. This would allow us to define a set of land types. Given that *different* types of labor elicit *different* factor payments, while *similar* types of labor elicit the *same* factor payments, we might be excused from thinking that the same regularities would apply to land. In fact, land of similar quality would elicit substantially different rents according to location. Generally, for example, we would expect rents to be higher in the more densely populated parts of the country than in the less densely populated sections. Land close to a very large city would tend to let for a higher rent than land at a similar distance from a smaller city (figure 3.4). Also rents would decline with increasing distance from a given city.

INTERNATIONAL INCOME GEOGRAPHIES

Variation in per capita income is also apparent—perhaps more so—among different nations. Certainly in terms of average incomes the range between the poorest and the wealthiest nation on the globe far exceeds the range between the poorest and the wealthiest county in the United States. The qualifications we inserted when discussing income geographies at the *intra*national level, however, are even more important at the *inter*national. There is no doubt, for example, that the income in kind of the population of India far exceeds cash income.

Table 3.1   Average Hourly Earnings of Adult Male Manual Workers by Selected Region, United Kingdom, October 1972

	National Average	Northwest	North	Scotland	Wales
	p*	p*	p*	p*	p*
Food, drink &	77.05	75.80	71.89	76.79	69.22
tobacco	*100.00*	*98.40*	*93.30*	*99.70*	*89.80*
Chemicals	83.19	86.50	89.23	81.70	81.71
	100.00	*104.00*	*107.30*	*98.20* ·	*98.20*
Metal manufacture	85.13	80.71	83.55	85.36	92.92
	100.00	*94.80*	*98.10*	*100.30*	*109.20*
Mechanical	79.84	77.19	83.49	85.07	78.38
engineering	*100.00*	*96.70*	*104.60*	*106.60*	*98.20*
Electrical	79.45	81.05	81.64	78.31	82.32
engineering	*100.00*	*102.00*	*102.80*	*98.60*	*103.60*
Vehicles	98.42	94.60	84.98	94.95	91.85
	100.00	*96.10*	*86.30*	*96.50*	*93.30*
Clothing &	71.13	68.50	73.41	69.42	69.64
footwear	*100.00*	*96.30*	*103.20*	*97.60*	*97.90*
Paper & printing	92.19	91.31	91.72	82.28	80.42
	100.00	*99.00*	*99.50*	*89.30*	*87.20*

NOTE: Italicized figures are wage rates as percentages of wage rates in the nation as a whole.
SOURCE: Reprinted from E. Victor Morgan, "Regional Problems and Common Currencies," *Lloyds Bank Review*, no. 110, October 1973, p. 24, by permission of the publisher.
*p = pence per hour (the wage rate).

The price structure faced by the inhabitants of less-developed countries is also very different. Food and housing in particular are likely to be much cheaper; nevertheless, the differences in income remaining after taking these considerations into account would be stark indeed.

Within occupational groups there is furthermore no homogeneity of wages to brighten the picture. While within the United States a coal miner in Utah may earn pretty much the same wage as a coal miner in Pennsylvania, both would earn far more than a coal miner in India or Nigeria. At the international level only profits are equalized among locations. Quite why this should be so requires a look at the forces accounting for the geographies of private income.

Geographies of Private Income:
Generating Forces

In explaining the geography of residential quality we drew on three major determinants operating jointly: the locational choices of individuals; those policies of governments that affect, either purposely or inadvertently, locational choices; and the juridical context regulating both individual locators and the range of policy that can be drawn on to limit those choices. This is also the explanatory strategy adopted with respect to private income.

INDIVIDUAL LOCATION PROCESSES

Factor payments or the prices that the different factors of production can command are determined in much of the world by relative scarcities; and these scarcities are, in their turn, determined by the supply of, and demand for, the different factors. Where labor is more scarce, therefore, it will tend to be more expensive. This scarcity may result from conditions of expanding demand for labor, or it may result from some bottleneck in the supply of labor—perhaps in the educational system or in the issuance of work permits to foreigners. Whether scarcity is attributable to circumstances of demand or supply, the result is the same: Employers have to pay more in wages to attract labor away from competing employers. At the same time, the labor deficit signifies that laborers will not have to undercut each other in the wages they demand in order to find work. As supply increases, however, and demand wanes, then labor, or a particular type of labor, becomes less scarce and employers can pay less in order to secure its services. In brief, factor payments are determined by relative scarcities, which are, in their turn, determined by the competitive behavior of buyers and sellers of labor in a so-called labor market. Such a market system prevails over large areas of the globe, and even in the so-called Communist countries there is considerable interest in its possibilities.

The scarcity of some factor of production and, hence, its price is determined, then, by supply-and-demand conditions. Demand-and-supply conditions, however, are determined by locational choices. As persons migrate into an area, so the labor supply increases; and, other things being equal, labor will become less scarce and wages will be forced down. If, however, entrepreneurs are moving into the area and increasing the demand for labor at a rate faster than that at which labor is moving into the same area, then labor will become more scarce and wages will go up. Similar impacts on labor scarcity stem from outmigration: as labor leaves small towns, for example, labor scarcity there increases and employers have to pay more for workers.

Figure 3.4   Prices of Residential Land per Acre, England, 1965–1969

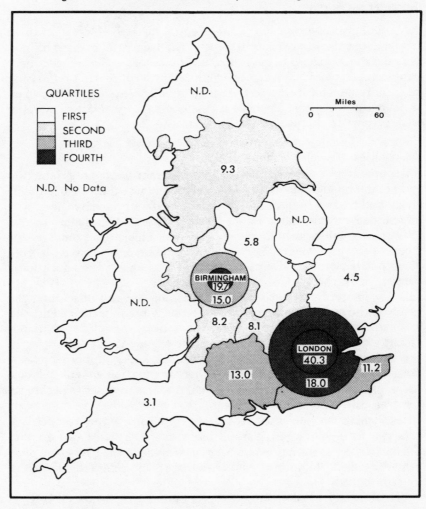

NOTE: Prices are in thousands of pounds per acre. Note the distance decay effects around London and Birmingham.

SOURCE: After John McAuslan, "Price Movements for Residential Land, 1965–69," *Chartered Surveyor* 102, no. 3 (September 1969).

Consider likewise the market impacts of the locational decisions of business investors. As more and more furniture stores are established in a particular town, so the rate of profit on capital invested in furniture stores there will deteriorate. On the other hand, as landlords disinvest from inner city housing by, say, failure to offset deterioration in its physical fabric, and housing ultimately becomes more scarce as a result of boarding up and abandoning the property, the return to capital investment increases for the landlords still remaining in business there.

Generally, of course, labor tends to move from lower to higher wage areas and capital tends to shift from low- to high-profit areas. While these shifts have implications for wages and profit rates in areas of origin and destination, respectively, they also have impacts on land rents. As labor leaves small towns, for example, so the demand for land for building purposes declines; land for building becomes less scarce and landlords are forced to accept lower rents. In larger cities, however, the demand from labor for housing and from entrepreneurs for new business sites makes land more scarce and increases the rent landlords can demand.

In sum, factor payments are determined by relative scarcities determined, in their turn, by supply-and-demand conditions. These, however, are determined by locational behaviors motivated by differences in factor payments. This mode of analysis has some interesting implications for our understanding of the geography of private income:

1. *The homogeneity of factor payments within markets.* Consider a two-region country where labor moves freely between the regions. Assume that doctors are more scarce in region 2 than in region 1. As a result we can expect doctors to shift from region 1, where they receive less for their services, to region 2, where they receive more. The supply of doctors will consequently increase in region 2, making them less scarce and driving the price they can command down; meanwhile, in region 1 the continuing outmigration of doctors makes them more scarce and drives up the prices *they* can command for their services. While we began with higher wages for doctors in region 2 than in region 1, therefore, the effect of the relocation of doctors from region 1 to region 2 is to make wages more similar between the two regions. Ultimately we can envisage a situation in which so much migration has taken place from one region to the other that doctors are equally scarce in both and wages are the same; hence, there is no remaining incentive for further migration: the markets in doctors would have achieved equilibrium by means of a locational adjustment process. Within an area where there is unimpeded mobility of labor, therefore, we would expect the monetary returns to a particular type of labor to be the same from one town to another and from one region to another.

A similar logic applies to profit rates. Differences in profit rates from one region to another reflect differences in the scarcity of capital: high profit rates reflect a capital shortage, while low profit rates reflect a capital surplus. Businessmen in low-profit areas will tend to disinvest and invest both the money so saved and their profits in the high-profit area. As they do this capital becomes more scarce in the low-profit region, forcing profit rates up; in the high-profit region, however, the entry of new firms into the market results in a competing away of high profits. The result is a tendency to interregional equalities in profit rates analogous to the homogenization of wages occurring in the market for a particular type of labor.

Rents, however, show only very limited tendencies towards homogenization. Within a metropolitan area rents for central city land may be 1,000 percent higher than land of similar quality at the edge of the city. It is true that there may be some homogenization of rents as individuals vacate the central city in search of lower land costs. Such locational behavior, however, is likely to occur only as peripheral land becomes more accessible to the central city and the real transport costs associated with it decline. This underlines the fundamental reason for the failure of rents to homogenize: land is immobile. Demand for land is higher in some areas simply because of its accessibility; it is lower in others because of inaccessibility. There is no way in which the owners of low rent land can move it to areas where high rents prevail, increasing the supply of land there and forcing its price down. Only as transport improves and relative location acquires less significance in the bids land users make for land will the rents for pieces of similar-quality land homogenize over space.

2. *Heterogeneity of factor payments between markets*. Geographically a market may be designated as an area within which a given factor has unimpeded mobility resulting in an interregional equilibrium of factor prices. Consider now the case of separate markets between which there are impediments to geographical mobility. Labor markets, for example, tend to coincide with nation states. For a variety of reasons American labor is much more mobile *within* the United States than it is *between* the United States and other countries: similar remarks would apply to French or German labor or that of most other nation states. Impediments to the movement of labor are partly institutional; for example, immigration quotas or labor permits. They are however also cultural. British shipyard workers are unlikely to be as happy living in Hamburg as on Clydeside: the cultural environment is quite alien to them. Although the European Common Market has eliminated institutional barriers to movement, it has not eliminated cultural barriers.

As a consequence of such isolated labor markets, international movements of labor will do little to homogenize the relative scarcities of a given type of labor from one country to another. Shipyard workers may be more scarce in West Germany than in Scotland, forcing up the wage there relative to that in Scotland. Such a differential, however, is unlikely to precipitate a movement of shipyard workers from Scotland to West Germany. As a consequence shipyard workers will continue to earn more in West Germany than in Scotland.

Capital, on the other hand, is much more mobile from one country to another. It is far more valid to speak of a global capital market than of a global labor market. Capital restlessly searches out areas of higher profit, competing away the excess profits there and forcing profit rates up in those areas now facing a capital scarcity rather than surplus. The result is substantial homogeneity in rates of return to investment from one country to another. Attempts to limit the global mobility of capital—for example, by placing restrictions on the operations of multinational corporations—may however fragment capital markets and destroy this global equilibrium.

3. *Integration and expansion of the market.* Our analysis thus far suggests that locational adjustments within a set of known market alternatives allows some to increase their incomes over what they had before: doctors moving to a doctor-scarce region will be rewarded by higher wages; landlords disinvesting from inner city properties and investing in suburban areas where demand for new housing is intense will receive higher rents on their buildings. At some point, however, a continuation of such locational adjustments establishes an equilibrium factor payment level: at that point no one can increase his or her income by relocating within the set of known market alternatives. Only by the *expansion* of market alternatives can incomes be increased. The search for new market alternatives by entrepreneurs and labor has two conceptually distinct, though concurrent, effects: integration of hitherto independent markets and spatial expansion of existing markets.

The search for cheaper sources of raw materials, higher wages, and the like leads to some information on comparative factor price structures between one market and another. Where the differential is sufficiently steep to provide possibilities of gain, some movement of goods, capital, and labor is likely to take place, stimulating a demand for the development of those facilities enhancing mobility between existing markets: transportation infrastructure; facilities for migrants (such as those provided by West Germany for migrants from Turkey and Yugoslavia); new transportation technologies lowering the price of commodity transport between two markets; media for transmitting job information from one market to another. As mobility barriers are overcome in response to this demand, factor prices in the two previously independent markets converge on an equilibrium value. It was partly in this way that a national labor market was established in each of the European countries in the nineteenth century. Previously isolated regional labor markets were linked until, for example, the wage a coal miner was receiving in South Wales was the same as that of a Scottish miner.

Integration of national markets in the nineteenth century also proceeded along transatlantic lines. Innovations in oceangoing transportation gave American grain farmers entrance to the British market and allowed them to undercut high-cost British grains. This had repercussions on both land and labor markets. On the one hand land prices in the hitherto "cheap land" areas of the North American grassland went up and converged on the declining British rents. Farm labor—deprived of its means of existence as a result of the collapse of the British farm labor market—migrated in large numbers to the North American continent; this served to raise agricultural wages in Britain and depress them in North America.

Alternatively the search for new markets, new raw materials, fertile, cheap land, and cheap, docile labor promotes an expansion of the market into areas the economies of which were hitherto organized along the quite different lines of subsistence and barter. Early merchant activity in South and Southeast Asia, coastal Africa and the Caribbean created new demands on the part of native populations that could be met only by increased production and trade. At the same time exploration unearthed new products to titillate the Western Europeans: tea, coffee, and spices, for example, or alternative sources of cheaper raw materials such as sugar cane instead of the expensive honey and cotton instead of flax. Contact with subsistence societies outside Western Europe, therefore, created entirely new and lucrative fields for capital investment.

What is evident, then, is a system of spatial relationships in which individual factor returns are much affected by the locational choices of others. Not, however, that the individual is entirely a victim of his spatial circumstances. Labor and capital are often able to achieve some improvement in income by moving among a given set of market alternatives; there are also possibilities of income expansion flowing from the integration and expansion of markets.

The implications of such a system of locational interdependencies for the political process are serious for at least three reasons: First, it is clear that as markets become integrated and expand, individual welfare is affected by market events at greater and greater distances. The juridical relationships and public policies designed to coordinate those events and distribute the product in a socially just manner must therefore satisfy the preferences of an increasing number of persons. These preferences moreover are likely to be increasingly diverse as the locational relationships different individuals have become more and more varied.

Nor will it be easy to devise a juridical context agreeable to all, for a second implication of the system of spatial interdependencies described above is that of income redistribution. For example, as workers migrate from a low-wage area to a high-wage area, the wages of those in the destination area will fall, while those in the origin area improve—a result hardly likely to recommend itself to the migrant's host population. Trading relations consequent to relocations have similar implications. The development of an export trade in textiles from India to Britain, for example, is fraught with serious consequences for high-wage British labor. Conflict then seems likely to be endemic in the system of spatial interdependencies in which the market enmeshes people.

Third, the idea of market expansion raises political questions. The market requires a certain body of law to sustain it. As the market expands into new areas it is unlikely that it will encounter compatible institutions of, for example, private property and freedom of contract. These, therefore, must be introduced and enforced—which, of course, is a large part of what imperialism was all about (Barratt Brown 1974, ch. 6). This, however, brings us to the broader topic of the juridical relationships and policies regulating those individual locational adjustments that, in turn, affect factor payments.

GOVERNMENTS AS LOCATORS

The locational adjustments we described above take place within the context of price-fixing markets: we have described, for example, how locational choices affect factor payments via their impact on demand and supply and hence on scarcity. Capital, for example, tends to move from areas of low profitability to areas of high profitability. This makes capital more scarce in its area of origin and so raises profit rates there; at the same time capital becomes less scarce in the area of destination, tending to depress profit rates there somewhat.

These movements of capital and labor, however, take place within, and are constrained by, a context created by government policies. These, as a result of the attractiveness variations they create, channel factor movements in certain directions and away from others, helping in no small way, therefore, to determine the ultimate geography of private income.

Within jurisdictions, for example, a wide range of policies calls for public investments of a localized character. These public investments exercise significant effects on rates of profitability in surrounding areas and, hence, exercise an upward effect on the demand for labor and land. This, of course, has implications for local wages and land rents. Construction of airports, new dock facilities, military installations, new irrigation works, and hydroelectric dams—all are examples of public investments generating local economic growth and increased factor returns in the private market. At smaller scales one can observe similar effects. The location by local public authorities of new highways, sewer lines and waterlines increases demand for land in some locations and lowers it in others. The impact on land rents is observable and, of course, is of critical interest to landowners.

Among jurisdictions policy helps to differentiate nation states in terms of their acceptability to capital. National educational and labor relations policy impacts on the productivity of labor and, hence, on the profitability of investment. Tax policies offering liberal terms for, say, the depreciation of plant have similar effects. All other things being equal, therefore, capital will tend to flow from nation states with policies that decrease profitability to those that increase profitability. As capital shifts, of course, so does the demand for labor, so that wages will tend to be bid up in those nation states able, by dint of policy, to attract capital from elsewhere.

Just as governments exercise effects on factor returns by attracting certain types of factor, so other policies exercise their effect by obstructing factor movements. Immigration policy may be used to exclude foreigners whose competition in the national labor market would tend to lower wages. Barriers to trade on the other hand may, paradoxically enough, stimulate an inflow of capital. Canadian imposition of tariffs on cars exported from the United States, for example, increased the relative profitability of producing them in Canada instead (Tatham 1956, p. 339).

JURIDICAL CONTEXT

All of these policies, damming up market movements "here" and deflecting them "there," occur within a juridical context constraining the policies of governments and the locational responses of individuals to policy outputs. Most critical for individual locational choice are the laws governing access to, use of, and the transfer of the resources needed to create wealth.

Central to the concept of private property is exclusivity of access to, and use of, property. An individual's land is his with which to do whatever he likes, and his right to the use of that land and its product is protected by the law of trespass. As a consequence he has an incentive to use his resources so as to increase their yield to him. This is in sharp contrast to a common property rights system, where individuals share rights of access to, and of use of, a resource (Dales 1972). Such a system was common in medieval Europe (Hardin 1968) and still characterizes use of the high seas for fishing purposes (Christy &

Scott 1965). The result is a limit on investment in yield-raising technologies, since part of the payoff will leak to others and reduce the
rate of return.

Next is the right of transfer of property. Under a private property
rights system the individual landowner can sell his or her property to
any interested party at whatever price the two can agree on. Individual capitalists can sell their fixed capital and lend their liquid
resources to whomever they please and for whatever price they
negotiate. The equivalent for the laborer is freedom of contract: the
right to sell his or her labor to any employer for whatever the two can
agree on. This has obvious and important implications for locational
behavior and for resultant factor payment equilibria. Without freedom of transfer, for example, interregional flows of investment funds
would dry up for want of the right to buy land and fixed capital.
Without freedom of contract, labor would be impeded from moving in
the direction of the highest wage.

Clearly such a juridical context is not the only one feasible for
solving the production problems faced by individuals in society: altering it, however, would affect the locational flexibility that permits
price-fixing markets to function. This is clear from a comparison with
pre–market law and the implications it had for that flexibility. While
it is difficult to generalize about pre–market societies, medieval European societies had a good deal in common and they provide an
illuminating contrast with present-day Western societies. Two
features can be referred to as providing a critically different juridical
context:

1. Rates of exchange between buyers and sellers in medieval societies were fixed according to custom and statute and were not open to
bargaining. This applied not only to the prices at which goods could
be sold but also to wages, rents, and interest: anti-usury laws, for instance, were common in medieval societies. This is in sharp contrast
to the market-determined fluidity of exchange rates characteristic of
present-day market societies. The fixity of exchange rates moreover
served to inhibit relocations in search of higher wages or higher
returns on capital. This parochiality of the horizons of resource
owners was apparent in other respects.

2. There were limits on the freedom of contract for owners of labor
and land and also for sellers and buyers of goods. As we have seen in
(1) above, freedom of contract was limited in terms of the price that
could be arrived at. It was also limited, however, in terms of those
with whom one could exchange. Laws placed severe limits on the sale
of land. The mobility of labor was likewise limited by laws tending to
tie the worker to the parish responsible for his welfare if he should
have recourse to the poor laws—laws, incidentally, that incited the

wrath of Adam Smith. Trade was also limited by laws designed to protect the welfare of local residents. It was not until the mid–nineteenth century, for example, that laws permitting French communes to limit export of wheat to other parts of France until local needs were met were finally abolished. The fact that the creation of a national grain market in this way resulted in riots in certain areas as bread prices rose suggests that such parochial laws had not been without their functions for local populations.

Medieval societies, therefore, were characterized by a parochiality of economic relations long since superseded. Even so, one should not forget that remnants of this parochiality are still apparent, albeit at a larger geographic scale. In 1975 American labor unions opposed grain export to the Soviet Union, ostensibly on the grounds that it would increase bread prices for the American consumer. This is vaguely reminiscent of controversies at the commune level in nineteenth-century France. Likewise, there are limits, say, on labor migration and ownership of land by foreigners, which limit spatial adjustments at the larger scale, just as they were limited at smaller scales in earlier periods of history.

There is, therefore, a set of constraints, enshrined in property rights, on the ability of individuals to take advantage of policy-induced variability in market opportunities. In addition to these constraints, however, are those aspects of the juridical context that govern the nature of policies, themselves. Constitutions, and their subsequent amendment and supplementation by statute, tie governments to a particular range of policy discretion. The U.S. Constitution, for example, forbids the states to interfere with interstate commerce. As a consequence the old industrial states of the Midwest and the Northeast have been unable to counter the drift of industrial investment away from them and towards the South and the West.

This is in sharp contrast to the situation at the global level. Attempts to establish textile industries in less-developed countries, for example, have been frustrated by developed countries' erection of tariff barriers to protect their own textile industries. Since the developed countries provide the larger fraction of the global market for textiles, this action has served to sustain the profitability of textiles in those countries relative to their profitability in less-developed countries. In the United States the older industrial states provide the larger fraction of the national market, yet their constitutional inability to impose tariffs on goods produced in the West and South has prevented them from maintaining their competitive advantage.

Market processes and the private incomes they generate, however, are not of interest only for their own sake and for their direct expression in the political process. They also receive an indirect expression in the political process as a result of their impacts on public provision and externalities, in particular, and on residential quality, in general. We are also in a position now to consider the implications of variations in residential quality for differences in private income. It is to the mutual relationships of residential quality and private income, as they play themselves out in a locational context, and over time, that we turn in the last section of this chapter.

Residential Quality and Private Income
IMPACT OF INCREASING PRIVATE INCOMES ON RESIDENTIAL QUALITY

As indicated in the last chapter, the major determinants of residential quality are the externalities we are exposed to and the levels of public provision we experience. Turning attention initially to the externality component of residential quality, most diagnoses regarding the impact of increasing private income would tend to be rather pessimistic. To a considerable degree, and given the prevailing juridical context, it would appear that private incomes can be increased only at the expense of environmental quality. Looking at societies at large and ignoring small-scale geographical variations, a private income/residential quality trade-off is evident: real private incomes, in terms of the consumption of goods and services, can be increased only with some deterioration in residential quality.

This is the *costs-of-economic-growth* argument advanced by, among others, E. J. Mishan (1969). The argument may be stated briefly. Under existing definitions of property rights the generation of increasing real private incomes is attainable only with the generation of negative externalities. A large variety of industries and the work forces they sustain depend on the sale of products whose production or use entails uncompensated costs on others: air pollution, water pollution, reduced life spans, noise, and the like (figure 3.5). Internalization of such costs by producing industries would result in increased costs of production, higher prices, reduced demand, lower levels of production, and, hence, reduced demand for labor and lower private incomes.

The argument is highly plausible. Attempts to reduce air pollution from automobiles and to increase their safety inevitably raise costs of production. Increased costs will be passed on to consumers in the form of increased prices and, other things being equal, will result in a reduction in demand for automobiles. This type of cost-in-

Figure 3.5   Urbanization, Water Pollution, and Cancer Mortality

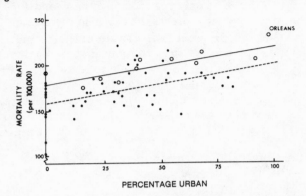

PERCENTAGE URBAN

NOTE: The figure refers to a set of parishes in Louisiana and shows that cancer mortality rates are higher in more urbanized parishes. Orleans parish, in which the city of New Orleans is located, has the highest rate of all. At the same time water pollution exercises an effect of its own. Parishes drawing water from the polluted Mississippi (open circles) tend to have higher cancer mortality rates than parishes drawing their water from other sources (closed circles). The two lines are regression lines, the thick one referring to eleven parishes drawing their water from the Mississippi and the dashed one referring to the fifty-three parishes not using Mississippi water.

SOURCE: After Talbot Page, Robert H. Harris, and Samuel S. Epstein, "Drinking Water and Cancer Mortality in Louisiana," *Science* 193, no. 4247 (July 2, 1976): 55–57.

creasing, employment-reducing argument has been frequently, effectively, and, in many cases, realistically employed by business when resisting pollution control legislation: legislation, for example, that would result in internalization of the negative externalities associated with the production technology or with the product, itself.

The trade-off between private consumption and residential quality, however, is not made evident to all members of society to the same degree: generally speaking those with higher incomes are those most able to escape the noxious side effects of industrial technology and products. The variable incidence over space of negative externalities such as noise, air pollution, and traffic hazard influences the geography of residential attractiveness: presumably those areas least affected by these negative externalities will be residentially more desirable. Competitive bidding for residential sites will proceed, however, not only on the basis of residential attractiveness—more desirable sites will elicit higher bids—but also on the basis of income: those with higher incomes will be prepared to bid more for a given site than those of lower income. As a consequence there is a certain perverseness in the allocation of residential sites: those benefiting most from the existing juridical context in terms of private income also benefit most in terms of environmental quality.

A similar logic applies to the public provision component of residential quality. What governments are able to do in the way of public provision—education, flood control, building inspection, creation of recreational facilities—depends to a substantial degree on the magnitude of the tax base. And the magnitude of the tax base, of course, is related to income—either directly through an income tax or indirectly by the taxation of some item (e.g., real property, sales of certain goods) whose consumption is directly related to private income. Wealthier populations, therefore, generally provide themselves with more education, more elaborate public parks, and more highway systems and public health facilities than do poorer populations.

Distributionally we find, again, a rather perverse consequence. Generally speaking, nation states are subdivided into local-level jurisdictions, the governments of which will be more-or-less responsible for the provision of services such as education, highway maintenance, and public safety. Even assuming that individuals with different incomes are distributed randomly with respect to these local jurisdictional boundaries, some jurisdictions will have larger tax bases per capita than others: for a given level of public provision, therefore, tax rates will be lower in some areas than elsewhere. As a consequence the geography of residential desirability is again altered, low tax rate jurisdictions eliciting higher bids than those with high tax rates. Those able to bid the most for residential sites in low tax rate jurisdictions, of course, will tend to be wealthier: builders, recognizing the attraction of a low tax rate, will tend to build housing in those jurisdictions appropriate to the tastes of the upper income. As a consequence there is a perverse allocation of fiscal resources to individuals: the poorer tend to live in jurisdictions with the more meager tax bases, while the wealthier tend to live in those more amply endowed. And, to the extent that the real estate market fails to keep out the poor, the majority will have an interest in exclusionary zoning ordinances and other techniques that provide a deterrent additional to that deriving from the market.

IMPACT OF RESIDENTIAL QUALITY ON INCOME

Not only does increasing private income affect residential quality, but there are also reverse effects. These tend furthermore to reinforce the distributional perversity we noted above.

Residential quality receives an expression in both wages and income from land. The educational process for which local government is responsible no longer produces the "well-rounded individual." Rather, it is now a matter of investing in "human resources." Job prospects are intimately tied to educational training and credentials, and parents know it. Residential location is fraught with important consequences for the future income prospects of children; this adds to the premium placed on housing in what are regarded as "good" school districts. The poor cannot afford to live in these school districts, and their children are therefore consigned to the "bad" schools; thus is poverty inheritable.

Residential quality also affects land income. This may be long term in the form of rents or it may be highly irregular in the form of capital gains from land sales. The value of land, however, reflects the quality of the immediate environment: land in unpolluted, quiet, middle-class neighborhoods will tend to sell for more than land in run-down neighborhoods; it will also tend to show a higher capital gain over time. Yet once again it is land in neighborhoods of this character that tends to fall into the hands of the wealthy, reinforcing the inequalities discussed in the previous paragraph.

Concluding Comments

We started this chapter by examining the concept of private income. Generally it is defined as the sum total of factor payments of wages, interest, and rents. This definition leaves something to be desired, however, since it ignores the contributions to private income of the subsistence sector and the effects of taxes and cost of living on purchasing power. Variations in private income nevertheless generally connote substantial differences in individual welfare.

Private income moreover tends to vary both among regions within nations and between nations. Within nations, however, and for particular occupational types there is considerable interregional similarity, suggesting that interregional variation in average private incomes is partly due to variations in occupational mix. We also alluded to tendencies towards interregional homogenization in profit rates, but we say that such interregional convergence did not extend to rents.

At the international level variations in private income among nation states vastly exceed those among regions *within* nation states. Furthermore, since there are substantial international variations in wages for the same occupation, little of the international variation in private incomes can be attributed to differences in occupational mix.

In explaining geographies of private income recourse was made to the three forces identified when explaining the geography of residential quality: locational processes regulated by public policies, with both these forces, in their turn, constrained by the juridical context. Locational processes include labor and capital shifts among regions. Since these tend to be from areas where they are less scarce to areas where they are more scarce, the overall effect of such movements is a leveling of interregional differences in profit rates and in wages within occupations. As a result of the immobility of land, however, there is no analogous leveling of land rents. And where labor is immobile as a result of institutional or cultural barriers the geographical homogenization of wages within occupations will tend to be frustrated.

Locational choices of this character are constrained by the political process. Politics have spatially differentiating effects raising factor returns in some areas and lowering them in others. Policy discretion, however, is constrained by the juridical context: this helps to determine the ability of a government to protect its markets from external competition. The juridical context also determines the ability of individuals to adjust to the attractiveness differentials so created. Of major significance in market societies are private property rights; rights of exclusive access, use, and transfer. Without the right to lend one's capital or sell one's services to whomever one pleases at a negotiated price, there would be no incentives to seek out those locations where factor returns could be maximized. As a consequence interregional equilibria in labor and capital markets would not be attained.

Finally we remarked on the relations between private income and residential quality. Increases in private income tend to be obtained at the expense of residential quality. This results from the negative externalities associated with increased production. In addition private incomes affect public provision via their impact on the tax base. Jurisdictions with relatively wealthy populations tend to have relatively large tax bases per capita: as a consequence they can provide themselves with public goods at a considerably lower tax rate— or more public goods at the same tax rate—than can poorer populations. These effects have additional feedback effects. Children in more affluent jurisdictions tend to have more money spent on their education, providing them with competitive advantages in labor markets.

Select Bibliography

Carter, Charles F. *Wealth.* Harmondsworth, Middlesex: Penguin, 1971.

Douty, H. M. "Regional Wage Differentials: Forces and Counterforces." In C. McConnell, ed. *Perspectives on Wage Determination,* pp. 207-17. New York: McGraw-Hill, 1970.

Easterlin, Richard A. "Does Money Buy Happiness?" *Public Interest,* no. 30, winter 1973, pp. 3-10.

Freeman, A. Myrick. "Income Distribution and Environmental Quality." In Alain C. Enthoven and A. Myrick Freeman, eds. *Pollution, Resources and the Environment,* pp. 100-106. New York: Norton, 1973.

Krutilla, John V. "Some Environmental Effects of Economic Development." In Alain C. Enthoven and A. Myrick Freeman, eds. *Pollution, Resources and the Environment,* pp. 253-62. New York: Norton, 1973.

Mishan, E. J. *The Costs of Economic Growth.* Harmondsworth, Middlesex: Penguin, 1969.

Quante, Wolfgang. "Flight of Corporate Headquarters." *Society* 13, no. 4 (May/June 1976): 36–41.

Scitovsky, Tibor. "Inequality: Open and Hidden, Measured and Immeasurable." *Annals of the American Academy of Political and Social Science* 409 (September 1973): 113–19.

Smolensky, Eugene. "Poverty, Propinquity and Policy." *Annals of the American Academy of Political and Social Science* 409 (September 1973): 120–24.

Young, George. *Tourism: Blessing or Blight?* Harmondsworth, Middlesex: Penguin, 1973.

Chapter Four

Location and Politics

So far we have briefly considered the forces generating the emergence of politics, in general, and of political intervention in location, in particular (chapter 1). We have also considered the impact of the political process on those flows of people and factors of production helping to determine geographies of residential quality and private income (chapters 2, 3). Clearly, movements have important implications for the welfare of localized groups. Yet to be discussed in depth, however, is the impact of these localized welfare outcomes on the continuing use citizens make of the political institutions they have helped to establish. How, therefore, do localized and impacted groups relate to politics?

A brief, opening review of the forces affecting the welfare of localized groups provides a context for this chapter's ensuing discussion. The second section identifies the various ways in which localized groups may react politically to welfare outcomes regarded as more-or-less unsatisfactory. We then shift to the output side of the equation and examine the ability of these groups to make the political process respond to their demands.

Political Process and Welfare in a Locational Context

Let us review the ideas presented so far regarding the impact of politics on location processes and, hence, on the welfare of localized populations. We will start with the body of constitutional and statutory law defining the juridical context.

Juridical relationships, we have seen, restrict and control government policies. These policies—for defense, energy, housing, and the like—in turn have tremendous implications for well-being. Public investments vary in their geographical incidence and so set up a geography of investment opportunity having implications not only for profits but also for wages and rents. On the other hand, public policies help to create geographic variations in residential desirability. The design of an urban highway network has immense significance for the congestion, air pollution, and noise experienced in different places. At larger geographic scales federal investment in military installations and irrigation works has served to improve tax bases and increase public provision in some western and southern counties (Fainstein & Fainstein 1976).

The degree to which individuals and businesses can adjust to these publicly created opportunities, however, also depends on the juridical context. Critical here are individual property rights. These regulate the ability of owners, for example, to sell property in less-desirable neighborhoods and relocate to more desirable ones. They also regulate the degree to which businessmen can take advantage of new, publicly created investment opportunities by disinvesting in one area and reinvesting in another.

The overall effect is to create a great deal of movement: of residents from less-desirable to more desirable areas, of labor from low-wage to high-wage areas, and of businesses from low-profit to high-profit areas. This, of course, has serious implications for the welfare of more stable elements in the population. As increased residential development takes place in some suburbs, there is a loss of tranquility and an increase in the congestion of schools and of other public facilities. The costs of expanding schools and highways have to be borne by old as well as new residents, tending to raise tax rates. Likewise as the geography of investment opportunity shifts, disinvestment creates unemployment, depleted tax bases, and increased welfare rolls in some areas at the same time that it creates employment, higher wages, and enhanced tax bases in others.

Movements of labor, residents, capital, and commodity flows therefore are, on the one hand, constrained by the state, working both through the juridical context and through public policy. On the other hand, they exercise important and far-reaching effects on the geography of welfare.

To some degree individuals adjust to these localized welfare impacts by relocating. Residents respond to neighborhood decline by moving to other, more desirable neighborhoods. Middle-class residents respond to rising central city tax rates by choosing to live in the suburbs. Corporations shift their headquarters, for example, from New York to Houston in response to similar tax differentials (Quante 1976). And gas-consuming businesses shift from states such as Ohio, where natural gas is no longer available, to states such as Texas, where it is still available—though at a price.

Alternatively, however, the possibilities of geographic substitution may be nonexistent, limited, or merely uneconomic. Firms may employ large amounts of fixed capital that is difficult to relocate and impossible to sell. How, for example, is a hospital or university to cope with surrounding neighborhood deterioration and the need for land for expansion? To what extent can poor blacks substitute more desirable environments for the ghetto? More generally residents develop ties to an existing neighborhood and to its residents, ties that cannot be taken along when moving.

The immobility of land poses particular problems: the landowner cannot respond to problems detrimental to the value of his land by moving it elsewhere. Clearly the environment itself must be changed by some alteration in the juridical context or in the policies constraining the locational adjustments that help to create that environment. The dominance of politics in the suburban fringe by large landowners is an important reflection of this.

At broader geographic scales it is the immobility of labor that limits the substitutability of locations. As capital investment patterns change at the global level, labor finds it difficult to adjust locationally. Not only are there the cultural ties that keep Americans in America and the French in France; there are also institutional barriers to international migration. Perhaps we should not be surprised, therefore, at lobbying by labor unions to limit capital export and to erect tariffs against foreign products.

Participation in the Political Process

Given this context, how—other than by relocation—might a population respond to some localized welfare impact of a negative character? They confront a situation in which locational choices have not redounded to local benefit: what would have been locally enhancing has gone elsewhere; while, conceivably, the only developments occurring within the locality have tended to be welfare detracting.

We have argued that the locational choices affecting local welfare are constrained by the juridical context and by the particular policies implemented by the government in accord with that context: policies, for example, that may affect the attractiveness of different locations for business investment or that may affect the residential desirability of different neighborhoods; and a juridical context that may inhibit locational adjustment to those differentials.

Clearly, therefore, modifying locational choices to the benefit of the local area—neighborhood, region, nation state—requires altering those aspects of the juridical context or policies affecting locational choice. This, however, requires some *participation in the political process:* some allocation of time, energy, and financial resources to secure the desired change. Necessary is some allocation of resources to lobbying legislators, bankrolling the election campaigns of those friendly to one's interests, and the like.

Participation in politics for local ends is most obvious in the formation of organizations uniting those with similar localized concerns. Precisely why organization is important need not detain us at this point. Suffice it to say that while for some (e.g., very large firms), organization may not be particularly important, for most it provides significant advantages. These include economies in presenting views to government and also the communication of a greater sense of threat to the government than, for instance, the odd random letter to the local member of Congress.

The organizations pressing for policies beneficial to their members are legion. At the national scale they include: political parties; labor unions; national associations of manufacturers such as the Confederation of British Industry; amenity societies such as the Sierra Club and the Audubon Society (in the United States); and the Council for the Preservation of Rural England, the Ramblers Association, and the National Trust (United Kingdom). At a local level organizations participating in the political process include: chambers of commerce; residents' associations; preservation societies, labor union locals; and local government bureaucracies.

Each organization has some geographical area of concern defined by the location of its members' interests. A chamber of commerce, for example, may be concerned about policies relating to the CBD. Neighborhood organizations will involve themselves in events in and around their specific neighborhoods. Labor unions, on the other hand, will focus on employment levels and employee benefits throughout the country. Organizations of manufacturing firms will center their interests on policies impacting on business confidence at the national level.

Each organization can be viewed as having some geographic area of interest, therefore, in which it would like to see developments—physical, social, or economic—beneficial to its members. These events are linked to the juridical changes or policy changes desired by respective organizations: an increase in the demand for the products of firms making up some manufacturers' association, for example, may be linked to the institution of a tariff on imports of foreign goods.

The demands of different organizations, however, are often competitive. This is most clear in the case of organizations concerned with different geographical areas (Molotch 1967). Chambers of commerce in different cities may compete for federal office buildings. The residents' organizations of adjacent villages often compete to keep a freeway a healthy distance from their doors, while in the city the respective organizations of adjacent neighborhoods may come into conflict over some traffic diversion scheme that takes traffic away from one neighborhood and debouches it in another.

Competition is also apparent among organizations that, while concerned with the same geographical area, have different views as to what local events are utility enhancing. At the local level one can envisage conflict between a chamber of commerce and an historic preservation society; controversy in this case might revolve around the appropriateness of different policies for enhancing the business district's attractiveness to visitors.

A useful classification of these organizations would be into *business, labor,* and *environmental interests.* The immediate antagonism of business and labor interests should be fairly evident. Business, for example, is interested in keeping the price of labor down by facilitating immigration of workers; labor, on the other hand, wishes to enhance its own scarcity value by keeping competing workers out. Environmental interests also oppose business on the grounds that it so frequently involves congestion, noise, pollution, and general degradation of landscape esthetics. These antagonisms nevertheless frequently resolve into a coalition of business and labor against environmental interests: for without any business investment at all the very means of physical survival are threatened.

What is therefore envisaged here is a set of organizations at a variety of geographical scales (1) trying, by some alteration of the juridical context or of prevailing policy, to attract into their relevant geographical areas, or turfs, that which its members regard as utility enhancing, or beneficial, and (2) trying to keep out what members regard as utility detracting, or harmful. Since neither the geographical areas organizations are concerned with, nor definitions of "utility enhancing" are common to, all members of society, the attempts of organizations to do the best by their members are bound to bring them into conflict with other organizations. In their attempts to attract the beneficial and keep out the harmful, therefore, some organizations necessarily have to compete with others, the members of which have either a different geographical environment of concern or different views of what will be advantageous.

In sum, individuals may express concern about developments in their locality. To the extent that a locational response is difficult or impossible, then changes in the juridical context and/or in prevailing policy become the only means of altering existing locational relationships in a utility-enhancing manner. These concerns, then, are frequently expressed in the form of organizations that intervene in politics. They represent memberships at a variety of geographic scales and areas and with a variety of conceptions as to what is utility enhancing. Consequently an organization's attempts to alter public policy or the juridical context in a given direction are likely to bring it into conflict with other organizations and their respective memberships. Which organizations, therefore, are likely to attain the objectives their members desire and, consequently, find their localized interests enhanced? An answer to this question is contingent on an examination of the role of government and the locational relationships in which government finds itself involved.

Payoff to Participation in the Political Process

Competing organizations, we have seen, press for some change that they believe will be ultimately enhancing to the localized interests they represent. The changes they lobby or campaign for may involve some change in policy or in the juridical context. And they will be changes likely to facilitate locational decisions to the advantage of respective localized interests. In the case of both a change in the juridical context and a change in policy, moreover, the payoff to participation is contingent on the same two considerations: the power the organization has with respect to the government and the juridical context constraining what government constitutionally may do. We consider in turn, therefore, the role of power relations and the juridical context.

POWER RELATIONS

Competing organizations confront a government responsible for formulation and implementation of policy. Governments moreover have their own interests, which may not coincide at all with those of the groups requesting change. One must presume that persons in government enjoy governing. The sources of their utility may be the exercise of power, public service, or—in a rather less-complimentary context—payoffs in money or in kind. In order to continue enjoying these benefits of office, however, governments must be reelected: they must retain the support of enough voters in order to ensure electoral success.

This has clear implications for those local interests desiring change: they must construct a coalition capable of commanding a majority of votes in the appropriate legislative or council chamber. In order to remain in office the government requires support in the form of popular votes or the votes of legislative representatives. To the extent that an interest group can plausibly threaten withdrawal of votes, therefore, its bargaining position is enhanced.

The bargaining resources at the disposal of an interest group may be the votes of members of the group itself or of its supporters. In Britain labor unions are able to exercise a good deal of power over the government through the votes of their members. Mobilized by union newsletters and discussion on the shop floor, labor unionists have demonstrated time and again their willingness to vote a union line. Likewise at the local level, the members of boards of zoning appeals are noticeably sensitive to the numbers of faces showing up to protest a particular rezoning request.

Other bargaining resources, however, may be of a more indirect nature; i.e., they do not consist of votes per se, but their withdrawal will indirectly affect support for the government. The electoral appeal of a national government, for example, is quite dependent on its ability to manage the economy, to sustain a high rate of economic growth, and to maintain full employment (Kramer 1971). Consequently, national governments are remarkably sensitive to the threats of different interest groups to withdraw the resources necessary for continued economic growth. Business lobbies stress the importance of maintaining the confidence of business through a favorable investment climate. This may be coupled with an explicit threat: policies less enhancing to business interests will provoke a flight of capital to countries with more appealing policies.

Similar threats are evident at more local levels. In a metropolitan area an office developer may threaten to locate a new office development elsewhere. Location may be made contingent on more flexible local government regulations regarding, for example, installation of sprinkler systems or provision of parking space. The bargaining resource in this instance, of course, occurs less through control of resources necessary to economic growth and more through control of resources contributory to the tax base. Local governments, particularly in the United States, generally conceive of the local electorate as tax-conscious. Attracting developments such as office buildings—which contribute more in tax revenue than the value of the public services they consume—is usually seen as facilitating a reduction in the local tax rate.

In many instances the range of discretion of the individual voter is consequently limited by the ability of other interests to withdraw resources vital to voter welfare. These are the resources vital to economic life; on questions of economic survival, concerns over residential quality tend to assume a different significance. If it is a question of jobs or pollution, for example, the interests controlling jobs will usually be in a powerful position.

This raises questions about the circumstances under which the voter's discretion is limited and the circumstances under which it is less so. It also raises important questions about the balance of power among capital, labor, and environmental interests. These questions can be resolved by a consideration of the locational relationships essential to local welfare at diverse geographical scales; i.e., at different scales of "locality."

Figure 4.1   Rhodesia in Its Current Context

NOTE: Rhodesia makes contact with hostile forces except in the south. The closure of the ports of Beira and Lourenco Marques has diverted most Rhodesian trade into a more circuitous route through South African ports such as Durban and East London.

International Level   At the international level major concerns are of a bread-and-butter character: generate sufficient personal income to enable one to live at his or her accustomed standard. This necessitates policies that will attract investment funds to the national turf.

It is not difficult to see why this should be necessary. At the international level relocation possibilities, for both cultural and institutional reasons, are extremely limited. If national policy fails to encourage investment, therefore, there are only slight possibilities of relocating to where capital *has* chosen to lodge. The absence of income redistributional mechanisms at the international level intensifies dependence on investment in the national turf. There is, for example, no international income tax. Failure to attract jobs therefore will not result in a compensating inflow of unemployment compensation from those countries that have been more successful in the competition for investment funds.

This, of course, gives substantial power to owners of capital. If appropriate national policies are not forthcoming, capital will threaten to disinvest and put its money into countries where policies are more appropriate. For labor this is a convincing argument and frequently provides for the margin of political victory over environmental lobbies.

In addition to capital, however, other interests of an external nature may find their power enhanced. Countries, for example, may face hostile neighbors posing a threat to security and necessitating burdensome taxes for national defense. Capital will tend to avoid these countries. Business people want low tax burdens, physical security for their investments, and secure and inexpensive communication links with the outside world.

In this regard the situations of Rhodesia and Israel are especially significant. Both countries are experiencing capital flight and capital avoidance due to serious problems with neighboring states; both are consequently being forced into negotiations with those capable of terminating hostilities and restoring a more propitious business climate.

In the Rhodesian situation, white minority rule has provoked the ire of dissident groups among the black majority. Neighboring states of Zambia and Mozambique (figure 4.1) have provided bases for black Rhodesian guerrillas spreading terror among whites. At the same time Mozambique has cut off a major trade link, forcing Rhodesian trade into a more circuitous route through South Africa, while Zambia has diverted its trade away from the Indian Ocean to the Atlantic, hurting the business of the Rhodesian railways. As a result of these specific acts and a more general international trade boycott, Rhodesia is no longer an attractive business location. Investment has dried up and firms are moving operations elsewhere, forcing the government to try to come to terms with the black majority.

In the case of Israel the immediate threat comes from Palestinian guerrillas operating largely out of Syria and Jordan (figure 4.2). In addition there is an internal threat of civil insurrection among the Arab populations of the West Bank. Perhaps more important still is the threat of invasion from Egypt on the one hand and Syria on the other. Guerrilla attacks have made everyday life hazardous for many Israelis. Massive military expenditures necessitated by Israel's international situation have resulted in very high taxes and runaway inflation. As a consequence both physical capital and human capital have

Figure 4.2   Israel in Its Current Context

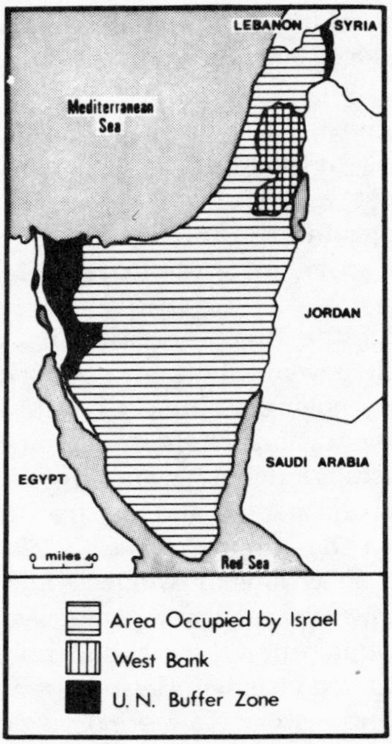

Area Occupied by Israel

West Bank

U. N. Buffer Zone

NOTE: Israel confronts guerrillas operating out of Lebanon and Jordan and the threat of invasion from Egypt and Syria. In addition there is the threat of civil insurrection among the Arab population of the West Bank.

tended to avoid Israel. Notably, for the first time in its history Israel is now losing population by outmigration. In Israel, therefore, the resources necessary for maintaining the current standard of living, let alone for improving it, are less and less at hand. Not surprisingly there is an increasing awareness of the need to come to terms with the Palestinian guerrillas and with neighboring Arab states.

Over the shorter time period, of course, the dominance of owners of capital in the political process may not be so evident. Environmentalists may win what appear signal victories, while labor may indulge in antibusiness policies of nationalization or high corporation taxes, for example. Over the longer term, however, those engaging in these policies will find both that disinvestment is slowly taking place and that the ability of the country to keep its physical stock of machinery and equipment in competitive shape is seriously vitiated. This has been the case in postwar Britain.

Intranational Level   At the intranational level, on the other hand, the trade-off between private income and residential quality concerns seems to be more in the direction of the latter. Local government may find itself under pressure to keep out industries that would be environmentally detracting in terms of noise, pollution, or esthetics. In other jurisdictions residents may oppose policies such as increased residential development that are promoted by local business interests: for instance, shopkeepers, public utilities, builders, and real estate developers.

It is not difficult to see why environmental groups should be more powerful at this level. Physical mobility means that the place of work can be spatially separated from the place of residence. Workers commute over long distances: in American metropolitan areas a fifteen-mile, one-way commuting distance is not unusual, while a minority may drive over fifty miles, one-way, to a distant metropolitan center. As a consequence protection of the environment with respect to the place of residence does not detract from the necessity for access to the means of physical survival.

Workers, of course, face problems if employment opportunities within commuting distance evaporate. The problem nevertheless is vastly different from that existing at the international level. They can, for example, relocate to other parts of the country where work is more readily available. Alternatively, unemployment compensation may provide a cushion while one waits for new business investment in the surrounding area. All this serves to drain off labor's antagonism toward environmental interests.

This is not to say that labor may still not find itself susceptible to the blandishments of industry. In one-industry towns or regions, for example, attempts to control air pollution have been met by industry threats to relocate elsewhere. Clearly this implies massive dislocation for the local labor force and for local business interests catering to their immediate consumption needs. In these cases labor has tended to ally itself with business interests, and environmental lobbies have been soundly defeated.

On the whole, environmental interests are nevertheless substantially more powerful at intranational levels. In some cases they may find their strength enhanced by labor and business groups outside their own geographical locus of interest. Keeping strip mining out of Colorado, Wyoming, and Montana, for example, is of interest not only to local amenity groups but also to West Virginia coal miners: concentrating national coal production in West Virginia's shaft-mining area improves the market position of coal mined there and allows miners to exert upward pressure on wages. Not surprisingly, federal attempts to pass legislation limiting strip mining in the West have met with strong support from West Virginia's congressional delegation.

In urban areas local environmental groups opposed to the construction of new suburban shopping centers may find a surprising source of support: operators of existing shopping centers and local chambers of commerce. Environmental interests, after all, limit the opportunities available for new business location. They therefore help to provide existing businesses and labor forces with a monopoly position translating into increased profits and wages.

Clearly, though, the intranational political arena does not exist in isolation from that at the international level. At the international level the major concern appears to be attracting business investment. At the local level major concerns appear to be trying to push it off onto other communities so as to maintain the tranquility, cleanliness, and healthfulness of the environment. Obviously there is an incompatibility here: if local communities are rejecting industrial development on environmental grounds, then the national government will have difficulty attracting investment. Sooner or later, through no fault of any particular local community, the national population will find, say, that its rate of economic growth is sluggish and unemployment is increasing.

Some mechanism is, therefore, required for reconciling national and local policies that could, apparently, be in conflict. In the United States the mechanism fulfilling this function is home rule. Local governments have to fund relatively large proportions of their spending from locally raised revenue. As a consequence tax base considerations loom large. In this respect business investment is, more often than not, rather attractive: it usually contributes more in revenue to local government than the value of the public expenditures its presence in the jurisdiction necessitates. In more middle-class jurisdictions this is a less-important argument. Middle-class households can be fiscally more self-sufficient: they provide more in revenue due to the larger amounts of real estate they consume; in addition, and in contrast to low-income households, they generate only small demands for local public safety and welfare expenditures. Voters in middle-class jurisdictions, therefore, exhibit increased discretion and are more likely to be influenced by environmental considerations of noise, congestion, and pollution than are low-income jurisdictions. As a result, business investment in American metropolitan areas, particularly the more environmentally obnoxious varieties, tends to lodge in more tax-base-sensitive and less environmentally conscious low-income jurisdictions (Williams et al. 1965, ch. 7; Peterson 1973, p. 131).

In Britain the mechanism for reconciling national policies of attracting investment and local policies of excluding the environmentally obnoxious is rather different. It consists of central government monitoring of local land use control policies. The central government has the right, as specified by the juridical context, to intervene in local government's land use decisions where it regards them as not in the national interest. In more cases than not, this intervention has been on the side of business interests rather than that of environmental groups. In these cases, therefore, local policies—and the interests whose bargaining power determines local policies—are frustrated by the juridical context.

JURIDICAL CONTEXT

Bargaining power, then, is a necessary but insufficient consideration in explaining the specific policies governments implement. Whether a preferred policy can be obtained is also limited by existing constitutional law. Powerful interests may desire various policies so as to attract the utility enhancing into their area; but only policies permitted within the existing juridical context are feasible. A local government, for example, may be able to respond to middle-class demands for an exclusionary zoning ordinance, since the states have delegated the land use control function to local governments. That same local government, however, may be unable to respond to the demands of the local chamber of commerce for a public works program simply because, for example, it has already reached the bonded debt limit mandated by the state.

Similar possibilities and preemptions are apparent at the state level. According to the U.S. Constitution, states may not engage in policies limiting interstate commerce. An attempt by the state of New York to cut back its welfare expenditures by imposing a residency requirement of one year on welfare applicants was struck down by the Supreme Court on precisely these grounds. States do however have considerable discretion over taxation policy, though their ability to introduce more progressive forms of business taxation is seriously limited by the bargaining resource considerations discussed earlier; i.e., businesses will threaten to move to states with more advantageous taxation climates (Alyea 1969).

Where preferred policies are precluded by the nature of the juridical context, the only feasible alternative for an interest group is to press for a change in that body of law. Under these circumstances power relations are again important—only more so.

In order to change the juridical context under which firms, individual households, and governments operate, construction of a winning coalition may be far more difficult. Such change frequently involves a constitutional amendment and, therefore, necessitates more than a simple majority in the appropriate legislature. In addition, vested interests grow fat under the status quo; they are, therefore, likely vigorously to oppose change. Changes in the juridical context are more radical and touch a wider range of interests in a more intense fashion than changes in policy. As a consequence, coalition building is a considerably more arduous task.

Under these conditions local organizations, which ordinarily find themselves competing with each other for policies allowing them to attract the utility enhancing onto their respective turfs, find that they have certain interests in common, but interests that are not shared by still other local organizations. At the state level, for example, the chambers of commerce and governments of all the central cities in the state may find that they have much in common when it comes to changing the rules governing land use control policy. Likewise, suburban local governments and respective chambers of commerce may find they have a quite different set of shared interests. Ordinarily local governments compete to attract the fiscally enhancing. Central city and suburban governments, therefore, have competed with each other. Overall, advantages have tended to lie with suburban local governments. This owes a great deal to the fact that discretion over land use control has been delegated by the state to local governments. This has allowed suburbs to zone land and hence to compete for fiscally advantageous business uses with central city governments; this, of course, is of interest to central city chambers of commerce, since it has provided unwelcome business competition for their members.

An alteration in the juridical context involving reallocation of the land use planning function to metropolitan planning boards would tend to alter these relationships. Central city interests—governments and chambers of commerce, for example—would now have some input into suburban zoning designations and rezoning decisions. The direction in which this input would go can easily be imagined.

As a result these proposals would be vigorously opposed by suburban local governments, suburban chambers of commerce, and all other interest groups gaining from the current decentralization of land use control. Advantages deriving from the juridical context are considerably more enduring and touch far more interests in a far more intense fashion than those deriving from policies conducted according to that corpus of law. As a consequence the coalitions involved in contesting it are likely to be considerably larger. They will of necessity consist of coalitions of different localized interests, each concerned about securing such change in the law as will facilitate its ability to attract the beneficial into its geographic area of interest.

Concluding Comments

The juridical context regulates government policies. These have important implications for welfare, since they set up both geographical differentials in investment opportunities in the private market and also differentials in residential quality. At the same time the juridical context permits individuals and businesses to respond to these differentials. The relocations subsequently set in motion result in localized welfare impacts on more stable elements of the population. Some of these elements may in turn relocate; others may be inhibited from so doing and will turn to the political process as a means of altering locational relations to their advantage once more.

Individuals, therefore, join with others who are similarly impacted to press for either a change in the juridical context or a policy change—one, moreover, that allows them to attract onto their respective turfs the utility enhancing and to keep out the undesirable. There is, therefore, a competition in the political process between interest groups representing different geographical areas and also between interest groups representing different conceptions of the utility enhancing. Business, labor, and environmental groups were the various interests referred to in this context.

Whether an interest group can secure the changes it wants will depend partly on the votes it can offer governments. The ability to obtain changes ultimately enhancing to local welfare depends in the first place on the ability to build a winning coalition. This may depend on the votes of interest group members themselves, or it may depend on the ability to manipulate resources crucial to the welfare of the voting population at large. At the international level business interests have considerable power, since they may threaten to invest their capital in other countries unless appropriate policies come forth. The immobility of labor with respect to international boundaries usually wins labor interest groups over to the views of business in this regard. At more local levels, however, the physical separation of work place and residence, made possible by physical mobility, permits a greater degree of voter discretion. As a consequence environmental groups are considerably more powerful here than at the international level.

The second consideration constraining the ability of interest groups to get what they want from governments resides in the juridical context. The ability of a government to respond in ways that interest groups would prefer is limited by law. The only way an interest group can get the policies it wants may be through obtaining a change in the juridical context that will, in its turn, make those policies possible. Changes in juridical provision, however, have much more intense effects on utilities than simple changes in policy. Attempts to change them, therefore, will necessitate the aggregation of like-minded local interest groups into broad coalitions capable of defeating the representatives of those localities happening to benefit from the status quo.

This chapter concludes the elaboration of our basic conceptual structure. We now turn and examine public problems, in both a descriptive and analytic mode, at international, intranational, and metropolitan scales.

Select Bibliography

Berkman, Richard L., and Viscusi, W. Kip. *Damming the West.* New York: Grossman, 1973.

Cuomo, Mario. *Forest Hills Diary: The Crisis of Low-Income Housing.* New York: Vintage, 1975.

Fellmeth, Robert C. *Politics of Land.* New York: Grossman, 1973.

Lineberry, Robert L. "Suburbia and the Metropolitan Turf." *Annals of the American Academy of Political and Social Science* 422 (November 1975): 1-9.

Miller, S. M., et al. "Creaming the Poor." *Trans-Action* 7, no. 8 (June 1970): 38-45.

Ridgeway, James. *The Politics of Ecology.* New York: Dutton, 1971.

Thane, Pat. "The History of Social Welfare." *New Society* 29, no. 621 (August 29, 1974): 540-42.

PART TWO

The International Level

Part 2 considers public problems arising from the interrelationships of nation states. Chapter 5 identifies and describes these public problems; the next two chapters attempt to explain them in terms of international competition structured by a juridical context observed unilaterally by individual nation states. Then chapter 6 examines the basis of such competition and the variety of national policies exemplifying it, and finally chapter 7 examines the outcomes of international competition.

Chapter Five

Location and Public Problems
at the International Level

This chapter identifies four major public problems: (1) international disparities in material welfare; (2) global resource problems; (3) problems of national self-determination; and (4) international jurisdiction problems. It should be made clear, however, that these problems are to some degree abstractions. Concrete world problems—such as relationships between the more industrialized nation states and the countries of the Third World—are frequently manifestations of more than one of the more general problems identified here.

International Disparities in Material Welfare

Most of the world's population lives in poverty alongside a rather wealthy minority concentrated in the nation states of North America, Europe, Australasia, and Japan. Some sense of these disparities can be gained rather quickly from the following facts: 70 percent of the world's population subsists on only 30 percent of the world's income. Other facts serve to underline this conclusion. An American baby consumes fifty times more of the world's resources than an Indian baby. In the poor countries per capita grain consumption averages about 400 pounds a year, little of which can be spared for conversion into animal protein. In the United States and Canada grain consumption is approaching one ton a year, of which only 150 pounds are consumed directly and the rest, as meat, milk, and eggs. Some sense of variations in levels of material welfare is provided by the differences in consumption levels from one nation to another presented in figure 5.1. Quite clearly the countries of North America, northwestern Europe, and Australasia are substantially better off than the rest of the world.

Internation disparities in private income are reflected in the tax bases of different countries and, therefore, in their ability to provide education and public health services. Consequently, when one speaks

Figure 5.1 Annual Consumption per Capita, by Nation, 1967 (in U.S. dollars)

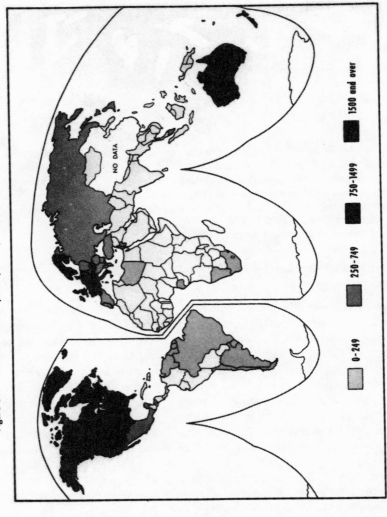

0-249 250-749 750-1499 1500 and over

SOURCE: After Coates et al., *Geography and Inequality*, p. 25.

of the less-developed countries (LDCs) of the world, one refers not simply to populations with lower incomes; in addition, their populations are illiterate and ill protected from the contagious diseases of cholera, smallpox, and typhoid, which were eliminated many years ago from the wealthier countries of the world. Figures 5.2 and 5.3 provide a clear illustration of these relations. Figure 5.2 identifies variations in infant mortality rates from one nation to another. Figure 5.3 provides some indication of the international geography of health provision. Note that both distributions reflect those variations in material welfare portrayed in figure 5.1.

Internation disparities in levels of material welfare and public provision of this character have been a source of growing discontent among the more articulate in LDCs. Many LDC spokesmen, for example, relate their own poverty to the existence of these disparities, claiming they are poor simply because the developed countries (DCs) are rich. A frequent argument is that the poverty of LDCs is a legacy of exploitation by more developed countries: exploitation that was first apparent in the nineteenth-century imperialistic ventures of Northern Hemisphere nations and that has since been apparent in the manipulations of multinational corporations and other forms of so-called neocolonialism (Cockroft, Frank & Johnson 1972).

The statistics used to demonstrate the magnitude of disparities in material welfare should nevertheless be regarded with some caution. The statistic commonly employed is the gross national product (GNP) per capita, or the value of all goods and services produced in a society divided by the total population of the nation. As a measure of national welfare this statistic—like the per capita consumption statistic on which figure 5.1 is based—may leave much to be desired and probably exaggerates differences in well-being between rich and poor nations. The observation that GNP per capita in the United States in 1967 was \$3,670 and in India only \$90 almost certainly overstates welfare differentials.

For a start, GNP includes only those goods and services entering into a money economy. LDCs, on the other hand, have large subsistence sectors and much trade is by barter. The value of most of the food consumed in LDCs, therefore, tends not to find its way into estimates of GNP, as it would in more developed nations.

A second problem with GNP is that, as a consequence of economic growth, many services are designed merely to offset the disadvantages of living in a rich and complex society. Can it reasonably be said, for instance, that medical treatment for injuries sustained in an auto accident or taxes paid for traffic control represent additions to social welfare? More logically, it would seem that they should not be counted at all, since without the *illfare* effects of economic development they would not have been needed.

Figure 5.2   Infant Mortality Rates by Nation, 1970 (deaths under one year of age per 1,000 live births)

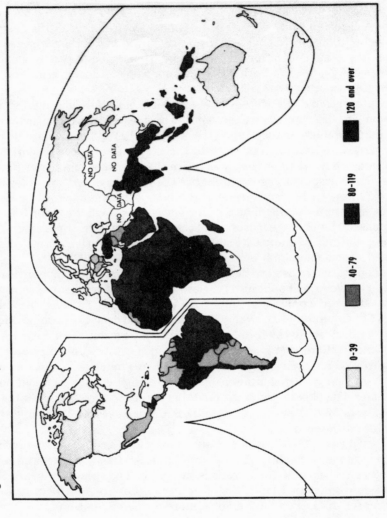

0-39   40-79   80-119   120 and over

SOURCE: After Coates et al., *Geography and Inequality*, p. 27.

Figure 5.3   Medical Care, by Nation, 1970 (population per physician)

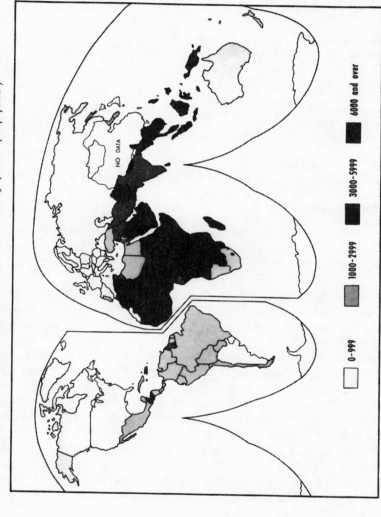

NO DATA

0-999

1000-2999

3000-5999

6000 and over

SOURCE: After Coates et al., *Geography and Inequality*, p. 29.

Table 5.1   Differences in Life Conditions According to Annual Income per Capita

	1	2	3	4	5	6
Annual Income in $ per head	1,000 +	576–1,000	351–575	201–350	100–200	100
Total population in millions	275	340	165	320	270	1,390
Life expectancy	71	68	65	57	50	45
Infant deaths in first year per 1,000 live births	24	34	68	75	100	150
Caloric consumption per head (in 1,000 units)	3.2	2.8	2.8	2.5	2.2	2.0
Carbohydrate content of food (%)	44	52	60	72	68	82

SOURCE: Reprinted from Paul Streeten, "How Poor Are the Poor Countries?" in Dudley Seers and Leonard Joy, eds., *Development in a Divided World* (Harmondsworth, Middlesex: Pelican Original, 1971), p. 73. Reprinted by permission of Penguin Books Ltd, © Penguin Books Ltd, 1970.

And, third, there is the problem of defense expenditure. This is largely concentrated in the wealthier nations of the globe and is one of the "services" the value of which is added to GNP. Can these expenditures, however, be regarded as additions to national welfare? Do Americans feel better off as a result of the vast amount of money spent on military equipment? Would they be better off if less were spent? Almost certainly they would be if other nations did likewise. Defense expenditures, therefore, may detract from national welfare rather than add to it, and their inclusion in measures of national product is dubious at best.

Despite these qualifications, it is clear that there are appreciable variations in material standards and that these have real and drastic effects on measures of welfare such as life expectancy and diet (Seers 1971; Streeten 1971). Table 5.1 presents some relevant data for nations classified into six groups according to income per capita in dollars. Not only is the variability appalling (infant mortality is 150 per 1,000 at live birth in the poorest countries, as compared to 24 in the wealthiest), but in addition the overwhelming majority of the world's population lives under these conditions. Not only is infant mortality higher; life expectancy is lower and caloric intake is substantially less. Even then diet in poorer nations is biased away from proteins and towards carbohydrates, giving rise to a variety of protein and vitamin deficiencies.

In a sense, however, these disparities are part of a broader global resource/population problem. For, even if there were no international disparities in levels of material welfare, the population of the world would still face critical resource problems, as we shall see in the next section.

Global Resource Problems

Global resource problems can be outlined briefly. The world's population is growing rapidly. While, as a result of cheap public health measures, death rates have been reduced drastically, birth rates continue at relatively high levels over much of the world but particularly in LDCs (figure 5.4). At present rates of increase (1978), world population will double in forty-one years. While the number of mouths to feed increases, however, world resources are finite. World production of food can be increased to cope with the increased demand but only over a short time period. As demand increases, the world will ultimately be unable to support the needs of its population. To increase food supply, for instance, increased use of fertilizers, irrigation, and insecticides will be required. This will mean more industrial output, which, however, depends on the availability of raw materials such as oil for fertilizers and metal for irrigation pipes: raw materials that will be in increasingly short supply as oil reserves and minerals are exhausted. At the same time industrial output creates pollution, which again reduces the livability of the planet. Oil spills and oceanic pollution eliminate the marine plants, which create 70 percent of the world's constantly renewed oxygen. As pollution of the ocean occurs, so its utility as a source of edible fish deteriorates.

Aggravating the global pollution problem is the fact that most of the nations of the world have opted for an industrialization approach to solving their resource problems. By investing in industry their hope is that not only can food be imported, but rising standards of living will also be possible on the basis of constantly rising productivity. This not only begs the question, Where is the food to be imported from if all nations seek to go the industrialization route without limiting their populations?; it also places a further burden on the world's finite mineral and energy resources.

This conjuncture of events has given rise to various forms of neomalthusianism: predictions that population will inevitably outstrip the life support system of the globe, resulting in widespread

Figure 5.4   Annual Rates of Population Increase, by Nation, 1971

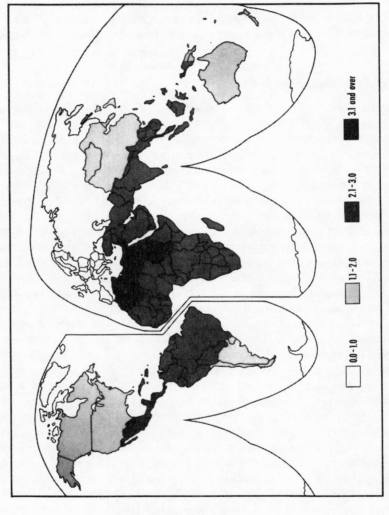

0.0 - 1.0   1.1 - 2.0   2.1 - 3.0   3.1 and over

SOURCE: After John F. Kolars and John D. Nystuen, *Human Geography* (New York: McGraw-Hill, 1974), p. 7.

Figure 5.5   Projected Relationship Between Global Population and Resources

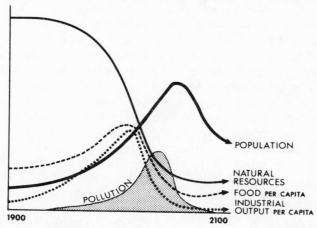

POPULATION

NATURAL
RESOURCES
FOOD PER CAPITA
INDUSTRIAL
OUTPUT PER CAPITA

POLLUTION

1900   2100

SOURCE: After *Time Magazine*, 24 January 1972, p. 32.

famine and health disasters until some new, lower level equilibrium
between population and resources can be achieved (Heilbroner 1974).
Figure 5.5 illustrates graphically one such neomalthusian scenario:
that associated with the study, "The Limits to Growth," sponsored
by the Club of Rome. Based on projected growth rates for population,
natural resources, food per capita, and industrial output per capita,
the study puts the cataclysm somewhere halfway into the twenty-
first century (Meadows & Meadows 1972).

Neomalthusian views call for a variety of national policies, all
designed to reduce pressure on world resources. Fundamentally,
these policies reduce to two: (1) population control through equalizing
birth and death rates; (2) a shift from a growth-oriented economy to a
no-growth economy. Current national economies, whether of the private capitalist or state capitalist variety, tend to have as their overall
effect an increase in the level of goods consumed per capita. Increasing consumption is based on increasing production: in turn, increasing production depends on the continuing extraction of nonrenewable
resources and on the increasing use of air and water for waste
disposal.

In a no-growth economy, however, the link between consumption
and the running down of nonrenewable resources and increasing
pollution would tend to be broken (Boulding 1966). This would be accomplished in a variety of ways. First, consumption levels would not
be allowed to increase; this would reduce pressure on production and
hence on nonrenewable resources. Second, the link between production on the one hand and pollution and the extraction of nonrenewable resources on the other would be weakened.

The latter could be achieved, for example, by shifting to nonexhaustible, nonpolluting resources like solar and tidal power. Recycling raw materials such as the lead in car batteries and the paper in newsprint represent other possibilities. Animal and human excreta would readily substitute as fertilizer for nonrenewable phosphates and other artificial fertilizers. Finally, consumer goods could be made more durable than they presently are. Currently, a major force for increased consumption and, hence, for increased production and exploitation of nonrenewable resources is the phenomenon of built-in obsolescence. In order to increase demand for its products, the market economy has tended to make use of strategies limiting product life. These techniques may include physical obsolescence; that is, the product wears out more quickly than necessary. It is rumored that, given current production technology, it is possible to produce an everlasting light bulb; clearly such an innovation is hardly in the interests of electric light bulb producers. Alternatively, shifts in fashion may serve to deflect demand away from the still-relatively-new-but-outmoded to that for which advertising has created an aura of increased desirability.

Obviously, shifting economies to a no-growth basis faces tremendous obstacles. Above, for example, we indicated the interest of the market economy in stimulating demand—a stimulation that is not consistent with the idea of a no-growth economy. This should not avert attention, however, from the fact that the consumer has become a willing conniver in the growth economy. Economic growth is the new god. People expect a continuing increase in their standard of living, and when they fail to get it governments suffer loss of popularity. In brief, any attempt to shift to a no-growth economy and hold consumption levels constant involves an immense re-education program to wean people away from their dependence on a consumer cornucopia. Given public sentiment in favor of growth, it seems unlikely that the vast sums needed for such a program could ever be appropriated.

There are, however, other more optimistic viewpoints on the global resource problem, viewpoints that those who would most suffer from a no-growth economy have been quick to embrace. A number of writers, among whom Wilfred Beckerman, the British economist, is one of the more prominent (Beckerman 1974), find the neomalthusian prognoses of doom far from proven and, in fact, likely to be controverted by the verdict of history. This rebuttal is based partly on what we know about the way in which market economies react to scarcity and partly on our knowledge of human reproductive behavior.

Market economies, for example, tend to react to scarcity of raw materials by an increased investment in the search for new sources or substitutes. Consequently, numerous neomalthusian scares of the past have not been substantiated by eventualities. A U.S. government study, published in 1944, for example, warned that the country would run out of tin, nickel, zinc, lead, and manganese by 1973. Clearly, this has not occurred. One can also foresee market reactions to the ultimate exhaustion of fossil fuels: the development of solar power, tidal power, and wind power. Already domestic solar power units are being marketed in the United States.

Likewise, increased pollution control will give industry incentives to devise less pollution-intensive technologies or shift to raw materials, creating less waste. To some extent, this may be happening already. According to Beckerman, pollution in London has been cut since 1960 by 85 percent, doubling the hours of winter sunshine and adding fifty-five species of fish to a hitherto lifeless river Thames.

There is also the issue of human reproductive behavior. A major role in the antimalthusian reaction is assigned to the concept of the *demographic transition* (Chung 1970). Studies of population growth and its correlates suggest that nation states typically run through a common scenario. At low levels of material welfare, birth rates tend to exceed death rates, resulting in the high population growth rates apparent today in South Asia and much of Latin America. As economic development occurs and urbanization takes place, however, death rates fall again; but birth rates fall still further (figure 5.6). As a result, according to Beckerman, population growth rates in more developed countries should have leveled off by the 1980s.

This antimalthusian viewpoint, however, is more than a feasible scenario of global development. It is also fodder for those who would lose from the implementation of no-growth policies: and many, particularly in LDCs, *would* lose. For a start, consider the context posed by the interdependence of nations. Nations depend on each other for certain products; and, given the connectedness of the world's oceans, water pollution in any given national jurisdiction ultimately affects persons elsewhere in the world. The success of no-growth policies in maintaining the long-term welfare of the world's population, therefore, depends on all nations' adopting them. Obviously, Sweden can clean up the Baltic Sea and restore its fish-producing capacity only if Denmark, East Germany, Poland and the other Baltic countries agree on antipollution policies. Likewise, an attempt to maintain real consumption in a particular nation state will be compromised if other nations continue to grow, raw materials become more scarce, and these scarcities are communicated by trade in the form of higher

Figure 5.6   The Demographic Transition

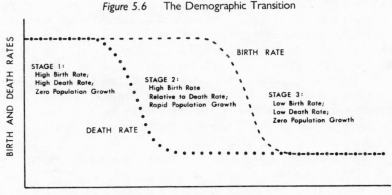

SOURCE: After Chung, "Space-Time Diffusion of the Transition Model," p. 222.

prices to the no-growth nation: under those circumstances real consumption levels in the no-growth nation would tend to fall.

Global agreement on no-growth policies, however, would be extremely difficult to attain. Freezing consumption levels would involve a bigger sacrifice for the population of LDCs than for those of DCs. As a consequence, no-growth policies tend to be seen by the LDCs as a serious threat to the future welfare of their peoples (Hines 1973, ch. 13).

Even adoption of no-growth policies by DCs alone is opposed to some degree. First, there is the problem that if environmental control policies are pursued at all seriously in DCs, there will be some substitution of environmental goods of clean air, clean water, and preserved landscapes for private goods. This will reduce rates of economic growth, thus reducing demand for the products of LDCs and at the same time exercising pressure on the funds available for aid programs. In LDCs there is, in fact, fear that the costs of environmental control policies will be absorbed by DCs in the form of reduced foreign aid commitments. Even if imports by DCs should continue to increase, moreover, there may be import pattern shifts that will hurt particular LDCs. Any reduction in the use of lead antiknock compounds in gasoline to reduce lead pollution, for instance, will have an immediate effect on the exports of lead-producing countries.

A second problem for LDCs is that they are dependent on DCs for the technologies they employ in agriculture and industry. New technologies currently being developed, however, reflect DC concern for environmental control. Technologies are likely to be substantially more expensive as a result, but LDCs will have to buy them, since nothing else will be available. As an example of this, it is quite conceivable that technology will develop in the direction of engine types in which considerable cost is incurred to keep emissions lower than DC clean air standards but much lower than LDCs would find optimal. It is considerations such as these that have led to the view that LDCs must attempt to develop and adopt, or be assisted in developing and adopting, more intermediate, less capital-intensive technologies more fitted to local needs and economic circumstances (Schumacher 1975).

With respect to a solution to the global resource problem, therefore, there is a clear antipathy between the interests of the more developed countries and those of the LDCs. In the attempt to persuade the other side, a case has to be made out in terms of global interest. LDCs are not likely to support DC no-growth policies unless DCs can show how they will have positive effects on the welfare of LDCs and vice versa. In this context, the viewpoints discussed here assume immense significance. Antimalthusian views, for instance, provide useful supporting arguments for the LDCs; they afford an opportunity of convincing the DCs that economic growth policies do not represent a challenge to their long-term welfare. Neomalthusian views, on the other hand, provide sustenance for those who argue that no-growth policies are in the best interests of not only the DCs but also the LDCs.

Apparently, therefore, national reactions to the global resource problem hinge critically on questions of national sovereignty. It is to such questions that we now turn.

National Self-determination

Nation states have policy goals. With respect to the private incomes of their citizens, these goals include a commitment to economic growth and redistribution of income. Other goals may concern public provision: for example, spending on education, public health and environmental quality standards, or the preservation of a national language.

To some extent failure to achieve these goals can be laid at the door of the individual nation state and its citizens, who may not be willing to be taxed for increased educational expenditures. Alternatively, public expenditures may be characterized by gross miscalculations as to future payoff: Concorde and other national misadventures fall into this category. Other sources of national failure may stem from inefficiencies in the economic system: monopolistic markets, imperfect information, or the failure of labor to adjust to changing product demands.

The problem nevertheless must also be viewed within a context of global interdependence. Frustration of national goals may be attributable to forces beyond jurisdictional boundaries and over which individual governments have limited control. A concern for implementing nationally preferred policies, therefore, often expresses itself as a concern for national self-determination and control of all those forces affecting national fortunes.

The threat to national self-determination takes two major forms: (1) *de jure* restrictions on national sovereignty and (2) *de facto* restrictions. With respect to the former, for instance, sovereignty may be limited by membership in international organizations. Membership in a common market implies some forfeiture of sovereignty with respect to trade policy and labor policy, a forfeiture that, in the event, may turn out not to be in a particular member nation's interests. The United Kingdom, for example, feels that it has experienced some disutility as a result of forfeiting control over trade policy to the European Common Market; the automobile workers of Britain who face serious competition on their home ground from French, Italian, and German cars would almost certainly agree.

Most obviously, the sovereignty of colonies is seriously limited by imperial countries. Colonies, for instance, have no control over foreign affairs, and domestic economic life may be closely regulated by the imperial power. Complicating the issue of national self-determination in these countries, however, is internal conflict over precisely what national goals would be given independence. Critical here is the role of white settlers, who more than likely will have views as to the future conduct of national policy that are quite different from those held by the indigenous population. It is no accident, therefore, that the excolonial countries receiving independence first have tended to be those with only small white settler populations. In the French empire, Tunisia and Morocco received independence before Algeria. In the British Empire, Ghana, Nigeria, Uganda, and Tanzania received their independence before Kenya, where settler-native problems were serious. Southern Rhodesia, of course, where these problems have been particularly intractable, has yet formally to gain its independence.

Alternative to de jure restrictions on national sovereignty, one can envisage a set of de facto restrictions. Major problems here derive from foreign ownership of capital equipment, land, and minerals. At present, these concerns find their locus primarily in the multinational corporation. A common feeling among host nations is that multinational corporations have goals, characteristic operating procedures, and obligations to the nation states in which they are headquartered that inhibit the implementation of national policy (Vernon 1968).

More tangibly, de jure and de facto restrictions on national sovereignty may be threatening to both public provision for, and the private incomes of, a nation state's citizens. Consider, for example, the implications of multinational corporations for national economic growth objectives. Some states impose embargoes on trade with other countries. The U.S. government, for instance, prohibits U.S. companies from trading with Cuba. Until quite recently, there were similar restrictions on trade with Communist China. Consider now the case of a branch plant in Canada whose corporate headquarters is located in the United States. Assume further that Canada has a particular interest in trade with Cuba and encourages all firms in Canada to participate in such trade. Should American branch plants operating in Canada participate and so help to achieve Canadian trade goals? Most American multinational corporations have assumed that the rules under which they work in the United States also apply to their operations elsewhere. The outcome has been a substantial frustration of host-nation trade policy (Litvak & Maule 1969).

This is an even more serious impediment than it might at first appear. The products of a multinational corporation branch plant may be components in the finished product of some other plant located in a country that does *not* impose embargoes. If there is a desire to export the finished product to a country embargoed by the nation state in which the multinational corporation is headquartered, what should be the posture of the multinational corporation? Should an American branch plant located in the United Kingdom sell its diesel engines for use in the fabrication of British locomotives, which will then be sold to China? Experience suggests that in such cases multinational corporation branch plants tend to err on the side of caution.

De jure limitations on sovereignty pose similar problems for private incomes. The issue of monetary union for the common market countries of Western Europe (the European Economic Community or EEC) is particularly interesting in this regard. At present all member nations of the EEC have their own currencies and control of monetary policy: exchange rate policy, interest rate policy, money creation, etc. More visionary protagonists of the common market ideal, however, have foreseen the need for monetary union. They have called for this to be achieved by 1980. The basis of the idea is the need to maintain competition between member nations of the EEC. Control of monetary policy can be used for purposes of national subsidy. Currency devaluation, for instance, makes a nation's exports cheaper overseas than those of its competitors and makes imports more expensive than the domestically fabricated product. It is, therefore, a useful—albeit somewhat temporary—means of gaining an international competitive edge. Monetary policy in general, through interest rates and money creation, is a major means of sustaining national demand and, hence, full employment.

For precisely these reasons, monetary policy is unlikely to be yielded to a supranational authority without a good deal of opposition. Almost certainly, for instance, it would result in widespread variations in levels of employment among nations—variations that could be eliminated only by an international mobility of labor from labor-surplus to labor-deficit nations that only the most optimistic could project (Cooper 1968, ch. 7). The logical consequence of monetary union, therefore, would be a call for a redistribution mechanism by means of which transfers could be made from those member nations of the EEC benefiting more from EEC policy to those benefiting less. Such redistribution does not now exist and is unlikely in the foreseeable future.

Common markets pose similar problems for other national policies. If common markets are to function as they were intended and eliminate all restrictions on member nation accessibility to commodity markets, labor markets, and capital markets, then an extremely detailed, painstaking standardization of national regulations must occur. Only in this way can unfair competition be eliminated or attempts to secure national monopolies be forestalled. In the area of commodity markets, this calls for standardization of regulations regarding product content. National regulations designed to protect consumer health and safety, for example, vary considerably from one nation to another. Failure to eliminate these regulations would create advantageous market positions for firms in nations that had historically observed more stringent standards: not only would they be able to sell their goods domestically, but their goods would also pass the more lax consumer regulations in other countries. Considering that national regulations and standards presumably reflect nation-specific tastes, this cession of authority and resultant homogenization of standards would likely result in some welfare loss for individual member nations.

In the United Kingdom threats to national welfare have been expressed in issues of environmental quality. This is implicit, for example, in attempts to impose common standards on trucks and detergents. In both cases, it is felt, British standards show more solicitude for environmental quality than those of the rest of the Common Market. The issue with respect to road transportation concerns regulations on truck and axle weight. Clearly, if these are not homogenized, nation states with highly restrictive standards could limit trade by excluding trucks from nation states with less-restrictive standards. National variation in standards also limits international competition in truck transportation: nations with more restrictive standards would be making their domestic market a protected preserve for their own trucking companies. EEC standards call for a limit of 40 tons on overall weight and an axle weight of 11 tons. Pre-Common Market, British standards called for a substantially lower overall weight of 32 tons and an axle weight of 10 tons. These restrictive British standards are rationalized in terms of the damage heavy trucks impose on highways, on buildings in the narrow streets of English towns, and also in terms of the general noise, physical danger, and vibration created.

Standards for consumer goods also create barriers to trade. In Britain, for example, household detergents are almost 100-percent biodegradable and can be broken down into nonfoaming products in ordinary sewage treatment plants. The EEC standard for household detergents, however, is only 80 percent. Clearly, continental detergent manufacturers, in the absence of Common Market-wide standardization, will be at a considerable disadvantage relative to British manufacturers. On the other hand, and just as clearly, British water quality will suffer a deterioration.

Both de facto and de jure limitations on national sovereignty, therefore, can pose problems for the achievement of national goals. The irony is, however, that these limitations are often traded, perhaps unwittingly, for increased economic growth. Nation states, for example, join common markets in expectation of the increased economic efficiency resulting from greater competition among firms in the different member nations. Apparently, then, these issues raise important questions about the evolution of market relationships and the ability of individuals or groups of individuals to determine the conditions of their own existence.

International Jurisdiction Problems

The final set of problems to be considered concern those arising from conflicts among nations regarding their respective sovereignty, or lack of sovereignty, over some land or water (Luard 1970). Historically, conflicts over the assignment of jurisdiction with respect to land have been most common. Some of the more publicized of these disputes involve West Germany and Poland and also Israel and neighboring Arab states.

The dispute between West Germany and Poland dates back to the Potsdam agreements following World War II. According to the treaty imposed on Germany, Poland was permitted to extend its boundaries westward to include large portions of what had hitherto been German territory (figure 5.7). These included the rich agricultural

Figure 5.7   Disputed Eastern Territories

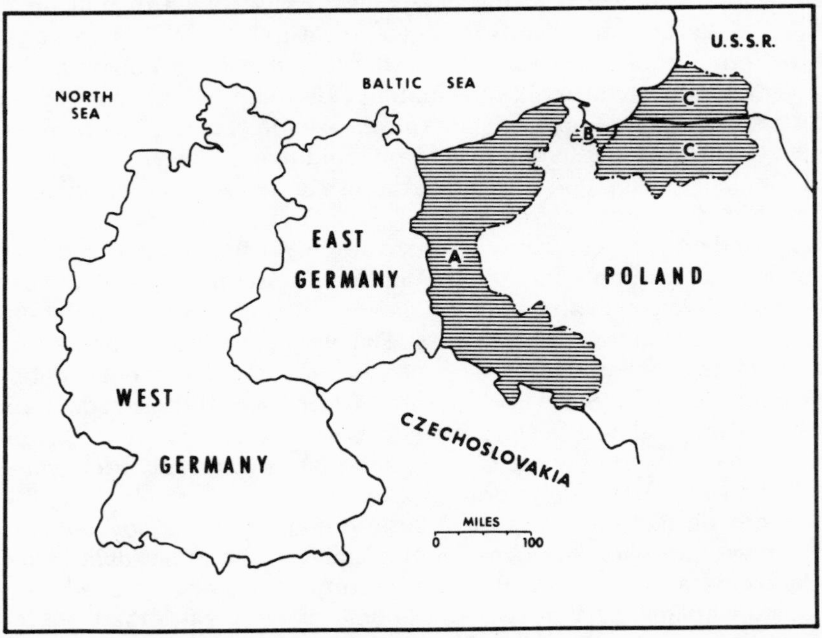

KEY: A = Pomerania and Silesia; B = Danzig; C = East Prussia.

lands of Silesia and lands in East Prussia symbolically significant to the Germans. At the time of this boundary extension, moreover, large numbers of Germans were expelled and made their way to refugee camps in East or, more frequently, West Germany. The latter has never accepted this boundary revision; and, to this day, official West German maps indicate the disputed territories as "Under Temporary Polish Administration." For right-wing political organizations and for refugee organizations in West Germany, the issue has been especially vexing (Wiskemann 1956).

In the case of Israel, the territorial disputants are several. The Palestine refugees claim much of the territory, since it was at one time the Arab state of Palestine. In 1948, however, with the declaration of the state of Israel and subsequent civil war, most of the Arab population of what had been Palestine were either expelled or they fled. Nearby Arab states such as Egypt intervened and began a long history of hostility marked by territorial gains by Israel. In addition to territorial disputes with the Palestine refugees, therefore, Israel now disputes land with the adjacent states of Egypt, Jordan, and Syria (figure 5.8).

Figure 5.8   Territorial Conflicts Between Israel and Adjoining States

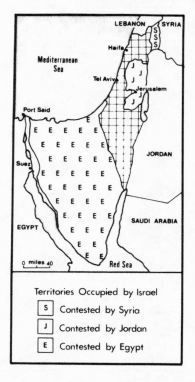

Territories Occupied by Israel

S	Contested by Syria
J	Contested by Jordan
E	Contested by Egypt

More recently, with the increasing exploitation of the world's oceans, conflicts over jurisdiction with respect to the sea have emerged as significant. One of the more publicized of these has been the dispute between Iceland and the United Kingdom. Iceland, extremely dependent on its fishing industry, has claimed an extension of its territorial waters to 200 miles. This would give the Icelandic fishing industry rights of exclusive access to the cod in that area; but it would also spell the demise of the British fishing industry, since the coastal zone around Iceland is the major source of British cod.

Peru and the United States have been locked in a similar dispute, though the issue is tuna rather than cod. The California tuna-fishing industry is heavily dependent on the coastal waters off Peru. Unfortunately, so is the Peruvian fish meal industry. Recent claims by Peru to a 200-mile fishing limit have, understandably, met with the opposition of California fishermen. For the U.S. government, however, the situation is rather more complicated. Although Californian fishing groups would like it to make an unequivocal stand in favor of, say, a 12-mile limit, the government has been under pressure, from

Figure 5.9   Bolivia's Struggle for an Ocean Outlet

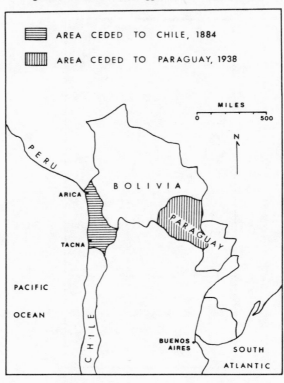

NOTE: Bolivia was not always cut off from navigable water. A war fought with Chile (1882–84) cut her off from the Pacific, while a war with Paraguay (1932–38) reduced her access to the navigable waters of the Paraguay that lead to the South Atlantic.

other parts of the country, to opt for the 200-mile limit. In New England, in particular, fishing fleets, dependent on coastal waters, have experienced intense competition from the Russians' long-distance fishing fleets. In 1977, therefore, the United States extended its fishing limits to 200 miles.

Clearly, many of these jurisdictional conflicts have a strong economic base. West Germany and Poland have disputed agricultural land; Iceland and Britain, rich coastal fisheries; Morocco and Spain, phosphate-rich areas of the Sahara. Bolivia meanwhile has fought wars with both Paraguay and Chile in its attempts to secure a trade outlet to the sea (figure 5.9) (Goblet 1936, ch. 8). What makes many of these territorial disputes particularly intractable, however, is the dependence of one or other of the protagonists on the real estate in question. The cod fisheries are absolutely vital to Iceland: over 80 percent of Iceland's exports come from exports of fish and fish products. Without control of the cod breeding grounds, Icelanders fear that the source of their wealth would be dissipated through overfishing by the British.

In other cases, where the offended parties have made adjustments in their economic life, the dispute has tended to lose much of its intractability. This has been so, for example, with the dispute between West Germany and Poland. The West German government spent large amounts of money on the assimilation of the refugees into the fabric of its economic life. Although revanchist organizations enjoyed considerable popularity among the refugees in the late 1940s and early 1950s, that support waned considerably with the West German economic miracle (Wiskemann 1956).

The dispute between Israel and the Palestine refugees provides an interesting contrast. In that instance, the displaced Arab populations have been grouped into refugee camps that, far from disappearing as in the German case, have grown by natural increase. The states within which the refugee camps are located—Syria, Jordan, Lebanon, and (at one time) Egypt—have neither tried to assimilate the refugees nor have their economies grown at a rate able to absorb the displaced populations. The result has been the continuing rancor, not to say bloodshed, with which we are all familiar.

Concluding Comments

At the international level, four major public problems have been identified. These include international disparities in material welfare; global resource problems; national self-determination; and problems of international jurisdiction.

The usual measure employed to indicate levels of material welfare is the GNP per capita. Although this probably exaggerates the degree of variation in welfare levels between poorer and wealthier nations, differences in life expectancy and infant mortality are, nevertheless, of a dramatic rather than modest character. These differences, moreover, are a source of growing discontent in LDCs. More articulate groups there relate the poverty of their countries to the wealth of other countries in a variety of theories of exploitation.

Problems of welfare disparities are further complicated by the global resource problem. Populations currently growing at a rapid rate look particularly ominous for the future of mankind when contrasted to the increasing depletion of the world's nonrenewable resources. One response to this problem has been neomalthusianism, emphasizing the need for programs of birth control and no-growth policies. By recycling of raw materials, the substitution of solar energy for nonrenewable energy resources, and re-education away from the blandishments of a consumer society, it is thought that the global population can live within the limits of a finite earth. Economic growth is, however, a double-edged sword. While for wealthier nations its resource-depleting effects may be most apparent, for poorer nations it represents the possibility of escape from poverty. LDCs, therefore, have shown themselves more willing to embrace anti-malthusian views of the future. These views emphasize the ability of the market mechanism to respond to shortage and the tendency for population growth to level off at higher levels of material welfare.

The third problem discussed was that of national self-determination. Nations are clearly limited in their ability to achieve policy goals by the restrictions of other nations or of international organizations. Two forms of restriction on national sovereignty were identified. Sovereignty may be limited in a de jure sense, as in common markets where there are attempts to limit national policies so as to eliminate national interference with the free play of commodity, labor, and capital markets. Alternatively, one can envisage de facto restrictions. These are associated with the operations of multinational corporations, the policies of the host country often coming into conflict with those of the country where the multinational corporation is headquartered. Ironically, however, such impediments to national self-determination are often traded, perhaps unwittingly, for an increase in economic growth and, hence, in national welfare overall.

Finally, we discussed problems of international jurisdiction. These involve conflicts over both terrestrial and oceanic resources. Most of them relate to the other problems discussed above in that they have an economic basis. They have proved especially intractable where one or other of the protagonists is particularly dependent on the contested resource.

Select Bibliography

Benoit, Emile. "The Attack on the Multinationals." *Columbia Journal of World Business* 7, no. 6 (November/December 1972): 15-22.

Dunning, John H. "The Future of the Multinational Enterprise." *Lloyds Bank Review*, no. 113, July 1974, pp. 15-32.

Hardin, Garrett. "The Tragedy of the Commons." *Science* 162 (December 13, 1968): 1243-48.

Heilbroner, Robert L. *An Inquiry into the Human Prospect.* New York: Norton, 1974.

Litvak, I. A., and Maule, C. J. "Conflict Resolution and Extraterritoriality." *Journal of Conflict Resolution* 13, no. 3 (September 1969): 305-19.

Robock, Stefan. "The Case for Home Country Controls over Multinational Firms." *Columbia Journal of World Business*, summer 1974, pp. 75–79.

Vernon, Raymond. "Problems and Policies Regarding Multinational Enterprises." In *United States Economic Policy in an Interdependent World: Papers Submitted to the Commission on International Trade and Investment Policy*. Vol. 1, pp. 983–1006. Washington, D.C.: Government Printing Office, 1971.

Chapter Six

International Competition: Basis and Process

In this chapter we consider the processes that could conceivably generate the problems identified in the last chapter. The view presented is that much insight can be gained by looking at processes of international competition for investment funds. Capital is important if governments are to achieve their goals of economic growth and job creation. Yet capital is volatile. On the other hand national populations are relatively immobile; and the harsh impacts of competition are not cushioned by a system of income redistribution among nations. These facts lend added urgency to the need to have capital lodge within the national boundaries.

In the first section of the chapter we briefly outline the global context of private markets and capital mobility, to which national policies represent an adjustment. We then examine the bases of international competition in terms of, for example, widely held national goals and the immobility of national populations. The third and final section looks at some of the specific policies designed to entice capital into the national confines.

Global Context

At the international level a context for an understanding of public problems is provided by the organization of the global economy. To a very large degree this is according to the dictates of private markets. Increasingly, real incomes are determined by market forces: wages, profit rates, rents, and commodity prices are the outcome of supply-and-demand conditions at an international scale. Wages for cotton textile workers in the Piedmont are affected by the price of cotton textiles produced in Hong Kong; rents for wheat land in the Great Plains are affected by grain prices in Western Europe; the profitability of a synthetic rubber plant in Akron, Ohio, is affected by the magnitude of the Malaysian rubber crop.

These supply-and-demand relationships moreover link government buying agencies into one global network, just as much as they link individuals. To an increasing degree the so-called "socialist"

countries of Eastern Europe, China, Cuba, and the USSR are tied into the world market system. Whether Russians will queue for bread is
more and more dependent on world wheat prices; and these are more
and more a function of harvests in Canada, the United States,
and—to a lesser degree—Australia and Argentina. Likewise the economic prospects of the Cubans depend both on the magnitude of the
sugar crop in the rest of the Caribbean and on the size of the U.S.
sugar beet crop.

Global prices and factor returns, therefore, are determined by
movements of goods and capital, evening out scarcities in different
countries in the manner described in chapter 3. A relative scarcity of,
for example, grain in Western Europe compared with North America
increases the price American grain merchants can get on the Western
European market relative to what they can get in North America.
The result is a flow of grain across the Atlantic: this makes grain
more scarce in North America, driving prices up, and less scarce in
Western Europe, driving prices down.

The most significant movements for an understanding of international problems, however, are those of capital: this is true whether the
capital is private or public, liquid or embodied in the form of human
skills. Private capital in the form of liquid assets, for example, is
mobile among national jurisdictions (Dunning 1972). A company
headquartered in one country may invest in a plant in another. Individuals may purchase shares in foreign firms or banks may lend
money to foreigners.

There is, of course, a pattern to capital flows. Private capital restlessly seeks out those national jurisdictions where returns to capital
will be maximized and forsakes those where profitability rates are
reduced. As a consequence, it tends to be attracted into those nation
states where business enterprise has some sort of cost advantage in
global markets; where labor is cheap and disciplined—for instance, as
in Singapore and Hong Kong; or where there is an abundance of mineral wealth, as in Canada. Capital, therefore, tends to leave nation
states where profit rates are low and, hence, where capital is less
scarce for countries where profit rates are higher and, therefore,
where capital is more scarce. The result of this movement is the
equalization of profit rates discussed in chapter 3. There are exceptions to this: Israel, for instance, attracts some capital for purely
sentimental reasons. More importantly there are differences in profit
rates that stem from differences in risk. These will be discussed
below.

Of course, *private* international investment is less important now
than it was, say, seventy-five years ago; and *public* international investment is considerably more important (Dunning 1972, ch. 2). Low

interest loans, interest-free loans and, occasionally, outright grants from international banks established by DCs are not an insignificant source of capital for LDCs. Similar commercial criteria nevertheless tend to apply in the disbursement of such funds as in private capital movements. Agencies often lend for specific projects and, given the finite resources at their disposal, they will be eager to put their money where expected rates of return are highest and, hence, where they can be reasonably sure of getting their money out (Payer 1974).

Liquid assets account for by far the largest fraction of the capital that moves from one country to another. In considering the context of public problems at the international level, however, it would be shortsighted to ignore the role of capital embodied in human form (Committee on International Migration of Talent 1970). The concept of "brain drain," according to which labor is educated and trained at public expense in one country and then moves to another country offering a higher wage, is an important one. Brain drains represent a significant source of capital gain for some nation states and of capital loss for others (figure 6.1). Between 1949 and 1967, for example, the United States imported 100,000 doctors, scientists, and engineers from developing or developed nations. This equaled an educational and training cost of $4,000 million. It has been estimated that this foreign aid to the United States is greater than the total U.S. aid to foreign countries over that period of time. In medicine alone foreign doctors account for 20 percent of annual additions to the U.S. medical profession (Titmuss 1968, p. 126).

International shifts of human capital are more important than they might at first appear. Maintaining preeminence in global markets depends more and more on developing new products over which a country can claim a monopoly—however short-lived that monopoly might turn out to be. As a result technically skilled manpower is increasingly at a premium.

Flows of this nature, however, merely provide the backdrop for specific national policies designed to divert them to parochial ends. But what are those ends and how can we explain their parochiality?

International Competition

The major fact about the relationships between nation states is their competition to attract capital investment. The ultimate goals of this exercise are twofold: economic growth and jobs.

Economic growth is a goal apparently universal across the nations of the globe; it is pursued by socialist and capitalist economies, poor nations and rich nations, alike. Certainly increasing wealth, far

Figure 6.1   Brain Drain Flows into the United States

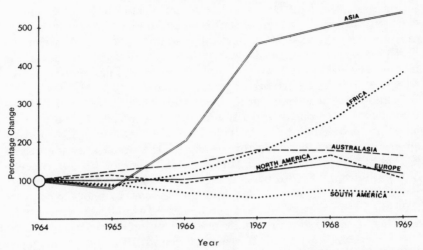

SOURCE: After Committee on International Migration of Talent, *Modernization and the Migration of Talent*, p. 26.

from dissipating the desire for material satisfactions, seems to augment it. Indeed the wealthier nation states are probably the more aggressive in their competition for more economic growth.

In the more developed nations competition for economic growth is allied with *competition for employment* (Cooper 1968, ch. 6). With the welfare state legislation of the 1930s and after, full employment became a primary goal of economic policy in those countries. This is not a concern shared to the same degree by LDCs. There the problem is likely to be one of underemployment rather than unemployment; typically the displaced industrial worker in the LDC returns to his native village and is reintegrated into the subsistence agricultural sector. In addition, full employment policies do not have the political urgency in LDCs that they have in DCs.

A more recent consideration injecting some complexity into the competition of wealthy nations for economic growth and employment has been the emergence of clean air, clean water, and landscape esthetics as important policy goals. This is likely to diminish somewhat the aggressiveness with which nations compete for economic growth (Walter 1972).

The goals of economic growth and jobs, moreover, are locationally qualified. Populations are not indifferent to the locations where capital investment lodges. Rather, investment is seen as worthwhile only if it locates within one's jurisdictional boundaries. National governments, therefore, pursue policies designed to attract capital into their jurisdictions; and this brings them into competition with each other. We consider first the geographically parochial basis of these policies and then their competitive nature.

GEOGRAPHICAL PAROCHIALITY

The goal of governments is to make things happen on the national turf. It seems reasonable that this should be a reflection of popular desires. Why, however, should needs be so locationally qualified?

In brief, people are tremendously dependent for their life chances on what goes on in their national jurisdiction, and for at least two reasons. First there is the typically chronic immobility of people between national jurisdictions. Most migration is within nations rather than between. The major reason for this is simply attachment to a distinctive national society not duplicated elsewhere. Moving to a different country confronts the individual with difficulties he would rather avoid: language is the most obvious of these, but there is also the exposure to alien values and national symbols, to strange places, and—quite simply—to social behaviors that are unpredictable and consequently perplexing.

It might be objected that international immobility of labor can be explained in large part by jurisdictional barriers. Undoubtedly this has some validity but it is emphatically only a partial explanation: the lifting of barriers to labor mobility within the Common Market, for example, does not appear to have produced any radical upswing in international movement. The British seem as addicted to their lukewarm tea, sausage rolls, cricket, and other idiosyncratic features of their culture as they were before joining the Common Market.

There is, however, a second reason for concern with what goes on within the jurisdictional boundaries of the nation state: the absence of any formal redistributional system at the international level. Consider, for example, the relationship between two British counties: say, Yorkshire and Lancashire. Let us assume that Yorkshire gets most of the new investment, and private incomes increase there; while in Lancashire investment languishes and wages are static or decline. The implications for welfare in this *intra*national situation provide an interesting counterpoint to the *inter*national level.

At the intranational level the nationally levied progressive income tax will tend to take a bigger bite out of higher Yorkshire incomes than lower Lancashire incomes. Furthermore this money will tend to be redistributed by the national exchequer in a manner benefiting the county—Lancashire—that has been least successful in competition for investment. Money will go to pay unemployment compensation, for example, and to subsidize schools and public works. At the intra-national level, therefore, there is a redistributional system that cushions localized populations against the unfortunate consequences of failure to attract investment.

The contrast with the international level is striking. Apart from some foreign aid there is little that is analogous to the redistributional system operating within nation states. There is, for example, no progressive income tax levied by the United Nations and redistributed to the nation states of the world according to need. The national level of expenditure on, say, education, public health, or recreation is therefore highly dependent indeed on the respective government's ability to attract capital investment and generate economic growth.

COMPETITION

Why, however, do these parochial policies generate competition among nations? Two facts are important: (1) the locational volatility of capital; (2) the goal of economic growth shared by all nations. As a consequence national policies are directed towards manipulating capital flows to national advantage. This, however, means directing capital away from some other nation and hence frustrating the ability of some other government to achieve its goals of economic growth. Failure to compete for mobile capital implies a loss of economic growth: failure to compete in terms of, for example, tax breaks for new business ventures will result in a diversion of investment funds elsewhere. There are, however, other strategies in the kitbag of tools used in international competition. It is to a consideration of these that we turn next.

Techniques of International Competition

Investors of capital are interested in maximizing profits over a more-or-less lengthy period of time. Investment will be embodied in the form of some physical equipment—factory buildings, railroads, power stations—yielding a stream of revenue into the future. It is from this stream of revenue that the original cost of the investment will be defrayed. In selecting a national jurisdiction for investment, therefore, it seems reasonable to surmise that investors try to estimate returns to investment over a number of years into the future.

Estimating rates of return for future years is dependent on a variety of calculations in each of which the firm will have a variable degree of confidence. It may be possible, for example, to establish the extent of reserves of some mineral or the likelihood of adverse weather for agricultural production. Long leases and loan agreements may allow the firm accurately to estimate rents and interest charges for future years.

Yet there are a number of events that are extremely difficult to predict but on which the realization of a given rate of profit is quite dependent. National policies with respect to taxes, trade, or labor provide instances of these. Less-structured events such as civil disorder may pose insuperable obstacles to profitable operation.

To any investment, therefore, there is an element of *risk* attached. Given the information that it has at hand, the firm may be able to project future profits only with a certain likelihood of realization. Critical to the likelihood of realization is the degree of certainty regarding future political conditions in the nation state at issue. Where conditions are uncertain or civil disorder is rife, likelihoods will be low and risk commensurately greater. Where political conditions are more stable, however, the risk attached to investment will be considerably less.

In sum, it seems likely that investors in evaluating alternative investment opportunities in different countries will have to consider two factors: (1) profit rates and (2) the risk attached to the investment. Investors will be attracted to countries with less-secure political conditions only where profit rates are unusually attractive. Politically stable countries on the other hand will continue to attract capital, even though profit rates may be somewhat lower.

This, of course, has important implications for national policies designed to attract investment funds. Clearly if the argument outlined above has any validity national governments have to address themselves to two types of policies: (1) those designed to maximize rates of return to private investors and (2) those designed to provide security for the investment and hence minimize the risk attached to it. The latter condition, in turn, involves attention to two problems: that of public control, or controlling dissidents or externally based hostile forces by physical force, incarceration, etc., and that of enhancing the legitimacy of the private market system among the population at large. By policies of income redistribution, job protection, and unemployment compensation, the population at large must be convinced of the fairness of the distribution of the national pie determined by the operation of private markets.

Reflection, however, suggests that there is a contradiction here. Improving profit rates can be secured by policies that reduce the share of labor in the national pie: for example, low corporation taxes and legal restraints on labor unions and on the use of the strike weapon. Such policies, however, which increase the rate of return to capital at the expense of labor, tend to threaten profits over the long term by undermining the legitimacy of the market system in the eyes of labor and, hence, by increasing the risk of investment. For any government, therefore, implementing national policy is like walking a tightrope: if it errs too much on the side of increasing profit rates, the legitimacy of the system will be reduced, risk will be increased, and, hence, profit realization will be threatened. The same result may occur if the government errs in the direction of redistribution: welfare policies, for instance, are carefully scrutinized by international bankers called in to bail out the governments responsible on the grounds that the policies may involve rates of taxation that reduce rates of return to capital and hence discourage investment (Payer 1974). Let us consider now in greater detail first those policies whose aim is to enhance profit rates and then those policies whose aim is to enhance the security of investments and minimize risk.

POLICIES TO ENHANCE PROFIT RATES

Domestic   A variety of domestic policies are designed to attract investment by improving profit rates. These range from manpower and market development policies to the treatment of capital investments per se. All nations, for example, have manpower policies. As research and development investments become increasingly important, so governments emphasize the national importance of investment in scientific and technical training. Evidence of another nation's superiority in the form of sputniks, for example, stimulates phases of national breast beating and soul searching. These are ultimately followed by a variety of policies designed to restore a nation to its deserved place in the technological sun.

The supply of labor is also affected by regulating inflows and outflows. In many nations the outflow of skilled labor has become a major national economic problem. In Portugal, for example, it has taken the form of a drain of skilled tradesmen—plumbers, carpenters, electricians—to other nations of Western Europe, especially France. Consequently the Portuguese government has imposed a minimum Portuguese residency period on all those skilled workers who have acquired some professional qualification at public expense.

Inflows of labor also provide possibilities. The problem is to organize the inflow of labor from other national jurisdictions so as to maximize economic growth without jeopardizing full employment. This may be achieved by a policy of labor permits or quotas on migrants. Alternatively there are more positive approaches. Australia has for a long time attempted to encourage Britishers to settle in Australia by offering cheap $14 air fares to Australia. Only if the immigrant returns within three years would he be liable for the full air fare.

A problem, of course, is that inflows of labor may prove to be liabilities, should economic conditions deteriorate. West Germany has

Table 6.1   Percentage of Investment in New Plant and Machinery Allowed to Be Written Off for Tax Purposes

	In 1st Year	By 5th Year	Cumulative Total over Asset Life
Belgium	22	92	
Canada	30	71	100
France	25	76	100
Germany, F.R.	20	67	100
Italy	25	100	
Japan	43	68	
Netherlands	26	86	110
Sweden	30	100	100
United Kingdom[a]	55	91	130
United States[b]	29	78	114

SOURCE: Reprinted from Richard N. Cooper, *The Economics of Interdependence*, p. 166. Copyright ©1968, McGraw-Hill Book Company. Used with permission of McGraw-Hill Book Company.

[a] Including an investment allowance of 30 percent, replaced by grants in 1966.

[b] Including an estimate for the effect of an investment tax credit of 7 percent.

developed appropriate policies in this regard. Labor is hired in, for example, Turkey, Yugoslavia, and Spain on renewable two- or three-year contracts by agencies of the West German government. If recession should intervene not only is recruiting activity suspended but contracts are not renewed; without a valid contract the immigrant is unable to secure work or access to West German social services.

Nations also compete in investment policy and market development (Cooper 1968, ch. 6). Subsidies are offered for particular purposes: countries eager to develop their tourist industries, for example, may offer this sort of stimulus as a carrot to international hotel chains. Alternatively the carrot may take the form of tax write-offs for investment in new plants and machinery: these are extremely common and competitive among the more industrialized countries (table 6.1). Tax holidays for new investors are frequently resorted to.

Governments also play a role in developing the domestic market for new investments. National tourist boards help to generate a demand from foreigners for, say, new hotels or car hire operations. Likewise a well-conceived tariff policy may help to divert investment from some other country. At the beginning of this century, Canada had little manufacturing of its own, importing its manufactured goods from the United States and Britain. The erection of a tariff around that market, however, altered the investment calculations of entrepreneurs in favor of supplying the Canadian market from within rather than from without (Tatham 1956, p. 339).

Figure 6.2   The European Economic Community and the European Free Trade Area

Foreign   Other policies designed to maintain or enhance profit rates find their locus outside the national jurisdiction. Nineteenth-century British imperialism, for example, has been interpreted as an attempt to prevent other countries from getting there first and excluding British traders.

In more contemporary times expansionism has assumed the form of attempts to carve up the continental shelf for purposes of oil extraction and fishing. Britain, therefore, expects her North Sea oil resources to stimulate a domestic boom: lower energy costs will enhance the country's attractiveness for investment and generate an inflow of funds. The recent attempts of Iceland to extend its fishing limits can be seen in the same light. Cod fishing provides the economic base of Iceland and presumably, without that base, the Icelandic market would deteriorate, followed by capital flight and a falling standard of living.

Perhaps most important today, however, is the formation of international trading blocs and international monopolies. Each merits extended treatment.

Trading Blocs   A *trading bloc* is a group of nations among which barriers to trade, labor movement, and capital movement are progressively reduced. These blocs assume two major forms. There is, first, the common market among the member states, of which (1) all barriers—tariffs, subsidies, price supports—to the import and export of goods are progressively reduced and (2) barriers to the movement of labor and capital are gradually eliminated. To nonmember nations the common market presents a common tariff wall, typically an average of the preexisting tariffs of the member nations. An example of a common market, of course, is the EEC, consisting of France, Italy, West Germany, Luxembourg, Belgium, the Netherlands, the United Kingdom, Ireland, and Denmark (figure 6.2). The EEC has still a long way to go before it assumes the idealized form described above; but, on the other hand, considerable progress has already been made.

A second type of trading bloc is the free trade area. Internally this is similar to a common market, all barriers to trade being eliminated. Externally, however, individual nation states retain preexisting tariff barriers with respect to nonmembers of the bloc. This has an important implication: if a member nation applies a high tariff to a good while another member nation applies a low tariff to the same good, nonmember nations exporting the good in question can elude the high tariff. This can be accomplished by exporting to the low tariff country, whence it can be taken tariff free into the high tariff country. Examples of free trade areas include the Latin American Free Trade Area (LAFTA), consisting of Mexico, Venezuela, Ecuador, Colombia, Peru, Bolivia, Brazil, Chile, Argentina, Uruguay, and Paraguay (figure 6.3).

The supposedly competitive virtue of the trading bloc can be summed up in three ideas: economies of specialization, economies of scale, and innovation (Swann 1970, ch. 2). Elimination of international trade barriers, it is argued, will expose inefficient industrial organization to the draughts of competition. This will result in more rapid adoption of cost-cutting techniques, concentration of ownership, increasing productivity, and hence increasing real incomes.

The elimination of barriers to trade also provides plants with the possibility of serving a much larger market without the uncertainties introduced by the threat of trade interference from tariffs and quotas. Instead of serving the British market of 55 million, for example, the British automobile industry, as a result of British membership of the EEC, will ultimately have access to a market of 240 million persons, tariff free. This permits total plant output to expand to a point at which it is possible to take advantage of internal economies of scale: increased specialization within the plant, vertical integration with suppliers and distributors, technological economies of scale, etc. The result again is reduced product costs, increased productivity, and higher wages.

Figure 6.3   The Latin American Free Trade Area

Finally there are the economies resulting from increased national specialization. Nations, so the argument goes, have comparative advantages in particular lines of production. By concentrating on and exporting those lines and by importing products in which they do not enjoy a comparative advantage, the total costs accruing to the set of nations involved would be reduced, productivity would again increase, and consequently so would wages (Ingram 1970, ch. 2). So long as nations protect industries in which they do not enjoy a comparative advantage, these economies will remain unexploited.

The proponents of trading blocs, however, go beyond this simple enumeration of arguments. As productivity and real wages within the trading bloc expand, the market becomes increasingly attractive for foreign investors. Some evidence for this is provided by investment flows during the period when Britain was not a member of the EEC. The United States, for instance, diverted a considerable amount of foreign investment from the former to the latter in order to take advantage of the larger market (Dunning 1972, p. 379). For Britain this was an important factor in deciding to reconsider its earlier refusal to join the EEC. In the late 1960s, for example, U.S. firms in Britain were contributing three times as much to exports as were indigenous manufacturing firms.

Second, the overall cost reduction and improved productivity have implications for the penetration of foreign markets. Briefly, products from the trading bloc will have cost advantages allowing them to undercut foreign competitors. This provides a further stimulus to the economic growth of member nations of the trading bloc.

That the formation of trading blocs is a response to international competitive pressures is evident from chronology. At the time of the formation of the EEC in the 1950s, for example, other Western European countries that, for a variety of reasons, did not wish to affiliate with the EEC formed the European Free Trade Area (EFTA): Austria, Denmark, Norway, Portugal, Sweden, Switzerland, and the United Kingdom. This was conceived largely as an institutional framework for bargaining with the EEC regarding, for example, the common tariff barrier to be instituted by the EEC countries against nonmembers (figure 6.2).

International Monopolies   Sellers or buyers of products can exercise an independent effect on world market prices if they account for a sufficiently large percentage of sales or purchases. In fact, a feature of growing significance in world trade in the mid-1970s was the emergence of international agreements between commodity-producing nations, agreements concerning output, pricing, and/or shares of the global market. They provide a means of expanding national revenue and hence enhancing market size and attractiveness for investment.

Possibly the most familiar example is OPEC, the Organization for Petroleum Exporting Countries, consisting of the Middle Eastern states of Iran, Iraq, Saudi Arabia, Kuwait, Abu Dhabi, Algeria, and Libya as well as of Nigeria, Venezuela, and Indonesia (figure 6.4). In the mid-1960s, prior to the formation of this producers' cartel, the oil companies were rather free to do as they pleased with respect to the terms at which they arrived with the producing countries. Favorable concessions could be obtained, for example, by playing one producing country against another. In 1969 OPEC was formed, the member countries of which produce more than 80 percent of world oil exports, more than 85 percent of Western European oil, and 90 percent of

Figure 6.4   Major Cartels in Global Commodity Markets

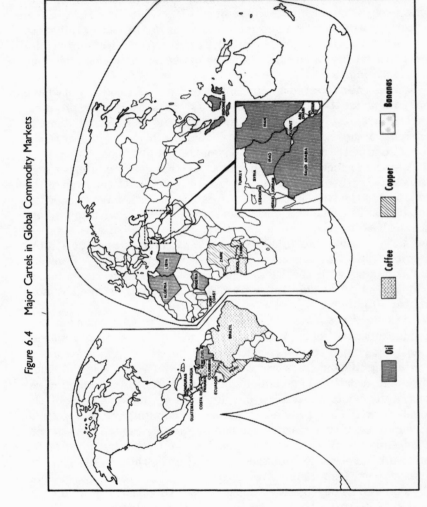

NOTE: The copper cartel is still in the discussion stage and has yet to be implemented.

Japan's. Given this strong monopoly position and demonstrating considerable cohesion, OPEC has managed to extract much higher prices from the consumer nations and also to limit output: the latter, of course, serves only to drive prices higher still.

The success of OPEC has stimulated similar activity on the part of nations specializing in other commodities. Brazil, Colombia, the Ivory Coast, and Angola, which together produce 60 percent of the world's coffee, already have agreed to establish a multinational company to control supply and hence prices. The banana trade has also been affected, while rumblings have been heard from producers of minerals (figure 6.4).

Monopoly arrangements, of course, are not likely to be effective in the case of all commodities. Where substitutes are readily available to consuming nations, the degree to which producers can determine prices will be severely limited. Attempts by producers of cane sugar to drive up prices by limiting supply would be met only by increased sugar beet production in consuming nations. Even in the case of Middle Eastern oil the advantages to be gained from monopolistic pricing are limited to some degree. Electric companies are now lobbying for the development of coal resources in the American West to relieve pressure on oil as a source of energy; oil exploration of offshore areas outside the Middle East is proceeding apace; and the industrial nations of the world are showing increased interest in nuclear energy as a source of power.

POLICIES TO ENHANCE INVESTMENT SECURITY

Domestic   Broadly, the security of investments can be threatened in two ways. On the one hand the legitimacy of the market system and those private property institutions on which it is based may be called into question: this may involve anything from the threat of nationalization to a full-scale revolution. On the other hand, private property and investment may be threatened by forces that are not calling the legitimacy of market institutions into question. Invasion or civil wars between separatist groups, which recently occurred in Nigeria or Northern Ireland, are just as threatening to capital productivity as are more revolutionary activities.

Confronted by threats of this nature governments have two major options:

1. They can attempt to co-opt dissident groups. This might be achieved by instilling in them a belief that the institutional status quo is a fair one and operates so as to eliminate any inequities that do emerge. A strategy of this nature may involve various conces-

sions to demonstrate, for example, that the market is not inhumane or that separatists do have something of a case.
2. To the extent that such a *legitimizing policy* is ineffective, then force will have to be resorted to; i.e., a *coercive policy*. Civil liberties will be limited and a secret police apparatus will be introduced; the military will gain ascendancy and civil order will be imposed rather than induced.

A glance at the nations of the world suggests that legitimizing policies have not been that successful: the number of military dictatorships in Africa and South America bears witness to this. Unfortunately a coercive policy is expensive in terms of manpower and it does not seem to have enduring effects. The termination of dictatorship—whether in Portugal, Argentina, Venezuela, or elsewhere—merely seems to be followed by a return of the chaos that had induced adoption of a coercive policy in the first place.

Consider, as a second option, the range of policies designed to legitimize political and market institutions in the eyes of the population. These may include policies of redistribution from the rich to the poor: a progressive income tax, welfare benefits, land reform, equality of opportunity in education, the nationalization of health care, and unemployment compensation. They may also include policies aimed at stemming discontent in particular regions of the country: subsidies to local industries, government orders to regional industries, increased state grants for regional spending on education, concessions on the use of regional languages.

Foreign   Domestic profit rates, we have seen, depend partly on events overseas; for example, access to foreign markets, access to foreign raw materials. Not surprisingly, then, it is also possible to identify some domestic, risk-minimizing effects of foreign policy.

Consider the idea that political instability increases risk: this places a premium on foreign policies that reduce domestic political instability. The linkage between domestic political stability and overseas expansion was frequently made by politicians and publicists during the Industrial Revolution and formed a major rationalization for imperialism (Polanyi 1957, ch. 18).

The Industrial Revolution resulted not only in vast social dislocation, but it also led to serious social polarization between the property-owning minority, who had managed to do quite well during it, and the vast, propertyless majority. During the nineteenth century the propertyless came increasingly to see themselves as exploited by the property-owning classes. This took a tangible form in the emergence of socialist movements challenging the property rights status quo, nationalization of private assets, and redistribution of income.

The emergence of this challenge to the property rights status quo induced fears among the property-owning classes: fears not only of revolution but also of a working class so enamored of the idea of internationalism that it would refuse to fight to defend the homeland.

Imperialism was seen as a way out of this impasse. The creation of colonies, for example, could provide land for resettlement of surplus population, reducing the downward pressure on wages. Earlier in the nineteenth century Madison in *The Federalist Papers* had clearly understood the implications of settlement: by the acquisition of western territories from the Indians and the Spaniards and the consequent provision of cheap land, the dangers of class warfare resulting from unequal distribution of property could be postponed (Stedman-Jones 1972, p. 216).

In addition imperial expansion would provide markets for domestic industry and sources of cheap raw materials. Towards the end of the nineteenth century, with the emergence of the United States and Germany as major industrial powers, these concerns became an obsession in Britain. Imperial expansion, however, not only implied an area for settlement, but it was also felt that increased economic growth in the imperial country would permit redistribution of income to the working classes. Cecil Rhodes typified much of this view linking overseas expansion to domestic tranquility:

> "I was in the East End of London yesterday and attended a meeting of the unemployed. I listened to the wild speeches, which were just a cry for 'bread', 'bread' and on my way home I pondered over the scene and I became more than ever convinced of the importance of imperialism. . . . My cherished idea is a solution for the social problem, i.e., in order to save the 40,000,000 inhabitants of the United Kingdom from a bloody civil war, we colonial statesmen must acquire new lands to settle the surplus population, to provide new markets for the goods produced by them in the factories and mines. The Empire, as I have always said, is a bread and butter question. If you want to avoid civil war, you must become imperialists" (Lenin 1939, p. 79).

Concluding Comments

To a very large degree incomes are determined by price-fixing markets operating on a global scale. To the extent that they participate in world trade this will be, and is, in fact, true of the countries of the so-called "socialist bloc." In a locational context, the supply-and-demand curves whose intersection determines prices and incomes are sensitive to movements such as those of goods from one country to another, migrations, and so forth. Most significant for understanding international problems, however, are movements of capital; for it is capital that provides the wherewithal for raising productivity and, therefore, national wealth.

Given that the major goals of governments are economic growth and employment generation, diverting investment flows into the national jurisdiction becomes a major policy goal. The jurisdiction where capital ultimately lodges is of supreme significance to a national population and hence to its government. Internation immobility signifies that investment in some other country will be of limited value. The urgency with which attracting investment flows is viewed is compounded by the absence of an international redistributional system: At a global level there is no progressive income tax by which countries successful in the competition for investment would provide a financial cushion for the less successful.

Given that investors are interested in rates of return over a lengthy period of time, policy designed to attract capital must be oriented to both enhancing rates of return now and minimizing the risk of loss in the future. National government hence must provide not only attractive cost structures, market accessibilities, and other enhancements to profits but also a certain degree of security for the foreseeable future. Both domestic and foreign policy are oriented towards these goals.

On the domestic side manpower training programs, government subsidies, and market development may enhance profit rates. With respect to the security of investment a major problem is that of forestalling domestic turmoil. In the eyes of the propertyless the legitimation of the market system by redistributional programs is important in this context.

In terms of foreign policy a major tool of international competition is the formation of common markets: cooperation with a few other nations so as to compete more effectively with the rest. International raw material cartels may also be useful in widening domestic markets and hence attracting investment. The problem of domestic political stability also receives its reflection in foreign policy. We suggested, for example, that nineteenth-century imperialism served to dampen revolutionary ardor in industrializing countries by providing their peoples with settlement opportunities overseas and possibly also by providing new markets large enough to sustain domestic redistribution policies.

In this chapter, therefore, we have attempted to situate national policies with respect to the market mechanism and the problems experienced in adjusting to market shifts at the global, international level. In the next chapter these policies are related to the problems outlined in chapter 5. These include problems of international inequality, the depletion of global resources, and national sovereignty.

Select Bibliography

Green, Reginald H., and Seidman, Ann. *Unity or Poverty? The Economics of Panafricanism.* Pt. 1. Baltimore: Penguin, 1968.

Hardin, Garrett. *Exploring New Ethics for Survival: Voyage of the Spaceship Beagle.* Baltimore: Penguin, 1973.

Knight, C. Gregory, and Wilcox, R. Paul. *Triumph or Triage: The World Food Problem in Geograph-ic Perspective.* Association of American Geographers Resource Paper no. 75-3. Washington, D.C., 1976.

Landsberg, Hans H. "Assessing the Materials Threat." *Resources,* no. 47, September 1974, pp. 1-3.

Schreiber, Jean-Jacques Servan. *The American Challenge.* Pts. 1-4. Harmondsworth, Middlesex: Penguin, 1969.

Chapter Seven

International Competition:
The Outcome

We have now considered public problems of international economic development, global resource scarcity, and international conflict. In the last chapter we isolated processes of international competition for investment as the major forces underlying these problems. In this chapter we attempt to link those processes with the problems described in chapter 5.

The chapter is divided into four major sections: First we examine the implications of international competition for the distribution of welfare outcomes across the nation states of the world. Second we examine the role of international competition in the geographical expansion of national economies: this will help us to understand conflicts such as those surrounding multinational corporations. Third we look at the relationship between international competition and the global resource problem. Finally, we look at the juridical context that constrains international competition and helps to bias its outcomes.

Distributional Implications

Distributionally the operations of international competition tend to be of most benefit to DCs and of least benefit to LDCs. Apparently, DCs are able to compete more effectively for capital investment. A number of considerations enhance their ability in this regard, including: (1) the distribution of physical and human capital; (2) access to markets; (3) culture; (4) political stability. The LDCs are not totally without advantages: they do have, for instance, important reserves of strategic raw materials and minerals at a time when DCs are exhausting their domestic supplies. We discuss each of these considerations in turn.

DISTRIBUTION OF PHYSICAL AND HUMAN CAPITAL

Generally speaking, investments in DCs have more human and physical capital with which to work than do investments in LDCs.

The greater availability of skilled labor and physical infrastructure is especially significant in that it is likely to enhance the productivity of any new capital investment. Location of investment in a developed economy is location with respect to suppliers of components, skilled manpower, piped water, highways, electric power, etc. In LDCs, new investment may have its rate of return qualified by the absence of component suppliers, the need to import or train skilled labor, or the need to invest in an electric power plant or water supply. In DCs different industrial and agricultural activities exchange economies simply by being adjacent to one another; and these economies cut costs of production. In LDCs, on the other hand, economies of this nature are less likely to be present, and profits will consequently be reduced.

ACCESS TO MARKETS

One approach to identifying market access is to examine each nation's domestic market. Generally, two factors contribute to this: (1) GNP and (2) literacy. While GNP is self-explanatory, literacy is less obvious; its significance derives from the role of advertising in market penetration. Those nation states having larger national products and more literate populations tend to have larger markets for both consumer and capital goods.

Given that larger markets tend to attract investment, the DCs have clear advantages. They have the more literate populations; as a consequence, these tend to be far more accessible through advertising and promotional literature than are the populations of LDCs. Next, nations with large GNPs are more likely to be DCs than LDCs. At first blush this might seem rather surprising; there are some poor countries such as India, China, and Indonesia that have rather large GNPs. Although poor, they are also populous, so that when their characteristically low product per capita is multiplied by their large respective populations, the result is a relatively high GNP. Despite exceptions such as these, the tendency is for the countries that are wealthier in terms of GNP per capita also to have the higher GNPs. A rank correlation coefficient calculated for a random sample of twenty-one nation states between GNP per capita and GNP turned out to be a rather respectable .57. Perhaps we should not be too surprised by this. After all, many LDCs are quite small indeed in terms of population size: this is the typical condition throughout Africa, Southeast Asia, and Central America.

Alternatively it might be argued that by examining domestic market size alone, we have exaggerated the advantage of DCs with respect to attracting new investment. Simple measures of domestic market size tend to overlook trade: in order to service a particular national market, an investment in physical plant does not necessarily have to be located there. Market access therefore is also a function of locational relations with respect to markets of different size. Two aspects of those relationships are important here: (1) the trade barriers erected by nation states (tariffs, quotas) and (2) distance relations. Unfortunately when we examine the impact of these considerations on market access, our gloomy prognosis for LDCs is confirmed rather than relieved.

Generally LDCs find a variety of trade barriers interposed between them and DC markets (Braun 1971; Frank 1968). First, there are barriers against primary products; exports of primary commodities constitute 85 percent of the export earnings of LDCs, so these barriers are of great significance. The more severe restrictions are those on temperate agricultural products: sugar, cereals, meat, wheat, and dairy products. There are also restrictions on semi-competitive commodities such as tobacco, cotton, wool, and vegetable oil seeds. The importation of some minerals into the United States furthermore is subject to quota restrictions: oil and copper are cases in point (Johnston 1967, ch. 5).

In addition, there are barriers against labor-intensive, technologically unsophisticated consumer goods. A major target of DC restrictionism has been cotton textiles (Johnston 1967, ch. 6). This industry has been especially important to the developing economies of India, Pakistan, South Korea, and Hong Kong. DCs, however, continue to have large cotton textile industries of their own. Quotas and tariffs on imports of cotton textiles have therefore been the order of the day. This problem moreover is one aspect of a more general problem: the tendency of DCs to impose higher tariffs on processed than on raw products (table 7.1). While there is a tariff on cotton yarn, the tariff on raw cotton itself is zero. The tariff on hides and skins is also zero; but, as those hides and skins are converted into more processed forms prior to export, so the tariff rises. This, of course, exercises an important dampening effect on the growth of manufacturing industry in LDCs.

Compounding this serious trade problem is the fact that LDCs tend to discriminate against each other as much as DCs discriminate against them; elimination of customs barriers and formation of regional customs unions could have substantial beneficial effects (Green & Seidman 1968). For a start, it would result in a widening of the domestic market for new industries, allowing advantage to be taken of economies of scale. The lower costs resulting from exploitation of economies of scale and technical innovation would permit increased competitiveness overseas: this would be in spite of the barriers that DCs erected.

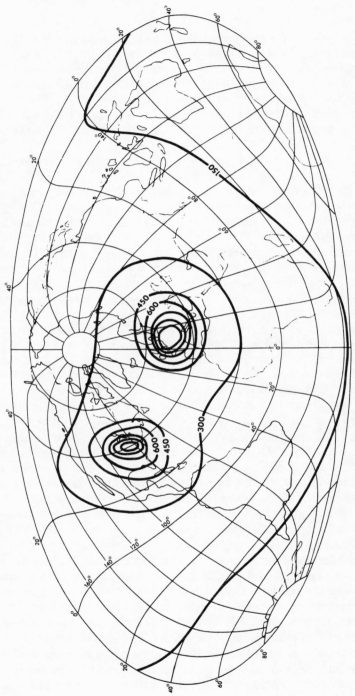

Figure 7.1 Global Distribution of Income Potential (in millions of U.S. dollars per square mile)

NOTE: Income potential is a measure of accessibility to consumer markets.

SOURCE: After William Warntz, "The Pattern of Patterns: Current Problems as Sources of Future Solutions," in Ronald Abler et al., eds., *Human Geography in a Shrinking World* (North Scituate, Mass.: Duxbury Press, 1975), p. 83.

Table 7.1   Tariff Rates in United States and Europe, by Commodity and Stage of Processing

Commodity	Tariff Rates (%)		
	EEC*	U.K.	U.S.
Cotton			
Raw	0	0	0
Yarn	8	8	14
Jute			
Raw	0	0	0
Yarn	10	13	20
Cocoa			
Beans	9	1.5	0
Powder	27	13	4
Iron & Steel			
Ore	0	0	0
Pig iron	7	4	9
Finished articles	9	14	10
Leather			
Hides & skins	0	0	0
Leather, finished	7	13	10
Leather footwear	16	15	13

SOURCE: Reprinted from James C. Ingram, *International Economic Problems* (New York: Wiley, 1970), p. 104, by permission of the publisher.

*The tariff rates given here represent the common external tariff rates for the six member nations.

The record however is not encouraging. In less-developed areas there has been some attempt at common market formation such as the East African Common Market, the Central African Federation, Guinea-Ghana, and the LAFTA; but these have been largely unsuccessful. The exploitation of the advantages provided by common markets requires considerable investment in intramarket transportation networks; currently, most internal transportation in LDCs is oriented towards coastal locations and export to DCs (Green & Seidman 1968, ch. 3). A second problem is that common markets tend to promote concentration of economic development in some member nations to the detriment of others. In the East African Common Market the gains were quite unevenly divided; Kenya and Uganda gained, but Tanzania lost (Nye 1963). Only strong internation labor mobility could offset these problems. But labor mobility tends to be weak, leading to international income divergence within common markets.

Figure 7.2   Income per Capita and Income Potential by Country

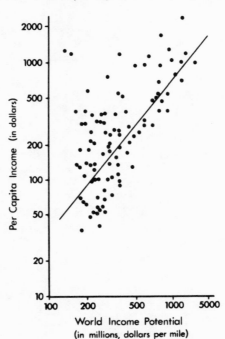

World Income Potential
(in millions, dollars per mile)

SOURCE: After William Warntz, "World Population Potential and International Crises," *Papers, Peace Research Society* (International) 4 (1966): 123.

The significance of these trade barriers for LDCs cannot be exaggerated. Export markets not only provide an incentive for investment in whatever production is fueling exports, but competition in export markets also prevents production inefficiencies that might emerge as a result of a monopoly of the domestic market. Given the small size of many domestic markets, monopolies are highly likely. In addition expanded markets permit plants in LDCs to obtain economies of scale in production—again, this is critical in LDCs due to the limits of the domestic market (Green & Seidman 1968).

Distance relations are also critical to market access. LDCs close to DCs have tended to benefit somewhat from their proximity: Mexico, for example, has an edge over other LDCs in exporting certain tropical products to the United States. Some measure of access to global markets is provided by a map of income potential (figure 7.1). This is a measure of access to wealthy populations and hence of market accessibility. It is readily apparent from figure 7.1 that market access is highest in North America and Western Europe.

Generally speaking, therefore, the wealthier countries of the world tend to be those more accessible to global markets as measured by income potential (figure 7.2). As a consequence, locations in the existing agglomerations of productive activity and wealth provide considerable advantages of profitability.

CULTURE

Within nation states, absence of the social values sustaining market relationships may pose problems. In many LDCs, people tend to be relatively unresponsive to market incentives. Investors in LDCs, therefore, may face problems of labor supply and also of disposing of the finished product. To some extent this is a function of the limited penetration of values of acquisitiveness. To some degree it is also due to a social structure emphasizing communalism rather than individualism: the fact that the individual worker may have to share his market fortunes with distant relatives is distinctly dampening to the acquisitive spirit.

With respect to the mobilization of labor in LDCs, much has been written regarding the *backward-bending labor supply curve* (Boeke 1953; Berg 1961). The idea is that as hourly wages rise, instead of eliciting more labor as one expects in a developed economy, laborers will work less and maintain their wages at the existing level rather than work the same amount of time and earn more (figure 7.3). When the price of coconut is high, the likelihood is that less of the commodity will be offered for sale; when plantation wages are raised, it is perfectly feasible that less work will be done.

This has been ascribed to a low profit motive and limited wants; and though it has recently received closer and somewhat negative scrutiny, it probably has a good deal of applicability. It is true, for example, that the African who works in the mines and then returns to his village to invest his wages in his plot of land is exhibiting commercial behavior of a sort. Is it, however, of the utility-maximizing sort that would lead the African to continue more remunerative mining work?

POLITICAL STABILITY

We saw in the last chapter that maximizing profits is contingent on risk minimization. A major source of risk, of course, is political instability and uncertainty. If a country lives in constant threat of insurrection, then it is unlikely to provide a particularly enhancing location for private capital.

As a general tendency, it seems reasonable to assume that investments in LDCs are more at risk from civil disorder than in-

Figure 7.3   Backward-bending Labor Supply Curve

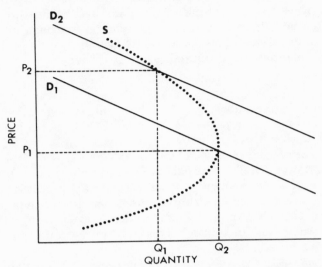

NOTE: As demand increases from D_1 to D_2, the units of labor offered (S) diminish from Q_1 to Q_2. The wage per unit of labor has increased from P_1 to P_2, so that wages can be sustained with less labor. Only where labor actually wants to increase its wages—as in an acquisitive society—will the labor offered increase as demand for labor increases.

vestments in DCs. Wealthier countries such as Sweden, Switzerland, Canada, and France tend to be politically stable and are characterized by democratic competition among political parties that really do not differ that much on, for example, how private property should be treated (Cutright 1963). In fact, they are likely to be somewhat *more* favorable towards private property. The poorer countries of the so-called Third World, on the other hand, tend to experience successions of more-or-less dictatorial governments, each varying substantially in its attitudes towards private property and the activities of foreigners. Alternatively the problem may be one of civil war—as seen over the last decade in Nigeria, Pakistan, the Sudan, Lebanon, and Angola—disrupting the market relationships on which profitable investment depends.

That this intuitive picture is not without more objective statistical support is suggested by figure 7.4. Generally speaking, democratic institutions and the political stability that tends to go with them are far more typical of the DCs than of the LDCs.

NONRENEWABLE RESOURCES

It is sometimes argued that LDCs do have one trump card: with the depletion of nonrenewable resources (coal, oil, nonferrous metals) in DCs, demand will inevitably switch to the hitherto little-exploited

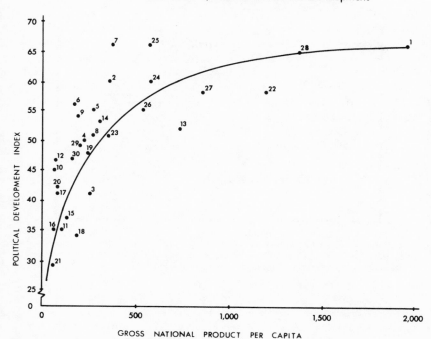

Figure 7.4   Political Development and Economic Development

NOTE: The index of political development is designed to measure the degree to which political institutions are democratic in different nation states. The thirty countries represent a random sample
from the non-Communist countries for which Phillips Cutright measured degree of political development in 1963 (Cutright, "National Political Development," pp. 253–64).

KEY TO NATION STATES: 1. Canada; 2. Costa Rica; 3. Dominican Republic; 4. El Salvador; 5.
Mexico; 6. Nicaragua; 7. Chile; 8. Colombia; 9. Peru; 10. Burma; 11. Cambodia; 12. India; 13.
Israel; 14. Japan; 15. Jordan; 16. Laos; 17. Pakistan; 18. Saudi Arabia; 19. Turkey; 20. South Viet-
nam; 21. Yemen; 22. Belgium; 23. Greece; 24. Iceland; 25. Ireland; 26. Italy; 27. Netherlands; 28.
Sweden; 29. Honduras; 30. Ceylon.

resources of LDCs. There is some merit to this view. Of the twelve
basic materials considered critical for modern industry, the United
States imports relatively large amounts of seven of them: 53 percent
of its zinc needs, 56 percent of its tungsten, 80 percent of its nickel, 83
percent of its tin, 89 percent of its bauxite, 97 percent of its manganese, and 100 percent of its chrome requirements. As for LDCs, some
of them already account for large proportions of world trade in certain minerals. Eighty percent of the world's copper exports, for instance, comes from Zaire, Zambia, Chile, and Peru; while 70 percent
of the world's tin exports originates in Malaysia and Bolivia.

Depletion, moreover, is only one force that could feasibly induce a
shift in DC demand for these resources towards LDCs. The exploitation and refining of minerals are often associated with air and water

Figure 7.5   Silver Bay in Its Regional Context

NOTE: Deposit of waste from taconite conversion activities at Silver Bay in Lake Superior has posed a threat to the health of people in the adjacent city of Duluth. Duluth draws its water from the lake; taconite waste contains fragments of asbestos, which is a carcinogen.

Figure 7.6   U.S. Production and Net Imports of Crude Petroleum, 1960–1975

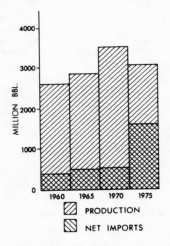

NOTE: Until sometime around 1970 U.S. production of crude petroleum was able to keep pace with increasing demands. Since then resource depletion has resulted in a marked reduction in annual production levels. Given increasing demands for oil in the United States, the deficit has had to be made up by increasing imports from overseas. In 1960 net imports as a percentage of total U.S. consumption of crude petroleum was 13.4 percent. By 1975, however, the same statistic was a dramatic 34.1 percent.

SOURCE: *U.S. Statistical Abstract, 1976* (Washington, D.C.: Government Printing Office, 1977).

pollution, interference with wildlife in wilderness areas, and land-scape despoliation by mining gear, excavation, and spoil heaps. Among the DCs of Western Europe and North America, therefore, it has generated considerable opposition from environmental conservation groups such as the Sierra Club, the Audubon Society, the Council for the Preservation of Rural England, and the National Trust. In some cases their opposition has had a purely delaying effect: this was the case with the Alaska pipeline. In other instances, mining and smelting activity has been prevented: this was so with recent requests for permission to develop copper resources in Wales (Searle 1975). In still other instances, the issue remains in doubt. An outstanding case of this involves the taconite refining activities of the Reserve Mining Company at Silver Bay, Minnesota. Dumping of tailings into Lake Superior has been shown to pose a serious health hazard for populations—such as that of Duluth—drawing their drinking water from the lake (figure 7.5). Federal lawsuits call for an end to the dumping; Reserve Mining Company, however, claims that inland waste disposal will impose crippling costs on the company's operation and it will make the whole iron ore and processing operation uneconomic.

In LDCs mineral exploitation and refining activity apparently generate no such concern. Quite possibly, therefore, the demand, for example, for iron ore, which cannot be met by the Reserve Mining Company as a result of environmental opposition, will be displaced to LDC iron ore producers such as Brazil, Mauretania, and Venezuela. Likewise if development of western energy resources in the United States is seriously limited, in all likelihood dependence on the oil and coal of LDCs will increase.

As a result of the depletion of minerals in DCs or, alternatively, opposition to their development, it is perfectly conceivable that LDCs will improve their ability to turn investment flows in their direction. This will be particularly so if LDCs can create raw material cartels such as OPEC to drive up the prices of their minerals.

Geographic Expansion

International competition has expansionary effects of a geographic character. As we saw in the previous section, nations tend to rely increasingly on other nation states for raw materials; foreign markets become an important condition of existence for domestic industry; and both forces encourage expansion of overseas investment.

Effective competition with the enterprises of other nations is dependent partly on minimizing costs of operation. Raw materials may represent one such cost. As domestic sources of, for example, oil, coal, and iron ore are worked out or at least the cheaper, more exploitable sources are, firms will tend to look overseas for their raw materials. As the United States has become progressively less self-sufficient in oil, therefore, it has had to look to the Middle East and Venezuela for a growing fraction of its energy needs (figure 7.6). Similarly, Britain ran out of cheap nonferrous metals fairly early in the Industrial Revolution and must now import tin from Malaysia, copper from Zambia, and lead and zinc from Australia. Even the remaining reserves of British iron ore are lean and expensive to work; as a consequence, the country obtains most of its iron ore from Spain, Sweden, and North Africa.

Rising populations also have their effects on geographic expansion. Domestic food production may be outstripped so that foreign sources of wheat, animal products, corn, and fruit become increasingly important. This occurred in Britain during the nineteenth century and led to a great increase in trade with the food-producing countries of Canada, the United States, Argentina, Australia, and New Zealand (Peet 1969). Increasing standards of living have the same effect: people demand more meat and, given the inefficiency of animals as food converters, this increases reliance on imports of grain from overseas. A vegetarian Britain, for example, would import far less grain than it does at present; a growing fraction of British grain imports is destined for animal feed rather than for flour.

On the market side economic growth also contains an imperative for expansion beyond national boundaries. Economic growth depends, as we have seen, on investment; hence, some of the national product must be saved rather than returned to the worker in the form of wages for consumption. In order to invest, consumption must be thwarted. If consumption is thwarted and demand lags, however, where is the incentive for investment? Exports provide an important means of resolving this dilemma.

Expansion outside the domestic economy, either on the market side or for raw material procurement, is also likely to be accompanied by foreign investment. The development of foreign sources of food and raw materials may involve investment in railroads, public utilities, and perhaps some processing activity. When the Midwest and the Great Plains became important sources of British food in the nineteenth century, they also became important objects for British investment in railroads: for without the railroads, there would have been no food for the British, and alternative sources of investment capital were very limited.

On the market side, we see a similar phenomenon. Expansion into foreign markets often provokes retaliation in the form of tariff barriers: the basis for this will be the harm imposed by trade on indigenous business and labor. One way of getting round the barrier, of course, as we saw in the Canadian case, is to export capital instead of goods and construct a branch plant to service the now-protected foreign market. Given the narcotic effect of economic growth, this investment is likely to be viewed in less-than-hostile terms by the receiving country.

Nation states, therefore, become economically interdependent. National welfare depends on access to foreign markets and sources of raw materials, and these interdependencies will be more-or-less mutual. But the emphasis must be on the "more or less." Some nations may be mutually dependent, so that gains from trade and from increases in trade are approximately equal. This type of configuration of events is the one most likely to give rise to common markets and free trade areas: where gains from trade are likely to benefit all parties equally rather than, say, one at the expense of others, then some pooling of sovereignty seems a reasonable and acceptable approach to enhancing the conditions for economic growth.

Geographical expansion on the other hand may have an asymmetric quality about it such that gains accrue disproportionately to one nation state at the expense of others—or so it is viewed by some of the countries involved. Nation states may develop spheres of interest consisting of those other nations providing them with markets, sources of raw materials, investment outlets, and possibly cheap labor. The United States, for example, has a sphere of interest that includes Canada and Latin America: certainly there are strong feelings both to the north and south of the United States that the value of present trade and investment relations accrues disproportionately to the United States. Likewise Japan has a sphere of interest in Southeast Asia including Taiwan, Indonesia, Malaysia, and, to some extent—though its people would be loath to admit it—Australia (Halliday & McCormack 1973). Some of these spheres of interest, of course, may be imperial in character or originate in imperial relations of a bygone era: this seems to be the basis of British relationships with much of Africa, India, and Australasia. Asymmetric interdependencies of this character are particularly likely to emerge between, on the one hand, industrial nations and, on the other, nations whose economic fortunes depend largely on the export of foodstuffs and minerals.

To some degree it can be argued that interdependency is in the interests of global efficiency: foodstuffs and minerals should be produced in those countries having a comparative advantage in their production—and likewise for manufactured products. Investment should move in the direction of higher profit rates and away from lower profit rates. Even given the parochial goals of nation states discussed in the last chapter, the resultant interlocking of the global economy nevertheless does provide an environment conducive to conflict. Foreign capital, for example, may pose an insuperable competitive challenge for domestic businessmen; if its techniques are relatively capital-intensive, then domestic labor may also incur net losses from unemployment.

Much of the conflict between national standards and common market standards in the EEC can be traced to this type of concern. In chapter 5 we discussed the problem of weight and axle length limits for trucks. The British trucking lobby is clearly not without some parochial interest in the outcome of the issue; if national standards could be preserved, the British trucking industry would be able to maintain its present monopoly of the British trucking market.

Foreign investment poses other problems for host nations of the sort reviewed in chapter 5. Canada, it will be recalled, faces particularly difficult problems due to the strict adherence to U.S. business legislation of American multinational corporations operating there. The result is a tendency for governments of host nations to feel that their sovereignty has been undermined either in a de jure or in a de facto sense.

Yet the trade-off nature of the problem forbids easy solution. If they exercise greater control over foreign investment (e.g., by nationalization or by strict limits on profit repatriation) or over foreign trade (e.g., by the imposition of tariffs), then this may set in motion shifts in international investment flows to their disadvantage. Trade interference, while it might in some cases stimulate capital imports attempting to leap the barrier, might incur retaliation from the affected nation states. It is quite difficult for Britain, for example, to impose severe trade restrictions on the United States simply because the American market is more important to the British than vice versa—and the Americans know it. Further, if British goods are shut out of the American market, that makes Britain a much less-profitable location for investment. Similar problems occur in the control of multinational corporations: while repatriation of profits may appear to be a serious problem for the host country, any attempt to place restrictions on their investments may simply frighten away others considering investing there. Policies of nationalization may incur additional penalties such as the freezing of assets in countries where the capital originated.

International Competition and
Global Resources

While international competition can hardly be said to have done much for the welfare of LDCs (i.e., welfare variations over geographical space), its continued operation also calls into question the future welfare of mankind as a whole (i.e., welfare variations between generations). Generally speaking, international competition for growth-inducing investment has tended to increase demands on global resources at the same time that it has worked systematically to diminish those resources. We will consider demand-increasing effects first and then resource-depleting effects.

DEMAND-INCREASING EFFECTS

We have seen that investment is attracted by market capacity. Given the desire of governments to attract in job- and growth-creating investment, we should not be surprised at attempts to stimulate market expansion. Generally, and particularly in the DCs, any flagging of domestic demand is bound to be followed ultimately, if not immediately, by calls for tax cuts, public works programs, and deficit spending designed to put purchasing power back into the economy. The result, of course, is more economic growth and increased pressure on resources.

Population policy also plays a role in enhancing demand. As we shall see shortly, economic growth occurs within a juridical context observed by individual nation states and enforced bilaterally. Clearly this body of international law has been to the advantage of some and to the disadvantage of others. It is, therefore, in the interests of each nation state to maintain some sort of global military presence with a view to preserving or obtaining a juridical context enhancing to its particular national interest. In brief, national military power is regarded as important in preserving or achieving conditions enhancing to national economic growth.

Population policy expresses this concern for national power. With regard to mankind as a whole, the urgent need is to reduce birth rates relative to death rates, so that rather than increasing, world population can actually decrease; but few nations in fact have explicit policies aimed at limiting population. There are some exceptions to this among nation states that have had or now have severe population problems. In India the third five-year plan promulgated in 1966 called for a large-scale program of education and motivation for family planning. This program involved the provision of birth control and contraceptive supplies, the establishment of family planning clinics in rural areas, and the provision of family planning services at urban health centers (Eldridge 1972).

By and large, however, such policies are exceptional. Where national population has declined or remained static, governments have actually introduced pronatalist policies. Perhaps most extreme in this regard has been France, which has had an explicit policy aimed

Figure 7.7   Impact of the Contraceptive Pill on Number of Live Births in Britain, 1951–1974

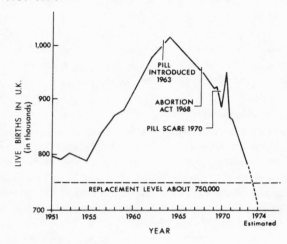

NOTE: Replacement level assumes no emigration.
SOURCE: After *Sunday Times*, 14 July 1974, p. 57.

at increasing its population since 1940. Incentives for families include allowances for all families having two or more children aged less than fifteen years. Allowances for third and subsequent children are higher. In addition, birth control propaganda, the sale or advertisement of contraceptives, and incitement to abortion—all are illegal (Eldridge 1972).

The actual impact of these measures is not well understood. In France the birth rate continues to fall in spite of generous cash incentives for big families. Likewise when family allowances were introduced in Canada after 1945, as though nothing had happened the birth rate continued to parallel that in the United States, which has no family allowance (Eldridge 1972). This is not to imply that policy measures have no effect on population growth at all. The evidence from Britain, for example, is that widespread private dissemination of the contraceptive pill has exercised a strong depressing effect on the national birth rate (figure 7.7). At the very least, this suggests that national birth control policies based on such technology might well achieve dramatic results.

As it is, explicitly antinatalist policies seem to be more the exception than the rule. A major problem here is the perceived link between population size and national power. Even in an age of nuclear warfare, Communist China has propounded the view that a large national population would ensure some survivors in a nuclear holocaust to pick up the pieces in some national interest. As a consequence few nation states regard a decline in the birth rate with complete equanimity. The consequences for global population growth and, therefore, pressure on resources are obvious.

RESOURCE-DEPLETING EFFECTS

Increasing demands resulting from economic growth and concomitant population growth, therefore, work to increase pressure on global resources. At the same time, international competition has still other effects that work in the direction of systematically reducing global resources. In brief, existing global demands could be met by policies that are less destructive of the resource base.

National economic growth, we have seen, depends on investment. Attracting investment is partly contingent on the national cost structure. National economies with low labor costs, raw material costs, and so forth will provide competitive advantages in marketing the finished product. Clearly some nation states provide more competitive cost structures than others.

As we saw in chapter 2, however, costs can be *internalized*, in which case they will show up in firm accounts and consequently detract from net revenues, or they can be *externalized*, in which case they will be imposed on others but be unaccounted for by the firm. To an important degree, therefore, the cost structure a nation state is able to offer a firm depends on the extent to which the national government will force it to internalize all its costs of operation.

To a considerable degree, then, nation states are forced to compete in environmental policy. Lax standards with respect to air and water pollution, for example, are attractive to firms. Clean air and clean water ordinances that put the burden of cleaning up on the individual firm add to production costs and hence serve to reduce the marketability of the finished product. As a consequence international competition for investment may be said to be a direct cause of the levels of air and water pollution experienced in those nation states "successful" in the competition. Pollution moreover serves to deplete natural resources. Land is effectively sterilized by industrial fumes. Agricultural yields may fall as a result of acid seepage from strip-mining operations. Or, if shaft mining is the norm, subsidence will disturb surface drainage and drastically lower the productivity of agricultural land. Water pollution kills off freshwater fish resources and reduces supplies of potable water. Both air and water pollution reduce life expectancy and so serve to deplete human as well as natural resources.

These external effects are not confined to the nation states where they originate. Chemically contaminated water drains into oceans, reducing their ability to support fish populations. This has effects on

Figure 7.8   Pollution Problem in the Lower Colorado Valley

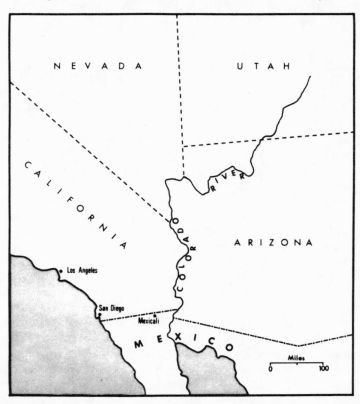

NOTE: The waters of the Colorado are used extensively for irrigation in Arizona and California. Much of the runoff from this irrigation process acquires a high saline content, which is collected into a canal system and deposited into the Colorado just before it enters Mexico. This seriously reduces the utility of the Colorado for irrigation in Mexico.

populations in no way responsible for the lax environmental standards producing contamination in the first place. In other cases water pollution affects international freshwater bodies, reducing their potability or irrigation potential for wholly innocent populations. This is true of international lake systems such as the Great Lakes of North America or some of the large European lakes such as Lake Geneva or Lake Constance (International Joint Commission of Canada and the United States 1970). The drainage basins of rivers also frequently have an international quality about them. Pollution upstream may impinge on foreigners downstream. A case in point is provided by the Colorado River (Berkman & Viscusi 1973, pp. 41–45). See also figure 7.8.

The problem would not be nearly so serious as it is if the external effects of industrial and agricultural activity were internal to the nation states in which the offending activities are located. Within states, governments have a political incentive to adopt some sort of environmental policy to make firms internalize their externalities. There is, therefore, some trade-off between policies that will encourage investment and those that will husband natural resources.

Externalities of air and water pollution, however, are also international. Here there are no political incentives for cleanup operations. The utility of congressional members is highly dependent on the satisfactions of U.S. voters, but it depends not at all on the satisfactions of Mexican or Canadian voters. At the international level the trade-off between attracting investment and resource conservation policies is biased heavily in favor of attracting investment. The result is a slow degradation of the globe's water and atmospheric envelopes with immense significance for its ability to sustain life.

Juridical Context

A variety of global problems, therefore, can be related in a plausible manner to international competition for investment. Nation states engage in a number of policies in an attempt to manipulate global investment flows to their advantage. These policies, however, are not carried out in an institutional vacuum: the outcomes of international competition for investment are in part dependent on the juridical context in which competition is carried out.

An important aspect of that juridical context is provided by international law. Of major significance is *national sovereignty*. One can conceive of a variety of hypothetical jurisdictional organizations of the globe in which the powers of nation states to tax and to provide public goods would be limited to a lesser or greater degree. These hypothetical jurisdictional organizations would have differing implications for the intensity and outcome of international competition. At present jurisdictional organization at the global level is about as decentralized as it could possibly be. In international law, nation states have virtually complete sovereignty over their citizens and the resources contained within their jurisdictions.

Private property rights provide a second facet of the relevant juridical context. Generally, outside the Communist countries individual rights to private property are guaranteed by the state. These rights are subject to some national variation: taxation, for example, or restrictions on ownership by foreigners. But by and large the basic private property institution is an observable reality. Consider now the implications of national sovereignty and private property rights in some detail.

NATIONAL SOVEREIGNTY

Nation states have ultimate power over the allocation of resources within their respective jurisdictional boundaries. They also have the power to control comings and goings of both goods and persons across national boundaries. There are virtually no ultimate sources of institutionalized power other than the nation state: each is literally sovereign with respect to its national jurisdiction and those who live within it. This sovereignty has important implications for the distributional effects of international competition.

We have seen that investors confront a set of investment opportunities varying in attractiveness from one nation state to another and that these investors naturally tend to put their money into countries where, subject to risk, profits are higher rather than lower. Much of the inequality in investment opportunities among states, however, can be traced to the highly decentralized form of jurisdictional organization currently dominant. Indeed, national sovereignty with respect to tariff policy, immigration, access to tax base, and disposition of state revenues tends to exacerbate rather than ameliorate international inequality in investment opportunities. This is in clear contrast to the situation within nation states. At that level the absence of any regional equivalent of national sovereignty tends to facilitate greater geographic equality of welfare.

Earlier in this chapter, for example, we noted that part of the enhanced effectiveness with which DCs can compete for investment can be traced to market accessibility advantages. Much of this variation from one nation state to another depends on domestic purchasing power as constrained by national taxation. *Within* nation states, on the other hand, national taxation of the progressive variety works to smooth out variations in purchasing power among the regions, decreasing the likelihood that already wealthy regions will continue to attract most future investment. Obviously there is no equivalent instrument at the international level designed to smooth out purchasing power variations from one nation state to another.

Tariff policies also interfere with market access. Clearly the advantage lies with those nations that have something to protect—generally, the DCs with their higher levels of purchasing power. We saw earlier in this chapter that tariff policies inhibit the hiving-off of labor-intensive industries such as cotton textiles to poorer, cheap labor LDCs. Within nation states, however, there is no equivalent regional sovereignty with respect to trade. In the United States the result has been a relocation of the cotton textile industry from the high-cost labor areas of New England to cheap labor areas of the South.

A similar logic can be applied to inequalities in the availability of that human and physical capital with which investment must work if it is to be productive. National sovereignty tends to limit the spread of capital among nations. At the *intra*national level, however, there are strong tendencies for interregional diffusion of funds for, say, education, highway construction, or dam building. National taxation and spending responsibilities have some equalizing effect on investment in education and public health among different regions. There is a similar tendency with respect to the availability of that publicly supplied infrastructure so important to private investment; for example, highways, irrigation works, flood control works, port facilities, and harbor development.

In addition interregional diffusion of human capital is achieved by on-the-job training of migrants. The existence of skilled labor in Georgia and Alabama owes much to the previous acquisition of skills in northern industrial cities. Generally at the international level barriers to migration inhibit the acquisition of job skills in this way by LDC populations. U.S. immigration policy, for instance, emphasizes skill and kin relationships with those already living in the United States. Prior to that the Immigration Acts of 1919 and 1924 established immigration quotas on the basis of the ethnic composition of the population in 1890; that year, of course, was before the movement from eastern and southern Europe had swollen to its 1913 peak. Migration into the United States between 1919 and the early 1960s, therefore, was heavily biased towards immigrants from the richer northern European countries of Britain and Germany and those of Scandinavia and against the poorer from elsewhere.

In Canada there is a policy similar to that of the United States. Kin links are again important. For those without a relative in Canada to sponsor them, admission is contingent on the compilation of points based on education, skill, age, and other factors.

It might of course be argued that foreign aid from DCs to LDCs does something to alleviate inequalities in the availability of human capital and physical infrastructure between rich and poor countries. Aid can easily be criticized, however, both in terms of its form and in terms of its quantity (Caustin 1970). Quantitatively the general feeling among development economists is that aid is both on too insufficient a scale and at terms that are too arduous for economies attempting to reach a point of self-sustaining economic growth. Consider for instance the gap between the actual level of aid required and current levels of aid. One U.S. economist's estimate places the annual capital flow need of LDCs for 1961–71 at a level exceeding by over 50 percent comparable flow in 1961 (Bhagwati 1966, pp. 210–14). In addition, most recipients of foreign aid encounter repayment problems even at soft rates of interest.

The *real* value of the resources transferred from DCs to LDCs is also reduced by the attempts of donor nations to monopolize resultant trade. Many transfers are for example accompanied by a stipulation that the money be spent on goods produced in the donor or lending nation or that the goods be shipped by liner companies incorporated in the donor nation (Bhagwati 1966, p. 207). The ability of LDCs to make their purchases of capital equipment in a competitive market is therefore reduced.

PRIVATE PROPERTY RIGHTS

Over much of the world individuals, firms, and other corporate entities are guaranteed certain basic private rights to property: rights of use, access, and transfer. These rights have a variety of effects of immense significance for international competition.

The most important is that they allow the creation of private markets. Accordingly global commodity prices are determined by the intersection of supply-and-demand curves, and capital gravitates to its highest return, irrespective of location. Generally this has had detrimental effects on the welfare of LDCs; this is especially apparent in the tendency for capital to shift from those countries where it was created to those where it will yield the most profit.

Under any circumstances private markets tend to have unequal results in the distribution of private incomes. In a geographic context, some of this inequality will be defined across localized populations. This has led to an institutional superstructure—the sovereign state—in which each localized population through its government attempts to deflect, divert, and regulate generally the flows of funds, labor, and commodities to its own advantage. This is particularly apparent in the erection of barriers to trade and to the migration of labor.

There is nevertheless a limit to state regulation, one defined by the tremendous profits to be made from investment under free market conditions by those with money to spare. As a result of these possibilities there is continual pressure on governments to assert "the rights of private property" and "to protect individual liberty from the encroachments of big government." In concrete terms this is manifested in pressure on government to maintain the freedom to export capital.

The bargaining resources available to capital assure it of a sympathetic hearing. Governments are warned of the danger of losing business confidence by interfering in market operations. In particular they are warned of the serious deterrent effect on capital imports of restrictions on the repatriation of profits. Even if government should attempt to restrict capital flight, there is no assurance that it will be invested within the national jurisdiction. Owners of capital are wealthy enough to wait: capital can be stored away in relatively unproductive forms—land, buildings, jewelry, art—until government sees the error of its ways.

Even with legislation hostile to capital mobility, in the face of some market incentive it is extremely difficult for government authorities to prevent it (Kindleberger 1970, ch. 14). Not only is there the simple expedient of smuggling money out—a not-too-absurd alternative given the denominations of some banknotes—but there is the equally effective method of purchasing some commodity, exporting it, and investing receipts in the country to which the commodity was exported.

The result is a mobility of capital that tends to transfer funds from LDCs, where political instability and limited investment opportunities deter investment, to DCs. Not surprisingly, therefore, there is a sentiment among some segments of the populations of LDCs in favor of breaking away from the global market system, so that the surplus generated within the national jurisdiction will be reinvested for the benefit of its citizenry. The only way this can be done effectively, however, is to abolish private property. It is conceivable, for example, that a country might prohibit all capital flows across its boundary. Unfortunately, as we have seen, that alone would not ensure investment for the benefit of those who had created the surplus. The resolution of this dilemma is state ownership of property as in Cuba and China.

To many this solution will appear unpalatable. The fact that state capitalism tends to be associated with restriction—if not abrogation—of individual freedom poses serious moral questions. It is legitimate to ask whether the populations of DCs should indeed stand by while large numbers of their fellows are subjected to the rigors of totalitarian regimes. The problems for DCs, however, are not only moral; there are also bread-and-butter issues. The abolition of private property and the institution of various forms of state capitalism, for instance, have serious weakening effects on the "matter of factness" of the private market system where it continues to survive. In an absence of alternative models, the private market system is taken for granted as natural. The emergence of alternatives demonstrates that economic systems are social creations; this tends to reduce the legitimacy of the status quo in the eyes of many of the citizens of DCs. In addition the establishment of socialist regimes provides important infrastructural support for the international labor movement throughout the world. The general effect of the replacement—albeit localized—of the private market system by various forms of state ownership is to increase redistributional pressures in DCs. Foreign aid therefore becomes a weapon in the "war of ideas" (Kindleberger 1970, ch. 9). Revolution in any one country will almost always be subject to international pressures as the DCs provide succor for the ruling class and attempt to avert the overthrow of the private market system.

Concluding Comments

In this chapter we attempted to relate the problems outlined in chapter 5 to the political processes described in chapter 6. The major political process identified was international competition for growth-inducing investment. In the present chapter we have examined the implications of this process for the redistribution of welfare between one nation state and another, for overseas investment, and for the global resource problem. We concluded by looking at the juridical context that constrains processes of international competition and investment flows and hence contributes towards the creation of observable welfare configurations.

Distributionally the outcomes of international competition tend to be of most benefit to DCs and of least benefit to LDCs; capital for investment in new factories, agriculture, and other areas tends to flow towards DCs; capital created in LDCs is likely to be invested ultimately in a DC. The advantages of DCs for investment are several. Their resources of physical and human capital make investment far more productive than it would be in an LDC. They tend to be more accessible to the larger markets of the world. Their populations tend to have cultural norms appropriate to a market society; the norm of acquisitiveness is especially important. DCs also tend to be politically more stable.

LDCs are not totally disadvantaged. As DCs continue to grow economically, they deplete their own scarce mineral resources and must look elsewhere. To an increasing extent, LDCs are the only countries where some raw materials can be found. Even when these are available in DCs, however, domestic opposition to the environmental despoliation resulting from their development may make LDC sources more attractive.

Increasing reliance on overseas sources of raw materials, of course, is one of the ways in which DCs relate increasingly to LDCs: international competition results in resource depletion, which leads to investments in LDCs for purposes of procuring the necessary raw materials. International competition also results in expansion into overseas markets and further rounds of overseas investment for purposes of serving those markets on the spot. International investment by existing firms, however, is likely to result in conflict with labor and business in the receiving countries.

The continued competitive operations of nation states also call into question the future welfare of mankind. Through a concern for national power, we were able to link international competition to continued population growth and hence to increasing demands on the globe's finite resources. At the same time international competition has reduced that resource base in other ways. Competition for investment tends to result in lax standards of pollution control and hence much higher degrees of air and water pollution than would otherwise exist.

A variety of global problems, then, can be related to international competition. The welfare outcomes of competitive policies, however, are dependent on the juridical context within which they are carried out. The two most significant aspects of that body of law are national sovereignty and private property rights. National sovereignty confines redistribution mechanisms to within the boundaries of nation states. This, of course, intensifies internation variations in attractiveness to investors and hence contributes substantially to inequalities in the competitive outcome.

Private property rights are defined and protected by most governments in the world. They allow the creation of price-fixing markets and encourage capital to shift from less-profitable to more profitable nation states. Since some states consequently become net exporters of capital, this is clearly not in their interest. They have, however, stopped short of prohibiting the export of capital. This is due to the ability of owners of capital to refuse to invest unless they have a congenial institutional framework. Even if limits on capital exports are instituted, they are quite difficult to implement. As a consequence, the only real solution many LDCs have to capital leakage is the abolition of private property rights.

This concludes our discussion of international problems. In the next three chapters, we reduce our scale somewhat and look at public problems occurring as a result of geographic relationships *within* nation states.

Select Bibliography

Borgstrom, Georg A. "The Dual Challenge of Health and Hunger—A Global Crisis." In Quentin H. Stanford, ed. *The World's* *Population,* pp. 176–86. Toronto: Oxford University Press, 1972.

Brown, Lester. "Rich Countries and Poor in a Finite, Interdependent

World." In Mancur Olson and Hans H. Landsberg, eds. *The No-Growth Society,* pp. 153–64. New York: Norton, 1973.

Cole, Lamont C. "Our Man-made Environmental Crisis." In Quentin H. Stanford, ed. *The World's Population,* pp. 159–66. Toronto: Oxford University Press, 1972.

Frank, Isiah. "The Role of Trade in Economic Development." *International Organization* 22 (1968): 44–71.

Nye, Joseph S. "East African Economic Integration." *Journal of Modern African Studies* 1, no. 4 (December 1963).

FURTHER READINGS

Bhagwati, Jagdish. *The Economics of Underdeveloped Countries.* New York: McGraw-Hill, 1966.

DeSouza, Anthony R., and Porter, Philip W. *The Underdevelopment and Modernization of the Third World.* Commission on College Geography Resource Paper no. 28. Washington, D.C., 1974.

Hensman, C. R. *Rich Against Poor.* Harmondsworth, Middlesex: Penguin, 1971.

Seers, Dudley, and Joy, Leonard, eds. *Development in a Divided World.* Harmondsworth, Middlesex: Penguin, 1971.

PART THREE

The Intranational Level

In part 3 we shift our scale of observation from the international level to the intranational level. From a concern with variations of well-being between nations we switch to an examination of similar problems between cities and regions. We will find that the processes operating at this scale bear a remarkable similarity to those producing problems at the international level.

Chapters 8 and 9 set out the public problems we regard as important at the intranational level. These are fourfold: (1) urban size problems; (2) the conflict of amenity and development; (3) regional disparities in income and public provision; (4) local autonomy. Chapter 10 identifies a set of political processes generating these problems, and chapter 11 then links process and problem.

Chapter Eight

Urban Size and the Conflict of Amenity and Development

Progressive urbanization has been a major geographic feature of Western societies over the past two hundred years or so. This process has been distinguished by, among others, two complementary relationships: the concentration of population in larger cities and the pressure on land resources within those cities and in their immediate hinterlands. Both of these relations generate a variety of public problems that places them from time to time in the spotlight of public policy. Increasing urban size brings in its train problems of congestion, crime, long-distance commuting, and so on. Pressure on land resources introduces problems of allocation to competing uses—problems that, given the pervasiveness of externalities, are not always efficiently or equitably resolved by the market mechanism. This chapter addresses both of these relationships: the first section considers the problems of urban size, while the second section examines land use conflicts with particular reference to those between developer and amenity interests.

Urban Size Problems

The typical tendency in more developed countries of the world is for larger cities to account for increasing proportions of respective national populations; small towns, on the other hand, may decline in size and will certainly account for decreasing fractions of those same national populations. More and more persons are living in bigger and bigger cities; fewer persons are living in smaller towns (table 8.1).

This shift in population generates a variety of public concerns (Alonso 1968). It is often claimed, for instance, that big cities are too big. Since they are associated with congestion, pollution, crime, and so forth, it is suggested that they are too big for their own populations. And since, according to some, cities have to be subsidized by the country as a whole, it may also be argued that they are too big for the country as a whole (Alonso 1968).

At the other end of the urban hierarchy the decline of the small town presents problems. Decreases in population make it difficult to

Figure 8.1   Britain's New Towns

SOURCE: After Clawson and Hall, *Planning and Urban Growth*, p. 203.

attract doctors. Public transport services may also be withdrawn. Pervading the urban size argument in many countries, however, is a certain moral strain: the idea that the small town, rural population is the repository of the strong beliefs and virtues that "made the country what it was," while the growth of large towns encourages a dissipation of moral fiber (Glass 1972).

Whatever the complexities of the motivations underlying these concerns, they have led in a number of countries to the beginnings of explicit urban size policies. These are designed to limit the growth of the larger cities. In Britain these are surrounded by Green Belts

Table 8.1   The concentration of population in larger urban agglomerations in the United
States, 1940–1960

	1940 (%)	1950 (%)	1960 (%)
3,000,000 +	22.6	28.9	28.1
1,000,000–3,000,000	22.3	18.6	26.4
500,000–1,000,000	15.2	16.2	17.0
250,000–500,000	16.5	17.0	14.0
100,000–250,000	16.6	15.7	12.8
Under 100,000	6.9	3.6	1.6

NOTE: Percentages in a given year add up to 100 percent (apart from rounding errors) and refer to
the percentage of the American population in SMSAs of a given size. Larger SMSAs tend to be obtaining
larger shares of total SMSA population than the smaller SMSAs.
SOURCE: Reprinted from Kevin R. Cox, *Man, Location and Behavior: An Introduction to Human
Geography* (New York: Wiley, 1972), p. 336, by permission of the publisher.

within which residential development is virtually prohibited; it is
therefore exceedingly difficult for them to grow by lateral expansion
(Clawson & Hall 1973, ch. 5). Programs of New Town construction
(figure 8.1) and town expansion (figure 8.2) have also been introduced
as a means of siphoning off population from the country's largest
cities, London, Birmingham, Glasgow, and Manchester. Relocation
not only reduces the size of those cities, it also allows reconstruction at
lower population densities (Clawson & Hall 1973, ch. 6).

In France urban policy has mainly concentrated on attempts to
limit the size of Paris. These have taken the form of restrictions on office development in the city along with attempts to divert growth to
eight major provincial cities defined as *métropoles d'équilibre* (figure
8.3) (Clout 1970; Boudeville 1966, ch. 7).

To what extent, however, are policies of this type addressing
themselves to real problems? To what extent would people be better
off if more lived in smaller cities and fewer lived in larger cities? Here
we consider in turn: (1) the welfare advantages of life in big cities as opposed to life in smaller cities; (2) the welfare disadvantages; and (3) the
net welfare effect of urban size.

WELFARE ADVANTAGES OF LARGE CITIES

On the positive side, urban size appears to be related to increased
money earnings. Table 8.2 presents ratios of average income within
cities of different size to average income in the nation as a whole.
Results are presented for four regions for 1959 and 1969. For both
years, and in all regions, the trends of these ratios exhibit
remarkable consistency: ratios tend to increase with city size.

Figure 8.2   Town Expansion Projects in England

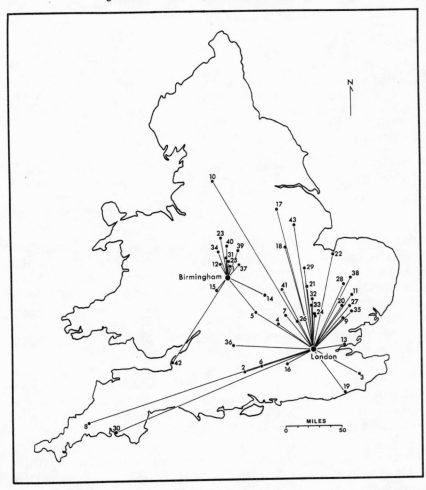

NOTE: Larger cities in Britain have been encouraged to conclude town expansion agreements with small towns in their hinterlands. Under these agreements the small towns construct public housing and reserve it for households from the large city desirous of reducing its population. For its part the large city agrees to contribute towards the expansion of public services in the small town. This map shows the receiving towns for the cities of London and Birmingham as of 1972.

KEY TO RECEIVING TOWNS: 1. Aldridge-Brownhills; 2. Andover; 3. Ashford; 4. Aylesbury; 5. Banbury; 6. Basingstoke; 7. Bletchley; 8. Bodmin; 9. Braintree; 10. Burnley; 11. Bury St. Edmunds; 12. Cannock; 13. Canvey Island; 14. Daventry; 15. Droitwich; 16. Frimley; 17. Gainsborough; 18. Grantham; 19. Hastings; 20. Haverhill; 21. Huntingdon; 22. King's Lynn; 23. Leek; 24. Letchworth; 25. Lichfield; 26. Luton; 27. Melford; 28. Mildenhall; 29. Peterborough; 30. Plymouth; 31. Rugeley; 32. St. Neot's; 33. Sandy; 34. Stafford; 35. Sudbury; 36. Swindon; 37. Tamworth; 38. Thetford; 39. Tutbury; 40. Uttoxeter; 41. Wellingborough; 42. Weston-Super-Mare; 43. Witham.

Table 8.2   Average Income for SMSA Population Classes Relative to U.S. Average, 1959–1969

Region and SMSA*	1959	1969
Northeast		
125	0.95	0.94
375	0.95	0.99
750	0.98	1.02
2,000	1.09	1.06
North Central		
125	1.02	1.00
375	1.02	1.04
750	1.10	1.07
2,000	1.15	1.12
South		
125	0.88	0.84
375	0.93	0.89
750	0.95	0.92
2,000	1.05	0.96
West		
125	1.00	1.00
375	0.99	1.05
750	1.04	1.08
2,000	1.13	1.14

SOURCE: Irving Hoch, "Urban Scale and Environmental Quality," in Ronald G. Ridker, ed., *Population, Resources and the Environment* (Washington, D.C.: Government Printing Office, 1972), p. 243.
*Size in thousands.

Similar relationships, though not quite so strong, are evident in Canada (Ray & Brewis 1976).

A second major advantage of the larger city as compared with the smaller one is the former's *more diversified employment structure.* At least there does seem to be a fairly strong relationship between industrial diversification and urban size. Using data for 1950, for example, it has been shown that industrial diversification increases with urban size, the correlation coefficient being a fairly respectable + .55 (Rodgers 1957, p. 22). Hence it is the Garys, the Flints, the Arvidas, and the Oshawas of this world that tend to be single-industry or even single-firm towns. Larger cities such as Chicago and Toronto are not only more diversified due to the addition of a large service sector to their local economy, but they are also more diversified in their industrial structures. The same generalizations appear to apply to cities elsewhere such as in Britain and France.

Figure 8.3   France's Eight Provincial *Métropoles d'Equilibre*

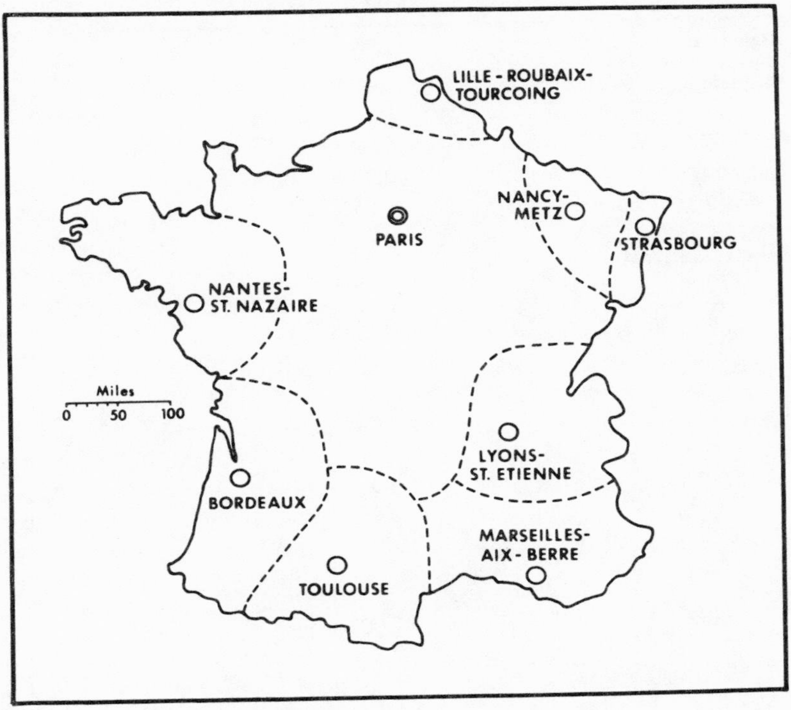

NOTE: Dashed lines indicate spheres of influence.
SOURCE: After Boudeville, *Problems of Regional Economic Planning*, p. 165.

This seems to provide some clear advantages for the populations of larger cities relative to those of smaller ones. Theoretically, for example, it should result in lower rates of unemployment. Different sectors of the urban economy tend to undergo business cycles that are somewhat unrelated; as some sectors are undergoing a cyclical deterioration in trade, therefore, and releasing labor, others may be experiencing expansion and recruiting additional workers. As a consequence the populations of larger cities should be cushioned against periodic unemployment. Unfortunately there is not a great deal of statistical verification for this relationship.

Diversification, however, has other advantages. Diversified urban economies are more likely to offer employment opportunities for women than are the more specialized economies of smaller towns. The word *likely* is important, however, for some small towns such as those specializing in textile production do employ large numbers of women in the labor force; still other smaller towns such as those specializing in the production of steel or automobiles offer few jobs for women. Larger cities on the other hand offer a greater certainty of employment for women. The greater probability with which big city families have two breadwinners rather than only one, therefore, may be an important reason accounting for variations in income per capita, though not in wage rates per capita.

A final advantage of diversification is more difficult to quantify; but it is nonetheless real, and there is a good deal of evidence of a casual nature to support it. Briefly, a more diversified employment structure enhances the bargaining power of both labor in the wage determination process and of the population at large in the political process. In small towns with their single dominant firm or single dominant industry, labor has few employment alternatives with which to play one employer against another. Firms have a monopoly of the local demand for labor and are therefore in a stronger position to determine wages than firms in larger cities. Similar influences carry over into the more general political process; in the small town the impact of the single firm or industry on the local economy provides it with considerable leverage in opposing, for example, environmental policies that would impose expense on it. In the larger city single firms or industries have substantially reduced leverage simply because the industrial structure is, in all likelihood, far less monolithic.

A third advantage of the larger city is that it tends to offer a *much more varied array of consumer goods and services in both private and public sectors* of the urban economy. In the private sector, central place theory (Berry 1967) has shown that as city size increases, so thresholds for increasingly higher order goods and services are satisfied. Larger cities, therefore, tend to be much more varied in their retail structures, catering not only to more mundane tastes but also to the more exotic. Consequently big cities tend to offer a much greater variety of private entertainment—cinemas, theaters, restaurants, private art galleries, and nightclubs—than smaller cities. They also tend to be more cosmopolitan: one can find both clubs catering to the more unusual tastes and also ethnic restaurants and ethnic-specific institutions.

In the public sector there is similar diversity. School systems are large enough to take advantage of some economies of scale and so will be able to offer more varied curricula: the proportion of school children taking Russian, for example, would probably show a direct relationship with city size. Finally, consider recreational programs. How many small towns have public golf courses and public parks as compared with larger cities?

A fourth more speculative advantage is believed to reside in *the more competitive provision of private goods and services in larger cities* as opposed to smaller cities. In the private economy the number of purveyors of a given function increases with urban size; for example, the number of grocery stores and banks. Theoretically this should allow customers to trade off one retailer against another. The consequently greater competitiveness should be apparent in the price of the average shopping basket or in mortgage terms for housing loans. There is, however, no systematic evidence available on these points.

Less speculative is a fifth advantage of urban size: the *availability of health care services*. Generally as urban size increases the availability of health care services increases. This is less true of general practitioners than it is of other health care professionals (table 8.3). Medical specialists are in particularly short supply in rural areas dominated by small towns when compared with larger metropolitan areas (figure 8.4). Inability to attract physicians is a critical problem for many of the smaller towns. Rural counties frequently have more hospitals than urban counties, but they are usually much smaller, more often inadequately staffed, poorly equipped, and deficient in outpatient and extended care facilities. The proportion of hospitals accredited by the Joint Commission on American Hospitals in 1966 was, therefore, much lower in nonmetropolitan counties (45 percent) than in metropolitan counties (78 percent).

WELFARE DISADVANTAGES OF LARGE CITIES

Major problems of the central city concern *congestion* of common facilities and of common resources like air, water, and highways. *Air pollution* is one of the more widely recognized of these congestion phenomena. There can be little doubt either of the aggravating effects of urban size on air pollution or of its serious implications for health. As table 8.4 shows, three types of pollutant—particulates, sulphur dioxide, and nitrogen dioxide—show fairly regular increases in concentration with city size. There are exceptions, of course, with towns less than 10,000 in size showing somewhat higher pollution levels in sulphur and nitrogen dioxide than towns somewhat larger. Interestingly enough the town credited with having the worst air pollution problem in the United States—Steubenville, Ohio—has a population of about 11,000.

Conclusions regarding the health effects of air pollution are frightening. If air pollution levels in major urban areas were halved, for instance, the incidence of diseases such as bronchitis and lung cancer could be drastically reduced (table 8.5). Table 8.5 also provides estimates of the actual monetary cost of air pollution-induced disease. These include not only the direct costs of hospital and nursing home care but also indirect costs such as the earnings foregone by those who are sick, disabled, or prematurely deceased.

Table 8.3   Urban Size and the Availability of Health Care (health personnel per 100,000 population)

	GPs (1966)	Dentists (1964)	Active Nurses (1962)	Pharma- cists (1962)
Greater metropolitan counties*	34	70	328	81
Lesser metropolitan counties**	28	52	340	65
Counties next to metropolitan areas	35	39	254	51
Isolated semirural counties†	36	39	243	56
Isolated rural counties	33	27	126	45

SOURCE: *Health Care in Rural America*, U.S. Department of Agriculture Economic Research Service ERS–451 (July 1970).

*1,000,000 + inhabitants.

**50,000–1,000,000 inhabitants.

†At least one township with 2,500 inhabitants.

One of the more apparent manifestations of big city congestion, however, is *highway congestion*. As figure 8.5 shows, both average trip length and duration of journey-to-work increase with city size. Perhaps a more sensitive indicator of congestion costs is the actual travel-to-work speed: operational speeds are about 22 percent higher in U.S. cities with less than one million in population than in larger cities. There is no doubt that this also exacerbates the air pollution problem of large cities by increasing the length of time over which exhaust fumes are emitted in a given area.

A big city problem as equally appreciated as that of congestion is *crime*. Per capita crime rates are almost always higher in larger cities than in smaller ones, whether they are in Britain, France, Canada, West Germany, or the United States. The urban size effect however appears to be particularly strong in the United States (table 8.6).

A third set of negative effects of urban size concerns *increased costs of living* (table 8.7). A particularly critical component of this increase concerns housing costs. With increasing size and the increasing population density that accompanies it, demand for a relatively inelastic supply of accessible land increases with consequent increases in land costs. There is no doubt that housing in small towns is a bargain, though this does not seem to be sufficiently appreciated to stimulate a return to them.

Finally, on the debit side, as cities increase in size we can recognize certain changes in overall urban spatial structure. These changes may have serious implications for environmental quality, especially as it is experienced by different subgroups of the population at large. In particular, *jurisdictional fragmentation increases with city size* (figure 8.6): as population increases, so subgroups of the population

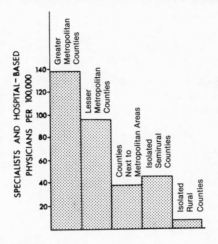

Figure 8.4   Urban Size and Access to Medical Specialists, 1966

SOURCE: Irving Hoch, "Urban Scale and Environmental Quality," in Ronald G. Ridker, ed., *Population Resources and the Environment* (Washington, D.C.: Government Printing Office, 1972), ch. 9.

Table 8.4   Pollution Concentration and Urban Size, 1969–1970

Class Number & Population Class	Concentration			No. of sites
	TSP*	SO²	NO²	
1. Nonurban	25	10	33	5
2. Urban <10,000	57	35	116	2
3. 10,000	81	18	64	2
4. 25,000	87	14	63	2
5. 50,000	118	29	127	9
6. 100,000	95	26	114	37
7. 400,000	100	28	127	17
8. 700,000	101	29	146	9
9. 1,000,000	134	69	163	2
10. 3,000,000	120	85	153	2

SOURCE: Irving Hoch, "Urban Scale and Environmental Quality," in Ronald G. Ridker, ed., *Population, Resources and the Environment* (Washington, D.C.: Government Printing Office, 1972).

*Total suspended particulates.

Figure 8.5   Average Auto Driver Work Trip Length, Duration, and Population (twenty-three cities)

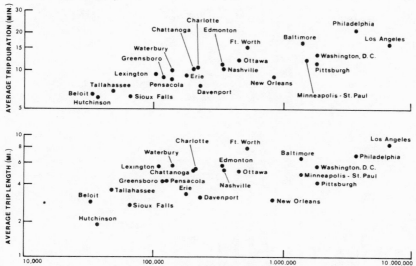

SOURCE: Irving Hoch, "Urban Scale and Environmental Quality," in Ronald G. Ridker, ed., *Population Resources and the Environment* (Washington, D.C.: Government Printing Office, 1972), ch. 9.

Table 8.5   Health Effects of a Fifty-percent Reduction in Air Pollution

Disease	Decline in Incidence (%)	Cost Saving/Yr*
Bronchitis	25–50	$250–500
Lung cancer	25	33
All respiratory diseases	25	1,222
Cardiovascular disease	10–20	468
All cancer	15	390

SOURCE: Irving Hoch, "Urban Scale and Environmental Quality," in Ronald G. Ridker, ed., *Population, Resources and the Environment* (Washington, D.C.: Government Printing Office, 1972).

*Millions of dollars.

Table 8.6   Crime Rates by City Size per 100,000 Inhabitants, 1967

City Population*	Homicide	Rape	Robbery	Assault	Burglary	Larceny	Auto Theft
>250	11.8	14.8	95.1	130.0	229.1	376.7	122.3
100–250	7.2	8.2	36.5	77.6	180.4	418.6	102.0
50–100	3.5	5.6	25.9	56.4	152.7	385.3	83.1
25–50	2.9	4.9	18.0	49.7	135.2	362.9	69.9
10–25	2.8	4.4	12.5	45.9	122.9	314.3	58.4
<10	2.1	3.8	7.3	47.6	114.6	253.4	52.0
Suburban areas	3.2	6.1	18.4	44.1	132.6	245.1	61.1
Rural areas	4.3	6.5	9.1	33.9	110.8	116.0	37.0

SOURCE: U.S. Federal Bureau of Investigation, *Crime in the United States—Uniform Crime Reports, 1967* (1968), pp. 116–17.

*In thousands.

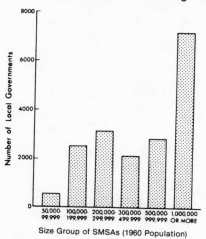

Figure 8.6   Urban Size and Jurisdictional Fragmentation

Size Group of SMSAs (1960 Population)

SOURCE: Benjamin J. Frieden, *Metropolitan America: Challenge to Federalism* (Washington, D.C.: Government Printing Office, 1966), p. 23.

Table 8.7   Cost of Living Index by Population Size and Region, 1966

Size*	North-east	North Central	South	West
5	.935	.923	.875	.930
50	.970	.954	.894	.960
125	.987	.968	.903	.978
250	.999	.979	.910	.990
375	1.007	.986	.914	.997
750	1.021	.999	.921	1.011
1,000	1.027	1.004	.925	1.016
2,000	1.042	1.018	.933	1.031
5,000	1.064	1.037	.945	1.052

SOURCE: Irving Hoch, "Urban Scale and Environmental Quality," in Ronald G. Ridker, ed., *Population, Resources and the Environment* (Washington, D.C.: Government Printing Office, 1972).
* In thousands.

Figure 8.7   Urban Size and Residential Segregation

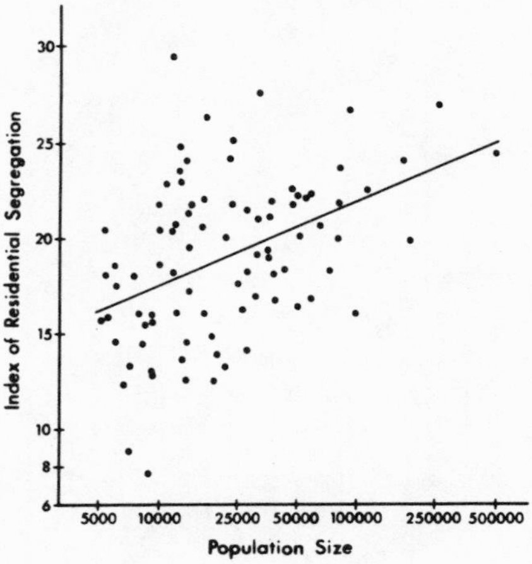

SOURCE: Irving Hoch, "Urban Scale and Environmental Quality," in Ronald G. Ridker, ed., *Population Resources and the Environment* (Washington, D.C.: Government Printing Office, 1972), ch. 9.

preferring particular packages of public provision—education, public safety, distances from other subgroups—increase in size to the point at which it is economically feasible for them to organize collectively as new jurisdictions (Cox 1973, ch. 2). This tendency towards fragmentation has serious implications for coordination on metropolitan areawide problems. It furthermore provides a necessary context for the emergence of inequalities in public provision and in tax rates between central city and suburban jurisdictions (Cox 1973, ch. 3).

In addition, *residential segregation increases with city size* (figure 8.7): to some extent this is a function of jurisdictional fragmentation and, in the U.S. context, the land use control rights that accompany municipal incorporation and facilitate residential exclusion of groups regarded as undesirable (Danielson 1972; Cox 1973, ch. 3). Even within jurisdictions, however, there are forces facilitating increased residential segregation. As jurisdictional population increases, for example, the number of high schools multiplies, providing the possibility of segregated pupil compositions if the population can arrange itself residentially to take advantage of it.

NET WELFARE EFFECT

It is possible, therefore, to assemble a wide variety of evidence regarding the negative and positive effects of urban size on welfare. Presumably, however, these effects exercise an impact *together* rather than individually; we are, therefore, faced with the task of specifying the relationship between urban size and welfare *in toto*. In addition what will be a desirable environment for certain subgroups of the population may provide disutility for other subgroups with different sets of preferences and/or resources. We are, therefore, also concerned with specifying the relationship between urban size and welfare for different segments of the population (Alonso 1968).

With respect to the population as a whole, a common assumption is that welfare initially increases with urban size, the benefits of city size exceeding its costs; ultimately, however, costs exceed benefits and utilities decline as a city continues to grow (Alonso 1968). The point of inflection in the curve (figure 8.8) then would represent an optimal city size. A fair amount has been written in the literature concerning what that optimal size is (Richardson 1972, p. 30). A number of authors have suggested that a city of about 250,000 is close to the optimal size. If the urban size-welfare relationship is characterized by an inflection, however, the position of the inflection is likely to vary with factors such as age of city and occupational composition; younger cities, for example, would have more efficient sewage and transportation systems than older cities, allowing them to grow to a larger size before encountering net disutilities.

It has also been hypothesized that the form of the relationship varies somewhat for different subgroups of the population (Thompson 1972, pp. 100–101). Lower income families in particular benefit from more competitive retailing and increasing competition among employers for labor. As cities grow in size, however, they are also the ones suffering most from growing crime levels, congestion, air pollution, and noise. The middle class, on the other hand, is able to escape the problems—largely of the central city—by relocating to the suburbs. At the same time residential segregation and jurisdictional fragmentation work to the benefit of the wealthier and to the disadvantage of the poorer. Those of higher income also benefit far more from the cultural amenities characteristic of larger cities. The inflection, therefore, typically lies further to the right for the middle class than for the lower class. Cities optimally sized for the middle class are consequently too big for those of lower income (figure 8.9).

All these arguments are of course somewhat hypothetical in character and make no reference to what people actually want as opposed to what we assume they want. In this respect the results of a recent public opinion survey are remarkable (Maizie & Rawlings 1973). Respondents throughout the United States were asked, Where would you prefer to live? On a farm, open country (not on a farm), in a small town, in a small city, in a medium-size city, in a large city, in a suburb of a medium-size city, in a suburb of a large city? Major results of interest can be found in table 8.8, where preferred urban size of

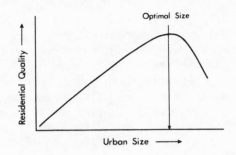

Figure 8.8   The Concept of an Optimal City Size

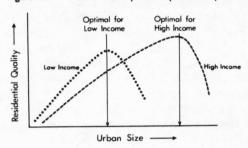

Figure 8.9   Income Group and Optimal City Size

residence is cross-classified by actual city size of residence and a variety of individual characteristics such as race and education. In brief, the outstanding results are:

1.   Fifty-three percent of the respondents preferred a rural or small town location, while only 13 percent preferred a large urban location. Yet in actuality only 32 percent lived in rural and small town locales, while 28 percent lived in big cities.
2.   Preference for small town life is considerably greater among those currently living in small towns (88 percent) than for those living in big cities (34 percent); even so, a majority of those currently living in big cities (60 percent) would prefer not to.
3.   There were some interesting racial differences. Blacks apparently show stronger preferences for big cities than whites. Since about as many blacks as whites were raised in nonmetropolitan contexts, this suggests that they do not share white nostalgia for small town, rural existence.
4.   The less educated and the poorer showed a strong preference for small towns. This bias was also apparent in the preferences of the more educated and the wealthier, but it was not nearly so strong.

Table 8.8   Where Would You *Prefer* to Live?

	Rural or Small Town (%)	Small Urban (%)	Large Urban (%)	No Opinion (%)	No.
National	53	33	13	1	1,708
Residence					
Rural or small town	88	10	2		473
Small urban	39	55	6		753
Large urban	34	26	39	2	478
Region					
Northeast	58	28	14		371
South	57	30	12		583
North Central	46	37	17		480
West	50	38	12		274
Age					
Under 30 years	56	28	15		468
30 years & over	52	34	13	1	1,219
Color					
White	54	33	11		1,362
Black	33	34	33		320
Education					
Less than high school	57	30	12	1	641
High school complete	54	32	13	1	542
Some college	47	38	14	1	300
College complete	40	38	22		206
Income					
Under $5,000	57	32	10	1	402
$5,000–9,999	53	34	12		487
$10,000–14,999	45	29	11		344
$15,000 or more	45	34	21		255

NOTE: *Rural* or *small town* includes the farm, open country, or small town responses. *Small urban* represents small city or medium-size city and suburb. *Large urban* includes the large city and its suburbs.

SOURCE: Maizie and Rawlings, "Public Attitudes Towards Population Distribution Issues," p. 605.

Figure 8.10   National Parks, Areas of Outstanding Natural Beauty, and Green Belts in England and Wales

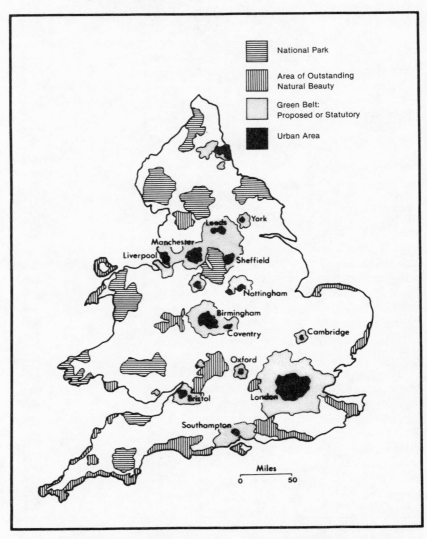

SOURCE: After James H. Johnston, ed., *Suburban Growth* (New York: Wiley, 1974), pp. 61; 70.

This is consistent with our earlier suggestion that the optimally sized city for those of lower income is somewhat smaller than that for those of higher income and/or more sophisticated tastes.

In addition to the evidence supplied by public opinion polls, however, there is other evidence suggesting that people find larger cities really rather distasteful to live in. We demonstrated earlier, for example, that wage rates per capita tend to increase with city size. It has been suggested that the additional wage earned in a larger city is of a compensatory nature; i.e., it is needed in order to induce labor to live and work in an environment that, on grounds not related to the availability of work, people find undesirable (Hoch 1972).

Amenity vs Development Conflicts

A sustained perusal of national and local newspapers impresses one with the frequency of conflicts between what we may loosely define as "amenity interests" and "development interests." These conflicts range in diversity from the issue of whether a pipeline should be constructed across Alaska to local issues such as those stemming from proposals to flood farmland in order to provide nearby cities with water.

Concerns of this nature are evinced at the policy level in a variety of planning legislation. In Britain, for example, land use is strictly controlled in areas designated as National Parks, Areas of Outstanding Natural Beauty, or as Green Belts around major cities (figure 8.10). In these areas it is generally extremely difficult to obtain permission to do anything other than use the land for agricultural purposes (Clout 1972); as a consequence new residential construction and mineral and industrial development are negligible.

Similar zones have been established in some of the U.S. states. Two major examples include regulation of coastal land use in Delaware and California. In 1971 Delaware passed a law—the Delaware Coastal Zone Act—that bars a variety of industrial activities from a coastal strip approximately 2 miles wide and 115 miles long (figure 8.11). The activities include oil refineries, steel mills, superports, and petrochemical plants. More recently California has taken steps towards state regulation of coastal land use. In 1972, by means of a statewide referendum, Proposition 20 provided for the establishment of a state coastal zone conservation commission and six regional commissions to regulate land use within 1,000 yards inland from the mean high tide mark. The work of the commissions will be to consider and grant permits, review environmental impact statements, and prepare a coastal land use plan.

Figure 8.11   The Delaware Coastal Zone

NOTE: The cross-hatched area on the map indicates the coastal zone now put off limits to heavy manufacturing by controversial Delaware law.
SOURCE: After *Business Week*, 2 March 1974, p. 71.

The federal government, on the other hand, has tended not to exercise such geographically localized and restrictive policies. Generally if the federal government wished to forestall what was regarded as undesirable development, existing owners were bought out. U.S. National Parks derive from such purchases and from lands never granted to private owners. In fact, the federal government owns close to one-third of the land area of the United States; and even outside National Parks, commercial use for grazing, timbering, or mining operations is strictly regulated (figure 8.12). An exception to this control-through-purchase policy, however, concerns federal payments to the states for interstate highways: the federal share has been marginally higher if a receiving state agreed to establish along either side of the interstate a zone within which advertising would be prohibited.

The conflicts these policies are designed to resolve or anticipate occur among a variety of protagonists (Gregory 1971; Smith 1975). Development interests, for example, include: mining companies wishing to prospect for or develop mineral resources; water companies whose goal might be to flood a valley in order to provide water for a distant city; property developers interested in building housing on the edge of the city or erecting office blocks in the center of the city; and State Transportation Departments eager to construct freeways.

Amenity interests, on the other hand, include groups concerned with the protection of wildlife or wilderness areas: in the United States, the Audubon Society, the Nature Conservancy, and the Sierra Club; in Britain, the Youth Hostels Association, the Ramblers' Association, the National Trust, and the Council for the Preservation of Rural England. In other cases of open space preservation the interests involved may be more of an ad hoc nature: for example, the Little Bledington Defence League. Amenity interests, however, are not confined purely to rural locales. In Britain, for example, just about every town of 10,000 population or more has its civic society, which both tends to oppose the demolition of any historical or architecturally meritorious physical fabric and also monitors the activities of local planners (Lowe 1977).

Clearly there are incompatibilities between development and amenity interests. Residential development tends to obstruct views and increase traffic and noise levels. Industrial and mining development generates air pollution and peppers hitherto esthetically attractive landscapes with smokestacks and spoil heaps. Office construction furthermore can detract from the visual pleasures afforded by historic monuments.

At the same time, it should be clear that there would be no incompatibility if developer interests valued areas different from those valued by amenity interests. Unfortunately both tend to value the same locations. Within a city, for example, the architecturally worthy buildings—the cathedrals, Victorian railway stations, Victorian town halls, sixteenth-century almshouses—are likely to be close to the business district. This, of course, is precisely the area where redevelopment pressures from office developers are likely to be strongest. Similarly residential developers tend to find their most profitable locations close to existing development: highway access along with public utilities is already provided. It is exactly there, however, that developers will come into conflict with existing residents anxious to preserve adjacent open space.

The same is apparent in wilderness and mountain areas. Generally valued for recreational purposes, the rocks that are associated with rugged, awe-inspiring terrain and wilderness tend to be mineralized heavily. As figure 8.13 shows, for an instance, there is a good deal of correspondence in Britain between the country's National Parks and Areas of Outstanding Natural Beauty and those areas containing

Figure 8.12   Percentage of Land Owned by the Federal Government, 1974

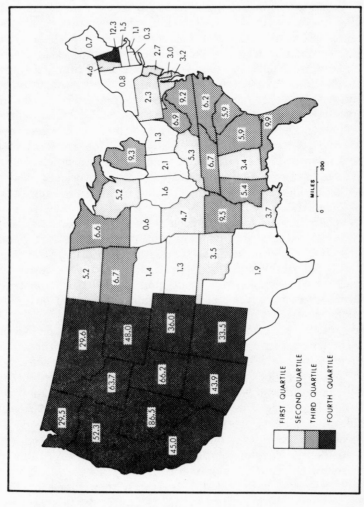

NOTE: The federal government owns large acreages in the form of National Parks, National Forests, grazing land, and military and air force bases, for example. Federal ownership is particularly important in the West, where in a number of states the federal government owns over half the land. This, of course, gives the federal government a good deal of power in regulating land use.

SOURCE: *U.S. Statistical Abstract, 1975* (Washington, D.C.: Government Printing Office, 1975), p. 203.

known deposits of nonferrous metals. As a consequence there have been a number of requests from mining companies to develop sites there. These have included requests to develop copper in the Snowdonia (North Wales) National Park; potash deposits in the Yorkshire Moors National Park; and oil deposits in the Dorset Area of Outstanding Natural Beauty. In each case substantial controversy has ensued as a result of the opposition of various amenity interests.

Similar problems occur in the United States. These have been highlighted by the country's recent energy crisis and awareness of dependence on foreign oil. The Rocky Mountains are justly famous for their natural beauty and large areas of virtually primeval wilderness. Unfortunately the Rockies also constitute a highly mineralized zone. Large deposits of oil shale are found in Colorado, while Montana and Wyoming contain over half of the country's strippable low-sulphur coal. In all, the Rocky Mountain area contains about half of the nation's remaining energy resources (figure 8.14). As in the British case, attempts by mining companies to purchase mineral rights and by the federal government to lease lands for prospecting have generated a great deal of resistance from conservation and amenity groups.

Outside highland zones, other locations that are typically under stress are those close to major, expanding metropolitan centers. Proximity creates incompatible demands for these locations. On the one hand, tranquil rural villages will be particularly valued for their combination of ready access and buccolic retreat. On the other, proximity to the city also makes those locations particularly valuable for new airports, reservoirs, rock festivals, garbage dumps, sand and gravel pits, new highways, and additional residential development.

There are, therefore, good reasons for expecting conflict between developer and amenity interests. It would be a mistake, however, to regard such controversies simply in those terms. Most of these conflicts, for example, appear to have strong class correlates; in addition, they appear to pit insiders against outsiders.

Development means construction work and a growth in the local economic base as population increases and retail sales expand. This is an especially attractive proposition in small communities where, with agricultural mechanization, employment opportunities decrease and young people have to migrate in order to find work. Development interests therefore typically find allies not only in the local chamber of commerce but also among local construction unions. The amenity interests, on the other hand, are more likely to be middle-class retirees or second-home owners of some substance who derive their incomes from outside the area and have chosen it for its quiet and unspoiled tranquility. Consequently the amenity interest can also be characterized as outsiders as opposed to the local prodevelopment forces that

Figure 8.13   Landscape Esthetics and the Occurrence of Minerals

SOURCE: After *Sunday Times*, 11 July 1971.

tend to have long-standing roots in the area. The result is a cleavage that can destroy any sense of community the town or village might have developed. Since the outsiders are likely to call on higher levels of government for help in resisting development, the locals are likely to dredge up old calls for home rule; and it is, in fact, to issues such as these that we turn in the next chapter.

Figure 8.14   Energy Resources in the Rocky Mountain Area

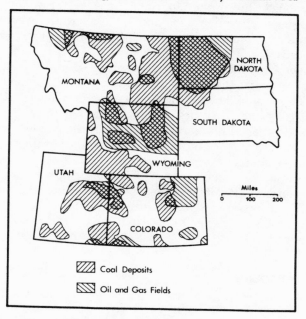

SOURCE: After *Newsweek Magazine*, 26 August 1974, p. 65.

Concluding Comments

This chapter considered urban size problems and conflicts between amenity and developer interests. That there is indeed an urban size problem is suggested by the explicit city size policies adopted by countries such as France and the United Kingdom. On the other hand, only an exhaustive examination of the empirical evidence allows one to decide whether increasing urban size has serious negative effects on welfare.

As it is, apparently to some degree people in larger cities are better off. They tend to earn higher incomes and they enjoy both a greater diversity of services offered at more competitive prices and also greater access to health care services. They furthermore have more diversified employment structures affording increased employment opportunities for women and some insulation from business cycle vicissitudes.

There is however no doubt that large cities are also more congested, more polluted, more costly to live in, and certainly more dangerous. To some degree, moreover, big cities may be worse places for poorer persons to live in than for richer ones. Increased levels of residential segregation and jurisdictional fragmentation permit better off elements of the community to insulate themselves to some degree from typically big city problems.

When we examine the net welfare effect of city size, a common presumption is that the optimally sized city is one of about 250,000 persons. This would suggest that many living in larger cities would prefer not to; survey evidence confirms this.

The second set of problems examined in the chapter were those associated with conflicts between amenity and developer interests. Many of these conflicts stem from the fact that the two opposing sets of interests tend to value the same locations. Supporters of the two tend to be socially dissimilar, amenity interests generally attracting more middle-class people. They are also less likely to be indigenous to the area they are concerned about than are protagonists of development interests.

Select Bibliography

Barr, John. "Durham's Murdered Villages." *New Society,* 3 April 1969, pp. 523–25.

Clawson, Marion. "The Future of Nonmetropolitan America." *American Scholar* 42, no. 1 (winter 1972–73): 102–9.

Drachman, Roy P. "Land Use Under Current Restraints." *Appraisal Journal* 42, no. 2 (April 1974).

Elgin, Duane, et al. *City Size and the Quality of Life.* Washington, D.C.: Government Printing Office, 1974.

Healy, Robert G. "Controlling the Uses of Land." *Resources,* no. 50, October 1975, pp. 1–3.

Lamm, Richard D. "Urban Growing Pains: Is Bigger Also Better?" *New Republic* 164, no. 23 (June 5, 1971): 17–19.

Lindsay, Sally. "Showdown on Delaware Bay." *Saturday Review,* 18 March 1972, pp. 34–39.

Lukas, J. Anthony. "The Devel-opers Are Coming." *Saturday Review* 55, no. 43 (October 21, 1972): 58–64.

Mayer, Harold. "Politics and Land Use: The Indiana Shoreline of Lake Michigan." *Annals of the Association of American Geographers* 54 (December 1964): 508–23.

Morrison, Peter A. "Population Movements: Where the Public Interest and Private Interests Conflict." In the *Commission on Population Growth and the American Future.* Vol. 5, *Population Distribution and Policy,* pp. 335–52. Washington, D.C.: Government Printing Office, 1973.

Smith, Peter J., ed. *The Politics of Physical Resources.* Harmondsworth, Middlesex: Penguin, 1975.

Ullman, Edward L. "The Nature of Cities Reconsidered." *Papers and Proceedings of the Regional Science Association* 9 (1962): 7–23.

Chapter Nine

Regional Disparities and
Local Autonomy

Urbanization takes place within a context of regions, and relationships at this level impose a further wrinkle on the domestic policy concerns of national governments. Regions tend to vary in terms of wealth, and this receives expression both in levels of disposable income and in the public spending of regional-level governments. There are, therefore, policies and juridical reforms designed to alleviate these inequalities. At the same time inequalities may be reflected in demands for increased autonomy: these demands are frequently intensified by a regional consciousness enhanced by cultural distinctiveness. These, then, provide the spectrum of concerns for this chapter. We first consider regional disparities in income and public spending; and we then turn to a consideration of issues of local autonomy.

Regional Disparities

At a regional level there are problems involving disparities in per capita income and public provision. In the more developed countries these have elicited policy responses. All the industrialized countries of Western Europe, for instance, have depressed area policies designed to attract industrial investment into areas of persistent unemployment and low incomes (Ezra 1973). In Britain there are substantial subsidies to those industrialists choosing to establish plants in depressed areas like Northeastern England, Northern Ireland, or Central Scotland. These are coupled with restrictions on plant expansion in those areas of the country such as Southeastern England that are regarded as already well provided for (Manners 1962; McCrone 1969). There is no equivalent legislation in the United States. The federal government did however establish an agency, the Appalachian Commission, designed to stimulate industrial investment in the low-income areas of Appalachia (figure 9.1). Although the commission has the power to make grants for public works expansion (airports, sewage treatment, waterworks), its major effect has in fact been limited to highway construction.

Table 9.1   The Value of Canadian Tax-sharing Arrangements, by Province, Fiscal Year Ending March 31, 1971

| | Per Capita Tax Abatements & Equalization Payment | | | | Total Tax Abatements plus Equalization Payments | | Per Capita Personal Income 1970 (est.) | | Population June 1970[3] |
	Federal Income Tax Abatement[1]	Provincial Share of Federal Estate Tax	Equaliza-tion Pay-ment to Provinces[2]	Total	Amount (millions)	As a % of Gross Provincial General Revenue	Amt.	Rank	(est.)
Newfoundland	$ 53	$ 1	$173	$227	$ 117.8	33.8	$1,759	10	518
Prince Edward Island	45	3	196	244	26.8	32.8	2,000	9	110
Nova Scotia	72	5	116	194	148.3	32.9	2,513	7	766
New Brunswick	63	2	132	197	122.7	29.3	2,258	8	624
Quebec	105[4]	9	86	201	1,208.0	31.9	2,794	5	6,013
Ontario	155	13		168	1,284.0	25.7	3,562	1	7,637
Manitoba	105	5	40	151	147.8	26.3	3,066	3	981
Saskatchewan	83	4	42	129	121.6	21.3	2,620	6	942
Alberta	118	5		123	197.2	19.3	3,059	4	1,600
British Columbia	139	9		148	315.7	24.8	3,322	2	2,137
All provinces	123	9	41	173	3,690.5	27.3	3,091		21,328

SOURCE: D. B. S., *Provincial Government Finances, Revenue and Expenditure 1970 (Estimates);* Canadian Tax Foundation, *The National Finances, 1970–71;* and *Report on the Economic Situation to the Ministers of Finance and Provincial Treasurers by the Continuing Committee on Fiscal and Economic Matters, 7–8 December 1970.*

[1]Individual and corporation income tax.

[2]Including stabilization payments.

[3]In thousands.

[4]Does not include value of extra abatements (22 income tax points) to Quebec as compensation for "opting out" of certain federal aid programs.

Figure 9.1   Appalachian Counties, 1967

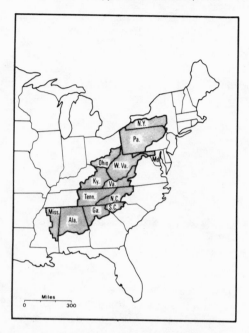

SOURCE: After Niles M. Hansen, *Rural Poverty and the Urban Crisis* (Bloomington: Indiana University Press, 1970), p. 60.

Inequalities of per capita income tend to be reflected in local tax bases. Another set of government policies, therefore, has aimed at subsidizing the revenues of poorer provincial, state, and local governments. In Canada, for example, there are explicit revenue equalization payments from the federal government (Advisory Commission on Intergovernmental Relations 1971, ch. 2). See table 9.1.

We now turn to consider, in turn, interregional income disparities and variations in public provision.

INTERREGIONAL INCOME DISPARITIES

In chapter 3 we noted the existence of substantial interregional disparities in per capita income in both Britain and the United States; we could have done the same for Canada, Italy, Spain, France, West Germany, or any number of other countries. We also observed that much of this variation is due to occupational mix: regions with an occupational mix biased towards lower paying jobs tend to have lower per capita incomes than regions with an occupational mix biased towards higher paying jobs.

Table 9.2   Migration by Redevelopment Area

	Redevelopment Area		Not a Redevel-
	5A[1]	5B[2]	opment Area
% moved away over 5-year period	14.6	13.5	13.2
No. of cases	303	436	3,615
Place of residence at time of interview			
% moved during year following interview	4.0	5.0	5.0
No. of cases	384	199	1,009

SOURCE: Peter A. Morrison, "Population Movements and the Shape of Urban Growth," in Maizie and Rawlings, *Population Distribution and Policy*, p. 307.

[1]High unemployment area.

[2]Low income area.

In addition inequalities in income are related to other inequalities in economic opportunity. Areas of lower per capita incomes tend to have relatively high unemployment rates and meager opportunities for female employment. Movement out of areas of high unemployment and lower income, therefore, might also provide the opportunity of dual incomes for a household. In general, however, movement from areas of more constrained economic opportunity into areas where incomes are higher and demand for labor is stronger is very limited. According to table 9.2, for example, it would seem that living in a depressed area—whether one of high unemployment (5A areas) or low income (5B areas)—exercises no obvious impact on the rate of outmigration as compared with that from other areas. There are almost no differences in outmigration rates either over a five-year or a one-year period, at least in the United States.

These aggregate relationships, however, conceal a great deal of variation across subgroups of the population. As table 9.3 shows, movement rates of the unemployed out of depressed areas are greater among the younger, the better educated, and the more white collar. To some degree differences in migration rates by education and occupation may relate to levels of information about jobs elsewhere. As figure 9.2 shows, white-collar employees, for example, are more dependent for job information on special trips, employer contacts, and, to a lesser degree, newspaper advertisements. Blue-collar employees are much more reliant on friends and relatives. Variation in movement rates may also have something to do, however, with the

Table 9.3   Demographic and Economic Characteristics of Unemployed Workers Who Did and Did Not Move in the Last Five Years

	Moved (%)	Did Not Move (%)
Age		
Under 35 years	56	33
35–64 years	42	64
65 years & over	2	3
Education		
Grade school	24	39
High school	50	53
College	26	8
Occupation		
Professional, technical	14	1
Other white collar	14	6
Blue collar	66	90
Other	6	1
Occupational preferences		
Security oriented	39	55
Achievement oriented	39	19
Other	22	26
County of residence*		
Live in SMSA	53	74
Do not live in SMSA	47	26
Race		
White	93	82
Black	7	18
No. of cases	117	201

NOTE: Workers represent heads of families in the labor force who had some unemployment.

SOURCE: Reprinted from John Lansing and Eva Mueller, _The Geographic Mobility of Labor_ (Ann Arbor, Mich.: Survey Research Center, Institute for Social Research, 1967), tab. 22, by permission of the publisher.

*_Movers_: place of origin of most recent move; _nonmovers_: current place of residence.

Figure 9.2   Sources of Job Information by Major Occupational Categories

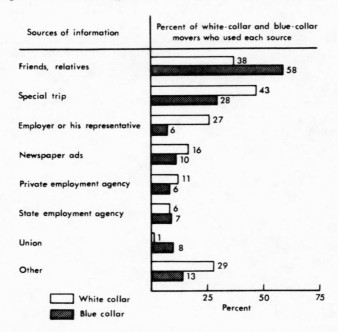

SOURCE: Peter A. Morrison, "Population Movements and the Shape of Urban Growth: Implications for Public Policy," in Maizie and Rawlings, *Population Distribution and Policy*, p. 306.

availability of savings to cushion relocation; certainly one would expect the typical white-collar employee to have more savings than the average blue-collar worker.

Occupational and educational differences in mobility moreover have important implications for interregional variations in per capita incomes. It has been found, for instance, that migration of the more educated is more responsive to interregional differences in per capita income than is migration of the less educated. As a consequence we should expect wages of more educated, professional groups to be bid down in areas of destination and bid up in areas of origin, resulting in convergence of wage rates between different regions. Less-well-educated labor, on the other hand, is less responsive to differentials in wage rates: continuing geographical wage differentials, therefore, should be a result of labor shortage in areas of higher wage rates and of labor surplus in areas where wage rates are lower.

There is in fact some evidence that interregional wage differences are greater for the less educated and the more blue collar than for the more educated and the white collar (Carnoy & Katz 1971; Wertheimer 1970). Similar relationships should help to explain the localization of unemployment and its concentration among more blue-collar, less-educated groups. Given their mobility rates they are slower to adjust to geographical variations in economic opportunity than more professional, more educated groups. As a result regional labor markets for blue-collar workers will be characterized by either excess supply and unemployment or excess demand and shortage. Regional labor markets for more professional occupations, at the same time, should exhibit greater degrees of equilibrium. When we turn and examine the reflection of these interregional variations in per capita income in levels of public provision, however, disaggregation by social group is much less relevant.

VARIATIONS IN PUBLIC PROVISION

Within nation states local governments are responsible for the provision of a variety of public services: these usually include education, public safety, public health, highway maintenance, land use planning, recreation, and cultural amenities such as museums, art galleries, and civic theaters. In order to fulfill their obligations in this regard they are given certain rights to raise money. The most important of these is the right to tax. Generally speaking these rights are largely confined to the taxation of property values, though local income taxes are used in some countries. Additional revenue-raising rights may extend to the right to borrow money, to sell bonds for local public works, and to set prices for local water and sewage services. Local government expenditure, however, is not entirely dependent on locally raised revenue; to varying degrees local governments may be able to call on central government for outright grants or cheap loans. In some countries a system of central government grants accounts for the larger part of local spending.

In federal countries, of course, the pattern is complicated somewhat by the insertion of an intermediate tier of governments: those of the states (in Australia and the United States) and of the provinces (in Canada), for instance. The rights of these intermediate governments to provide and to tax are defined constitutionally; local governments derive their rights to spend and raise money from the state and provincial governments. Like local governments in unitary states, however, states may have rights to call on revenues from the federal government.

The geographical reflection of these relationships is a set of jurisdictions—states, local governments—varying in levels of public provision and tax rates. There is, in brief, a geography of public provi-

Figure 9.3 Relative Fiscal Gaps, 1960

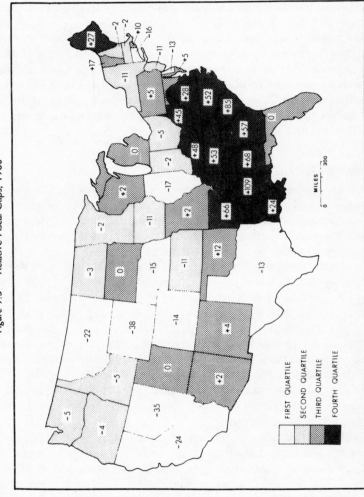

NOTE: Positive gaps indicate a deficiency of revenue relative to needs.

DATA SOURCE: Richard A. Musgrave and A. Mitchell Polinsky, "Revenue Sharing—Critical Review," in *Financing State and Local Governments*, Federal Reserve Bank of Boston Conference Series no. 3 (June 1970). p. 46. tab. 3.

sion that has important implications for individual welfare. Let us consider first the degree of inequality actually existing and then the dependence of that inequality on institutional constraints.

Interjurisdictional Inequality   Within nation states a critical problem of inequality at the interjurisdictional level *may* be that of *fiscal disparities:* a discordance between the geography of need for public services and the geography of public resources from which to satisfy those needs.

Consider, in this context, figure 9.3. The map presents indices of the negativeness or positiveness of the fiscal disparity for each of the fifty states. Fiscal disparity is assumed to be some measure of the difference between expenditure needs and fiscal capacity. In this case, expenditure needs have been evaluated as the cost of supplying average performance levels for the existing mix of state and local programs in the United States; fiscal capacity, on the other hand, has been taken as the yield of a representative state and local tax system not allowing for transfers from the federal government. The percentages appearing on the map have been computed by taking the difference between capacity and needs as a percentage of needs. Negative percentages imply an excess of capacity over needs, while positive percentages imply the reverse. Clearly a number of severe assumptions have been made in these computations. The range of variation depicted by the figures, however, is almost certainly of the correct order of magnitude.

Twenty-one of the fifty states have an excess of expenditure needs over fiscal capacity. The size of this deficiency is greatest in the low-income states of the South, though there are also deficiencies in West Virginia, Maine, and Vermont. Fiscal capacity tends to exceed needs, however, in wealthier states such as California and Illinois. The total pattern, therefore, suggests a strong explanatory role for tax base geography; the rank correlation between fiscal disparities and income per capita is − .64, suggesting a fairly close relationship with per capita tax base (figure 9.4). This, of course, assumes that income per capita is a reasonable index of per capita tax base.

Turning from general to more specific concerns, consider now: (a) interstate variations in welfare payments and (b) variations in educational spending at state and local levels.

Geography of Welfare Payments   The issue of variation in welfare payments can be treated relatively briefly. We focus in particular on the form of welfare payment subsumed by Aid to Families with Dependent Children (AFDC). AFDC payments vary appreciably from state to state (figure 9.5). In 1970, for instance, the average monthly payment per recipient was $15.15 in Alabama, $19.80 in Louisiana,

Figure 9.4   Relative Fiscal Gap and Income per Capita, 1960

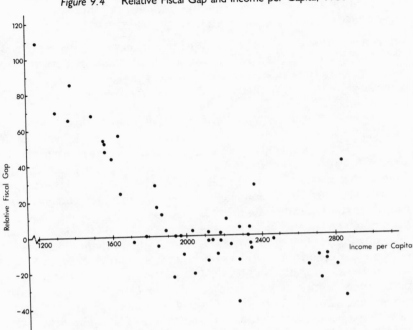

DATA SOURCES: *Relative fiscal gap data:* Richard A. Musgrave and A. Mitchell Polinsky, "Revenue Sharing—A Critical Review," in *Financing State and Local Governments,* Federal Reserve Bank of Boston Conference Series no. 3 (June 1970), p. 46, tab. 3; *income data* U.S. Bureau of the Census, *Statistical Abstract of the United States, 1972* (Washington, D.C.: Government Printing Office, 1972), p. 319, tab. 519.

and $13.95 in Mississippi; in New York, on the other hand, the average monthly payment per recipient was $77.70; in Michigan, $62.10; and in Illinois, $58.40. These differences can in turn be traced back to interstate differences in tax base. Although subsidized by the federal government the poorer states have little incentive to provide large payments. The federal government pays 5/6 of the first $18 and then 50–65 percent—in inverse ratio to state per capita income—of the balance. As a consequence poorer states tend to spend little at all above the first $18; wealthier states with greater fiscal capacities, on the other hand, do. As indicated in figure 9.6 the percentage of a state's AFDC payments financed by the federal government declines with increasing state per capita income. As a consequence there are substantial differentials in welfare payments between poorer and richer states.

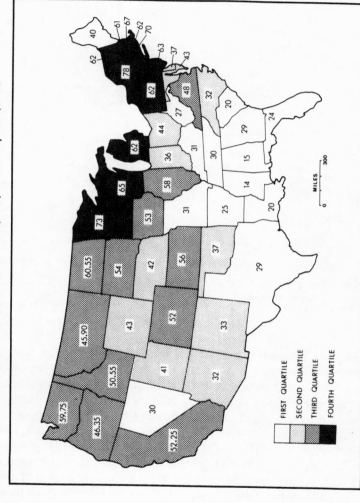

Figure 9.5   AFDC Payments per Recipient per Month by State, 1970

SOURCE: National Center for Social Statistics, AFDC: Selected Statistical Data on Families Aided and Program Operations (Washington, D.C.: Government Printing Office, 1971), item 30.

Figure 9.6   Percentage of AFDC Payments Federally Financed, 1970, and Personal Income per Capita for the Fifty United States, 1971

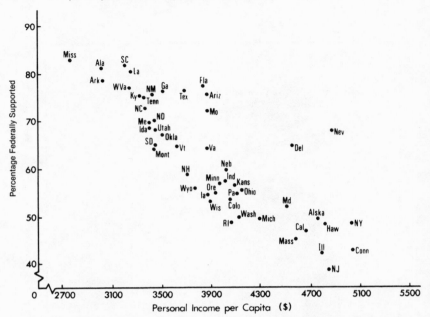

DATA SOURCES: *AFDC data:* National Center for Social Statistics, *AFDC: Selected Statistical Data on Families Aided and Program Operations* (Washington, D.C.: Government Printing Office, 1971), item 30; *income data:* U.S. Bureau of the Census, *Statistical Abstract of the United States, 1972* (Washington, D.C.: Government Printing Office, 1972), p. 125, tab. 194.

Geography of Education   The dependence of public provision on tax base geography, however, is perhaps most apparent in education (Coons, Clune & Sugarman 1970; Michelson 1972). When all educational spending within states at elementary and secondary levels is aggregated and per pupil expenditures are computed, considerable variation is apparent. The most free-spending state, New York, spent $1,466 per pupil in 1972; but Alabama—the state spending least— spent only $543 per pupil. At the state level, then, the most spent per pupil by a state exceeded the least spent by a state by a ratio of about 2.7:1. Within states somewhat larger disparities in per pupil expenditure may exist among school districts. In California in 1969–70, per pupil outlays ranged from a low of $474 to a high of $1,733—a ratio of 3.6:1.

To a considerable degree, variability of this sort is a result of tax base geography. States spending less per pupil tend to have less-substantial per capita tax bases. At the local level the question becomes one largely of variability in the *property* tax base. In a recent case

Figure 9.7   Fiscal Capacity and Expenditure per Pupil for California School Districts, Classified by Fiscal Capacity

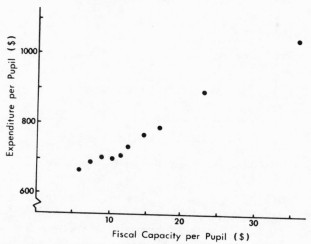

DATA SOURCE: Weiss and Driscoll, "Comparative School Finance Data."

before the California Supreme Court, for instance, two school districts—Baldwin Park and Beverly Hills—were compared. In 1968–69 the Baldwin Park school system expended only $577 to educate each of its pupils, while in the same year the Beverly Hills School District, just a few miles away, spent $1,232 per pupil. Variability in the assessed valuation of property per pupil was even greater: $3,706 in Baldwin Park and $50,885 in Beverly Hills—or a ratio of 1:13.

Clearly, to spend as much as they did the citizens of Baldwin Park would have had to have taxed themselves more severely than the citizens of Beverly Hills. In fact the Baldwin Park rate was $5.48 per $100 of assessed valuation, while in Beverly Hills it was only $2.38 per $100: a ratio of over 2:1. In a recent study the school districts of California were arranged into deciles according to fiscal capacity or assessed property valuation per pupil (Weiss & Driscoll 1972). For each decile median fiscal capacities per pupil, median expenditures per pupil, and median school tax rates were computed. Figure 9.7 indicates graphically the relationship between fiscal capacity per pupil and expenditure per pupil, while figure 9.8 indicates the relationship between fiscal capacity per pupil and school tax rates in mills. Both graphs are as we might expect and have a good deal of generality with respect to the nation.

Of course the pertinence of these statistics may need to be qualified. In particular the data reported here should not mislead us to the

Figure 9.8   Fiscal Capacity and School Tax Rates for California School Districts, Classified
by Fiscal Capacity

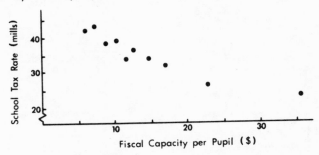

Fiscal Capacity per Pupil ($)

DATA SOURCE: Weiss and Driscoll, "Comparative School Finance Data."

point of inferring that per pupil educational expenditures are
necessarily redistributionally perverse. It is true that, in general,
poorer persons live in jurisdictions with lower assessed value per
pupil, where local governments, therefore, raise less revenue per pupil
than those of largely middle-class jurisdictions; but there are exceptions. Many low-income jurisdictions have rather healthy tax bases
resulting from the location of industrial or commercial land uses
(Peterson & Solomon 1973, pp. 62–65).

Significance of Institutional Constraints   The degree to which tax
base geography is translated into serious variations in tax rates and
public provision depends on the other hand on a variety of institutional considerations. In particular we can point to the role of the level
of geographical aggregation of local governmental jurisdictions and
also to the role of intergovernment transfers.

Level of Aggregation   There can be no doubt that the geographical
aggregation of jurisdictions can usually go a long way towards
eliminating variability in tax base and hence in public revenue per
capita. In the United States, for example, interstate variation in tax
base accounts for only a portion of interjurisdictional tax base
variation *in toto*, and the more severe extremes actually occur *between*
school districts *within* states. In Massachusetts the richest school
district in terms of assessed property valuation per pupil has 10.4
times as much money as the poorest. In Illinois, New York, and
Kansas comparable ratios are 20.1:1. 84.2:1, and 182.8:1, respectively.

In the United States proposals for combining school districts or
for shifting funding responsibility from local to state level have been
one outcome of recent court cases dealing with inequality in access to
educational resources. The fundamental constitutional question is,
Does unequal access to resources for education violate equal protec-

tion under the law as specified by the relevant state or federal constitution (Long 1973)? In some cases, as in New Jersey and California, only review of this question by the state supreme court is required. In some other cases, however, it must go to the Supreme Court. An example is the Texas case, *Rodriguez vs San Antonio Independent School District.* In that instance the Supreme Court ruled that education is not one of the rights guaranteed by the Constitution. In many states activities on this issue nevertheless continue, and it is likely that far-reaching changes in funding arrangements will come forth.

In Ohio, for example, the department of education is acting as an intermediary in encouraging consolidation of school districts within counties so as to eliminate some of the more glaring tax base disparities. By far the most widely touted solution, however, is for the state to assume all responsibility for school funding via a state-administered property tax or state income tax increase, the funds to be disbursed on an equal per pupil basis. This is essentially the system operating in the Canadian province of New Brunswick (Advisory Commission on Intergovernmental Relations 1971, ch. 4).

As of 1967 the provincial government in New Brunswick assumed the entire burden of financing public elementary and secondary education throughout the province. Historically the situation had been quite similar to that in the U.S. states. Constitutionally education in Canada is a provincial responsibility; the administration of public schools, however, had been delegated to local school boards, which proceeded to raise revenue on the basis of a locally administered property tax. As in the United States, property tax geography had a powerful effect on the resources invested in the education of children in different school districts, and the problem was exacerbated in New Brunswick by the existence of Anglo-French ethnic conflicts.

These inequalities have been largely eliminated in legislation going far beyond the finance of education alone. The local property tax has been replaced by a uniform, provincewide, real estate tax levied at a rate of 1.5 percent of market value. With respect to the disbursement of funds to local school districts the provincial minister of education sets the budget after negotiations with local school boards as to their needs and requirements. Funds are distributed in a way so as to achieve per pupil equality of resources.

A major problem nevertheless remaining has been the hiring of teachers. A provincewide salary scale has been introduced to eliminate salary competition for teachers. Teaching staffs, however, differ widely in their experience and qualifications, so that there is some variation among school districts in the amount spent per pupil. While the introduction of a provincewide salary scale does allow poorer districts to attract the better teachers on a basis equal to the richer

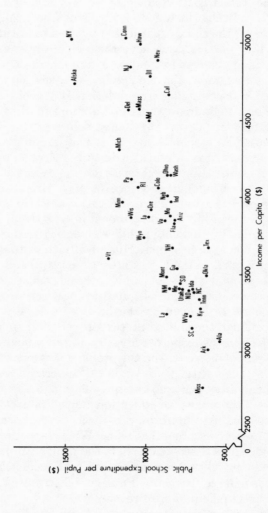

Figure 9.9   Public School Spending per Pupil, 1972, and Income per Capita for the Fifty United States, 1971

SOURCE: U.S. Bureau of the Census, *Statistical Abstract of the United States, 1972* (Washington, D.C.: Government Printing Office, 1972), p. 125, tab. 194.

Figure 9.10   Spending per Pupil on Primary and Secondary Education by English and Welsh Counties, 1969–1970, as a Function of Assessed Valuation per Pupil

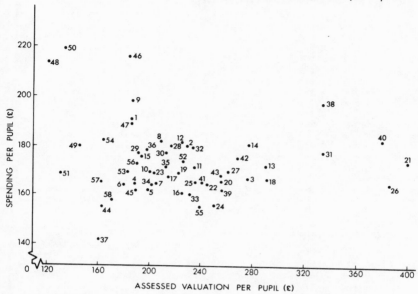

NOTE: Revenue raised per pupil by a tax rate of one penny per pound of assessed value (one pound in 1969–71 = 240 pennies).

DATA SOURCE: *Institute of Municipal Treasurers and Accountants, Education Statistics 1969–70.*

KEY TO COUNTIES: 1. Rutland; 2. Westmorland; 3. Isle of Wight; 4. Holland; 5. Hereford; 6. Kesteven; 7. E. Suffolk; 8. Huntingdon; 9. Cumberland; 10. E. Yorkshire; 11. W. Suffolk; 12. Oxford; 13. Bedford; 14. Cambridge; 15. N. Yorkshire; 16. Northampton; 17. Salop; 18. Dorset; 19. Cornwall; 20. Lindsey; 21. E. Sussex; 22. Devon; 23. Norfolk; 24. Worcester; 25. Leicester; 26. W. Sussex; 27. Berkshire; 28. Wiltshire; 29. Northumberland; 30. Gloucester; 31. Buckingham; 32. Somerset; 33. Warwick; 34. Nottingham; 35. Derby; 36. Stafford; 37. Durham; 38. Hertford; 39. Hampshire; 40. Surrey; 41. Cheshire; 42. Essex; 43. Kent; 44. W. Yorkshire; 45. Lancashire; 46. Radnor; 47. Merioneth; 48. Montgomery; 49. Cardigan; 50. Brecon; 51. Anglesey; 52. Pembroke; 53. Caernarvon; 54. Carmarthen; 55. Flint; 56. Denbigh; 57. Monmouth; 58. Glamorgan.

districts, there may still be some perverse allocation. It is likely that the better teachers are more attracted to more middle-class or urban school districts. Given a scarcity of better qualified teachers, therefore, and even with a provincewide salary scale, there are bound to be some interdistrict variations in the resources invested per pupil. This is clearly a problem that U.S. states currently considering statewide financing for education will have to take into account; that is, if they are to succeed in their mission of eliminating inequalities in access to resources in education.

Intergovernment Transfers   An alternative response to fiscal disparities, however, is provided by government grants, either from federal to state or local governments or from central to local governments.

Figure 9.11   Relative Fiscal Gaps With and Without Federal Transfers, 1960

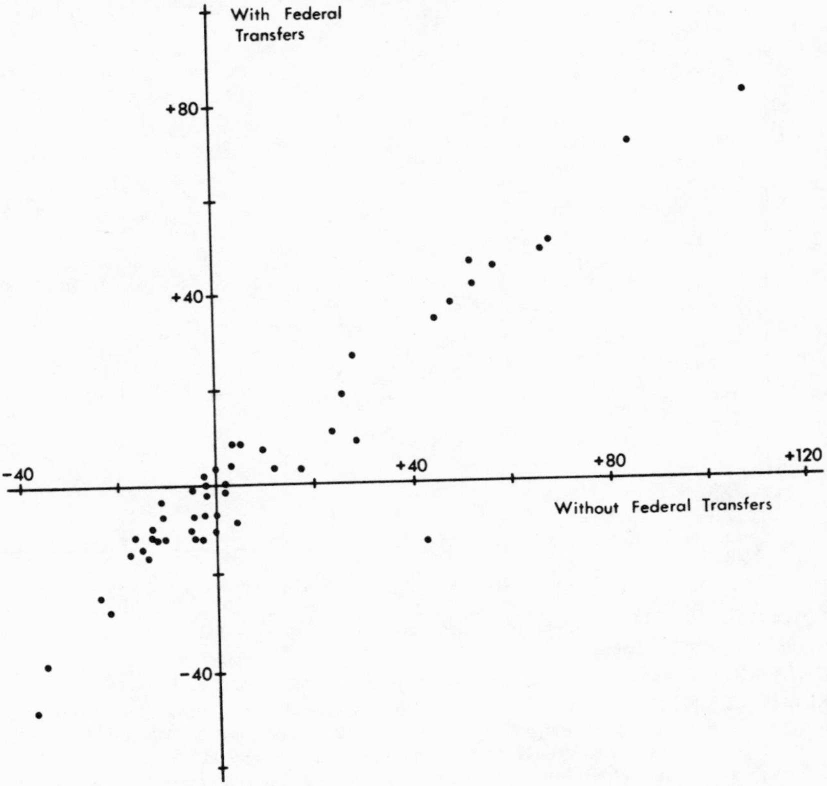

NOTE: There is a low degree of equalization achieved by federal transfers.
DATA SOURCES: Richard A. Musgrave and A. Mitchell Polinsky, "Revenue Sharing—A Critical Review," in *Financing State and Local Governments*, Federal Reserve Bank of Boston Conference Series no. 3 (June 1970), p. 46, tab. 3.

These can exercise a substantial equalizing effect on local revenues relative to needs. Educational funding in the United States and the United Kingdom provide an interesting contrast and case in point. Figure 9.9 indicates the relationship between public school spending per student in the United States and per capita income across the fifty states; per capita income is intended as a crude measure of tax base. It is obvious that there is a substantial relationship between these two variables. The rank correlation, in fact, is + .79.

Figure 9.10 provides analogous data for the fifty-eight counties of England and Wales. Plotted on the vertical axis is a measure of per pupil spending on elementary and secondary education, while the horizontal axis shows a measure of per capita tax base. This measure is the revenue per pupil that a tax of one penny per pound of assessed value would generate. In this case, however, there is obviously no relationship at all. Having a more favorable local tax base does not appear to have the same positive effect on per pupil expenditures that it has in the United States. In fact the rank correlation in the case of England and Wales is almost zero.

The relationships in the two countries then are starkly different. The fundamental reason for this lies in the nature of educational funding. In the United States the role of the federal government is modest: in 1968 barely 9 percent of total public school spending originated in the federal government. As a consequence one can expect little amelioration of what are substantial interstate differences in fiscal capacity. By comparison, in England and Wales central government assistance is on a generous scale indeed. Though it would be difficult to quote a reliable figure, it seems likely that at least 40 percent of the money spent by local education authorities originates with the central government.

There are two forms of central government assistance. First there are *general grants*, which make special allowances where large numbers of school children, declining population, and low population densities necessitate additional expenditures on busing. More important, however, are the so-called *rate deficiency grants*, which have a strongly equalizing effect on local authority revenue. The idea here is that local per capita tax bases below the national average should be supplemented by central government subsidy until they attain the national average. There is therefore a fairly comfortable lower fiscal floor below which a local authority—no matter how unsuccessful its efforts to improve its tax base—may not sink.

When we look at state expenditures *in toto* in the United States, it is apparent that the equalizing effects of federal transfers are modest at best. Earlier in this chapter, for instance, we attempted to provide some estimate of the fiscal disparity experienced by each of the fifty states. Those estimates did not take into account the impact of federal transfers on state resources. Consider now figure 9.11, which graphs fiscal disparities assuming federal transfers on the ordinate against fiscal disparities assuming no federal transfers on the abscissa. If federal transfers were truly equalizing with respect to the resources needed to satisfy state needs, then the points would lie on a straight, horizontal line; if there were absolutely no equalizing effect at all the points would lie on a line at 45° to the point of origin of the graph. In fact, there is some equalization but it is not particularly strong.

Figure 9.12   Major Contrasts Between Northern and Southern Sudan

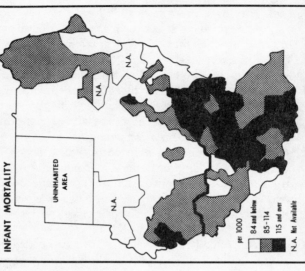

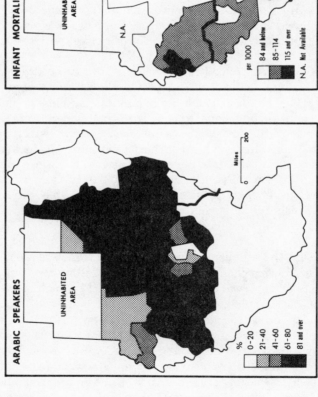

NOTE: The more Arabic and Muslim north tends to be characterized by higher levels of material welfare than the non-Arabic, Christian south. This is apparent in the contrast in infant mortality rates. The heavy black line indicates the division between north and south.

SOURCE: After K. M. Barbour, "North and South in Sudan, A Study in Human Contrasts," *Annals of the Association of American Geographers* 54, no. 2 (June 1964): 210; 221.

Local Autonomy

Major issues in some countries have concerned the degree of autonomy local, state, or provincial governments should have. Demands for increased autonomy may range from a desire to have a local language taught in public schools or to preserve, say, racially segregated institutions to, at the other end of the spectrum, independent statehood.

In some countries separatism is a real threat. This is particularly so in the LDCs of Africa and Southeast Asia, where bloody civil wars have been fought between dissident, localized minorities and the nation state as a whole. In Nigeria the Biafran war pitted the tribal groups of the southwest and north against the minority Ibo of the southeast (Schwartz 1966). In the Congo achievement of independence from Belgium was followed by the attempt of tribal groups in the remote southeast to form an independent state of Katanga. In Sudan a protracted and bloody civil war between the Arab and Muslim north of the country and the black, Christian south has just ended (Kyle 1966). See also figure 9.12. Nor are separatist attempts always unsuccessful. One is reminded, for example, of the recent establishment of the new state of Bangladesh out of what was formerly the eastern wing of Pakistan.

Strong separatist movements are not confined to LDCs. Figure 9.13 details some of the more important movements in Western Europe. Separatist groups are especially apparent in Spain, where culturally distinct groups in Galicia, Catalonia, and the Basque Country all vie for a measure of independence from the majority Spanish. In Spain separatist movements have been violent. This is also true of the Croatian movement in Yugoslavia. Rivalry with the majority Serbs has been both bitter and murderous: in 1941, for example, Croats, with the compliance of Germany's occupying forces, massacred a half million Serbs.

Separatist movements elsewhere in Western Europe are somewhat recent and more pacific. The movements for Welsh and Scottish independence provide examples. The Scottish separatist movement is particularly strong, the Scottish Nationalist party gaining 30 percent of the total Scottish vote in the general election of 1974 (Brand & McCrone 1975). Movements for autonomy in Brittany and Corsica are similarly recent and, apart from occasional arson, relatively peaceful.

In North America, with the exception of the drive for an independent Quebec in Canada, autonomist movements are rather modest affairs. The United States, for example, has a history of attempts to establish new states by partitioning old ones. Notable among these has been the effort to create a new state of Superior out of Michigan's Upper Peninsula: some adjacent counties in Wisconsin have also asked

Figure 9.13   Separatist Movements in Western Europe

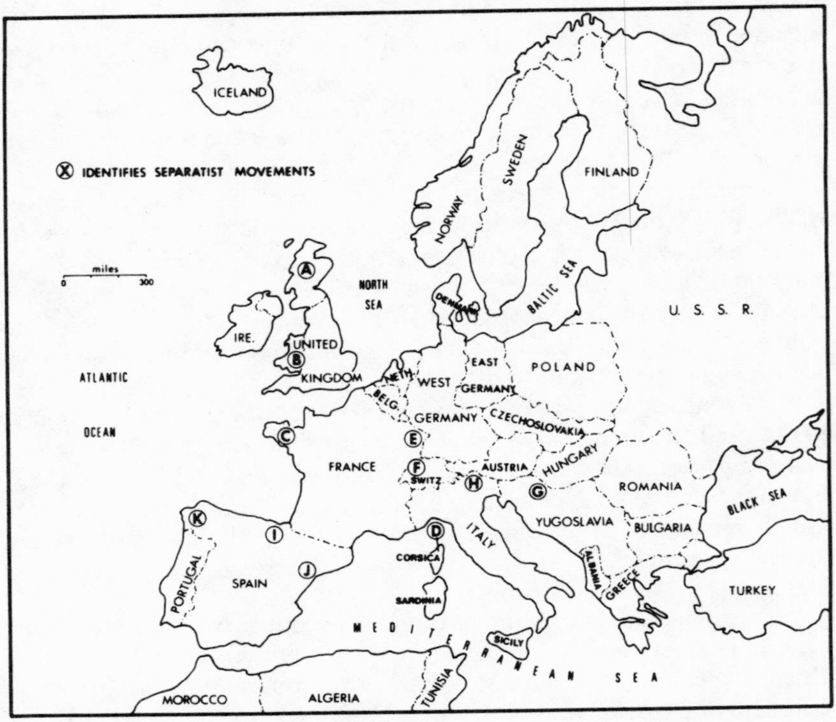

KEY: A. Scotland; B. Wales; C. Brittany; D. Corsica; E. Alsace-Lorraine; F. Swiss Jura; G. Croatia; H. Alto Adige; I. Basque Country; J. Catalonia; K. Galicia.

to join (figure 9.14). As recently as 1965 there was an attempt to divide California into two states, North and South California. The major thrust for this came from Northern California, which feared domination by more populous Southern California.

All separatist movements have a great deal in common. In particular, local populations demanding increased autonomy see themselves as relatively deprived in an economic and/or cultural sense. In the ideologies they develop to rationalize their demands this deprivation is related to their minority political status; i.e., they constitute a minority of the total national population.

In many cases indeed, hotbeds of autonomist sentiment tend to coincide with populations that, by national standards as a whole, are rather poor. In the United Kingdom, Wales and Scotland are two of the poorer regions, and unemployment levels there are typically well above the national average. In France incomes in Corsica and Brittany are 72 percent and 82 percent, respectively, of national per

Figure 9.14   Proposed State of Superior

capita incomes. Unemployment levels are again relatively high: four times the national average in Corsica, for example. To some degree, of course, a stagnant regional economy may pose doubts about the viability of, for example, an independent Scotland or Wales. Not surprisingly, therefore, the catalyst to the growth of separatism is often the discovery of some resource—oil in Scotland (Brand & Mc-Crone 1975) or Biafra, for example—dramatically altering these calculations and dissolving doubts.

In other instances, however, the localized populations demanding increased autonomy occupy relatively privileged economic statuses. In Spain the Basque provinces and Catalonia are two of the wealthier areas of the country. In Yugoslavia, Croatia ranks second in wealth of the seven republics into which the country is divided. The conception of exploitation, however, remains the same. In those cases where the local population is relatively worse off lower incomes are attributed to minority status. In wealthier Croatia, Catalonia, and so forth, the charge is that the government is not providing public services equivalent in value to the taxes the regions pay; again this is attributed to their minority status. Croatian nationalists, for instance, have been especially concerned about the use of the higher taxes they pay to fund development in the poorer Yugoslavian republics of Macedonia and Montenegro.

A second major feature of separatist movements is their sense of cultural deprivation. The localized populations among which autonomist feeling is most likely to occur tend to be distinguished by a relatively unique culture of which they are, moreover, highly conscious. This is not true of all separatist movements. It is however true of some of the strongest: the Quebec national movement and the Breton movement in France, as well as the efforts of the Welsh, the Basques and Catalans in Spain, and the Croatians in Yugoslavia. In LDCs the cultural distinctiveness of separatist groups is especially apparent, tribal affiliation often providing the touchstone of cultural expression.

Culture is mediated through language, which therefore tends to be a central political issue for separatist groups. In some cases teaching of the minority language is forbidden in public schools; this is a major source of discontent among Breton, Basque, and Catalan nationalists. In other cases the use of language on public broadcasting media may be significant: this applies to Wales, where a major grievance is the British Broadcasting Corporation's refusal to have more than a minuscule fraction of its Welsh programs in the Welsh language. In all cases the threat to cultural integrity and preservation is laid at the door of political institutions in which the aggrieved elements of the population are but a minority voice.

A final feature of separatist movements is concern over the intrusion of alien elements. In cases where the localized population is relatively poor and the alien population is represented by a relatively rich stratum, the sense of grievance tends to be heightened. This is so in contemporary Quebec. In large national corporations headquartered in Montreal there were in 1973, at the $10,000 to $15,000 salary level, three English speakers for every French speaker; the proportion was four to one at the $15,000 to $22,000 level and six to one above $22,000 (Astrachan 1973, p. 16). There is no doubt that traditionally the anglicized have formed the basis of Quebec's business elite and have been overrepresented in the province's middle class. This is not atypical of those relatively poor areas that sustain separatist movements: charges of colonialism will be common and have a certain plausibility.

Concluding Comments

The first section of this chapter looked at regional welfare disparities. There are interregional differences of appreciable magnitude in per capita income in countries such as the United States, Canada, and Britain. To some extent these are explicable in terms of occupational mix. To some degree, however, labor markets fail to adjust to the changing location of job opportunities: this is especially apparent among the less educated, the blue collar, and the older. The failure of these groups to move out of areas of declining opportunity could be due to inadequate information about job alternatives elsewhere or to lack of funds for relocation.

Geographical variations in per capita incomes are reflected in tax bases and consequently in levels of public provision. These variations are particularly clear in U.S. educational provision. In other countries such as Britain transfer payments from central government have done much to mitigate inequalities in provision at the local level. In other cases the shifting of funding responsibilities upwards from local to provincial or state levels may help to smooth out the more extreme geographic variations.

The second and briefer section of the chapter examined local autonomy issues. In many LDCs separatism, often associated with tribal affiliations, is a real threat. Even in Western Europe and North America, however, similar demands are expressed. Demands for autonomy tend to be linked to a relatively deprived economic status within the nation state as a whole. In addition autonomist sentiment is often characterized by a sense of cultural deprivation: status as a religious, ethnic, or cultural minority is a typical concern. Not surprisingly language teaching and language use tend to be major issues with groups seeking increased autonomy.

These then are the problems we have chosen to focus on at regional and local levels. The following two chapters attempt to develop some explanation for their existence.

Select Bibliography

Brand, Jack, and McCrone, Donald. "The SNP: From Protest to Nationalism." *New Society,* 20 November 1975, pp. 416–18.

Douglas, Jack D. "Going Broke the New York Way." *New Society,* 11 December 1975, pp. 593–96.

Ezra, Derek. "Regional Policy in the European Community." *National Westminster Bank Quarterly Review,* August 1973, pp. 8–21.

Weinstein, Bernard L. "What New York Can Learn from Texas." *Society* 13, no. 4 (May/June 1976): 48–50.

Chapter Ten

Political Processes at the Intranational Level

This chapter examines the processes regarded as underlying public problems at regional and local levels. Critical to the argument is the idea that local, state, and other levels of government attempt to control investment and concomitant population flows to their own advantage: to the advantage of the local tax base or job market, for example. The first section, therefore, considers the context of investment flows and associated population movements. These have welfare impacts that provide the stimulus for local policy; since local governments have substantially the same sorts of goals in mind when they attempt to control flows to their own benefit, they find themselves competing with one another. These relationships are discussed in the second section. The final section identifies and exemplifies the competitive techniques local governments employ.

Investment Flows and Population Movements

It is impossible to understand local policies outside of that locational flux and volatility the control of which is the object of local policy. It will be argued that the objective of local policy is to control locational shifts so that the utility enhancing locate within jurisdictional boundaries, while the utility detracting are deflected elsewhere.

The locational shifts at issue occur within both the private and public sectors of the economy, new public or private investment projects sparking off population shifts. Private capital, for example, is locationally footloose, ever searching out the profit-maximizing location in response to market shifts, technological change, the running down of resources, and central government regulation. Private investment moreover tends to be cumulative, locators at one stage of the process providing incentives for others to locate there at later stages. It is these economies of agglomeration that result in the tendency for big cities to grow at the expense of small cities (see chapter 8).

Figure 10.1   Value of Construction Contracts as a Percentage of Bank Deposits, 1974

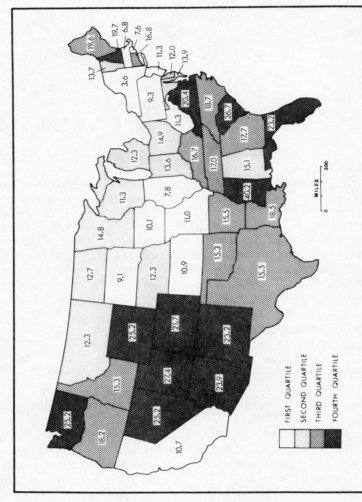

SOURCE: U.S. Bureau of the Census, *Statistical Abstract of the United States, 1965* (Washington, D.C.: Government Printing Office, 1965), pp. 454; 748.

Public capital, while not so locationally versatile, also shows shifts over space. To some degree this has been a result of the tendency to follow and complement the activities of private capital. Roads, reservoirs, airports, and so forth, will be constructed in and around a particular city because that is where private capital has chosen to locate. Likewise freeways will tend to be built between the larger cities. In the past, as today, an implicit rule of public decision makers seems to have been to put the public works where congestion was greatest.

Today this takes more explicit shape in the application of *cost-benefit analysis* (Lichfield 1964). This involves computation of the respective benefits and costs yielded by locating, say, an airport at different locations (Hall 1970; Self 1970): that location showing the greatest excess of benefits over costs is then chosen. The result, however, tends to be the same, since costs and benefits will be contingent on the locational patterns produced by the private sector of the economy.

All these shifts in public and private capital investment tend to spark off population migration. Expansion of employment in a large city results in migration from surrounding towns. Declines in a regional resource base lead to outmigration not only of capital but also of population as people seek new jobs.

Shifts of this nature occur at a variety of geographical scales. A detailed breakdown of capital investment by state would show that some states have been net savers while others—such as Florida—when experiencing investment booms have tended to be net investors (figure 10.1). Within states there are similar patterns: the money that is placed in a savings account in a small country bank may be invested in new housing in an adjacent town. Quite clearly, these scale variations are likely to be paralleled by shifts in population distribution. Within the United States there are broad redistributions from east of the Mississippi and north of the Ohio rivers to the rest of the country (figure 10.2). The West has tended to be a net gainer. Some western states, however, have gained more than others. Within states even smaller scale shifts can be identified: redistributions of population from smaller towns to larger towns, for example.

Basis of Local Policy

This locational volatility and scale variation would have little interest for political geographers if it were not for its welfare impacts. As it is, shifts in investment and population have implications for both residential desirability and private incomes. These, in turn, affect in-

Figure 10.2   Percentage Change in Population by State, 1970–1975

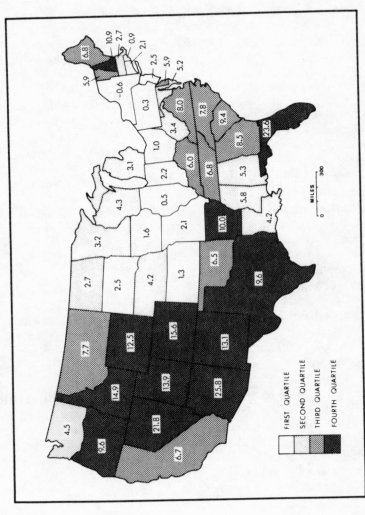

FIRST QUARTILE
SECOND QUARTILE
THIRD QUARTILE
FOURTH QUARTILE

MILES
0   300

SOURCE: *Population Estimates and Projections, Current Population Reports*, Series P-25, no. 615 (Washington, D.C.: U.S. Bureau of the Census, 1975).

volvement in local political processes, local policy formation, and the ways in which local governments relate to each other.

WELFARE IMPACTS ACROSS LOCATIONS

Interjurisdictional shifts of population and investment, for example, affect tax bases and the service demands made on those tax bases: these effects will have implications for tax rates and/or public provision. The decline in the population of small towns, for example, has left many of them with the problem of paying off past debts for capital expenditures—schools and street lighting, for instance—from a deteriorating tax base. The result is inevitably either an increase in tax rates and/or a cutback in public service levels. Those cities experiencing a large increase in capital-intensive investments on the other hand find their fiscal position enhanced: the tax base has increased without any commensurate increase in public service burden.

Public investments also have effects, but their net effect on the fiscal status of a local government is not clear. Since public buildings and publicly owned land are exempt from local property taxes, they might be regarded as fiscally negative: it is for this reason that some counties will attempt to keep out, say, state parks or new reservoirs. Public investments of this nature however often have beneficial impacts on private investment: a state park may stimulate a local tourist trade, which in turn enhances local property values and the tax base.

Other aspects of residential and environmental quality include externality effects. New capital investment may impose nuisances of noise, air pollution, and traffic to the detriment of residential desirability. The growth of population likewise may convert erstwhile bucolic retreats into rows of little boxes. The construction of a new highway may deluge the inhabitants of some particularly picturesque area with day visitors, whereas construction of new bridges may relieve congestion and make life a little more bearable.

As indicated in chapter 3, capital investments and population shifts impinge on private income prospects. To some extent these are a function of the impact of residential desirability on changes in rent. Construction of a new highway, for instance, increases access and therefore rents. Construction of an airport may depress rents; if, however, the property in question is located out of hearing range the impact may be an *increase* in rents as the relative scarcity of quietness increases.

Impacts on private income, however, are likely to be more significant than these. Investment increases the demand for labor and, to the extent that supply is inelastic over the short term, wages will increase. Yet in areas of disinvestment, labor demand will flag and wages will consequently decline. Shifts of population reorder labor market calculations, however, so that wages will tend to be bid down in areas of high inmigration and bid up in areas of high outmigration. Changes in population also affect market distributions and hence profits. One would not wish, for example, to own a grocery store or a real estate business in a town that was losing population.

Since—as we saw in the last section—the processes redistributing utility in this way occur at different scales, changes in residential desirability and private income show similar scale variations. Some processes redistribute residential utilities over short distances: the location of an airport, for example, would have almost purely intra-jurisdictional effects on property values, raising them in some neighborhoods and lowering them in others. The net fiscal effect for the local government in question, therefore, would probably be negligible. Other shifts, however, redistribute utilities *among* local jurisdictions, enhancing the tax base of some and reducing that of others: shifts of capital investment from small to large towns provide cases in point.

WELFARE IMPACTS ACROSS INDIVIDUALS

Across individuals, households, and firms at the same location, however, a given set of migration and business shifts, for example, may have substantially different welfare implications. Two explanations may be adduced: First the scale of the area within which events critical to individual welfare occur varies from one individual to another. Events at the regional level, therefore, may impinge on some, while the welfare of others is almost totally dependent on what goes on at a local level. Second there is the fact that individual preferences vary: what is utility enhancing to some is an anathema to others.

Individuals, households, and firms are dependent for their welfare on events with geographic locations: the noise from the adjacent airport; the variety of goods offered by the nearby supermarket, city, or state parks; or perhaps taxes levied at the municipal and state level. Theoretically, at least, it should be possible to plot the locations of these events on a map. It seems reasonable to assert that the maps would be quite dissimilar from one household to another and from one firm to another.

Some firms, for example—and the labor forces they employ—are oriented almost entirely to the local market. Realtors or insurance agents in Columbus, Ohio, are therefore deeply concerned about the growth of the Columbus market: what happens in the rest of Ohio or in adjacent states is a matter of relative indifference. Other firms—such as steel distributors—on the other hand may be dependent on a more regional scale market, selling products not only in Ohio but in the surrounding states of Indiana, Kentucky, and West Virginia. Columbus will be a relatively small fraction of the total market, so that the profitability of the firm does not depend a great deal on what happens there. As a final instance, one can consider firms oriented to national markets: a food processor or a textile firm, for example. Obviously what will excite the national-level firm will not necessarily interest a regional- or local-level firm.

Similar distinctions may be made with respect to households. It might be feasible in this case, however, to argue that the rich are less locality-dependent than the poor. Wealthier households are likely to have second homes that allow them to escape big city ills. For recreation they may be less dependent on city parks and more on state parks or even weekend trips to New York or Las Vegas.

Fiscal arrangements also seem important. If local governments must raise most of their revenue locally, then there will be much greater concern about the sort of fiscal externalities that are being introduced into the local jurisdiction. Local zoning issues will likely excite more interest on fiscal grounds than in the case where local government expenditure is made up largely of subsidies from higher levels of government. In some states such as North Carolina, where locally generated revenue is a relatively small proportion of local expenditure, we should expect households to be less concerned about local fiscal policy than, say, those in New Jersey, where fiscal home rule is still a reality (figure 10.3). Likewise in Canada, given the relatively large grants flowing from provincial to local governments, we should expect concern with local fiscal policy to be much less than in the United States. Perhaps this helps to account for the large degree of popular opposition in Canada to central city redevelopment (Lorimer 1970): the fiscal stakes are rather insubstantial.

More generally we have a situation in which individuals and firms are dependent for their utility on events at different geographical scales. We also have a hierarchy of governments corresponding to different geographical scales. As a consequence the groups concerned with strictly local policy will often be different in their composition from those concerned with state or provincial policy. The interests that lobby federal governments may be different again. Within a single city, for example, a locally oriented business such as a real estate firm will be highly concerned about municipal policy, particularly as it affects residential construction and development. At the same time a large concrete manufacturing firm may be more in-

Figure 10.3   Percentage of State and Local Revenue Raised by Local Governments, 1973

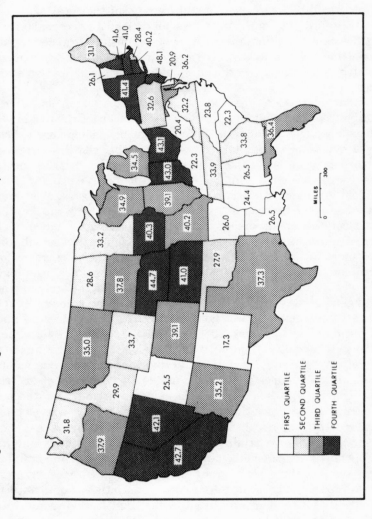

FIRST QUARTILE

SECOND QUARTILE

THIRD QUARTILE

FOURTH QUARTILE

MILES

0   300

SOURCE: U.S. Bureau of the Census, *Statistical Abstract of the United States, 1975* (Washington, D.C.: Government Printing Office, 1975).

terested in state public works policies (highways and port development, for example), while a large manufacturing firm located in that
same city but having national or even worldwide markets will concentrate on negotiations at the federal level.

Welfare impacts also vary across individuals, however, since they
have different preferences for what events they would like to see
around them: what is utility enhancing and what is utility detracting
varies from one individual to another. Especially significant in this
regard is the trade-off between residential desirability and private income discussed in chapter 2. Labor unions, particularly construction
unions, may be eager to see mining, industry, and other sources of
construction work in the vicinity. In this they may be joined by the
local chamber of commerce. These are not activities, however, that
local middle-class households would find utility enhancing. If these
households occupy second homes in the community, they are going to
be concerned especially with maintaining the environmental attributes that attracted them to it in the first place. In their view residential expansion and construction and mining activity are likely to
detract from the values they place on the location.

Other conflicts separate producers and consumers. In a number of
British towns, for instance, chambers of commerce have opposed applications to local planning authorities to construct large shopping
centers in suburban locations (Hall 1976). Although this opposition is
usually veiled with arguments that "the town is already well provided with retail facilities," their monopolistic self-interest should be
readily apparent; that is, suburban shopping centers will be utility
detracting. This is not likely to be the interpretation placed on the
issue by local consumer groups who stand to gain from increased
competition in the form of lower retail prices.

INVOLVEMENT IN THE POLITICAL PROCESS

As suggested earlier in this book, individual responses to these welfare impacts can take two broad forms: First, locational relationships
can be changed by shifting locations. Firms, for example, can—and
do—respond to increasingly adverse market conditions by relocating
where the market has shifted. Labor moves out of depressed areas
where the demand for its services is limited to areas where business is
booming; and along state boundaries residential choices may be affected by relative tax rates. Many New York City commuters, for example, live in adjacent Connecticut in order to avoid punitive New
York State taxes.

Alternative to such a relocational strategy is one that attempts to change locational relations not by shifting locations but by changing the events at the locations critical to individual welfare: strategies include altering the local tax base, the pupil composition at local schools, and the local demand for labor. The method depends on some involvement in the political process, some attempt to alter local policy in a direction that will surround one with the utility enhancing rather than the utility detracting. This might be achieved by gerrymandering neighborhood school boundaries or keeping out the fiscally undesirable by exclusionary zoning, for example.

What, however, determines which strategy will be undertaken? Is it possible to predict which elements of an impacted population will tend to relocate and which fractions will tend to become involved in the local political process? One approach to this question is based on the assumption of rationality in individual choice. If individuals are rational, then presumably choice will be based on a comparative analysis of the costs and benefits associated with alternative strategies. For some, for example, the costs of shifting to a new location are likely to be especially high. At a regional level members of minority cultures may be critically affected. Language, for instance, imposes disabilities on the French speakers of Quebec in competing for jobs elsewhere in Canada. Migration data provide some evidence on this. Thus while in Canada intraprovincial migration rates are quite similar for English- and French-speaking groups, the interprovincial rate is almost nine times higher for the English speaking than for the French speaking (Stone 1969, p. 82). The unique nature of the French-speaking community with its strong emphasis on church and family would also serve to make relocation elsewhere in Canada a particularly disorienting experience. Even where linguistic differences are less apparent, attachment to region-specific cultures—as in Wales, Scotland, Brittany, or Corsica—may inhibit relocational strategies and increase the attractions of political strategies.

At more local levels other forces come into play. An important source of income for landowners, for instance, is rent; and rent is dependent on events in the immediate vicinity: highway construction, sewer line and waterline extension, railroad service, irrigation works, in particular, and public works, in general. Given the immobility of land, landowners cannot adapt to the location of public works. The distribution of public works must be altered to conform to the interests of landowners; and it is through the political process that attempts to secure conformity are made.

Another immobile resource is local repute. The stock-in-trade of retailers, insurance agents, and realtors is a local reputation and notability. Yet these are not easily transferred to another location. For them, as for landowners, local market growth is imperative. Not surprisingly, therefore, this group, along with the landowners, form the core of local booster lobbies inciting local government to ever greater efforts to "Build a Better Community" (Salisbury 1964).

LOCAL POLICY FORMATION

At a given jurisdictional scale, therefore, the parties contending for control of local policy may have different conceptions of what is beneficial to the locality, what is harmful, and, consequently, what policy should be adopted. Broadly, three major interests can be identified: environmental groups, labor groups, and business groups. Environmental groups include not only national lobbies such as the Sierra Club or the Council for the Preservation of Rural England but also civic amenity groups or ad hoc neighborhood associations emerging to contest a particular rezoning request. Labor groups include labor unions at a diversity of scales from the union local through to the national organization. Business is an especially diverse interest. It includes not only landowners, retailers, merchants, and the chamber of commerce, in general, but also local producer interests: a fruit cooperative, a dairyman's association, or perhaps the California Tuna Boat Association. As a result of this diversity, consensus can be elusive: the local tourist industry, for instance, may be anxious about mining activity in the vicinity and hence oppose demands for expanded mineral exploitation.

Local policy will be the outcome of the attempts of these groups to persuade each other that what they want is for the good of all and should therefore be adopted as general policy. Bargaining resources—those whose withdrawal can plausibly be threatened—therefore become important. To some extent this is a matter of votes. In this regard constituents have an advantage over nonconstituents; the enfranchised residents have advantages over the unenfranchised transient. Occasionally this is apparent in policy. When conflict over Main Street parking arises between local shopkeepers and through traffic, the local shopkeepers inevitably win and Main Street parking is retained. The speed traps operated by some small town police departments would not survive in a world in which out-of-towners had the local vote. Nor should we be surprised to find that local governments are astonishingly insensitive to the needs of gypsies for campsites (Sibley 1976) and also of migrant workers for public health care.

While on most issues votes are the ultimate weapon, however, their decentralized nature may mislead as to the true sources of community power. In many local government jurisdictions a single large employer can wield tremendous power over local policy by, for example, threatening to take jobs elsewhere if local government adopts what is regarded as a hostile policy. The firm moreover does not have to be located within the jurisdiction as yet: the threat may simply be to relocate the plant elsewhere than the jurisdiction in question unless local policies are congenial. If the local government is also highly dependent on its own locally raised revenue, then contributions to tax base will constitute another effective bargaining resource. Considerations like these help to explain the continuing high levels of air and water pollution in one-industry towns such as Gary, Indiana (Greer 1974), and Youngstown and Steubenville, Ohio (Zwick 1972, pp. 173–74).

The final bargaining resource to be discussed here is campaign funds. More than ever not only national elections but also local elections are bought (Drewry 1975; Fellmeth 1973, ch. 12; Mintz & Cohen 1971, ch. 4). Television and radio advertising, newspaper splashes, and canvassing are effective—but they are costly. Every successful candidate for office has financial backers. These may range from a single wealthy benefactor to a local labor union. Campaign support, however, is obviously not disinterested: failure to heed policy advice will be punished by switching future campaign funds to more pliant candidates.

One implication of all this is that business and labor interests are frequently in coalition against environmental interests. Development often means destroying historic buildings or pleasant landscapes. To the developer, however, it means profit, and to the worker it means jobs. Construction of a reservoir for a distant city may be opposed by locals on amenity grounds; but if business interests claim that jobs depend on an increased supply of water, local labor interests will soon voice support for the reservoir (Smith 1975, ch. 5).

This does not mean that there are no situations in which amenity lobbies can secure their objectives. Much, for example, depends on the geometry of the jurisdiction relative to a particular policy decision. If a jurisdiction is structured so that most of its population is middle class and white collar, then within the jurisdiction development interests will have no labor lobbyists on whom to call. It is at least partly for this reason that a number of suburbs have succeeded in introducing no-growth policies.

At a larger scale there are situations in which the beneficial impact of a development has a field of effects smaller than that associated with existing amenity values (figure 10.4). In these cases

Figure 10.4   Hypothetical Fields of Effects of Developing a Site or Preserving It for Amenity Purposes

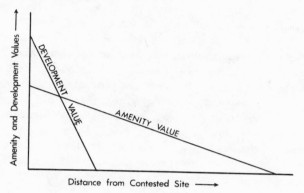

moving decisions up to higher levels of the jurisdictional hierarchy will strengthen amenity interests. This seems to have been true in the case of the 1972 California referendum on Proposition 20. The object of this proposition was to halt all further development of the California shore line within 1,000 yards landward of the mean high tide line, absent the approval of a special coastal commission to be established by the state. It seems plausible that coastal counties would be the main losers in terms of jobs and tax revenues from such a ruling; but populations of noncoastal counties would benefit from access to the coast for recreational purposes. In fact a study showed that when holding a number of other significant variables constant, the support of coastal counties for Proposition 20 was less than that of interior counties by about eight percentage points (Campbell 1974, p. 19). It seems perfectly feasible that if the vote on Proposition 20 had been limited to coastal counties alone, developmental pressures would have prevailed and it would have been defeated.

In other cases it may be that richer jurisdictions are more willing to forego tax base and job advantages in order to preserve the environment. Accordingly, in voting on Proposition 20, wealthier coastal counties were substantially more likely to support it than were poorer ones (Campbell 1974, pp. 19–20).

Another case in this context is the contrast between the outcome of the Colorado Winter Olympics issue and the Alaska pipeline issue. In the Colorado case the question was whether the state should hold and subsidize the Winter Olympics in 1976. Federal monies were also contingent on this funding decision. Although the subsidy was strongly supported by tourist interests, airlines, public utilities, ski resorts, and all the other interests standing to benefit directly, local residential populations were strongly opposed. Their argument was that the Olympics would serve only to increase developer pressures in Colorado, creating that congestion the absence of which was one of the state's great virtues. A referendum sustained the amenity interests.

In Alaska the issue was the construction of a pipeline from north to south to carry oil from the North Alaska slope to ice-free Pacific waters. Although opposed on amenity grounds by the Sierra Club, the Audubon Society, and other groups, support in Alaska for the pipeline was almost universal. An important consideration here was the state's relative poverty and high unemployment rate.

Contrary to these instances, we nevertheless find local governments by and large pursuing similar policies with respect to regulating locational decisions. They therefore compete with each other.

COMPETITIVE LOCAL POLICIES

Local governments attempt to attract into their jurisdictions that which their constituents regard as beneficial and to keep out those social groups, activities, and land users regarded as utility detracting. To the extent that local governments have similar conceptions of the beneficial and detracting and, therefore, similar goals, this will likely bring them into competition with each other. Exclusionary policy on the part of one local government will only deflect demand elsewhere and induce pressures for exclusion there, too. The attempts of the Rocky Mountain states to put barriers between the energy companies and development of the region's oil shale and coal have increased pressure on Pacific and Atlantic coastal states to develop the reserves of oil and natural gas thought to lie offshore. This has resulted, in turn, in attempts by the state governments of New Jersey, Delaware, Maryland, California, and other coastal states to forestall development. Since the Constitution allocates land use regulation to the states, they furthermore would have every right to impede development by, for example, refusing to allow construction of new storage tanks or refineries onshore.

Similar relations characterize small village communities in Britain. Typically they oppose new residential development on amenity grounds. As one succeeds in turning back the tide, however, so the pressure on adjacent villages increases, provoking, for example, the formation of local action committees, heated exchanges in parish council meetings, and demonstrations.

To some extent, then, what one local government gains, others will lose. It is a competition, moreover, that is carried on at a variety of geographic scales. States compete with respect to the development of energy, for example. City governments compete for federal or state office buildings. And within counties towns have competed for the privilege of being the county seat (Schellenberg 1970). In fact, on any one issue competition is often markedly hierarchical. States may compete for a federally subsidized coal gasification plant, for example, while counties compete for it within states.

It is however likely that in some cases the losses from competition will be spread out across all competitors rather than be concentrated locationally. If each state in the United States is equally effective in keeping energy development out, then presumably imports will increase and the nation as a whole will feel the loss in terms of a deterioration in the flexibility of U.S. foreign policy.

Techniques of Competition

In competing to attract the utility enhancing and keep out the detracting, local governments have two broad choices: (1) they can implement policies permissible within the constraints of existing constitutional and statutory law (i.e., the juridical context) or (2) they can set about changing that body of law either so that what are regarded as more effective policies will become legally feasible or, alternatively, so that individual locational choices will be constrained into locally more advantageous channels. We examine first, then, policies implemented in accordance with the prevailing juridical context. We then turn and look at attempts to alter that context.

COMPETITION WITHIN THE PREVAILING JURIDICAL CONTEXT

In order to deter undesirables and to attract private locators regarded as acceptable, local governments can draw on a range of policies. Some of these are purely of a public relations nature. Local governments may, for example, advertise their charms for industry in the classified advertisements of the *Wall Street Journal*. Some advertising is intended to discourage rather than attract. Some years ago the state of Oregon had a well-publicized campaign aimed at keeping the state in its present uncongested condition. This advertising emphasized the more undesirable features of the state such as its relatively heavy rainfall (figure 10.5).

Since 1947 a number of states have attempted to increase their attractions for industry by introducing anti-union legislation. Between 1947 and 1967 twenty-one states passed so-called right-to-work laws prohibiting union shops, so that nonunionists could be employed. Generally this was regarded as a step in the direction both

Figure 10.5   Negative Advertising by the State of Oregon

Figure 10.6   Right-to-Work Laws and Unionization Levels, 1960

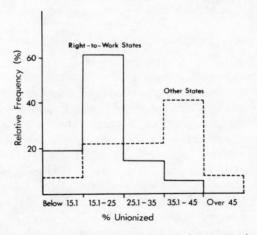

NOTE: Two histograms are shown. One indicates the relative frequencies of states with Right-to-Work laws according to a classification by degree of labor force unionization; the other indicates relative frequencies of other states according to the same classification.

DATA SOURCE: Palomba and Palomba, "Right-to-Work Laws," p. 483.

of improving industrial relations and labor productivity and also of keeping wages down (Palomba & Palomba 1971). These laws were usually introduced in poorer states, where existing unionization levels were low and, as a consequence, union opposition was trivial (figure 10.6). Interestingly enough, however, such legislation does not seem to have made the affected states any more attractive for industrial investment (Palomba & Palomba 1971, p. 482).

Local governments may also use public works programs to attract the enhancing and keep out the undesirable. We have already seen how withdrawal of state subsidies effectively excluded the 1976 Winter Olympics from Colorado. Elsewhere local governments have deferred investment in sewage systems in order to deter new residential development. In other cases the willingness of a local government to provide public works may tip the scale in the other direction. A few years ago in New York State, when Chrysler was considering shifting a plant from a cramped site in Syracuse to Auburn, Syracuse officials were able to offer an acceptable alternative by locating a site and making available the necessary rezonings, sewer lines and waterlines, and highway access (Martin 1968, pp. 254-59). A great deal of course was at stake in terms of payroll and tax base contributions: it is unlikely that the city would have done the same thing for a small employer.

With respect to residential development, withholding required permits may provide the necessary entrée to desirable land use control. A few years ago the town of Petaluma, close to San Francisco, attempted to limit its rapid rate of expansion by cutting down to negligible numbers the building permits issued (Rose 1974). In Britain local planning authorities in rural areas have used their control over permits for residential construction to prevent the expansion of small villages into large dormitory towns catering to the needs of nearby cities (Clawson & Hall 1973, ch. 5).

If land use regulation does not prevent development, however, purchase may. Many local governments own a surprisingly large amount of land and hence are able to exercise appreciable direct control over development; but in order to secure local government goals, *outright* purchase may not be necessary. Certain of the landowner's rights can be purchased, limiting him or her as to land use and achieving the essential goals of policy without the expense of complete purchase (Whyte 1970, ch. 5). Suffolk County on Long Island, subject to intense developmental pressure from New York City, has recently purchased the development rights over large tracts of land in order to retain its rural character—and to keep people out. If a farm is worth, for example, $5,000 per acre to a developer and $2,000 as farming land, the farmer has to be paid the difference of $3,000 per acre. This adds a few cents to local taxes but nothing like the increase that would occur with dense residential development.

Figure 10.7 Defense Contract Awards in Dollars per Capita by State, 1972, 1973

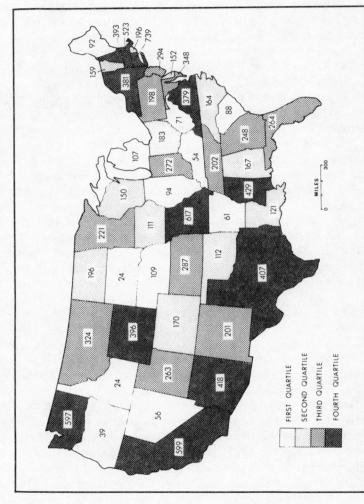

FIRST QUARTILE
SECOND QUARTILE
THIRD QUARTILE
FOURTH QUARTILE

MILES
0   300

SOURCE: U.S. Bureau of the Census, *Statistical Abstract of the United States, 1974* (Washington, D.C.: Government Printing Office, 1974), p. 313.

Thus far comments in this section have been confined to attempts to regulate and deflect the locational decisions of the private market sector. National policies, however, also have diverse positive and negative effects for different areas: a major focus of local governments, therefore, is to attract those public works and government orders that enhance the tax base and local employment and to keep out those that do not. Consider, for instance, the significance of defense policy. Defense departments make large orders for military equipment, orders that can do a great deal for the economic health of communities with plants manufacturing military hardware (Clayton 1962). Figure 10.7 shows the location of military orders by state in the United States. Obviously some states such as California receive disproportionate shares of these expenditures. The Department of Defense also locates military installations, air bases, and naval facilities. Again, at a local level these can provide a significant boost to the local retail market—certainly enough to cause a chamber of commerce to become concerned about imminent closure of a base.

Government largesse is apparent in other forms. In the United States cities compete for state and federal office buildings. In Britain small towns compete for bypasses to relieve their traffic miseries. Where industries are publicly owned, governments come under a variety of other pressures. In Britain attempts by the nationalized steel industry to close small, uneconomic plants have met with substantial resistance from the local communities affected. Location of new investment is also subject to local pressure. Recent competition for a new sheet strip mill from Wales and Scotland was finally resolved by dividing the spoils between the two locations.

ATTEMPTS TO ALTER THE JURIDICAL CONTEXT

All these instances of competition are ones where the body of law constraining local policy and individual locational choice goes unchallenged. It is clear, however, that the juridical context does have crucial implications for locational decisions, for the abilities of governments to influence those decisions, and, hence, for local welfare. For example, the unconstitutionality of state residency requirements may have imposed on some northern states welfare payment burdens that could have been avoided if a residency requirement for eligibility had been permissible. The argument here is that relatively large AFDC payments in states such as New York have stimulated migration of the poor from the South (Kain & Persky 1968; Glantz 1973). These poor households have simply added to the welfare burden in some northern states. This has necessitated increasing tax rates that have, in their turn, stimulated tax base erosion as middle-class households relocate out of the state.

We could construe a similar argument with respect to state right-to-work laws. It is only since 1947 and the Taft-Hartley Act that states have had the right to introduce such legislation. That the poorer, less-industrialized states have taken up the option suggests that they saw it as one means of attracting industrial investment away from the more industrialized, more heavily unionized states.

We should not be surprised, therefore, that states or local governments occasionally enter into coalition in order to secure some constitutional amendment or new statute providing them with a competitive advantage and altering geographic attractiveness gradients in their favor. In addition to considering the outcomes of competition within the constraints of existing law, therefore, we must also consider the outcome of attempts to change that law. We will confront these issues in chapter 11.

Concluding Comments

Shifts of capital in both private and public sectors provide the context for local and regional policy. These shifts have implications for tax bases and jobs. Since they tend to generate population shifts, other welfare impacts relating to congestion or to depopulation may be at issue. These redistributions of investment and persons occur, and consequently have welfare effects, at a variety of geographic scales.

A given locational process, however, may have substantially different welfare impacts for those at the same location. To some degree this is a function of the scale of area on which their utility is dependent. Appropriately enough jurisdictional organization caters to this diversity of scale-specific interests by providing local governments and respective jurisdictions at a variety of geographic scales. Welfare impact, however, is also affected by differing definitions as to what is utility enhancing and what is utility detracting.

Individual responses to these welfare impacts take two broad forms. Individuals may alter their locations with respect to the utility enhancing and utility detracting by shifting their absolute locations. Alternatively they may remain where they are and attempt to alter the nature of events at adjacent locations so that they are enhancing rather than detracting to utility. This usually requires some involvement in the political process.

As a result of differing conceptions of the enhancing and detracting, local policy formation is often subject to substantial dissensus.

Three major interests can be identified: environmental, labor, and business groups. Business groups have advantages in terms of control of jobs, tax base, and campaign funds and are frequently in coalition with labor groups. Though some local policies clearly represent victories for environmental interests, these are relatively unusual.

On the whole, local governments pursue remarkably similar policies with respect to manipulating locational relationships to the advantage of their constituents. As a result they frequently come into conflict with each other. Much local policy, therefore, is highly competitive: what one local government aims in terms of, say, tax base, another loses.

Techniques of competition are twofold: First, local governments can implement policies permissible within the constraints of existing constitutional and statutory law. They can therefore advertise, offer public works inducements to firms, enact labor legislation attractive to investors, lobby for public investments, and so forth. Alternatively, they can join with similarly impacted local governments and attempt to change those laws, so that investment and population flows move into channels more enhancing to their constituents.

Select Bibliography

Clayton, James L. "Defense Spending: Key to California's Growth." *Western Political Quarterly* 15 (1962): 280-93.

Molotch, Harvey. "The City as a Growth Machine: Toward a Political Economy of Place." *American Journal of Sociology* 82, no. 2 (1976): 309-32.

"The Second War Between the States." *Business Week*, 17 May 1976, pp. 92-95.

Winnick, Louis. "Place Prosperity vs. People Prosperity: Welfare Considerations in the Geographic Redistribution of Economic Activity." In *Essays in Urban Land Economics*. University of California Real Estate Research Program. Los Angeles, 1966.

Chapter Eleven

The Competitive Outcome of Local Political Processes

This chapter attempts to link the system of competitive relations outlined in the last chapter with the public problems identified in chapters 8 and 9. The immediate focus is the differential ability of local governments to attract the beneficial, or utility enhancing, and keep out the utility detracting. This, however, provides the basis for understanding problems of geographical inequality in incomes and public provision, the differential growth of cities of different size, conflicts between amenity and developer interests, and conflicts between regional and national interests.

Recall from the last chapter, however, that local governments compete in two different senses: they compete within the constraints of the juridical context and they also compete—albeit as members of larger coalitions—to alter that context. This chapter therefore is divided into two major sections: initially we consider the effectiveness of those local policies carried out within the constraints laid down by higher levels of government; then we review the possibilities of changing those constraints.

Competition Within the Juridical Context

Some local governments are obviously more effective in competing for the utility enhancing than others. They are able to attract activities enhancing to the local tax base while they are able, for example, to push off onto less-fortunate local governments environmentally noxious heavy industry and mining activity. Some local governments are able to attract clean, capital-intensive jobs in new, shiny factories, while other local governments languish in the refuse—both human and physical—of another, grimier industrial age. Explanation of this differential effectiveness in competition reduces to three fundamental considerations: (1) the local government's environmental context—more specifically, the site and situation attributes of locations within its jurisdiction; (2) local power, which affects the ability of local governments to secure desirable policies from higher levels of government; and (3) the juridical context constraining local governments and individual locators.

ENVIRONMENTAL CONTEXT

Consider the attractiveness to locators of places within a local government's jurisdiction. On considerations of site and situation hinge much of the ability of a local government to attract the utility enhancing. Yet these attributes—physical and human resources, market accessibility, mineral resources—are facets of physical and economic geography that local government cannot change to even the most modest degree except, perhaps, over the very long term. These environmental considerations, therefore, are ones whose existence must be assumed rather than challenged and ones that will critically constrain the ability of a local government and the local population it represents to achieve their goals.

When we consider site attributes, for example, major attention must attach to resource base constraints. Obviously the local governments of jurisdictions within which there are, for example, extensive oil deposits will have little difficulty attracting activities enhancing to the local tax base. Jurisdictions in areas of high agricultural productivity like the Central Valley of California are also likely to achieve their fiscal goals. Consider, however, the problems of communities whose resource base has been depleted, whose coal has been exhausted, timber cut, or soils eroded. To the extent that the populations of these jurisdictions have failed to adjust to a changing distribution of job opportunities, local unemployment problems will compound problems of public provision from a deteriorating tax base.

The human resource base is perhaps equally important: the degree to which local labor is educated, well-trained, and nonmilitant is an increasingly important locational consideration as the value of finished products more and more converges on the value added by labor. Areas dominated by minority cultures may be at a disadvantage in this regard. Linguistic differences can limit labor productivity by inhibiting communication between management and labor. The violence accompanying separatist movements in areas like Quebec or northern Spain may inhibit investment. The prospect of separatist success and ensuing problems of market fragmentation are equally discouraging.

As a consequence of these considerations, some jurisdictions will not be chosen by the types of private and/or public investment their local governments would like to attract. For example, Northeast Scotland has long been an economic backwater of the British Isles. It is only with discovery of North Sea oil and the establishment of onshore facilities in Aberdeen, Dundee, and Peterhead that the dearest hopes of local chambers of commerce have been realized.

At the same time some jurisdictions will be chosen for investment, even though, perhaps, a majority of their inhabitants are not in favor of it. A recent case in point is provided by attempts to locate facilities in the United Kingdom for the construction of deep-sea drilling platforms. Feasible locations are adjacent to the deep water of some extraordinarily beautiful sea inlets along the coast of Northwest Scotland (figure 11.1). Local inhabitants and their local governments would prefer to keep development out: it would result in some deterioration of local esthetics, wear and tear of roads built only for light tourist traffic, and Sunday working in an area where sabbatarianism is taken seriously. Demand from elsewhere for construction of platforms in the area is, however, intense. These locations represent virtually the only ones in the United Kingdom where construction is possible. Otherwise drilling platforms will have to be bought from Norway to the considerable distress of the ever-sensitive British balance of payments. If the central government authorities in Britain have their way, therefore—and they have the power to have their way—the people of Northwest Scotland will get drilling platform construction on their doorstep whether they like it or not.

Similar statements could be made about the role of situation. In attracting employment-creating investment and investment enhancing to the local tax base, accessibility to expanding markets and economy of agglomeration considerations are obviously important. Small towns in the Great Plains, surrounded by areas from which population is draining, clearly have tremendous problems in competing with towns located in expanding areas such as the Texas shore or Florida.

A measure of market accessibility is provided by population potential (Stewart 1950). Areas of high population potential tend to be areas where industrial employment and value added in industry are both relatively high. As figure 11.2 indicates for the United Kingdom, areas of high population potential also tend to have relatively high per capita incomes.

It is significant that a number of the areas noted for separatist sentiment have relatively low population potentials: Wales and Scotland, for instance. Problems are doubly acute for these areas, however, since distinctive local cultures tend to retard outmigration and labor market adjustment. Attachment to the Welsh way of life, for instance, tends to inhibit relocation in search of jobs, thus producing local labor surpluses, unemployment, and economic hardship.

Accessibility considerations, of course, account in large part for the ability of large cities to attract investment away from small towns. Large cities are generally located at hubs in the national

Figure 11.1   The Vulnerable Sea Lochs of Northwest Scotland

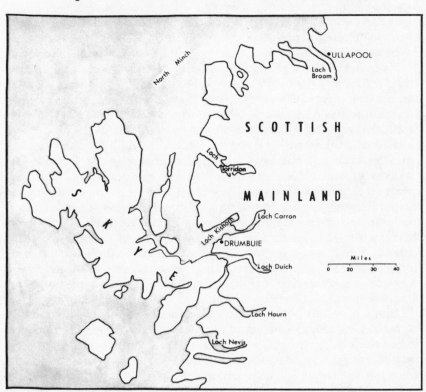

NOTE: The Atlantic coast of Northwest Scotland is penetrated by numerous deepwater oceanic inlets known as *sea lochs*; a number of these are shown here. They are particularly attractive for the construction of drilling platforms for the North Sea oil fields. Two sites—one near Ullapool on Loch Broom and one near Drumbuie on Loch Kishorn—have attracted attention. Since construction work would detract from the esthetics of the area, however, local opposition to such construction work has been intense.

transportation network and have a variety of activities to which the investor's firm will be complementary. Location in a large city is more often than not a location minimizing distance from component suppliers; small town locations, on the other hand, impose inconveniences of supply, which investors would rather avoid. In addition urban size provides one important indicator of local demand.

Public authorities are probably as sensitive to access considerations in their locational choices as are private investors. Federal office buildings, therefore, are located in larger cities, which have easy airline communication with Washington, D.C., and are centrally located with respect to existing consumer travel patterns. Likewise when schools are reorganized to take advantage of economies of scale in education, it is commonly local village schools that are closed, while larger schools in nearby larger towns are expanded. Given changes in population distribution, location in larger towns is clearly movement-cost minimizing.

As a consequence of situation considerations like these, some jurisdictions will not be chosen by public or private investment, even though they may want to be. A major issue in rural areas in Britain has, in fact, been the closure of small village schools. Local residents claim that closure will destroy community life.

Then again, some jurisdictions will be chosen, even though they would prefer not to be. As discussed in chapter 8, small villages close to metropolitan centers become subject to a variety of developmental pressures threatening to their rural or small town tranquility. As large cities grow, they place increasing demands on more and more extensive hinterlands. The commuter belt expands inexorably outward, disturbing small rural villages that are accustomed to and enjoy their sparse populations. As a consequence amenity-development conflicts have a wavelike geographic form occurring at ever-increasing distances from large cities as developmental pressures expand outwards.

LOCAL POWER

Some local governments are more effective in obtaining what they want from central government than others. Critical variables here include: (1) the degree of access the local government enjoys to those concerned with making final decisions regarding the location of public and other facilities and (2) bargaining resources.

Access to Government Decision Makers   There can be no doubt that having local representatives on strategic committees at the national level can be important for what comes the way of a local jurisdiction happening to lie within the relevant constituency. Some years ago a South Carolina congressman named Mendel Rivers was associated with a congressional district positively bulging at the seams with military installations (Greenberg 1974, p. 79). Rivers was chairman of the House Armed Services Committee. Little wonder, therefore, that his electioneering slogan was "Rivers Delivers."

Nor are these events confined to the United States. In the early 1970s a minor stir was created in France when Ford Motor Company decided to locate in Bordeaux after having first announced it would locate in Charleville in northeast France. Chaban Delmas, the French premier at the time, was also mayor of Bordeaux!

Figure 11.2   Population Potentials and Relative Income Levels in the United Kingdom

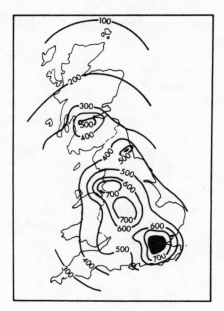
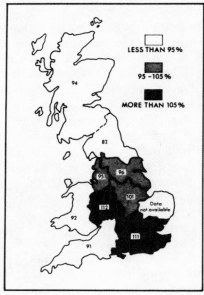

SOURCE: After Kevin R. Cox, *Man, Location and Behavior: An Introduction to Human Geography* (New York: Wiley, 1972), pp. 179; 182.

More generally it is a recognized fact that congressional representatives who want certain types of federal public works or expenditures in their congressional districts are more likely to succeed if they are on the appropriate committees. As a result Senate and House committees tend to be dominated by legislators from states most affected by the deliberations of those respective committees. The Senate Interior and Insular Affairs Committee, for example, occupies a strategic position with respect to the authorization of Bureau of Reclamation projects; i.e., irrigation projects. In the Ninety-second Congress (1971–72) all but two of the sixteen members were from those western states to which the bureau's operations are statutorily restricted (figure 11.3).

Bargaining Resources   Critical bargaining resources are related to population size, which connotes votes in state and national assemblies, in referenda, and in electoral colleges. Within states more populous areas have advantages in referenda on public works programs having strictly localized benefits. The California Water Plan, for example, is intended to bring water by canal and aqueduct from water surplus areas of Northern California to subarid Southern

Figure 11.3   States with Senators on the Senate Interior and Insular Affairs Committee,
1972–1973

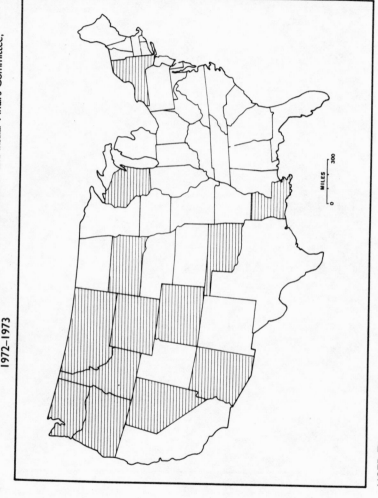

NOTE: There is a dominance of states west of the Mississippi.

Figure 11.4   The California Water Project

NOTE: As a result of climatic variation water is more readily available in Northern than in Southern California. By damming the Feather River in its upper reaches the idea is to create additional water supplies for Southern California that are to be delivered by an aqueduct system almost 700 miles long.

California (figure 11.4). As figure 11.5 indicates, rates of support for the project were higher in Southern California. More significant still was the fact that the relatively large population of Southern California permitted these favorable voting rates to be translated at the state level into a majority in favor of the water project.

To some extent the ability of large cities to continue to attract new employment-creating activities is a function of their bargaining power with central governments. Often contributing relatively large delegations of legislators to central legislative assemblies, they also make vital contributions to the national economy. Environmental Protection Agency attempts to limit automobile use in Southern California, for example, can be countered by perfectly plausible scenarios of the impact they would have on the economic life of the area: and the contribution of Southern California to the nation's economic welfare is by no means insignificant.

More recently we have the example of federal guarantees of loans to New York City (Alcaly & Mermelstein 1977, ch. 3). Without loan guarantees, default on a variety of loans seemed imminent in 1975. Since New York City accounted for such a large fraction of all municipal loan finance in the United States, default could have dealt a devastating blow to the confidence of lenders in the municipal bond market, making it exceedingly costly for local governments to fund capital projects. Clearly if it had been, say, Tulsa, Oklahoma, in danger of defaulting, federal assistance would have been less likely.

The construction of a strong public interest argument can also help in marshalling support for local public works projects. Majority support can be generated to the extent that those most likely to benefit directly from a project can argue that construction will provide benefits to the nation as a whole. A case in point is provided by the French government's recent decision to construct a canal between the Saone and Moselle rivers, thus linking up the French Mediterranean coast with the Low Countries and West Germany (figure 11.6). The populations benefiting most directly from this will be those in the immediate vicinity of the canal: they will gain from construction money poured into the area. The cities of Lyons and Marseilles also stand to gain from increased trade. Proponents of the plan have gone further than this, however, arguing that the link is important in the international battle for Middle Eastern trade. With the imminent construction of a canal between the Danube and the Rhine a navigable water link will extend all the way from the Low Countries to the Black Sea, providing easy access to the eastern Mediterranean. This, it is argued, will divert traffic from French Mediterranean ports to the detriment of the French rate of economic growth.

Figure 11.5   Voting in the California Feather River Project Referendum, 1962

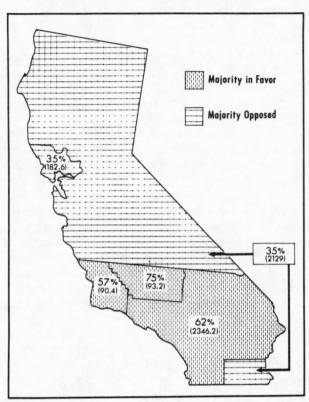

NOTE: Percentages refer to the yes-vote as a proportion of all voters. Figures in parentheses in-dicate total numbers voting (in thousands). In the state as a whole the bond squeaked through by a very narrow margin (51.5 percent). Without the large yes-vote from the populous area of the state (Southern California), which stood to gain most from the project, it would clearly have been defeated.

DATA SOURCE: Norman Plotkin, "A Social Choice Model of the California Feather River Project," Public Choice 12 (spring 1972): 84.

While local populations and their representatives may articulate arguments like this, they may also receive support from national interest groups. Undoubtedly in the case referred to above, support for the canal has been forthcoming from French barge operator associations. In the United States construction unions and highway and bridge constructors have provided similar galvanizing power for local or regional lobbies pressing for highway improvements.

Figure 11.6   The Projected Saone-Rhine Canal

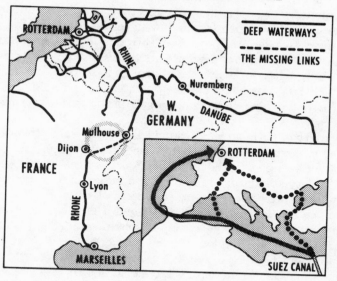

NOTE: Construction will clearly benefit populations in eastern France, particularly around Lyons, Dijon, and Marseilles. The populations have been able to sell the idea to the French government by pointing out the trade implications of a plan for linking up the Rhine system with the Danube; much trade from the Middle East would be diverted from French ports, while construction of the Saone-Rhine Canal would enhance their competitive position.

JURIDICAL CONTEXT

Some local areas and local governments are clearly favored and others just as clearly are disadvantaged by the provisions of constitutional and statutory law. There is no doubt, therefore, that this body of law has also contributed to the emergence of regional and local problems of a public character; for example, spatial disparities in wealth and public services, locational conflicts, or demands for local autonomy. These provisions pertain both to the rights and obligations of local governments to, say, raise revenue, spend, and plan land use. We will consider first constraints on the locational choices of individuals as laid down by central government. Then we will examine the role played by constitutional and statutory constraints on the activities of local governments.

Central Government and the Individual Locator   Constitutional law and much of statutory law as it pertains to individuals is locationally indifferent: people have to pay their taxes wherever they are located; trespassers will be prosecuted in both town and country; all children irrespective of location must attend some school approved by the ministry or department of education. Despite its apparent locational neutrality, much of this law nevertheless is not indifferent with respect to locational processes. Introduction of apparently innocent statutes may in fact generate attractiveness gradients between places and greatly influence the ability of local governments to attract the utility enhancing and keep out the undesirable. The definition of *national minimum standards* is particularly informative in this regard.

A variety of national legislation is directed towards the establishment of minimum standards. More specifically this may take the form of, for example: (1) the minimum hourly wage an employer must pay; (2) safety standards in factories and mines; and (3) minimum air quality standards for effluent producers. Unfortunately, as well meaning as this legislation might be—and it is not always that well meaning—it can often have extremely detrimental effects on the employment of the less skilled, the casual worker, and those with no alternative but to work in relatively unhealthy mining conditions.

Take the case of minimum wage legislation (Peterson & Stewart 1969). Wage labor tends to vary in quality from place to place. In some areas it is highly skilled and productive. In others there may be large numbers of high school dropouts or older workers requiring expensive retraining: the legislated minimum wage may be far more there than what the typical worker is worth to his or her employer. The alternatives for the firm are twofold: break the law or terminate business. The result is (1) a diminution of employment opportunities in those poor, backward areas where employment needs are greatest and (2) further concentration in those areas and larger cities where labor *is* worth the minimum wage.

Safety standards have similar implications. In mining areas the economic feasibility of adhering to national standards may depend on the nature of the underlying geology and on the size of operating units. In areas where geological structures are heavily faulted and safety hazards are greater, adherence to a national safety standard may be quite unprofitable. Likewise larger mines with their economies of scale may be able to afford the expenditures more than smaller mines. A likely result would be the closure of small mines and a decimation of the small town populations dependent on them.

That the imposition of national standards may have detrimental effects on the economic prospects of small towns relative to those of larger cities is evident in a number of other instances. The attempt in Britain to create nationally homogeneous standards for the hiring and firing of longshoremen provides an excellent case in point. In 1946 a so-called "national dock labor scheme" was legislated. This

Figure 11.7   Dock Labor Scheme and Non-scheme Ports in the United Kingdom

provided workers with greatly improved job security, fringe benefits, and higher pay rates, and it terminated casual employment. The dock labor scheme, however, applied only to the country's major ports (figure 11.7). To most small ports enjoying only limited trade, these rules did not apply; these ports have generally been associated with smaller towns serving relatively rural areas (figure 11.7). As a result of staying out of the dock labor scheme they have enjoyed lower wage bills: hourly wage rates are lower and severance payments are not required. There is now an attempt to extend the expensive dock labor scheme to all ports in the country. In non-scheme ports the effects would likely be devastating. Increased labor costs would be especially onerous. In particular the termination of casual labor would mean that labor would have to be paid for the whole week, when at present in many small ports existing demand is satisfied by two or three days of work.

The effect of extension would, therefore, likely erode the economic base of numerous smaller ports. At the same time it would enhance the competitive position of the country's major ports. Indeed the attempt to extend the scheme is a result of pressure from heavily unionized dockers in London, Liverpool, and other major ports. As a result of the reduced labor costs of small ports, trade has been leaving London, Liverpool, Southampton, and other larger cities.

In addition to minimum standards other aspects of centrally administered law critically constrain and channel individual locational choice. Of major significance is the role of compensation arrangements. In a mobile society uncompensated costs and benefits are rife. Poorly educated persons migrate from Alabama to New York, for example, and impose welfare costs on the cities receiving them. As towns grow in size, so the new arrivals must be catered to in terms of public works: widened roads, new school facilities, additional water supplies. Yet these are costs that are spread out over both old and new residents. In brief, new residents impose costs on existing residents and do not compensate them for those costs.

Consider, however, a hypothetical situation in which migrants would be liable for compensation. Where they imposed costs on destination populations and had to pay compensation for the privilege of residing among them, the incentive to migrate would be considerably reduced. Migration to large cities would slow down and, quite likely, so would the rate at which population is being concentrated in larger cities.

The same situation holds with respect to origin cities. Outmigration imposes particular hardships on small towns with a history of depopulation. Consider, however, the likely impact of a tax on leavers. This would provide a disincentive for outmigration. The overall result of a compensation policy, therefore, would be a slowing down in the movement of population from small to large towns and an urban size hierarchy somewhat more in accord with what people profess to prefer.

The compensation issue also sheds light on amenity-development conflicts. Development often detracts from local amenities, causing hardship to existing residents. This may be apparent in noise, pollution, and traffic and in the more tangible form of declining property values. At present developers have little incentive to locate their reservoirs, new residential developments, airports, and freeways where they will least disturb existing populations. If they were liable for compensation to those populations, however, the result would be rather different. The added cost of developing close to existing residential areas would prompt a new evaluation of alternatives and guide new land use into locations where it would be least obnoxious.

Minimum standards and compensation arrangements have no explicit locational objective. There are national statutes, however, that are clearly locational in their intent. Permission from planning authorities to carry out certain activities, for example, may be area-specific, as may be certain subsidies. Developed nation states, particularly in Western Europe, are a patchwork of Green Belts, National Parks, Areas of Outstanding Natural Beauty, Development Areas, Conservation Areas, and Grey Areas; location within each area is subject to area-specific regulations and/or qualifies for some sort of public subsidy. These designations have obvious effects on locational choice. Green Belts around large cities, for example, tend to deflect developer interest to the outer edge of the Green Belt to the dismay of residents and to the delight of landowners (figure 11.8). French restrictions on industrial and office development within sixty to seventy miles of Paris have produced similar competitive advantages for towns located just beyond that radius (figure 11.9). Restrictions on development within British National Parks, on the other hand, make it difficult for towns there to compete for jobs with towns elsewhere. The drawing of a line on a map, then, bestows competitive advantages. This is apparent from the degree to which towns will fight to be included in a Development Area with all the national subsidies it makes available for new industrial development. The gradual geographic extension of the areas qualifying for this aid (figure 11.10) is an eloquent expression of the attractiveness of these locational advantages for the towns lying within them.

Central Government and Local Government   The rights and obligations of local governments as laid down by state, federal, or central governments are also critical to the outcome of competition among them. Consider, for example, the case of revenue sources. To the extent that local governments are dependent on revenue raised within their own jurisdictions, those jurisdictions with relatively healthy tax bases will, all other things being equal, have something of a relative attraction for new locators. As a consequence, there is some tendency for the advantages of fiscally well-endowed local governments to be cumulative: low tax rates attract capital-intensive industry, permitting further tax rate reductions, attracting still more capital-intensive industry, and so on.

Figure 11.8   The Effect of Green Belts on Property Development

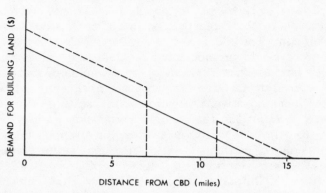

DISTANCE FROM CBD (miles)

NOTE: The solid line represents bids for building land at varying distances from the center of a large city. Imposition of a Green Belt between seven and eleven miles results in bids for building land within the Green Belt falling to zero, while property developers are now willing to pay more (indicated by the dashed line) for building land in the city and beyond the Green Belt.

Yet continuing attractiveness and maintenance of tax base will be dependent on ability to exclude those who would detract. Decentralization of control over land use planning from central to local government may provide exactly the appropriate tool. In the American case it has allowed local governments to establish local zoning ordinances having exclusionary effects: by zoning for large lots or "single-family residential" the poor may be excluded and competitive advantages maintained.

Under these circumstances variations in public provision will tend to reflect tax base geography. To the extent that a jurisdiction is poor, it will spend relatively less per pupil on education than, say, a wealthier jurisdiction. A critical correlate of per capita tax base, of course, is private income. Income taxes collect less per capita from poorer populations than from wealthier ones. Poorer persons live in lower valued homes, so that property tax collections at a given tax rate will be less. As a consequence, place-to-place variations in per capita income will tend to be reflected in public provision: states with generally poorer populations will spend less on education, recreation, and highways than states with generally richer populations.

Not surprisingly, therefore, localized poverty may come to have a certain inertial quality about it. Poorer populations spend less on the education of their children. Consequently the productivity of their children and the ability of the area to attract in high-paying, capital-intensive industries remains weak. A further round of low incomes results.

Figure 11.9   The Location of Decentralized Industries in France, 1950–1958

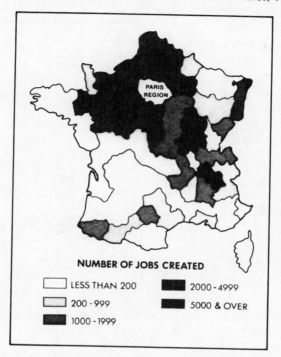

NUMBER OF JOBS CREATED

- LESS THAN 200
- 200 - 999
- 1000 - 1999
- 2000 - 4999
- 5000 & OVER

NOTE: A ban on new industrial development within forty to fifty miles of Paris has led to some relocation from Paris of firms seeking to expand. Locations just beyond this limit, however, have proven much more attractive than those more peripheral westerly locations in France most in need of industrial development.

SOURCE: After Kevin R. Cox, *Man, Location and Behavior: An Introduction to Human Geography* (New York: Wiley, 1972), p. 239.

Where local governments or states are heavily reliant for their spending on local tax resources, however, conflicts between amenity and development interests are likely to be considerably weaker. Development will be seen as enhancing the local tax base and reducing tax rates—at least over the long term. It will, therefore, be regarded by many as in the public interest; but in countries like Britain, where local governments are much less dependent on locally generated revenue, a "tax base enhancement" argument will be much less convincing. To a considerable degree this must account for the peculiarly dogged resistance to additional residential development, in those countries, of small town and village residents.

Another important aspect of the decentralization of powers to a system of local governments is the degree to which central govern-

Figure 11.10   The Progressive Extension of Areas Qualifying for "Depressed Area Aid" in the United Kingdom

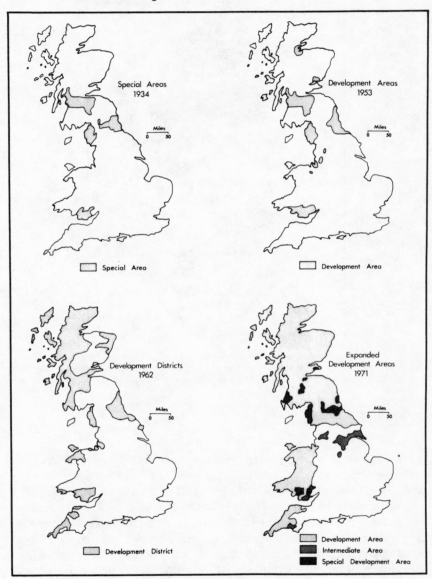

SOURCE: After Graham Hallett, Peter Randall, and E. G. West, *Regional Policy for Ever?* (London: Institute of Economic Affairs, 1973), pp. 20; 26; 31; 35; 44.

ments retain veto or override powers with respect to local policy. In Britain central government retains and uses important discretionary powers over local land use planning decisions. Local residents or other concerned interests may appeal a particular local planning decision to the central government, which will then send an inspector to either investigate the pros and cons of the case himself or hold a public inquiry. Inspectors can and often do make recommendations to the central government reversing local government decisions.

The argument here is that planning decisions, while made locally, may be on issues of national significance and, therefore, of interest to central government. As a consequence of the resultant central government override powers, however, local populations may find that their ability to keep out the utility detracting is considerably limited. This will be so where something obnoxious to locals is of positive significance to the nation as a whole. Local residents, therefore, may object to the establishment of a large airport in their vicinity on the grounds of noise. Clearly, however, such a development may also serve a wider and more beneficial purpose and may be seen in this light by central government authorities.

This, of course, has implications for demands for local autonomy. Where local preferences are especially intense the imposition of some national policy and the frustration of local sentiment may have local welfare effects that are far from trivial. In Britain national land use planning legislation aimed at preserving Areas of Outstanding Natural Beauty has had particularly unfortunate effects on the Welsh. Wales is a desirable location not only for the Welsh, for whom it represents emotional attachments, but also for the English, who find it increasingly attractive and who see it as an ideal location for second homes or for retirement homes. Planning constraints on the availability of land for building in the more picturesque areas of Wales, however, have increased housing market competition between the indigenous Welsh and the English arrivals. By inducing a scarcity of building land, land use planning control has increased the price of housing to a level that only the wealthier second home and retirement home seekers can afford. As a result of housing shortage, therefore, the Welsh are slowly displaced from their own land by the—increasingly resented—English.

Changing the Juridical Context

Site and situation are largely beyond the control of local government policies. The bargaining power local governments are able to exercise with respect to the locational decisions of central government agencies may also be a constraint that they have to live with. The body of constitutional and statutory law governing the activities of local governments and individual locational choice, however, is less static. Rules are altered. In a real sense, therefore, the effectiveness of a local government in attaining its goals depends on its ability to secure a congenial juridical context.

The locus for change is that higher level in the jurisdictional hierarchy responsible for constitutional and statutory law. This will be the central government in unitary systems and state and federal governments in federal systems. The ability of a local government to secure change congenial to its objectives, however, is contingent on the construction of coalitions. This is particularly so in the case of constitutional law, since constitutional amendments usually require more than a simple majority vote in appropriate legislative assemblies.

The organizations and interests entering into these coalitions are likely to be of a highly diverse nature. National legislators will come under pressure not only from groups of local governments but also from business, labor, and amenity lobbies affected in some way by the changes pending. The bureaucracies of the central government also are not unbiased spectators. Changes in the law may affect the difficulty under which they work or their professional rewards, and the value of securing their approval may be evident in the voting process.

Clearly, existing constitutional and statutory law—i.e., the juridical status quo—is of benefit to some local governments, to some local groups, and to some national or statewide lobbies. Any attempt to change those rules will therefore likely be opposed. An excellent example is provided by the fate of current proposals in a number of U.S. states to shift funding of education from local school districts to the state. Specifically most of these proposals call for a statewide property tax and disbursement of funds on a per pupil basis to existing school districts (Peterson & Solomon 1973). This would replace present arrangements, in which local school boards levy a property tax and are consequently quite dependent for what they can spend on the opulence of the local tax base.

Generally, as we saw in chapter 9, wealthier school districts spend more per pupil with a lower tax rate than do poorer school districts. The effect of a statewide property tax would be (1) to raise tax rates and possibly decrease per pupil spending in wealthier school districts and (2) to lower tax rates and increase per pupil spending in poorer school districts. This would suggest that wealthier school districts would be opposed to statewide funding—and indeed they are (Meltsner 1972). Also opposed are mineral and agricultural interests in rural areas; mineral and agricultural wealth frequently makes for a large local tax base. Small rural populations, however, result in relatively low tax rates. The effect of statewide funding would be to raise tax rates in such areas to the cost of mineral and agricultural interests.

Other lobbies opposed to statewide funding include dealers in state and municipal bonds. For them a major source of income comes from dealing in school district general obligation bonds. Obviously statewide taxation would eliminate that taxing power, placing the activities of bond dealers somewhat in jeopardy. On the other hand, teacher unions have tended to support statewide funding, presumably because they feel it will facilitate pay raises.

Any attempt to change the juridical context, therefore, will be hotly contested by those likely to lose. Bargaining resources become important and a variety of public interest arguments designed to neutralize the opposition and to place a veil over blatant self-interest will emerge. Opponents of statewide educational funding, for example, will argue that local funding provides advantages for all. An abundance of resources in *some* schools facilitates innovation that is of benefit to *all* school districts, rich and poor. Local funding, it will also be argued, ensures local accountability and control of teacher performance; statewide funding results in responsibility to a large, remote state bureaucracy unconcerned with educational tastes that, it is urged, are bound to vary from one school district to another; i.e., considerations that attempt to swing both rich and poor school districts behind the funding status quo will be emphasized.

The obstacles to changing the juridical context, therefore, are substantial. It would nevertheless be untrue to say that there have been no such changes. Overall in more developed countries there has been a long-term and progressive erosion of local government powers. This has been as true of federal as of unitary states. It is apparent in at least two developments: the tendency for funding local public services to be increasingly centralized at central government levels (Mushkin & Adams 1966; Robson 1966) and the emergence of central standards of private and public provision as norms that local governments may be called on to implement but over which they have no control. We focus here upon the centralization of funding.

For a variety of reasons central governments account for increasingly large proportions of local government spending: in federal states this applies both to the state-federal relationship and to the local-federal relationship (tables 11.1 and 11.2). Similar trends are apparent in unitary states such as Britain (figure 11.11).

The theoretical rationale for this development is usually couched in terms of the presence of interjurisdictional externalities and their depressing effects on public provision (Olson 1969). Education provides a particularly useful context for a discussion of interjurisdic-

Table 11.1   Ratios of State and Local Revenue from Own Sources to Federal Grants, 1946–1964

	State	**Local**
1946	6.8	114.8
50	3.9	45.4
54	4.7	45.7
58	3.8	47.9
62	3.3	35.0
64	3.1	31.6

SOURCE: Mushkin and Adams, "Emerging Patterns of Federalism," p. 236, tab. 6.

Figure 11.11   Rates (locally raised property taxes) as a Percentage of Central Government Grants plus Rates in Britain, 1907–1954

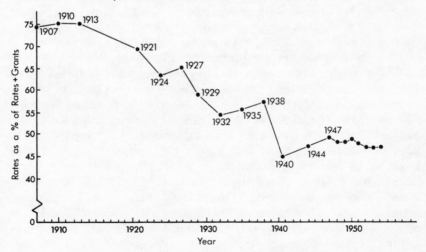

NOTE: Data for 1950–54 are for England and Wales and omit Scotland and Northern Ireland.
DATA SOURCE: R. M. Jackson, *The Machinery of Local Government* (London: MacMillan, 1958), p. 207.

Table 11.2   State Aid to Local Governments, Selected Fiscal Years, 1902–1964

	General[a] ($)	State Aid ($)	State Aid[b] (%)
1964	30,256	12,873	42.5
62	26,705	10,879	40.7
56	16,238	6,590	40.6
46	6,082	2,092	34.4
40	5,007	1,654	33.0
27	5,298	596	11.2
02	798	52	6.5

NOTE: Dollar amounts in millions.

SOURCES: U.S. Bureau of the Census, Governments Division, *Governmental Finances in 1903–04*; Census of Governments, 1962, *State Payments to Local Governments*, vol. 6, *Topical Studies*, no. 2.

[a] Revenue from local sources.

[b] As a percentage of general revenue from own sources.

tional externalities and their impact on public provision. For example, there is no doubt about the national effects of what goes on in the schoolroom. Population migrates from the district where it was educated to jurisdictions in which it ultimately chooses to settle, providing benefits in the form of educated manpower or costs in the form of illiterate manpower. There are also gains—or losses—to the nation as a whole. An individual's education is a reasonably good indicator of future income prospects and hence of ability to contribute towards federal revenue via the federal income tax. Education is also a prerequisite for national military service. The military administers intelligence tests, and there appears to be an inverse relationship between failure rates and investment in education across the fifty states (figure 11.12).

The presence of these interjurisdictional externalities is widely regarded as inducing underinvestment in the public service in question (Weisbrod 1965). Public expenditure decisions, for example, should bear some relationship to taxpayer welfare. If manpower educated at taxpayer's expense leaves the spending jurisdiction for somewhere else, then clearly the taxpayer is getting less than he might in terms of, say, additions to local tax base. The public authority responsible for educational funding, therefore, will have less incentive to spend than it otherwise would. And certainly it has no incentive to consider the impact of its educational policies on the welfare of those jurisdictions receiving its migrants.

To what extent, however, do these considerations actually exercise a depressing effect on educational provision? A test of the idea is

Figure 11.12   Educational Expenditures and Mental Disqualification from Military Service, 1971

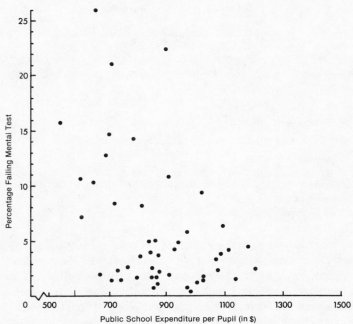

SOURCE: U.S. Bureau of the Census, *Statistical Abstract of the United States, 1972* (Washington, D.C.: Government Printing Office, 1972), tabs. 194; 434.

not difficult. If, for example, there is some effect, communities experiencing greater rates of net outmigration should, all other things being equal, be more reluctant to spend on education than communities that are not. A recent examination of this question related current public education expenditures per pupil to net outmigration rates across the continental United States (Weisbrod 1965); at the same time a variety of other significant variables such as per pupil personal income and percentage of the school age population in public schools were held constant.

It appears that net outmigration is indeed related to educational expenditures. On the average a one-point increase in the percentage of the population net outmigrating is associated with a $4.04 decrease in public education expenditure per student. This suggests that Arkansas, for example, which had 22-percent net outmigration over the relevant period, would have spent 22 × $4.04 = $89 more per student if it had had no net outmigration, all other things being equal. It actually spent $242 per student, so that the $89 represents a reduction of 27 percent from the presumed zero outmigration expenditure rate of $331 ($242 + $89). It would seem, then, that migration out of a state may lower educational investments. Consequently there is a distinct possibility that without countermeasures such as federal subsidies to education, states would produce less education than would be optimal for the United States as a whole.

Problems such as these provide the *theoretical* rationale for conditional grants-in-aid and a number of other forms of subsidy to local governments (Boehne 1969). Consider, for example, a central government confronted by a set of constituent local governments that, from the national standpoint, are not providing as much of some service as they should; this underinvestment, we will assume, is due to the existence of interjurisdictional externalities. One method of inducing local governments to consider the national interest in their investment decisions is to provide a matching grant for the activity in question. Thus, it is argued, the states of the United States have little interest in providing interstate highways, since much of the benefit devolves to those beyond respective state boundaries. In order to persuade them to invest in these highways, therefore, the federal government provides the states with $9 for every dollar they spend. Not all such matching grants are so generous; for the construction of four-year colleges by state education departments, for example, the federal share has been 33⅓ percent and for the urban renewal program, 66⅔ percent.

To summarize the argument so far, interjurisdictional externalities provide the theoretical rationale and ostensible reason for central government grants to local governments. The real reasons for the introduction of conditional grants-in-aid, however, are rather more complex. For a start, from the viewpoint of the spending local government, conditional grants-in-aid permit expenditures with only limited accountability to the local electorate; money can be spent while minimizing the risk of charges that the local taxpayer's money is being wasted or misallocated. Conditional grants-in-aid therefore provide a means to *externalize* costs of local programs.

A second consideration is that conditional grants-in-aid permit large increases in those types of expenditures eagerly sought by special interest groups. Lobbying by these groups on behalf of new conditional grants-in-aid programs or funding of existing ones is likely to be intense. The interstate highway program, for example, does not benefit only car drivers (Mowbray 1969, chs. 1, 2). Major beneficiaries include construction unions and manufacturers of concrete, bitumen, and structural steel. State departments of transportation also stand to gain in terms of an expansion of their respective bureaucracies and of their power vis-à-vis other state agencies. In simi-

lar manner a grant-in-aid program for education will be supported by
teacher unions, which see it as a means of increasing salary scales;
and grants-in-aid for dam construction and irrigation works in the
West will be supported by the Bureau of Reclamation, whose general
existence depends on a continuing stream of such projects (Berkman
& Viscusi 1973).

Considerations such as these help to explain the unrealistically
high level of central government contributions to local spending.
Ideally central government-local government matching ratios for
conditional grants-in-aid should be in proportion to the division of
benefits between the higher level jurisdiction making the grant and
the lower level jurisdiction receiving it. If 60 percent of the benefits of
investment in education accrues to the jurisdiction of the local government making the investment and 40 percent accrues to the higher
level jurisdiction, then the matching ratio should be $4 of nonlocal
funds for $6 of local funds.

Generally, however, the actual matching ratio is far too high from
the national viewpoint. It seems absurd that 90 percent of the benefits from interstate highways, as implied by the federal matching
criterion, accrues to national populations outside the state making
the investment. It is also unlikely that the same ratio would apply to
all states. Is it reasonable to expect, for example, that the *national*
benefits from constructing a given length of interstate highway in
Montana are equal to those from constructing the same length of
highway in Ohio? Likewise in terms of education the ratio of national
to local benefits logically is greater for local-level jurisdictions, which
experience more outmigration. The appropriate national-local ratio,
therefore, should be greater, say, for Arkansas than for Maryland or
for Mississippi than for California.

Opposition to conditional grant-in-aid programs is nevertheless
usually limited, and rarely are there complaints that the federal contribution is too high. The reason is plain: all local governments,
states, and special interest groups see themselves gaining from the
grants. The real loser is the federal taxpayer. Although in a context of
economic growth conditional grants-in-aid do not result in increased
federal tax rates, neither do they result in decreased tax rates. Any
popular concern that does emerge, however, can be effectively
neutralized by the "interjurisdictional externality" bromide.

Concluding Comments

The ability of local governments to attract the utility enhancing and
keep out the utility detracting depends on a triad of circumstances:
environmental context, local power, and juridical context. Environ-

mental context in the form of site and situation attributes provides local governments with advantages—or disadvantages—in attracting private investment. Variations in accessibility seem particularly important in explaining the emergence of some regions as relatively wealthy and also in understanding the tendency for large cities to grow at the expense of small towns and rural areas. The growth of large cities, of course, places developmental pressure on hinterlands and increases the likelihood of conflict with amenity interests.

The power that local government has within central government is also significant in obtaining public decisions enhancing to local welfare. To some degree this is a function of the links enjoyed by the local government, through its representatives, with the system of national legislative committees and public agencies having discretion over these decisions. In addition the bargaining resources local governments can resort to may be important. It is perhaps for this reason that public decisions frequently favor large cities: national economic welfare is quite dependent on the continuing viability of big city environments for business purposes.

The final member of this triad is the juridical context: that ensemble of constitutional and statutory constraints on individual location and local government policy. In the first place central governments implement laws that, although ostensibly indifferent with respect to location, do have serious locational effects of an inadvertent character. Minimum wage legislation, therefore, will tend to divert business from more rural areas and small towns, where labor is perhaps less well trained and consequently not worth the minimum wage, to big cities and areas of the country, where labor is better trained. The absence of compensation for those adversely affected by the locations of others was also seen as affecting the ability of local governments to attract the enhancing and keep out the detracting. In a world where compensation payments were mandated the distribution of population between large and small cities would look quite different from what it is today.

In the second place the rights and obligations of local governments also affect their competitive abilities. To the extent that local governments have to raise most of their own revenue, those with large tax bases will be able to provide a given set of services with a lower tax rate, the lower tax rate affording a competitive edge.

Maintaining that competitive edge, however, depends on keeping out the utility detracting: local control over land use was seen here as especially important. The end product of such a regime would be substantial inequality among jurisdictions in public provision and tax rates. Dependence on local tax base, however, would tend to increase the power of developer interests relative to amenity interests.

The juridical context, of course, is not immutable. It is nevertheless not that easy to change. In order to alter statutory and constitutional law coalitions must be formed at the national level not only with similarly impacted local governments but also with those national interest groups standing to gain from reform. Given that change of this nature will adversely affect the welfare of other groups, progress is slow and difficult.

Not that there have been no changes. Major ones in Western democracies include increased centralization of funding of locally provided goods and services. The theoretical rationale for grants-in-aid from central to local governments is usually framed in terms of that underprovision by local governments that results when they provide positive externalities to each other. By the same token certain interests other than the national interest are fulfilled by conditional grants-in-aid: local governments obtain revenue without any corresponding obligation to the local electorate: and special interest groups may gain from the spending associated with a grant-in-aid program.

Select Bibliography

Berkman, Richard L., and Viscusi, W. Kip. *Damming the West.* New York: Grossman, 1973.

Boehne, Edward G. "Making Economic Sense Out of Grants-in-Aid." *Philadelphia Federal Reserve Bank Business Review,* February 1969, pp. 3–9.

Clawson, Marion. "Economic and Social Conflicts in Land Use Planning." *Natural Resources Journal* 15 (July 1975): 473–89.

Manners, Gerald. "Regional Protection: A Factor in Economic Geography." *Economic Geography* 38 (1962): 122–29.

Roe, Charles. "Land Use: The Second Battle of Gettysburg." *Appraisal Journal* 42, no. 2 (January 1974): 90–102.

FURTHER READINGS

Fellmeth, Robert C. *Politics of Land.* New York: Grossman, 1973.

Harriss, C. Lowell, ed. *The Good Earth of America.* Englewood Cliffs, N.J.: Prentice-Hall, 1974.

Reilly, William K., ed. *The Use of Land.* New York: Crowell, 1973.

Whyte, William H. *The Last Landscape.* Garden City, N.Y.: Doubleday Anchor, 1970.

Zwick, David, with Benstock, Marcy. *Water Wasteland.* New York: Bantam, 1972.

PART FOUR

The Metropolitan Level

Characteristic of metropolitan areas is a third cluster of public issues. These result from the relations households have with their neighborhoods, municipalities, and with the actors responsible for events impacting on household welfare at those geographic levels: local governments, real estate interests, banks, school boards, and so on. Chapter 12 is essentially descriptive and focuses on variations in residential desirability within metropolitan areas. Chapter 13 attempts to identify political processes that could conceivably generate these inequalities and all the problems with which they are linked. In particular we arrive at a conception of competitive local policies in which locally based groups compete with each other to control the forces making for residential desirability. Chapter 14 shows how these competitive processes act to produce the observed geographical inequalities.

Chapter Twelve

Public Problems in Metropolitan Areas

In this chapter we consider geographical variations in residential desirability in metropolitan areas. These are considered at two distinct levels: that of the neighborhood and that of the municipality. At the neighborhood level externalities of a behavioral and physical character combine with variations in public services to produce a variation in residential attractiveness: one, moreover, that is mirrored in the geographical distributions of income groups, the better off living in the more attractive neighborhoods and the less well off consigned to the more undesirable areas.

A second set of variations derive from the typical fragmentation of the American metropolitan area into numerous municipalities, each with its own powers of public spending and revenue raising. Public provision and tax rates vary substantially from one municipality to another. These differences provide a further basis for residential sorting by income. But first we consider variations at the neighborhood level.

Variations in Neighborhood Residential Desirability

What makes some neighborhoods within a municipality more environmentally appealing and therefore more residentially attractive than others? Why are we prepared to bid more for the privilege of residing in one neighborhood than in another? Abstracting from individual preferences major reasons attach to the externalities, or uncompensated benefits and costs, that residents provide for each other, that nonresidents provide—or impose—and that agencies of local government make available.

SOURCES OF EXTERNALITIES

Local Residents   Consider first the externalities that individuals make available for each other. One of the more impressive facets of the distribution of these externalities within urban areas is their localization. Certain neighborhoods, for instance, are characterized by low crime rates, high levels of maintenance of residential property, and generally desirable public behavior. They are the sort of neighborhoods where parents believe their children will be able to mix with the "right sort of child." Other neighborhoods, on the other hand, are notable more for high rates of crime and delinquency, public insobriety, household noise, and "the wrong sort of child." This characterization, of course, will be recognized as separating more middle-class neighborhoods from more lower class neighborhoods. To the extent that blacks are more lower class than whites, then segregation by race accomplishes a similar and unequal distribution of the benefits and burdens implied by behavioral externalities. Residential segregation by social class and by race, then, is a fundamental fact in Western cities and one fraught with serious implications for the distribution of residential desirability (Downs 1973).

It is sometimes suggested, however, that everyone prefers residential segregation and that therefore there are no serious welfare inequalities resulting from it. To some extent there may be an element of truth in this. Many recent immigrants to the United States, for example, prefer to live in distinct ethnic ghettos (Bourne 1974; Lopata 1967; Gans 1962). Not only are there questions of language and customs, but agglomeration permits the achievement of thresholds for ethnic-specific services: restaurants, groceries, churches, and cultural groups. Segregation may also permit certain public economies to be attained: school curricula emphasizing the interests of a particular group or ethnic school teachers, for example. In addition segregation in the context of a ward electoral system may facilitate representation in local government.

The evidence by and large, however, is not particularly convincing. Only a small proportion of the urban population in North America or in Western Europe prefers the ethnic or religious enclave. Generally the pattern of segregation by social class prevails. And in this context the most significant fact is that lower class individuals prefer middle-class neighborhoods almost as much as middle-class individuals do. In Columbus, Ohio, for example, individuals of widely differing socio-economic status were asked in a survey administered by the author to rank three neighborhoods in order of residential preference, assuming that they had the money to live anywhere they pleased: a relatively drab though respectable working class district; a long-settled, middle-class neighborhood; and a highly affluent and spacious suburb. For the vast majority (70 percent), and irrespective of socioeconomic status, the rankings were the same: what one would regard as the more attractive neighborhoods were preferred to the less-attractive neighborhoods.

Nonresidents While residential segregation establishes the unequal distribution of one set of externalities across residential neighborhoods, others are defined by the activities of nonresidents. The residents of some neighborhoods tend to experience higher levels of air and noise pollution than others. Residents in other neighborhoods may experience car parking problems and greater levels of congestion in neighborhood streets. Generally these problems tend to be most critical towards the center of the city; their symptoms decline in incidence with distance from the CBD.

Air pollution is typical of these externalities. Generally, for example, it reaches a peak in downtown areas and decreases towards the suburbs; this is apparent in carbon monoxide levels and is associated with automobile traffic patterns, the auto being the major source of carbon monoxide fumes within cities. Philadelphia (figure 12.1) is typical of this configuration.

Given this pattern we should not be surprised to find that it is those of lower income who experience higher exposure to air pollutants. Figure 12.1, for example, includes dashed areas: these are areas considered by the U.S. Office of Economic Opportunity to be poor areas. Correlation with high levels of air pollution is quite evident.

Table 12.1 provides similar data in tabular form for Kansas City, St. Louis, and Washington, D.C.: in the case of each of these there is a monotonic decrease in exposure to air pollutants with increasing income. Apparently, then, there is a strong pro-rich bias in the distribution of less-polluted air. The health effects of this are not trivial (Lave & Seskin 1970).

LOCAL AGENCIES: DISTRIBUTION OF PUBLIC SERVICES

The activities of nonresidents therefore provide a geographic distribution of externality impacts that generally favor more middle class over lower class populations. Residential quality, however, is also a function of public provision: for example, street lighting, highway quality, speed limits on streets, school quality. Rather surprisingly access to these services varies markedly from one neighborhood to another. This is despite the constitutionally mandated criterion of equal public services for all.

Evidence of locational bias in the provision of municipal services is widespread. Recent evidence emerging from a legal suit concerning the small city of Shaw, Louisiana, is typical also of much larger American cities (Ratner 1968, pp. 1–63). Though applying to relatively mundane services, the list of inequities is a depressing one. Almost 98 percent of the houses fronting on unpaved streets in Shaw are

Figure 12.1 Relative Carbon Monoxide Emissions in Philadelphia

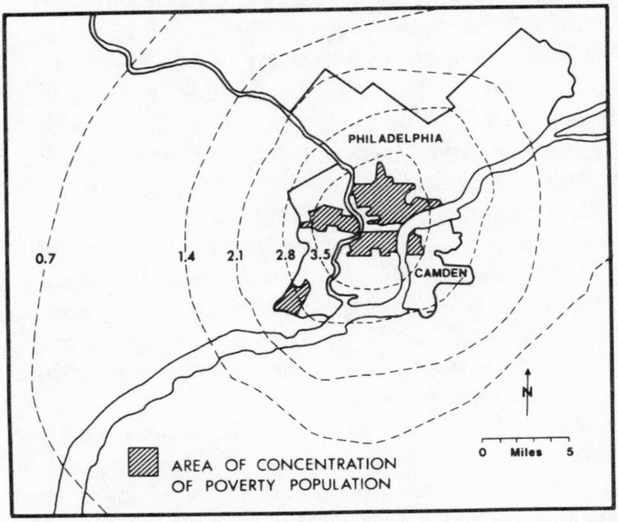

SOURCE: *The Inner City Environment and the Role of the Environmental Protection Agency* (Hearings Before the Subcommittee of the Environment of the Commerce Committee, U.S. Senate, 92d Cong., 2d Sess. on the Inner City Environment and the Role of the Environmental Protection Agency, February 4, April 7, and May 8) (Washington, D.C.: Government Printing Office, 1972), p. 33.

black occupied; 97 percent of the houses not served by sanitary sewers are in black neighborhoods. All modern street lighting fixtures of the mercury vapor variety are confined to white neighborhoods; these neighborhoods also have operational storm sewers and drainage ditches. Disparities between white and black neighborhoods extend, in addition, to the provision of fire hydrants, stoplights, and water main size.

Possibly the most obvious of inequalities in public provision, however, are those in education. Generally children attending schools in whiter, more middle-class areas of a school district tend to have more experienced teachers, to be taught in newer, more up-to-date buildings, and to use the newest textbooks and equipment. Quite the reverse applies in black and lower class areas of the city (Sexton 1961; Baron 1971). Yet it is precisely in these areas that the need for educational services is greatest: lower class parents tend to make a far more modest monetary and personal investment in the informal education of their children—books, travel, verbal interaction, guidance on which tv programs to watch—than do more middle-class parents. In addition, application of the neighborhood school principle—assignment of children to schools on a geographic proximity basis—in a

Table 12.1   Air Pollution Indices by Income Size Class

Income Class[a]	Suspended Particulates[b]	Sulfation[c]	Mean
Kansas City			
0–2,999	76.7	0.22	1.16
3,000–4,999	72.4	.20	1.09
5,000–6,999	66.5	.18	0.98
7,000–9,999	63.5	.17	0.93
10,000–14,999	60.1	.15	0.86
15,000–24,999	57.6	.14	0.80
25,000–over	58.1	.12	0.76
St. Louis			
0–2,999	91.3	.97	1.19
3,000–4,999	85.3	.88	1.10
5,000–6,999	79.2	.78	1.00
7,000–9,999	75.4	.72	0.93
10,000–14,999	73.0	.68	0.89
15,000–24,999	68.8	.60	0.82
25,000–over	64.9	.52	0.74
Washington, D.C.			
0–2,999	64.6	.82	1.19
3,000–4,999	61.7	.82	1.16
5,000–6,999	53.9	.75	1.04
7,000–9,999	49.7	.69	0.96
10,000–14,999	45.5	.64	0.88
15,000–24,999	43.2	.58	0.82
25,000–over	42.0	0.53	0.77

SOURCE: Reprinted from A. Myrick Freeman, "Distribution of Environmental Quality," in A. V. Kneese and B. T. Bower, eds., *Environmental Quality Analysis: Theory and Method in the Social Sciences* (Baltimore: Johns Hopkins Press, 1972), p. 205, by permission of the publisher. Published for Resources for the Future by Johns Hopkins Press.

[a] In dollars.
[b] μgms/ml.
[c] mg. SO_3/100 cm$_2$ per day.

residentially segregated environment results in disparities in exposure to middle-class peer environments. As will be seen shortly, this can be highly significant. In summary, however, the problem of inter-school disparities can be discussed from three viewpoints: disparities in teacher quality, in the capital equipment required by the education process, and in access to middle-class peer groups.

There seems little doubt that, based on a variety of criteria, pupils at schools with more middle-class, white enrollments tend to get higher quality teachers than schools with more lower class and/or black enrollments (Owen 1972). *Quality* refers both to the intellectual capacity of the teacher and teacher experience. Verbal skills, for example, are commonly regarded as a good index of IQ; by relating student social class to the verbal skills of their teachers it is possible to test for inequality. A study of the Detroit city school district disclosed that there was a very strong relationship between teacher verbal skill and student social class; students of higher social class were being exposed to teachers of higher verbal skill and, therefore, presumably teachers of greater intellectual capacity (Guthrie et al. 1970, p. 3458).

Disparities of a similar geographical incidence are also evident in data on teacher experience and qualifications. A study carried out in Chicago in 1963 ranked public high schools by the socioeconomic status of the population of surrounding neighborhoods and found that in the ten lowest ranking schools about 37 percent of the teachers were not fully certified and the median teaching experience was approximately four years. In contrast, in the ten highest ranking schools less than 1 percent of the teachers were not fully certified and the median teaching experience was over twelve years (Kerner et al. 1968, p. 428). The socioeconomic contrast, of course, also corresponded with a racial contrast. Similar inequalities have been found in other cities.

These disparities in experience and qualification are largely responsible for variations in per pupil expenditures across schools (Owen 1972). Generally pupils attending schools in poorer neighborhoods tend to have less spent on their education than do pupils attending schools in wealthier neighborhoods. More qualified and experienced teachers tend to command higher salaries, thus boosting expenditures at those middle-class schools to which they tend to gravitate. Further there is good reason to believe that these disparities are not of minor significance in their impact on student achievement. Many empirical studies have verified a relationship between teacher experience and student performance on standardized achievement tests (Guthrie et al. 1971, pp. 79–84).

Similar disparities exist in availability of the capital equipment necessary for education. These interschool disparities have been exhaustively documented for elementary schools in a northern central city school district, and our discussion draws heavily on those findings (Sexton 1961). Disparities were identified by differences in the treatment of four groups of schools, each defined according to the average family income of the population in the neighborhood of the school. Specifically the groups were defined as follows: Group I, $3,000-4,999; Group II, $5,000-6,999; Group III, $7,000-8,999; Group IV, $9,000 and over. It was found that schools in the lower income groups—I and II—were considerably older than schools in the upper income groups. The mean ages of the schools were: Group I, 45 years; Group II, 46 years; Group III, 26 years; Group IV, 25 years. On average, therefore, schools in poorer neighborhoods tended to be almost twice as old as schools in wealthier areas of the school district.

These differences in age are clearly associated with deficiencies in the specific facilities available at schools in different types of neighborhoods. Fifty percent of the Group I schools and 46 percent of the Group II schools lacked a science facility, for example, while less than 5 percent of the schools in more affluent neighborhoods in the same school district had such a deficiency. Similar disparities were apparent in the provision of conservatories, instrumental music, and speech.

Such disparities clearly demand implementation of some type of equalization policy either by federal or state authorities. Equalization policies, however, have tended to be ineffective. Where federal funds do reach the more needy school districts, they often tend to be reallocated by local school district authorities in a way so as to benefit middle-class children as well as, or instead of, the poorer children for whom the aid was originally intended. The perverse reallocation of Elementary and Secondary Education Act Title I funds at the local level has received extensive press publicity in this regard (Cox 1973, p. 79).

Finally a variety of policies have as their end product a reduction in the exposure of lower class children to middle-class peer environments. School location and pupil assignment policies may be used to maximize the white, middle-class nature of pupil enrollments at some schools and, consequently, maximize the black, lower class pupil composition at other schools. With respect to pupil assignment, excellent examples have been unearthed in recent congressional hearings on equality of educational opportunity. In Pasadena, for example, there have been numerous cases in the past in which white middle-class students have been assigned to a more distant school with a predominantly white enrollment rather than to a closer school with a largely black enrollment (Cox 1973, p. 79).

Variations in peer group environment, moreover, seem particularly significant. Recent evidence on the factors affecting educational achievement suggest that peer group effects are important. Indeed, the major finding of the Coleman report on equality of educational opportunity in the United States was that family background was the most significant determinant of student arithmetic and verbal achievement; the second-ranking variable, however, was the peer group family background (Coleman et al. 1966). When lower class children have middle-class peer groups, therefore, they tend to do much better in school than when their peer group is confined to

Figure 12.2   Jurisdictional Fragmentation in the St. Louis Metropolitan Area, 1960

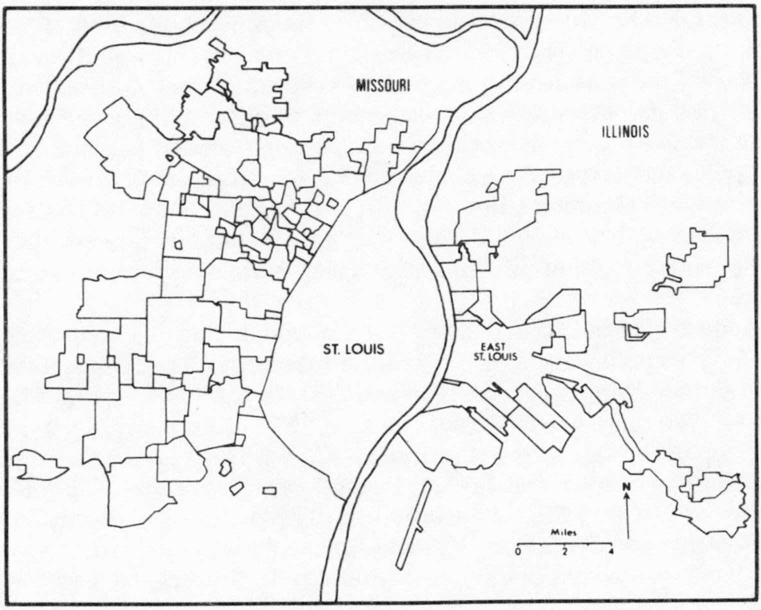

children from the lower class. So long as middle-class children remain in a majority in a school, the presence of lower class children furthermore has no adverse effect on *them*. It is this finding that is most significant, since it suggests that if larger numbers of lower class children were placed in dominantly middle-class schools, overall achievement rates would rise substantially. So long as residential segregation combined with the neighborhood school concept persists, however, this is not going to happen. This argument, of course, is an important one in the armory of those who would like to see abolition of the neighborhood school concept and its replacement by busing of children from low-income neighborhoods to dominantly middle-class schools.

Inequalities of this nature, however, with the wealthier gaining at the expense of the poorer, find a mirror image at the jurisdictional level. It is to inequalities at this larger scale that the second half of this chapter is devoted.

Variations in Jurisdictions and Residential Desirability

In the United States, metropolitan areas are divided into a multiplicity of municipalities, school districts, nonschool special districts and counties—each with its own powers to provide services and raise revenues. The average number of local government units per metropolitan area is eighty-seven. Clearly, however, larger metropolitan areas have more local government units. In some cases this number is quite high: the Chicago metropolitan area, for example, has over 1,000 local government units. Some idea of the intense jurisdictional fragmentation prevailing in larger cities is provided by figure 12.2 (the St. Louis area).

Jurisdictions in metropolitan areas moreover differ substantially in residential desirability. There can be no doubt that in U.S. metropolitan areas most households regard themselves as better off living in suburban jurisdictions than in the central city. Of course, some suburbs are residentially more attractive than others: there are industrial suburbs that are less desirable and bedroom suburbs that are more desirable (Logan 1976). But by and large the characterization is a valid one.

The residential advantages of independent suburbs are several. They result from public provision, tax rates and the behavioral externalities experienced in suburbs. With respect to public provision the most notable feature of local government spending patterns in the suburbs is the relatively large amount spent on education. Table 12.2 provides some indication of differences in per pupil spending between a number of central cities and selected suburbs. Although these particular suburbs are unusually affluent and differences in per pupil spending are correspondingly large, this is illustrative of a more general tendency (Cox 1973, p. 31). And as table 12.2 shows, differences in spending furthermore translate into quite tangible differences such as those in pupil-teacher ratios. In addition the financial resources of independent suburbs and their generally more motivated pupils give suburban school districts a competitive edge in attracting the more experienced and stable school teacher.

Tax rates also differ between central city and suburban ring. In 1965 local taxes in the central cities of the thirty-seven largest SMSAs amounted to 7.6 percent of the personal income of residents, compared with 5.6 percent in the suburban ring (Advisory Commission on Intergovernmental Relations 1967, p. 80). This does not mean that suburban residents were paying lower taxes, however. Since they were almost certainly paying taxes on a higher individual tax base, absolute taxes were, in fact, probably higher.

These contrasts are symptomatic of a much more profound fiscal problem in metropolitan areas: the segregation of tax base from demand for public services (Cox 1973, ch. 3). As a result of the suburbanization of capital-consuming individuals and businesses within metropolitan areas the assessed valuation of property per capita—the most significant element in the local tax base—is now higher in the

Table 12.2　Per Pupil Expenditures and Pupil Teacher Ratios for Selected Central Cities and Suburbs, 1967

City and Suburb	Pupil-Teacher Ratio	Per Pupil Expenditures
Los Angeles	27	$ 610
Beverly Hills	17	1,192
San Francisco	26	693
Palo Alto	21	984
Chicago	28	571
Evanston	18	757
Detroit	31	530
Grosse Pointe	22	713
St. Louis City	30	525
University City	22	747
New York City	20	854
Great Neck	16	1,391
Cleveland	28	559
Cleveland Heights	22	703
Philadelphia	27	617
Lower Merion	20	733

SOURCE: *Hearings Before the Select Committee on Equal Educational Opportunity of the United States Senate*, p. 3357.

suburbs than in central cities. In order to yield the same amount of revenue per capita, therefore, central city local governments generally have to tax at a rate higher than their suburban counterparts.

In actuality central city revenue needs are greater than those of the suburbs. In addition to demands for education, which suburban local governments also confront, central cities have particularly onerous burdens in the area of public safety. Crime, associated with the generally lower income populations of central cities, induces demands for police spending on a level substantially higher than in the suburbs. Rising demands for services and a narrowing tax base result in a serious fiscal squeeze.

In addition some have argued that as a result of their large daily influxes of commuters and shoppers, central cities must provide for public safety and for additional services such as street maintenance. The suburban beneficiaries of these services, however, pay nothing in taxes; rather, the additional services have to be funded by the hard-pressed central city taxpayer (Hawley 1951; Neenan 1972). This argument is particularly forceful in the case of cultural and recreational amenities such as symphony orchestras, art galleries, and zoos, which are enjoyed by central city and suburban resident alike but are subsidized only by the central city taxpayer.

Table 12.3   Changes in Central City: Suburb per Capita Expenditure and Revenue Gaps,
1957–1965

	Education Expenditure ($)	Noneducation Expenditure ($)	Tax Revenue ($)
Per capita gap			
1957	− 25	+ 69	− 38
1965	− 47	+ 100	− 48

SOURCE: Advisory Commission on Intergovernmental Relations, *Fiscal Balance in the American Federal System*, vol. 2, p. 87.

Table 12.4   Robbery Rates per 100,000 Population for Selected Central Cities and
Metropolitan Areas

Area	Central City	Metropolitan Area
Chicago	420.8	244.3
Newark	379.8	109.4
Washington	358.8	153.2
Miami	241.2	164.2
Los Angeles	293.4	189.1
Cleveland	213.4	101.1
Houston	135.3	95.5
Dayton	129.6	55.2

SOURCE: Advisory Commission on Intergovernmental Relations, *Fiscal Balance in the American Federal System*, vol. 2, p. 48.

While the argument has not gone uncontested (Cox 1973, pp. 67–68), it has provided the basis for a number of central city policies aimed at including suburban populations within the central city tax base. The most important of these is a municipal income tax levied not only on persons who live in the central city but also on those who work there. Municipal income taxes are common in the metropolitan areas of both Ohio and Pennsylvania.

An additional burden for central cities is their relatively large share of tax-exempt property. Public buildings such as state and federal offices and the offices of charitable, religious, and educational groups are exempt from the local property tax, even though they generate large influxes of clients who require locally funded public safety and highway services. Central cities, as a result of their advantages of access to the metropolitan area as a whole, generally have a disproportionate share of such property. In Detroit 30 percent of the

Table 12.5   Proportion of Metropolitan Population in Suburbs by Race and Family Income, 1969

Family Income ($)	All Races*	White*	Black*
Under 5,000	41.8	48.9	19.0
5,000–9,999	51.6	56.3	20.2
10,000–14,999	61.0	63.7	23.0
15,000–19,999	63.2	65.5	25.7
20,000–24,999	64.4	66.1	29.3
25,000 & over	65.5	66.0	34.5

NOTE: Wealthier families are more likely to live in the suburbs than poorer people. But at a given level of income blacks are less likely to live in the suburbs than whites.
SOURCE: U.S. Bureau of the Census.
*Percentage in suburbs.

land area is exempt from the local property tax. In Boston the equivalent figure is an incredible 60 percent. The negative impact of this on the tax bases of many central cities is substantial.

In dynamic terms the metropolitan fiscal disparities problem is deepening: any counteracting forces are overwhelmed by the housing market and business location forces described above (Cox 1973, p. 31). Table 12.3 exemplifies the problem in terms of per capita gaps between central city and suburb in the period 1957–65. In 1957 central city per capita tax revenue was $38 less than in the suburbs; in 1965 it was $48 less, despite the greater tax efforts made by central cities. This clearly indicates the way in which the redistribution of businesses and middle-class residents out of the central city and into the suburbs has brought benefits to suburban populations at the expense of those remaining in the central city. The problem of noneducational expenditures for public safety and welfare services, for example, also appears to be increasing. While the expenditure gap has moved in favor of the city in noneducational expenditure, quite the reverse has occurred in educational expenditure.

Nor can central cities easily borrow their way out of this situation. To some degree they are constrained by state bonding limits. In the municipal bond market interest rates reflect risk. Clearly municipalities experiencing fiscal problems are riskier propositions. Consequently for those public works that will make them more attractive to middle-class resident and business alike, central cities in general can obtain loans only at relatively high interest rates.

In addition there are substantial differences between suburban and central city jurisdictions in resident exposure to various behavioral externalities. Notable among these is crime. Table 12.4

gives some indication of the differences at issue in the area of robbery rates. These differences, of course, result in vastly increased central city expenditures on public safety: expenditures that suburbs are consequently fortunate to escape.

Other significant behavioral externalities occur in education. As remarked earlier in this chapter, major educational resources include the child's peer group. Middle-class peer groups apparently are a more valuable input for attaining higher achievement scores than are lower class peer groups. Compared to central city schools, of course, suburban schools are much more middle class.

These differences in residential quality would be of little importance if they did not reinforce other inequalities in society. Generally suburbanites already have access to more substantial private resources in the form of income, capital assets, and savings than does the average central city dweller. While we should be careful not to impute to central city dwellers' uniformly low incomes, there can be no doubt that average incomes are lower; and in some cities such as Cleveland, St. Louis, and Newark, the variance of incomes around that average is also minimal. When one takes into account the fact that most blacks are poor and live in the central city, one sees that income inequities are compounded by racial ones (table 12.5).

Of course some argue that while jurisdictional fragmentation is associated with considerable variation in public provision, tax rates, and associated behavioral externalities, albeit of a redistributionally perverse character, it does allow tailoring of public policy to individual tastes. Assuming variation in preferences for public policies, individuals—in a context of many local governments—can match their preferences with appropriate policies by their choice of residence (Aronson 1974).

To some extent this may be true. Older, possibly retired persons who do not want to see their taxes raised in order to pay for education may cluster into a jurisdiction where local government actually spends very little on it. The greater the proportion of the population of the jurisdiction that is old, of course, the less will be the local need for educational spending. In other cases preferences may involve the location of shopping centers: some households may prefer shopping centers because of their favorable impact on the local tax base; others may wish to keep shopping centers at a distance because of the traffic they generate. Where there is jurisdictional fragmentation and local control of land use, the preferences of both groups can, in principle at least, be satisfied.

By and large, however, the taste-diversity argument is not a particularly convincing justification for jurisdictional fragmentation. There are at least two counter-arguments. First, while tastes may be fairly uniform within smaller, individual suburban municipalities, this is far from true in more populous central cities: preferences there vary between, for example, black and white, young and old, or one ethnic group and another.

This sheds some doubt on the idea that households sort themselves out among jurisdictions according to their public policy preferences. Significant in this regard is the fact that the variety of preference apparent in central cities is one of the bases of demand for some measure of neighborhood control there.

Second, and certainly most important, the argument relating diversity of preference to jurisdictional fragmentation depends on individuals being able to act on those preferences in their residential choice behavior. The capability to relocate, however, is usually contingent on income. There are many central city, low-income families, for example, who would prefer to live in middle-class suburbs. Housing prices there, however, are beyond their means.

Concluding Comments

This chapter has reviewed, with particular reference to the United States, variations in residential desirability in metropolitan areas. These variations tend to be distributed quite perversely. At both neighborhood and jurisdictional levels wealthier households enjoy residentially more attractive environments than do poorer ones.

At the neighborhood level low-income households tend to live in neighborhoods where their neighbors are less than considerate in their public behavior. Levels of crime tend to be higher and standards of property maintenance lower than in middle-class neighborhoods.

Nonresidents may also have undesirable impacts on residential attractiveness. A variety of such problems—air pollution, noise, congestion, car-parking difficulties—seem to have their greatest incidence close to the CBD and to decline with distance therefrom. To the extent that neighborhoods closer to the downtown tend to be occupied by those of lower income, these impacts have perverse distributional consequences. Much clearer in their distributional effects are interneighborhood variations in public services. These are particularly apparent in education. Physical facilities, teacher experience, teacher turnover rates, and peer group composition—all work to the disadvantage of children in lower income neighborhoods.

Similar distributional perversities are apparent at the jurisdictional level. A major dichotomy here is that between central cities and independent suburbs. Independent suburbs tend to spend more per pupil on education than central cities, but most central cities must tax their citizens at higher rates. Fiscal inequality furthermore is associated with inequality in exposure to behavioral externalities. Having more middle-class neighbors means that residents of independent suburbs are far less likely to be exposed to crime than residents of the central city. Of course, a major reason why middle-class people choose to live in independent suburbs may be precisely these differentials in tax rates and crime rates. But that would be to anticipate what follows in chapters 13 and 14.

Select Bibliography

Boal, F. W. "Territoriality on the Shankill-Falls Divide, Belfast." *Irish Geography* 6, no. 1 (1969): 30-50.

————."Territoriality and Class: A Study of Two Residential Areas in Belfast." *Irish Geography* 6, no. 3 (1971): 229-48.

Brazer, H. E. "Some Fiscal Implications of Metropolitanism." In Benjamin Chinitz, ed. *City and Suburb.* Englewood Cliffs, N.J.: Prentice-Hall, 1964.

Coleman, James S. "Equal Schools or Equal Students?" *Public Interest,* no. 4, summer 1966.

Fellman, Gordon; Brandt, Barbara; and Rosenblatt, Roger. "Dagger in the Heart of a Town." *Trans-Action* 7, no. 11 (September 1970): 38-47.

Fitch, L. C. "Metropolitan Fiscal Problems." In Benjamin Chinitz, ed. *City and Suburb.* Englewood Cliffs, N.J.: Prentice-Hall, 1964.

Frieden, Bernard J. "Toward Equality of Urban Opportunity." In H. Wentworth Eldredge, ed. *Taming Megalopolis,* pp. 507-35. Garden City, N.Y.: Doubleday Anchor, 1967.

Levin, Henry M. "The Coleman Report—What Difference Do Schools Make?" *Saturday Review,* 20 January 1968.

Sexton, Patricia C. *Education and Income: The Inequality of Opportunity in Our Public Schools,* pp. 23-25; 113-36; 211-23; 227-38. New York: Viking, 1961.

Chapter Thirteen

Local Policy in Metropolitan Areas

In this chapter we begin the task of explaining the inequalities in residential desirability identified in chapter 12. More specifically we identify the critical processes that will have to be related to the geography of residential desirability in chapter 14. These are processes of competition between local governments and neighborhood organizations attempting to attract the utility enhancing and to keep out the utility detracting. The argument is that the urban land development process has welfare impacts critical to localized populations at neighborhood and jurisdictional levels in metropolitan areas. Involvement in the political process at both levels represents a defense mechanism: local residents attempt to control and deflect the urban land development process to their own benefit.

The chapter starts, therefore, with a consideration of the functioning of the urban land development process and its impacts on resident welfare at neighborhood and jurisdictional levels. In the second section we consider the implications of these impacts for participation in the political process. Finally described are the diverse techniques that neighborhood organizations and local governments employ to manipulate the development process to their own advantage.

Basis of Local Concern

CONTEXT

At the *inter*national level we saw that the critical context for national policy was created by international investment flows bringing with them the prospects of jobs and economic growth. At the *intra*national level local governments were concerned with the impact of analogous flows and concomitant population movements on local job markets, tax bases, and physical amenity. At the urban level the critical context is provided by the local impacts of the urban land development process. It is the urban land development process, therefore, as it operates in particular subareas of the city, as it links one neighborhood with another and the inner city with the suburbs, that provides the ultimate source of those welfare impacts critical for local political processes in metropolitan areas.

271

The urban land development process is the process by which urban land is created and shifted (Woodruff 1974) from one use to another. It includes, therefore, the conversion of raw suburban land into housing estates, drive-in theaters, or shopping centers; the extension of factories into surrounding vacant land; the demolition of downtown structures and their replacement by parking lots or office buildings; and the conversion of housing from single-family residential to apartments.

To some degree, therefore, it is a physical process involving additions to or alterations in physical structures. At the same time it is a social process, as the use of existing structures alters with ongoing social change. A group of once smart downtown hotels becomes the nucleus of skid row. A city park becomes less a place of recreation for local residents and more a place to be avoided as junkies and hoodlums take over (Simon 1976). Or an erstwhile middle-class neighborhood becomes more lower class in its social composition (Wolf & Lebeaux 1969, pt. 1; Molotch 1972).

In part the urban land development process is a market process: urban land is bought and sold in a market in which sellers compete against one another and buyers do likewise. But it is only partly a market process. Local government is a *necessary* participant in the creation of urban land and, often enough, in changes in the use of urban land. The creation of new residential areas on the edge of a city, for example, depends on waterline and sewer line extensions. Large downtown redevelopment projects may depend on the ability of the developer to induce local government to implement new traffic schemes or mass transit systems (Beagle, Haber & Wellman 1971).

Here we consider urban land development under three headings: commercial land development; residential land development; and the relationships between the two. In the cases of both commercial and residential development, a mixture of market forces and public sector activities are in evidence. Market forces dominate on the demand side, but the supply of urban land is dependent on cooperation between public and private agencies.

Commercial Land Development   To some degree the development of land for commercial purposes is a function of demand forces. Certain locations within the metropolitan area represent more profitable sites for factories, office buildings, stores, and warehouses. Consequently more money can be made from developing those sites for commercial purposes than from developing sites elsewhere. Within the metropolitan area a premium tends to be placed on locations that maximize accessibility to the remainder of the metropolitan area: nodes in the transportation network, for example. For industrial plants and offices it is a question of accessibility to the metropolitan labor market; for stores and service industries such as cinemas and restaurants, nodes on the transportation network represent points of maximum access to the consumer market.

Clearly, however, points of maximum accessibility to the metropolitan area are relative to specific modes of transportation (Schaeffer & Sclar 1975). In the late nineteenth century the major mode was the streetcar, with streetcar lines focusing on the downtown area. At that time the "centrality" of the CBD was more than apparent. Mass diffusion of the automobile and the construction of a highly connected and decentralized network of fast highways has, however, altered calculations of accessibility. No longer does the CBD enjoy the clear pre-eminence of centrality that it once did. While still at the center of the urban transportation network, new nodes enjoying high levels of accessibility to the metropolitan area have emerged at the intersections of freeways and major highways. These have proven highly attractive locations for manufacturing plants and what is now, in North America at least, the ubiquitous suburban shopping center.

Other forces have also played an important role in increasing the relative attractiveness of suburban sites for commercial development. An effect of the CBD-oriented city was the tendency for land rents to decline with distance from the CBD (Yeates 1965; Brodsky 1970). As technologies have changed and commercial developments have expanded their land needs, so the lower land prices of suburban locations have appeared more attractive. One widely touted change has been the shift in industrial technology from land-economizing vertical structures to land-extensive horizontal ones. The widespread use of the automobile has added another dimension to the space consumption needs of commercial developments: parking space requirements for shoppers and for workers must now enter into land need calculations.

Other changes in technology have tended to increase the indifference of the commercial developer towards CBD locations. The use of the telephone has reduced the premium offices used to place on close physical proximity to, say, law offices, advertising agencies, and other offices and service industries. At the same time the truck has released manufacturing from dependence on downtown railroad yards.

It would be misleading, however, to regard new commercial development as spread evenly throughout a given suburban ring. Locators of, for example, new stores, office buildings, and service industries are subject to a good deal of uncertainty as to which locations will be most profitable. As a consequence they tend to be attracted to those areas with a proven track record: those that already have a good deal of commercial development. The result is the agglomeration with which we are all familiar in the modern urban landscape: the commercial strip, the proliferation of stores, cinemas, and restaurants around pre-existing shopping centers, and the like. There are also supply constraints, however, and it is to those that we now turn.

A major problem for commercial development on the supply side is land assembly. Commercial activities tend to agglomerate: stores tend to be located close to one another; manufacturing plants exist cheek-by-jowl in many downtown areas; universities tend to be surrounded by retailing uses or other institutional uses such as hospitals. With economic growth many of these activities will wish to expand, and the most economic direction of expansion will be horizontal. Expansion, however, is likely to be difficult. Adjacent land is, in all likelihood, already developed under various forms of durable structure, the owners of which will be seeking a price equal to that of the land plus the undepreciated balance of the cost of the improvements. At the same time adjacent owners may be unwilling to sell, since they cherish expansion plans of their own. Adjacent retailing outlets may covet each other's land as the site for a new parking garage, for example. Even if adjacent sites should be vacant, there will be problems of assembling them into a cohesive block. Expansion will permit increased productivity and hence rent. Each of the landowners involved has monopoly powers with respect to implementation of land assembly, however, and is likely to hold out for a lion's share of the increased rent. Price gouging of this nature represents a substantial deterrent to land assembly (Woodruff 1974, pp. 51–54).

To some degree expansion may take place by intensification of the use of existing land. Usually this involves some vertical expansion as in the highrise office or skyscraper. For many activities, particularly manufacturing plants, however, current technologies will make this solution uneconomical. The result is a tendency to seek out new sites in undeveloped suburban areas, where land comes in large blocks eliminating the assembly problem and where the firm can purchase enough land to satisfy its expansion plans well into the foreseeable future.

The creation of urban land of course is not simply a market process. The establishment of suburban industrial plants or shopping centers depends on a wide variety of public actions: the provision of sewerage, water, and highway access, for instance. The necessity of rezoning or some form of development permission increases this dependence. In the United States local governments have been more than pliant in providing the infrastructure and development permission necessary for peripheral expansion. In Canada and Britain this has been less the case and, as a consequence, CBDs have been able to retain more of their monopoly of office and retail activity. Britain is a particularly interesting case, since downtown retail interests have ac-

Table 13.1   Nonresidential Uses of Urban Renewal Land as of 1971

	Floor Space*	All Nonresidential Land (%)
Public		
Schools	37,186	9.9
Hospitals	11,280	3.0
Other government	53,654	14.2
Other institutional	18,162	4.8
Private		
Retail	76,308	20.3
Wholesale & distribution	10,734	2.9
Office buildings	62,848	16.7
Other commercial	73,979	19.7
Industrial	32,239	8.6
Total	376,390	

SOURCE: *The Central City Problem and Urban Renewal Policy* (Washington, D.C.: Government Printing Office, 1973), p. 67.

*Thousands of sq ft.

tively intervened in the planning process to oppose the establishment of new suburban shopping centers (Hall 1976). Generally speaking, local government has supported existing commercial interests for fear of tax base erosion. The fact that both British and Canadian cities lack freeway networks of the intricacy and density common in U.S. cities of similar size is also significant.

In U.S. cities, therefore, local governments have substantially stimulated suburban expansion of commercial development. At the same time there have been attempts to intervene in the central city land market and enhance the possibilities of land assembly and redevelopment there. A major weapon in this effort has been federal urban renewal legislation (Woodruff 1974, pp. 54–60; Netzer 1970, pp. 110–18). This provides local governments with the right of eminent domain: more specifically the legislation provides local governments with the right to condemn existing properties, purchase them at a negotiated price, clear the land in question, and sell to developers. The result has been a moderate amount of office expansion in U.S. downtowns along with expansion of hotels, retailing, and some institutional uses (table 13.1).

In the creation of urban land for commercial purposes, however, there are close, if not always clear, relations between supply-and-demand forces. We remarked earlier on the forces of uncertainty, on the demand side, creating agglomerations of commercial activity in

suburban locations. As these agglomerations increase in size congestion will occur and there will be pressure on local government for new
highways capable of easing the pressures and for rezonings that will
permit additional parking space development. As these occur and the
supply of commercial land in the area increases, new businesses will
be encouraged to move in, recreating the congestion problem and necessitating more ameliorative action on the part of local government.

Residential Land Development   To some degree the development
of land for housing or a shift in the use of existing housing is contingent on demand forces (U.S. Department of Housing and Urban
Development 1976). Prices for residential land and housing, for example, will be bid up in areas regarded as residentially attractive.
Their residential attractiveness may derive from certain neighborhood advantages such as good schools, quiet, lakeshore sites, or distant views. Considerations that vary across jurisdictions may also be
significant; some jurisdictions have lower tax rates and their local
governments spend more on education. For areas that are already
completely built up the quality of the housing stock may serve to differentiate demand; bids for areas where residential property is newer
and more in accord with contemporary tastes and needs, may elicit
higher bids than property in older parts of the city.

The competitive bidding mechanism helps to direct flows of residents and funds. Wealthier households, for example, outbid poorer
ones for property in low tax suburbs or in more attractive parts of the
city. The result will be an allocation to the wealthy of housing at
those more attractive sites, while the poor are able to purchase housing only in less-desirable locales.

Major shifts of this nature that take place in U.S. cities are those
relating inner city to suburb on the one hand and deteriorating neighborhoods to gentrifying ones on the other. Housing units in inner city
areas are often the least attractive units in the least attractive
neighborhoods; they also tend to be in jurisdictions where tax rates
are relatively high and where education is short-shrifted, so that more
money can be spent on public safety. Housing units in suburban
areas, however, are usually much newer, barely deteriorated if at all,
more adequate to modern tastes, and located in less densely occupied
neighborhoods with good schools, few public safety problems, and
relatively low tax rates. While suburban housing markets boom, in
many cities the bottom has dropped out of the inner city housing
market. For the least attractive residential properties, people are not
prepared to pay much compared with what they are willing to pay for
suburban properties. The distribution of abandoned housing in inner
cities is eloquent in this regard (figure 13.1). The wealthy furthermore

Figure 13.1   The Relationship Between Housing Abandonment and Residential Quality in
St. Louis

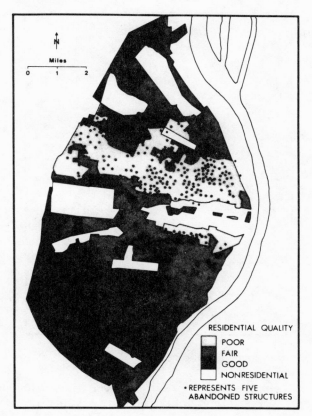

SOURCE: U.S. Department of Housing and Urban Development, *Abandoned Housing Research: A
Compendium* (Washington, D.C.: Government Printing Office, 1973), pp. 64; 65.

will outbid the poor for the more attractive suburban properties. The
result is a tendency for inner city populations to be relatively poor
and for housing investment money to be diverted from inner city
markets, where demand is weak, to suburban areas, where it is more
than buoyant.

Other shifts of residents and investment funds link deteriorating
and gentrifying neighborhoods. Deteriorating neighborhoods involve
a displacement of erstwhile middle-class residents by lower class
residents (Wolf & Lebeaux 1969, pt. 1; Molotch 1972; Cox 1973, pp.
85–86). As areas deteriorate in residential quality middle-class households considering purchase there are prepared to pay less than before;
ultimately they may be outbid by lower class households or landlords

Figure 13.2   Perception of Investment Possibilities in Housing by Three Professional Landlords, Baltimore, 1971

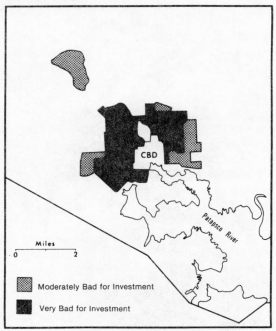

SOURCE: After Harvey, *Society, the City and the Space-Economy of Urbanism*, p. 40.

bidding on their behalf. The result is a shift of occupancy and a decline in the physical fabric of the housing commensurate with the ability to pay of the new lower income residents.

Gentrifying neighborhoods represent the other side of the coin: within certain geographically restricted areas of U.S. central cities, middle-class households are displacing lower class households (Ash 1967; Cox 1973, pp. 83–85; U.S. Department of Housing and Urban Development 1975). Presumably such areas have undergone an increase in their residential attractiveness. Previously lower class households outbid middle-class households because the middle-class evaluation of the area was so low. With increased residential attractiveness middle-class households ultimately outbid lower class households. Properties change hands at higher prices, therefore, and landlords invest in the refurbishment of their properties, reflecting the increased willingness to pay of middle-class households.

Demand, however, is only one aspect of the story. There are also certain supply forces that critically constrain the directions in which investments move and hence the opportunities available to those considering purchase or rental of housing at any one time. In any city there is a group of business activities whose sole raison d'être is involvement on the supply side of the housing market. We may call this group of business activities the *housing interest*. Generally its core consists of builders, land developers, land companies, apartment landlords, savings and loan companies, mortgage bankers, and realtors. The housing interest tends to see the city as a geography of investment opportunity: rates of return to investment in new construction and conversion to rental are greater in certain parts of the city than in others (Harvey 1972, pp. 38–44). Figure 13.2, for example, suggests that in Baltimore, at least, landlords see suburban locations as more attractive for investment in apartment buildings than inner city locations.

In terms of new construction there is no doubt that suburban locations provide opportunities for increased profits. To some degree this is a function of land costs. Unit land costs are much higher in the central city than in suburban locations. This is an especially critical consideration, given shifts in demand towards the more space-consuming, single-story ranch house.

It is also, however, a function of supplying desirable neighborhoods. As we observed earlier, consumers are bidding not only for housing but for neighborhoods. The investor in housing may be able to affect that environment in a more-or-less costly way, depending on the location of the investment within the metropolitan area. Considering the case of new housing development, it is possible that the demands of the more middle class could be satisfied by a restructuring of the central city environment. This would involve large-scale clearance of old housing structures and replacement by new housing developments over areas extensive enough that the middle-class occupants would be able to share out their externalities and minimize contact with lower class residents of the inner city.

The major problem here is land assembly. Ownership of housing structures in the central city is highly fragmented. Assembly of land is a long, slow—and therefore costly—process. In the case of older owners, for instance, purchase may be possible only after death. In other cases there will be leases of varying length. Most importantly, as in commercial land development, there is the possibility of monopolistic exploitation by sellers. In an attempt to assemble contiguous plots of land over a wide area, sale by *all* owners is essential. Owners often realize this and refuse to sell except at an extortionate price. This, of course, increases greatly the costs and hazards of central city land assembly.

In the suburbs, on the other hand, costs of land assembly are much more modest. More likely than not land covering a sufficiently large area can be purchased from a single farmer or landowner, eliminating the problems of price gouging so typical of central city land deals. It is in the suburbs, therefore, that one finds the new housing development homogeneous in price and therefore appealing to a relatively homogeneous income group, the members of which are eager to share out their positive externalities.

Similar considerations apply to the investment of money in existing housing for the purposes of supplying new, possibly more profitable, markets. Typically ownership of adjacent properties is fragmented. Provision of a more attractive environment as well as more attractive housing is consequently contingent on purchase and refurbishment of surrounding properties as well. As a consequence investment by landlords may not take place and deterioration occurs.

Investment in new or existing housing also depends on the ready availability of finance. Builders usually build on the basis of construction loans. Households purchase with a mortgage loan typically repayable over a period of twenty years or more. Households may also take out loans for repair, renovation, or maintenance purposes. Credit worthiness of a new development or an existing property, therefore, becomes an important constraint on supply. Property in neighborhoods where capital values are appreciating is a much better risk than property in neighborhoods where capital values are declining. In the former case, and in the event of foreclosure, the lending institution can recover the value of its loan and more. In the latter case, however, since property values are declining over time, foreclosure would be much more of a disaster for the lending institution, since resale of the property might not allow the full value of the original loan to be recovered.

Additional variables of significance in this context include the availability of fire insurance for properties and the availability of Federal Housing Administration (FHA) mortgage insurance. In order to protect their investment in a residential property, lending institutions insist that it be insured against fire. In some areas of a city, however, fire risk is so great that insurance companies refuse to insure (Syron 1972). Typically, of course, these areas of the city are the more deteriorating neighborhoods. Without fire insurance mortgage finance is not forthcoming and so the demand for such neighborhoods declines.

FHA activities reinforce this pattern (Harvey 1972, pp. 45-46). The FHA guarantees mortgages to lending institutions. The FHA in each city, however, decides which properties in which sorts of neighborhoods will be insured. These locational discriminations clearly tend to reinforce those choices that the lending institution makes independently on the basis of its own judgments of neighborhood credit worthiness and those that are forced on it by fire insurance considerations.

The end product is that bids for housing tend to be deflected from declining and deteriorating areas of the city, where risks are regarded as high, into middle-class suburbanizing or gentrifying areas of the city, where investments are regarded as much more secure (Bradford & Rubinowitz 1975). The effects on property values in different neighborhoods as a result of this spatial displacement of demand can easily be imagined: windfall gains for owners in areas regarded as "safe" by lending institutions and serious losses for owners in areas that have been redlined (Naparstek & Cincotta 1976).

Finally it goes without saying that the creation of new residential land in the city is dependent not only on the forces of the private market but also on the actions of local government. Urban renewal for residential development, for example, may necessitate new schools, public parks, and street layouts. In suburban areas the infrastructural investments of local government are typically heavy: sewerage, water, and highways, in particular. Given the low densities of most suburban residential development, per household infrastructural costs tend to be higher than in the more densely settled areas of the city.

Relationships Between Commercial and Residential Land Development The commercial and residential land development processes, of course, are not isolated from each other. On both demand and supply sides there is substantial complementarity. Suburbanization of employment opportunities stimulates demand for suburban housing; but suburban residential development also increases the attractiveness of suburban sites for shopping centers. At the same time on the supply side the extension of infrastructure to commercial developments increases the likelihood of residential development in the vicinity. So to some degree the metropolitan area may lose some of its mononuclear character and dissolve into more of a polynuclear form, areas of residential land use surrounding agglomerations of retailing and employment located throughout the city.

Commercial and residential uses come into competition with each other and land uses shift according to the ability of one use to bid the land away from the other. Commercial developments, for example, may lower the value of land in the vicinity for residential purposes but increase its value for commercial purposes, hastening the sale of properties by home owners to commercial developers. Likewise around airports a variety of commercial enterprises may—rezoning permitting— be more than willing to buy land away from home owners—and at a substantial price (Crowley 1972). This example, however, suggests that land uses may not always be compatible and that, in fact, residents may experience substantial discomfort as a result of land use change in their vicinity. It is the welfare impacts of the urban land development process that we consider next.

WELFARE IMPACTS

The urban land development process can and often does result in dramatic land use changes: commercial uses displace residential ones, or an erstwhile middle-class neighborhood shifts to lower class occupancy. These transformations, directly traceable to events in the urban land development process, have important and serious implications for the welfare of existing residents.

Neighborhood Level   At the neighborhood level commercial development can have serious negative effects on those who happen to live in the vicinity. New shopping centers, for example, reorient traffic flows, creating congestion, noise, and air pollution where hitherto there had been none. As highways are widened to speed up the traffic, residents along the streets involved are impacted by increased traffic hazard. Even modest shopping and service developments can create problems. Gentrification is often accompanied by an expansion of antique stores, restaurants, and taverns catering to those who, while not being able to live in the neighborhood itself, would like to at least sample some of its attractions. Resultant parking problems and sounds of midnight revelry do not endear them to local residents, however.

Other types of commercial development create their own problems. Industrial land uses are often malodorous and may pollute both air and water. Shift work gives rise to problems of noise around the clock. Heavy trucks servicing the facility deteriorate highways and create hazards for children.

New housing developments or conversions of existing ones bring their own distinctive problems with them. While apartment buildings are often opposed by existing middle-class residents on the grounds of the congestion they create, the real reasons are likely to be somewhat different. Generally speaking average tenant incomes are substantially below those of home owners. This provides a cue for home owners, who are then able—often realistically—to relate apartment buildings or conversion of housing to apartments, to all sorts of undesirable consequences. Construction of apartment buildings, new public housing projects, and conversion of existing housing to apartments do indeed appear to be associated with a syndrome of pathologies.

The poorer are seen as less law abiding than the wealthier and indeed poorer neighborhoods do have higher crime rates. Likewise schools in poorer neighborhoods are likely to have security problems totally unknown to schools in wealthier sections of the city. In addition the children of poorer families tend to have less-desirable behavioral traits: poor motivation in school and lower aspiration levels that tend to be contagious (Wilson 1959). We have already discussed, for example, the role of peer groups in the educational process (see chapter 12).

New commercial and residential land development, therefore, have important effects on the welfare of existing residents. These effects moreover tend to be intensified by market forces. Commercial developments tend to agglomerate, for example: parcels of land in the immediate vicinity increase in value to the point where commercial developers can bid them away from housing developers. The result is further commercial development, congestion, fumes, traffic hazard, and parking problems for those happening to be unfortunate enough to live nearby.

Changes in residential desirability also stem from changes within the residential land development process, itself. As neighborhoods become congested or decline in terms of income composition, so the level of demand for residential property there will decline. Decline may proceed to the point where lower income households, or landlords catering to lower income tenants, are able to purchase property from middle-income occupants (U.S. Department of Housing and Urban Development 1976). The neighborhood therefore becomes more lower income in its residential composition, with further repercussions for public safety and local schools.

The market, therefore, intensifies the unfortunate welfare impacts of commercial development and of certain types of residential development. At the same time existing residents may experience a decline in their property values. This is particularly likely for those whose property is in residentially deteriorating neighborhoods. Where the source of the welfare impact is commercial development, however, there is a strong possibility that values will increase as residential property becomes more valuable for commercial purposes.

Jurisdictional Level   At the jurisdictional level critical welfare concerns involve not only the behavioral externalities important at the neighborhood level but also public provision levels and tax rates (Gaffney 1973). An important concept at the jurisdictional level, therefore, is that of "fiscal externality."

The urban land development process has fiscal effects. A commercial or residential development brings a certain amount of capital into the jurisdiction the assessed value of which will be reflected in property tax collections. At the same time such developments impose on local government requirements for public services. Shopping centers require police surveillance, alterations to access roads, and water supply. Residential developments require public safety expenditures and, in addition, any children living there will have to be educated, all at public expense.

In brief a given development has a net revenue impact on the local municipality. Where that impact is positive, so that revenues exceed the value of services provided, existing taxpayers will, in effect, receive a subsidy, and property tax rates can be reduced. Where the net revenue impact is negative, tax rates will have to be raised to provide the same level of public services that existing taxpayers enjoyed hitherto.

Generally speaking shopping centers are extremely attractive fiscally. Their service demands are modest and there are no children to be educated. Where a sales tax is in force local government revenues will be further augmented—often at the expense of neighboring jurisdictions where shopping center patrons live. Industrial developments are similarly attractive, particularly if the local government levies an income tax on those who, while working in the plant, are not residents in the jurisdiction. The fiscal attractiveness of industrial developments, however, has to be traded off against their frequently detracting effect on local amenities. Clean industries are obviously more desirable.

The fiscal attractiveness of housing developments varies a great deal. Large houses on large lots tend to provide more revenue per capita than small houses on small lots. Single-family homes are therefore preferable to apartments. And single-family luxury homes are better than the standard tract development. In addition, one-bedroom apartments are more attractive than two-bedroom apartments, since the former are unlikely to have children that need to be educated at public expense.

Public housing is fiscally the least desirable form of housing development: residents are likely to impose new demands for public safety expenditures, and public housing projects do not pay property taxes. The federal government makes payments in lieu of property taxes, but these invariably fall short of expenditure needs.

As at the neighborhood level market forces tend to intensify these effects somewhat. Capital-intensive commercial developments tend to be property tax sensitive. They tend to be attracted to low property tax rate jurisdictions. As they move in property tax rates are reduced (while those elsewhere increase), adding incentives for other commercial developers to locate there. As a consequence the property tax bounty of commercial developments tends to be spread in a most uneven manner across the metropolitan area. "To He Who Hath Shall Be Given" seems to be an apt characterization of this process.

Participation in the Political Process

In the U.S. context the welfare impacts reviewed above are particularly important. Compared with his British or Canadian counterpart the American faces serious threats to utility as a result of the functioning of the urban land development process. At the jurisdictional level this is attributable to the greater significance of locally generated revenue. As we have seen in previous chapters, local governments in the United States are much more dependent on revenue generated from within their jurisdictional boundaries than are local governments in either Canada or Britain. As a result negative fiscal externalities are much more serious. Establishment of some activity that adds little to local revenue while imposing large demands on local provision can have serious effects on local taxes. In the British context, meanwhile, central government payments will offset this deterioration and hence sharply attenuate the negative character of the fiscal externality involved.

At the neighborhood level welfare impacts can be related to other institutional variables. Especially significant is the neighborhood school concept. Since, according to this, children attend the school nearest to their residence, neighborhood social composition has critical implications for children's peer groups and educational quality. This is in sharp contrast to the British case. Historically at least British school children have been allocated to different schools at the age of eleven, less on the basis of residence and more on the basis of academic ability. Since academic ability is related to social class it has been perfectly feasible for middle-class and lower class children from the same neighborhood to attend quite different schools, each dominated by children from their respective social class.

Related to the schools issue but also having a broader impact of its own is the issue of public safety. For what appear to be historically unique circumstances U.S. cities and the American urban lower classes, in particular, are characterized by unusually high crime rates. Neighborhood deterioration in the U.S. context, therefore, involves disutilities on existing middle-class residents of a magnitude totally outside the experience of urban populations in Canada or Western Europe. The public safety impacts of dislocation in urban housing markets provide a uniquely American source of concern, and an intensity of feeling about neighborhood deterioration that is absent in cities elsewhere.

Welfare impacts of the type described have distinct loci at neighborhood and jurisdictional levels. Given this localized character, and also their intensity when compared with similar welfare impacts in Canada and Western Europe, we should expect in the United States some involvement in the political process at both neighborhood and jurisdictional levels. At the neighborhood level, for example, we should anticipate participation in neighborhood organizations attempting to manipulate and control the land development process to their own benefit. To some degree this control can be exercised through politics. Rezoning requests, if unopposed by neighborhood groups, may threaten the residential desirability of a neighborhood and, therefore, its ability to continue to attract middle-class residents. Protest by neighborhood groups may also be effective in deflecting other public actions detrimental to the neighborhood: for example, public housing projects, one-way streets, and conversion of culs-de-sac into through streets.

Similar remarks also apply to the jurisdictional level. Here, however, the instrumentality attempting to control land development is the local government rather than a neighborhood organization; and the beneficiary is the jurisdictional population rather than the population of a single neighborhood. Local governments, therefore, may employ their land use control powers to keep out land uses imposing fiscal externalities of a negative rather than positive character.

These local-level policies, however, have a strong "zero-sum" element: what one neighborhood gains another loses and vice versa. In the case of the location of public housing, for instance, location in a certain neighborhood may depress property values there by making it less residentially attractive. Other neighborhoods that were successful in deflecting the public housing, however, gain. Consequent to location of the project, neighborhoods without public housing acquire a new scarcity value: distance from public housing. Those who would otherwise have chosen to live in the neighborhood that eventually received public housing, transfer their bids to other neighborhoods, forcing up property values there.

In some cases this zero-sum character is apparent, indeed, to the households, neighborhood groups, or local governments affected. In London traffic diversion schemes have created quiet neighborhoods (Hillman & Henderson 1973). These neighborhoods have become much more attractive residentially, leading to increasing property values and the sort of gentrification process described earlier in this chapter. Traffic, however, is merely diverted onto streets a few blocks away, inducing traffic hazards and noise there (figure 13.3).

Neighborhood organizations and local governments, therefore, see themselves as competing. Neighborhood organizations wish to attract the utility enhancing and keep out the utility detracting (Molotch 1967). The utility enhancing in the form, say, of middle-class residents, however, have a number of neighborhoods from which to choose. Gaining some edge in attractiveness by, for ex-

Figure 13.3   Impact of a Traffic Diversion Scheme

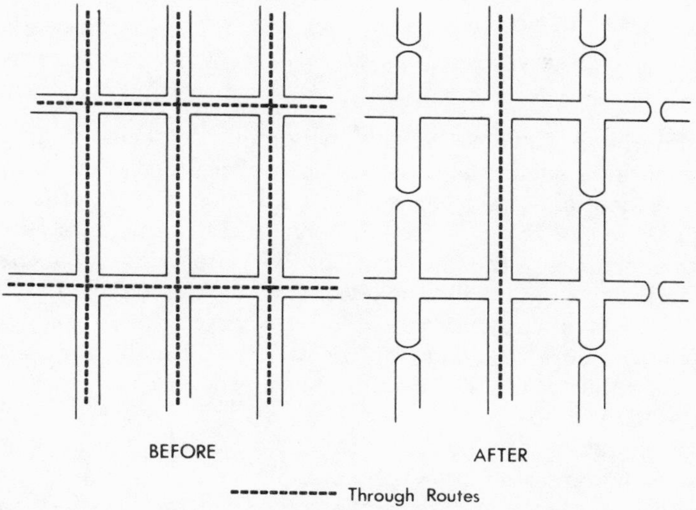

BEFORE   AFTER

----------- Through Routes

NOTE: Blocking off some streets and converting them into culs-de-sac concentrates through traffic on a few streets only. Those living on the newly created culs-de-sac enjoy increased quiet and an absence of fumes at the expense of those living on the few remaining through routes.

ample, keeping out public housing or traffic congestion is therefore important to obtaining residential choice decisions beneficial to the neighborhood. A similar logic applies to the jurisdictional level. Here, however, the fiscal assumes significance, and an important goal of local governments is attracting those land uses that will be fiscally enhancing and keeping out the fiscally detracting (Gaffney 1973). Attracting capital-intensive business may permit a lowering of tax rates not available to those local governments less effective competitively. It is to the variety of competitive strategies employed that we turn next.

Techniques of Competition

As at the intranational level, then, groups compete to attract to their vicinity or jurisdiction the utility enhancing and to keep out the utility detracting. Likewise local groups have available to them two broad policy options: (1) they can compete with one another within the broad constraints of constitutional and statutory law laid down by governments at higher levels in the jurisdictional hierarchy or (2) recognizing that this juridical context may favor some at the expense of others, local groups, local governments, and others may work to alter it. Each option is considered in turn at both neighborhood and jurisdictional levels.

COMPETITION WITHIN THE PREVAILING JURIDICAL CONTEXT

Neighborhood Level   At the neighborhood level neighborhood organizations engage in a variety of policies designed to maintain local residential attractiveness (Wolf & Lebeaux 1969, pt. 1; Molotch 1972). Many of these policies involve attempts to intervene in the political process at the municipal level or, alternatively, to ensure the local efficacy of municipal policy.

We have already remarked on the attempts of neighborhood groups to secure rezoning treatment that will maintain the residential desirability of the neighborhood. In addition neighborhood groups may lobby local school boards for a variety of policies designed to make local schools more attractive. These attempts may range from requests for new physical plants or, say, classes in French in grade schools through to requests for an alteration of school catchment area boundaries designed to maintain or enhance the middle-class character of pupil composition.

Neighborhood groups seem particularly important in the gentrification process. In the attempt to attract middle-class residents and private capital into the area, neighborhood organizations may lobby city council for environmental improvements: tree plantings, new street lighting, the creation of vest pocket parks, or the diversion of traffic. Particularly important, however, is the securing of policies more directly related to housing investment. A common antecedent of gentrification is declaration of the neighborhood as a code enforcement area for which low-interest improvement loans will be available. Generally speaking housing codes in poorer neighborhoods tend not to be enforced. Since enforcement would often result in landlords having to raise rents above the level current tenants can pay, a conspiracy between landlord, tenant, and housing inspector results in continued physical deterioration. The availability of low-cost loans, however, along with some assurance that neighboring property owners will also be investing, alters landlord calculations. Since improvement throughout the code enforcement area makes the area attractive to middle-class tenants and buyers, the original lower class tenants lose out anyway.

Neighborhood groups may also cooperate with local government to ensure the effectiveness of public provision in the local area. In deteriorating neighborhoods, for instance, cooperation of local residents with police may attain unusually high levels (Molotch 1972). Local resident groups may form their own cruiser patrols linked by radio with local police stations to supplement existing patrols. Alternatively and somewhat less ambitiously neighborhood organizations may flood the area with literature designed to sensitize residents to the importance of reporting any crime or delinquency they observe.

Cooperation with other public services may also be apparent. Monitoring of adherence to city ordinances is an expensive business. Neighborhood groups may provide useful supplemental assistance by, for example, reporting housing code or zoning code violations in the neighborhood. Conversion of erstwhile residential use to, say, business or entertainment use will be particularly provocative to local residents.

Neighborhood organization activities, however, are not confined to lobbying local government or providing assistance to local government agencies; neighborhood groups may also become more directly involved in the private market aspects of the land development process. This is likely to be especially apparent in deteriorating neighborhoods (Wolf & Lebeaux 1969, pt. 1; Molotch 1972). Major concerns there involve the activities of realtors. Commonly they are accused of *steering* and *blockbusting*; these are related activities.

The blockbusting phenomenon refers to a process by which realtors attempt to stimulate housing turnover in neighborhoods regarded as ripe for a change in occupancy from middle to lower class. These neighborhoods usually consist of rather older housing stock adjacent to low-income and/or ghetto neighborhoods. By introducing a few low-income or black residents into the area realtors are able plausibly to argue with existing residents that the area is changing and that they should sell out now before everyone else tries to do so. By panicking existing residents about neighborhood prospects unscrupulous realtors may be able to purchase housing at low prices and resell to new residents at substantially higher prices. The effectiveness of the policy, however, depends in large part on the degree to which people can be plausibly persuaded that the neighborhood is changing.

To some degree this can be done by overt soliciting of residents. It must also be apparent to residents, however, that the area is indeed no longer attracting desirable residents. Realtors achieve this goal by the practice of *steering*. This involves showing prospective middle-class buyers properties only in other neighborhoods or telling them that such-and-such neighborhood is changing and it would be inadvisable to purchase there.

Neighborhood responses have been twofold: first, blockbusting may be neutralized by counterinformation policies. Neighborhood organizations may hold block meetings, for instance, at which local residents will be advised of the unscrupulous tactics of realtors; of the misleading nature of the information they are spreading; and, most importantly, of the fact that if all agree not to sell, the blockbusting effort can be defeated and realtor attention will be deflected elsewhere.

The steering problem is less easily handled. In a significant number of cases, however, it has stimulated neighborhood activists to establish their own real estate organizations that can neutralize or even reverse steering by other realty firms. Undesirables, for example, may be advised that suitable housing in the neighborhood is not presently available.

Jurisdictional Level By their lack of power neighborhood groups are seriously limited in what they can do. They lack the power, for example, directly to control land use or public provision within the neighborhood. This is less true of local governments with respect to their jurisdictions.

In competing for desirable developments—either commercial or residential—a local government must find some competitive edge. It must make its jurisdiction attractive to the desirable by providing them with what they in turn desire: low tax rates, good schools and good teachers, public safety. Clearly in order to offer these goods the local government must be able to keep out the undesirable: those developments that add little to the local tax base but impose large burdens on local public services such as education and public safety.

In sum, competition involves making the jurisdiction attractive to the utility enhancing; this implies keeping out the utility detracting. To some extent market forces may suffice; if a jurisdiction contains only new, up-to-date, single-family housing structures, the market will ensure that only the more affluent who can afford such structures will live in that suburb. If such market forces do not already exist then local governments dispose of a wide variety of discretionary powers that can enhance the residential attractiveness of the jurisdiction in question. Most of these powers are of a negative, exclusionary character.

By far the most publicized power available to local governments is the zoning power (Sagalyn & Sternlieb 1972, ch. 1). This can be used to exclude the fiscally and behaviorally undesirable in at least two ways. Perhaps most common is large lot zoning: land is zoned for housing units standing on lots of a minimum acreage. Usually the minimum acreage is relatively large: an acre or half acre, for example. This forces buyers to consume more land than they might otherwise want and, more importantly, excludes those who cannot afford these lots. In some areas the extent of large lot, or so-called "minimum lot size," zoning is quite daunting. In Cuyahoga County, surrounding

Cleveland, Ohio, two-thirds of the undeveloped land zoned for single-family residential construction in the late 1960s was zoned for minimum lots of half an acre. In adjacent Geauga County 85 percent of residentially zoned land had to be developed with single-family homes on lots of an acre or more.

An alternative approach is to zone land for single-family residences rather than for apartments. Apartment tenants consume relatively less capital than home owners and contribute less on a per capita basis to local revenues. Since an apartment is a relatively cheap housing option apartment tenants are likely to be less affluent and hence less desirable as neighbors. If apartments are to be permitted it is better that they be for the old—at least they don't have children to burden local schools.

Subdivision regulations may achieve similar exclusionary goals. In drawing up the rules governing subdivision by developers, local governments may call for relatively expensive investments in the form of, for example, roads, curbing, and dedication of land for schools and parks. All these costs, of course, have to be spread across the ultimate purchasers of the housing, inflating housing prices and filtering out those of lower income.

In still other cases the local government may not have to do anything. Simple avoidance of certain policy options may result in excluding the fiscally burdensome. In the undeveloped suburban fringe households may rely on septic tanks for sewage and on well water. These are facilities requiring private investment of a substantial nature and, again, work to keep out those of lesser means. Local governments may however be more than eager to extend sewer lines and waterlines if it means capturing some large business investment or shopping center strengthening the tax base.

Some local governments, of course, are less able to take advantage of these tools. They may contain no undeveloped land from which the undesirable can be excluded by zoning or subdivision regulations. In addition the possibility of annexing undeveloped land may have been precluded by the incorporation of surrounding communities: as a result of the competitive annexation policies of adjacent local governments, jurisdictions may find themselves cut off from unincorporated land. Clearly in these cases a different set of competitive policies becomes mandatory. One policy engaged in by central city governments is urban renewal.

A major goal of central city governments is to attract businesses and middle-class residents who will add more to tax base and impose less pressure on public services than existing low-income residents. A major problem in attracting such capital into already built up areas is the land assembly problem discussed earlier in this chapter. Commer-

Figure 13.4   Impact of Urban Renewal on the Poor and Blacks

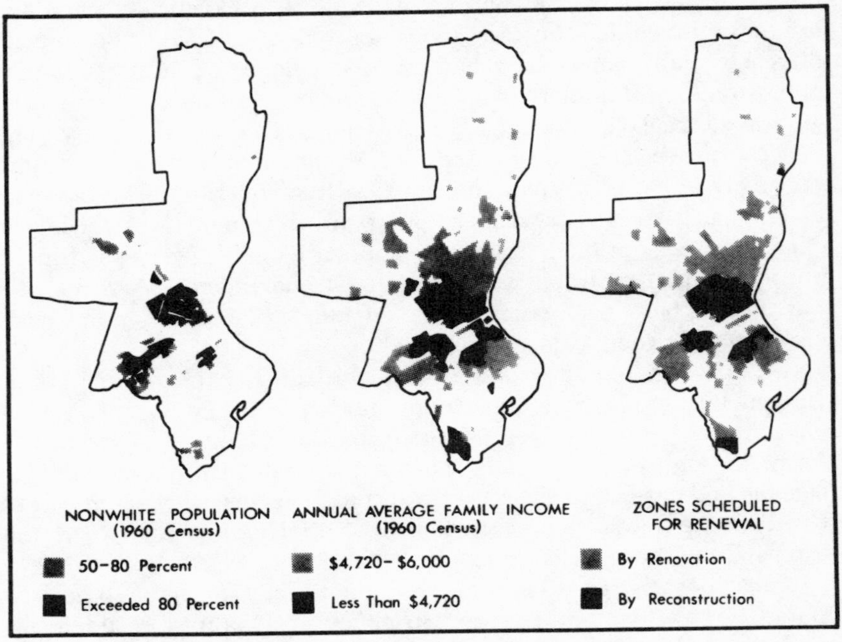

NONWHITE POPULATION
(1960 Census)

■ 50–80 Percent

■ Exceeded 80 Percent

ANNUAL AVERAGE FAMILY INCOME
(1960 Census)

■ $4,720– $6,000

■ Less Than $4,720

ZONES SCHEDULED
FOR RENEWAL

■ By Renovation

■ By Reconstruction

NOTE: Areas for which renovation and reconstruction are planned tend to be those in which the poor and/or the black are concentrated.

SOURCE: After Nathan Glazer, "The Renewal of Cities," *Scientific American* 213, no. 3 (September 1965): 203.

cial developments want sites tailored precisely to their needs. Middle-class persons want to live in relatively middle-class neighborhoods, insulated and secure from central city public safety problems. Hotel, restaurant, department store, and office building owners have similar desires for their customers. Urban renewal provides an answer—and a subsidized one at that—to the land assembly problem.

Federal legislation in the United States has given municipalities the right of eminent domain in blighted areas: the right, that is, to condemn blighted property and purchase it at a price to be negotiated or, if negotiation proves impossible, to be imposed by the local urban renewal authority. The procedure then is for the local urban renewal authority to clear the area of structures, relocate residents, and prepare land for redevelopment. The land is then sold or leased to private or public developers. The whole process is subsidized: two thirds of the total cost net of receipts from the sale of land to ultimate redevelopers is reimbursed by the federal government. This of course provides an incentive for local governments to negotiate less than market prices with developers, providing a further stimulus to redevelopment.

Urban renewal has several attractions for local government. It affords a means of replacing low-value with high-value structures and hence of enhancing the city tax base. In addition it may alter the social composition of the city in a fiscally desirable direction. To the extent that urban renewal results in the erection of luxury apartments, a more middle-class population imposing fewer demands on local government may be attracted back into the city. Since the middle-class populations most likely to assume residence are unlikely to have children—middle-class parents are frequently wary of inner city schools—or to send their children to private schools, their fiscal attraction is increased. At the same time urban renewal demolishes the dwellings of low-income residents (figure 13.4) with their public safety and welfare problems.

ALTERING THE JURIDICAL CONTEXT

On the other hand we should not ignore alternative strategies that local groups and local governments may engage in to secure their objectives. Their ability to compete effectively for the utility enhancing depends to a considerable degree, after all, on the man-made rules controlling the operations of, for example, realtors, bankers, and land developers.

To the degree that neighborhood groups and local governments are able to conceptualize the role of the juridical context in this way, they will have taken the first step to secure a change in those rules in their favor. Consider, for example, an erstwhile middle-class neighborhood that is experiencing the first pangs of deterioration, decline in social class, and perhaps racial integration. In considering the source of these problems members of the appropriate neighborhood organization may come up with diverse diagnoses. To the extent that realtor steering or blockbusting bears the burden of their animus, then the solution may be seen as the establishment, by the neighborhood organization, of its own realty company, as discussed above. To the extent that the location policies of city government—highway location, code enforcement—are seen as the problem, then the solution suggested may be increased lobbying and pressure on appropriate city agencies.

To the more perceptive, however, other diagnoses and, consequently, alternative solutions may be arrived at. To the extent that the diagnosis is one of inadequate neighborhood power with respect to city government, for example, the solution may be to press for the establishment throughout the city of neighborhood commissions with which city government must consult when considering the location of some facility. The diagnosis may however be based on knowledge of the land development process as it affects the neighborhood: residents may arrive at a conception of realtor blockbusting and steering, for example, deriving less from the avariciousness of realtors and more from the failure of the city to enact an open housing ordinance giving the city attorney power to prosecute in cases of racial discrimination in the sale of housing (Wolf & Lebeaux 1969, ch. 3). The argument here would be that concentrated racial invasion is a result of the inability of blacks to buy housing in the same locations as whites of equivalent income: that discrimination by sellers, mortgage lenders, and realtors tends to channel blacks into only a few neighborhoods, which consequently bear a welfare impact that would be otherwise spread out over all residents.

A similar line of reasoning may be applied at the jurisdictional level. Local governments may arrive at a diagnosis in which their ability to compete is seen as constrained by a set of constitutional or statutory rules that are less than absolute in character. The problems of a central city in attracting commercial development, for example, may be related to the rules governing the sale of bonds for public works. The city government may see its competitive ability constrained by a low level of investment in highways, airports, public buildings, and perhaps schools and water and sewage facilities. This may be related to state limits on the city bonded debt, in which case the solution would be to secure an increase in that bonded debt limit. Alternatively it may be seen as a function of failure to obtain passage of bond referenda by the local electorate, in which case salvation may lie in the direction of increasing the amount of bonded debt, for which local government does not have to seek electoral approval.

It must be emphasized, however, that the ability to conceptualize the role played by the juridical context in producing local predicaments is only the first step. Although juridical relationships are less than absolute in nature, changing them involves securing majorities in appropriate state legislatures or city councils; and this can present major problems. As we have seen at the national level, securing majorities involves building coalitions with other affected interests that can outlobby those interests gaining from the status quo. The latter, however, may be powerful indeed. To the extent that blockbusting allows realtors to make unusually large profits, realtors and realty boards will oppose open housing ordinances and, for example, legislation designed to facilitate the monitoring of housing sales for evidence of discrimination. Likewise city government bureaucracies—the traffic department, the zoning commission—are unlikely to sit idly by as a set of neighborhood commissions restricting their discretion are legislated into existence. Precisely how the juridical context affects the competitive outcome and the degree to which that context has been effectively challenged is reserved for the next chapter.

Concluding Comments

At the urban level the critical context for local politics is provided by the urban land development process. This is the process by which urban land is created and shifted from one use to another: broadly it involves both commercial and residential development.

To some degree urban land development is a private market process. This is particularly so on the demand side. On the supply side, however, local government is also important. The conversion of raw agricultural land into urban land is critically dependent on the extension of water pipes and sewerage by local governments. Building permits and rezonings are also important, as indeed they are in a shift from one type of urban use to another.

Market forces, however, tend to dominate the urban land development process. There will be no infrastructural extensions or permits unless private entrepreneurs request them. Consequently as market demands change, so the spatial expression of the urban land development process changes, altering the character of neighborhoods and creating new shopping developments in previously agricultural areas. Major manifestations of the urban land development process, therefore, are neighborhood change, suburbanization, and the abandonment of inner city areas.

Clearly these shifts in the spatial focus of the urban land development process have significant effects on the welfare of existing residents. These localized welfare impacts are especially important in the United States. Reliance on locally generated revenues increases fiscal concern at the jurisdictional level. Within neighborhoods crime and the neighborhood school concept combine to make residents intensely concerned about who their neighbors are. The result is an involvement in the political process through neighborhood organizations and local governments designed to manipulate the urban land development process to the advantage of the local turf.

Resultant local policies, however, have a significant zero-sum element: what one neighborhood group or jurisdiction gains, another to some degree loses. Consequently neighborhood groups and local governments see themselves as more competitive with each other in their respective arenas, competing to attract the utility enhancing and to keep out the utility detracting.

As at the national level local groups have two broad policy options: they can compete within the constraints of the existing juridical context or they can dispute over exactly what that context should be. Within existing constitutional and statutory constraints, neighborhood groups may oppose rezoning requests regarded as threatening to the neighborhood, lobby for local public improvements, or even become involved directly in the housing market by forming their own realty company. Local governments have substantially more power to control their future than neighborhood groups. Major tools here include exclusionary zoning, zoning-in commercial developments, subdivision regulation, and—for those cities with little in the way of still-to-be-developed land—urban renewal.

Alternative diagnoses of their troubles may however lead local governments and neighborhood groups to select other alternatives. Pointing in a somewhat radical direction, for example, is the formation of coalitions with other neighborhood groups or local governments in order to secure a change in the juridical relationships governing competition.

Select Bibliography

Brown, Lenore Egan. "Victorian Village." Columbus Monthly 1, no. 1 (June 1975): 20–27.

Harrison, Paul. "The Life of Cities." New Society, 5 December 1974, pp. 599–604.

Hillman, Mayer, and Henderson, Irwin. "Towards a Better Kind of Environmental Area." New Society, 12 July 1973, pp. 75–77.

Molotch, Harvey. "Toward a More 'Human' Human Ecology: An Urban Research Strategy." Land Economics 43, no. 3 (1967): 336–41.

Weinstein, Jerome I. "Negative Property Values: The Problem of Abandoned Buildings." Appraisal Journal 41, no. 3 (July 1973): 395–403.

Wolf, Eleanor P., and Lebeaux, Charles N. Change and Renewal in an Urban Community. Pt. 1. New York: Praeger, 1969.

Chapter Fourteen

The Competitive Outcome in Metropolitan Areas

The last chapter identified a set of competitive policies relating metropolitan-area local governments and neighborhood groups to one another. In this final chapter we examine the effectiveness of these competitive policies and the forces limiting it. The first two sections examine the effectiveness of competition at the neighborhood and jurisdictional levels. We then consider challenges to the juridical context that make competition fruitful for some and not so for others. Finally we explore some of the outcomes of competition for the employment and housing prospects of low-income groups in the central city.

Neighborhood Level

ENVIRONMENTAL CONTEXT

Each neighborhood in the city may be regarded as comprising a set of locations with site and situation attributes evaluated as more-or-less desirable by a variety of interests. Depending on these attributes, therefore, neighborhood organizations may find it more-or-less easy to regulate to local advantage the urban land development process in both its social and physical aspects.

Residents, for example, may find themselves competing with non-residential uses harmful to residential desirability. Neighborhoods may include locations attractive to city planners designing a freeway or a network of one-way streets. This will be a particular threat to inner city neighborhoods where traffic congestion is most severe and new highway plans most applicable. Additional traffic speeds, noise, or local traffic burdens resulting from implementation of the highway plan will make these neighborhoods even more residentially undesirable than they are already.

Alternatively neighborhoods may include prime business locations. Development for business purposes, however, may clearly detract from the residential amenities of the area. The parked automobiles of business clientele may overflow into adjacent

297

residential streets. This may be especially true of business operations such as cinemas or restaurants. Taverns or nightclubs may, in addition, introduce an unwelcome element of late-night rowdiness.

And within the housing market itself, the immediate constellation of site and situation attributes may prove sufficiently attractive to residential developments to pose problems for existing residents. New housing, for example, tends to be attracted to the vicinity of existing residential developments, since the necessary urban infrastructure—highways, sewer lines, waterlines and gas lines—will already be available there. Neighborhoods adjacent to undeveloped land, therefore, tend to have an uncertain future; new high density construction may well take place, creating traffic, additional housing, and noise where previously there had been tranquility and vistas over surrounding countryside. Not surprisingly housing in these semi-developed areas tends to elicit lower bids than similar housing in already developed areas: buyers hedge their bets.

Within already developed areas, however, residents may be threatened by changes in residential use. Proximity to a university may stimulate conversion of owner-occupied homes to apartments and lead to social changes that are far from comforting to long-standing residents. Older housing may be less easy to move on the owner-occupied market, stimulating conversion to apartments.

Land use changes of this character create market differentials that serve to intensify already existing variations in residential desirability. A new apartment building may make a middle-class neighborhood less desirable through its impact on local traffic levels and through the impact of its residents on local schools and public safety. As a consequence the value of housing in that neighborhood may fall to a level at which lower income persons can purchase property there, thus nudging the locality further in the direction of what many middle-class home purchasers will regard as undesirable social change.

More generally housing in dominantly low-income neighborhoods or close to low-income neighborhoods will elicit rather weak bids from middle-class households. Residence will involve exposure to a variety of antisocial behaviors both in the neighborhood and, what is perhaps more important to parents, in local schools as well. As a result the competitive bidding mechanism will tend to allocate housing there to lower income families.

At the same time some housing will continue to elicit strong bids from middle-class households, even when the neighborhood is adjacent to a low-income housing development or undesirable commercial land uses. To some degree this may be a function of the insulating character of natural or artificial barriers. A freeway or railroad embankment may serve to isolate middle-class households from the traffic congestion or social threats beyond; it may also serve as a "natural" boundary for local school catchment areas. In fact it may well be that one of the effects of freeway building in cities has been to create such protected pockets for middle-class occupancy.

Alternatively proximity to undesirable developments may be traded off against other housing attributes. It may be, for example, that housing units enjoy lake views and breezes or panoramic views of the surrounding city. Housing along Chicago's North Shore, for example, has remained stubbornly middle and upper class in its occupancy, despite the deterioration that has gone on within a quarter of a mile from the lake. Housing may also enjoy advantages of accessibility to the downtown area, increasing what middle-class households are prepared to bid. Yet other housing may have a certain esthetic or historic merit appealing to middle-class tastes.

Such a combination of elements, offsetting the disadvantages of proximity to low-income neighborhoods or the problems of inner city congestion and pollution, often helps to explain gentrification in American cities. In certain neighborhoods small nuclei of middle-class households, often in coalition with property developers, have managed to engineer a social transformation resulting in the displacement of lower class by middle-class households. While public action is often important in increasing the attractiveness of the area—tree plantings, low interest loans, code enforcement, for instance (Cox 1973, pp. 83–85)—the advantageous nature of the raw material should not be overlooked. Most gentrifying neighborhoods, for example, tend to enjoy advantages of accessibility to downtown and have appealing historical associations and/or local architecture. German Village, within a ten-minute walk of downtown Columbus, Ohio, provides a case in point. Still-cobbled streets and an unusual architecture provide additional compensations for abutment against the deteriorated areas to the east. In Cincinnati, Ohio, the gentrification of the Mt. Adams neighborhood pinpoints a similar set of advantages:

> The primary reason rehabilitation has succeeded in the Mt. Adams area is the neighborhood's unique location. *Located minutes from downtown* Cincinnati, *with a beautiful view,* and *geographically isolated by its elevation,* Mt. Adams appeals to young, upper-middle income families who are willing to pay high rents for the aesthetics and conveniences of the neighborhood.
>
> The Mt. Adams area is marked by attractive commercial renovation and distinctive, new residential units as well as rehabilitated structures. A new performing arts center has been constructed in a park adjacent to the neighborhood and the area has acquired a Bohemian, yet dignified character (U.S.

Department of Housing and Urban Development 1975, p. 233).
(Emphasis added.)

While locations within certain areas may be attractive for these uses,
however, the level of confidence in the neighborhood may be insufficient to generate the necessary investment. But by requesting status
as a code enforcement area or conservation area eligible for low interest loans, the requisite confidence may be induced. In addition
local residents' associations may request tree plantings or traffic
diversions designed to enhance the residential attractiveness of the
area and hence increase the possibilities of rehabilitation for middle-
class use.

By appealing to existing zoning laws or licensing laws local
residents' associations may also be able to block commercial development and the neighborhood blight that it often presages. But
whether a neighborhood group will be successful depends on the
degree of power it has with respect to city council, local public agencies, and local public officials.

LOCAL POWER

The ability of a neighborhood interest group to regulate urban
development to the advantage of the local turf depends, all other
things being equal, on its ability to obtain public decisions in its
favor: on its ability to dissuade the city highway department from a
road-widening scheme through the middle of the neighborhood; on its
ability to persuade the city board of education to add new facilities to
the local school; on its ability to steer public housing projects into
other areas; and on its ability to overturn rezoning applications that
would filter in undesirable commercial developments. The power of
neighborhood groups therefore becomes important: they must have
political resources providing advantages over other neighborhood
groups who would equally like to keep out the residentially detracting; furthermore, the degree of power a neighborhood group has with
respect to other interests vying for control of neighborhood turf—a
local university, a business group, a shopping center or manufacturing firm—is also of critical significance.

The political resources neighborhood groups are able to bring to
bear on their projects may be classified as *accessibility resources* and
bargaining resources. Undoubtedly the residents of some neighborhoods and some neighborhood groups enjoy greater degrees of access to public officials and to representatives on local governing
bodies. This facilitates both the flow of information and the degree to
which local needs will be given a sympathetic hearing. Local politicians and public officials, for example, have a range of nonpolitical
contacts in, say, the Rotary Club, the chamber of commerce, or in

Figure 14.1   Residences of Detroit School Board Members

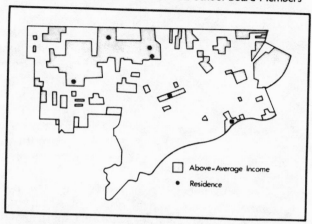

☐ Above-Average Income

● Residence

NOTE: There is a general coincidence with areas of above-average income.
SOURCE: After William Bunge et al., "A Report to the Parents of Detroit on School Decentralization," in Paul English and Robert Mayfield, eds., *Man, Space and Environment* (New York: Oxford University Press, 1972), p. 516.

their own neighborhood, local PTA, or golf club. These contacts facilitate the flow of information between politicians and officials and others not involved directly in local politics. In these ways, for instance, the chamber of commerce may be able to keep abreast of council developments relevant to its interests; alternatively a member of the chamber of commerce may be able to make some request of a local councilor in a highly informal and unobtrusive manner during a weekly golf game. Within particular neighborhoods residents may benefit from the fact that one of their coresidents is, say, chairman of the local housing committee: he may be able to provide them with information relevant to their neighborhood long before it becomes public. Such a dual role—chairman and neighbor—also facilitates the funding of requests for special neighborhood amenities.

In addition, however, councilors and public officials share with others, to a greater or lesser degree, a set of ideological predispositions making them more-or-less *receptive* to particular demands. A belief in the virtues of property ownership may make the city council rather more sympathetic to the demands of a *private* housing estate for a community center than to the demands of tenants of a *public* housing estate for increased police protection or improved landscaping of public spaces. Belief in the virtues of self-help may make the council less likely to fund a methadone treatment center in an inner city neighborhood and more likely to provide low interest loans for a code enforcement program.

As a consequence those residents who share a community of contacts and sentiment with public officials and local representatives have advantages. To the extent that public figures are white and middle class it will be white, middle-class neighborhoods that have the advantages. Some idea of the links that do in fact exist is provided by figure 14.1. Clearly members of Detroit School Board tended to reside in more middle-class neighborhoods of the city. This arrangement is not atypical of big city school boards and almost always provides middle-class neighborhoods with considerable advantages of either an intended or inadvertent character. These links may result, for example, in a new physical plant or in redrawing school district boundaries, both to the advantage of white middle-class neighborhoods.

In any particular instance other interests may also enjoy the balance of those contacts and ideological sympathies that make accessibility a real and, indeed, mutual affair between constituent and public official. Universities, for example, have substantial interests in their surrounding neighborhoods, which expanding universities look on as potential sites for new labs or basketball arenas, for example (Parsons 1967). In having the surrounding area declared an urban renewal area, however, they may be opposed by existing middle-class residents who regard their properties as far from deteriorated. In such a case university alumni on city councils and in city housing departments may provide both the contacts and loyalties necessary for effecting redevelopment.

In addition to accessibility resources bargaining resources may also give a neighborhood group an edge over its rivals. In U.S. central cities more middle-class neighborhoods enjoy advantages due to the positive fiscal balance their residents contribute to the city as a whole. Occupying valuable residential properties and generating little demand for public safety or welfare expenditures, such residents are viewed as assets to be cosseted. Loss of middle-class residents to surrounding suburbs and their replacement by lower income residents is regarded by public officials as an important source of the fiscal crisis besetting so many big U.S. cities. The significance of these bargaining resources may be apparent in *inaction* as well as in action. City boards of education, for example, may refuse to intervene in a teacher hiring process by which the better qualified teachers gravitate to schools in more middle-class neighborhoods. Alternatively city tax assessments may fail to keep pace with increasing capital values in gentrifying neighborhoods, thus providing a subsidy to the process (Peterson et al. 1973).

Again, however, this is not to say that the advantage always lies with middle-class neighborhood groups. In the surrounding area a large manufacturing firm may have interests that bring it into con-

Table 14.1 Income and Community Activism (percentages answering in the affirmative to selected questions)

1. Have you ever worked with others in this community to solve any community problem?

Income ($)	% Yes
6,000 & under	14
6,000–9,999	17
10,000–14,999	25
15,000–24,999	39
25,000 & over	47

2. Have you ever taken part in forming a new group or a new organization to try to solve a community problem?

Income ($)	% Yes
6,000 & under	10
6,000–9,999	10
10,000–14,999	13
15,000–24,999	19
25,000 & over	28

SOURCE: *Benchmark* (Columbus, Ohio: Academy for Contemporary Problems, 1974).

flict with residents. These conflicts may involve smoke emission levels or the desire of the firm to acquire land for expansion. In cases like these the balance is likely to lie with the firm: contributions to local jobs and tax base will usually be too large for local government to ignore.

All of this, however, assumes that there are neighborhood organizations and concern for the neighborhood on the part of residents to begin with. Clearly to the extent that neighborhoods lack some sort of representation or monitoring of activities significant to their welfare, they will become the depressed areas of the city: the repositories for all the flotsam and jetsam—both physical and human—rejected by those other neighborhoods that have in fact made their views known. By and large the neighborhood organization is a feature of middle-class and wealthier areas of the city (table 14.1). Where most residents are black and/or lower class the neighborhood is unlikely to have a voice. To some degree this must account for the unattractive surroundings of poor white and black neighborhoods and for their failure to keep out public housing, one-way streets, and all those other features of the urban landscape detracting from residential attractiveness.

JURIDICAL CONTEXT

To some extent, however, the exercise of local power presupposes some set of institutional arrangements that local government is empowered to implement and that can be mobilized by neighborhood

Figure 14.2   Social Class and Support for Zoning in Houston, Texas

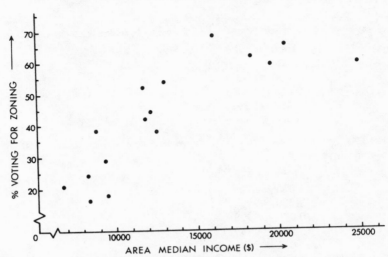

NOTE: Voting represents the outcome of a straw vote taken in 1962.
DATA SOURCE: After Bernard H. Siegan, *Land Use Without Zoning* (Lexington, Mass.: D. C. Heath, 1972), pp. 28–29.

groups to the advantage of their respective neighborhoods. The utility of opposing rezonings, for example, depends on the nature of the zoning ordinance that local government is empowered by the state to enact. There are therefore statutes and ordinances that local government is empowered to administer and that provide, albeit inadvertently, certain neighborhoods with advantages for attracting the utility enhancing and excluding the utility detracting. They permit the establishment of attractiveness gradients between neighborhoods so that some neighborhood groups will be relatively successful in regulating neighborhood change and development to local advantage, while other neighborhoods will remain residentially unattractive. The statutes and ordinances of particular relevance in this neighborhood context include *zoning ordinances* and the *neighborhood school concept.*

Zoning Ordinances   These were originally established to separate nuisance activities, particularly commerce and industry, from residential land uses (Babcock 1966). In their origin, therefore, they were not seen as providing any particular advantage for any specific group in society: rather they would provide benefits for all. Residents would gain from zoning as a result of their separation from noise, congestion, and industrial odors; business operations would certainly not lose and might even gain as a result of the avoidance of expensive liti-

Table 14.2   Zoning and Housing Costs; Price of Vacant Lots by Residential Zoning
Category, Montgomery County, Md., 1967

Minimum Lot Size(ac)	Median Sales Price
2.00	$18,000
.92	11,800
.46	7,650
.34	5,400
.21	4,000
.14	3,600

SOURCE: U.S. National Commission on Urban Problems, Building the American City (Washington, D.C.: Government Printing Office, 1968), p. 214.

gation brought by enraged residents. As zoning ordinances have become more and more specific with respect to the type of land use permitted in certain areas, however, a distinct class bias has become apparent.

In particular, subdivision of residential land uses into, for example, multifamily residential; high density, single-family residential; and low density, single-family residential tends to facilitate the emergence of socially homogeneous neighborhoods. Gradations of residential land use can easily be designed so that they correspond to levels of housing consumption (table 14.2); since housing consumption tends to increase with household income a relationship between residential land use zone and household income can be engineered. It is not unreasonable to expect to find higher income families in low density, single-family residential zones, since in these areas increased land consumption will increase housing prices; nor is it unreasonable to expect to find lower income families in multifamily housing. A carefully conceived zoning ordinance, therefore, can be effective in insulating middle-class families from lower class ones. Not surprisingly it would seem that middle-class households are more in favor of zoning than those of the lower class. Houston, Texas, is one of the few cities where there is no land use zoning. A recent straw vote there showed substantially higher levels of support for a zoning ordinance in middle-class neighborhoods (figure 14.2).

The effect of zoning, then, is to create attractiveness differentials between neighborhoods: some neighborhoods will tend to be middle class and some lower class. Rezonings constitute major threats to this structure of relationships. Not surprisingly a major focus of animus of neighborhood groups in middle-class areas of the city is the application to rezone for multifamily apartments, higher density housing, or commercial developments. The zoning ordinance therefore works to protect middle-class neighborhoods from the utili-

Table 14.3 Percentage of Changes in Employment in Thirty-nine Metropolitan Areas: Cities and Suburbs

	Manufacturing		Retail Trade		Wholesale Trade		Selected Services	
	A*	B†	A*	B†	A*	B†	A*	B†
1948–54	3.1	24.3	4.6	68.7	– 4.7	34.2	54.6	86.9
54–58	– 9.3	3.1	3.6	– 0.1	3.9	46.4	16.2	40.5
58–63	– 1.0	17.1	– 10.2	10.0	– 3.0	39.3	3.0	26.5
63–67	7.3	25.9	2.2	22.5	3.7	29.1	3.0	19.2

SOURCE: Gold, "The Mismatch of Jobs and Low-Income People in Metropolitan Areas," p. 454.

*Central cities.

†Suburbs.

ty detracting and assists them in maintaining their overall residential attractiveness.

Neighborhood School Concept   Effective as zoning ordinances might be in controlling neighborhood social composition, they nevertheless do nothing directly to control the education available to children from households in particular neighborhoods. After all, education and school problems are a major concern of neighborhood groups in their struggle to maintain the desirability and middle-class status of their respective neighborhoods. The major weapon in their fight here has been the neighborhood school concept (Downs 1970). Children generally attend the school nearest their place of residence. This tends to minimize travel. In a context of residential segregation, however, it also tends to minimize mixture of the races and of the social classes—which is precisely what white middle-class households would prefer (Downs 1970). While the neighborhood school concept may have been predicated originally on a desire to minimize student travel, therefore, segregation of pupil compositions has certainly been its effect. That this has been to the advantage of white populations in general and middle-class whites in particular is apparent from their opposition to court-ordered busing for racial balance. This opposition receives expression in demonstrations and violence in the inner city white neighborhoods of cities such as Boston. Much more significantly it is apparent in the flight of white middle-class families to the suburbs (Coleman & Kelly 1976, pp. 234–55): eloquent testimony, therefore, to the important function the neighborhood school concept has performed for the white middle class.

Consequently at the neighborhood level we have a pair of institutional arrangements—the zoning ordinance and the neighborhood school concept—that clearly work to the advantage of white middle-class neighborhoods. They permit the middle class to exclude undesirable development from their neighborhoods and this, of course, provides them with a continuing advantage in competing for the utility-enhancing resident. We will find that similar patterns prevail at the jurisdictional level.

Jurisdictional Level

In broad outline we can fashion a similar argument with respect to competition at the jurisdictional level: some local governments are more effective than others in attracting utility-enhancing urban land developments. At this level, however, considerable attention focuses on the ability of local governments to attract the *fiscally* enhancing and to keep out the fiscally detracting. We examine in turn the roles in this competition of environmental context, local power, and the juridical context.

ENVIRONMENTAL CONTEXT

Each jurisdiction in the city consists of a set of locations with site and situation attributes evaluated as more-or-less attractive by the fiscally more-or-less desirable. Land in some jurisdictions, for example, will continue to elicit strong bids from the fiscally desirable as a result of certain characteristics of accessibility, housing stock, and the like.

Commercial developments are especially significant for tax base. Typically industries, offices, and public utilities pay far more in local taxes than the value of the services they directly consume. They are therefore courted assiduously by local governments. Suburban local governments offer speedy extensions of waterlines and sewer lines; central city governments may speed up the necessary rezonings and permits. A major criterion for business location, however, is that of accessibility to the rest of the metropolitan area. Retailers want to be near the center of the consumer market; industries want to be accessible to the labor market. Historically, of course, as was indicated in the last chapter, the most accessible point in the metropolitan area was the CBD, located near the geographical center of the city and at the hub of the railroad and streetcar lines. Automobiles, freeways, and outer belts have tended to reduce this advantage; and this goes quite a long way towards explaining the growth of retailing and industry in the suburbs, their decline in the central city (table 14.3), and the attrition of the central city tax base.

In many metropolitan areas the old CBD has nevertheless remained at the geographical center of the urbanized area. In cities such as Denver, Fort Worth, Dayton, and Pittsburgh the CBD has continued to attract retail and office investment enhancing to the central city's tax base. This is not true of all metropolitan areas, however. In lakeside, riverside, or oceanside cities the metropolitan area has tended to grow away from the CBD. In cities such as Chicago, Boston, Cleveland, Detroit, or St. Louis the CBD was originally established along and has tended to remain near the navigable water that was an original source of the city's growth. With suburbanization, however, the CBD has tended to become increasingly *ec*centric with respect to the metropolitan area as a whole (Ullman 1962, p. 19). The geographical center of the urbanized area has tended to shift away from the central city towards the suburbs. This is particularly so when the geographical center is weighted by purchasing power: the more affluent suburbs pull it in their direction.

As a consequence in metropolitan areas like these the central city

Figure 14.3   Impact of CBD Centrality on CBD Share of Metropolitan Area (SMA) Retail Sales

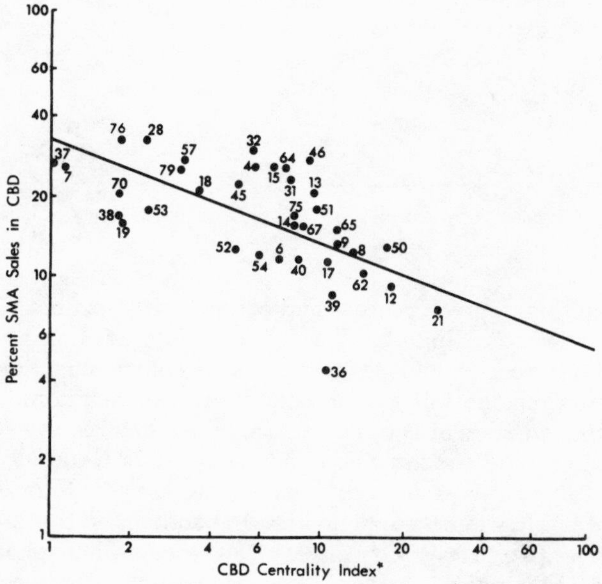

*miles from CBD x log. urbanized area in square miles

SOURCE: After Ronald R. Boyce and W. A. V. Clark, "Selected Spatial Variables and Central Business District Retail Sales," *Papers and Proceedings of the Regional Science Association* 11 (1963): 177.

KEY TO CITIES: 4. Atlanta; 6. Baltimore; 7. Birmingham; 8. Boston; 9. Buffalo; 12. Chicago; 13. Cincinnati; 14. Cleveland; 15. Columbus; 17. Dallas; 18. Dayton; 19. Denver; 21. Detroit; 28. Fort Worth; 31. Houston; 32. Indianapolis; 36. Los Angeles; 37. Louisville; 38. Memphis; 39. Miami; 40. Milwaukee; 45. New Haven; 46. New Orleans; 50. Philadelphia; 51. Phoenix; 52. Pittsburgh; 53. Portland; 54. Providence; 57. Rochester; 62. St. Louis; 64. San Antonio; 65. San Jose; 67. Seattle; 70. Syracuse; 75. Washington, D.C.; 76. Waterbury; 79. Worcester.

in general and the CBD in particular have lost much of their attraction for retail, office, and industrial business. In some cities suffering from this problem new CBDs are emerging in the suburbs to challenge the hegemony of the historic CBD. One is Clayton, Missouri, to the west of St. Louis (Kersten & Ross 1968).

One measure of the attractive power of the CBD as a business location is the degree to which it monopolizes metropolitan-area retail sales: as a CBD becomes more and more eccentric with respect to its metropolitan-area market, we should expect this dominance to deteriorate. Figure 14.3 suggests that this is precisely what happens. CBD retail sales as a proportion of total metropolitan-area sales appear on the horizontal axis. Centrally located CBDs like those in Pittsburgh and Fort Worth clearly tend to have retained their retail

Table 14.4   Acceptability of Different Housing Types to Suburban Leaders, New Jersey

Housing Type	Desirable*	Undesirable*
Single family, large lot	79	20
Single family, small lot	49	48
Garden apartment	46	52
Highrise apartment	27	70
Mobile home	9	91

SOURCE: State of New Jersey, County and Municipal Government Study Commission, *Housing & Suburbs: Fiscal & Social Impact of Multifamily Development*, 9th Report (Trenton, 1974), p. 78.
*Percentage of total sample.

dominance to a degree greater than eccentrically located CBDs such as those of Detroit, Philadelphia, Chicago, and St. Louis.

While business provides the greatest fiscal surplus, however, certain types of residential development are not to be ignored. In particular the folk wisdom of U.S. city officials emphasizes the advantages of upper and middle-income housing (table 14.4). Generally of higher assessed value the residents of these houses are also regarded as low-cost citizens: they generate little in terms of demand for public safety or welfare expenditures. Of course if low-income households should displace middle-income residents housing values would decline to the detriment of the jurisdictional tax base. Maintaining a continuing flow of middle-income residents is therefore crucial.

Raw, accessible land ripe for development is important in this regard. New housing tends to be more expensive and therefore available only to those of higher income. Suburbs with large areas of undeveloped land and perhaps a new freeway or outer belt linking them with the rest of the metropolitan area have tended to gain in this respect. Age of housing stock is however also important in a more general sense. Newer housing tends to elicit higher bids than older housing. As a consequence it is the older, inner suburbs that are more likely to be threatened by middle-class flight and fiscal deterioration than the newer, outer ones.

To some degree local governments also may be able to alter jurisdictional boundaries so that they include locations attractive to the fiscally desirable. A major weapon here is annexation. As commercial developments find suburban locations more attractive, to what extent can central cities retain them for the central city tax base by annexing the land on which they stand? As the central city housing stock ages and its population alters in the direction of the fiscally less desirable, to what extent can the city alter its fiscal balance by extending its boundaries and, figuratively speaking, lassoing new middle-class housing developments or undeveloped residential land in prime locations?

Unfortunately not all local governments are able to annex unincorporated land (Danielson 1972, pp. 148–50). The major problem here is that by state law a local government can annex such land only if it is contiguous to its jurisdiction. In the case of many central cities for this reason annexation is not feasible. Boston, for example, has the same boundaries today that it did in 1873. Other cities that are cut off from unincorporated land include St. Louis, Cleveland, Chicago, and Detroit. The inner suburbs of such cities tend to be in a similar predicament.

Fiscally this is of the utmost significance. Instead of enhancing the central city's tax base as a result of annexation new business development will enhance the tax base of some suburb. This will allow that suburb to be even more fiscally attractive to businesses or middle-class residents contemplating relocation from the central city. A recent comparison of large U.S. central cities with fiscal crises and those without found that a major difference was annexation history: those with fiscal problems were no longer able to expand by annexation, while those without could annex and had (Muller 1975).

Given the significance of annexation it should not surprise us that it is highly competitive. Local governments in the same metropolitan area vie for control of unincorporated land to which they are contiguous. A major weapon in this competition may be the ability of a local government to offer low-cost sewer and water services. Columbus, Ohio, has had a particularly aggressive annexation policy. One of its advantages has been its low-cost water supply and sewage treatment service. This has encouraged independent suburbs to purchase water and sewage service from Columbus, but at a cost: a binding determination of the maximum geographical extent of a given jurisdiction for which the services will be provided.

A major tactic in competitive annexation is to encircle one's competitors. This not only secures unincorporated land, but more importantly it also cuts off a competitor from other unincorporated land. Figure 14.4 illustrates a particularly devastating annexation by the city of Columbus that virtually destroyed the possibility of future annexations by the city of Worthington. By such means do municipalities attempt to preserve their fiscal positions.

LOCAL POWER

Power relations, particularly in the independent suburbs, may make it difficult to exclude the fiscally undesirable. Developer interests may enjoy a degree of access and indirect control over local government encouraging land development irrespective of its fiscal consequences for existing residents. Local landowners and realtors sym-

Figure 14.4   Competitive Annexation Strategies, Columbus and Worthington, Ohio

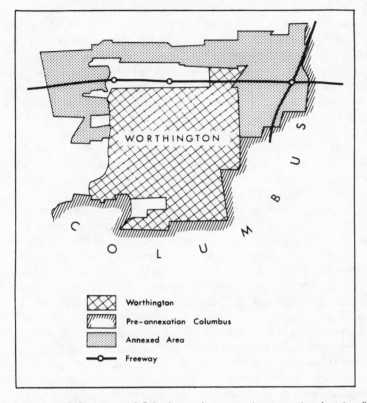

NOTE: In the late 1960s the city of Columbus made one massive annexation that virtually pre-empted the expansion of the independent suburb of Worthington. The annexation was facilitated by the fact that the annexed area included only thirteen property owners: this simplified negotiations between them and the city. The annexation also included prime commercial and residential property close to freeway interchanges.

pathetic to developer interests, for example, may dominate local councils. Alternatively or in addition, developer interests may control resources that are enhancing to councilor utility. Large land companies and builders, for example, tend to be prominent in the funding of local election campaigns in the suburban fringe.

Dominance by land development interests is particularly apparent in earlier stages of development in a suburb. Residential growth is, as yet, limited; and the negative fiscal consequences of development have yet to be made apparent to residents. As residential growth increases, however, and schools experience overcrowding, tax rates increase and open space disappears, so local residents will become more and more concerned. Developer interests on local councils will then have to contend with increasing opposition. Results of such a changing balance of power include the enactment of exclusionary zoning ordinances, sewer moratoria, and deceleration in the rate of annexation.

This is not to say, however, that new development comes to a halt. One of the more interesting characteristics of suburban housing markets is the way in which some development will continue despite exclusionary zoning ordinances. An explanation for this might take the following form. First, recognize that exclusionary zoning increases the supply of land for low density buildings and reduces supply of land for the excluded land use—say, multifamily dwellings and high density residential uses. As a result of scarcity of land for the excluded uses the price of land zoned for those uses in a metropolitan area increases dramatically. Now consider the pressures on the property developer contemplating construction of apartments. If he purchases land already zoned for apartments he will have to pay a high price. Alternatively he may purchase land zoned for low density use that is, in all likelihood, therefore, considerably cheaper, and he may seek a rezoning to apartments. If the rezoning is granted the value of the land skyrockets immediately, redounding to the profits of the property developer (Hagman 1974, p. 116). There is, however, a risk involved, for we have no reason to believe that the local zoning commission will not be as exclusionary in practice as their zoning ordinance is in intent. It is at this point that bribery and corruption assume an important role (Hagman 1974, p. 114). That bribing of zoning officials by developers occurs is a well-known fact (Balk 1966; Downie 1974, p. 90), and we can now appreciate why. The stakes for the developer requesting a rezoning are high indeed: he is therefore prepared to share some of it with local zoning officials in order to gain the greater part.

JURIDICAL CONTEXT

The ability of local governments to continue to attract the utility enhancing depends on establishing an attractiveness gradient between their jurisdiction and other jurisdictions, an attractiveness gradient that is apparent in, among other things, tax rates, school spending, and school pupil compositions. Establishing this attractiveness gradient, however, depends on the power to exclude, the power to provide services, and the power to fund services from local sources. These powers are delegated to local governments by the states.

Municipalities have important statutory responsibilities for the provision of public services. Table 14.5 provides some idea of the divi-

Table 14.5 Financing of Selected Urban Services, 1970–1971

Selected Urban Services	Amounts Spent by Governments Actually Providing the Services (in billions)			How State-Local Spending Is Financed[a]		
	State ($)	Local ($)	State & Local ($)	Federal Funds (%)	State Funds (%)	Local Funds (%)
Income-redistribution activities						
Welfare	10.5	7.7	12.2	54	35	11
Health & hospitals	5.4	5.8	11.2	7	47	46
Housing programs	–[b]	2.5	2.6	63	5	32
Public schools	0.5	41.3	41.8	10	39	51
Resource-allocation activities						
Police, correction, & fire	2.0	7.4	9.4	2	22	76
Transportation (except highways)	0.3	3.4	3.7	5	11	84
Water supply & water treatment	–[c]	6.1	6.1	8	2	90
Local parks & recreation	–[c]	2.1	2.1	2	5	93
Sanitation (except sewerage)		1.4	1.4			100
Libraries	0.1	0.7	0.8	10	13	77
Total	18.8	78.5	97.3	18	32	50

NOTE: Because of rounding, detail may not add to totals.

SOURCE: Adapted from U.S. Census Bureau releases.

[a]These columns describe the source of funds for the state-local direct expenditure shown in the preceding columns. The federal government also makes the direct expenditure for federal programs, for example, for the air-traffic-control system. The federal funds shown in this table include only federal aid to state and local government.

[b]Less than $50 million.

[c]There is some direct state-government expenditure for urban water supply and for urban parks, but it is small and difficult to separate from published data.

sion of public responsibility between local and state governments with respect to funding. The table lists the proportion of local funds constituting state-local expenditures on selected urban services from 1970 to 1971. Fiscally, local governments are particularly responsible for services such as public safety, sanitation, water supply, parks, and recreation; they enjoy diminished responsibility in the areas of welfare and education. As the second column of the table shows, in *absolute* terms the amount of money local governments must raise for educational purposes is nevertheless especially onerous. Hence the significance of a healthy local tax base—an advantage that, as we have seen above, can be attained by use of the zoning power. These funding and spending powers moreover provide considerable scope for the creation of attractiveness differentials. To the extent that a jurisdiction includes high value land uses with residents imposing only modest public service burdens, tax rates can be kept low and education can be funded at an attractive level.

Decentralization of schooling is critical for the creation of attractiveness gradients in another sense. As busing for racial balance has been introduced in more and more U.S. central cities, so, in the eyes of the white middle class, suburban school districts have acquired a new virtue: whiteness (Coleman & Kelly 1976).

Creating attractiveness gradients is one thing: maintaining them is another. How, for example, is a low-tax-rate, middle-class community to maintain its fiscal advantages? How can it possibly turn back the threat of lower class housing development within its jurisdictional confines: lower class housing development, moreover, that would probably generate more demand for public services than it would provide in terms of additional property tax revenues?

Of major significance is the delegation of land use planning and control by the state to the municipality. Since zoning power is largely vested in municipalities and counties the act of incorporation assumes a critical importance for communities wishing to regulate their local land use environment by, for example, the promulgation of exclusionary zoning ordinances. That this power is a major incentive to incorporation is occasionally revealed with unusual clarity. Such a case concerned the community of Blackjack, Missouri, just north of St. Louis (Danielson 1976, pp. 31–33). Early in 1970, a nonprofit corporation organized by the Methodist church in St. Louis drew up plans to construct, with federal subsidy and at a density of just over eight per acre, townhouses for lower income groups in the then-unincorporated community of Blackjack. Later that year, after the announcement of these construction plans, the community incorporated and obtained the power to zone; two months later the new city of Blackjack rezoned the projected building site so as to impose a minimum lot size of one-third of an acre, thus effectively quashing the project.

Other exclusionary powers accrue by default. Provision of public housing, for example, is a local privilege and *not* a responsibility. If a local government desires to keep out public housing tenants with all their problems, it simply decides not to establish a local public housing authority. Alternatively if charity overwhelms it, it may decide to erect some token public housing. In all likelihood though it will be housing for the elderly: few of the retired have children in school and still fewer create difficulties for the local police.

The necessary concomitant of the exclusionary policy is inclusion. Local governments zone little or no land for undesirable uses but large fractions of their turf for desirable ones. Typically, for example, there is a tendency to underzone for apartments and overzone for those commercial and office uses enhancing to the local tax base.

All this of course assumes that a bit of real estate can be fenced off from the rest of the world as the jurisdiction of a new local government: a bit of real estate the tax resources of which will be shared only among local residents and from which the undesirable can be excluded by, say, a zoning ordinance. To what extent, therefore, does state law permit the creation of new local governments?

The proliferation of local governments and their respective jurisdictions in U.S. metropolitan areas is a function of the favor shown by state law to two mutually exclusive processes: incorporation and annexation (Cox 1973, pp. 20–22). To the extent that annexation is facilitated relative to incorporation a central city government and existing independent suburbs may be able to annex land and nascent suburban communities beyond their jurisdictional boundaries, thus forestalling further fragmentation. Clearly to the extent that state law casts a friendly eye on incorporation rather than annexation, then suburban communities attempting to escape the fiscal and behavioral problems of the central city or of existing independent suburbs will incorporate. Ultimately they will form a noose of independent jurisdictions around the central city and older independent suburbs, preventing them from expanding by annexation. As a result of the concentration of fiscal and behavioral problems there, however, the implications of this have been especially serious for central cities.

Prior to 1900, annexation was relatively easy and it accounts for the large areas covered by most of today's central cities. Since then areal growth of central cities has slowed down appreciably and most of the growth of metropolitan areas has been associated with the incorporation of new independent municipalities. Much of the responsibility for this locational pattern devolves to the state juridical context; after 1900 this favored the incorporation of new suburban municipalities rather than annexation. By a variety of devices state legislatures, increasingly dominated by a coalition of legislators from rural and suburban areas, attempted to reduce the likelihood of central city annexation of their constituencies. Power in annexation procedures therefore was often shifted away from the central city toward suburban areas. At the same time that annexation was made more difficult for central cities, the legal procedures for municipal incorporation remained extremely favorable to small, unincorporated suburban communities. In particular they continued to allow tiny communities—often fewer than 500 in population—to incorporate and establish municipal governments. The result was the high degree of jurisdictional fragmentation, with a large central city surrounded by smaller independent suburbs, observable today.

More recently there have been efforts to change the juridical context in favor of central cities, though in many cases this has been too late, since they are already surrounded and cut off from unincorporated territory by suburban rings. A number of states including Ohio, Georgia, Arizona, and North Carolina have passed "anti-incorporation" laws. These contain the idea of creating around a municipality a belt of land in which new incorporations cannot take place unless the existing municipality agrees to the incorporation or refuses to annex an area when asked to do so. In Arizona, for example, the belt is three miles in width around municipalities of fewer than 5,000 and six miles in width for larger towns and cities. No new incorporation can take place in these belts unless the existing municipality agrees or refuses to annex when petitioned.

Challenging the Juridical Context

Institutional arrangements therefore play an important role in stabilizing middle-class neighborhoods and also in helping communities to develop those differentials of locational desirability that allow them to continue to attract utility-enhancing developments and to leave the detracting to others. Obviously certain groups suffer from this. It should not surprise us, therefore, if the losers from the competitive struggle attempt to alter the rules under which it is played.

We have already referred, for instance, to changes in state annexation and incorporation law. To some degree altering the statutes so as to facilitate annexation rather than incorporation can be interpreted as a pro–central city policy; central cities can more easily prevent tax base attrition by reincorporating within the city businesses and households that may have relocated into unincorporated areas. Unfortunately for many central cities already hemmed in by suburbs, the legislation has come too late.

One could also refer to the abolition of the neighborhood school concept. The attack on racial segregation in the schools has led to integration plans in a variety of cities. In some cases these plans are merely designed to forestall litigation by co-opting the disinherited. City school boards, for example, may adopt open enrollment policies allowing children to enroll in any school they wish, so long as the change improves racial balance in the sending and receiving schools (McAdams 1974). The most devastating form of attack on the neighborhood school concept, however, is court-ordered busing. This is usually a consequence of litigation on the part of the National Association for the Advancement of Colored People (NAACP) and other black pressure groups. It results not only in increased racial integration in the schools but also in the busing of white middle-class children out of their neighborhoods into schools in black, low-income neighborhoods. In general, however, litigation has been confined to big central city school districts; most suburban school districts have few blacks and there has been little basis there for developing a case against racial discrimination. The general effect, therefore, has been for white households and especially the middle class to alter their residential location plans in favor of independent suburbs.

These changes in the statutes or reinterpretations of existing statutory and constitutional law, however, have merely tended to reemphasize the significance of the remaining advantages accruing to middle-class neighborhoods and independent suburbs. The failure of changes in annexation law to ease the fiscal plight of cities cut off from unincorporated land, for example, has served only to underline the significance of exclusionary zoning and dependence on the local tax base (Muller 1975). It is also apparent that busing within central city school districts has been counter-productive: while the initial effect may have been some increased racial integration, white flight to independent suburbs has served to resegregate pupil compositions (Coleman & Kelly 1976). This, then, has served to focus attention on the need to attack educational home rule.

Attempts to alter these institutional arrangements have come more in the form of major attacks through the courts than as proposed statutory and constitutional amendments. The important point is that according to some interpretations of constitutional or statutory law existing institutional arrangements have effects that are, in fact, already unlawful; all that is necessary is a court judgment and an order for redress. Unfortunately so far in this attack through the courts results have not been notably successful.

In the exclusionary zoning area one of the more important of recent Supreme Court rulings is *James vs Valtierra* (Danielson 1976, pp. 180–86). In actuality the case concerned the location of public housing rather than exclusionary zoning per se. Forces opposed to exclusionary zoning, however, fear that the ruling may have sufficient generality to adversely affect their efforts also. The background to the case is the requirement of the California state constitution for a local referendum on public housing proposals: this requirement, of course, has worked substantially against the expansion of low-income housing in suburban locations, and it was challenged successfully in a federal district court, the grounds being the denial to blacks and the poor of equal protection under the Fourteenth Amendment to the Constitution. This decision in turn, however, was appealed and overturned by the Supreme Court on the grounds that the requirement of a referendum for public housing proposals cannot be said to rest on "distinctions based on race." While it can be said to rest on distinctions of income, this is not unconstitutional.

This ruling has served to deflect the anti-exclusionary effort into demonstrating the racially discriminatory character of exclusion. Given that it is also income discriminatory and most blacks are poor, however, this is not easy. A recent case in point is provided by the legal challenge to the Blackjack exclusionary zoning action described above. In order to overturn it in the courts the prosecution had to show that it was racially discriminatory (Glazer 1974, pp. 109–10; Danielson 1976, pp. 184–86). Evidence used, therefore, included data on disparities for similar income groups in the housing conditions of blacks and whites in St. Louis. Not surprisingly, given the difficulty of isolating motives, the federal court refused to overturn Blackjack's decision to exclude high density housing.

A second landmark decision reemphasizing the virtues of local autonomy and protecting suburban strongholds from the (as they see it) barbaric forces from without may be the 1974 decision concerning busing *between* school districts for purposes of racial balance. Major problems in the achievement of racial balance by busing have been twofold. First, courts could order busing only to undo the effects of specifically de jure segregation on school pupil compositions; this might be, for example, where segregated housing patterns could be proven to have resulted from government-enforced restrictive covenants preventing white home owners from selling to blacks. De facto segregation is not a sufficient basis for ordering busing. The second problem is that busing to achieve racial balance is of little utility within many central city school districts, since their pupil compositions are already largely black: 86 percent of pupils in

Figure 14.5   Racial Imbalance and School Districts in the Richmond Metropolitan Area

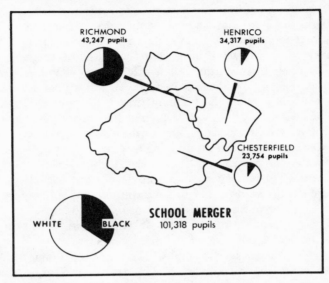

NOTE: Richmond School District has an enrollment that is almost 69 percent black; busing, therefore, does little to rectify racial imbalance. In an enlarged school district including adjacent Henrico and Chesterfield school districts, enrollment would be over 65 percent white. Busing in such an enlarged school district would go a long way to correcting racial imbalances.

Washington, D.C., are black, for example, while in Detroit, Michigan, and Richmond, Virginia, the respective figures are 65 percent and 70 percent. A related problem, as we have already seen, is that where busing has been instituted white parents have adjusted and escaped its effects by relocating to suburban jurisdictions. This has been particularly common among middle-class, white households.

As a result of the latter it has become increasingly apparent that interracial balance in pupil compositions in the public schools of many larger cities could be achieved only by busing on a metropolitanwide basis. In order to do this, however, there had to be some rationale tracing the whiteness of independent suburbs and the blackness of central cities to acts of de jure segregation. This rationale is now emerging. Federal courts in Detroit and Richmond, for example, have found that de facto segregation has been condoned and even fostered by official state policy to a degree such that one could justifiably label the outcome as de jure segregation. In Richmond, therefore, the judge held state officials responsible for affirmative action to reverse the situation and produce meaningful integration, even if it meant busing between school districts.

The federal district court judge in Richmond ordered consolidation of largely white suburban school districts with the largely black central city school district (figure 14.5). In Detroit the court ordered inter-school district busing to be implemented. The Detroit case has been appealed to the Supreme Court and the inter-school district busing plan has been rejected. This is widely regarded as a serious blow for similar cases pending in cities such as Indianapolis, Indiana; Wilmington, Delaware; and Louisville, Kentucky.

There can of course be no doubt that devolution of responsibility for public provision and funding has important and continuing support from those benefiting from it. This is most apparent at those catalytic moments when local autonomy is either challenged or used to evade problems confronting particular communities. Some of these cases are outstanding.

In the exclusionary zoning literature an example underlining the significance of home rule for keeping out the unwanted is the Black-jack case. In fact much suburban incorporation is of the defensive variety aimed (1) at keeping out those imposing undesirable behavioral externalities or (2) at sequestering fiscal resources from the poor in order to keep tax rates down.

The self-interestedness of support for local autonomy derives much of its impetus from educational considerations. It should not surprise us therefore that although for most purposes, for example, the population of Marion County, Indiana, has the same metrogovernment as Indianapolis, in the area of education the suburban populations have retained—by popular choice—their long-standing local school districts.

As suggested above the threat of busing is a powerful motive for support of suburban home rule in education. In Denver residents have not adjusted to busing only by relocating in school districts outside Denver; in addition they have lobbied for and obtained a state amendment preventing Denver from annexing the unincorporated territory into which they have moved and, hence, from bringing them back into the city. Opposition to busing between school districts is symptomatic of the same forces. In this context it is useful to recall that the Detroit case described above was appealed to the Supreme Court by the state acting in conjunction with two of the threatened suburban school districts.

Outcome of Competition

Residential location in an urban area is important to one's welfare. It will affect local tax rates and the amount of money spent on a child's education. It will affect the degree of public safety, the discipline

Table 14.6   Household Income and Experience of Neighborhood Problems in Columbus, Ohio

	Income (%)				
	Under $6,000	$6,000–9,999	$10,000–14,999	$15,000–24,999	$25,000 & over
Drugs	40	40	33	28	21
Unsafe places for children to play	41	38	29	19	12
Juvenile delinquency	34	34	25	18	17
Lack of financial support for schools	28	27	18	20	16
Air pollution	23	22	16	11	7
Torn-up street	22	18	14	10	5
Abandoned houses/ buildings	17	13	7	4	3

NOTE: Percentages refer to the percentage in an income group responding that the problem mentioned is a "very serious" problem in their neighborhood.
SOURCE: Benchmark (Columbus, Ohio: Academy for Contemporary Problems, 1974).

problems encountered in local schools, and the safety, cleanliness, and amount of traffic of local streets.

Generally speaking we have seen that these aspects of welfare tend to be closely correlated with household income. Wealthier households live in better neighborhoods and are also more likely to live in an independent suburb with its typically lower tax rate and more opulently endowed school system. Lower income households, on the other hand, live in the less-desirable neighborhoods and in jurisdictions the local governments of which are most likely to be experiencing fiscal constraint (table 14.6).

These are important outcomes of the competitive processes identified in chapter 13. In the present chapter we have attempted to show why middle-class neighborhoods are generally successful in attracting the utility enhancing and keeping out the utility detracting: they tend to have the ear of local government and are certainly favored by the juridical context. We have also attempted to show why suburban local governments have been more effective in fiscal competition: particular emphasis was placed on access to undeveloped land and hence on annexation and that corpus of law that allows middle-class suburbs to, in effect, zone out lower income groups and zone in commercial and the more desirable residential developments.

Competition, particularly fiscal competition, however, has other effects on welfare that are less related to residential desirability and more related to job markets and housing prices. This chapter concludes, therefore, with a consideration of the effects of competition on: (1) the housing problems of low-income, inner city populations; (2) the employment problems of low-skill, inner city populations (usually identified as "the transportation and poverty problem"). In both cases there is some evidence that fiscal competition again results in the poor getting less than they otherwise would.

INNER CITY HOUSING PROBLEMS

There is some indication of a link between local government fiscal competition in metropolitan areas and the housing prices faced by low-income residents. Attention has mainly focused on the effects of urban renewal problems. Recall that urban renewal has provided a major tool for central cities in enhancing their fiscal position. It allows elimination of areas of low assessed value properties and their replacement by higher value properties; and fiscally undesirable residents who impose heavy demands on public services may be replaced by higher income families, thus reducing public safety expenditure and welfare expenditure needs. This, however, will depend on where the displaced low-income residents go, whether renewal assumes a residential form, and what the precise nature of that residential form will be.

An overall effect of urban renewal as it has been implemented, however, has been, according to a number of observers, a deterioration in the supply of low-income housing (Gans 1965; Edel 1972). Large numbers of low-income residences have been demolished; but they have not been replaced by structures at rents within the budget of low-income households. Table 14.7, for example, compares the degree to which housing demolition was accompanied by the construction of public housing for low-income families before and after 1949, a critical year, since it was then that urban renewal legislation (Housing Act of 1949) was introduced, paving the way for federally subsidized urban redevelopment. Clearly before 1949 the pattern was one of net accretion in the housing stock available to low-income families. Since then units demolished have tended not to be replaced by public housing. There are exceptions to this, of course. The massive and ill-destined Pruitt-Igoe project in St. Louis was built on urban renewal land (Rainwater 1971). By and large, however, any new

Table 14.7   Comparison of Public Housing Constructed with Dwelling Units Demolished for Public Housing or as a Result of Urban Renewal

	Before 1949 Housing Act			1949–57		
	Demolished	Built	Gain/Loss	Demolished	Built	Gain/Loss
New York	12,545	14,171	+ 1,626	43,869	50,462	+ 6,593
Chicago	3,467	8,483	+ 5,016	27,929	24,479	– 3,450
Los Angeles	529	3,468	+ 2,939	5,801	5,819	+ 18
Philadelphia	2,862	3,248	+ 386	19,279	12,471	– 6,808
Detroit	424	4,879	+ 4,455	12,063	3,301	– 8,762
Baltimore	4,242	5,021	+ 779	13,229	5,314	– 7,915
Houston	2,210	2,251	+ 41	0	348	+ 348
Cleveland	3,977	5,179	+ 1,202	3,977	2,279	– 1,698
Washington	563	3,147	+ 2,584	8,505	6,909	– 1,596
St. Louis	1,318	1,315	– 3	9,860	5,430	– 4,430
Milwaukee	0	615	+ 615	4,126	2,415	– 1,711
San Francisco	179	1,741	+ 1,562	8,591	4,142	– 4,449

Boston	5,619	5,102	− 517	11,767	5,871	− 5,896
New Orleans	3,837	5,381	+ 1,544	576	6,889	+ 6,313
Newark	2,075	2,711	+ 636	6,928	8,180	+ 1,252
Cincinnati	1,675	3,818	+ 2,143	10,421	2,404	− 8,017
Louisville	2,671	3,005	+ 334	7,967	1,957	− 6,010
Minneapolis	0	464	+ 464	7,669	2,825	− 4,844
Pittsburgh	2,659	4,463	+ 1,804	7,862	4,771	− 3,091
Atlanta	3,466	5,188	+ 1,722	8,264	3,794	− 4,470
Providence	173	1,056	+ 883	5,777	1,916	− 3,861
Dayton	712	1,191	+ 479	4,309	1,143	− 3,166
Norfolk	0	730	+ 730	6,043	2,990	− 3,053
New Haven	724	1,035	+ 311	3,994	1,092	− 2,902
Total*	76,895	126,496	+ 49,601	320,392	230,795	− 89,597

NOTE: Listed are the twelve largest cities and twelve others with major urban renewal programs.

SOURCE: National Commission on Urban Problems (Douglas Commission), *Building the American City* (Washington, D.C.: Government Printing Office, 1969).

*Total represents that for seventy-four cities.

residential construction in urban renewal projects has tended to be for middle-class families: developments such as Detroit's Lafayette Square spring to mind in this context (Wolf & Lebeaux 1969, pt. 2).

This is not to say, however, that the result has been homelessness for low-income families displaced by urban renewal; rather the illfare effects have been apparent in increased housing costs (Hartman 1964). Urban renewal has tended to reduce the supply of low-income housing, necessitating that low-income households spend more to obtain housing. Some of the increased supply has, in fact, come from erstwhile middle-class neighborhoods. As noted earlier, one result of urban renewal is that low-income households will be prepared to outbid middle-income households for housing at the boundary between middle-income and low-income neighborhoods. Market accommodation to changes in supply induced by urban renewal is therefore achieved, but at the cost of considerable social dislocation.

TRANSPORTATION AND POVERTY PROBLEMS

The shift of employment opportunities to the suburbs and the increasing isolation of those of lower income in central cities may pose problems of access to employment opportunities. This has been a problem generating considerable concern at the level of both government and research, a number of writers postulating a relationship between relatively high levels of unemployment in the central city and decreasing accessibility to jobs (Kain & Meyer 1970; Gold 1972).

The argument can be stated briefly. Employment opportunities have been leaving the central city. Those requiring little training have been suburbanizing fastest. In the central city itself job markets are increasingly biased toward white-collar positions requiring higher levels of skill and education.

Conceivably there are a number of ways in which the less skilled of the central city might adjust to this changing distribution of job opportunities. They could, for example, commute to jobs in the suburbs. Problems here, however, include relatively low levels of auto ownership and the inadequacies of metropolitan mass transit systems. Among the city's very poor, auto ownership rates are surprisingly low: for family units earning before-tax incomes from $2,000–2,999 in 1967, for example, only 53 percent owned an automobile.

Nor does mass transit provide a feasible source of relief. The spread of the automobile throughout the population as a whole has seriously eroded the market for mass transit services. Increasing geographical dispersion of places of work and of residence has furthermore increased per passenger costs of operation. As a result there are few metropolitan mass transit systems that are not in financial jeopardy and attempting to cope with these problems by paring down services to the bare minimum.

An alternative to commuting, of course, is residential relocation: the poor of the central city could move into housing closer to suburban job opportunities. We have already seen above, however, that suburban jurisdictions generally tend to be able to screen out the poor. Not only do they have a relatively expensive housing stock; but their reserves of developable land are also protected from development of housing for low-income groups by exclusionary zoning, "gold-plated" subdivision regulations, and the reluctance of suburban local governments to embark on public housing projects.

As a consequence, the argument concludes, central city, lower income groups are faced with serious problems of job access. Not only does the mobility problem hinder retention of a suburban job, but it also makes job search arduous. Even if commuting is a possibility the costly journey to work reduces the monetary return from a job as compared with the monetary return from welfare payments. The result is unemployment or job instability as workers shift from one more-or-less unsatisfactory job to another. To the extent that the municipality is responsible for welfare payments, as in a few states, these costs generally are passed on to the central city taxpayer.

There is in fact considerable circumstantial evidence regarding the mobility problems of the central city poor and their relationships to unemployment. In many cities, for example, we know that blacks have substantially longer journey-to-work trips than whites. In Chicago the average black work trip is eight miles, compared to six miles for whites. Also there is no doubt that the black mobility problem lends itself to all types of extortion by unscrupulous entrepreneurs. In Los Angeles transportation-cum-employment agencies have sprung up to recruit black domestics and transport them to and from the middle-class suburbs where they work, charging the middle-class client $16 per day and paying the employee $10 (*Time Magazine*, 6 April 1970, p. 48).

There are also some outstanding cases in which suburban relocation of employment has resulted in loss of jobs by those for whom mobility—either of the residential or journey-to-work variety—poses significant problems. When the National Bureau of Standards vacated its Washington location and moved to suburban Gaithersburg, Maryland, although total employment increased by 125, black employment decreased by 75 (*Time Magazine*, 6 April 1970, p. 48).

The problem nevertheless has also been a source of considerable debate among geographers, regional scientists, and urban economists. It is clear that for whites accessibility is a determinant of income and unemployment rates: whites living in the suburbs have lower rates of unemployment and higher incomes than whites of equivalent education and job skills living in the central city (Harrison 1972). For blacks, however, there is apparently no such contrast: job discrimination may shut the door of suburban opportunity, even when they can relocate closer to jobs. Clearly this is a problem requiring considerably more research before we can come to definitive conclusions.

Concluding Comments

This chapter has explained the outcomes of competition among localized groups in metropolitan areas to regulate urban land development to local advantage. At both neighborhood and jurisdictional levels ability to compete effectively was related to three critical variables: environmental context; local power; and the juridical context.

At the neighborhood level certain aspects of site and situation may serve to maintain residential desirability. This may be a question, for example, of enduring physical amenity or of insulation by artificial or natural barriers from surrounding developments that would otherwise detract: public housing developments or shopping centers, for example. These aspects of site and situation moreover enter into market calculations and the competitive-bidding mechanism: areas that are residentially more attractive on these grounds will therefore attract more middle-class residents with their felicitous implications for local schools and public safety.

Alternatively a neighborhood may also be attractive to commercial developments. This will make the area less residentially desirable and perhaps precipitate neighborhood deterioration. Whether nonresidential uses can penetrate one neighborhood rather than another, however, depends on power relations. Critical here is (1) the accessibility of neighborhood residents to city councilors and public officials and (2) the bargaining resources they have vis-à-vis others interested in the neighborhood turf. The fiscal balance of particular land uses is especially crucial to the land use bargaining process in U.S. cities.

The exercise of local power, however, presupposes the existence of a set of institutional arrangements that local government is empowered to implement and that can be mobilized by neighborhood groups to the advantage of their respective neighborhoods. Especially important here have been the zoning ordinance and the neighborhood school concept. The zoning ordinance has provided advantages to neighborhoods zoned for single-family rather than for multifamily housing, for instance. The neighborhood school concept has provided some neighborhoods with a competitive edge they would lack if neighborhood school pupil compositions comprised a greater cross-section of the different social classes.

A similar argument was presented to explain the outcome of competition at the jurisdictional level. At this level, however, major goals attach to attracting the fiscally enhancing and to excluding the fiscally detracting. For reasons having to do with site and situation certain local governments may have more difficulty in doing this. The increasing eccentricity of many CBDs has deterred commercial development there and consequently hurt a number of central city fiscs. To the extent that a city can expand by annexation such considerations may be less important; many central cities and inner suburbs, however, find themselves cut off from unincorporated land by other, more suburban municipalities.

Many outer suburbs consequently find themselves well placed to attract fiscally enhancing shopping centers, offices, and luxury housing developments. Local power considerations, however, may make it difficult to exclude fiscally detracting multifamily apartment developments. This is especially likely in the early stages of suburban development, when landowning interests predominate in the local political process.

And finally there is the juridical context. The ability of local governments to continue to attract the fiscally enhancing depends on establishing an attractiveness gradient between their jurisdiction and others. Critical here is the devolution of responsibility for funding and provision to local governments: this allows the initial establishment of attractiveness gradients based, perhaps, on random variations of tax base. Maintenance of the attractiveness gradient, however, depends on the power to exclude undesirable developments and to include the desirable. This power is obligingly provided by the states in the form of local discretion over land use zoning.

The outcome of these competitive processes is, of course, rather unequal: some neighborhoods are pleasant to live in, others are not; some jurisdictions have high tax rates, still others have low ones. Residents, however, are not necessarily lacking in control. The institutional constraints imposed on local government by federal and state governments are important to the competitive outcome, but they are by no means immutable. There have therefore been a number of attempts to alter them. Notable among these is the attack on the neighborhood school concept led by black interest groups and recent attempts to overturn exclusionary zoning in the courts. The vested interests gaining from the status quo, however, are strong; and change is likely to be gradual rather than radical.

Finally we saw how competition, particularly fiscal competition, has other effects on welfare that are less related to residential desirability. Exclusionary zoning in combination with suburbanization of job opportunities has posed serious problems of job accessibility for the central city poor. Central city urban renewal policies, designed to mitigate the central city's fiscal situation, have tended to increase the scarcity of low-income housing and so increase the rents low-income groups must pay.

Select Bibliography

Balk, Alfred. "Invitation to Bribery." *Harper's Magazine* 233, no. 1397 (October 1966): 18–24.

Danielson, Michael N. "Differentiation, Segregation, and Political Fragmentation in the American Metropolis." In A. E. Keir Nash, ed. *Governance and Population: The Governmental Implications of Population Change*, pp. 143–76. Washington, D.C.: Government Printing Office, 1972.

Davidoff, Linda; Davidoff, Paul; and Gold, Niel. "The Suburbs Have to Open Their Gates." *New York Times Magazine,* 7 November 1971.

Epps, Richard W. "The Appeal of Black Capitalism." *Philadelphia Federal Reserve Bank Business Review*, May 1969, pp. 9–15.

Gerard, Karen. "The Locally Inspired Fiscal Crisis." *Society* 13, no. 4 (May/June 1976): 33–35.

Hayes, Edward C. *Power Structure and Urban Policy.* Ch. 5. New York: McGraw-Hill, 1972.

Kain, John F., and Persky, Joseph J. "Alternatives to the Gilded Ghetto." *Public Interest,* no. 14, winter 1969, pp. 74–87.

Kuttner, Bob. "Ethnic Renewal." *New York Times Magazine,* 9 May 1976, p. 18.

Lorimer, James. *A Citizen's Guide to City Politics.* Toronto: Lewis & Samuel, 1972.

Lowi, T. J. "Apartheid U.S.A." *Trans-Action* 7, no. 4 (February 1970): 32–39.

Meyer, John, and Kain, John F. "Interrelationships of Transportation and Poverty." *Public Interest,* no. 18, winter 1970.

FURTHER READINGS

Alonso, William. "Urban Zero Population Growth." In Mancur Olson and Hans H. Landsberg, eds. *The No-Growth Society*, pp. 191–206. New York: Norton, 1973.

Chinitz, Benjamin, ed. *City and Suburb*. Englewood Cliffs, N.J.: Prentice-Hall, 1964.

Cox, Kevin R. *Conflict, Power and Politics in the City: A Geographic View*. New York: McGraw-Hill, 1973.

Downs, Anthony. *Opening Up the Suburbs*. New Haven: Yale University Press, 1973.

Harvey, David W. *Society, the City and the Space-Economy of Urbanism*. Association of American Geographers Commission on College Geography Resource Paper no. 18. Washington, D.C., 1972.

Liston, Robert A. *Downtown*. New York: Dell, 1968.

Muller, Peter O. *The Outer City: Geographical Consequences of the Urbanization of the Suburbs*. Association of American Geographers Resource Paper 75-2. Washington, D.C., 1976.

BIBLIOGRAPHY

Advisory Commission on Intergovernmental Relations. *Fiscal Balance in the American Federal System.* Vol. 2, *Metropolitan Fiscal Disparities.* Washington, D.C.: Government Printing Office, 1967.

————. *In Search of Balance: Canada's Intergovernmental Experience.* Washington, D.C.: Government Printing Office, 1971.

Alcaly, Roger E., and Mermelstein, David, eds. *The Fiscal Crisis of American Cities.* New York: Vintage, 1977.

Alonso, William. "Urban and Regional Imbalances in Economic Development." *Economic Development and Cultural Change* 17, no. 1 (October 1968): 1–14.

————. "Urban Zero Population Growth." In Mancur Olson and Hans H. Landsberg, eds. *The No-Growth Society,* pp. 191–206. New York: Norton, 1973.

Alyea, Paul E. "Property Tax Inducements to Attract Industry." In Richard W. Lindholm, ed. *Property Taxation U.S.A.* Madison: University of Wisconsin Press, 1969.

Aronson, J. Richard. "Voting with Your Feet." *New Society* 29, no. 621 (August 29, 1974): 545–47.

Ash, Joan. "Residential Rehabilitation in the U.S.A." *Urban Studies* 4, no. 1 (February 1967).

Astrachan, Anthony. "The Cultural Revolution on Our Doorstep." *Saturday Review,* 25 September 1973, pp. 14–19.

Babcock, Richard F. *The Zoning Game.* Madison: University of Wisconsin Press, 1966.

Balk, Alfred. "Invitation to Bribery." *Harper's Magazine* 233, no. 1397 (October 1966): 18–24.

Baron, Harold M. "Race and Status in School Spending: Chicago, 1961–66." *Journal of Human Resources* 6, no. 1 (1971): 3–24.

Barr, John. "Durham's Murdered Villages." *New Society,* 3 April 1969, pp. 523–25.

Barratt Brown, Michael. *The Economics of Imperialism.* Harmondsworth, Middlesex: Penguin, 1974.

Beagle, Danny; Haber, Al; and Wellman, David. "Rapid Transit: The Case of BART." In David M. Gordon, ed. *Problems in Political Economy: An Urban Perspective.* Lexington, Mass.: D. C. Heath, 1971.

Becker, Howard S. "Career Patterns of Public School Teachers." In Blaine E. Mercer and Edwin R. Carr, eds. *Education and the Social Order.* New York: Holt, Rinehart & Winston, 1957.

Beckerman, Wilfred. *In Defence of Economic Growth.* London: Cape, 1974.

Benoit, Emile. "The Attack on the Multinationals." *Columbia Journal of World Business* 7, no. 6 (November/December 1972): 15-22.

Berg, E. J. "Backward-sloping Labor Supply Functions in Dual Economies—The Africa Case." *Quarterly Journal of Economics* 75, no. 3 (August 1961).

Berkman, Richard L., and Viscusi, W. Kip. *Damming the West.* New York: Grossman, 1973.

Berry, Brian J. L. *Geography of Market Centers and Retail Distribution.* Englewood Cliffs, N.J.: Prentice-Hall, 1967.

Bhagwati, Jagdish. *The Economics of Underdeveloped Countries.* New York: McGraw-Hill, 1966.

Boal, F. W. "Territoriality on the Shankill-Falls Divide, Belfast." *Irish Geography* 6, no. 1 (1969): 30-50.

————. "Territoriality and Class: A Study of Two Residential Areas in Belfast." *Irish Geography* 6, no. 3 (1971): 229-48.

Boehne, Edward G. "Making Economic Sense Out of Grants-in-Aid." *Philadelphia Federal Reserve Bank Business Review*, February 1969, pp. 3-9.

Boeke, J. H. *Economics and Economic Policy of Dual Societies, as Exemplified by Indonesia.* New York: Institute of Pacific Relations, 1953.

Borgstrom, Georg A. "The Dual Challenge of Health and Hunger— A Global Crisis." In Quentin H. Stanford, ed. *The World's Population*, pp. 176-86. Toronto: Oxford University Press, 1972.

Boudeville, J-R. *Problems of Regional Economic Planning.* Edinburgh: At the University Press, 1966.

Boulding, Kenneth E. "The Economics of the Coming Spaceship Earth." In Henry Jarrett, ed. *Environmental Quality in a Growing Economy.* Washington, D.C.: Resources for the Future, 1966.

Bourne, Richard. "The Cubans of Miami." *New Society* 29, no. 618 (August 8, 1974): 347-50.

Bradford, Calvin P., and Rubinowitz, Leonard P. "The Urban-Suburban Investment-Disinvestment Process: Consequences for Older Neighborhoods." *Annals of the Academy of Political and Social Sciences* 422 (November 1975): 77-86.

Brand, Jack, and McCrone, Donald. "The SNP: From Protest to Nationalism." *New Society*, 20 November 1975, pp. 416-18.

Braun, Oscar. "Trade and Investment." In Dudley Seers and Leonard Joy, eds. *Development in a Divided World.* Harmondsworth, Middlesex: Penguin, 1971.

Brazer, H. E. "Some Fiscal Implications of Metropolitanism." In Benjamin Chinitz, ed. *City and Suburb.* Englewood Cliffs, N.J.: Prentice-Hall, 1964.

Brodsky, Harold. "Residential Land and Improvement Values in a Central City." *Land Economics* 46, no. 3 (August 1970): 229-47.

Brown, Lenore Egan. "Victorian Village." *Columbus Monthly* 1, no. 1 (June 1975): 20-27.

Brown, Lester. "Rich Countries and Poor in a Finite, Interdependent World." In Mancur Olson and Hans H. Landsberg, eds. *The No-Growth Society*, pp. 153-64. New York: Norton, 1973.

Campbell, Alan J. "An Analysis of Preferences for Environmental Preservation." Master's paper, The Ohio State University, 1974.

Carnoy, Martin, and Katz, Marlaine. "Explaining Differentials in Earnings Among Large Brazilian Cities." *Urban Studies* 8, no. 1 (February 1971): 21-38.

Carter, Charles F. *Wealth.* Harmondsworth, Middlesex: Penguin, 1971.

Caustin, Harold. "Aid." In Dudley Seers and Leonard Joy, eds. *De-*

velopment in a Divided World. Harmondsworth, Middlesex: Penguin, 1970.

Chinitz, Benjamin, ed. *City and Suburb.* Englewood Cliffs, N.J.: Prentice-Hall, 1964.

Christy, Francis, and Scott, Anthony. *The Common Wealth in Ocean Resources.* Washington, D.C.: Resources for the Future, 1965.

Chung, Ray. "Space-Time Diffusion of the Transition Model: The Twentieth-Century Patterns." In George J. Demko, Harold M. Rose, and George A. Schnell, eds. *Population Geography: A Reader,* pp. 220–39. New York: McGraw-Hill, 1970.

Clawson, Marion. "The Future of Nonmetropolitan America." *American Scholar* 42, no. 1 (winter 1972–73): 102–9.

———. "Economic and Social Conflicts in Land Use Planning." *Natural Resources Journal* 15 (July 1975): 473–89.

Clawson, Marion, and Hall, Peter. *Planning and Urban Growth.* Washington, D.C.: Resources for the Future, 1973.

Clayton, James L. "Defense Spending: Key to California's Growth." *Western Political Quarterly* 15 (1962): 280–93.

Clout, Hugh D. "Industrial Relocation in France." *Geography* 55, pt. 1 (January 1970): 48–63.

———. *Rural Geography.* Ch. 6. Oxford: Pergamon, 1972.

Coates, B. E.; Johnston, R. J.; and Knox, P. L. *Geography and Inequality.* New York: Oxford University Press, 1977.

Cockcroft, James D.; Frank, Andre Gunder; and Johnson, Dale L. *Dependence and Underdevelopment: Latin America's Political Economy.* New York: Anchor, 1972.

Cole, Lamont C. "Our Man-made Environmental Crisis." In Quentin H. Stanford, ed. *The World's Population,* pp. 159–66. Toronto: Oxford University Press, 1972.

Coleman, James S. "Equal Schools or Equal Students?" *Public Interest,* no. 4, summer 1966.

Coleman, James S., and Kelly, Sara D. "Education." In William Gorham and Nathan Glazer, eds. *The Urban Predicament.* Washington, D.C.: Urban Institute, 1976.

Coleman, James S., et al. *Equality of Educational Opportunity.* Washington, D.C.: Government Printing Office, 1966.

Committee on International Migration of Talent. *Modernization and the Migration of Talent.* New York: Education & World Affairs, 1970.

Conkling, Edward C., and Yeates, Maurice. *Man's Economic Environment.* New York: McGraw-Hill, 1976.

Coons, J. E.; Clune, W. H.; and Sugarman, S. D. *Private Wealth and Public Education.* Cambridge: Harvard University Press, 1970.

Cooper, Richard N. *The Economics of Interdependence.* New York: McGraw-Hill, 1968.

Cox, Kevin R. *Conflict, Power and Politics in the City: A Geographic View.* New York: McGraw-Hill, 1973.

Crowley, R. W. *The Effects of an Airport on Land Values.* Ministry of State for Urban Affairs Working Paper A.72.4. Ottawa, 1972.

Cuomo, Mario. *Forest Hills Diary: The Crisis of Low-Income Housing.* New York: Vintage, 1975.

Cutright, Phillips. "National Political Development: Measurement and Analysis." *American Sociological Review* 28, no. 2 (April 1963): 253–64.

Dales, J. H. "Land, Water and Ownership." In Robert Dorfman and Nancy S. Dorfman, eds. *Economics of the Environment.* New York: Norton, 1972.

Danielson, Michael N. "Differentiation, Segregation, and Political Fragmentation in the American Metropolis." In A. E. Keir Nash, ed. *Governance and Population: The Governmental Implications of Population Change,* pp. 143–76. Washington, D.C.: Government Printing Office, 1972.

———. *The Politics of Exclusion.* New York: Columbia University Press, 1976.

Davidoff, Linda; Davidoff, Paul; and Gold, Niel. "The Suburbs Have to Open Their Gates." *New York Times Magazine,* 7 November 1971.

Davis, Kingsley. "The Sociology of Demographic Behavior." In Robert Newton, Leonard Broom, and Leonard Cottrell, eds. *Sociology Today.* New York: Harper & Row, 1959.

deSouza, Anthony R., and Porter, Philip W. *The Underdevelopment and Modernization of the Third World.* Commission on College Geography Resource Paper no. 28. Washington, D.C., 1974.

Douglas, Jack D. "Going Broke the New York Way." *New Society,* 11 December 1975, pp. 593–96.

Douty, H. M. "Regional Wage Differentials: Forces and Counterforces." In C. McConnell, ed. *Perspectives on Wage Determination,* pp. 207–17.   New York: McGraw-Hill, 1970.

Downie, Leonard, Jr. *Mortgage on America.* New York: Praeger, 1974.

Downs, Anthony. "Residential Segregation by Income and Race—Its Nature, Its Relation to Schools and Ways to Ameliorate It." In *Hearings Before the Select Committee on Equal Educational Opportunity of the U.S. Senate, Ninety-first Congress, Second Session on Equal Educational Opportunity.* Pt. 5, *De Facto Segregation and Housing Discrimination,* pp. 2966–80. Washington, D.C.:

Government Printing Office, 1970.

———. *Opening Up the Suburbs.* New Haven: Yale University Press, 1973.

Drachman, Roy P. "Land Use Under Current Restraints." *Appraisal Journal* 42, no. 2 (April 1974).

Drewry, Gavin. "The Price of a Vote." *New Society,* 13 November 1975, pp. 367–68.

Dunning, John H. "The Future of the Multinational Enterprise." *Lloyds Bank Review,* no. 113, July 1974, pp. 15–32.

Dunning, John H., ed. *International Investment.* Harmondsworth, Middlesex: Penguin, 1972.

Easterlin, Richard A. "Does Money Buy Happiness?" *Public Interest,* no. 30, winter 1973, pp. 3–10.

Edel, Matthew. "Planning, Market or Warfare? —Recent Land Use Conflict in American Cities." In Matthew Edel and James Rothenberg, eds. *Readings in Urban Economics,* pp. 134–51. New York: Macmillan, 1972.

Eldridge, Hope T. "Population Policies." In Quentin H. Stanford, ed. *The World's Population,* pp. 117–27. New York: Oxford University Press, 1972.

Elgin, Duane, et al. *City Size and the Quality of Life.* Washington, D.C.: Government Printing Office, 1974.

Enthoven, Alain C., and Freeman, A. Myrick, eds. *Pollution, Resources and the Environment.* New York: Norton, 1973.

Epps, Richard W. "The Appeal of Black Capitalism." *Philadelphia Federal Reserve Bank Business Review,* May 1969, pp. 9–15.

Ezra, Derek. "Regional Policy in the European Community." *National Westminster Bank Quarterly Review,* August 1973, pp. 8–21.

Fainstein, Susan S., and Fainstein, Norman I. "The Federally Inspired Fiscal Crisis." *Society* 13, no. 4 (May/July 1976): 27–32.

Fellman, Gordon; Brandt, Barbara; and Rosenblatt, Roger. "Dagger in the Heart of a Town." *Trans-Action* 7, no. 11 (September 1970): 38–47.

Fellmeth, Robert C. *Politics of Land.* New York: Grossman, 1973.

Fitch, L. C. "Metropolitan Fiscal Problems." In Benjamin Chinitz, ed. *City and Suburb.* Englewood Cliffs, N.J.: Prentice-Hall, 1964.

Frank, Isiah. "The Role of Trade in Economic Development." *International Organization* 22 (1968): 44–71

Freeman, A. Myrick. "Income Distribution and Environmental Quality." In Alain C. Enthoven and A. Myrick Freeman, eds. *Pollution, Resources and the Environment,* pp. 100–106. New York: Norton, 1973.

Frieden, Bernard J. "Toward Equality of Urban Opportunity." In H. Wentworth Eldredge, ed. *Taming Megalopolis,* pp. 507–35. Garden City, N.Y.: Doubleday Anchor, 1967.

Gaffney, Mason. "Tax Reform to Release Land." In Marion Clawson, ed. *Modernizing Urban Land Policy,* pp. 115–29. Washington, D.C.: Resources for the Future, 1973.

Gans, Herbert J. *The Urban Villagers.* New York: Free Press of Glencoe, 1962.

——. "The Failure of Urban Renewal." *Commentary,* April 1965, pp. 29–37.

Gerard, Karen. "The Locally Inspired Fiscal Crisis." *Society* 13, no. 4 (May/June 1976): 33–35.

Glantz, Frederick B. "Migration and Economic Opportunity: The Case of the Poor." *New England Economic Review,* March/April 1973, pp. 14–19.

Glass, Ruth. "Anti-urbanism." In Murray Stewart, ed. *The City:*

Problems of Planning. Harmondsworth, Middlesex: Penguin, 1972.

Glazer, Nathan. "On Opening Up the Suburbs." *Public Interest,* no. 37, fall 1974, pp. 89–111.

Goblet, Y. M. *The Twilight of Treaties.* London: Bell, 1936.

Gold, Neil N. "The Mismatch of Jobs and Low-Income People in Metropolitan Areas and Its Implications for the Central City Poor." In Sara Mills Maizie, ed. *Population Distribution and Policy,* pp. 441–86. Washington, D.C.: Government Printing Office, 1972.

Green, Reginald H., and Seidman, Ann. *Unity or Poverty? The Economics of Panafricanism.* Baltimore: Penguin, 1968.

Greenberg, Edward S. *Serving the Few: Corporate Capitalism and the Bias of Government Policy.* New York: Wiley, 1974.

Greer, Edward. "Air Pollution and Corporate Power: Municipal Reform Limits on a Black City." *Politics and Society* 3 (1974): 483–510.

Gregory, Roy J. *The Price of Amenity.* London: MacMillan & Co., 1971.

Guthrie, James W., et al. "Educational Inequity, School Finance and a Plan for the '70s." In *Hearings Before the Select Committee on Equal Educational Opportunity of the U.S. Senate, Ninety-first Congress, Second Session on Equal Educational Opportunity.* Pt. 7, *Inequality of Economic Resources,* pp. 3451–500. Washington, D.C.: Government Printing Office, 1970.

——. *Schools and Inequality.* Cambridge, Mass.: MIT Press, 1971.

Hagman, Donald G. "Windfalls for Wipeouts." In C. Lowell Harriss, ed. *The Good Earth of America.* Englewood Cliffs, N.J.: Prentice-Hall, 1974.

Hall, Peter. "Roskill's Felicific Calculus." *New Society,* 19 February 1970, pp. 306–8.

———. "Hypermarkets." *New Society* 37, no. 721 (July 29, 1976): 236.

Halliday, Jon, and McCormack, Gavan. *Japanese Imperialism Today.* Harmondsworth, Middlesex: Penguin, 1973.

Hardin, Garrett. "The Tragedy of the Commons." *Science* 162 (December 13, 1968): 1243–48.

———. *Exploring New Ethics for Survival: Voyage of the Spaceship Beagle.* Baltimore: Penguin, 1973.

Harrison, Bennett. "The Intrametropolitan Distribution of Minority Economic Welfare." *Journal of Regional Science* 12, no. 1 (April 1972): 23–43.

Harrison, Paul. "The Life of Cities." *New Society,* 5 December 1974, pp. 599–604.

Harriss, C. Lowell, ed. *The Good Earth of America.* Englewood Cliffs, N.J.: Prentice-Hall, 1974.

Hartman, Chester W. "The Housing of Relocated Families." *Journal of the American Institute of Planning* 30, no. 4 (November 1964).

Harvey, David W. *Society, the City and the Space-Economy of Urbanism.* Association of American Geographers Commission on College Geography Resource Paper no. 18. Washington, D.C., 1972.

Hauser, Phillip M., and Duncan, Otis Dudley. *Study of Population.* Chicago: University of Chicago Press, 1959.

Hauser, Phillip M., and Kitagawa, Evelyn M. *Differential Mortality in the United States.* Cambridge: Harvard University Press, 1973.

Hawley, Amos. "Metropolitan Population and Municipal Government Expenditures in Central Cities." *Journal of Social Issues* 7, nos. 1, 2 (1951): 100–108.

Hayes, Edward C. *Power Structure and Urban Policy.* Ch. 5. New York: McGraw-Hill, 1972.

Healy, Robert G. "Controlling the Uses of Land." *Resources,* no. 50, October 1975, pp. 1–3.

Hearings Before the Select Committee on Equal Educational Opportunity of the U.S. Senate, Ninety-first Congress, Second Session on Equal Educational Opportunity. Washington, D.C.: Government Printing Office, 1970–71.

Heilbroner, Robert L. *The Worldly Philosophers.* New York: Simon & Schuster, 1967.

———. *An Inquiry into the Human Prospect.* New York: Norton, 1974.

Hensman, C. R. *Rich Against Poor.* Harmondsworth, Middlesex: Penguin, 1971.

Hillman, Mayer, and Henderson, Irwin. "Towards a Better Kind of Environmental Area." *New Society,* 12 July 1973, pp. 75–77.

Hines, Lawrence G. *Environmental Issues.* New York: Norton, 1973.

Hoch, Irving. "Income and City Size." *Urban Studies* 9, no. 3 (October 1972): 299–328.

Hoover, Edgar M. *The Location of Economic Activity.* New York: McGraw-Hill, 1948.

Ingram, James C. *International Economic Problems.* New York: Wiley, 1970.

International Joint Commission of Canada and the United States. *Pollution of Lake Erie, Lake Ontario and the International Section of the St. Lawrence River.* Washington, D.C.: Government Printing Office, 1970.

Johnston, Harry G. *Economic Policies Toward Less-Developed Countries.* Washington, D.C.: Brookings Institution, 1967.

Kain, John F., and Meyer, John R. "Transportation and Poverty." *Public Interest,* no. 18, winter 1970, pp. 75–87.

Kain, John F., and Persky, Joseph J. "The North's Stake in Southern Rural Poverty." In the President's National Commission on Rural Poverty. *Rural Poverty in the United States,* pp. 288–308. Washington, D.C.: Government Printing Office, 1968.

——. "Alternatives to the Gilded Ghetto." *Public Interest,* no. 14, winter 1969, pp. 74–87.

Kerner, Otto, et al. *Report of the National Advisory Commission on Civil Disorders.* Washington, D.C.: Government Printing Office, 1968.

Kersten, Earl W., Jr., and Ross, D. Reid. "Clayton: A New Metropolitan Focus in the St. Louis Area." *Annals of the Association of American Geographers* 58, no. 4 (1968): 637–49.

Kindleberger, Charles P. *Power and Money.* New York: Basic Books, 1970.

Knight, C. Gregory, and Wilcox, R. Paul. *Triumph or Triage: The World Food Problem in Geographic Perspective.* Association of American Geographers Resource Paper no. 75-3. Washington, D.C., 1976.

Kramer, Gerald H. "Short-Term Fluctuations in U.S. Voting Behavior, 1869-1964." *American Political Science Review* 65, no. 1 (March 1971): 131–43.

Krutilla, John V. "Some Environmental Effects of Economic Development." In Alain C. Enthoven and A. Myrick Freeman, eds. *Pollution, Resources and the Environment,* pp. 253–62. New York: Norton, 1973.

Kuttner, Bob. "Ethnic Renewal." *New York Times Magazine,* 9 May 1976, p. 18.

Kyle, Keith. "The Southern Problem in the Sudan." *World Today,* December 1966, pp. 512–20.

Lamm, Richard D. "Urban Growing Pains: Is Bigger Also Better?" *New Republic* 164, no. 23 (June 5, 1971): 17–19.

Landsberg, Hans H. "Assessing the Materials Threat." *Resources,* no. 47, September 1974, pp. 1–3.

Lave, Lester B., and Seskin, Eugene P. "Air Pollution and Human Health." *Science* 169 (August 21, 1970): 723–33.

——. "Air Pollution and Human Health. *Annual Report, 1973,* pp. 15–26. Washington, D.C.: Resources for the Future, 1973.

Lenin, V. I. *Imperialism: The Highest Stage of Capitalism.* New York: International, 1939.

Levin, Henry M. "The Coleman Report—What Difference Do Schools Make?" *Saturday Review,* 20 January 1968.

Lichfield, Nathaniel. "Cost-Benefit Analysis in Plan Evaluation." *Town Planning Review* 35 (1964): 160–69.

Lieberson, Stanley. *Ethnic Patterns in American Cities.* New York: Free Press of Glencoe, 1963.

Lindsay, Sally. "Showdown on Delaware Bay." *Saturday Review,* 18 March 1972, pp. 34–39.

Lineberry, Robert L. "Suburbia and the Metropolitan Turf." *Annals of the American Academy of Political and Social Science* 422 (November 1975): 1–9.

Liston, Robert A. *Downtown.* New York: Dell, 1968.

Litvak, I. A., and Maule, C. J. "Conflict Resolution and Extraterritoriality." *Journal of Conflict Resolution* 13, no. 3 (September 1969): 305–19.

Lloyd, Peter E., and Dicken, Peter. *Location in Space: A Theoretical Approach to Economic Geography.* New York: Harper & Row, 1972.

Logan, John R. "Industrialization and the Stratification of Cities in Suburban Regions." *American Journal of Sociology* 82, no. 2 (1976): 333–48.

Long, David C. "The Property Tax and the Courts: School Finance After Rodriguez." In George E. Peterson, ed. *Property Tax Reform.* Washington, D.C.: Urban Institute, 1973.

Lopata, Helena Znaniecki. "The Function of Voluntary Associations in an Ethnic Community: 'Polonia.' " In Ernest Burgess and

Donald J. Bogue, eds. *Urban Sociology.* Chicago: University of Chicago Press, 1967.

Lorimer, James. *The Real World of City Politics.* Toronto: Lewis & Samuel, 1970.

————. *A Citizen's Guide to City Politics.* Toronto: Lewis & Samuel, 1972.

Lowe, P. D. "Amenity and Equity: A Review of Local Environmental Pressure Groups in Britain." *Environment and Planning A* 9 (1977): 35–58.

Lowi, T. J. "Apartheid U.S.A." *Trans-Action* 7, no. 4 (February 1970): 32–39.

Luard, D. Evan. *The International Regulation of Frontier Disputes.* New York: Praeger, 1970.

Lukas, J. Anthony. "The Developers Are Coming." *Saturday Review* 55, no. 43 (October 21, 1972): 58–64.

McAdams, John. "Can Open Enrollment Work?" *Public Interest,* no. 37, fall 1974, pp. 69–88.

McCrone, Gavin. *Regional Policy in Britain.* London: Allen & Unwin, 1969.

Maizie, Sara Mills, and Rawlings, Steve. "Public Attitudes Towards Population Issues." In Sara Mills Maizie, ed. *Population Distribution and Policy,* pp. 599–630. Washington, D.C.: Government Printing Office, 1973.

Manners, Gerald. "Regional Protection: A Factor in Economic Geography." *Economic Geography* 38 (1962): 122–29.

Martin, Roscoe. *Decisions in Syracuse.* New York: Greenwood, 1968.

Mayer, Harold. "Politics and Land Use: The Indiana Shoreline of Lake Michigan." *Annals of the Association of American Geographers* 54 (December 1964): 508–23.

Meadows, Donella H.; Meadows, Dennis; et al. *The Limits to Growth.* New York: Universe, 1972.

Meltsner, Arnold J. "Political Feasibility and Policy Analysis." *Public Administration Review* 32, no. 6 (November/December 1972): 859–67.

Meyer, John, and Kain, John F. "Interrelationships of Transportation and Poverty." *Public Interest,* no. 18, winter 1970.

Michelson, Stephen. "The Political Economy of Public School Inequalities." In Martin Carnoy, ed. *The Political Economy of Education: New Approaches to Old Problems.* New York: McKay, 1972.

Miller, S. M., et al. "Creaming the Poor." *Trans-Action* 7, no. 8 (June 1970): 38–45.

Mintz, Morton, and Cohen, Jerry S. *America, Inc.* New York: Dell, 1971.

Mishan, E. J. *The Costs of Economic Growth.* Harmondsworth, Middlesex: Penguin, 1969.

Molotch, Harvey. "Toward a More 'Human' Human Ecology: An Urban Research Strategy." *Land Economics* 43, no. 3 (1967): 336–41.

————. *Managed Integration: Dilemmas of Doing Good in the City.* Berkeley and Los Angeles: University of California Press, 1972.

————. "The City as a Growth Machine: Toward a Political Economy of Place." *American Journal of Sociology* 82, no. 2 (1976): 309–32.

Morrison, Peter A. "Population Movements: Where the Public Interest and Private Interests Conflict." In the *Commission on Population Growth and the American Future.* Vol. 5, *Population Distribution and Policy,* pp. 335–52. Washington, D.C.: Government Printing Office, 1973.

Mowbray, A. Q. *Road to Ruin.* New York: Lippincott, 1969.

Muller, Peter O. *The Outer City: Geographical Consequences of the Urbanization of the Suburbs.* Association of American Geographers

Resource Paper 75-2. Washington, D.C., 1976.

Muller, Thomas. "Growing and Declining Urban Areas: A Fiscal Comparison." Washington, D.C.: Urban Institute, 1975.

Mushkin, Selma J., and Adams, Robert F. "Emerging Patterns of Federalism." *National Tax Journal* 19, no. 3 (September 1966): 225–47.

Naparstek, Arthur J., and Cincotta, Gale. *Urban Disinvestment: New Implications for Community Organization, Research and Public Policy.* Washington, D.C.: National Center for Urban Ethnic Affairs and the National Training and Information Center, 1976.

Neenan, William B. *Political Economy of Urban Areas.* Chicago: Markham, 1972.

Netzer, Dick. *Economics and Urban Problems.* New York: Basic Books, 1970.

Nye, Joseph S. "East African Economic Integration." *Journal of Modern African Studies* 1, no. 4 (December 1963).

Olson, Mancur, Jr. "The Optimal Allocation of Jurisdictional Responsibility: The Principle of 'Fiscal Equivalence.' " In Robert H. Haveman, ed. *The Analysis and Evaluation of Public Expenditures: The PPB System,* pp. 321–31. 3 vols. Washington, D.C.: Government Printing Office, 1969.

O'Sullivan, P. M. "Accessibility and the Spatial Structure of the Irish Economy." *Regional Studies* 2 (1968): 195–206.

Owen, John D. "The Distribution of Educational Resources in Large American Cities." *Journal of Human Resources* 7, no. 1 (1972): 26–38.

Page, Talbot; Harris, Robert H.; and Epstein, Samuel S. "Drinking Water and Cancer Mortality in Louisiana." *Science* 193, no. 4247 (July 1976): 55–57.

Palomba, Neil, and Palomba, Catherine. "Right-to-Work Laws: A Suggested Economic Rationale." *Journal of Law and Economics* 14, no. 2 (October 1971): 475–83.

Parsons, K. C. "The Role of Universities in City Renewal." In H. Wentworth Eldredge, ed. *Taming Megalopolis.* Vol. 2, pp. 979–1001. Garden City, N.Y.: Doubleday Anchor, 1967.

Payer, Cheryl. *The Debt Trap.* Harmondsworth, Middlesex: Penguin, 1974.

Peet, Richard C. "The Spatial Expansion of Commercial Agriculture in the Nineteenth Century: A Von Thunen Explanation." *Economic Geography* 45 (October 1969): 283–301.

Peterson, George E., and Solomon, Arthur P. "Property Taxes and Populist Reform." *Public Interest,* no. 30, winter 1973, pp. 60–75.

Peterson, George E., et al. *Property Taxes, Housing and the Cities.* Lexington, Mass.: Lexington Books, 1973.

Peterson, George E., ed. *Property Tax Reform.* Washington, D.C.: Urban Institute, 1973.

Peterson, John M., and Stewart, Charles T., Jr. *Employment Effects of Minimum Wage Rates.* Washington, D.C.: American Enterprise Institute for Public Policy Research, 1969.

Polanyi, Karl. *The Great Transformation.* Boston: Beacon, 1957.

Quante, Wolfgang. "Flight of Corporate Headquarters." *Society* 13, no. 4 (May/June 1976): 36–41.

Rainwater, Lee. *Behind Ghetto Walls.* Harmondsworth, Middlesex: Penguin, 1971.

Ratner, G. "Inter-neighborhood Denials of Equal Protection in the Provision of Municipal Services." *Harvard Civil Rights-Civil Liberties Law Review,* fall 1968, pp. 1–63.

Ray, D. Michael, and Brewis, Thomas N. "The Geography of Income and Its Correlates." *Canadian Geographer* 20, no. 1 (spring 1976): 41-71.

Reilly, William K., ed. *The Use of Land.* New York: Crowell, 1973.

Reiner, Thomas. "Organizing Regional Investment Criteria." *Papers and Proceedings of the Regional Science Association* 11 (1963): 75-84.

Richardson, Harry W. "Optimality in City Size, Systems of Cities and Urban Policy: A Sceptic's View." *Urban Studies* 9, no. 1 (February 1972): 29-48.

Ridgeway, James. *The Politics of Ecology.* New York: Dutton, 1971.

Robock, Stefan. "The Case for Home Country Controls over Multinational Firms." *Columbia Journal of World Business,* summer 1974, pp. 75-79.

Robson, Brian T. *Urban Analysis.* Cambridge: At the University Press, 1969.

Robson, W. A. *Local Government in Crisis.* London: Allen & Unwin, 1966.

Rodgers, Allan. "Some Aspects of Industrial Diversification in the United States." *Economic Geography* 33, no. 1 (January 1957): 16-30.

Roe, Charles. "Land Use: The Second Battle of Gettysburg." *Appraisal Journal* 42, no. 2 (January 1974): 90-102.

Rose, Jerome G. "Recent Decisions on Population Growth Control: The Belle Terre, Petaluma and Madison Township Cases." In James W. Hughes, ed. *New Dimensions of Urban Planning: Growth Controls.* New Brunswick, N.J.: Rutgers University Center for Urban Policy Research, 1974.

Russell, Clifford S., and Landsberg, Hans H. "International Environmental Problems—A Taxonomy." *Science* 172 (June 25, 1971): 1307-14.

Sagalyn, Lynne B., and Sternlieb, George. *Zoning and Housing Costs.* New Brunswick, N.J.: Rutgers University Center for Urban Policy Research, 1972.

Salisbury, R. H. "Urban Politics: The New Convergence of Power." *Journal of Politics* 26 (1964): 775-97.

Schaeffer, K. H., and Sclar, Elliot. *Access for All.* Harmondsworth, Middlesex: Penguin, 1975.

Schellenberg, James A. "County Seat Wars: A Preliminary Analysis." *Journal of Conflict Resolution* 14, no. 3 (1970): 345-52.

Schreiber, Jean-Jacques Servan. *The American Challenge.* Pts. 1-4. Harmondsworth, Middlesex: Penguin, 1969.

Schumacher, E. F. *Small Is Beautiful.* New York: Perennial, 1975.

Schwartz, Walter. "Tribalism and Politics in Nigeria." *World Today,* November 1966, pp. 460-67.

Scitovsky, Tibor. "Inequality: Open and Hidden, Measured and Immeasurable." *Annals of the American Academy of Political and Social Science* 409 (September 1973): 113-19.

Searle, Graham. "Copper in Snowdonia National Park." In Peter J. Smith, ed. *The Politics of Physical Resources.* Harmondsworth, Middlesex: Penguin, 1975.

"The Second War Between the States." *Business Week,* 17 May 1976, pp. 92-95.

Seers, Dudley. "Rich Countries and Poor." In Dudley Seers and Leonard Joy, eds. *Development in a Divided World.* Harmondsworth, Middlesex: Penguin, 1971.

Seers, Dudley, and Joy, Leonard. *Development in a Divided World.* Harmondsworth, Middlesex: Penguin, 1971.

Self, Peter. "Nonsense on Stilts: The Futility of Roskill." *New Society,* 2 July 1970, pp. 8-11.

Sexton, Patricia C. *Education and Income: The Inequality of Oppor-*

Smith, David M. *The Geography of Social Well-Being in the United States.* New York: McGraw-Hill, 1973.

Smith, Peter J., ed. *The Politics of Physical Resources.* Harmondsworth, Middlesex: Penguin, 1975.

Smolensky, Eugene. "Poverty, Propinquity and Policy." *Annals of the American Academy of Political and Social Science* 409 (September 1973): 120-24.

Sopher, David E. "Place and Location: The Spatial Patterning of Culture." *Social Science Quarterly* 53, no. 2 (September 1972): 321-37.

Stedman-Jones, Gareth. "The History of U.S. Imperialism." In Robin Blackburn, ed. *Ideology in Social Science.* London: Fontana, 1972.

Stewart, John Q. "Potential of Population and Its Relation to Marketing." In R. Cox and W. Alderson, eds. *Theory in Marketing,* pp. 19-39. Chicago: Irwin, 1950.

Stone, Leroy. *Migration in Canada: Regional Aspects.* Ottawa: Dominion Bureau of Statistics, 1969.

Streeten, Paul. "How Poor Are the Poor Countries?" In Dudley Seers and Leonard Joy, eds. *Development in a Divided World.* Harmondsworth, Middlesex: Penguin, 1971.

Swann, Dennis. *The Economics of the Common Market.* Harmondsworth, Middlesex: Penguin, 1970.

Syron, Richard F. "The Hard Economics of Ghetto Fire Insurance." *New England Economic Review,* March/April 1972, pp. 2-11.

tunity in Our Public Schools. New York: Viking, 1961.

Sibley, David. "The Location and Layout of Gypsy Caravan Sites: Notions of Deviancy in Official Policy." *Antipode* 8, no. 1 (March 1976): 83-87.

Simon, Donald E. "A Prospect for Parks." *Public Interest,* no. 44, summer 1976, pp. 27-39.

Tatham, George. "Canada: Economic Aspects." In W. Gordon East and A. E. Moodie, eds. *The Changing World.* London: Harrap, 1956.

Thane, Pat. "The History of Social Welfare." *New Society* 29, no. 621 (August 29, 1974): 540-42.

Thomas, Brinley. "The International Circulation of Human Capital." *Minerva* 5, no. 4 (1967): 479-504.

Thompson, Wilbur R. "The National System of Cities as an Object of Public Policy." *Urban Studies* 9, no. 1 (February 1972): 99-116.

Time Magazine, 6 April 1970, p. 48.

Titmuss, Richard. *Commitment to Welfare.* New York: Pantheon, 1968.

Turvey, Ralph. "Side Effects of Resource Use." In Henry Jarrett, ed. *Environmental Quality in a Growing Economy,* pp. 47-60. Washington, D.C.: Resources for the Future, 1966.

Ullman, Edward L. "The Nature of Cities Reconsidered." *Papers and Proceedings of the Regional Science Association* 9 (1962): 7-23.

U. S. Department of Housing and Urban Development. *Neighborhood Preservation.* Washington, D.C.: Government Printing Office, 1975.

———. *The Dynamics of Neighborhood Change.* Washington, D.C.: Government Printing Office, 1976.

Vernon, Raymond. "Economic Sovereignty at Bay." *Foreign Affairs,* October 1968, pp. 110-22.

———. "Problems and Policies Regarding Multinational Enterprises." In *United States Economic Policy in an Interdependent World: Papers Submitted to the Commission on International Trade and Investment Policy.* Vol. 1, pp. 983-1006. Washington, D.C.: Government Printing Office, 1971.

Wagner, Philip L. *Environment and Peoples*. Englewood Cliffs, N.J.: Prentice-Hall, 1972.

Walter, Ingo. "Environmental Control and Patterns of International Trade and Investment: An Emerging Policy Issue." *Banca Nationale del Lavoro Quarterly Review*, no. 100, March 1972, pp. 82–106.

Weinstein, Bernard L. "What New York Can Learn from Texas." *Society* 13, no. 4 (May/June 1976): 48–50.

Weinstein, Jerome I. "Negative Property Values: The Problem of Abandoned Buildings." *Appraisal Journal* 41, no. 3 (July 1973): 395–403.

Weisbrod, Burton. "Geographic Spillover Effects and the Allocation of Resources to Education." In Julius Margolis, ed. *The Public Economy of Urban Communities*, pp. 192–206. Washington, D.C.: Resources for the Future, 1965.

Weiss, Steven J., and Driscoll, Deborah. "Comparative School Finance Data, New England States vs. California." In Federal Reserve Bank of Boston. *Financing Public Schools*. Boston: Federal Reserve Bank of Boston, 1972.

Wertheimer, Richard F. *The Monetary Rewards of Migration Within the U.S.* Washington, D.C.: Urban Institute, 1970.

Whyte, William H. *The Last Landscape*. Garden City, N.Y.: Doubleday Anchor, 1970.

Williams, Oliver P., et al. *Suburban Differences and Metropolitan Policies*. Philadelphia: University of Pennsylvania Press, 1965.

Wilson, Alan B. "Residential Segregation of Social Classes and the Aspirations of High School Boys." *American Sociological Review* 24 (1959): 836–45.

Wingo, Lowdon. "The Quality of Life: Toward a Microeconomic Definition." *Urban Studies* 10, no. 1 (February 1973): 3–18.

Winham, Gilbert. "Attitudes on Pollution and Growth in Hamilton, or 'There's an Awful Lot of Talk These Days About Ecology.' " *Canadian Journal of Political Science* 5, no. 3 (September 1972): 389–401.

Winnick, Louis. "Place Prosperity vs. People Prosperity: Welfare Considerations in the Geographic Redistribution of Economic Activity." In *Essays in Urban Land Economics*. University of California Real Estate Research Program. Los Angeles, 1966.

Wiskemann, Elizabeth. *Germany's Eastern Neighbors*. London: Oxford University Press, 1956.

Wolf, Eleanor P., and Lebeaux, Charles N. *Change and Renewal in an Urban Community*. New York: Praeger, 1969.

Woodruff, A. M. "Recycling Urban Land." In C. L. Harriss, ed. *The Good Earth of America*. Englewood Cliffs, N.J.: Prentice-Hall, 1974.

Yeates, Maurice H. "Some Factors Affecting the Spatial Distribution of Chicago Land Values, 1910–1960." *Economic Geography* 41, no. 1 (1965): 57–70.

Young, George. *Tourism: Blessing or Blight?* Harmondsworth, Middlesex: Penguin, 1973.

Zwick, David, with Benstock, Marcy. *Water Wasteland*. New York: Bantam, 1972.

INDEX

PSYCHOLOGY

for

LAW ENFORCEMENT OFFICERS

A Monograph in

THE POLICE SCIENCE SERIES

Edited by

V. A. LEONARD

Department, Police Science and Administration
The State College of Washington
Pullman, Washington

Ninth Printing

PSYCHOLOGY
FOR
LAW ENFORCEMENT OFFICERS

By

GEORGE J. DUDYCHA

Professor of Psychology
Wittenberg University
Springfield, Ohio

With Contributions by

F. K. BERRIEN

DON W. DYSINGER

PETER JAN HAMPTON

A. R. LAUER

ALFRED R. LINDESMITH

HAROLD LINDNER

DONALD B. LINDSLEY

NORMAN C. MEIER

WILSON L. NEWMAN

Police Science Series

CHARLES C THOMAS · PUBLISHER
Springfield · Illinois · U.S.A.

Published and Distributed Throughout the World by

CHARLES C THOMAS • PUBLISHER

Bannerstone House

301-327 East Lawrence Avenue, Springfield, Illinois, U.S.A.

© *1955, by* CHARLES C THOMAS • PUBLISHER

ISBN 0-398-0482-X

Library of Congress Catalog Card Number: 55-6111

First Printing, 1955
Second Printing, 1960
Third Printing, 1966
Fourth Printing, 1967
Fifth Printing, 1970
Sixth Printing, 1971
Seventh Printing, 1973
Eighth Printing, 1973
Ninth Printing, 1976

With THOMAS BOOKS *careful attention is given to all details of manufacturing and design. It is the Publisher's desire to present books that are satisfactory as to their physical qualities and artistic possibilities and appropriate for their particular use.* THOMAS BOOKS *will be true to those laws of quality that assure a good name and good will.*

Printed in the United States of America

R-1

CONTRIBUTORS

F. Kenneth Berrien, Ph.D.
Professor of Psychology
Rutgers University

George J. Dudycha, Ph.D.
Professor of Psychology
Wittenberg University

Don W. Dysinger, Ph.D.
Professor of Psychology
University of Nebraska

Peter Jan Hampton, Ph.D.
Associate Professor of Psychology
University of Akron

Alvah R. Lauer, Ph.D.
Professor of Psychology
Director, Driving Research Laboratory
Industrial Science Research Institute
Iowa University of Science and Technology

Alfred R. Lindesmith, Ph.D.
Professor of Sociology
Indiana University

Harold Lindner, Ph.D.
Clinical Psychologist
Mount Vernon Junior College

Donald B. Lindsley, Ph.D., D.Sc.
Professor of Psychology
University of California

Norman C. Meier, Ph.D.
Professor of Psychology
Director, Bureau of Audience Research
State University of Iowa

Wilson L. Newman, M.A.
Formerly Supervising Psychologist
Illinois Department of Public Safety

PREFACE

THERE was a time when psychology was largely speculative, theoretical and academic. In the last half century, however, interest has shifted more and more in the direction of applied psychology and the problems of daily life. This trend has been so marked, in fact, that at the present time more than half of the members of the American Psychological Association are employed in such ways that they are quite properly called *applied psychologists*.

This marked interest in the application of psychological facts, principles and procedures to the day-to-day problems of life has led to the publication of many volumes in such areas as: education, nursing, personnel work, advertising, salesmanship, industrial relations and numerous others. Singularly enough psychologists have devoted comparatively little attention to the application of psychology in the area of law enforcement. This unfortunately is true even though a major part of a law enforcement officer's work is directly concerned with people and hence is fundamentally psychological in nature. In spite of the fact that psychologists' interest in law enforcement work is not as great as some of us would like, psychology does have much to offer law enforcement officers in that it gives them insight into the nature and peculiarities of human behavior.

It is the purpose of this volume to present some of the well-established psychological facts and principles that are of particular interest and value to law enforcement officers, with the hope that law enforcement officers will thereby have a better appreciation of human nature, and as a result be more effective in dealing with people and in the execution of their duties.

The writer is indebted to the several authors, editors and publishers who so generously granted permission to use previously published material and illustrations, and to Mr. David Burris and Prof. Frank White for their kindness in preparing several additional illustrations. I am especially indebted to the nine contributors to this volume without whose contributions it would not have become a reality, and to Prof. Arthur E. Wood, of the University of Michigan, for his critical reading of Chapter 10 and helpful suggestions given.

Springfield, Ohio   GEORGE J. DUDYCHA

CONTENTS

ix

PSYCHOLOGY

for

LAW ENFORCEMENT OFFICERS

Chapter 1

WHAT IS PSYCHOLOGY?

By

GEORGE J. DUDYCHA

WHAT PSYCHOLOGY MEANS TO JOHN DOE

PSYCHOLOGY is very often a magic word to John Doe and his friends. Naturally it is not quite like hocus-pocus or abracadabra, for that is childhood magic. Psychology, for John Doe, is something more than that. Of course he does not call it "sophisticated magic" nor "intellectual magic," in fact he does not dare call it magic at all, lest his friends think him primitive. Nevertheless many a John Doe thinks of psychology as a mysterious way, if not a magical way, in which things can get done. All one needs to do, says John Doe, to win friends, sell goods, make children good, keep adults in the straight-and-narrow path, and prevent motorists who signal right from turning left, is to *use psychology*.

Psychology means yet other things to John Doe. He thinks of it as something that gives one complete knowledge of the "mind," or as something that gives one x-ray eyes to see another's thoughts, desires and inner-most secrets. At other times he regards psychology as a power exerted by one person over another as in hypnosis. Moreover psychology lends him a certain sophistication when he speaks of "the psychological moment" or of "the psychology" of some event.

Common Sense and Psychology

There are those friends of John Doe who tell us that psychology is really nothing more than common sense. This is not entirely true, if we mean by common sense those things that many people believe. The writer has learned that one-third of the stu-

3

dents entering college believe that the shape and prominences of the head indicate one's character, and that one can estimate very accurately an individual's intelligence by looking at his face. Furthermore, one student in four thinks that an expectant mother can influence the character of her unborn child by thinking. Every fifth student thinks that men are more intelligent than women, and that the children of first cousins are always feeble-minded. Although these are commonly held notions, all are false from the point of view of science. Commonly held notions, or that which frequently passes for *common sense*, are not necessarily true. Truth does not depend upon majority judgment. Nor is psychology a collection of old-wives' tales that are commonly believed.

How Common Sense Differs from Psychology

There are several important differences between what generally passes for common sense and what is scientific psychology. These can be stated briefly as follows:

Common sense is based on uncritical observations. Because some crooks are shifty-eyed it does not follow that anyone who avoids another's gaze is dishonest. More research on the problem might reveal that embarrassment, rather than dishonesty, causes the lack of eye steadiness. Thus this judgment is based on inadequate observation. In contrast to this procedure, psychology examines all the phases of a problem before a conclusion is drawn.

Common sense jumps to conclusions. A person who refuses to talk must be guilty. This idea is commonly held. And certainly at times it may be true, but to jump to the conclusion that it is always true, without considering the other factors that may lead to blocking, indicates a lack of scientific restraint. Psychology uses the scientific method and that means that one must suspend judgment until the facts fairly speak for themselves.

Common sense acts on prejudice. The notions that men prefer blondes, or that red-haired women become angry easily, are readily accepted by men who have had pleasant experiences with blondes and frustrating ones with red-heads. It is abundantly evident that one's emotions often have a way of coloring one's judgments so that the truth is obscured. Such biases, however, can not be tolerated if one hopes to be scientific.

Common sense lacks organization. Common sense most usually consists of isolated statements that attempt to stand or fall on their own authority, rather than on the way in which they fit into the larger picture or scheme of things.

Common sense is regarded as that which is reasonable. It is quite likely that, in the main, you are in agreement with the above points, with this reservation. Common sense may mean to you that which is reasonable. And this is an important point. But to whom is that which you are considering reasonable? Is it just reasonable to you? Is it just reasonable to someone? Or is it reasonable to many people who have examined the idea with great care and from many points of view? What may appear reasonable to one person does not to another. Scientific psychology always tries to find that which is reasonable through the experience of many people.

THE MEANING OF SCIENTIFIC PSYCHOLOGY

Ways in Which Psychology Is Defined

In recent years psychology has been defined in several ways. Sometimes it is regarded as the study of human nature, at other times as the science of the nature and development of living organisms, or as the science of mind and of consciousness. Some writers merely define it as the study of the activities of individuals; others think of it as the science of experience and behavior.

These and other similar statements of definition notwithstanding, there is considerable agreement among psychologists as to what modern psychology is and does. The one word that summarizes and gives unity to these various definitions is the word *behavior*. Briefly, psychology can be defined as *the science of the behavior of living organisms*.

What Is Behavior?

By the word *behavior* psychologists mean simply *any activity* of an organism. Some of these activities are such as involve the whole organism. Hence psychologists are interested in the co-

ordinated responses of the airplane pilot, the truck driver, or of
the skilled mechanic operating a complex machine. Some of these
activities involve only parts of the body. Hence psychologists
measure the speed with which a motorist can depress a brake
pedal after perceiving danger, the time it takes a dark-adapted
eye to adjust to a bright light, or the strength of a man's grip.

Some behavior is social, as that of strikers on a picket line;
other behavior is essentially non-social, as learning to assemble
the parts of a gun in the dark. Some behavior is normal, as that
of the motorist who abides by traffic signals at a busy intersection;
other behavior is abnormal, as that of the frustrated woman who
calls the police nightly because of the prowler under her bed.

The Purpose of Psychology

Psychology seeks to accomplish several things. On the one
hand it aims to be theoretical, that is to discover the general principles of behavior. It seeks to learn what is generally true of people;
it seeks to find the basic ideas in terms of which the particular
things that people do from day to day can be understood. Psychology, however, is not concerned with the theoretical alone.
It seeks to be practical as well. Psychologists are constantly finding ways in which their theoretical knowledge can be put to use
in the solution of day-to-day problems. Aptitude and achievement tests are used to discover the assets and shortcomings of
juvenile delinquents so that they can be trained in that which is
useful. Psychological tests are also used by transportation companies to discover accident-prone drivers. Psychology is applied
to lie detection, to interviewing, to the treatment of offenders,
to parole, as well as to many other areas having less to do with
law enforcement work.

In general, we can say that the purpose of psychology is to
understand people, to predict their behavior from day to day,
and to effect a measure of control for their own and the public
good.

Psychology as a Method

Objectivity is the key word. Objective observation, and objective experimentation are the key methods. Objective observation and experimentation are unbiased, rigorously controlled, repeatable procedures. Such objectivity is always difficult to achieve and hence sometimes it is achieved imperfectly. Psychological tests of various types, some of which will be mentioned later, are attempts to get at psychological problems in an objective and controlled manner. The recording of physiological responses, such as are used in lie detection, is an attempt to get at dishonest behavior objectively. So also is the attempt to trace the salient or outstanding events in a person's past life, known as the case history method, a method that helps us understand why some people are arrested so frequently and for the same offense. Besides these there are still other objective psychological methods some of which will be referred to in the succeeding chapters of this book.

The Value of Psychology

There are many values derived from knowing psychology that can be listed, but three need to be stressed.

Understanding others. "I just can't understand him." This comment is frequently heard. It shows that there is a desire to understand others, but that insight into the perplexing problems that people present is lacking. Psychology does help in this regard in that it does give some insight into what makes other people "tick." It helps one to understand other folks' problems, emotions, conflicts, hopes, aspirations, assets and limitations.

Understanding one's self. This is by far the more difficult thing to achieve, yet it is essential if we are to understand others who are like or different from us. "Know thyself" is an old motto — a goal that too few people achieve to any great measure.

Better human relations. This is the keystone of the other two. What is the value of knowing others better and of understanding ourselves more completely, unless this knowledge brings us closer together in more harmonious living? Certainly more insight into interpersonal relations will help us prevent some of the people we rub elbows with from committing the offienses against society that they might otherwise commit, and will equip us to aid those who have already committed such offenses to become useful citizens again.

Psychology and Law Enforcement

Many applications of psychology are made to teaching, business, industry, advertising, personnel relations and other areas of our work-a-day world. Psychology is also applied to nursing, to propaganda analysis and to public opinion polling. Unfortunately its application to police work, to court procedures, to the treatment of offenders and to other phases of law enforcement work is more limited. Nevertheless, significant advances are in progress and psychologists are becoming more and more interested in law enforcement problems.

In the following chapters we shall present some of the applications of psychology to such things as the measurement and selection of police officers, the psychological methods of obtaining information, lie detection, and psychology in the courtroom. Space will also be given to the psychology of dealing with and controlling people, the characteristics of abnormal people commonly encountered by law enforcement officers, and to the service that psychology offers offenders in the way of adjustment and rehabilitation. It is the purpose of this book to present that which modern psychology knows about law enforcement problems.

INDIVIDUAL DIFFERENCES

When arrests are made, people react very differently. Some are calm, collected and cooperative; others are disturbed, violent, profane or just plain fighting mad. Some are sad and full of self-reproach whereas others are hilarious and exhilarated. One finds them talkative or mute, menacing or subdued, rational or irrational. One thing is certain, no two of them behave just alike.

People Differ One from Another

That no two people are just alike is an obvious fact. Each differs from the others in not one but in many ways. Even when the differences are not too readily apparent, as in the case of identical twins, closer scrutiny invariably reveals differences. Either the one twin talks more than the other, is more aggressive in social situations, has a mole that the other lacks, or differs in other ways.

Of the many illustrations of individual differences in behavior from which one can select, one that is familiar to all is that of motorists' responses to boulevard stop signs. Although the law requires each motorist to come to a complete stop before entering a through street, there are those drivers who do not conform to the full intention of the law. True, many motorists do come to a full stop, but there are those who merely slow the car down so that it is scarcely moving and then drive on. Then there are those who slow down as they approach the intersection but continue on their way at a speed of six or eight miles per hour without pretending to stop. There are even a few people who ignore the traffic sign completely and drive through without so much as slackening their speed. It is even conceivable that some people are so callous to the welfare of others that they speed by at an accelerated rate. The extent to which motorists actually differ in this regard is pictured in Figure 1.

72%   24%   3%   1%
Full Stop   Nearly Stop Reduce Speed Same Speed

Fig. 1. The responses of motorists to a boulevard stop sign.

Men Differ from Women

That men and women differ organically and functionally is very evident. All of the differences between the sexes, however, are not as evident as the physical ones. There are many less apparent differences that often escape notice, such as the dissimilarity of fingerprint patterns found in men and in women, that are illustrated in Figure 2. The "arch" design appears more commonly in women; the "whorl" type appears more frequently in men.

The differences of a behavioral sort between men and women are, for the most part, quantitative rather than qualitative. They are differences in amount rather than in kind. Both men and women have strength of grip, but men, on the whole, excel women in this regard. Likewise, both men and women can write, but women tend to excel men in the neatness and legibility of their penmanship.

A few of the many differences between men and women that are of interest are presented in tabular form below:

SOME COMPARISONS BETWEEN MEN AND WOMEN

MEN	WOMEN
General information more extensive	Greater command of language
Greater ability to use numbers	Learn to talk earlier
Excel in arithmetic reasoning	Use longer sentences
Swifter runners	Greater ability to memorize
Faster swimmers	Take suggestions more easily
Greater group variability with regard to most things	Pulse rate faster
More impatient as motorists	As motorists, poorer in judging distance
Most accident prone at age 21	Most accident prone at age 37
Three times as many speech defects	As motorists, panic easier
Five to eight times as much colorblindness	Show more courtesy on the road
Twenty-three times as many sent to penal institutions per year	
More juvenile delinquents	

People Differ from Day to Day

One day we are "sitting on top of the world"; the next day we may be sitting on its bottom side. One day we are optimistic, enthusiastic, confident; by the next our enthusiasm has waned and our self-confidence has ebbed away. Not only does our mood change, our interests, our ambitions, and even our skills and abilities change. In one sense we are in a constant flux.

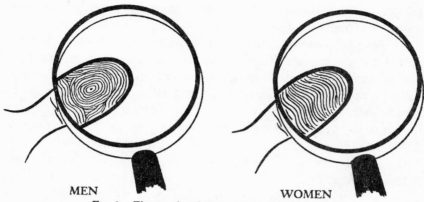

MEN   WOMEN

FIG. 2.   Fingerprint designs in men and women.

Over a period of time, the changes in an individual may reveal a process that has direction—a process that indicates growth or decline. As one passes from infancy to youth, to maturity, to old age, many changes occur in spite of the continuity that one feels or experiences. Older automobile drivers, when tested, show less alertness when steering, slower recovery from glare, and less quickness when braking. These are evidences of decline that may be more than compensated for by the fact that older drivers often drive more slowly, exercise more caution, control their emotions more effectively, and exercise better judgment. As younger drivers they probably exercised less caution and care.

Children, on the other hand, grow in stature, perfect their skills and learn new things. In fact these changes may be so pronounced, even over a short period of time, that if we are out of contact with the children for a time, we scarcely recognize them as being the children we knew.

Thus, we see that from day to day and over the years a person is an ever-changing pattern of action and of behavior. These ways in which a person differs from time to time are most important for anyone whose business it is to deal with people.

The Nature of Differences

A more systematic approach to the classification of individual differences results in placing them in several general divisions or groups. The following classification may be regarded as more suggestive than exhaustive.

Physical differences. Physical differences are the most obvious and the ones that usually suggest themselves first. Such factors as height and weight are important in determining behavior. Who has not observed that the short, slight person has a tendency to stand when speaking and to rise up on his toes to give him added height and possible prestige. Here size is a factor in behavior. In contrast a person who is large or one who is tall (whose bones present quite a different leverage ratio) of necessity behaves differently. In addition to these more obvious features, more subtle physical differences add their contribution to the complex pattern of behavior characteristic of the people one meets. We are what we are, in part at least, because of the type of organism we have.

Differences in ability and skill. For many people every lock clicks just like every other lock. There are those people, however, who have a discriminating touch and a keen sense of hearing that enables them to pick any lock they care to open. Most people are somewhere in between these limits. Ability to discriminate colors, and brightnesses and forms also varies. Some people can distinguish an object at night only if it is three or four yards distant, others can distinguish the same object equally well even though it is thirty yards distant. Variations in this regard are well illustrated in Figure 3.

As for skills, there seems to be no limit as to their number and variety. Moreover the extent to which these many skills are developed in various people varies considerably. Take the skill of marksmanship as an example. Some people are accurate marksmen regardless of the handicaps, others are competent only under favorable conditions, and still others miss the target entirely much of the time. There are men who apply manual holds so skillfully that the person they seek to restrain can not move, and on the other hand there are people who are all thumbs when they try the

→

FIG. 3. Differences in the ability to see an object at night. (Adapted with permission from: U. S. War Department: *Personnel Classification Tests*, TM 12-260 War Department Technical Manual, 1946.)

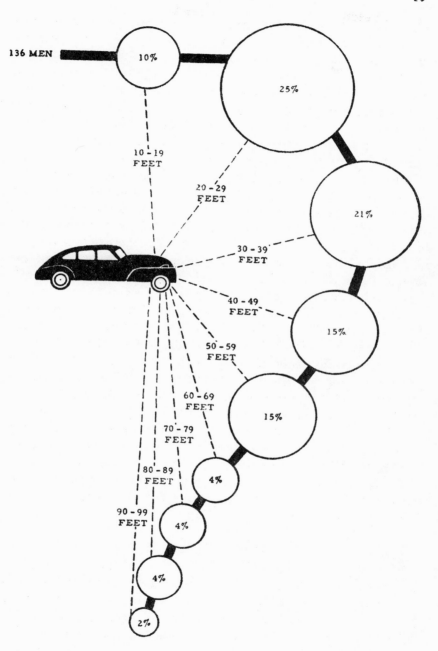

same thing. Although this list of ways in which skills and abilities differ could be greatly extended, these illustrations emphasize the point that such variations exist.

Personality differences. Consider a group of suspects, seen through a one-way vision screen, passing in review for identification. Better yet, recall the group of people placed in the jail late last Saturday night. One can not help noticing the ways in which such people differ from each other. These differences are more than differences in appearance; they are differences in behavior. No doubt you observed that some of these people stood or sat motionless, others gestured vigorously and somewhat meaninglessly, still others talked continuously and at times incoherently. Some were emotional, some were disoriented and confused, and others were rational and extremely logical in their thinking.

Some of these ways in which people differ from others are characteristic of them. The very talkative person may be characteristically talkative and hence may seldom be sullen and almost never mute. He has a pattern of behavior that is just as different from that of others as his facial features differ from those of others. These behavior differences are personality differences.

Differences in intelligence. One commonly thinks of people as gifted, superior, average, dull or feebleminded. This, of course, is a general classification on an intellectual basis. People differ intellectually in more specific ways too. For example, some are exceptionally able to deal with numbers, or with words, or with people, or with machines and things mechanical, whereas others have these abilities to a much lesser degree. Moreover, some people are clever with many things; many are clever with a few things, and some seem to lack cleverness in most areas. These differences are differences in intelligence.

The Causes of Individual Differences

Heredity is a cause. By heredity we mean all the pre-individual determiners, or all those characteristics that one receives from past generations through the germ cells from which one grew. Jim may be said to have eyes like his mother's, a chin like his father's, a voice like Uncle Bob's, a nose like grandmother's and to be colorblind like grandfather. Structural characteristics, or physical traits of this type, are easier to identify as hereditary than functional or behavioral characteristics are. One's learning aptitude, for example, is without doubt largely dependent on heredity, but just how much of it is dependent on heredity, we do not know with certainty. One thing is certain, however, some of our differences are hereditary differences.

Environment is a cause. By environment we mean all those things, activities, or stimuli in the world *that we respond to* in one way or another. Nothing is a part of our environment *unless we respond to it*. For example, a blind person can not read ink-print, and therefore it is not a part of his environment; nor can a deaf person hear a symphony, and therefore it is not a part of his environment either. Anyone may on occasion fail to see an overhead traffic signal or an obscured road sign, and at that time these are not a part of that person's environment, regrettable as that failure may be.

Physiological conditions, which are a part of our physical environment, are important factors in determining what we do. That gnawing pain in our "middle" or that splitting headache may make us unpleasant companions or difficult husbands. Decreased air pressure, as at high elevations, when we are accustomed to lower altitudes, may render us unsafe drivers. An abscess in the head may make one violent; alcohol may make one unsteady, and a lack of morphine may make one vicious. These are physical conditions that determine behavior.

The cultural or social aspect of our environment is also of tremendous importance. A man, for instance, who has quarreled violently with his wife or with his boss may exceed the legal speed limit when driving a car, deliberately run down a stray dog, or ignore the safety of jay-walking pedestrians. He behaves this way because of an intensely unpleasant social experience that has given rise to frustration and emotion. On the other hand, because of social environment, one is very apt to bring his car to a dead stop on a village street where there is a "thru street" sign, even though it is three o'clock in the morning and the bitter cold has driven all the villagers off the street. This behavior is the result of social living that has disciplined the person to respond in specific ways to signs and symbols.

Reasonable uniformity in social behavior is essential to community life. We must learn to respect the rights of others, and even to seek their welfare, in order that our rights are honored and our welfare secured. In fact, the reason we need law enforcement officers in our communities is because there are those among us who have not learned, or are unwilling to learn, to live harmoniously with others and to submit to the will and welfare of the group.

The Importance of Individual Differences to Law Enforcement

In general, laws are made to apply to all people alike. Allowances are seldom made for particular people who break a law unless such allowances are specified in the law. This is as it should and must be. Laws can not be interpreted differently according to the offender's standing in the community, or according to some peculiarity that he may have. Because of this, one may ask: Why should law enforcement officers be concerned with individual differences? Is not an effective officer one who is impartial, one who treats all people alike? From one point of view we must answer this question in the affirmative, and that is when we are thinking of the *enforcement* aspect of police work.

Modern concepts of law enforcement work carry us beyond this more limited view. Any officer who is service-minded goes beyond mere enforcement. He does not wait until a crime is committed before he is willing to act; instead he seeks to take such action as will decrease the likelihood that the crime will be committed or will be prevented entirely. A competent officer who observes a group of boys participating in such activities as are likely to result in a violation of a law or in injury to others deals wisely and promptly with this situation. He may enlist the cooperation of playground directors, social workers, teachers, ministers or priests, parents or interested citizens who attempt to deal with the potentially delinquent behavior before it develops to a point where drastic legal action must be taken. This officer is engaging in crime prevention work. It is here that individual differences can and must be taken into consideration. When the social service motive enters into law enforcement work people are dealt with as individuals. We need more of this type of attitude and hence we need more insight into the ways in which people differ one from another and the significance of these differences.

THE MEASUREMENT OF INDIVIDUAL DIFFERENCES

We have been thinking about the *fact* that people differ, and hence our approach was qualitative. Merely to note that Jim, John and Jerry differ, however, is not enough; we also need to discover how much they differ one from the other. To accomplish this we must measure them with some type of measuring instrument. Therefore, to discover their differences in weight we use a scale; and to ascertain their differences in height we use a yardstick. But suppose that we want to learn how much they differ in intelligence, or in aggressiveness, or in freedom from mental peculiarity, or in marksmanship, or in knowledge of police science, then how shall we measure them? When we deal with variations in knowledge or behavior, rather than with physical variations, we use some type of test that measures, more or less well, the trait that interests us.

What Is a Test?

A test of knowledge of police science may consist of a series of factual questions that must be answered by the testee—the person being tested. In this case, the measure of the testee's knowledge is in terms of the number of questions that he answers correctly. A person's marksmanship is measured by having him shoot from a certain position at a target of known distance, and the score obtained from the target is the objective measure of his marksmanship. In the first instance we are dealing with a set of typical questions; in the second case we are using a standard situation. In both cases we have an objective basis for comparing one person's performance with that of another. Thus a test is a typical situation, or a group of such situations, that is representative of a more general area of knowledge, skill or behavior, and that affords some numerical or quantitative evaluation of a person's performance in the larger area of activity.

All aspects of a person's behavior are not as easily measured as in the two illustrations given above. Nevertheless psychologists have devised fairly adequate tests for getting at some of the more important behavior traits. Among these are tests that measure the tendency toward mental peculiarity or neuroticism and that give us a "trouble score" for the person. Some tests throw light on such traits as dominance and self-sufficiency that are important in leadership. Still other tests measure motor coordination, skills of various types, the perception of depth and detail, and many other types of abilities and aptitudes. However the trait that has received most attention is intelligence, and hence there are many tests from which to choose. A later section in this chapter will discuss this type of testing more fully.

Results of Group Testing

If one measured every tenth man in a city of some size one would find that the majority of men are around five feet seven and one-half inches tall. Naturally all are not of this height; some are taller and others are shorter. Furthermore the farther one gets away from this average height the fewer men one finds, and at the extremes there are exceedingly few. There are extremely few who are eight or more feet tall (one of the tallest on record was nine feet and three inches), and there are equally few who are around three feet tall. In height, then, people cluster about an average, and the greater the deviation from the average the fewer there are. This fact is true whenever people are measured for any physical or behavior trait. And when the obtained results are plotted, the curve is bell-shaped. This curve is known as a *normal probability curve*. It is on the basis of the properties of this curve that psychologists base much of their reasoning concerning tests and test results.

Merely obtaining test results or scores is not enough. Scores must be given meaning and there are several things that help in giving them meaning. First, one needs to know what the average score is, because this is the base from which one must start. Suppose that one gives a standard intelligence test to a large group of applicants who are seeking to enter law enforcement work.

To give meaning to the scores that these applicants earn it is advisable to classify them into several groups, such as: exceptionally superior, superior, average, inferior, and poor. Now how many applicants can one expect to find in each one of these groups or categories?

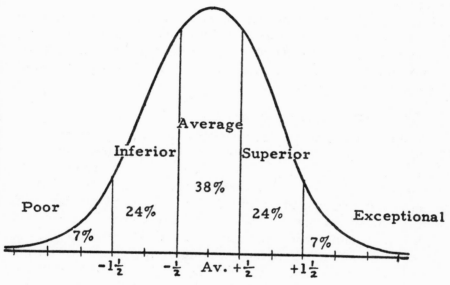

FIG. 4. The normal probability curve.

The procedure of breaking-up a group into five categories or divisions, illustrated in Figure 4, can be stated briefly as follows: First one must find the average of the group which is the average score. Then one measures off in both directions from this average score distances in terms of *standard deviations* (a statistical measure of the variation of the group that must be computed), going out one-half a standard deviation in both directions from the average. This gives the scores that are the limits of the average group, which includes about 38 per cent of the whole group. Thus the 38 per cent of the applicants who are in the middle of the group are average. Next one must determine the limits of the superior and inferior groups. This is done by going one standard deviation above the upper limit of the average group and also going one standard deviation below the lower limit of the average group. These two groups, the superior and the inferior, each include about 24 per cent of the whole group. Beyond the outermost limits of these two groups one finds the exceptionally superior and the poor groups, each of which includes about 7 per cent of the whole group.

It is true that this distribution of percentages holds only when the group is perfectly normally distributed, and most groups only approximate a normal distribution, but the concept is still a serviceable one. One can use these percentages as guides when breaking-up a group into subgroups.

The Interpretation of Test Scores

The types of scores. Psychologists use several types of scores. One of these is the *raw* score which often is the total number of correct responses or answers on a test that has many items. The raw score may also be the correct answers multiplied by certain numerical weights and added together. Because of the difficulties that raw scores present, they are usually converted either into *percentile* scores or into *standard* scores. This is done because one can not compare directly the raw scores earned on one test (which may range from 29 to 76) with the raw scores on another test (which may range from 52 to 162). Suppose that a person gets a score of 60 on the first test and one of 109 on the second test. How do these two scores compare? There is no direct basis for comparison until both are converted into some common measure. To attempt to do so may be just as absurd as comparing pounds with inches.

Percentile scores result when one converts raw scores to a percentage basis by finding the percentage of people who exceed and who fall below a certain score. Now since both scores in the above illustration are converted into percentiles, a common unit of measurement, the raw score of 60 becomes a percentile score of 56, and the raw score of 109 becomes a percentile score of 51. It is now evident that the raw score of 60 is actually a little higher than the raw score of 109, and that the person did slightly better on the first test than he did on the second. It is further evident that on both tests he was only slightly better than average which is always at the fiftieth percentile. Percentile scores always extend from 1 to 99 with the average at 50.

Standard scores differ from percentile scores in the way in which they are determined, but they are like them in that they give a common basis for comparing test scores. Standard scores are based upon standard deviations, which were mentioned briefly in an earlier section. Standard scores range essentially from 20 to 80 with the average at 50. Thus a standard score of 65 on one test is the same as a standard score of 65 on a second test, even though the raw scores earned on the two tests may have been 81 and 212 respectively. To put it another way, to get a raw score of 81 on the first test is the same as getting a raw score of 212 on the second test.

The need for norms. If a man is given a personality test that measures the traits of "dominance" and of "sociability," and he earns a raw score of 20 on each of these, what does the score of 20 mean in each case? Does it mean that he is equally dominant and sociable, or equally lacking in these qualities? This question can not be answered until the earned scores have been compared with acceptable norms or standards.

Norms are derived from the scores of a large number of people who have taken the same test. The scores they earn are converted into percentile scores or into standard scores, and these scores are then used as the basis with which an individual's score is compared. By comparing the score of 20 earned on the dominance test with the norms for adult men, we find that the percentile score is 29. This means that this person is very much below the average in dominance and that 71 men in every 100 are more dominant than he. Likewise his score of 20 on sociability, when compared with the norms, is a percentile score of 65. This means that he is above average in sociability and that only 35 men in every 100 are more sociable than he. In this way meaning is given to test scores, and comparisons between scores on different tests are made.

Applications to Law Enforcement Work

Standardized tests are widely used in the selection and promotion of law enforcement officers. Not only are they used by the United States Civil Service Commission, but by state and municipal governments as well. Some of the advantages of standardized tests are that they have been tried out in use; each person is measured in the same way; the scoring is objective and impartial, and each person's performance is compared with that of many people. In the following chapter practical aspects of testing as applied to law enforcement work will be presented at some length.

CONTROLLING PEOPLE THROUGH MOTIVATION

"Stop!" shouts a policeman, and the motorist stops. This officer is controlling the motorist's behavior by the force of a command. At another time a motorist is unwittingly attempting to park in a restricted area. An officer approaches, saying, "I'm sorry, sir, you may park here only momentarily, but you will find a very fine municipal parking area in the next block and to the right." In this case the officer is also controlling the motorist's behavior, but largely by suggestion. In both cases the officer's purpose is to effect certain responses in the motorist, and to get him to do things that are desirable or needful. In so far as the officer is successful, his motivation is effective.

Motivation means the use of those factors that activate a person toward a goal. Motivation implies something other than the use of force; it is more subtle than that. It usually implies that one uses somewhat indirect methods to achieve his goal. The police officer in the above illustration did not want the motorist to park his car where he was; the officer wanted him to use the parking area in the next block. He achieved his end, not by a command, but by releasing the *motorist's tendency to do that which officers suggest*. Therefore this officer was in control of the situation, but the motorist was less aware of it than had the officer ordered him in a gruff voice to park in the next block. The officer took the chance that the motorist had such a tendency, and since he was correct in his assumption, he secured the desired action with a minimum of resistance.

This illustration emphasizes that successful motivation of other people depends on one's knowledge of people, the tendencies to action that they possess, and the goals that they seek.

Basic Tendencies

One of the most widely quoted lists of human motives or basic tendencies is the one given by W. I. Thomas, the sociologist. This list includes four fundamental wishes or desires: the desire for *new experience*, for *security*, for *response*, and for *recognition*.

The adolescent boys and girls who participate in exciting hot-rod races on busy highways, play such games as "chicken" or "Russian roulette," go to their first "junk" party, or smoke their first "reefer" are seeking excitement and new experience. This desire for new experience can be exceedingly insistent and that which satisfies it is not always legal or socially desirable. This is not to say that this drive is seldom satisfied in socially acceptable ways. Enrolling in the FBI Academy, attending a traffic institute, going on a trip, and scores of other things that one may do, are motivated in part, if not in large part, by a desire for new experience.

Evidences of the desire for security can be seen everywhere. Our insistence on retirement plans, tenure in office, dismissal with a fair hearing, and many similar practices characteristic of our society grew out of man's desire for security. Sometimes people are so strongly motivated by the desire for security that they exhibit peculiar or abnormal behavior. Old people sometimes hoard enough food, clothing, money, or just plain junk to last an ordinary person several life-times. Advancing age sometimes stimulates a fear of the future that leads people to hold fast to that which they have.

The desire for security is being used wisely by a law enforcement officer when he says to a resisting offender, "It will be easier for you in the future, if you come along with me now."

In the stressful, annoying, confusing and frustrating situations in which people find themselves, the desire for response is unusually strong. When people are in trouble, they demand action. Rarely do they sit idly by and let events take their course. "Why doesn't someone do something?" "I want to see my lawyer." These are common demands—demands for action—for response.

Ranks, titles, insignia, uniforms appeal quite generally because of the desire for recognition. Any representative of the law prefers to be addressed as "Officer" rather than "Say, Flatfoot." The former shows honored recognition, the latter derision. This desire for recognition is characteristic of all people to a greater or lesser extent, and hence the need for being alert to this drive when dealing with other people. If law enforcement officers are to aid in achieving a higher level of morale in our society, which in part is one of their functions, the desire for recognition can not be ignored. If by morale we mean self-confidence on the part of people, contentment with that which they are doing, and discipline determined by the desire and welfare of society, then this can be achieved more fully by being cognizant of the desire for recognition that motivates people so strongly. This an officer does when he says to a protesting offender, "Tell it to the Chief." In effect this officer is saying, "I am just an officer of the law, but you are important, and hence you must discuss this matter with my superior who is also important." "I'll say I'm important," thinks the offender, and he goes along with the officer willingly because his desire for recognition has been appealed to. This officer accomplishes his task because of insight into the operation of a fundamental human desire.

Derived Needs

The four fundamental desires just discussed are common to all people. It is true that they vary in degree from person to person, but they are essentially characteristic of all. This universality must not lead us to suppose that they are the only human drives. There are other human needs, the needs that come as a result of learning. They are the desires that are characteristic of our family, our community, and our society. They are the things that we come to need because we learn to need them.

The desire to conform may be taken as an illustration. Many people learn through childhood to conform to the behavior standards set by parents and by people in the neighborhood and community. In fact so well is this learned that the desire to conform may become very compelling. Hence people are motivated by habit to thank their host and hostess for a "delightful evening" even though the entertainment was boring, the food mediocre and the company dull. This need to conform is a learned need and hence a derived need.

Just as there are those people who learn to conform to society, there are those who learn *not* to conform to social standards and the laws of society. Non-conformity, like conformity, grows out of one's home and community life. Both may be strong and compelling in their determination of behavior. The fact that non-conforming behavior may be undesirable and even socially detrimental does not mean that it is any less compelling. One person may experience just as strong a need to break a law as another feels the need to obey it. The difference is in the direction of their motivation rather than in the mechanism of motivation.

If one is to understand behavior of this type, and if one is to have insight into that which lies behind the desirable actions of some people and the antisocial acts of others, one must take into account the desires, tendencies, and learned pre-dispositions that lead to action. And if one hopes to control the actions of others with any degree of effectiveness, he must learn how to manipulate these drives so as to secure the desired action. This task is not at all easy.

HOW WE LEARN

The old adage says, "You can't teach an old dog new tricks." Perhaps the reason many people believe this is because they have never tried to teach an old dog a new trick. Not having tried, they assume that it is impossible. Too many people naively accept the idea that learning is limited to children and young people. Yet a little reflection soon convinces one that many middle-aged and old people learn too. Just try to count the number of things that you have learned since leaving school and you will be amazed at the length of the list. That people continue to learn throughout life is a fact, and that this fact is accepted is indicated by the common adage, philosophically stated, "Well, we live and learn." Yes, we do live and learn for learning is characteristic of living. In fact it is something that we can not avoid.

What Is Learning?

Many people associate learning with ideational or book learning. Therefore they think of all learning as improvement, as doing something better, as knowing more. This view of learning is correct in part, but it is not the whole story. A careful driver sometimes *learns* to be careless. Thugs do learn to blow open safes with a single charge. Pickpockets develop such skill that they are not detected. Learning is not always in the direction of improvement, nor in the direction of that which is socially desirable. In fact some of the time it is just the reverse.

What, then, is learning? Careful examination of Figure 5 should lead to a discovery. Do not be satisfied with seeing the obvious; look for something more. Continue studying the figure until it takes on new meaning.

FIG. 5.   What do you see? (Reproduced with permission of General Electric Co.)

What did you see in Figure 5? Without a doubt you immediately thought: "G-E," "General Electric," large corporation light bulbs, or something similar. Perhaps you were puzzled that the two symbols were alike and that they were separated by "or." It is quite likely that you thought that this figure makes little sense, and the only reason you continued to examine it is because you assumed that there must be a catch in it somewhere. No doubt you repeated the letters "G-E" then the word "or" and then the letters "G-E" several times. Then you said it faster, "G-E or G-E" followed by "G-E o-r G-E," followed by "G-e-o-r-g-e." Then something clicked and you had it: "George!"

This illustration gives one some insight into the nature of learning. Learning is, in part, seeing new relationships. Now you have learned to think of "G-E," not only as a symbol for a large corporation, but as the beginning and end of a common given name. "G-E" has a new meaning. Something new has been learned.

There is another fundamental fact about learning: it progresses from the known to the unknown. Learning never develops out of nothing, it always comes from something—something that one already knows or can do. The new idea you discovered in Figure 5 developed out of that which you knew and recognized immediately. Hence now you have the new idea that George is two "G-E's" separated by "or."

Another illustration is your present skill in typing. This did not develop out of nothing either. Skill in typing grows out of the earlier control that one has over his fingers. If your fingers are stiff with arthritis, you can not learn to type; and if you have no fingers, it certainly is impossible. But having fingers, and having certain control over them, you have integrated these finger activities into new ways which you now call skill in typing. This integration of responses, which one is already capable of making, into new patterns and combinations is the process of learning. There is one other feature of learning, not yet mentioned, that is important, that is, that these modifications and new integrations of behavior are retained for some time.

When Do We Learn?

We learn when there is a need for learning. This *need* implies that there is motivation. As infants we learned to suck more and more efficiently (to suck less air) because there was a biological need that we call hunger. As adults, however, many of our needs are learned needs—they are needs that grow out of social life. We need to get to work quickly, hence we learn to drive a car. We feel the need for a raise in rank or rating, so we learn more about police science and law enforcement.

It must be noted further, however, that the mere presence of a need is no guarantee that learning will result. Learning results when the need is a felt or a recognized need. In other words, learning occurs when there is an *intention to learn*. Many police officers could improve their marksmanship, but they do not because they have no strong intention to do so. Even practice will not assure improvement unless there is the intention to improve. It is clear, then, unless a person is motivated to learn, no learning results.

Helping Others to Learn

Sometimes the term "Peace Officer" is used in preference to "Law Enforcement Officer." The implications in the two are different, and in some ways the former has much to commend it. The officer's duty is as much to preserve the peace as it is to enforce laws. Preserving the peace suggests that it is the officer's function to aid people, young, middle-aged, and old, to *learn* to do that which is in keeping with the standards of our society, or those things that are regarded as right. To accomplish this, the officer needs to know something about the process of learning and the ways in which he can effect learning in others.

Psychologists have formulated a number of fundamental principles of learning that can be used as guides in one's own learning or as aids when directing the learning of others. Space does not allow a comprehensive examination of these principles, and hence only a few of the more fundamental ideas can be presented. What may be called the *tell-show-do-praise method* brings together several of these essential ideas.

The tell-show-do-praise method. Very often people expect others to learn how to do something as a result of merely being told how to do it. Although it is possible to learn from such a verbal description, it is less likely to result in success in the case of most people, and in any event it is apt to be found very difficult. Just recall the experience that you had when trying to assemble a complex machine by merely reading the directions provided. It was not easy.

Language is symbolic; it consist of signs that stand for things and actions. When the clues to learning are limited to language clues, learning is apt to be slow, devious and hence discouraging.

One reason for this is that people do not pay close attention when verbal or written instructions are given.

As an example of the shortcomings of learning based on "telling" alone, consider the following illustration. A very inexperienced person was sent, with three rounds of ammunition, to a pistol range to demonstrate his skill. He was told, not once but several times, just how to shoot. The description given was very adequate, but no effort was made to go beyond the description. Did the person make a perfect, or even a satisfactory score? The answer is apparent.

Some instructors take the second step. They not only tell the person how the task is done, but they show him as well. This is certainly much better than merely telling a person what to do. However it is not enough either. For even though the description is adequate and the demonstration excellent, the learner is not an expert from that moment on.

Learning depends largely on *doing*. Telling and showing are important aids, but one learns most when he tries to do the thing himself. It was pointed out above that learning is integrating responses into new combinations or patterns. The only way in which this can be accomplished is through one's own activity. There is no substitute for practice. But practice under the guidance of a competent instructor, who tells and shows repeatedly, results in the gradual elimination of faulty responses and in ultimate mastery.

To speed the process of learning, emphasis must be placed on the fourth aspect of the tell-show-do-PRAISE method. Learning can occur without praise, it is true, but it is much more rapid and lasting when praise is used. Praise motivates one, it strengthens the intention to learn, it facilitates the doing, it brings achievement closer.

Use the tell-show-do-praise method of learning. Stress each of its phases. Be patient with the learner, for since learning is a growth process it takes time. Do not expect mastery from the beginning, for it comes only as the result of repeated trials which are most effective when separated by intervals of rest from practice. Therefore, for best results supplement the tell-show-do-praise method of learning with the practice-rest-practice-rest method and you will be impressed with the results.

INTELLIGENCE

The word intelligence is a very common word that has some meaning for everyone. Usually it suggests the ability to do something well, or knowledge that is unusual or exceptional. It must be pointed out, however, that although very intelligent people often do achieve a high degree of skill and exceptional knowledge, such achievement must not be confused with intelligence. If the two are regarded as identical, then young children can hardly be said to be intelligent. A further difficulty with the above view is that it compels one to regard all who excel in any function, no matter how limited, as intelligent. Occasionally one finds a feeble-minded person who has exceptional facility with numbers or one who has a phenomenal memory for certain types of details, yet all things considered these people are feebleminded.

Psychologists define intelligence in various ways. Some regard it as synonymous with abstract thinking, others with learning. Still others emphasize flexibility and versatility in the use of symbols and in meeting novel or new situations. From the point of view of many intelligence tests, emphasis is placed on the speed and accuracy with which people adjust to new situations. In general, intelligence may be regarded as the ability a person has to use his past experiences in such ways as to meet new situations quickly and effectively.

In view of this definition, a law enforcement officer demonstrates the degree of his intelligence by the extent to which he brings his past experiences, of whatever sort, to bear on a present problem, and relates them in such ways as to gain insight into the problem and to achieve a satisfactory solution.

Types of Intelligence

Intelligence is sometimes thought of as being of three broad types: abstract, social, and mechanical. Abstract intelligence is the type that is used when one solves problems, learns academic material, or deals with symbols. Social intelligence is insight into or understanding social situations and people. It is what is sometimes called social sense. Mechanical intelligence is the insight people have into things mechanical, the ability to deal with things skillfully.

Testing Intelligence

The intelligence test. The intelligence test is a device used to measure a person's intelligence in terms of that which he has learned and knows. There is no known way in which one can measure what is commonly called *native intelligence*, meaning that which is inherited from our ancestors. Two important facts concerning intelligence tests need to be understood: an intelligence test presents sample situations to which the person tested tries to respond; and second, it measures intelligence in terms of the person's adaptability to these sample situations. This view seems to suggest that the tests measure intelligence indirectly. This is not entirely the case. If intelligence is regarded as something that a person *can do*, rather than as something he *has received*, then the tests are measuring this, in that they throw light on what the person can do in the sample situation.

The kinds of intelligence tests. Intelligence tests were first used early in this century. However, it was not until shortly before World War I that the real value of intelligence tests was recognized. The first intelligence tests were individual tests, that is, one person was tested at a time. But with the coming of World War I, and the necessity of placing large numbers of men in a civilian army, the first group tests, called Army Alpha and Army Beta, were made. With these tests over 1,750,000 men were tested. These tests, being group tests, had the definite advantage that many people could be tested in a short time. During the period between World Wars I and II many new group tests appeared, new techniques were introduced, procedures were refined, and tests were devised for various types of groups. Although there are excellent individual tests for children and for adults, group tests are very widely used because of their cheapness and ease of administration and scoring.

Two other types of tests must be mentioned, these are *speed* tests and *power* tests. Of the two, speed tests are used more widely. In the speed test there is a time limit within which the person tested tries to accomplish as much as possible. The power test, on the other hand, has no time limit, but the test items are arranged in the order of difficulty from easy to difficult. Intelligence is indicated in terms of the difficulty-level to which the person achieves successfully. Hence this test measures intelligence in terms of power instead of speed. Each test has its advantages. In the speed type of test all the people start and stop together, hence it is easy to administer. In the power type of test, some people work much longer than others, but each is satisfied with the opportunity to attempt all the items he desires.

The meaning of test scores. We hear a great deal about IQ's, and even about a Dr. IQ, yet most people have a rather vague idea of what is meant, beyond the fact that it indicates intelligence. IQ is a ratio of a person's *mental age* (usually determined by an individual type of test) to his *chronological age*. The formula is: mental age divided by chronological age (both in months) multiplied by 100, so as to make it a whole number. Since the result is a ratio, it can be compared directly with another person's IQ, even though the two people differ considerably in age. Furthermore, if one's mental and chronological ages are alike, then the IQ is 100 and the person is average. If the mental age, however, exceeds the chronological age, then the IQ is above 100; if the reverse is true, then the IQ is less than 100.

Group tests of the speed type, that are so widely used, do not give us IQ's. The scores obtained on these tests are raw scores that are converted into percentile scores[1] which can be compared with similar scores obtained with other tests. The intelligence of older children and adults is most usually recorded in terms of percentile scores that run from 1 to 99 with the average at 50.

The Distribution of Intelligence in the Population

It was pointed out above that when many people are measured with some measuring device, as a test, the measures distribute

---

[1]For a discussion of percentile and standard scores see pages 20-21.

themselves in a characteristic, bell-shaped curve that is called the normal distribution curve. In such a distribution there are few very high scores, more that are moderately high, many that are average, fewer that are moderately low, and very few that are extremely low. When large groups of children or adults are measured with intelligence tests, bell-shaped curves are also obtained. This is evident in the distribution of IQ's obtained with the Stanford-Binet test in which 16 per cent are superior, 10 per cent very superior, and 1 per cent near genius. On the other side of the distribution similar percentages are found: 16 per cent are low normal, 8 per cent borderline, and 3 per cent feebleminded.

Of the various intelligence tests used during World War II, the Army General Classification Test (AGCT) was used most widely. During 1940-1945 more than twelve million inductees were given the AGCT. The scores they obtained are distributed in five grades in terms of standard scores (not IQ's) in Figure 6

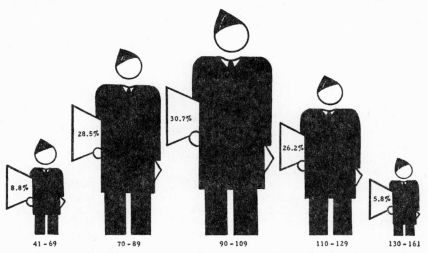

FIG. 6. Distribution of AGCT scores for army inductees in terms of standard scores. (Adapted, with permission, from Walter V. Bingham: Inequalities in Adult Capacity—from Military Data, *Science, 104:* 147-152, 1946.)

as follows: Grade I with scores of 130 and above, 5.8 per cent; Grade II with scores between 110 and 130, 26.2 per cent; Grade III, the average group, with scores between 90 and 110, 30.7 per cent; Grade IV with scores between 70 and 90, 28.5 per cent; and Grade V with scores below 70, 8.8 per cent.

It is clear from these results that intelligence is not uniformly distributed in the population. Characteristics other than intelligence are also distributed in a similar way, as was pointed out in an earlier section.

Intelligence and Occupation

Not only does one individual differ from another in intelligence, but one occupational group differs from others as to the *average* intelligence of its members. This does not imply that all the people employed in a given way are identical, or even closely similar, in intelligence. Within any group there are individual differences, and in some groups these differences are much greater than in others. Furthermore, the overlap between one occupational group and another is usually great. When one takes the averages, however, one can arrange occupations in order from those whose members, on the average, earn high intelligence test scores on down to those who earn much lower scores.

TABLE I

Intelligence of Occupational Groups*

Occupational Group	Number	First Quartile	Average	Third Quartile
Accountant	216	121	129	136
Teacher	360	117	124	132
Lawyer	164	118	124	132
Bookkeeper, General	302	114	122	129
Chief Clerk	297	114	122	131
Draftsman	139	109	120	127
G-Man	72	114	120	124
Clerk-Typist	616	110	119	126
Postal Clerk	377	109	119	126
Manager, Production	94	111	117	124
Salesman	859	107	115	125
File Clerk	119	105	114	123
Gunsmith	53	100	112	119
Shipping Clerk	408	101	111	121
Machinist	617	99	110	120
Policeman	172	96	109	118
Electrician	435	96	109	118
Machinist's Helper	429	96	108	118

TABLE I (Continued)
Intelligence of Occupational Groups*

Occupational Group	Number	First Quartile	Average	Third Quartile
Sheet Metal Worker	462	95	107	117
Shop Maintenance Mechanic	280	92	106	117
Riveter, Pneumatic	113	91	106	115
Utility Repairman	305	91	105	116
Structural Steel Worker	107	88	104	119
Foreman, Construction	281	88	104	118
Plumber	222	87	103	114
Automotive Mechanic	1,693	89	102	114
Bricklayer	213	88	102	114
Carpenter, General	1,004	86	101	113
Chauffeur	358	87	100	113
Truck Driver, Heavy	3,473	83	98	111
Crane Operator	128	87	96	111
Laborer	7,805	76	93	108
Miner	502	75	87	103
Farm Worker	7,475	70	86	103
Lumberjack	236	70	85	100

*Adapted from Stewart, N.: AGCT Scores of Army Personnel Grouped by Occupations, *Occupations*, 26:1-37, 1947.

In Table I a number of occupations are listed in order according to the average AGCT scores earned by inductees who had previously been employed in these various ways. Besides the average score, the table shows the first and third quartile points between which 50 per cent of the people in the group fall. Above the third quartile, there are 25 per cent of the people tested, and below the first quartile there are 25 per cent of the people. Several of the occupations listed are of interest to law enforcement workers. Information on many other occupations than those listed is available.

THE MEANING OF PERSONALITY

"She is bulging with personality." "He hasn't any personality whatsoever." Such comments as these are very common. They imply that personality is something that one has, or lacks, or has to a certain degree. It is regarded as a possession similar to the other possessions that one has. This view is not limited to personality; other aspects of the person are regarded as possessions also. One person is said to *have* character, another is regarded as *having lost* his mind, or even his soul. This point of view raises a very fundamental question, namely, if personality, mind, soul, and character are things that a person has, then what or who is the person? Who is the owner of these various things?

What do people mean by the phrase, *has personality?* Usually the following things are uppermost in their thinking: tact, affability, social grace, superior intelligence and other such desirable characteristics. Fundamentally these are ways of behaving, and it is behavior that should be central in our thinking. What, then, is personality? It is the pattern of behavior that we find in a human being. *Personality is not something that one has; it is something that one is.* Moreover, this pattern of behavior that one is, is essentially a unique pattern.

How Does One Come to Be What He Is?

There are several factors that determine the pattern of behavior that one is. First among these is heredity. Heredity is all those potentialities for development that one inherits from his ancestors. This includes the kind of organism one is, the way in which it functions, and the aptitudes and capacities that one can develop. The kind of person one is depends in part on heredity.

Moreover, the kind of person one is depends on the way the body functions. Sometimes it functions smoothly and well; then again it may function badly. Perhaps some endocrine gland, such as the thyroid, functions too much or not enough, thus throwing the whole organism out of balance and markedly changing behavior. The loss of a hand, or of an eye, or some type of crippling, not only handicaps the person, but often changes his outlook on life. Illness, deafness and many other physical conditions all contribute to making us what we are.

A third and very important factor that contributes to personality is daily experience. These are the day-to-day experiences that result in joy or sorrow, achievement or frustration, success or failure. Although the major experiences are more apt to be remembered and the minor ones forgotten, each contributes much or little to the pattern of behavior that one exhibits thereafter.

There was the time you disobeyed your parents, or defied your boss, or had an argument with your best girl, and you have not been the same since. There was also the time you won first place in a contest, was voted the most valuable employee, or received an unexpected inheritance, and these things changed you too. How does one come to be what he is? The answer is this: One comes to be what he is by a process of interaction between those potentialities and assets that one has, and the situations that one experiences from day to day. Hence a person is an ever-changing pattern of behavior with certain features abiding through the years. Personality IS the person.

Frustration, Conflict and Adjustment

Generally life does not flow along smoothly and without interruption and difficulty for long. Perhaps there are two chief reasons for this. For one thing, the world in which we live is not fixed and constant; nor in the second place, are we the same from day to day. Each day unexpected situations arise that demand adjustment and problems that need solution. Our mood, our physical vigor, and even our knowledge and skill are different from time to time. All this makes for more or less rough going, or a feeling of frustration, of conflict in response, and of difficulty in adjustment.

The feeling of frustration is the experience that we have when the drive to do something is strong and a barrier or obstruction is encountered. When life flows along smoothly, tasks are completed, and goals are achieved, there is little or no feeling of frustration, and hence the emotion experienced is one of pleasantness rather than one of bewilderment or anger. Here is a common illustration. A law enforcement officer strongly desires to achieve a higher rank, this is his goal. For a time no frustration is experienced, but if the appointment is delayed long, or someone else is appointed in his stead, or he learns of an unfavorable rating given by a superior, frustration is quite certain to follow. And the stronger the desire for the appointment the more keenly is the frustration felt. On the other hand, had the desire been much less strong, or only vaguely defined, frustration might not have resulted at all.

Conflict is also experienced when the drive is strong, but the situation that gives rise to it is somewhat different from the above. Conflict results when there are alternate goals with the drive toward each equally strong. An officer when observing a minor violation of the law, may experience a mild conflict as to whether he should arrest the person or let him go with a mild reprimand. A motorist may experience a conflict that is more intense when

Fig. 7. A situation that causes conflict.

confronted with the types of situations represented in Figures 7 and 8.

FIG. 8. A conflict-arousing situation.

The experiences of frustration and the presence of conflicts can not be eliminated entirely from daily life. This being the case, the important fact is not that we have these experiences, but the way we adjust to them.

Types of Adjustments

Naturally not all people adjust to frustrating situations and to conflicts in the same way. Fortunately there are those people who find satisfactory solutions for their problems, either through personal resources that they possess or through assistance from others. Unfortunately, however, there are many people who are less successful in meeting life's problems, and some of the ways these people use are of importance to law enforcement officers.

Rationalization. This is a most common type of adjustment. It is most commonly known as "excuse giving." When one rationalizes he attempts to make his own acts seem right and acceptable in the eyes of another. It is an unsound kind of reasoning. The motorist who excuses his responsibility for an accident by saying, "I couldn't help it; my brakes didn't hold," is rationalizing, since he expects to be absolved of all blame. Obviously he still is responsible for the condition of his brakes.

Regression. When an arrested person cries, screams, stamps his feet, tears his hair, or throws himself on the floor, he is having a temper tantrum like that of a child. He has returned to an infantile form of behavior that may have worked when he was a child, but which is most inappropriate for an adult.

Repression. Another attempt to meet a difficulty is by ignoring or forgetting it, or even denying that it exists. Law enforcement people encounter this type of adjustment in its more extreme form. The person with amnesia is of this type. He has repressed so thoroughly that he has forgotten not only his difficult and unpleasant problem but also his name and the circumstances concerning his recent experiences as well.

Projection. The person guilty of arson who serves as a willing informer and who points an accusing finger at others may honestly think that those whom he accuses, and not he, are guilty. Likewise, the person who accuses law enforcement officers of using dictatorial methods may be projecting his own desire to be dictatorial into the behavior of the officers. Projection is reading one's own behavior and motives into the behavior of others. Because the motivation behind it is often subtle, it is difficult to detect, and one is easily misled by the person's apparent sincerity.

Compensation. This type of adjustment is perhaps less significant from the point of view of law enforcement. Compensatory adjustments include such things as: identifying one's self with another to gain power or prestige, daydreaming, belittling others and their accomplishments, or carrying some perfectly normal activity to a ridiculous extreme. For instance when a law violator informs an arresting officer that he is an intimate friend of the mayor, in order to escape blame, identification is being used. When a person defames another's character he is compensating by belittling, for what he is trying to do is enhance his own worth at the expense of the other person.

REFERENCES

ANDERSON, J. E.: *The Psychology of Development and Personal Adjustment*, New York, Henry Holt and Company, 1949. This book is broader in its coverage than most texts in the general field.

GARRETT, H. E.: *Psychology*, New York, American Book Company, 1950. This book presents the minimum essentials of psychology.

MUNN, N. L.: *Psychology, The Fundamentals of Human Adjustment*, Second edition. New York, Houghton Mifflin Company, 1951. An excellent presentation of psychological principles and experimental results is found in this text.

RUCH, F. L.: *Psychology and Life*, Fourth edition. Chicago: Scott, Foresman and Company, 1953. This book appeals to the general reader.

Chapter 2

RATING AND TESTING POLICEMEN

By

GEORGE J. DUDYCHA

T HE NOTION that anyone can do any job well was discarded long ago. It is common knowledge that to do a task well, or even acceptably, requires some ability, skill, or special aptitude. Hence the selection of people for various jobs, including police work, must be according to the assets they possess. If this selection is to be made intelligently, two things must be considered. First, there are the requirements of the job. What must the person do? How do his duties or tasks vary? What is required of him most often, and what least often? These questions are answered by a job analysis that not only enumerates but evaluates the tasks assigned to the worker. One must first know what the job is before a suitable worker can be found to do it.

The second, and equally important factor in placement is knowing the assets of the worker. Actually this is a much more difficult task than that of job analysis. It is difficult because completely adequate ways of evaluating abilities and aptitudes are not available. It is true that some of the methods devised by psychologists are of considerable help, but they must be applied with caution and skill.

Traditional Methods of Evaluation

The interview. One of the commonest methods used to select people for job placement is the interview. Unfortunately the interview is too often an unsystematic period of questioning during which an employer "sizes up" a prospective employee. Decisions are often made on the basis of vague impressions, unfounded prejudices, or the answers to two or three trick questions. Although confidence in such unsystematic and unscientific methods is often high, results of their use, when measured against on-the-job success, are often disappointingly low.

This is not to say that the interview is an utterly hopeless method of obtaining information. On the contrary, it is a valuable method when used systematically. The interview is effective when the interviewer employs carefully phrased questions, that are presented in an order that is directional (leads to a goal or end) and that reveal pertinent information. Like many other things, interviewing is a skill that produces results in proportion to the skill of the user. Hence the value of interview data depends, to a great extent, on the interviewer.

The personal data sheet. A second common method of gaining information about an applicant is the personal data sheet. The information obtained by this procedure includes such items of personal data as age, physical characteristics and handicaps, marital status, etc., educational training, and work history. Information of this type is of little value in the selection of applicants unless the significance of the various items is known. For instance an applicant from which age group makes the most effective policeman? Are married men preferable to single men? Are men with families more desirable than married but childless men? More specific information with regard to these and related questions is needed. Hunches are not enough.

That personal data can be of considerable value in the selection of applicants was found in a study of insurance salesmen. In one group of superior salesmen, 94 per cent were married and only 6 per cent were single. Futhermore those successful salesmen averaged about 2.5 dependents, and hence had one or more children, whereas unsuccessful salesmen had fewer dependents. Personal data of this type can be significant.

Although personal data have long been collected and used as a partial basis for the selection of law enforcement officers, little scientific evidence of the significance of such data seems to be available. More careful follow-up work of applicants who are accepted is needed so that the future selection of officers can be more scientific and efficient.

Information testing. Another widely used method of selecting law enforcement officers is information testing. These tests, using multiple-choice, true-false or short answer questions, reveal the applicant's general information and knowledge of the local situation. Information given by these tests must, without a doubt, be given appropriate weight in the selection of law enforcement officers, for knowledge of laws, ordinances and local places is essential for their success.

Valuable as information tests are in the selection of law enforcement officers, undue emphasis should not be placed on them to the near exclusion of other methods of selection. It is possible that a man might make an excellent score on an information test and yet make an undesirable officer. Another man with less information but possessing other desirable qualifications not measured by an information test might be an outstanding success. Information is not the sole criterion of success. A deficiency in information can be remedied, but one of intelligence or personality can not. Other things equal, a man who has the required information is preferable to one who does not have it, but a man who lacks specific information must not be discarded too quickly, especially if he possesses other assets that will make him a valuable officer.

RATING PROCEDURES

The Purpose of Rating Scales

Rating scales are aids used to get systematic evaluations of a person's character, personality and behavior traits. They are not tests. They are merely devices that guide the person making the evaluation in his thinking and facilitate the recording of his judgment. It is in this regard that ratings are superior to letters of recommendation. Several letters of recommendation written concerning the same person may cover very different points, no two of them commenting on the same personality or behavior trait. Hence any evaluation in the one letter is not corroborated by statements in the others. In the rating scale, on the other hand, each trait is evaluated by each of the persons making a rating and hence there is comparability of judgment.

Rating procedures are used for various purposes. Sometimes they are used to obtain information concerning applicants for a position, and at other times to secure information that can be used as a partial basis for promotion. Sometimes ratings are compared with previous ratings on the same person to indicate progress made. They are also used to make comparisons between individuals engaged in the same work. Whatever use is made of them, they must include those traits that give pertinent information. It is useless to rate a police officer on interest in puppet making, since puppet making is unrelated to police work. However, to rate him on his promptness in completing assignments, his dependability in executing orders, his skill in dealing with adolescents, and other similar things related to police work, is logical.

Rating procedures are means to an end. To achieve that end one must first clearly define the problem. If the problem is one of selection and placement, it is one thing; if it is a problem of promotion in rank, it is another. The purpose determined, the next step is to select pertinent traits. This can be done only after an adequate job analysis is made. The number of traits selected should be kept at a minimum with no unnecessary traits or "deadwood" included. When these principles are observed a usable instrument is developed.

The Types of Rating Procedures

Rank-order procedure. One of the simplest, but not the best, methods of evaluating people is the rank-order method. This is always a matter of comparing each person in a group with every other member and placing them in order from the one who is the most outstanding on down to the one who is least outstanding. Hence the rank-order method applies only to groups; it is impossible to rank one person. Generally it is easier to place the people at the head and the foot of the list than it is to evaluate those who are between. Certainty in the evaluation of the people in the middle is often low. Therefore when many people must be placed in rank order it is advisable first to group them into five or six general groups and then to arrange the people in each subgroup. This may not greatly increase the value of the ratings, but it does facilitate the task.

Check-list scales. This evaluation technique is constructed in either of two ways; either a list of pairs of adjectives is used, or a series of graded phrases or statements is employed. In either case the rater checks the items in the series or the pair that in his judgment best describe the person rated.

Category scales. Several very similar scales can be listed here, all of which are alike in that the person rated is placed in one of several groups or categories, of which usually there is an odd number. The *alphabetical scale* consists of a series of letters, often A to E, in which A indicates much of the trait, C an average amount, and E little. The *numerical scale* is the same except that numbers are substituted for letters. The *descriptive-adjective scale* uses a series of descriptive words or phrases, such as, very superior, superior, average, inferior, very inferior. The *percentage scale* employs a series of percentages extending from zero to 100, in steps of 10's in which 50 is average.

In each of the category scales the number of categories used varies from three to many, but five or seven seems to be satisfactory for most purposes, with nine or eleven as the maximum. When the number is too small the rating is too rough and undiscriminating. When, on the other hand, many categories are used, raters are apt to be confused.

Advantages and disadvantages. The rating procedures described above have this in common: they are easy to construct, simple to administer, quick to give, and the results are easily tabulated. In spite of these advantages, they have these drawbacks: Categories often are not well defined and hence interpreted differently by various raters. These scales tend to invite casual evaluation and arbitrary judgment. Furthermore, since the categories are discrete or separate, they too often imply that there is a real, and perhaps substantial, difference between one category and the next, which is not always the case.

THE GRAPHIC RATING SCALE

All things considered, the most acceptable rating scale is the graphic rating scale. It consists of a line, usually about five inches long, that is divided into a large number of small divisions so that it looks much like a foot-rule. Beneath this line is a series of descriptive words or phrases that indicate different degrees of the trait rated. At the left of this graphic line and series of descriptive words and phrases, is the name and brief description of the personality or behavior trait considered. At the right is a space in which the rater can indicate that he has had no opportunity to observe the ratee with regard to this trait. The advantage of this latter feature is that it encourages the rater to judge the ratee only when he is competent to do so. When the rater is sufficiently acquainted with the ratee to make a judgment, he places a check-mark somewhere along the line nearest to the descriptive word or phrase that in his judgment best describes the person under consideration.

The number of traits rated at any one time by this method varies with the purpose and the information desired. Usually at least six traits are listed and often the number is as large as 12 to 14. Obviously it is unwise to require a rater to indicate his judgment on 30 or 40 traits. Hence the number should be limited to those that are essential and that can be judged reasonably well. Generally only those traits are included in a rating scale that can not be evaluated by objective tests. Whenever tests can be used they are preferable to ratings because test data are generally more reliable than ratings.

A final comment concerning the construction of the graphic rating scale concerns the descriptive words and phrases used. Several items need emphasis. First, the number of descriptive words or phrases should seldom, if ever, be fewer than four. Too few categories gives too little opportunity for discriminating judgment. Also it is best to have an odd number. If there are five or seven degrees of judgment, the middle one is taken as the average. More than this number of categories, as nine or 11, become increasingly cumbersome to use and force the rater to attempt finer discriminations than he may feel able to make. Furthermore a large number of degrees of difference can not be placed conveniently under a five-inch line, and even if they are, some of them will be used seldom.

A second caution with regard to the descriptive words and phrases is that they must represent different degrees of only *one* *trait*. It is all too easy, when selecting the descriptive phrases, to shift from one trait to another as one progresses from one extreme of the scale to the other. Finally, one must make certain that the categories selected do indicate different degrees of the trait rated.

The Reliability of Graphic Rating Scales

Types of raters' errors. There are two common errors of judgment found among raters. The first is the *perseveration error* (also called halo effect) in which the rater persists in judging a person as high, or average, or low with regard to all traits, largely because he thought of him as high, average, or low on the first trait. True a person may be exceptional in a number of traits, but consistent rating of an individual as exceptional with regard to all, or nearly all traits, should make one alert to the possible presence of bias in the rater's judgments. To say that because a person is very intelligent, he should know enough to be dependable; and because he is dependable, he must be honest, etc., strikes one as a case of perseveration error.

A second rating error is known as the *generosity error*. It is true that a rater can only rate people with whom he is acquainted. This acquaintance, however, may bias him favorably (or unfavorably) toward the person rated, and hence he may regard him more favorably than he should. In other words, he is generous in his ratings. This is even more true when self-ratings are used.

Increasing the value of ratings. The first essential in securing reliable ratings is using trained raters. Raters who are uninformed as to the essential principles of rating, are almost certain to give less reliable ratings. Among other things attitude is important. The rater must seek to give his considered judgment rather than an impulsive one. Furthermore the rater's judgment must be discriminating. He must recognize that most people are average with regard to any trait and that the farther one departs toward extremes, the fewer people should be so rated.

When rating a person on such traits as cooperativeness, punctuality, interest in people and other similar traits, the rater should recall as many instances in which these traits were exhibited as possible. Ratings based on vague recollections are of little value. However, ratings based on knowledge of Patrolman Johnson's willingness to accept difficult assignments, to collect information when off duty, and to volunteer for dangerous and difficult tasks, are valuable because they are based on specific information.

A final caution deals with perseveration and generosity errors. These can be avoided, in part, by forcefully calling raters' attention to the nature of these errors and the need for avoiding them. Besides this two other things are done. The first is to stagger the scales for the several traits by placing the high or desirable end of the scale for the first trait to the right, that for the second trait to the left, for the third trait to the right, etc. This breaks the raters' tendency to place all checks at the right or left ends of the scales.

Another way to eliminate perseveration errors is to scramble the descriptive words or phrases describing the degrees of a particular trait. Thus instead of the weakest description being at the left and the strongest at the right, with intervening ones showing a continuous graduation, the descriptions are scrambled so that adjacent descriptions are not continuous. This forces the rater to search for the best descriptive word or phrase and hence discourages perseveration errors. On the whole this method is not preferred by raters because it is confusing and also because fine gradations of judgment can not be indicated. In effect it is a scrambled category scale, and hence loses some of the value of a graphic rating scale.

A final way to increase the value of ratings is to secure judgments from several raters who are about equally well acquainted with the person whose traits are rated. In this way a composite judgment can be obtained that, in most cases, is more reliable than a single judgment.

Interpretation of Ratings

Determination of scores. The value of ratings can be increased by converting the raters' estimate into scores and then determining the total score for all the traits. The method of scoring ratings varies somewhat with the type of rating procedure used. In the case of the rank-order method, for example, all one needs to know is the position of any given individual in the group, and the size of the group. When using the alphabetical scale, arbitrary values are assigned to the letters which makes it similar to a numerical scale. In the case of the descriptive-adjective scale, values, in steps of 10, are assigned to the various descriptive terms of the scale, thus treating it as a percentage scale. The numerical values used in any of the separate scales are then cumulated, or averaged for the various traits, and this number is the final score for the person on the total scale.

Preference for the graphic scale was indicated above. One of the reasons for this is the method of scoring generally used. When using the graphic rating scale, the rater places a check-mark somewhere along the line of the scale to indicate his judgment. Since this check-mark need not be placed immediately above a descriptive word or phrase, but in an intermediate position between them, the rater can be more discriminating in his judgment. In other words, he need not place the person in one of several categories, as in the category scales, but places him somewhere along a continuous scale that extends from one extreme of the trait to the other. The usual method of scoring this scale is to measure the distance (in terms of millimeters) that the check-mark is from the lower end of the scale. When the scale is divided into 100 to 130 divisions, marked at 10-point intervals, the scoring is greatly facilitated. If a total score on all the traits combined is desired, an average of the scores for the several traits can be determined. On the whole this is somewhat questionable. It is better to compare individual traits than averages.

Evaluation of scores. We pointed out above that the judgments of several raters, preferably three, are superior to the evaluation of a single rater. This is particularly true when the raters agree fairly well in their individual judgments, but when they do not agree reasonably well, discretion must be used.

As an illustration, let us take the case of a patrolman who was rated by three superior officers. All three officers agreed very closely concerning the patrolman's initiative in that each of them rated him as very superior in this respect. Their close agreement strengthens one's confidence that the patrolman is outstanding in this regard. As to leadership, however, two of the officers rated the patrolman as moderately superior in leadership, but the third officer rated him as definitely inferior. If these three ratings are averaged, the patrolman's leadership score is about average, in spite of the fact that two of the raters judged him as superior. In this case it may be better to accept the judgments of the two raters who agree closely, as representative, rather than the composite of all three. On the trait of dependability the patrolman was rated as very superior, average and very inferior by the three raters. Averaging these three ratings gives the patrolman an average rating on dependability, but slight confidence can be placed in this average since the three raters disagreed so markedly. The best approach in this case is to secure additional ratings from one or more competent judges and see how their judgments compare with the first three. Then if some agreement is present between the ratings of several of the judges, their ratings can be accepted as possibly more representative than that of the original raters.

Sometimes raters are requested to indicate their confidence in their own ratings. When this is done, these estimates of confidence are used as a means of weighting ratings when marked disagreements between raters develop.

Police Rating Scales

The type of rating scale used in police work at any given time depends, in large part, on the purpose for which it is used, the type of information desired, and the opportunity for rating. Whether the purpose is one of selection, evaluation, or promotion is also of major importance. No matter which type of rating scale is used, the value of the results obtained depends on the care with which the rater makes his judgments, the extent of his acquaintance with the person rated, and his competence in observing the behavior of others. It must be remembered that any rating device is merely an aid used to obtain an evaluation of a person in a systematic way. The following rating scales, adapted for police work, incorporate some of the features regarded as effective and desirable.

POLICE RATING SCALE
The Selection of Patrolmen

Name of person rated_____ Date_____

Address_____

When first acquainted with ratee?_____

Nature of contact with ratee_____

Are you related to ratee?_____If so, how?_____

Rater's signature_____

Position_____

Address_____

Listed below are several traits generally accepted as essential to success as a patrolman. You are requested to give your careful and considered evaluation of the above applicant concerning these traits. Before making your judgment concerning each trait, recall as many specific incidents as possible in which the trait was observed in the applicant. Indicate your judgment by placing a check-mark (√) somewhere along the line of each scale nearest the word or phrase that best describes the applicant. Intermediate positions between the descriptive categories may be used. If you have had no opportunity to observe a given trait in the applicant, check the blank marked "unknown."

I. *Initiative.* Ability to get results through original and somewhat uncommon adaptations of experience. Attitude toward adopting improved methods.

Very original	Often resourceful.	Accepts new ideas willingly. Occasionally suggests new ideas.	Routine worker. Needs direction.	Very unprogressive. Needs constant direction.	UNKNOWN

II. *Practical Judgment.* Ability to grasp a situation, think clearly, and arrive at conclusions.

Poor grasp of situation. Recommendations more wrong than right.	Misinterprets some facts. Makes occasional errors in judgment.	Judgment usually sound and reasonable in ordinary circumstances.	Grasps situation quickly. Thinks logically.	Exceptionally logical thinker. Exceptional grasp of essential factors.	UNKNOWN

III. *Ability to Learn.* Quickness and ease in learning new skills, methods and ideas.

Exceptionally quick learner.	Learns quickly but with effort. Mastery good.	Learning speed average. Mastery fair.	Slow to learn. Mastery below average.	Very slow to learn. Mastery poor.	UNKNOWN

IV. *Ability to Follow Directions.* Speed and accuracy in executing written and oral instructions.

Follows only simplest directions without help.	Follows ordinary directions with help.	Follows directions reasonably well with few errors.	Follows complex directions with occasional help.	Follows complex directions accurately without help.	UNKNOWN

V. *Social Sense*. Insight into social situations and behavior. Understanding of people.

Exceptionally adept in meeting and dealing with people.	Meets most people well and understands their intentions.	Adjusts well in most social situations with which familiar.	Somewhat awkward in social situations. Misunderstands intentions of some people.	Commits many social blunders. Frequently misinterprets people's intentions.	UNKNOWN

VI. *Cooperation*. Ability to work well with others.

An obstructionist.	Indifferent to others' needs and wishes.	Cooperates much of the time and fairly willingly.	Works harmoniously with others. A good team worker.	Outstandingly cooperative. Actively promotes harmony.	UNKNOWN

VII. *Attitude Toward Others*. Fairmindedness and courtesy.

Intensely interested in welfare of others, even beyond the call of duty.	Actively concerned for the welfare of others.	Shows conventional concern and courtesy.	Self-interest strong. Often discourteous.	Callous to the needs and welfare of others.	UNKNOWN

VIII. *Attitude Toward Work*. Interest in work; desire to do well; industry.

Does least possible. Complains much.	Disinterested plodder.	Moderately interested. Work fairly satisfactory.	Interested in most aspects. Takes pride in work.	Exceptional in interest, application and achievement.	UNKNOWN

IX. *Emotional Control.* Ability to control emotions under ordinary conditions of stress.

Exceptionally even-tempered.	Seldom angry or depressed. Regains control quickly.	Emotional control satisfactory except when under stress.	Becomes angry or depressed easily. Recovers slowly.	Emotionally uncontrolled. Often angry or depressed.

UNKNOWN

X. *Dependability.* Extent to which he can be relied upon to complete tasks acceptably and promptly.

Requires supervision. Seldom completes work on time.	Easily satisfied with quality of work. Often behind schedule.	Usually completes tasks acceptably and promptly. Some supervision necessary.	Reliable. Gives attention to details. Occasional supervision needed.	Completes all assignments most satisfactorily. Gives close attention to details.

UNKNOWN

XI. *Accuracy.* Ability to avoid error when completing an assignment.

Always accurate and precise.	Makes few errors and corrects most.	Usually accurate but unaware of some errors.	Makes errors. Assumes errors are unimportant.	Shows slight concern for accuracy.

UNKNOWN

INTELLIGENCE TESTING

Application to Police Officers

Although the first attempt to measure intelligence was made a half century ago, it was not until our entrance into World War I that any systematic effort was made to measure the intelligence of adults. It is significant that soon after the close of that war, when the Army Alpha Intelligence Test was given to civilian groups variously employed, that policemen were among the first tested. Thurstone, in 1922, published some of the first data on the intelligence of policemen. In the three decades since this first venture in testing the intelligence of policemen, many communities have adopted the intelligence test as a standard instrument for the selection of police officers. Less scientific techniques are still used, however, and the intelligence test is not used as a screening device nearly as widely as it should be.

Recommended Intelligence Tests

The following tests[1] are some of those more widely used for testing civil service applicants. These are not listed in an order of merit because the features each has may make it more desirable in one case and less desirable in another.

The *Army General Classification Test* (AGCT), that was administered to more than twelve million inductees during World War II, is now available in a "Civilian Edition." This test aims to measure general learning ability by testing for several factors: verbal factor (vocabulary), number and reasoning factors (arithmetic word problems), and space factor (block counting). The working time for this test is 40 minutes, and the raw score can be converted into standard or into percentile scores. This test has definite possibilities in police work.

Another recently developed test, well suited for testing adults, is the *New California Short-Form Test of Mental Maturity*, Advanced Form.

The *Ohio State University Psychological Test* (Form 21) differs from many other intelligence tests in that it has no time

[1]For a list of names and addresses of publishers see Appendix

limit and is a power test. The testee is encouraged to attempt all the items of the test and to take as much time as is needed. Since this test emphasizes difficulty rather than speed, it is well suited for testing people who are slower and more deliberate in their thinking and action.

Another widely used series of tests is the *Henmon-Nelson Tests of Mental Ability*. Each test has 90 items arranged in the order of difficulty, with a time limit of 30 minutes. Either the high school or college forms can be used depending on the academic level of the applicants tested.

A group of tests that have proved valuable through long use are the Otis tests. The *Otis Self-Administering Tests of Mental Ability*, Higher Examination, that is also published under the title of *Otis Employment Tests*, has a working time of 30 minutes, but norms are also available for a 20-minute time limit. The *Otis General Intelligence Examination* is a self-administering test that requires approximately 30 minutes to complete. The *Gamma Test* of the *Otis Quick-Scoring Mental Ability Tests* also has a working time of 30 minutes. A mental ability test associated with the above, because items in some of the forms are taken from the Otis tests, is the *Personnel Test* by Wonderlic. This is one of the more recently constructed tests that is well received. Perhaps its chief advantage is that it has a short working time of 12 minutes. It can also be given with unlimited time if so desired.

The test originally used for testing policemen, and still used, is the *Army Alpha*, now available in several forms. Among these forms are: *Revision of Army Alpha Examination*, Forms A and B, that requires 30 to 40 minutes to complete; the *Revised Army Alpha Examination*, Forms 5 and 7, that requires 30 minutes, and the *Revised Alpha Examination*, Form 6, Short Form, that requires only 15 minutes.

The Intelligence of Policemen

Minimum requirements. How intelligent should a policeman be? Quite obviously this question has not been answered satisfactorily. Suggestions, in terms of Army Alpha scores, have been made from time to time, however. Vollmer, in the early 1920's, suggested that a raw score of 75 on the Army Alpha should be a minimum qualification for police work. A score of 75 is the lower limit of the C+ category that extends to a score of 104. Since C, or a score of 60, is average, he placed the minimum requirement slightly above that of the average of the population. In 1924, Telford and Moss, who suggested a number of tests for patrolmen, placed the lower limit at 65, but indicated that they preferred it at 95. Some large cities have set the minimum limit at 100. It is significant that all of these limits are in the C+ category.

Since the early 1920's the trend has been definitely in the direction of raising the minimum Army Alpha scores required. A score of 110 was suggested as desirable in a bulletin published by the International Association of Chiefs of Police in 1938. Some claim that the lower limit should be a score of 120. Both of these latter recommendations place the minimum at the B level. A more recent recommendation in an article in the *Encyclopedia of Vocational Guidance* places the lower limit at a score of 135, which is the lower limit of the A category of intelligence.

These figures indicate a definite and significant trend. It is true that all policemen are not as yet selected according to these high standards, but it is heartening that people are becoming increasingly aware of the fact that much is demanded of the police officer and that the effectiveness of his service to the community depends, in part, on his intelligence. Although we can expect a gap between what is recommended and what is required, the fact that higher and higher standards are recommended means that higher requirements will be demanded.

Results reported. No simple answer can be given to the question: What is the intelligence of policemen? Several things complicate the problem. Many of the studies report the intelligence test scores for applicants rather than for men in service. As already noted, minimum requirements are not uniform and hence the intelligence of police officers in different communities can not be compared directly. Length of service also seems to be a factor.

Reports on the Army Alpha scores made by policemen and by applicants in the 1920's give averages that range from 55 to 149.3, or all the way from a C to an A rating. A group of 64 applicants in San Diego had an average of 76.5, and another group of 113 in Palo Alto had 104.2. A group of 50 students in the Maryland State Police Training School had an average of 100, and a group of 321 students in the Police School in Los Angeles had an average of 116.1. An older study reports that Detroit patrolmen averaged, on the Army Alpha, 71.4, whereas sergeants and lieutenants averaged 55 and 58 respectively. Another early report from Cleveland indicated averages as low as 59 for detectives and as high as 98 for captains. On the other hand, a group of 15 policewomen in Washington, D. C. had an average Army Alpha score of 144, and a group of 26 men in the department in Berkeley an average of 149.3.

More recently the Army General Classification Test has been used. In Table I (see page 34), we observed that 172 policemen had an average AGCT standard score of 109, which is equivalent to an Army Alpha raw score of 70. In 1950, DuBois and Watson[2] reported on a group of 129 applicants selected as patrolmen in St. Louis who had an average AGCT score of 118, which is equivalent to an Army Alpha score of 96.

It must not be inferred that these results are necessarily typical of all police officers employed today. Moreover, we must remember when dealing with averages that a half of the cases fall above and a half fall below the average. Certainly these rather meager data suggest strongly the need for further systematic study of the intelligence of police officers.

PERSONALITY TESTING

The Need for Testing

The selection of policemen on the basis of intelligence alone is not enough. An applicant may be superior in this regard and still be a dismal failure as a police officer because of other traits he possesses. A single incident, reported to the author by a police chief,[3] is sufficient to illustrate this point.

---

[2]DuBois, P. H. and Watson, R. I.: The Selection of Patrolmen. *Journal of Applied Psychology*, 34:90-95, 1950.

---

[3]Personal communication from Chief Lawrence Abbott, Springfield, Ohio.

A group of men, who met specified requirements and passed certain tests, were appointed as patrolmen and assigned to the police school for training. After several days of instruction, a call came that a man was found dead in an entryway. To give the men of the school some practical experience in observing the gathering of data and in report making, the chief instructed that the students be taken out on the call in cars. At the scene they were deployed at such a distance so as not to interfere with the actual investigation. On arrival the officers found a man lying dead in a pool of blood in an entryway. Investigation revealed that the victim, an epileptic, was descending the stairs when he had an epileptic seizure which caused him to fall from a landing over a banister to the entryway. During the fall, the man struck his head, and the blow caused his death.

On the way back to the station, several of the student patrolmen observed that one of their number was not only acting peculiarly but that he was also saying odd and meaningless things. The next day the man's behavior was even more bizarre than the day before. He told a variety of tales, quite obviously false, that were so fanciful that even laymen were certain that something was wrong. The man spared the department further trouble and embarrassment because he was discharged immediately.

It is certain that this man was not good officer material, and it was fortunate for the department that this was discovered early. Had this man not been taken to the scene of the accident, which made his psychoneurotic condition evident, he might have continued as a patrolman for a considerable time with no one aware of his difficulty. Evidently a crisis situation, for which he was not prepared, would have made his abnormality apparent, but this situation might have been crucial for the welfare and safety of others. The hazard caused by this man's failure in a crucial situation can not be overestimated.

It is imperative, then, that people who are emotionally unstable, predisposed toward mental abnormality, or actually psychotic be eliminated early in the selection process. This, however, is not easy. People do not wear placards on their backs stating, "I am abnormal"; neither are there any identifying marks, nor do they "show it in their faces." The signs of abnormality are much more subtle; they are found in one's behavior.

Because a policeman works with people, some of whom are abnormal, he himself should be as free of peculiarities and quirks as possible. As a means of finding normal people for law enforcement work, a psychiatric examination is recommended. When the list of applicants is long, this procedure is time consuming and expensive, and hence quicker and less expensive screening devices must be used.

Approaches to Personality Testing

The neurotic patrolman in the above illustration showed his abnormality after being placed in a situation of considerable stress. Naturally it is not always possible to do this, nor will the same stressful situation precipitate abnormal behavior in the people who have such tendencies. In view of this, the *stress interview* originally used in Germany and to a limited extent with police officers here, has merit. The purpose of this method is to place deliberately the applicant in a situation that creates stress of a verbal and motor sort, and then to observe and rate the person on various characteristics. Although its use has been limited, the stress interview has possibilities and does merit further development.

A second approach, used to a limited extent in the selection of policemen, is the *Rorschach Test* which is a projective technique. It is a clinical instrument, consisting of a series of ink blots into which meaning is read, that throws light on personality traits and particularly on abnormal tendencies. A group of 25 New York City patrolmen participated recently in a research study in which the Rorschach test was used. More data are needed before generalization is possible. One of the chief disadvantages of this test is that a highly trained specialist must adminster, score and interpret it.

The most easily employed approach to personality testing is with the questionnaire-type of test. Tests of this type are widely used in both education and industry. One of their advantages, in addition to the light they throw on personality traits, is that they are easily and quickly administered to large groups, and that they are simple to score. Interpretation of scores, however, must be left to a competent and well trained person.

Some available tests. Although the list of tests from which one can select is long, all of the tests are not particularly suited to police work. Selection must be based on the traits important in law enforcement work. The desirability of eliminating applicants with tendencies toward emotional instability or mental abnormality was stressed above. A test specifically designed to accomplish this with army inductees during World War II, and which is now available for civilian use, is the *Cornell Index*. This test does not reveal the type of abnormality, but rather the presence of difficulty. It is recommended as a supplementary aid when interviewing.

Information concerning other types of personality adjustment than emotional instability or neuroticism is very desirable when selecting patrolmen. One test that throws light on five types of adjustment that are significant is *The Adjustment Inventory*, Adult Form, by Bell. This test measures home, health, social, emotional, and occupational adjustment. A police officer should be rather well-adjusted in his own home life so as to be better able to deal with the types of marital discord and family problems that a policeman encounters in the course of duty. Moreover, he should not be over-anxious about his health and not be a chronic complainer. He should be moderately aggressive in his social adjustment and emotionally stable. Although some dissatisfaction with employment can be expected among applicants, marked dissatisfaction should make one alert to the possibility of a chronic condition. Should an applicant's attitude prove to be one of chronic dissatisfaction, he should be rejected because of his possible influence on the morale of others.

The Personality Inventory by Bernreuter measures the following traits: emotional stability, self-sufficiency, introversion-extroversion, dominance-submission, confidence in oneself, and sociability. This test has been given to policemen, but more study of its value in law enforcement work is needed. The *Thurstone Temperament Schedule*, recently developed, measures seven temperament traits: active, vigorous, impulsive, dominant, stable, sociable, and reflective. Other tests have possibilities in this field of work, but much experimental work must be done before positive results can be cited.

SPECIAL APTITUDES

McCall, writing in the *Encyclopedia of Vocational Guidance*, lists seven psychological requirements that should be met by applicants for police work. The first of these is concerned with attention and memory: the ability to concentrate on oral instructions, to follow directions, and to have good auditory, and we might add, visual imagery. His second and third requirements deal with reasoning ability: the ability to reason arithmetically, and to make practical judgments in day-to-day situations. His fourth requirement is linguistic—vocabulary; fifth is the perception of relations; sixth is the ability to deal with numbers; and seventh, general adaptability. These are undoubtedly essential requirements. Now let us list some of the available tests that measure these qualities.

Tests for Special Abilities

Tests of attention and memory. The two mental processes of attention and memory are closely related in that the extent to which one remembers depends in part on the degree or clearness of attention. The abilities to attend and to remember are very essential in law enforcement work. Law enforcement officers are given instructions daily that must be remembered and directions that must be carried out. Therefore a good auditory and visual memory is essential for success.

It is a common practice, when measuring attention and memory, to give applicants a set of oral instructions that must be reproduced or followed. On the whole a more standardized procedure than this is preferable.

The *Social Intelligence Test*, of the George Washington University Series, is appropriate in this connection because it has a section on memory for names and faces. In all, the test has five parts that measure various aspects of one's social perception and judgment. Hence this test throws light not only on memory for names and faces, which is very important in law enforcement work, but also gives information concerning one's knowledge of people and of social situations. This test has had limited use in police work.

A simple method of measuring auditory attention and memory span is to read slowly a series of digits (as: 2 5 9 4 6 3 8) that is repeated immediately after presentation by the person tested. The average adult can repeat seven digits correctly. Repeating nine correctly shows superiority. A common method of measuring visual attention and memory ability is to show the person a drawing with many details (of a traffic accident or similar event) for a few seconds after which he is to recall as many of the items in the picture as possible. Sometimes the person's recall is measured in terms of his response to a list of questions based on the picture. Some police departments use a series of automobile license plates, exposed briefly one at a time, as a means of measuring attention and memory span.

Perhaps the chief difficulty with each of these tests is that they measure immediate rather than delayed recall. Although there is some delay in recalling the names and faces in the social intelligence test mentioned above, it is hardly long enough to duplicate a real-life situation. Perhaps rechecking the testee on this part of the test after several hours and again after a day would give more realistic information.

Tests of arithmetic reasoning and skill. Several different tests can be used to measure arithmetic reasoning, some of which are more comprehensive than others. The *Stanford Achievement Arithmetic Test*, Advanced Form, has a performance time of 50 minutes. The *Moore Test of Arithmetic Reasoning* requires only 30 minutes to give. If only a brief period of time can be devoted to this testing, the *Otis Arithmetic Reasoning Test*, that requires but six minutes, can be used. To measure skill in computation or knowledge of fundamentals the following tests can be used: *Schorling-Clark-Potter Hundred Problem Arithmetic Test*, and the *Rogers Achievement Test in Mathematics*.

Practical judgment. Perhaps the best test that can be recommended here is the *Test of Practical Judgment*, Form AH, by Cardall. This test was given to graduates of the Traffic Institute of Northwestern University who earned an average score of 212. This places their average at about the 75th percentile of the test. Another test that can be used to good advantage here is the *Social*

Intelligence Test, mentioned above, the first part of which deals with judgment in social situations.

Vocabulary and reading tests. There are several vocabulary tests from which to select. Among those more suitable for law enforcement officers are: *Columbia Vocabulary Test, Wide Range Vocabulary Test, Cooperative Vocabulary Test,* and the *O'Rourke Survey Test for Vocabulary.* Many of the reading tests measure vocabulary as well as speed and comprehension of reading. Suitable tests are: *Nelson-Denny Reading Test, Minnesota Speed of Reading Examination for College Students,* and the *Iowa Silent Reading Test,* Advanced Form.

The perception of relations. Two tests can be listed here. The first, which measures perception of spatial relations, is the *Revised Minnesota Paper Form Board.* The second, the *Minnesota Clerical Test,* deals with the perception of the similarities and differences between pairs of numbers and pairs of names. In both of these tests emphasis is placed on speed and accuracy in perception.

Adaptability. The one test specifically designed to measure the adaptability of policemen is the *Policeman Examination General Adaptability Test* by O'Rourke. This test has 100 items and requires one hour to administer.

Interest in police work. Long use of the *Strong Vocational Interest Blank for Men* (Revised) has demonstrated that success in a certain occupation depends, in part, on having interests like successful people in that occupation. This is no doubt just as true of policemen as it is of people engaged in other occupations. Since this test can be scored for policemen, it can be used as a means of determining whether an applicant's interests are like those of policemen or not.

REFERENCES

BITTNER, R. H. and WORCESTER, D. A.: The Selection of Men for the Nebraska Safety Patrol. *Journal of Consulting Psychology, 3:57-64,* 1939. Discusses the use of the Army Alpha and other tests.

BURTT, H. E.: *Principles of Employment Psychology,* (Revised edition). New York, Harpers, 1942. A comprehensive discussion of rating procedures in employment is found in Chapter 12.

DOOHER, M. J. and MARQUIS, VIVIENNE (Eds.): *Rating Employee and Supervisory Performance.* New York, American Management Association, 1950. This is a comprehensive discussion of merit rating in industry.

DUBOIS, P. H. and WATSON, R. I.: The Selection of Patrolmen. *Journal of Applied Psychology,* 34:90-95, 1950. Discusses the use of psychological tests in the selection of patrolmen in St. Louis.

KATES, S. L.: Rorschach Responses, Strong Blank Scales, and Job Satisfaction among Policemen. *Journal of Applied Psychology,* 34:249-254, 1950. This is a study of 25 New York City policemen.

MAHLER, W. R.: *Twenty Years of Merit Rating, 1926-1946,* New York: Psychological Corporation, 1947. An extensive bibliography on merit rating in various areas.

MERRILL, MAUD A.: Intelligence of Policemen, *Journal of Personnel Research,* 5:511-515, 1927. An early application of intelligence testing to the selection of policemen.

PATERSON, D. G.: Rating. *In* Fryer, D. H. and Henry, E. R. (Eds.) *Handbook of Applied Psychology,* Vol. I. New York, Rinehart, 1950. Selection 20, pp. 147-154. An excellent discussion of rating with several illustrations.

Chapter 3

THE PSYCHOLOGY OF INTERVIEWING
By
GEORGE J. DUDYCHA

WHAT IS AN INTERVIEW?

THE WORD *interview* is an old and familiar word that has considerable meaning for each of us. Perhaps the first thought that occurs to us when someone mentions the word is one person asking another person questions. Certainly asking questions is a very important feature of interviewing, but interviewing, as we propose to understand it, is much more than a process of questioning. To be more specific, interviewing is a formal process of interaction, or of communication, between one person and another (or several others) in which the interviewer[1] seeks to impart to or extract from the *interviewee* information and attitudes, for the purpose of directing the interviewee's action, of aiding him to adjust to a difficulty, finding a solution to a problem, or of determining a course of action. To put it simply, an interview is a "conversation with a purpose."

Interviews can be classified as fact-finding, informing, and motivating. Although all three types may overlap in any one interview, usually one predominates. In the employment situation the fact-finding and informing aspects predominate. The exit or termination interview used in industry is almost exclusively of the fact-finding type, so also are the public opinion poll and the market research interviews. All three types of interviews are used in counseling, with the motivating type predominating. Therapeutic interviews, however, are by-and-large motivating interviews. Interviews

---

[1]The interviewer is the person who directs the conversation or asks the questions; the interviewee is the person who is being interviewed.

67

used in criminal investigation, on the other hand, are largely of the fact-finding type.

INTERVIEWING AND LAW ENFORCEMENT

In the law enforcement field a distinction is commonly made between interviewing, as such, and criminal interrogation. Criminal interrogation, as the term seems to imply, is concerned with the legal aspects of questioning an offender. Because of its technical aspects, criminal interrogation is often treated apart from interviewing even though logically it is one of the types of interviewing. Due to the limitation of space, we shall confine our discussion of the interview to the broader aspects of interviewing and omit criminal interrogation as such. For a detailed discussion of criminal interrogation the reader is referred to the references listed at the end of this chapter.

That the interview is used extensively in law enforcement work, as well as in other areas of life, is abundantly evident. An important part of the law enforcement officer's task is to piece together information that reveals the facts of a case, the sequence of action, and the responsibility for acts committed. To accomplish this the law enforcement officer must question suspects and witnesses. Hence he uses the information-seeking interview. In addition to seeking information the law enforcement officer must also give information and direction to others. To make certain that his instructions are understood he often talks things over with his subordinates. Hence he uses the informing interview also.

The above two applications of the interview in law enforcement work are obvious and generally accepted. There is yet a third and very important application of the interview in this field and that is in the area of adjustment. At present its use is limited, but the need for extension is great. People need to become more aware of its possibilities as a means of *decreasing* violations of the law and of aiding those who are guilty of its infractions to become more law abiding. The law enforcement officer is not only charged with the duty of apprehending and arresting offenders, but of maintaining law and order as well. Too often law and order are maintained by the use of force, restraint and barriers where education and adjustment would be more effective. Restraint by force is negative; education and adjustment are positive in nature. Although restraint must be used, we need to place more emphasis on the positive approach than we do.

There is a definite place for the adjustment interview and for adjustment counseling in law enforcement work. Take the case of a man who speeds through a traffic signal thus endangering the lives of other people. An alert traffic officer arrests him for this violation and a police court fines him and possibly deprives him of driving privileges for a specified period. There the matter is dropped until this man is charged with a similar offense a short time later. The penalty is increased and so the cycle of violation and arrest continues. A counseling interview with this man would fairly quickly reveal the cause of his trouble—perpetual bickering with his wife, or frequent arguments with his boss. Because of his anger and frequent frustration, and his desire to fight back against his wife or his boss, in spite of the odds against him, he "takes it out" on the traffic light that can not "talk back." It is like kicking one's dog because of a nagging wife. As long as this man's frustration continues he may continue running through traffic lights without ever being aware of what motivates him to do so. Arrests, fines, and license revocations may have little effect until this man appreciates more fully his problem and adjusts to it more wholesomely.

A man once told the author that each time he is faced with a frustrating and seemingly insoluble problem, he jumps into his car and drives like mad over the countryside until he relaxes. Think of the hazard created by this one man. Certainly we have penalties for such behavior, but do they stop such insane acts? One thing is certain, as long as this man fails to learn a more safe and sane way of meeting his frustrations, he will continue to be an exceedingly serious road hazard menacing the lives of others.

Fortunately in the area of juvenile delinquency notable advances have been made in the direction of an intelligent and enlightened approach to the problems that lie behind a given child's delinquency. In these cases legal formalities are dispensed with as much as possible, and counseling procedures are substituted. Since the approach has proved effective with juvenile delinquents, it should be extended and adapted to alcoholics, drug addicts, prostitutes, shop-lifters, peeping Toms, kleptomaniacs, homosexuals, the chronic-complainers-to-the-police, and a score of others of this sort who are personality problems. Use of the counseling or adjustment interview over a period of time, supplemented with other therapeutic measures, would, without a doubt, go far toward reducing the incidence and severity of some of these offenses. It would also do much to aid some of these people to lead more socially acceptable, more productive, and more satisfying lives.

During the last several decades the philosophy of law enforcement has undergone some change. Though emphasis continues to be placed on retribution for crimes committed, interest in the offender's social history and personal experiences as a means of insight into his crime is growing. Interest seems to be shifting from the offense to the offender. Although the "understanding" approach has much merit, it must not be regarded as a substitute for punishment. What we are saying is that intelligent counseling and psychotherapy can lessen the likelihood that an offender will repeat his offense at a later time. This is particularly true in the case of minor crimes and offenses. Since this is the case, psychological counseling and psychotherapy should be developed as one of the phases of police work.

Two approaches can be used in the application of this method. One way is to have one or several people well trained in clinical psychololgy attached to the department who would do nothing but psychological work. The other method is to have a competent psychological counselor who would do some of the work and refer the more serious cases to appropriate services and agencies. Both of these approaches merit serious consideration.

GETTING SET FOR THE INTERVIEW

Importance of Favorable Physical Conditions

Law enforcement officers must interview in various places and sometimes under conditions that are not favorable to good interviewing. Police officers, for instance, interview the victims of a traffic accident, if their condition permits, at the scene of the accident. Detectives, when called to the scene of a serious crime, also question as many of the people involved as possible. Interviewing under these conditions is not easy. The physical surroundings are anything but conducive to answering questions with care. In these and similar situations, attention continually jumps from one thing to another and is not sustained; memory is poor; emotion is intense. As a result even the law enforcement officer is under considerable strain. Yet information must be obtained regardless of the conditions. Fortunately much of the law enforcement officer's interviewing can be done in more favorable surroundings.

Where to interview. The ideal place to interview is in a private office equipped for the purpose. It must be a place that is quiet, free from interruptions (as the telephone that rings every few minutes), that is conducive to relaxation, and that inspires confidence. If one is to accomplish the most possible during an interview, attention must be given to the psychology of the situation. Hence both physical and psychological factors must be employed to build good mutual feeling, or rapport, between the parties of the interview.

Privacy is of major importance. To try to interview someone over a counter in a lobby where telephones are ringing, other people are constantly interrupting, and strangers are eavesdropping, is hardly ideal. Yet these are the conditions under which law enforcement officers sometimes attempt to use the interview.

Eliminate barriers. The object of the interview is to establish the best possible relationship between the parties of the interview so that their interaction and exchange of information and attitudes contribute or result in the solution of a problem. This can be accomplished best when there are as few barriers between the interviewer and the interviewee as possible. Law enforcement officers must especially be aware of this need for eliminating barriers because many people are put on the defensive when questioned by them. Therefore even from the standpoint of the physical situation there should be few or no barriers. The counter separating the police officer from the person interviewed is such a physical barrier. If the interviewee must stand a step lower than the officer, the barrier is enhanced. Such barriers divide. They increase the social distance between the interviewer and the interviewee. They do that which in interviewing we want most to avoid.

When the interviewing is done in an office, the arrangement of the furniture should be such as to eliminate barriers. It is well to have at least two chairs between which the interviewee can select. If there is only one chair for him to occupy, he may feel forced to sit where he does not care to sit. Though this seems to be a trifling matter, it may result in unconscious antagonism and a show of resistance. Choice decreases the likelihood of resistance and eliminates the barrier.

It is also well not to have a desk beween the interviewee and the interviewer. The person interviewed should sit to the right or to the left of the interviewer's desk, whichever is more convenient and natural. Because nothing separates the parties of the interview, the arrangement suggests confidence, mutual trust, and the absence of fear. The attitude, "I like a piece of furniture between us," does just the opposite. To accomplish more in the interview, eliminate the physical barriers that inevitably create psychological barriers.

Prepare for Each Interview

To the inexperienced interviewer preparation for the interview may appear to be a waste of time. He assumes that the important thing is the "talk" that the one person has with the other, during which the interviewer applies certain specific techniques that produce the desired results. For him, knowing several rules-of-thumb is all that is necessary.

This is far ʿrom true. Nothing just happens of itself. The success of anything depends in large part on the amount and nature of the planning that goes into it. FBI officers never attempt to arrest a public enemy without carefully planning their method of attack to the smallest detail. A sheriff's posse does not attempt to smoke out a maniac barricaded in a farmhouse without some preliminary planning. Neither do police officers just descend on a strike-bound plant where there is labor trouble without plan or purpose. Planning is essential to any venture. Interviewing is not an exception to the rule.

Avoid being stampeded into an interview. In law enforcement work the need for interviewing is often urgent and immediate. One must admit that there are times when the opportunity for preparation is almost nonexistent. Even at such times a few moments of reflection may prevent some blundering in an interview. A partial substitute for preparation time is a learned technique for meeting unexpected situations. The officer who just happens to witness a traffic accident has no opportunity to get background data on the people involved, but he can be equipped with a technique for meeting this type of unexpected situation.

Office interviewing, on the other hand, always gives one an opportunity to prepare for the interview, and one should never allow himself to be stampeded into such an interview without preparation. If a suspect or a witness is unexpectedly brought to a police captain's office for examination and questioning, and the officer proceeds with the interview with little or no information, he is most likely to flounder about, create a poor impression, accomplish little or nothing, and waste his and the other person's time. Because the interview was unexpected he allowed himself to be pushed into it before he was ready for it. What an officer should do at such a time is to excuse himself after meeting the person briefly and perhaps formally, retire to another office, check such records and files as are available, question other officers who may be able to give some information, and then return to his office and proceed with the interview. It is far better to keep the interviewee waiting for 10 or 15 minutes and have a successful interview, than to begin immediately without control of the situation. The delay must not be regarded as lost time, but rather as essential for success.

How background material helps. A juvenile delinquent was brought to police headquarters for questioning. The officer assigned to interview the boy, knowing the importance of preparation, took time to get background data before proceeding with the interview. Hence when he came to the interview he already knew much about the boy. He knew more than his name and address.

He knew his father's name and his occupation, the number of brothers and sisters the boy had and their names, the boy's position in the family, and his general attitude toward his family. From the boy's teacher he learned about the quality of his school work, his attitudes towards others, his special abilities, and his outstanding personality traits. From the director of the settlement house in the boy's neighborhood, he learned about the boy's chums, their names, their activities and their interests. Thus when this officer came to interview the boy, he was able to say: "You are going on 15," rather than, "How old are you?" "You pitched a good game Friday," rather than ask, "What are your interests?" "Did you see Butch this morning?" rather than inquire, "What is your friend's name?"

The obvious completeness and accuracy of the interviewer's knowledge amazed the boy. Hence he thought: "If he knows all this, what doesn't he know?" Because the boy was impressed with the officer's seeming omniscience, he was more willing to volunteer information because he assumed that the interviewer knew it anyway. Thus the officer obtained the information he was seeking and at the same time developed a favorable and cooperative attitude in the boy.

Preparation for the interview pays-off in that it increases the interviewer's prestige, enhances his control over the situation, creates favorable attitudes, secures cooperation, and even saves interviewing time.

CONDUCT OF THE INTERVIEW

Opening the Interview

The success of any interview depends to a considerable extent on the initial interviewer-interviewee contact. If this first contact is strained or awkward, even momentarily, the success of the interview may be materially decreased. Therefore the interviewer must make a determined effort to elicit nothing but favorable responses from the interviewee, to develop good rapport, and to provide a situation that makes for relaxation and freedom of expression.

Getting acquainted. The greeting is the first step in getting acquainted. It must be friendly, sincere, and formal or informal, depending on the person interviewed. Addressing the person by name, sometimes by first name, breaks down the first barrier. The greeting must be followed by the seemingly spontaneous introduction of a topic for conversation that is of mutual interest. If it is introduced as a question, the interviewee is given an opportunity to talk, and talk he must if the interview is to be profitable and successful. In the selection of the topic for conversation, emphasis must be placed on the spontaneity of its presentation and on its interest value. Trite topics, such as the weather and one's health, leave one cold. People want to be treated as individuals and hence they like to talk about topics that are tailored to their interests and activities. They want to feel that this is their topic of conversation and not just a stock question that the interviewer asks everyone.

Developing rapport. Rapport means harmonious relationship. Anything that separates, divides or increases the social distance between the interviewer and the interviewee decreases rapport. Hence all barriers, of whatever sort, must be removed.

On the other hand, several things make for rapport. We have already noted the importance of the greeting and the opening conversation. Confidence is fostered by showing a genuine interest in the interviewee and his problem, by giving him one's undivided attention, by respecting him as a person, and by not registering surprise at what he says. Rapport is increased by putting the interviewee at ease, and by encouraging relaxation. Sitting accomplishes this to a degree. Our major emphasis, however, must be on understanding. An understanding attitude and insight, rather than one of superiority and condemnation, contributes much to good rapport.

INTERVIEWING TECHNIQUES

Restatement of Purpose

It was pointed out above that the purpose of the interview is to obtain information pertinent to a problem, to gain insight into a person's behavior, or to secure understanding and action on the part of the person interviewed. The interview is not an opportunity for the interviewer to "lord it over" the interviewee, nor to browbeat him, nor to condemn him. His chief purpose is to get the interviewee to talk and to react. By talking he gives information that may or may not be of value. Moreover, he concentrates his attention on what he is saying to such an extent that he does not attend to his gestures and other body responses. Not infrequently these are more revealing than what he says. Finally, by talking he gains insight into his own problem, recognizes his attitudes, and discovers solutions that he is willing to accept. Everyone will testify to the benefits derived from talking things over with a trusted friend, a personal counselor, a minister or a priest, a physician, or a lawyer. Since the law enforcement officer deals almost entirely with people in trouble, he too has the opportunity to accomplish much with these people by use of the interview.

Keep the Person Talking

One of the more important things that the interviewer must learn is to keep the interviewee talking and reacting as much of the time as possible. True the interviewer must talk too, sometime more and sometimes less, but his prime purpose is: *Keep the person talking and responding.* The inexperienced interviewer, on the other hand, finds it much easier to do the talking himself and hence he falls into the habit of lecturing. Too often law enforcement officers lecture people. Such an officer exhibits his lack of interviewing skill, or his domineering attitude, or both.

Since keeping the interviewee active is so important, several suggestions must be given as to technique. First there is the need for giving the interviewee the opportunity to continue talking, without interruption by the interviewer, even though he does so haltingly and without complete clarity. The inexperienced interviewer who finds himself in this situation has a tendency to share the interviewee's embarrassment and to put words into his mouth. This is illustrated in the following case.

A man who in a fit of anger severely beat his wife was interviewed by a police officer. Because of intense emotion during the questioning, the man experienced considerable difficulty expressing his thoughts and attitudes. He was completely blocked when he said:: "I - I - I -d - d - d, I - d—." To which the officer added, "despise your wife." Because the man was in a verbal morass, and because the officer's words gave him a quick way to freedom, he agreed. Yet what he was trying to say was that he *disliked* having his no-account brother-in-law in the house. Certainly the two thoughts are very different. On this occasion the officer failed to get the truth by not allowing the man to blunder on until he expressed his true attitude.

The use of long pauses. A second way to keep the interviewee talking is by the effective use of long pauses or periods of silence. The inexperienced interviewer is embarrassed by long pauses because he feels that it is his responsibility to keep the conversation going. Hence when there is a pause, he immediately jumps in with some comment that fills the gap. The interviewee soon learns this, and thus allows the interviewer to do it more and more often. What the interviewer must learn is that the long pauses (that seem much longer than they are) are just as embarrassing to the person interviewed as they are to him, and that the interviewee has the same cultural habit of filling in conversational gaps. Therefore if the interviewer waits long enough, the interviewee will in many instances volunteer additional information and comments just to break the embarrassing hiatus. Because of the pressure to continue talking that the interviewer thus exerts on the interviewee, by keeping quiet, the interviewee is very apt to relax his guard and express an idea or an attitude that he withheld earlier. Fortunately this somewhat subtle pressure exerted by the interviewer is resented much less than other more obvious methods are.

Disregard some comments. It is important not only to keep the interviewee talking, but to keep him talking about that which is pertinent to the problem. Some people intentionally and others as an unconscious defense mechanism, wander off into an aimless and unprofitable conversation. The interviewer must not allow himself to be led off on a tangent unless he believes that it will provide some profitable lead. In any case he must maintain direction of the interview which means that he must resist unprofitable leads suggested by the person interviewed. To do this he must learn to ignore some of the comments made by the other person. Every statement made by the interviewee does not merit or require a response from the interviewer. Some of them can and must be ignored.

The non-directive approach. A final suggestion for keeping the person talking is taken from the recently developed method of non-directive counseling. The non-directive method is a clinical approach to personality problems. It is a service method used for therapeutic purposes. Briefly its aim is to keep the client talking until he discovers a solution to his problem that is his own and that he is willing to accept and act on. The non-directive method of keeping the person talking is *repetition and restatement of the client's comments.* The following fragment from a police officer's interview with a delinquent boy illustrates the point.

Boy: "I hate my old man."
Officer: "You have a strong dislike for your father."
Boy: "Yeah, he makes me work and takes all my money."
Officer: "He doesn't allow you to keep any of your earnings."
Boy: "Naw, he takes it all to buy whiskey. And he beats my ma."
Officer: "You say your father is mean to your mother."
Boy: "Yeah, and he stole some money too."
Officer: "Your father stole money."
Boy: "Sure, and he's try'n' to pin the rap on me."

Note the techique used by the officer. He did not condemn the boy; nor did he ask questions; nor did he register surprise. He merely restated the boy's comment. The effect of this is that a further comment is drawn out of the interviewee without giving direction to his thinking, as is true in direct questioning. To such a rephrasing, the interviewee is very unlikely to come back with a simple "yes" or "no." Since the person's idea has already been repeated and accepted, he goes on to volunteer another idea, which in turn is repeated and accepted, and which elicits yet another statement. So the interview continues. It is like playing catch. Each time the officer threw the ball back to the boy, only to have him attempt a new curve. When the interviewee experiences blocking, as will happen, the interviewer can restate an earlier statement made by the interviewee, or ask a direct question, either of which will start the process going again.

The advantages of the non-directive approach are that the interviewer does not put words into the mouth of the interviewee (he allows the interviewee to direct his own thinking); he keeps the conversation moving, and he provides an opportunity for the free expression of attitudes. The non-directive method of interviewing can not always be used by law enforcement officers, but it is remarkable in how many situations it can be used when one learns the technique.

Suggestions for Questioning

The free narrative report. The free narrative report followed by questions has been found to be effective and reliable on the witness stand and elsewhere. This approach may be illustrated by the question: "Tell me all about the trouble you have been having with your neighbors." After the person has indicated adequately the direction of his thinking and his attitudes, further information can be obtained by direct questioning or by the use of the non-directive technique discussed above. The advantages of this technique are that it gives the interviewee the opportunity to talk freely, it puts some pressure on him to continue talking, and his thinking is self-directed.

When direct questioning is resorted to for the purpose of extracting further information or for verifying facts previously presented, the questions should be stated positively. This leads to less confusion than when negatives are used.

Avoid yes-no questions. One of the things to avoid when questioning during an interview is the yes-no type of question. Some questions can not be answered "yes" or "no." Take the question: "Do you still beat your wife?" If answered positively, the man admits that he was and still is a wife-beater. If answered negatively, the man admits that he was a wife-beater in the past but has discontinued the practice. The man who has never beaten his wife can not answer this question without explanation.

A further objection to the yes-no question is that people sometimes agree with the questioner just to be agreeable, or because they do not understand the question, or because they are afraid to disagree. Hence agreement does not mean that one is getting the truth. Furthermore this type of question determines what the interviewee will respond to and limits him to it. If the questions asked are irrelevant to the problem at hand, nothing is gained even though the answers are given. We must constantly keep in mind the purpose of the interview. The purpose is more than merely getting a response from a person. The purpose is to get a meaningful response, and that is somewhat less likely with the yes-no type of question.

Avoid too rapid questioning. A second thing to avoid when questioning is too rapid questioning. Rapid questioning causes excessive tension and emotion and these in turn produce disorganized responses. Sometimes this is done deliberately and with intention. It is then a modified third degree that does not fit in with the purpose of interviewing. The interviewer seeks information, insight or adjustment. These are not obtained by precipitating an emotional explosion nor by putting the person in a mental and motor straight-jacket.

Terminating the Interview

No interview should seemingly run on endlessly, nor should it just fade out. Just as the beginning of the interview is important, so also the ending is important. When one should begin to close an interview depends on the characteristics of the interviewee, what has been accomplished, and the need for supplemental information. In any case the process of closing must be orderly, definite, and not too abrupt.

To close an interview without warning with the words, "That's all," is entirely too abrupt. It comes as a shock to the interviewee. If he had anything more to say, he is completely blocked. Instead the interviewer should indicate that he is closing by the technique that he follows. He can use several things to indicate his intention. He can summarize briefly what has been covered or accomplished during the interview. Following this he can give the interviewee a final opportunity to express additional ideas, if he so desires. The

question: "Is there anything else that you wish to add or emphasize?" will accomplish this.

Indicate a course of action. Another closing technique is to suggest definite and alternative courses of action to the interviewee.
These alternatives should be the ones that were developed fully
during the interview. The following are illustrative closing statements.

One can say to the wife complaining of marital discord: "You
can meet your husband half way in any of the several ways we
discussed, or you can have him placed in jail. Consider the
alternatives and please let me know tomorrow which course of
action you prefer to follow." The interview with the juvenile
delinquent may be closed this way. "See Mr. Smith about your
chances of getting a position on the playground softball team,
and also see Jim Bradford, at the community house, about that
vacancy at Camp Chief Fleetwing. Let me know later today what
you learn."

Indicating a course of action to the interviewee releases him
from the interview situation; it gives him a feeling of accomplishment; it tends to remove the blocking or thwarting that he may
have experienced earlier, and it generates some hope that the plan
or plans of action discussed will result in the solution of a problem.
Because the person has a sense of closure, or that something has
been completed, he is now ready and willing to terminate the
interview.

THINGS TO LOOK FOR WHEN INTERVIEWING

Causes versus Symptoms

It is so easy when interviewing to observe only the symptoms
rather than the causes. It is like seeing the play rather than the
strategy of the game. Yet much of the time, what the person says,
the way he says it, and what he refuses to say, are symptoms
beyond which one must look if he is to understand that which
motivates the person. It has been emphasized repeatedly that one
of the purposes of the interview is to gain insight into or to understand the person interviewed. Insight comes with knowing what
motivates. Hence the interviewer must look for that which pre-

disposes the person to act in given ways, for his drives to action, and for his expressed and unexpressed ambitions and goals. Moreover the person's estimate of himself and of others, and the way in which he views life in general are fundamental to understanding him. Hence this attitude of looking beyond the symptoms is adopted by the competent interviewer.

The Theme Song

The interviewer who seeks to learn what makes his interviewee "tick" is interested in the person's emotions and attitudes. These are often revealed in the person's *theme song*—the idea, the feeling, the incident, or the bias to which the person continually returns. It is what lies behind the theme song that is significant. Law enforcement officers are very familiar with some theme songs, such as: "The cops are always trying to pin something on me." This and other similar conventional theme songs are of some, but less value. It is rather the *individual* theme song that gives insight into the person's motives.

Finding Sore Spots

Sometimes the interviewee suddenly unexpectedly shifts from one topic of conversation to another that is wholly unrelated to it. This usually indicates that a sore spot has been touched. Either the person has realized that the information he has given is much too damning, that it is much too personal, or too painful to pursue the topic further and hence he seeks to get as far away from it as possible. By shifting to something that is very remote, he unwittingly reveals that the first topic of conversation was definitely emotionally toned. Further probing may reveal the reason for the sore spot.

Attitude Signals

There are various bodily responses that are meaningful to the competent and alert interviewer. Among the more obvious are blushing and pallor. Generally the former indicates pleasantness and the latter fear or anger. These vascular changes are much more apparent in some people than in others. Anger is also indicated by raising the voice, by a change in inflection, by more labored breathing, and sometimes by a slight dilation of the nostrils.

Tension is evident in a "nervous" laugh, crossing and recrossing of the legs, awkward placement of the arms and hands, clasping the hands back of the head, twisting things, and biting finger nails. Scratching the ear or cheek indicates embarrassment, so also does lowering the eyes. Surprise is evident in raised eyebrows, wide-open eyes, and a quick, determined glance at the interviewer.

Gestures of the hands and other parts of the body are also valuable signals. Often the interviewee points in a direction without knowing that he has done so. Since the pointing may be very meaningful to the interviewer, it often reveals more than statements made at the time.

The reason these signals are valuable to the interviewer is that they are involuntary responses. The person is attending to what he is saying, not to what he is doing. He may control his statements by giving close attention to them, but he can not give equally close attention to his bodily responses at the same time. Therefore catching the person off guard in this way gives the interviewer the advantage.

SOME DO'S AND DON'T'S

The interviewer's task is complicated by the fact that he must not only attend to the interviewee's attitudes and responses but to his own as well. At all times the interviewer must be master of the situation. This is even true when the non-directive technique is used. Some do's and don't's that make for successful interviewing follow.

Be Responsive

Give your undivided attention to the person you are interviewing. Nothing is more annoying to an interviewee than to have the interviewer open his mail, make a telephone call, doodle on a blotter, search his file, manicure his finger nails, arrange things on his desk, or walk around the room while conducting an interview. Such half-hearted attention is frustrating and leads the interviewee to regard the whole affair as a gross waste of time. For the interviewer, an interview may be just another interview, and hence monotonous and uninteresting. For the interviewee, on the other hand, the interview may be vital and crucial and therefore he demands the interviewer's undivided attention.

On the other hand the interviewer must not go to the other extreme of feigning interest, over-acting, or being insincere in his attitude and manner. Such shamming is soon detected, and when it is observed, it is just as damaging to the success of the interview as the disinterested attitude is.

Responsiveness is perhaps most readily shown in the face. The interviewer shows his interest by looking, much of the time but not continuously, at the person he is interviewing. Changes in facial expression from time to time let the interviewee know that the interviewer is still listening. A dead-pan expression reminds one strongly of the telephone conversation with the silent listener. In that case one is prompted to say, "Are you there?" To the dead-pan interviewer, one would also like to say, "Are you there?"

Do Not Antagonize

Since the interviewer is trying to develop rapport, or to come into the best possible relationship with the interviewee, he must be on guard against antagonizing the person interviewed. Nervous habits such as constant clearing of the throat, adjusting glasses, twiddling thumbs, picking the teeth, and similar things may be very annoying to others and thus create an unconscious barrier between the two. Remember, annoying mannerisms antagonize.

Disagreements that lead to arguments are also dangerous barriers. During an interview an argument should be avoided at all costs because an argument puts each party on the defensive. Hence they draw apart, pull into themselves, and mistrust the other. This attitude defeats the interviewer's purposes and robs him of that positive attitude so essential for success. Since the interviewer is seeking information and insight, he must remember that the truth is told to a friend and lies to an enemy.

Avoid Prejudice

Prejudice is a matter of prejudging another, usually on the basis of some physical feature, behavior trait, or meager bit of information. That people with long noses are "nosey"; that people with full lips are "sexy," and that people with shifty eyes are dishonest, are common examples of such prejudices. The person who opens an interview with these and similar preconceived notions merely goes through the motions of an interview.

Closely related to the matter of prejudice is generalizing on the basis of a single or on limited experience. "Once a cheat, liar or thief, always a cheat, liar or a thief." This is a popular conclusion. But careful observation reveals that the girls who take jewelry from the "five-and-dime," or the boys who take pocket-knives do not necessarily steal everything on which they can lay their hands. Behavior tends to be specific rather than general. It tends to match specific situations rather than follow general principles. Therefore the interviewer must be careful not to overrate the importance of particular statements or experiences.

Interviewing Children

There are times when law enforcement officers must interview children, sometimes even very young children. Children who have witnessed crimes, have been molested, or have been involved in other ways with adults, must be questioned. The officer who interviews children must always remember that children are not small adults, and that therefore the methods used when interviewing adults are not necessarily appropriate when interviewing children.

A man was arrested because he indulged in some sex play with two small girls. He was taken to the police station for questioning and later the two girls were questioned. Since the incident was reported to the police in the evening, the questioning of the two girls was delayed until nearly midnight. Both girls were roused from deep sleep, brought to the police station and questioned for nearly an hour each. This was hardly the time or the place to subject these children to questioning. Even an adult roused from deep sleep is not apt to be alert, cooperative or even coherent, let alone a young child.

The police officers, in the above case, would have been far wiser had they postponed questioning the girls until the following morning when they were wide awake, rested, alert and cooperative. Moreover, questioning these children in their homes, where there was security, rather than in a police station, that aroused fear and worry, would have been far better.

To question children successfully one must take into account the child's nature and know his psychology. The approach to the child is different from that to an adult. The competent interviewer knows this and hence tailors his methods to the person interviewed; he takes into account the psychology of the interviewee.

RECORDING THE INTERVIEW

It is imperative that a record be made of each interview. This is particularly necessary when one interviews several people each day. No one can remember accurately the mass of details and observations encountered during a series of interviews, no matter how vivid they are at the time. Moreover the value of an interview increases when there are records to which one can return again and again at later times.

The Use of Recording Machines

The most accurate record of an interview is obtained by recording mechanically everything that is said. The chief advantages of this method are completeness and reproducibility. Not only is every word recorded, but all the inflections and exclamations as well. Therefore the actual interview can be shared by other people not present at the original interview, if that is desirable.

On the other hand, there are several disadvantages to this method. Unless the microphones are concealed, so that the interviewee does not know that a recording is being made, the interviewee may be suspicious and fearful of the reasons for recording the interview and hence not participate as fully and freely as he would were no recording made. There is also the time required and the expense incurred in making a full transcription of the interview. Furthermore, since a recording does not include the observations made by the interviewer at the time of the interview, the transcription, to be meaningful, must be supplemented by a summary of the interviewer's observations and an evaluation of the interview as a whole.

The Summary Report

A second and rather practical way of recording an interview is to write a complete and organized report of the interview immediately upon its completion. An alert interviewer should be able to remember the significant facts presented during the interview for a few minutes after it has been completed, and until he is able to record them. Likewise, he should have little difficulty remembering the attitudes he noted and the observations that he made. It is desirable to space interviews so that the interviewer can write an adequate summary, or make extensive notes at the close of each interview before beginning the next one. If this is not done, confusion of the interviews is almost inevitable.

Recording During the Interview

Taking notes during an interview is a very undesirable practice. The only time that it should be permitted is when highly factual information, such as, a telephone number, the name and address of someone mentioned during the interview, or similar data are presented. There are several reasons that make note-taking inadvisable. The primary reason is that it is apt to serve as a barrier between the interviewer and the interviewee. The interviewee is apt to be over-cautious in his responses since he knows that his statements can be checked against the record in the future. Recording hampers his spontaneity; it puts him on the defensive. A second disadvantage of this procedure is that it divides the interviewer s attention between the interviewee and the task of recording. This slows up the progress of the interview substantially, stereotypes the situation, and decreases rapport. Therefore note-taking during an interview should seldom, if ever, be permitted.

CONCLUDING STATEMENT

At the end as in the beginning of this chapter, we must emphasize that the purpose of the interview is to obtain information, to gain insight into the motivation and behavior of the interviewee, and to aid him to adjust better in social situations than he has in the past. These are the things that law enforcement officers should expect to accomplish by interviewing. These purposes, however, can not be achieved in any fortuitous or accidental way; interviewing is a technique that must be learned and carefully applied. And when the techniques of interviewing are thoroughly learned and diligently applied the results are rewarding.

REFERENCES

Bingham, W. V. and Moore, B. V.: *How to Interview*, 3rd Rev. Ed. New York, Harper & Bros., 1941. A general discussion of interviewing in various areas, such as, business, industry, professions, etc.

Dudycha, G. J.: A Suggestion for Interviewing for Dependability Based on Student Behavior. *Journal of Applied Psychology*, 25:227-231, 1941. Lists the kinds of questions that are apt to indicate aspects of dependability.

Erickson, C. E.: *The Counseling Interview*. New York, Prentice-Hall, 1950. This book presents many practical and easily comprehended suggestions.

Garrett, Annette: *Interviewing: Its Principles and Methods*. New York, Family Welfare Association of America, 1942. Chapters 1-7 discuss principles of interviewing, especially as applied to social work.

Inbau, F. E.: *Lie Detection and Criminal Interrogation*, Baltimore, Williams and Wilkins, 1948. An excellent discussion of the two subjects.

Mulbar, H.: *Interrogation*. Springfield, Illinois, Charles C Thomas, Publisher, 1951. An excellent book written for law enforcement officers.

Young, Pauline V.: *Interviewing in Social Work*. New York, McGraw-Hill, 1935. Chapters 3 and 4 are of general interest.

Chapter 4

THE PSYCHOLOGY OF LIE DETECTION

By

Donald B. Lindsley

Lying and deceit have been part of man's life and behavior from the earliest records of his activities in social groups. There are indications that man sought ways to deal with lying and criminal tendencies in his fellow man even in these early days. Among the various methods employed to determine guilt or innocence were: Trial by Combat, in which the winner was absolved; Trial by Torture, in which he who could withstand the greatest suffering was exonerated; Trial by Ordeal, in which certain reactions to severe stress were taken as indications of innocence. Actually these procedures were used less as trials than as persistent attempts to force confessions of guilt. Other methods of dealing with a suspect which did not seek to determine his guilt so much as to find a solution to the disposition of his case were: Benefit of Clergy, a form of parole under religious auspices; Sanctuary, usually a place of temporary refuge in a sacred and inviolable asylum, immune from law; and Compurgation, the clearing of the accused by oaths of others as to his innocence.

HISTORICAL ASPECTS OF LIE DETECTION

Ancient Methods

Larson has dealt extensively with the ancient methods of detection of guilt or innocence of the suspect, and Trovillo has provided an interesting survey of historical methods leading up to modern scientific procedures. Of the above mentioned ancient methods, the Trial by Ordeal, because of the presumed signs or symptoms of guilt, bears the closest resemblance to modern lie detection methods. For that reason a few examples will be given here to illustrate the recognition of the need even in early days to separate the guilty from the innocent, and to suggest that some of these early methods may have contained an element of psychological and physiological basis, though of course this was not recognized. Instead, superstition and religious faith seem to have been the principal bases upon which both the accused and the accusers looked upon the Trials by Ordeal and other methods.

Trial by ordeal. In India, Persia and Denmark one of the Ordeals was to place a red hot iron upon the tongue of the accused. If the tongue was burned the accused was put to death. This rigorous and torturing method may have had a physiological basis. Modern interpretation of this phenomenon suggests that in the guilty, superstition concerning his guilt and fear of the consequences might give rise to a predominance of sympathetic nervous system activity causing a dry mouth and greater chance of burning than in the moist mouth of the innocent.

Another procedure employed in Africa was to require a suspect to plunge his arm into cold water and then in boiling water. If, by the next day, the skin had blistered or pealed the person was assumed to be guilty. Here also there may have been a possibility that a physiological reaction could have preserved the arm of the innocent and made the arm of the guilty more vulnerable to burning and blisters.

Still another test was the Ordeal of Rice Chewing, employed in India and in various parts of Europe during the Dark Ages, and perhaps until the 15th or 16th century. The accused was compelled to chew a mouthful of rice or other dry food substance. If he was not able to swallow it or spit it out he was judged guilty. Again, the mucous-like secretion of the salivary glands activated by the sympathetic branch of the autonomic nervous system during fear, might tend to produce an especially dry mouth, in contrast to the more fluid secretion characteristic of the parasympathetic branch, which tends to predominate during relaxed and less apprehensive states such as might prevail in the innocent.

Development of Modern Methods of Lie Detection

Origin of physiological measures. During the Dark Ages all knowledge of science was stifled, but especially that related to anatomy, physiology and medicine. Consequently, it was only with the greatest of difficulties that Vesalius, the great anatomist, and Harvey, known for his work on circulation, together with others of their time, were able to learn about the parts and functions of man's body during the 16th and 17th centuries.

It was not until late in the 19th century that instruments for measuring and recording blood pressure and pulse rate were developed. In 1896 Riva Rocci developed the cuff method of measuring blood pressure and pulse variations indirectly. Erlanger, in 1904, improved upon this procedure and developed a method for the continuous recording of blood pressure. Prior to this however, Lombroso, during the latter half of the 19th century gained a great reputation as a criminologist and used some of the early methods of measuring blood pressure and respiration to assist in identifying criminal suspects. His student, Mosso, an Italian physiologist, also contributed to the refinement of the measuring instruments. As a result of the effort of these and other workers there gradually came into being instruments such as the *sphygmomanometer*, for measuring blood pressure and pulse rate; a chest *pneumograph* and recording tambours developed by Marey for measuring respiration; and the *plethysmograph*, for measuring changes in blood volume.

Since blood pressure, pulse rate, and respiration are major components of the polygraph lie detector, it may be seen that the gradual evolution of measuring techniques and the use of the measures in combination for various purposes, including lie detection, make it evident that no one can be directly credited with inventing or developing the "lie detector." Lombroso is probably the first to have used some of the measures for studying criminals. Subsequently, Münsterberg, a German psychologist, who came to Harvard early in the 20th century strongly advocated the use of physiological and psychological methods of studying deception. It was one of his students, Marston, who in 1915 undertook one of the earliest scientific studies of the validation of the blood

pressure and pulse methods of detecting deception. Marston subsequently devoted a great deal of his time to applying the technique
and serving as a consultant for deception tests in police and private
investigatory work. In 1938 he published a book entitled, *The
Lie Detector Test* in which he discusses primarily his own experience in using deception tests together with his opinion on applications and limitations. In a final chapter he gives practical suggestions in the use of the method based upon his own experience,
and the measures and indications he has found useful.

Apparently stimulated by Marston's work, Chief August Vollmer of the Berkeley, California Police Department in the early
1920's encouraged Dr. John A. Larson and others associated with
his department to use and further develop the polygraphic methods
of lie detection in police work. It appears that the practical use of
the lie detector in police investigation received great impetus from
the successful use made of it in the Berkeley police department.
Larson's book on *Lying and Its Detection*, which appeared in 1932,
describes much of this early work.

Leonarde Keeler, as a student at Stanford University became
acquainted with the work at Berkeley and carried on some experiments under psychologist Dr. Walter Miles, developing and
improving equipment. Later Keeler worked with the Scientific
Crime Detection Laboratory of the Northwestern University Law
School, which eventually became the basis for the Chicago Police
Scientific Crime Detection Laboratory. Keeler contributed a great
deal to the popularization and widespread use of the lie detection
technique, as well as to the practical validation of the method.
Keeler is particularly well known for his innovations in the use
of the method; for example, he is credited with introducing The
Hidden Key Technique or Peak of Tension Method, which will
be described later.

Among those who have been associated with the Chicago
Police Laboratory since its establishment prior to World War II,
are Inbau and Trovillo, both of whom have written extensively
on the subject and made significant contributions to the practical
applications of polygraphic lie detector methods. Inbau's book *Lie
Detection and Criminal Interrogation* is an excellent reference

book on polygraphic lie detection methods, as well as on interrogation methods. The Chicago laboratory is today one of the most progressive and extensive users of lie detector methods.

Despite the acceptance of the lie detector in police investigation and in private and governmental screening, it can be said that no truly scientific study of the varied measures which might be used in crime detection work has ever been conducted to validate the method carefully and thoroughly. True, some studies have been reported of its use in police work with suggestions as to the accuracy of prediction by using certain criteria, but by and large the interest has centered more in the practical details of the technique and methods of interrogation than upon careful definition of the procedure and statistical analysis of results. On the other hand numerous studies have been carried out in university and hospital laboratories where investigation of emotion and emotional reactions were being studied by one or more methods of physiological measurement. These studies have employed a variety of measures, some of which might well be used in lie detection work. In addition to the traditional blood pressure, pulse, and respiration records, these studies have employed singly or in combination some of the following: galvanic skin response, skin temperature, pupillary change, muscle tension, brain waves, etc. It has proved difficult to differentiate emotions in terms of the patterns of response in one or more of the measures mentioned. Whether this is due to the artificiality of laboratory emotions, or to extensive variability from individual to individual is not entirely clear. There are other reasons as well.

Association tests. Although physiologic measure of emotion and stress began earlier and gradually evolved into present day polygraphic methods of lie detection, an important development in psychological methodology also got its start during the latter part of the 19th century. Wundt in Germany and Galton in England began to experiment with the association of ideas along about 1880. This was about the time of the beginning of experimental psychology. Interest in learning, memory, perception and emotion lead naturally to the investigation of ideas, words, and things associated in the mind through experience. It was observed that the mention of a particular object or a word would immediately call to mind another which had been associated with it in experience. The psychologists of that time, and particularly those such as Wertheimer and Klein, Jung, and Münsterberg in the early years of the 20th century, were quick to realize the significance of this method for investigating mental content. It was a short step from studies such as these to the application of the technique to deception.

Münsterberg again was influential in proposing that association tests and other experimental methods of psychology be applied to the detection of guilt. Duprat in France utilized association methods to detect lying and develop a classification of liars. Langfeld published a study on the use of the association reaction time test to deception. Lists of words to be used in association tests for purposes of touching upon mental conflicts were developed by Jung and by Kent and Rosanoff. These, however, were primarily for clinical purposes in probing the minds of patients with psychiatric disorders. Each list contained a number of common, everyday words, of innocuous nature and a few interspersed "critical" words presumed to touch upon likely areas of conflict and emotional trauma. The nature of a subject's response to these critical words was the key to a "normal" or "abnormal" response. Reaction time, or the delay in his response to certain critical words was assumed to reflect conflict or preoccupation with matters related to the particular word. The giving of bizarre or unusual responses to such words was another indication of disturbance. In deception test situations it was presumed that "critical" words mixed with non-critical words would give rise to blocking or delay of response, sometimes unusually quick responses, uneasiness and uncoordinated speech and movements.

The use of drugs ("truth serum"). With many drugs, both stimulant and depressant, it is now well known that there may be a transient excitant phase in which the user becomes euphoric, talkative, and sometimes emotionally responsive. For example, it has been known through the ages that liquor or wine, containing alcohol, will loosen the tongue during an excitant phase and that a person who has imbibed sufficiently may reveal things he would not ordinarily discuss publicly. However, as is also well known, different people react differently under the influence of alcohol. Some become depressed and morose, whereas others become excited and volatile; some talk freely and others shut up like a clam. Similar reactions have been observed to different drugs, so that it is not always predictable just what type of reaction will be obtained.

In 1921, Dr. R. E. House, an obstetrician from Texas, observed in deliveries in which the mother had been given scopolamine, an alkaloid similar to hyoscine, that the mother in a certain stage of anesthesia or sedation might be talkative and reveal things she would not ordinarily discuss. This led him to consider the possibilities of scopolamine in the interrogation of criminal suspects. He gave many demonstrations throughout the United States, as a result of which newspapers quickly applied to the sedative drug he employed, the term "truth serum." According to Larson and others there is no such thing as a "truth serum." Scopolamine, like other anesthetics or sedatives, such as ether, nitrous oxide, chloroform, and the barbiturate drugs, will produce a condition in one stage of which a person may talk freely, but with a mixture of truth and falsehood. From a legal point of view it cannot be assured that the truth will be told, or that a bona fide confession will be obtained. However, in the proper stage of anesthesia or sedation, when inhibitions have been overcome, the responses to certain questions concerning a suspected crime may reveal important clues to be followed up later.

Since Dr. House's early experiments and demonstrations a great deal more has been learned about drug action, and many new types of sedatives have been compounded, especially the barbiturates used extensively in childbirth, for control of psychiatric disorders, epileptic attacks, and so forth. One of the uses to which such drugs have been put in psychiatry is that of securing repressed information presumably buried deeply in the subconscious mind of the patient and otherwise not readily subject to recall. Also during the last war a method known as "narcosynthesis" was used with hysterical patients undergoing war neuroses in order to allow them to transiently relive certain of their battle experiences believed to be a persistent cause of unconscious conflict. In schizophrenic patients of the catatonic type, who will not talk and therefore participate in psychiatric therapy or reveal any clues to life and emotional experiences which may underlie their disorder, sodium amytal has been used to facilitate communication with the patient. Typically, if it works, there is a transient phase which can sometimes be prolonged by slowly injecting the drug, during which the patient will answer some questions and reveal some of his conscious or unconscious problems. If the patient passes through this stage into a deeper stage of narcosis there may be another transient period of talkativeness as he recovers from the sedation or anesthesia.

The principle involved in the so-called "truth serum" is simply that a drug may, in one of the stages of anesthesia or sedation, temporarily give rise to a condition in which certain inhibitions and obstructions to memory and to questions consciously or unconsciously avoided, are removed. Because of the uncertainty of the truth or falsity of the statements, except as they can be subsequently checked by other sources of evidence, and because certain drugs may give rise to hypnotic and hallucinatory images and memories, the results cannot always be considered valid. The "evidence" thus revealed is not accepted in court and in general the procedure is not looked upon very favorably by the medical profession or by laymen.

Hypnosis. In general, hypnosis is not regarded as a satisfactory means of obtaining a confession of guilt or deception. A person under hypnosis can lie and does. He will not reveal things which prove seriously detrimental to his welfare. Furthermore, the high degree of suggestibility found in some subjects may give rise to false confessions, where the subject wishing to please or conform to the hypnotist's suggestions may actually confess to something he is only being questioned about, if the question carries a strong implication of his guilt. Like hypnotic drugs there is a certain measure of uncertainty involved in hypnotic performances or statements, but nevertheless important clues may be gained in this way.

Police methods. One hears a great deal about the so-called "third degree" which, in its most sensationally depicted form by certain newspapers and rumor carriers, is implied to be very similar to

Trial by Ordeal or Trial by Torture, in which confessions are enforced. Although it is undoubtedly true that the police in certain quarters have been guilty at times of subjecting a suspect to punishment, indecencies and threats, as well as to severe fatigue, strain and nervous exhaustion in an effort to "break" him and secure a confession, many of the alleged incidents are believed to be gross exaggerations.

The problem of attempting to secure a confession or accumulate important facts in the case is part of the police officer's job when a crime has been committed. First degree investigation is administered at the scene of the crime or at time of arrest. Second degree investigation is conducted at the place of confinement or at the time of booking at the police station. Third degree goes beyond the ordinary interrogation procedures in that it employs special psychological "props," and probes. Typical of the "props" are an isolated setting in a darkened room, with perhaps a bright spotlight thrown upon the accused making it difficult for him to see the accusers or to employ evasive mannerisms which depend for their success upon watching the reactions of those who observe them. Relays of interrogators may keep up a steady stream of questions employing different techniques of questioning, without letup for several hours, during which time the accused may be without food or rest and near a state of exhaustion. Questioning and cross-questioning as fatigue sets in may reveal inconsistencies the accused no longer has the strength or reason to deny. Eventually he may find himself caught up in a web of contradictions, when it is easier to confess and secure relief from the heat, brightness and constant harangue, than to go on denying his guilt. A confession should never be obtained in this manner; if a person's health or sanity has been jeopardized, it should not be allowed. Any confession thus obtained should be rejected in court upon trial and probably would be. False confessions are usually rejected, though confessions obtained by force, if verified, are often admissible as evidence.

Inbau in his book on *Lie Detection and Criminal Interrogation* devotes approximately half the space to criminal interrogation procedures, taking up in a very well written and explicit manner the conditions under which testimony under third degree or similar procedures is acceptable as evidence.

If the "third degree" is simply an intensive interrogation, constituting a battle of wits between interrogator and a suspect, and employing acceptable psychological methods of penetrating the defense for a crime, there should be no serious objection to it. Acceptable, means that there should be no vilification, punishment or torture, no threat to harm or mistreat, and no imposition of conditions such as withholding necessary nourishment, medical attention, necessary rest and so forth, when such conditions would endanger life, impose pain, or otherwise expose the accused to inhuman indecencies. The arrangement of an interrogation room and the conditions of questioning may well employ psychological advantages favoring the interrogator without becoming unacceptable in the sense defined above. Larson in his book has presented the opinions of various authorities, including police officers, lawyers, psychologists and others concerning the nature and limitations of third degree methods. In general these reflect the fact that there is often a misunderstanding on the part of the public concerning what is meant by "third degree," and that when it is stripped of undesirable and unacceptable features it constitutes an admissible procedure of police investigation.

POLYGRAPHIC LIE DETECTION MEASURES

What Is the Polygraph?

A polygraph, as the name implies, is a device which records multiple tracings or graphs. An apparatus which records multiple tracings therefore may be a polygraph, and of course does not have to be a lie detector. It is a lie detector apparatus only when the measures are appropriate and when an expert operator can detect signs in the record which are suggestive of deception. As discussed in the preceding historical account, certain physiological measures have been found useful in the detection of lies, and in discriminating between the reactions of the guilty and the innocent. The polygraphic lie detector does not make this discrimination itself. The trained operator must do this. Therefore one may not speak of a polygraphic apparatus as a lie detector per se. It simply records faithfully certain reactions of the subject which, if made under proper scientific conditions, enable an experienced operator to distinguish between truthful and untruthful responses.

Characteristic Lie Detection Measures

The typical lie detection measures are blood pressure, pulse rate, respiration, and sometimes the electrodermal or galvanic skin response. These are not the only measures which can be used, but since they are the principal ones which have been used most ex-

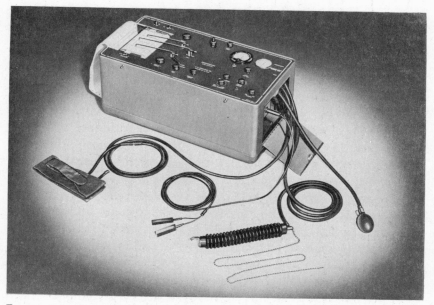

FIG. 9. A cardio-pneumo-polygraph. (Reproduced by courtesy of C. H. Stoelting Company, Chicago, Illinois.)

tensively and which the Stoelting, Keeler, Lee and other commercially made polygraphs usually provide for, they will each be described in some detail here. Other possible measures will be described later.

Blood pressure. In order to understand what fluctuations in blood pressure mean and what their significance may be relative to deception, it is necessary to discuss the function and control of circulation and the principles by which blood pressure is measured and recorded. The circulatory system consists of the blood vessels and the heart. The heart serves as a distributing and pumping station, forcing freshly oxygenated blood out through the arteries and smaller arterioles to the fine capillary beds in the tissues of the body. Small venules and larger veins return the deoxygenated blood to the right side of the heart where it is pumped into the pulmonary system of the lungs to rid itself of carbon dioxide and take up a fresh supply of oxygen. It is then returned to the left side of the heart from whence it is pumped out through the main arterial channels of the body.

Within this closed hydrodynamic system there is a definite pressure at all times in order that the blood may circulate. There is an average pressure level but it doesn't remain constant very long, for there are both brief and longer period variations in pressure. The arterial pressure varies with systole and diastole of the heart, that is, with the contraction and relaxation of the heart pumping system. Of these brief alternations in pressure, the maximum is reached at systole when the heart ventricle contracts and forces blood out to the peripheral vessels. With a finger on the wrist artery one can feel this pulse wave of pressure and count the heart rate. The minimum pressure in the system occurs during diastole, or when the ventricle relaxes and expands. If one measures these two pressure levels on a blood pressure indicator such as the physician uses, the point at which the systolic pressure just breaks through the resistance offered by the blood pressure cuff is known as *systolic pressure*. The point at which the pressure in the cuff no longer is great enough to offer resistance to the minimal pressure level in the artery is known as *diastolic pressure*.

The way in which blood pressure is measured by the indirect method is to place a rubber cuff around the arm just above the elbow, or around the lower leg just above the ankle. The cuff is connected to a rubber bulb with a screw valve. When the valve is tightened and the bulb pressed repeatedly the pressure in the cuff will increase to a point where it finally occludes or blocks the circulation in the limb, and where if one listens with a stethoscope placed over the artery just below the cuff he will no longer hear the pulse beat forcing itself past the resistance offered by the cuff pressure. In other words the pressure in the cuff exceeds that in the artery. One must not leave the pressure in the cuff at this level very long, otherwise it will cause pain, and if left long enough at a blocking level will deprive the distal part of the limb of its circulation and eventually will cause deterioration of the tissues. Once the pressure in the cuff has been pumped to a level exceeding the systolic or maximal fluctuating pressure, the valve on the bulb is turned slightly to release the pressure in the cuff very gradually. The cuff is attached to a mecury manometer, resembling a thermometer, which registers the pressure in the cuff in terms of how high it will force a column of mercury in its tube which is calibrated in millimeters.

Another type of indicator is the aneroid or dial type in which a needle rotates due to the pressure exerted on a small metal bellows. The needle position is read against the dial where pressure is calibrated also in terms of millimeters of mercury. Hence as the pressure in the cuff gradually comes down the column of mercury in the tube, or the needle on the dial, will show slight oscillations when the maximal pulse breaks through the resistance offered by the cuff. At this point the stethoscope will make audible the sharp tapping sound, associated with the maximal pressure of the heart beat. The blood pressure read at this precise point is known as an absolute measure of *systolic pressure*. As the pressure in the cuff diminishes still farther the pulse will be heard less distinctly until suddenly it develops a muffled quality—this is the point of absolute *diastolic pressure*, the minimal pressure during the heart cycle. The difference between systolic and diastolic pressures is known as *pulse pressure*.

Another more prolonged change in blood pressure, is due to the amount of resistance offered to the flow of blood in the arterioles, which are elastic and capable of constriction or dilatation. These smaller vessels of the peripheral circulatory system are under the control of the autonomic nervous system, and receive fibers from both the sympathetic and parasympathetic branches of the autonomic system. Since these branches of the nervous system are not generally under voluntary control, the action of constriction or dilatation is mainly reflex in nature, and for the most part we are unaware of it. In addition to the nervous control of the blood vessels, there is a humoral control, with an adrenalin-like substance known as sympathin producing a sympathetic-like control, and acetylcholine producing a parasympathetic-like control. These humoral substances may circulate in the blood stream.

As constriction of the arterioles occurs due to sympathetic nervous system action the resistance to flow of blood in the peripheral vessels is increased and the over-all pressure in the system is increased. Blood pressure rises. This tends to happen during action of the arm and leg muscles, as it does also during emotional states of anger or fear, whereas during pleasurable and relaxed states the peripheral vessels tend to relax and blood pressure falls.

We must be very careful in our interpretations of increasing and decreasing blood pressure or heart rate. Activity of a limb or a movement of the body may change blood pressure and most certainly causes a momentary increase in heart rate. Hence in lie detection work one must be sure not to let movement and activity interfere with response to questioning, or if it does occur be sure that it is noted on the record as movement so that it will not be misinterpreted as a significant response to an interrogation.

Most modern polygraphic lie detector units employ a dial manometer of the type known as Tycos, made by the Taylor Instrument Company. It is usually mounted in clear view on the top of the instrument board. Connected to the dial type indicator is the blood pressure cuff and a side tube with the pressure bulb for pumping up the pressure. After the cuff has been placed on the subject's arm or lower leg above the ankle, being wrapped and securely folded or hooked, it is gradually pumped up. One should explain to a subject beforehand that he will feel pressure on the arm or leg, so that he will not be frightened by the procedure. As the pressure is increased above systolic level, to a point where the needle is rising but not showing jerky pulse deflections, the valve on the bulb may be loosened very slightly so that the needle starts coming down very slowly. Watching it carefully the observer will detect at a given point a slight tremor of the needle as each heart beat makes itself felt—this is systolic level. Going down until the needle tremor with each beat stops, is diastolic level. Let us assume the systolic level was found to be 130 mm Hg (mercury) on the dial and the diastolic level was 70. The pulse pressure then would be 60.

The customary procedure in the use of the polygraph is to record continuously, except for occasional rest periods, with the pressure in the cuff pumped to a level just above diastolic pressure level. This is called "relative pressure" variation, since it is neither a measure of diastolic nor systolic pressure. Given the initial values of pressure for the subject as determined above, the pressure in the cuff when ready to interrogate and record would be pumped to about 80 or 90, 10 to 20 above the diastolic level. This is a comfortable pressure for the subject and at this point there is a distinct pulse beat shown in the dial needle's activity, and also in the pen or recording system. With the pressure in the cuff fixed at this point by tightly closing the valve on the bulb, any subsequent variation in the arm or leg artery will reflect itself as a rise or fall in the tracing. Any variation in pulse rate will be seen in the frequency with which the pulse deflections vary on the record; also any strengthening of the pulse will show in the size of the pulse deflections. There is usually a button or some device for regulating the pen's position on the paper, independent of the pressure in the system. The pen should be adjusted so that it is writing in its proper space.

The main things to look for in the blood pressure-pulse record are: (1) shifts in the level of the pressure line, especially those that occur immediately after a question is asked or a stimulus of some kind presented to the subject—these may be changes either up or down in pressure level; (2) changes in the number of pulse beats per unit of time on the record—these can usually be detected by observing the interval between successive beats, though they may require measurement with a millimeter rule. The beats usually speed up after a crucial question, but they might show a change in the opposite direction. The best rule with both blood pressure and pulse rate is to compare a given subject's reactions to a crucial stimulus with his reactions to a non-crucial stimulus, and also to the values for "resting" level between stimuli. If the critical stimulus or question shows a marked rise in pressure level and an increase in pulse rate, whereas the non-critical stimuli did not produce such a response it may be inferred that for him there has been a significant change in response to the critical question. If as the questioning has shifted from innocuous and everyday topics of conversation to questions related to the circumstances bearing more closely upon the offense of which he is suspected there may be a gradual or sudden shifting of the blood pressure upward, even necessitating adjustment of the pen to keep the tracing on the graph. Any such shift compared to the "resting" level or the level during non-critical questioning may be significant of increasing fear or emotion associated with guilt.

Cautions about blood pressure changes and shift of pulse rate. A subject should be put at ease and a reasonable degree of relaxation attained before the start of an experiment. A tensing up of the muscles of the arm, or a movement of the arm or any other part of the body may be sufficient to cause a change in blood pressure, and especially a change in pulse rate. Therefore, the subject should be observed constantly and when a movement occurs a suitable symbol for movement should be marked on the record, so that any response occurring at that time, even though it falls at an appropriate interval after a question or stimulus, will not be attributed solely to the stimulus. It might be an artifact of the movement and bear no relation to the stimulus. Sometimes a sigh, cough, clearing of the throat, or other fidgeting of the subject will produce such artifacts which must not be confused with blood pressure or pulse changes expected in relation to a stimulus or question. It is precisely this kind of misinterpretation made by an inexperienced operator which leads him to make errors in his evaluation of the records. It would be desirable to have some kind of signalling system recording simultaneously on the graph, by means of which a second observer doing nothing but watching for movements of the subject could indicate these disturbances. However, an operator after some experience can learn to watch his subject and manipulate the controls at the same time, indicating by a mark on the record when subject movements and other disturbances, such as unexpected stimuli, intrude. A door slammed in the hall, or a telephone ringing in the next office, might be the cause of a subject's response.

Respiration. With each inspiration and expiration of air the chest and abdomen move. A pneumograph placed around the chest or abdominal region and fastened snugly will be caused to expand or contract as respiration occurs. The pneumograph is a rubber tube partially inflated, or a rubber tube surrounding a flexible coil of wire. It is attached by means of a rubber tube to a Marey tambour and recording pen so that as pressure variations are caused in the pneumograph by expansion and contraction of the chest wall, the tambour will, through a lever system, rock the pen and make an oscillatory tracing on the paper graph.

The usual method of evaluating respiration by inspection, as the records are being taken, depends upon qualitative observations. For example, if respiration speeds up or slows down in rate, if it builds up or drops down in amplitude, if it blocks temporarily in some given phase of the respiratory cycle, if there is a sudden increase in speed and amplitude in one or more inspiratory cycles after a crucial question, or if there is a sudden shallowing of the respiratory waves, these may be taken as indications of change. Again these changes must be evaluated in terms of the given subject's previous pattern of respiration, his response to other stimuli which were non-critical, and so forth. If always after critical questions there is a shallowing for two or three respiratory cycles, but these shallow patterns do not occur after non-critical questions, one could take this as a significant indication in this subject. It does not follow that other subjects will respond in the same way to questions which affect them critically; instead another subject might take two or three quick and deep breaths after critical questions only; still another subject may show a different pattern. A subject must become his own "control," and by comparing critical versus non-critical periods a differentiation in the subject's response may be detected. Again a caution must be injected not to confuse movements, sighs, yawns, and so forth with bona fide responses, and not to confuse responses to extraneous stimuli with those to the experimental stimuli.

Galvanic skin response. The galvanic skin response, sometimes called electrodermal response, psychogalvanic reflex, skin resistance and so forth, is a part of some lie detection devices. It measures a phenomenon associated with the sweat gland membranes. Two readily accessible areas which are rich in sweat glands are the palms of the hands and the soles of the feet, consequently in order to measure the galvanic skin phenomenon electrodes are attached to the palm of the hand or the soles of the feet. It is desirable to have at least one electrode on the palm of the hand or the sole of the foot. The other electrode, usually a larger one may be placed on the wrist or around the ankle and in order to reduce the resistance at this point the skin under this "indifferent" electrode may be pricked in two or three places. It is also possible to record this phenomenon from the finger tips and some lie detector equipment comes with finger tip electrodes. Some investigators place one electrode on the palm of the hand and one on the back of the hand.

The phenomenon is measurable in two ways by the Feré and Tarchanoff methods. The Feré method involves the use of an external current, supplied by batteries, which is applied to the electrodes through a bridge circuit and a measurement of the resistance offered by the skin is made. Since the skin resistance for any given subject is unknown and also is variable depending upon the degree of relaxation, emotionality, and so forth, it has been found convenient to measure it by means of a Wheatstone bridge.

At the start of an experiment the subject's resistance is apt to be lower than a little later, if he is initially tense and apprehensive about the test. If we talk to him and try to put him at ease, and he relaxes a little more, his resistance level will rise. If he were to go to sleep it would rise considerably; however, we don't want him to go to sleep since we intend to question him about certain everyday affairs as well as about some things presumably related to the crime we may suspect him of having committed. After some preliminary adjustments of the resistance to compensate for preliminary changes in the subject's resistance level, in order to keep the galvanometer or pen position where we want it, we may begin. The first few questions, regardless of whether they are harmless and unrelated to the crime, are apt to give large deflections, therefore several stimuli such as "How old are you?" "Where do you live?" "Did you have breakfast this morning?" and so forth may be asked. Or if you wish to reserve some of these questions for "Yes" and "No" answers, because you know the answers and want to determine what his response will be when telling the truth, you might instead, for purposes of "warm-up" or getting the subject adjusted to the situation, ask him to respond to words which you will say to him, by giving the first word he thinks of. This is the so-called *free association procedure.*

It might go like this for several words, Grass—subject's response, Green; House—Barn; Cow—Pasture; Dog—Cat; and so forth. It will usually be noticed that after several such stimuli and responses by the subject, the size of the galvanic response or resistance change will diminish. When it seems to reach a stable level, critical stimulus words may be introduced such as, *Money*—(subject's association word); Sky—Blue; Water—Ocean; *Pocketbook*—(subject's association word). If the crime had been taking a brown pocketbook from a desk drawer which contained exactly five ten dollar bills and three ones, plus a check made out to John Brown, certain of these features could be worked into the association test, and both the nature of the association response and the galvanic skin response noted to the critical items. For example, additional stimuli could be, Sixteen dollars—(Response), *Fifty-three dollars*—(Response); Red—Green; *Brown*—(Response); Joe Smith—Bill Smith; *John Brown*—(Response), and so on.

If the suspect delayed unusually long in responding to critical (italicized) stimuli related to crime, or in some instances gave unusually prompt responses compared to the time for response to non-critical words, the association aspect of the procedure might itself be revealing. However, we are interested also in his galvanic skin response and if it was always larger on the critical words or stimuli compared to the non-critical stimuli we would have a right to consider that these indications suggested that he knew a number of the details associated with the crime and therefore should be probed further about it. Let us assume that other persons to be tested later, who were also under possible suspicion for this crime, did not give unusual association or galvanic skin response. To carry the probing of our principal suspect further, we could begin a series of questions such as those mentioned earlier concerning age, address, name, breakfast and other known facts concerning the subject and his activities. Interspersed with these at appropriate intervals we could ask, Did you take a pocketbook from a desk drawer? Answer, No. Did you take a pocketbook containing fifty-three dollars? Have you recently seen a check made out to John Brown? The exact form in which these questions may be put will depend upon the circumstances which surround the crime. Perhaps it would be better to attempt to be more subtle than the above questions indicate. The questions cited are just examples of the procedure which may be used and do not represent a carefully thought out approach in this case.

The writer has always found the galvanic skin response to be a very sensitive indicator of deception. Allow a subject to take a number between 1 and 10 which he will lie about when asked if it is 3, 7, 2, 4, etc., answering NO to every number, thus lying about *the* number selected. Almost without exception, after going through the list three or four times, there will be one number to which a sizable response is given consistently, whereas the smaller responses to other numbers usually completely disappear with repetition. Likewise, having a subject select a card from a deck of ten cards or more, and then shuffle them and return the deck to the experimenter may be used as a good initial test. As the experimenter mentions each card and asks, "Is this the card?" the subject lies and says, "NO" to every card. It is usually easy enough to demonstrate to him that you can name the card on the basis of his galvanic skin responses. It is a particularly good psychological move on the part of the experimenter to do a harmless lie test such as this before the "real" test for guilt in connection with a crime, for it convinces the subject that you really do have a means of telling when he is lying. Frequently a suspect will confess after a demonstration such as this, before the critical test procedure has been attempted, for he will realize that he is helpless in trying to conceal his deception and guilt.

Keeler apparently found the galvanic skin response very useful and incorporated it in his lie detector unit. Some other investigators have spoken disparagingly of it, stating that they felt the blood pressure and pulse indications much more useful. The writer wonders whether this may not have been due to the fact that the galvanic skin response is a measure which requires a good deal of care and patience, a goodly amount of experience, a reasonably good circuit and recording system, carefully attached electrodes and a subject who sits still and does not sigh, yawn, swallow or make other fidgety movements. Some investigators are disturbed by the fact that some subjects give a good many spontaneous galvanic responses, whereas others have a fairly steady tracing except for critical stimuli. Also some subjects have a naturally high and others a naturally low resistance level, and either of these may change during the course of the interrogation, necessitating rebalancing of the bridge circuit. Factors such as this and others very probably have prejudiced the judgment of some investigators who have used the galvanic skin response and did not like it or find it reliable.

The writer has used both the Feré resistance method and the Tarchanoff EMF or potential method and prefers the latter. Most commercial lie detectors employ the resistance method and some form of the Wheatstone bridge circuit, sometimes with amplification. The Tarchanoff method employs no bridge circuit and does not measure resistance—instead it measures a potential difference between the two electrodes in the palm of the hand, or wherever they are placed relative to the hand or foot. This requires about a three stage audio-frequency voltage amplifier and a power stage capable of driving some type of oscillograph pen. The amplifier may be a resistance-capacity coupled type, preferably with a time-constant of about one second in order to respond with reasonable fidelity to the slow EMF or potential changes. A DC or direct-coupled amplifier would be preferable, for it would provide a completely faithful record of the wave form and entire response. However, a faithful record of wave form is not necessary, and a resistance-capacity coupled amplifier system will provide a perfectly adequate response in terms of magnitude. The input impedance of the amplifier should be at least a megohm or more so that resistance changes of the skin under the electrodes will not appreciably affect the magnitude of the response. The advantage this type of measurement has over the resistance method of Feré is that the tracing maintains a relatively fixed position at all times, except for the few spontaneous changes in skin potential. From each of these discrete changes the tracing immediately assumes its original position of quiescence (see Figure 10). As this happens a new stimulus may be put to the subject. Thus there is no problem of constant adjustment or balancing of a bridge as in the resistance system. Some resistance

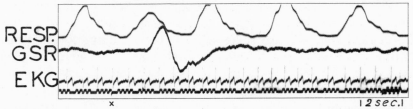

Fig. 10. Respiration, galvanic skin response and electrocardiograph recorded by Westinghouse Oscillograph. Stimulus presented at point marked (x). Note strong GSR one and one-half seconds later; also increased size and slowing of respiration, and slight speed-up of heart rate.

units employ an automatic balancing circuit, which of course would also eliminate this difficulty.

It is the writer's impression that more should be done with the galvanic skin response in lie detection. Its sensitivity and the discrete character of the response make it a readily detectable measure. Another advantage it has over blood pressure, pulse and respiration measures, is that it depends upon the sweat glands which have solely a sympathetic nervous system innervation, and therefore the response is apt to be less complicated than the blood pressure-pulse measures which depend upon so many reflex feedback systems, or than respiration which is under both reflex and voluntary control.

Other Measures for Lie Detection Work

What other measures of physiological and psychological nature might be employed in lie detection? Several kinds of measures have been used in the study of emotion, anxiety and conflict, and there is a possibility that some of them could profitably be used to supplement those already described. Because present day electroencephalography, the recording of brain waves, employs commercial apparatus with as many as eight recording pens and suitable amplifiers for magnifying minute electrical changes in the body, its possibilities will be described first. One of these 8-channel electroencephalographs (abbreviated EEG) costs about twice as much as one of the well known polygraphs with three or four recording pens. It will however record each of the phenomena handled by the polygraph, plus four other measures, simultaneously. For example, with an 8-channel EEG machine one could record the electrocardiogram (EKG) which would provide a measure of heart rate, galvanic skin response (GSR) by the Tarchanoff method, muscle action potentials as an indication of increasing muscle tension, electroencephalogram (EEG) or brain waves, eye movements and blink rate, skin temperature, blood pressure, respiration, tremors and perhaps even other phenomena. The last four measures would require some kind of device to transduce temperature change to electrical form, and pressure variations as in blood pressure, respiration and tremors to electrical form. Such devices have been developed and are commercially available, or could be made up by a technician with some mechanical and electrical skill.

Still other measures which might be employed are blood volume recorded by a plethysmograph, which measures the change in volume of a finger or a hand by the amount of fluid it displaces. Salivary secretions can be measured in the parotid gland and the chemical analysis of saliva can be made under various emotional conditions. Blood and urine can be analyzed chemically under the influence of various emotional stimuli. Metabolic rate, likewise might be studied under critical and non-critical conditions of questioning. Many of these measures are as yet impractical for application in the lie detection or deception situation, but they are mentioned here to indicate that there may be possibilities after further study and research.

Among psychological approaches to areas of conflict and anxiety such as a guilty person might harbor as a result of his crime, are the responses and reaction times to association stimuli. This area has not been explored as fully as it might be. The technique employed by Luria for studying the disorganization of motor responses and tremors of the fingers is another method which needs further study and exploration.

The utilization of any of these latter measures requires a good deal of background knowledge about the nature of physiological, psychological and neurological processes. The refinement and definition of these measures is the task of the expert in these fields; it is not to be presumed that a police officer or for that matter any other technically trained person without such a background could develop and apply these measures. They are discussed here not with that intent, but rather simply to inform about other possibilities which may at some future time be developed to a point where they could be applied after a better understanding of their mechanism has been worked out.

Some Practical Considerations in Lie Detection Work

The examining room. If possible, a special room should be set aside for interrogation and polygraphic lie detection. It should be a quiet place where outside noises from street or hall are at a minimum, and where interruptions are unlikely to occur. The room should be simply furnished with a minimum of distractions such as pictures, extraneous equipment and so forth. Chairs and a desk for the examiner plus only the essential polygraph and other equipment should be present. A comfortable chair for the subject should be provided in which he may relax and be put at ease. A large overstuffed leather chair with broad arms is suitable. An old style Morris chair with adjustable back and flat broad arms is often useful. A new modern type chair with back that tilts back and at the same time has a support which comes up and holds the legs is ideal.

If the polygraph equipment is placed on the desk it is desirable to have the subject facing the opposite direction with face toward a bare and non-distracting wall. In order for the examiner to be able to observe the subject a moderate sized mirror might be mounted on the wall out of the direct line of view of the subject but at a suitable angle for noting the subject's facial expression and movements.

The ideal situation is to have two rooms, one for the recording equipment and examiner, and one for the subject, with a one-way vision window suitably placed for watching the subject. With the examining room dark except for a small shielded lamp over the polygraph equipment, and with the subject's room lighted the window may be made to look like a mirror to the subject. The two rooms should be connected by a two-way communication system with the controls on the examiner's side. Thus he may press a switch and talk to the subject at any time, but at all other times can hear the speech, breathing or other noises or expressions made by the subject. If an extra observer is available for duty in the examining room he may watch the subject's movements and activities and by pressing a signal key impose a signal on the tracing being made, noting for each signal the nature of the movement which may later be transcribed on the record. This prevents artifacts in the record being misinterpreted as bona fide responses to questioning. If one wishes to record the exact time when the examiner speaks to the subject and in turn when the subject gives a verbal response (association reaction time) this may be accomplished by having the microphones in the two rooms, together with their amplifiers, so arranged that the voice response may be recorded on two separate recording lines on the polygraph along with the other tracings of physiological responses.

In lieu of two separate rooms, one for subject and one for examiner, the partial partitioning of a single room by a temporary wall and viewing window will suffice. The equipment and the manipulations of it by the examiner should be out of the subject's view. Noises of manipulating the equipment, throwing off switches, and so forth should be reduced to a minimum for a very slight noise made by a switch may be sufficient stimulus to cause a response which could be confused with the response to questioning. The observant examiner will soon learn what kinds of things constitute distractions to the subject.

Polygraph equipment. There are several commercially available types of lie detection polygraphs which seem to have reliable and adequate facilities for recording blood pressure, pulse, respiration and in some instances galvanic skin response. In addition some may have voice recording and other signalling devices. At least one type, the Stoelting polygraph, in some models has also had Luria type tremorgraph recording units. For the uninitiated it would probably be wise to get some expert advice on the different types of equipment before purchasing a unit. This might be obtained from other police departments where polygraphs of one or more types had been used extensively and where officers trained in polygraph work would be in a position to advise on advantages or disadvantages of particular equipment for certain uses. Another source of information might be from psychologists or physiologists in neighboring universities, who may have had extensive experience in recording autonomic responses in connection with emotion or other processes. At least such individuals should be able to advise on the suitability of described characteristics of the equipment.

When a polygraph has been purchased instructions should be studied very carefully and extensive instruction and practice in using it should be a rule before attempting to use it in a lie detection situation with a suspect. An instructional course or a period of apprentice training with skilled and expert operators, with a prescribed "check-out" procedure is most desirable.

Treatment of an examinee. Inbau, in his excellent book, has pointed out the importance of not attempting a test on a suspect who has been subjected to rigorous grilling by other police methods a short time before. The examinee in such an instance might be fatigued, disgruntled, uncooperative, and otherwise indisposed to taking the test. It is important that all suspects examined be treated with respect and introduced to the testing procedure gradually and quietly, so that they may be put at ease and not be frightened of the procedure. The examiner should not be looked upon by the examinee as a threatening person who is hostile, antagonistic and domineering. He should be made to feel that the test is important because if he is innocent it will help protect him and others who are not guilty of the crime; if he is guilty the test will help to define the nature and circumstances of his guilt. In many instances it is necessary to have the consent of the suspect before a lie detection test may be attempted, and this is highly desirable. The failure of a suspect to submit to a lie detection test casts considerable doubt on his innocence, and most subjects realize this;

however, it is questionable whether this should be used as a threat to enforce testing. Unless a suspect willingly submits to a test and cooperates with the procedure required during testing, it is fruitless to try to apply the polygraphic procedure. Under such circumstances constant movement, tension and other forms of resistance would completely invalidate the test results.

Planning a polygraphic test. The examiner should familiarize himself very carefully with all of the available details of the crime and the circumstances under which it was committed. Likewise he should know as much about each suspect to be tested as he can. With these and other facts at hand he should make an outline of the procedure he intends to employ and in general this should be somewhat standardized so that his experience in working with other cases will have taught him what to expect. First, it is desirable to get the suspect adapted to the procedure by a few trial runs during which the examiner decides what levels of sensitivity are suitable for each of the measures. The next step would be to explain to the suspect what the lie detection procedure means and what it is capable of revealing.

In order to make this impressive and convincing to the subject, a demonstration test with numbers may be conducted in which the examiner identifies the number between one and ten the subject has taken even though he has been instructed to lie about it, by saying, "NO," to each number. Another test is to identify a playing card selected from among several by the subject. It is well to have the subject write down on a slip of paper the number or card selected so that when the identification is made it can be checked. This should be done very carefully so that the examiner is sure it will come off as expected. To have the test backfire under such circumstances due to carelessness on the part of the examiner would be to lose a great psychological advantage right at the start. If it is successfully demonstrated to the subject that his deception in a harmless situation like this can be detected, it will prove a very strong psychological stimulus which will reinforce any subsequent lying on his part and make it more readily detectable. Furthermore, it is not unusual for a suspect to confess at this point that he is the guilty person, for often he will realize that it is hopeless to try to conceal his guilt.

With a prepared outline of the procedure, and after the preliminary adjustment and demonstration tests, one may proceed with the actual investigation. This might begin with the presentation of a type of association test, where words are presented which have no bearing on the crime, with other crucial words being introduced into the list. There should be a random order in which such words are introduced into the list, never every third word or other fixed position. The same procedure may be worked with questions, some of which are distinctly related to the crime and others not. This general method, which has proved very useful, is called the *Relevant-Irrelevant Word or Question Method*.

Another method introduced by Keeler is *The Hidden Key* or *Peak of Tension Method*. This involves presenting a list of words or questions, only one of which is definitely known to be crucial, and which no suspect, other than the guilty party, could recognize as a crucial factor. Sometimes such a procedure may be accentuated by telling the suspect there is one name and one name only in the following list which is important to the solution of this crime, if you are guilty you will recognize this name and respond to it. Or, among the following sums of money is one which is the actual amount stolen, if you are guilty you will know which amount is correct. In this procedure it is *not* necessary to require the suspect to respond verbally, which often has an advantage since the effort of speaking sometimes introduces artifacts that may be confused with the affective or emotional response to a stimulus.

The Status and Problems of Polygraphic Lie Detection

A recent Symposium on *The Polygraphic Truth Test* provides a very excellent survey of the present status of polygraphic lie detection. This symposium was held as a part of the Thirteenth Annual Law Institute of the University of Tennessee and the portion of it dealing with the polygraph test is reported in the *Tennessee Law Review*, February, 1953. All persons working with polygraph lie detection tests should read these articles carefully. William Wicker, Dean of the University of Tennessee

College of Law reviews the legal status of the lie detector test in an article entitled, *The Polygraphic Truth Test and the Law of Evidence*. Most court decisions as to the admissibility of polygraph test results as evidence hark back to a decision rendered by the Court of Appeals for the District of Columbia in 1923, in which the test results were held inadmissible because the procedure had not yet gained general scientific acceptance. During the past thirty years techniques have improved, the experience and training of operators is in general more rigorous and advanced, and improvements in equipment have been made. Wicker argues that the 1923 decision should not set the pattern for all subsequent decisions as it often does in substantive law, since this is a matter of procedural law in which the demonstration of how a fact may be proved or disproved is a matter of procedure. Wicker does imply that if polygraph test results are admitted to court as evidence, it is likely that the evidence will have to be presented by expert opinion testimony. This means that the expert is subject to cross-examining not only on his diagnosis of the results and his reasons for it, but upon his training and experience as well. It thus behooves any expert to have full qualifications and know his subject well.

The second article in the symposium is entitled, *A Consensus as to the Validity of Polygraph Procedures*, by Edward E. Cureton, Professor of Psychology, University of Tennessee. Professor Cureton sent out 1700 questionnaires to psychologists, polygraph examiners and observers and experimenters. He had about a 50 per cent reply to the questionnaire, in which 93 per cent of the psychologists felt that a polygraph operated by a well trained investigator had moderate or high validity; none held it to be invalid, 7 per cent had no opinion. Among observers, experimenters and examiners 95 per cent considered the procedure had moderate or high validity; none considered it invalid, 5 per cent had no opinion. Of examiners who actually use the technique in police investigation, 99 per cent rated the technique of moderate or high validity. These opinions by experts in the use of the technique, and by university psychologists, presumably unbiased since most of them did not use the test in police work, but instead were informed about the measures and their use in emotion and deception detection in the laboratory, speak very well for the test procedure. Many of the respondents emphasized that the qualified examiner must have background information, thorough training and experience with the technique, and above all a scientific and objective attitude.

The third article in the series is by Paul V. Trovillo, Director of Research, Russell Chatham, Inc., Personnel Consultants, Oak Ridge, Tennessee. It is entitled *Scientific Proof of Credibility*. This paper presents the need for scientific controls and further experimentation. Trovillo holds that it is a good method in qualified hands; he discusses the number of qualified operators in the country, where training may be obtained and other pertinent factors.

The symposium brought out some of the difficulties standing in the way of polygraphic application, and these are presented in a series of cartoons reproduced in Figure 11. These cartoons emphasize eight points: (1) Contested legality—the failure of general acceptance by the courts. (2) The police investigator who turns to the polygraph only as a last resort. (3) Newspaper and magazine writers who distort the news concerning use of the lie detector—both favorable and unfavorable distortion. (4) The fight against outmoded methods. (5) Examiners who are not competent and well-trained. (6) The adamant detective or police investigator who spurns help. (7) The civilian polygraph expert who considers himself a prima donna and no doubt offends experienced and skilled police investigators by his tactics. (8) The "quack" who pretends to be something he isn't in the way of an expert on polygraph work.

PSYCHOLOGY OF THE ACCUSED

As we have observed in the historical account, there have been through the ages attempts to judge guilt or innocence in terms of reactions and appearances of the accused. Knowledge of the consequences of being judged guilty, regardless of guilt or innocence,

→

Fig. 11. Cartoons illustrating some of the major problems facing the use of the polygraph as a technique and as legal evidence. (Reproduced from the *Tennessee Law Review*, 1953, Vol. 22, by permission.)

leads no doubt to *fear* of the consequences in the form of punishment, maiming or death. The assumption is that such manifestations of fear normally are greater in a guilty person with knowledge of his guilt than in an innocent person. However, such an assumption must be tempered by the fact that present-day investigation and study of emotional reactions of fear have shown that "normal" or average persons differ greatly in their reactions to stimuli calculated to arouse fear. Such reactions are a part of the life history of the individual and the many experiences he has undergone.

Obviously, no two individuals, even identical twins, have been subjected to precisely the same experiences throughout life with the result that no two individuals react exactly alike in the presence of any situation, even though superficial observation may suggest that they do. If sufficiently detailed experimental measures are made of their reactions and their physiological responses in muscles, the nervous system, circulatory system, and glandular function, individual differences will be evident.

Nature of fear. Fear is predominantly a learned response and depends upon painful and unpleasant experiences, through which a person learns of the consequences of certain situations to which he is exposed. A two year old child has no fear of a snake which will terrify his mother, nor is he afraid and wary of a hot stove until he has touched it and been burned. Thus through painful and unpleasant experiences, or through the observation of fearful reactions of others, a child may become conditioned to respond in a fearful manner to certain stimuli or even to the threat or anticipation of certain stimuli. Basically, the response mechanism from which a fear response stems seems to be unlearned and present at birth. Any strong, sudden and unexpected stimulus, such as a loud noise produces in the newborn infant a Moro reflex, which consists of a body jerk with extension of the limbs. Before the first year has ended this reflex response has been modified to a generalized flexion of body and limbs, and is known as the "startle response." This basic pattern of flexion or the startle response persists throughout life when a strong, unexpected stimulus such as a bright light, or loud sound suddenly is presented without warning. Accompanying the "startle response" which is a rapid overt flexion of body muscles, is a series of internal changes such as increased heart rate, a transient elevation in blood pressure, a brief gasp or change in respiration, and several other unobservable, but measurable responses if special measuring devices are employed. The early fear responses of the child are often related to pain and unpleasantness which is introduced suddenly by an intense stimulus.

If a big barking dog suddenly comes bounding up to a two or three year old child, the action and noise are apt to produce a fear reaction even though the dog is only being playful. If in its playfulness the dog should bump into the child and topple him over it will add to his general fear response. Thereafter the child may be frightened of all animals, especially large and active ones. This is a process known as conditioning and generalization of the fear response. Eventually a child learns to cope with such situations and because he is larger and is exposed to socialization in the presence of other children and adults who are not afraid of animals he loses his fear through closer association with them in harmless situations. However, other types of situations arise to which some of the basic fear responses may become attached. For example, from 6 to 12, a child learns that he must conform with some of the wishes of other children in cooperative play. He must conform to demands for discipline at home and in the school, for if he does not penalties and punishments resulting in pain and unpleasantness are apt to result. Now his fear responses extend to anticipated failure to conform or perform as he is supposed to do. He begins to learn that society with its rules, regulations, and laws, imposes restrictions and penalties; his parents and the church expose him to ideals and morals for which there are threatened penalties if he does not conform.

It is a complex process, but many of the original fear responses associated with physical pain and discomfort become associated with social and cultural demands and the possible penalties or punishments related to the failure to conform to acceptable standards. Among these social taboos are lying, stealing, injuring another person, and many other forms of misbehavior which are not socially acceptable. Consequently, with knowledge of the consequences of transgression in any of these areas, the actual commission of one of these acts leads to fear of being detected in the act or being found guilty of it at a later time. Furthermore, through exposure during the years to standards of right and wrong, even though a given individual may persist in taking the wrong path time and time again, such a person will develop a "conscience" about his deviations from the right. An inner conflict develops between a sense of judgment of right and wrong, even though the wrong may win out much of the time. Sometimes through compensatory processes such as rationalization the individual may try to convince himself and others that his "wrong" acts and transgressions against society and its codes are "right" and justified. Although he may be able to rationalize his acts and convince others of their justification, or perhaps even his innocence of the acts themselves, it is often more difficult to convince one's "self."

As in the case of other people, one may superficially convince one's self, but a deeper or subconscious memory of the situation remains indelibly recorded somewhere in the nervous system. Though this memory may be repressed much of the time by concern with other matters and distractions of various sorts which a person learns to employ to cover up things he wishes to forget or conceal, there is a constant tendency for such matters to well up in consciousness and even to reflect themselves in the form of action or behavior. The welling up of such thoughts we call "conscience" and this sort of process can initiate or reinstate old patterns of fear response. Sometimes the persistent recurrence of a bad conscience and the associated fear states accompanying it give rise to what we call *anxiety*, a kind of chronic worry, tenseness, restlessness, sleeplessness, interference with appetite and many other symptoms.

But it is not only the outward manifestations which may occur and be evident to others, it is the inner tensions and activity of the physiological system that cannot be seen, which are important from the point of view of the polygraph or "lie detector" study. A person may learn to repress, conceal or cover up external reactions which may be evident to him as well as to others, but he is handicapped in attempting to conceal reactions which are not evident to him and which may not be under voluntary control.

Such reactions are blood pressure change, heart rate, skin resistance and temperature changes, muscle tensions, tremors, respiratory changes, salivation or dryness of mouth, blanching or blushing responses of the skin, and many other signs of activity in the body which are under the control of the *autonomic* or *involuntary nervous system*. Some of these changes may be set off by any clue which automatically elicits a memory of the act which constituted the original transgression. It could be a word, an idea expressed, a picture, being confronted with a piece of the evidence such as the lethal weapon or the stolen piece of material.

The foregoing picture of the development of emotional reactions of fear from the earliest reflex patterns in infancy to the socialized response patterns of the older child and adult is obviously simplified for purposes of illustration, but it does seem to represent the nature of the process by which basic fear responses get perpetuated and related to new stimulus conditions, social attitudes and evaluations of consequences. The responses of a child growing up continue to be modified as he grows older. And eventually as a youth or an adult he learns to control many of the more exaggerated forms of reflex response. This is accomplished by voluntary means by those muscles under voluntary control. However many of the response mechanisms over which most persons have little or no voluntary control continue to respond similarly throughout life. For example, most people cannot control heart rate, blood pressure, sweating, digestive functions, blanching or flushing of the face, and tremors of the hands. Therefore some of these reactions will still manifest themselves even though a person has learned to control facial expression and bodily posture and has by mannerisms learned to cover up other uncontrolled responses.

Because a certain number of involuntary response mechanisms of which the subject may not even be aware, continue to function and are recordable and measurable by certain instruments such as those incorporated in the so-called "lie-detector" or polygraph, these kinds of uncontrolled responses can serve as reliable and valid indices of emotional arousal, despite a poker-faced facade on the part of the person concerned.

There may be a number of observable features of external

behavior which can be noted as telltale signs even without the aid of instruments if the observer is trained in observational methods which allow him to concentrate upon and look for the right things. This is often easier said than done. Actions are often part of a complex pattern of behavior and certain elements of the total picture are often transient and fleeting. It therefore requires a skilled observer operating under special conditions of experimentation and probing to bring out and note some of these otherwise masked signs. This is comparable to the physician observing certain signs in a patient which are not evident to the layman, because the latter does not by training and experience possess the powers of observation which direct his attention to the right things.

The contrast between the behavioral manifestations of a child and adult help one to realize the difference in astuteness required on the part of the observer. For example, a child who is accused of taking cookies from a jar, often shows by his shy looks, evasiveness, restless fidgeting, and so forth, a behavior which gives him away. Also because he is not experienced in concealing his reactions and has not learned ways of dodging or side-tracking the accuser, he will be more susceptible to accusation and breakdown. More than likely he will have no ready answers for his defense, or in any event will not be experienced in "alibi-ing" his way out of the accusation. Under the threat of authority he will often admit his guilt. Not so with the older adolescent child or adult, and even less so with the hardened, brazen, and experienced delinquent or criminal. Their defenses have been well learned through many similar practice experiences, and it is only through those media of response over which they have no control and of which they are not even aware, that their guilt can be evinced.

Fear in the guilty and in the innocent. If fear of consequences be accepted as one of the bases on which deception reactions depend, it must be recognized that consequences have different meanings and values for different individuals. Certainly the two- or three-time loser, who has been in and out of jails and has many times previously been before the police, a jury, and a judge, will have less fear and feel that less of a social consequence hangs on any given act and conviction for it, than will the innocent and respected citizen, who has a considerable reputation and esteem of his family, friends and others to consider. Although the innocent person and respected citizen may be more nervous, restless and emotionally upset about being questioned concerning a crime it is not this reaction in which the police investigator should be interested. Rather he should be concerned with those critical clue-items which there is good reason to believe are closely associated with the crime and which only the perpetrator of the crime could know about. It might seem that fear is not the exact term to apply to the situation of the criminal where capital punishment is not at stake. Yet despite this circumstance the criminal still does not wish to lose his freedom. Or perhaps he has come to believe, as many do, that he is smarter than the law and it is a mark of personal defeat to have to recognize that he can be outwitted. These and many other bases for his reactions could be classed as a kind of apprehension or fear of detection of guilt, and therefore be subject to the same involuntary and uncontrolled responses when confronted with guilt-evincing questions or subtle clue-reminding stimuli. It is upon this basis then that "lie-detection" depends for the most part.

REFERENCES

INBAU, FRED E.: *Lie Detection and Criminal Interrogation.* Baltimore, Williams & Wilkins, 1942. A very practical discussion of lie detection and criminal interrogation.

LARSON, JOHN A.: *Lying and Its Detection.* Chicago, University of Chicago Press, 1932. One of the early, comprehensive discussions of lie detection.

LEE, C. D.: *The Instrumental Detection of Deception,* Springfield, Illinois, Charles C Thomas, Publisher, 1951. A very practical discussion of lie detection.

MARSTON, W. M.: *The Lie Detector Test.* New York, Richard R. Smith, 1938. An interesting account with emphasis on procedure.

MULBAR, H.: *Interrogation.* Springfield, Illinois: Charles C Thomas, Publisher, 1951. An excellent discussion with much emphasis on procedure.

SYMPOSIUM: *The Polygraphic Truth Test.* Thirteenth Annual Law Institute of the University of Tennessee, Knoxville, Tenn. Nov. 14, 1952. *Tennessee Law Review,* February 1953.

Chapter 5

THE PSYCHOLOGY OF HUMAN RELATIONS

By

Norman C. Meier

ENVIRONMENT AND THE INDIVIDUAL

Environment Sets the Pattern of Human Relations

THE RELATIONS one has with other people, whether they be satisfying, unpleasant, or indifferent, have their bases in the kind of environment in which one lives. One's environment is not just the physical surroundings—the good neighborhood or the shabby one down by the tracks—but one's social surroundings as well—the kind of family one is born into, one's playmates, the school attended, the church, the gang, the clubs and many other groups that afford associations with others. All of these contacts affect one in some manner and contribute something toward setting the pattern of one's adult human relations.

These associations not only set the pattern, but they also provide, for the remainder of one's life, a means of identification. Therefore when anyone runs afoul of the law, clues are forthcoming from former associates. One may be located, when he disappears, by running down earlier ties, earlier experiences, former places of work or of residence and the like. One's life history is a permanent record, and one's known personality characteristics a means of identification.

Everyone has social ties. We are born into a family, under usual circumstances, and develop ties with parents, brothers and sisters, and with relatives, that normally last through a lifetime. There are, of course, exceptions. There is the child born out of wedlock, the waif abandoned during a disaster, the child unwanted by parents or relatives, and the one orphaned by an accident that took all others in the family. Since the family unit also embraces relatives, who may substitute for parents, one usually does identify himself with them even though the contacts are few and the circumstances that separate one from them strange and unusual. In fact it is difficult to conceive of a person as completely out of touch with everyone, and of a wanted man as not in some way or at some time in contact with some of the members of his family or the social units to which he formerly belonged. More often than not there is some one person to whom an individual turns in time of deep trouble. Sometimes it is the person's mother, or a former buddy, or a priest or minister, or a former employer.

Primary group relationships. In the home each person sees the others in a close face-to-face manner over a period of years. This is known as the primary group. It is the first to have its effect on the child and generally it is the most important. He hears the parents and other adults express their views on religion, politics, business, the next door neighbors, and about everything else of interest to the parents. Unwittingly, the child absorbs their views, their biases and prejudices, their opinions, attitudes and general outlook on life. It is small wonder then that the child in a Catholic home grows up to be a Catholic and perhaps a Democrat; or the child in a Protestant home emerges as a Baptist or Presbyterian.

As the child grows older and meets people outside the home, goes to high school or college, attends labor union meetings, sees movies, and attends lectures, some of the early acquired beliefs may be altered. The individual may leave the home environmnt, may align himself with even the opposite political party, or drift away from the faith in which he was reared. But more children, generally considered, follow the parental line of thought and belief than reject them. The initial strength of these early beliefs and attitudes are too well established to be abandoned easily.

Secondary group influences. Considerable numbers of younger persons and a large proportion of adults do not live at the home of parents nor have homes of their own. Still others are married but must live in transient quarters, owing to uncertainty of employment, housing shortages, inadequate income, or because they are engaged in seasonable employment or employment that requires living in out-of-the-way areas. The transient hotel or low-cost rooming house then becomes the locale of the person's immediate group relationships, replacing the early parental environment. These relationships may be close or very casual.

The individual will usually seek the best quarters his income will afford, ordinarily budgeted at one-fifth his income. Hence any extreme deviation from this ratio would indicate either that he is not living in accordance with his means or that proper housing is not available. Generally, however, the living quarters indicate the economic and personal competence of the individual. The cheap lodging house or transient hotel in a run-down section of a city or down by the tracks in a smaller community, will often be sought by the unfortunate who has drifted from job to job, never successfully mastering any trade or particular skill, and by those who have personalities that make it difficult for them to adjust to successful living in an age of industrialization. They have formed the attitudes and prejudices outside what home life they had and reflect the views of others similarly unfortunate in the economic struggle.

Indirect factors affecting human relations. Let us consider now the more stable person also uprooted from his primary group influences but under quite different circumstances. He has difficulty finding satisfactory employment in his home community, so migrates with his family to a distant city where he finds that overcrowding prevails.

Under such circumstances the primary group relations and also the secondary group associations are disrupted. The person and his family must readjust to a new environment, learn the prevailing beliefs and attitudes and perhaps modify his own to conform. If he does, he is accepted, and his newly established relations will be satisfactory. If he does not and still retains the beliefs and attitudes of his former community, he may find himself socially isolated. His prejudices may even get him into trouble. For law enforcement officers to understand persons in such situations, when the need arises, it is necessary to know something of the beliefs, attitudes, biases, and prejudices prevailing in the original community.

The importance of background for understanding human relations is well illustrated in the case of some children of Polish descent. In the public schools of a large midwest city, the school truant officer and specialists who handle troublesome children were unable to get a word out of some children of Polish descent. They simply shut up like clams. Inquiry into the family origins disclosed that the family had emigrated from a rural section of Poland. The peasants were forbidden to hunt on the baronal estates and hence resorted to poaching. When raids were made, seeking evidence, the peasants learned to give no information under any circumstances. The practice became so firmly ingrained that it remained with them after they migrated to America and the children continued it. Even shaking the children, threatening, or any amount of entreaty left them unwilling to talk.

The individual is thus a product of many influences, beginning with the family, and the family in turn reflects influences going back into the past.

Every one with whom we have more than casual contact is apt to affect, in some slight measure, the general pattern of our subsequent human relations. Americans are a generation of joiners —joining a church group, a political party, a lodge, a soft-ball club, or a sewing circle. What effects do these associations have on our patterns of human relations?

Group Identification

The moment a child joins a neighborhood "gang" or the YMCA or other like group, he stands to have his primary group influences modified because he will meet with others whose family inculcations are different from his. Naturally, the total effect of this will vary with the person, but it is always there. Some of this group identification is with social organizations, some with social institutions, and with publics.

Social organizations. With adults, and with younger people as well, joining a club, a lodge, a team or what not, will, so long as it is not exclusive and snobbish, tend to enlarge the individual's horizons. His earlier prejudices against Catholics or against Jews or against lawyers may be modified. He may become acquainted with a lawyer who once represented a widow without fee and, therefore, appears quite human. In discussions and contacts so afforded he acquires many new slants on problems about which he was meagerly informed.

Social institutions. Law and religion are institutions maintained by society for the good of all. Though the law may at times cause hardship and the devil quote scripture, by and large the greater good comes from respect for both. Yet both restrict what the individual may do. In one sense religion is man's own awareness that there is a power greater than any one man's no matter what his concept of that power may be. Likewise the law-abiding citizen feels that whatever restrains him from wilful acts contrary to law is for his *own* eventual benefit as well as that of others. The law-enforcement officer, an agent of society itself, is the safeguard whereby people can live together in peace and security.

Publics. The average citizen takes his political institutions more or less for granted. He may have to arrange for garbage collection, to pay taxes and assessments, to avoid creating a nuisance, and be responsible for the acts of his children or his dog. Whether he does these things grudgingly or willingly reflects his general attitude toward the community and its government. The "substantial citizen" takes all these obligations as a matter of course. For those who resent the operation of ordinances and other regulatory "impositions" on complete freedom, good human relations would suggest some education in the facts of group living.

Membership in civic groups, such as Parent-Teacher Associations, Civic Music enterprises and the like does much to promote identity with the general welfare of the community. It is a failing of the average citizen that he is quick to criticize bad city management or the national government, yet takes little or no part in the democratic process. So long as nothing happens to restrict his freedom he gives little thought to the political structure in which he lives; he is vaguely aware that it exists and he is prone to believe that it always will exist.

The political scene, however, does provide *interest outlets* for him. Being able to criticize enhances his ego. Hence his criticism is usually voiced among like-minded friends who assent readily.

This in turn leads him to assume that he is dead right in his views. Viewed objectively such behavior is understandable when we examine human relations more closely by learning more about the individual.

Group identification takes over where primary group influences decline. Identification with specific groups tends to satisfy the need for security and for prestige which are prominent motives in social relations. Identification with a labor union provides a measure of security against want or unfair treatment. Patriotism is an expression of group identification providing a feeling of security against loss from defeat in conflict; it also is an extension of the family group identification to a larger field. Identification with the Grange or the Farm Bureau gives the farmer a feeling of security and the prestige of considering himself a successful farmer. Without some opportunity for group identification the individual would feel lonely and insecure.

MOTIVATION IN HUMAN RELATIONS

To understand human relations in everyday living it is necessary to know what *motivates* the individual—why he acts as he does. Motives must be inferred. They cannot be observed directly. We may even at times fail to understand or to discern our own motives. Yet motives determine what interests us, what we do, how we feel about others and things in general. They influence the ideas we develop, the opinions we express and the beliefs we hold.

Motivation: General Principles

A motive is anything which energizes us toward an activity needed to satisfy some need, drive, or goal-objective. Motivating agents or factors may be: *biological drives or needs*, such as the need to satisfy hunger, either directly or by seeking employment; *emotions*, inner states such as fear or anger aroused by external situations; or *values and interests*, social in nature, as religious convictions or need for prestige.

When a strong motive is operating, as in a contest to outdo a rival, the mental processes are characterized by *intensity* or a high energy level. If a long-run objective serves as a goal-object, such as working toward a promotion, requiring energy to cope with both temporary successes and set-backs, it is characterized by *persistence*. Should progress be temporarily blocked, making it necessary to try different approaches, it is characterized by *variability*. Individuals differ in the three characteristics, but the characteristics usually found in some degree indicate the person's endeavor to satisfy needs, drives and goals, experienced in everyday living.

Biological drives, emotions and social motives, all of which must be inferred, will be discussed later. We now turn to a principle of motivation of simpler character, of wide application, and of great usefulness in dealing with others.

The self-interest principle. Generally considered the one person the individual knows most about is *himself*. He knows himself at close range; others must regard him at a distance. It is *his* tooth that aches; others can only imagine what it is like. He may have secret ambitions about which he confides to no one. It is his welfare that he is concerned with throughout life; no one else can be quite so completely interested. The psychoanalyst refers to this aspect as the *ego* and the constant concern as ego-enhancement. The ways of ego-satisfaction are many and devious, and even the individual may not at times realize the full nature of the workings of his own mind.

In almost all human relations, results are normally forthcoming when the appeal is made in accordance with the principle of self-interest. It is still better if it can be shown to be a matter of *mutual* self-interest, or that both parties will benefit. Modern effective advertising does not thrust an article at a buyer, it formulates an appeal on a personal note that makes the buyer *want* the item. The appeal outlines how his time will be saved by use of the item; or how he will be more successful in his work. The candidate for office is less likely to get votes by saying "vote for me" than he is by showing *how much better* the administration of affairs will be under his guidance.

The offender brought to traffic court for speeding can be made to accept his fine graciously instead of glumly if it is pointed out that some day another speeder may crash *him* at an intersection; that traffic regulations are designed to protect *his* life as well as everyone's, and that the few minutes saved are scarcely worth the gamble. Most persons do not see that the greater *self-interest* lies in another direction.

Self-interest is not to be confused with *selfishness, self-indulgence,* or *wilfulness.* Rather it refers to the elemental fact that the individual has needs, wants, drives, and aspirations which he is constantly striving to satisfy. Anything which helps him to satisfy these strivings will, if properly understood, be welcomed by the individual. His support will be won readily for any project when he sees what it may mean for himself, his family, his children, his community or his country. Hence the problem is to present the proposition in such a way that he can envisage how he may be affected, even though indirectly. *Self-interest is a primary principle of motivation.*

Self-regard and self-esteem. The normal individual strives constantly to think well of himself. He does not like to admit defeat, nor to recognize weaknesses. He will resort to all sorts of explanations, even self-deception, to escape such thoughts. He is inclined to dwell more on his successes. The time he gives to contemplation of his more satisfying achievements is far in excess of the fleeting moments he devotes to his humiliations and disappointments.

From his early days the child observes the effect of his own actions on those of adults. He enjoys praise and approval. Punishment defines to him what is not approved. The child who is wanted grows in self-esteem because he gets attention. Some, of course, get too much and develop a feeling of dependency. Instead of developing an individuality capable of self-reliant behavior, they want to be waited on, and to have every wish granted. In the dependency situation the self lags in development. Hence such persons need to have more occasions for fostering self-esteem, to be gratified that they—and not others—accomplished something.

The adult seldom contemplates any move without awareness of its presumed effect on others. Before a girl accepts a date with a young man of unsavory reputation she asks herself: What will people think? One does not appear in compromising situations if he values his reputation. The ambitious young man wants to drive a car somewhat above his income level, because he believes that being seen in the more expensive car will lead people to think he is successful. He may wear good, well-fitting clothes because he feels that not only do clothes make the man but that he will be judged by them when promotion is in the offing. The young un-married woman indulges in an expensive perfume with the anticipa-tion of what it will do to her general allure when she is with the young man of her choice, and at the same time enhancing her own self-esteem as a person of discerning good taste. The principle of self-esteem is closely related to that of self-interest.

Drives, Urges, Needs — Their Nature and Variety

The individual has physiological needs that must be satisfied: hunger, thirst, need for relaxation and rest, elimination of waste products, comfortable living conditions, etc. He also has drives of a social nature: to earn a living, marry and establish a home, to out-distance rivals, to win honors and recognitions. These con-stitute goals.

Drives, needs and tensions demand release or satisfaction. When a goal is recognized and sought, such as success in attaining a desired position, a state of mild tension is experienced, a kind of restlessness, which will continue until the goal is reached. As each stage toward the attainment of the goal is reached, some reduction in the tension occurs. If progress toward the goal is interfered with or blocked, the tension may increase. Individuals, of course, vary in the strength of their drives. Some will redouble their efforts to overcome the difficulty; others may modify the goal and try for a lesser objective, while still others may abandon the goal altogether.

Successful drives enhance self-esteem. The individual who is able to satisfy his basic needs only, has a low order of drive and is not particularly bothered by any more advanced goals. The individual, on the other hand, who has drives of both *basic-need* satisfaction and *social drives* for a better and better position in society has a succession of new goals always following one another. A patrol-man seeks to become a sergeant, then a lieutenant, a captain, etc.

As soon as he attains one rank he desires a higher one. New tensions cause him to strive toward the satisfaction of his revised goal. Attainment of a rank changes the picture. Perhaps his wife now wants to belong to the country club or to satisfy her expensive tastes. Therefore the officer tries for a more important position in the department. If in time he is successful, his self-esteem rises accordingly.

Blocking of drives requires adjustment. The "success-story" type of experience is not too frequently the case. More often needs are not easily satisfied. The person may lose his job and have difficulty in finding as good a one. Promotion may not come his way. He may have quit school in the sixth grade and hence finds himself unprepared for the demands of the work he would like to do. His sex drive may be frustrated when his girl marries another. He may have blundered into making a serious mistake in offending his supervisor. When these things occur tension increases without compensating progress toward the goal.

In all instances of blocking of drives, some form of adjustment is in order. The individual cannot go on except at considerable loss of peace of mind, disturbance to health, lessened self-esteem, a lessening of self-confidence or other effect on his mental outlook. If the blocking occurs in the basic needs, it can be more or less serious. If it concerns only the social drives, such as not "getting along" as rapidly as desired, or failing to make a social club or purchase a better automobile, the frustration is not serious and the person adjusts to the situation in a matter of time. Throughout life it is commonplace to be making such adjustments, beginning in the primary group. A younger brother realizes he cannot do everything his older brother does. An older sister in her early twenties sees a younger sister marry before she does. These are the "minor tragedies" of life; they are of lesser consequence in human relations.

Adjustment: Adequate or Inadequate

In the person's effort to reduce the tension set up by a blocked goal, many different things may be tried. Some of these are positive measures that result in adequate or reasonably satisfactory adjustment; others lead only to by-passing the difficulty. We are interested, however, in the achievement of adequate adjustment and therefore ask: How can it be attained? What are the principles?

The principle of equilibrium. A relatively simple resolution of a blocked drive is the acquiring of ideas, information, or skills needed to meet the situation. If the person has sufficient drive the learning will be accomplished, and the barrier (blocking) removed. What one must learn depends on the nature of the situation. One person may read a book, such as Dale Carnegie's *How to Win Friends and Influence People*, take a course in salesmanship, or join a class in effective speaking. Another may learn more about his job and so in time attract the attention of his boss.

The *principle of equilibrium* holds that the individual strives vigorously and persistently to maintain his progress toward his self-defined goals despite temporary frustrations and disturbances. On a simpler level this tendency is seen in a person's effort to be comfortable. If the room is too warm, he will open a window or turn off the heat. Or if he becomes aware of bodily discomfort, he removes his tie or his shoes, or tries something until he again feels comfortable—until he regains equilibrium. What one does, then, to maintain equilibrium should contribute to good adjustment.

The principle of dominance. When the individual finds himself confronted with several needs at once, and he cannot satisfy all of them, he gives his attention to the dominant one. If one is comfortably resting in bed after a hard day's work but smells smoke the need for personal survival becomes dominant over the need for relaxation. In other words, the relative importance of needs at any given time determines the nature of one's adjustment.

The principle of goal perception. When faced with difficult and complex demands, the decision may have to be made on the basis of another principle—that of *goal perception*. A man wants to get ahead in his occupation or profession. To do so he must make many decisions and answer many questions. Is he *vitally* interested in his present line of work? Is he best fitted for it? What would he do if he lost out in it now? What are his total resources in skills, training and general competence? Is he apt to go farther in some other field? Should he stake everything on the present goal? As indecision continues, tension mounts. Obviously this tension will not decrease until he has a clearer perception of his goal. Goal perception, therefore, does make for more adequate adjustment.

The principle of secondary reinforcement. Once the individual is engaged in goal perception he may be aided in his perception by various minor considerations which did not heretofore appear. He may find that the work now chosen will take him to a dry climate that is good for his asthmatic condition. Or he may find that his new occupation is one in which his wife has a strong related interest. In other words, many secondary things reinforce his chances for achievement and make for better adjustment.

Unusual or strange motives may sometimes provide a *clue* to crime commitment. In attempting to unravel an otherwise baffling case, some leads may be established by investigation of the individual's early life and particularly the considerations that led him to the choice of his life work. Did he have any particular idiosyncracies, hobbies, or strange interests? Did he take special pleasure in collecting and dissecting insects or small animals? Was he given to sadistic practices? Who may have influenced him? How did he *arrive* at his goal perceptions? What was his dominant motivation in going into the ministry? Or the law? Or to become a meat cutter? Had he at any time had any particular anxieties; strong, persistent tension periods; dominant and all-compelling drives; abnormal social or sex needs? How had he reacted to economic loss or family troubles? Why had he never married; why did he hate women? Had he been plagued with chronic illness or alcoholism? If he drank to excess or gambled excessively, what was the cause? What seemed to be the consistently dominant need in his life? Why was it never adequately satisfied?

The Motivating Function of Emotion

Emotion may be considered as a bodily state accompanying motivation or as a motivating agent itself, taking on the characteristics of a drive. Mild emotion, sometimes described as *affective tone* gives a quality or "color" to almost every experience. We "like" a particular person without knowing just why; we have a feeling of distrust or mild aversion to another, causing avoidance or withdrawal. We say certain colors or combinations are "warm" and that they attract us, while others, as mustard gray or some "dirty" yellow-greens, repel us. Emotional states are classified as positive or pleasant and negative or unpleasant states .

Emotion as reaction to drive satisfaction or frustration. When a drive is blocked, anger may result. If frustration is anticipated, there may be anxiety or fear, which in turn causes the person to be additionally motivated to prevent or to overcome the frustrating condition or situation. Rage, an extreme form of anger, mobilizes full energy to combat the obstacle, as a fighting man against a hated enemy viewed as a block to his goal of winning a war. Rage, in instances of extreme motivation as in the case of a person suffering a grave and rank injustice, may summon energy to precipitate great bodily injury on his adversary—even to murder. Great fear may mobilize supreme effort to escape, as "superhuman" speed in escaping from a wild animal or prodigious exertion in escaping from entrapment in a collapsing building or cave-in. Nature has provided for such emergencies by releasing maximum flow of blood sugar into the blood stream, greater secretion (outpouring) of adrenin, and a retarding of digestion and other bodily functions not needed in the struggle. Emotion as an energizer thus serves the organism in its struggle for survival. The emotion accompanying drive satisfaction, joy or elation, serves the purpose of relaxing the individual, releasing the tension, and increasing the feeling of well-being. Such emotion may normally be a mild sense of satisfaction with things in general, or a violent outburst expressed in a shout or wild action.

Intensity, variability and persistence. Emotion thus varies in intensity from mild states of liking or disliking to complete domination of the person, mobilizing every last ounce of energy and concentrating on a single goal—as escape, in panic. It may vary in the same person from mild dislike of another, to suspicion and strong dislike, and to jealousy followed by an extreme manifestation of aggression culminating in murder. It may be an accompaniment of slowly built-up feeling stemming from outraged conviction, leading finally to assassination, as in the political field. Murder not infrequently has its incentive or background in the emotion of fear—fear of a rival, fear of economic loss, or fear of exposure. In such situations it is a way out of a frustrating situation.

In more normal or ordinary human relations emotion takes the form of minor anxieties, minor instances of fear, or of anger, or less disturbing and more rewarding experiences producing elation or tension-reduction. The usual function of emotion is that of energizing the person—causing renewed motivation, new striving toward the goal, or toward overcoming the cause of the frustration or attaining a more satisfying equilibrium, denoting improvement in the total situation. It is normally characterized by considerable *variability*, depending upon the type of personality affected. Some permit anxiety and tension to persist some time before setting about to find ways and means of resolving or correcting the condition or situation. Others will try at once to overcome the frustrating circumstances, or, failing in that effort, will vary the tactics in a continued effort to attain the goal in some other way, or failing in that direction, may redefine the goal so that a reasonably satisfactory substitute can be ultimately attained.

The *intensity* of the emotional response is usually related to the speed or promptness with which the person will react. If violent anger ensues from the blocking of the drive, the greater will be the motivation to overcome the frustration. If only mild annoyance is incurred, and the person is a balanced, urbane individual, the longer the frustrating situation may persist.

Anger and aggression. Psychologists are inclined to regard anger as directly related to a characteristic type of response, namely *aggression*. Frustration normally leads to some form of resistance or combativeness against the cause of the frustration. The principle assumes that the frustration was caused by an act or a condition set up by another, either through malice, conflict of ambition, rivalry, or some other aspect of inter-personal relations. If the frustrated individual lays the blame on another, he then tends to act aggressively against that person or against the person or conditions believed responsible. He may openly challenge him or he may try to get even by some devious or indirect manner, as attacking his reputation or attempting to block his rival's effort toward *his* goal.

The anger of the soldier in Korea may be against Stalin but he has to take it out on North Koreans and Chinese. Hence anger and fear may be directed to realistic objects, as against the football player who, unseen by the officials, clips a player to avert a touchdown, or against a symbolic object as Truman or Stalin, in different circumstances and settings.

The role of learning. Fears are sometimes residual experiences from early childhood, explainable by the process of *conditioning*. A child is frightened by a loud noise at the same time she may be caressing a pet rabbit. The fear is hence transferred to the rabbit, or by *second-order conditioning* to any furry animal or her mother's fur neck piece. Or the child may have been badly frightened by a dark object which the parent identifies as a drunken Negro—hence she is fearful when meeting a Negro after dark. In later childhood she learns that her father had been defrauded by an unscrupulous lawyer and generalizes that lawyers are a crooked lot.

Severe punishment for minor mistakes or misdemeanors may cause a child to have persistent anxieties, which may be transferred to a fear of adults generally. Discussion in the home about "those awful Joneses" may lead to anxiety about being "mixed up" with "such people," in school or in social affairs. Young persons in homes where the adults talk constantly of some despised classes or neighborhood clan or of fears about possible change whereby a minority people may become a "menace" are apt to acquire fears and anxieties. In the deep South the early contact of the child with "keeping the nigger in his place" by poor white families, conditions the child to grow up with the same attitude. Such conditioning, unless a reconditioning takes place to modify the attitude, may make such persons, grown to adulthood, susceptible to acts of violence when and if the occasion and circumstances might some time afford. Attitudes such as these become a part of the social values, discussed in the following section.

Social Motives

The motivation discussed thus far has been largely concerned with the welfare of the individual himself: striving to satisfy his hunger needs, attract a mate, avoid frustrations to attainment of goals. *Social* motives look to the outside. If the individual seeks *prestige*, it is standing with reference to others; if he wants *security*, it is a relationship to some other person, as a parent, or the government. But, like emotion, social motives deal with symbols, as property is desired because it is a *symbol of prestige* and security.

Security as a social motive. The desire for security has its beginnings in the mother-child relationship. To the infant the mother provides relief from hunger and thirst, she removes *wet* and irritating clothes, protects the child from painful and frightening situations. Absence of the mother may produce anxiety, threat of loss of these satisfactions, expressed in crying.

The *secure* child is one who had these satisfactions in normal degree; his environment is regarded as safe and he generalizes that people are usually good. Th *insecure* child is one who was not cared for adequately: fed irregularly, neglected, and afforded little protection. He has little trust in the future and hence tends to grasp whatever is at hand; people are regarded as generally bad and he is not inclined to trust anyone.

The wish for security is present in both the secure and the insecure. Everyone seems to need someone to whom he can turn in time of trouble; to need acceptance in some group; to need warmth and friendship. The secure individual takes it for granted that he will get these, if not now, later. The insecure person tends to fear that these satisfactions will not be his and takes any little slight as a serious indication.

Among adult groups *collective security* is at times sought. The labor unions have sought to provide security for the factory worker against arbitrary discharge; they and industry and government have provided insurance security against aging, illness and unemployment. These and manifold other forms are outgrowths of the basic feeling of the security motive in the parent-child relationship.

Dominance and prestige. When the individual is accepted into a group he is thus assured of security so far as that group can contribute. His next goal may then be to attain *preferred* status within the group. If he has a strong dominance drive, perhaps stemming from earlier *insecurity*, he will run for an office or try to get on an important committee. Usually the drive had its antecedent in parental rewards and punishments. As a child he was admonished to make good grades, to stand up and fight for his rights, to eat his spinach so he can be strong and make the team later on. Some times the pressure on the child is a parental compensation for past frustrations of their own. The father never went beyond third grade: hence the son must go to college; to be able to go he is required to make good grades in high school. The drilled-in competitive attitude remains in the child as he grows to manhood and may appear as dominance in his lodge or country club. In extreme instances its may be so dominant that unworthy means are undertaken to gain an advantage which is not deserved, and the dominance motive may explain gangster alignments, in which rivals may use drastic means to resolve the situation.

Not all persons seek power over others. Some prefer to be favorably known among their associates, to be looked-up-to, to be regarded as experts or authorities. This form of dominance is known as *prestige*, and constitutes the form of dominance sought or enjoyed by men in science, writing, professional people generally and the persuasive type of political leaders. It is hence a socially more desirable manifestation of the dominance motive and is more generally conducive to good human relations.

Acquisitiveness. Psychology does not recognize any innate drive of acquisitiveness, yet the practice of accumulating wealth and personal possessions is widespread. As such it may be a special expression of the *security* motive, insurance-plus against hard times and adversity. In other instances it may be a form of prestige-seeking, having a "show-place" home or estate. Deprivation in early childhood may tend to explain the adult's interest in acquisitiveness beyond normal satisfactions. Advancing years may also cause the individual to continue acquiring things, always fearing he may never have enough to last out his lifetime. The not infrequent cases of persons found dead in the midst of poverty yet having minor fortunes is to be explained as perhaps cases of advancing senility, loss of interest in life, or inertia which causes them to keep on acquiring without thought of past acquisitions. The miser is often activated by no desire except to be left alone, all social motives once active now dormant, owing perhaps to an unfortunate traumatic experience. The shock of losing his wife, or being deserted by offspring was just too much. He could not adjust to a new orientation of his life.

Values and the individual. Social motivation, in addition to the functioning of the security, dominance, prestige or other derived motives, has an additional individual aspect, which determines which of the foregoing is most likely to have ascendance. Any goal which has especial significance for the individual, or any complex of goals, constitutes a special consideration, known as *values.* In his total orientation a person may place a higher regard for culture over financial success: he may then, when opportunity presents itself, resign his $40,000 a year position with a corporation or law firm to take a college presidency at $15,000 or even less. Or after he has attained reasonable security, may then devote his time to social reform.

Values tend to indicate what particular associations, group identifications, and religious interests will have the dominant influence on the individual's time and activity. With the individual who considers highly the association which membership in a service club affords, he will hold on to membership despite circumstances that otherwise might cause him to drop out, as being no longer able to afford the time and cost. If his interest lies in church activity he will let nothing interfere. If one of his highest values is having a host of loyal friends he may jeopardize his own business success in doing favors beyond ordinary expectation. Maintaining a healthy conscience, doing nothing ever to lead to self-reproach may be a paramount goal, a higher value to him than everything else.

The complexity of adult motives. To understand an individual's behavior adequately it is usually necessary to have some insight into his controlling motives. The biological motives are obvious enough: one has to satisfy the drives of hunger, thirst, rest and other biological needs. Likewise the functioning of emotion as energizers of these drives can be understood fairly readily if the circumstances are known. It is in the realm of the social motives that difficulty may be found, for the reason that the operation of these motives involves many conditions and experiences that are peculiar to the individual, and make each person somewhat unique. In any complete understanding the total life-history may need to be explored to find the key circumstances that explain present behavior. In difficult cases this calls for the services of the expert on human relations.

THE DEVELOPMENT OF NORMAL SOCIAL RELATIONS

Criteria of Normal Social Relations

The dominance problem. In normal social relations one individual is apt to assume dominance over the other or others. He may issue orders, make demands or merely lead a conversation. If he does this in an agreeable manner and his dominance stems from possession of superior knowledge, the other person adjusts to the relation amicably. In fact most persons do not care for responsibility; they would just as soon let someone else assume it. The successful leadership of a Franklin Roosevelt or General Eisenhower is explained largely by that circumstance. Each impressed people as a man who knew his business, leadership in government. For successful military operations, or the successful playing of a symphony by a large orchestra, the group must accept the dominance or leader role of one person. Otherwise there would be discord, ineffectual effort or even chaos.

It may happen at times that a person assumes dominance in a situation for which he is ill-suited or inadequately prepared either in knowledge, proper training or in personality. By early experience as a bully, or a leader among younger or weaker boys, he got the habit of playing the role of an autocratic and domineering person. In later years when he is with others more nearly his equal the dominance role may earn for him the ill-will of those he attempts to dominate.

Recognition of individuality and individual worth. The proper attitude toward others in social relations is a considerate regard for the other person. It is not always possible to know in advance whether the other person knows even more about the matter. If it becomes apparent after an interchange of ideas that such is the case, one should defer to the one with superior knowledge and experience and not press an earlier assumed dominance position. If the matter is the subject of committee discussion, the chairman should attempt to discover the contributions of all present and not impose his own ideas to the exclusion of others. Some individuals are modest to a fault and need encouragement to express the good ideas they may have. Others who are bothered with a feeling of inadequacy or insecurity may refrain from talking at all.

Ascendance-submission. Two terms express the social relationship more adequately than dominance-submission. By *ascendance* is meant a relationship that exists between two persons in which one leads while the other acquiesces, without necessarily assuming real dominance. If the doctor counsels the patient the latter listens carefully. But if the visit is followed by a brief chat about the weather, the physician assumes the submissive role, particularly if the patient happens to be the local weather forecaster. The president of the country assumes a submissive role when he asks the White House gardener to tell him about the roses being planted. *Ascendance-submission* thus is a relationship that may "shift without notice" whenever the conversation veers to something one knows better than the other. In most normal human intercourse anyone is apt to find himself in a situation where he is the one who knows more or most about a matter under consideration and more or less automatically assumes the ascendant role.

Establishment of rapport and cooperation. Before one can "do business" with another there must be a feeling of some degree of mutual trust. The word "rapport" expresses the relationship: a suspicious individual who does not "open up" must be encouraged to believe that he can talk easily and freely with the interrogator, who means well and wants to be helpful. Often a sympathetic attitude is helpful, manifesting a sincere interest in the person's trouble and giving assurance that everything will be done to help him when the matter is clearly understood. It is often helpful, therefore, to avoid a domineering manner. It is likewise desirable to avoid perfunctory or "officious" behavior. Cooperation is more likely to be won by being considerate and patient, and being fair in every way. Try to see things from *his* viewpoint, not your own.

Fostering of Desirable Human Relations

Control of egoistic tendencies. The desire to dominate varies with different persons but most individuals derive satisfaction from being in a position of dominance. It gives one a feeling of self-importance. The law-enforcement officer is no exception. The traffic officer issuing a summons or a warning is in a position of dominance. He represents the law. He may "throw his weight around" and exhibit downright satisfaction in "bawling out" the offender. This will provide considerable ego-enhancement; for he realizes he holds the upper hand in the situation and makes the most of it. The offender may be frightened, indignant (if his speedometer was off considerably), or filled with suppressed resentment if the infraction was of a minor nature. Of course there are times when harsh treatment is richly deserved, but better human relations are likely to be fostered when the patrolman is impersonal, calm and matter-of-fact, simply stating the facts and issuing the proper ticket, along with such information as may be in order. The citizen may then be aware that he alone is at fault and that the Law is an agency of society (including himself) in its effort to conserve life and property in everyone's interest.

Use of motivating devices. Appeals to *positive* interests, to *action*, are more effective than appeals to negative feelings and emotions or to inhibition. Suggestions to have one's speedometer checked, to inform oneself on certain traffic regulations recently in effect, or other suggestions, if in order, are better than sarcasm or imputations of driving ineptitude. Simple, concise words are likely to be more effective than abusive or wordy admonitions.

Arguments and considerations which fit in with the listener's *desires* are likely to be more effective than those which do not. Before persuasion can be used, however, it must be learned what the desires are. There are desires common to most individuals and an extended interrogation should uncover some on which one can work. In dealing with an inhibited, reclusive or defeated individual who is sullen and uncommunicative, his resistance may be broken into by probing for some activity in his past in which he excelled. It may be such an unusual thing as tattooing or arranging cock-fights, but a display of interest in it by the interrogator may elect a feeling of self-importance leading to better communication as he comes to respond to the interest shown in him. Any appeal to ego-enhancement, except to those already conceited, is a good approach in gaining rapport and cooperation.

Effective appeals. In everyday social relations, such as attempting to persuade another that his course has been wrong, recourse can be made to various appeals. He can be shown to hold a position that is *not* subscribed to by *experts*, persons who have given study to the matter and should have opinions commanding prestige and respect. He can be informed that "majority opinion"— that which is generally held by most people, differs from his. Some studies have shown that both these carry weight, the latter somewhat more than the former, on matters of general social import. There is good support for trusting the collective judgment or common sense of many persons. Gallup has found in his public opinion sampling of the whole population that on many issues the public "sensed" the course six months or a year or more before Congress got around to enacting it into law.

An appeal is more effective if it is presented in a modest manner. Often it is better to *suggest* the course believed good by putting it in the form of a question, along with the supporting argument. A position stated in simple terms, with effective use of voice and appropriate gestures when helpful, will go far toward making the proposition acceptable sooner, than it would be if the matter were presented in a too-assured, know-it-all manner. The person who is well-informed, is sure of his ground, and has something in reserve, need not be forward and pushing. He moves with confidence; he knows his facts and he is concerned mainly with presenting them fairly and adequately.

Avoidance of ineffective approaches. If one wants to influence another he must avoid antagonizing him. Labor leaders may have private opinions of the representatives of management with whom they are to deal, and vice versa. If they meet, however, with a degree of mutual respect, each feeling that all the right is perhaps not on one side, their relations are apt to get off to a good start. One should be ready to concede that his presumed facts and figures are, when shown to be, somewhat inaccurate, and then proceed again with the revision in mind, instead of stubbornly rejecting the facts.

Too much self-assurance, too much bluster, or too much arrogance is likely to antagonize the listener, making it more difficult to influence him favorably. In many instances it is the quiet, patient conferee who wins most of his objective in the end. Of course, one may challenge the status of a presumed "expert" who is quoted; one may refuse to be swayed by an emotional appeal devoid of much real substance, and one may flatly reject an argument when advanced. But one will be effective in turn if he calmly presents a "debunking" of the presumed experts, citing instances when he has been wrong or pointing out his faulty qualifications, shows the shallowness of the emotional appeal, or gives in detail his superior knowledge which moves him to reject the argument advanced.

Insight into biases and prejudices. As just about everyone has biases and prejudices it is difficult to recognize them. Even when they are brought to one's attention some persons resist believing they have them. They are acquired in the home, in reading, in listening to radio and in daily contacts. Strongly held biases may interfere with normal social relations. The individual is indeed fortunate who can detect bias in his own thinking and allow for it. Some rabid Democrats just "can't stand" to hear a Republican friend discuss politics and vice versa. An early experience with a lawyer in which one's father failed to get what was due him in an inheritance contest, prejudices the person against all lawyers. He will not admit that most lawyers make a living by fair and just charges for services conscientiously and honestly rendered. He "knows" lawyers, and "that's all there is to it."

Assuming the role of the other. While one may not be able to rid oneself of biases and prejudices or even make much headway in correcting for them, he may find it useful to try to place himself in the other person's position. He may see that it is reasonable for his friend to dislike Negroes because the friend had some early unpleasant experiences with Negroes (or Jews or Catholics or Italians or bankers) and he can relate to the friend how pleasant his own relations, on the other hand, have been with individuals in the group toward which the prejudice is directed. Or he can suggest that his friend imagine himself to be a member of a minority group—how would *he* then feel? Or he may grant to his friend that the Democrats have done much for the common people. In turn the friend may recognize some merit in Republican alarm at high taxes and other Republican views. The crux of the bias or prejudice is *lack* of adequate understanding of the other side. Few Whites know much about Negroes and vice versa. In industry where they work side by side, or at a baseball game, the prejudice is reduced and may vanish. Joe Louis or Jackie Robinson have drawn as many cheers from Whites as from Negroes. Where individual work and good character are concerned, prejudices based on accidents of birth tend to weaken.

Control over emotions. Finally, good human social relations are best furthered by fair-minded regard for the other person, accepting him for his individual worth rather than permitting pre-judgment to interfere. Distrust, prejudice emotionally aroused, and hatred engendered by tales of supposed acts or beliefs of others make satisfactory relations difficult. Where bias or prejudice exists emotions are more ready to erupt in violence or personal antagonisms. The old saying that a soft answer turneth away wrath is no idle observation; nor is the one that whom the gods would destroy they first make mad. It is many times difficult to maintain an even temper under repeated provocation, but the person who does will usually end up as the one having the advantage in any normal social relation.

REFERENCES

BRITT, S.: *Social Psychology of Modern Life*, 2nd Ed. New York, Rinehart, 1949. For general reading on social behavior.

GRAY, J., ED.: *Psychology in Use*, 2nd Ed. New York, American Book Co., 1951. Chapters 1, 3 and 11 discuss, respectively, psychological principles, influences of the home and means of influencing people.

KRECH, D., and CRUTCHFIELD, R.: *Theory and Problems of Social Psychology.*

New York, McGraw-Hill, 1948. Chapters 1-4 present theoretical aspects of behavior (motivation, perceiving). Chapters 5 and 6 show how beliefs and attitudes develop (somewhat technical).

NEWCOMB, T.: *Social Psychology*. New York, Dryden Press, 1950. This volume will repay general reading. Specifically recommended are Chapters 3, 4, 14 and 15.

SHERIF, M.: *An Outline of Social Psychology*. New York, Harper & Brothers, 1948. Part One on Motives, Chapter 6 (group membership) and Chapters 11 and 12 are recommended.

STAGNER, R., and KARWOSKI, T.: *Psychology*. New York, McGraw-Hill, 1952. Chapters 2-4 present an excellent account of drives, emotion, and social motives. Highly recommended.

VAUGHAN, W.: *Social Psychology*. New York, Odyssey Press, 1948. A readable text. Part V covers institutions.

Chapter 6

THE PSYCHOLOGY OF LEADERSHIP AND GROUP CONTROL

By

NORMAN C. MEIER

GENERAL ASPECTS OF LEADERSHIP

Leadership as a Function of Several Variables

U NDER normal conditions most people prefer a passive role in society, leaving leadership roles to others. With some individuals this attitude is an extension or projection of dependence upon the father to governmental officials. Most people are content to follow their own affairs, assuming that politics and leadership in government can be left to those who are interested or to those who aspire to such leadership.

Leadership is associated with personality types. Some people are fitted for it, while others are not. There are also those who are capable of leadership but who are not interested in exercising it until some particular occasion or need arises. This need may be for some citizen to take the initiative in organizing a movement for better government; or it may be the need to direct others at the scene of a serious accident. Leadership functions in a social situation that requires collective effort or group participation, and in which there is an aggregation of individuals or a public (affected by a common medium or media of communication), and a person (the leader) who possesses the requisite qualities and needed knowledge to direct the others. "The times," or a particular setting or complex of conditions, may determine the acceptability or suitability or selection of one leader over others equally competent. It is therefore impossible to generalize much about leadership, except

151

to say that it is a function of many factors all taken together: the individual, the need, the others, and the occasion.

No general type of leader. While leadership is a complex matter, varying with circumstances and individuals, some general observations are in order. Usually leaders of larger movements, governments, or institutions are persons of above average ability, energy or drive, and general intelligence. They are ordinarily fitted for some *specific* type of leadership; it is only rarely that a person is successful in a number of different fields. Shakespeare was a literary genius, but he probably would have failed dismally as a prime minister. Churchill may be a great prime minister but not an outstanding artist. A local politician without much formal education can be successful locally but he will hardly measure up to the demands of international statesmanship without help from others.

Circumstances frequently make the leader. In any nation or state there are at all times individuals with the capacity and the desire to assume leadership. Many senators and governors believe they could do a good job as president. Governors Dewey and Warren and Senators Taft and Russell undoubtedly know government at first hand. Circumstances, however, have thus far denied them the opportunity of being president. In Minnesota a Scandinavian name aids in the election of a governor, while in Boston an Irish name is of great advantage to an office seeker. Norman Thomas's qualities for high office were never put to test because he was identified with a minority party. On the other hand, Franklin Roosevelt appeared at a time when his particular qualities seemed to fit the needs of the times.

Potential leaders are those who fit the needs of the occasion. In a comparatively simple situation, such as a traffic jam or a serious accident, any individual who has knowledge of what should be done may assume leadership: it may be an officer in the first instance, or a doctor in the second—in case no doctor is around it may be anyone who knows first aid. In a more complex matter, as in choosing nominees for political office, the candidates are expected to be persons with the required qualifications. If the available candidates differ in background, experience and personality it is the responsibility of the people in a convention or a primary election to weigh the respective considerations. It may be that the one with the greatest appeal who also has the benefit of arduous and sagacious strategy on the part of backers wins out. In a close contest the final choice may be determined by some over-all consideration or by an unexpected turn of events. By and large, an effort is made to select the one among all those qualified who best fits the needs of the occasion or the long-run welfare of the people.

Types of Leaders

Institutional leader. By becoming a bishop the individual at once becomes an institutional leader; the followers of the faith look up to him for guidance, views, advice, opinions. The public generally recognizes his leadership. The president of a college or of a corporation is likewise in a position of leadership by virtue of the office he holds. Prestige attaches to the position, just as the officer's insignia carries authority among troops or members of a police force. Authority is maintained by hierarchies of rank.

The institutional or executive leader's chief aim is the furtherance of the institution, to gain support for it and then see that its programs are carried out. He usually tends to remain aloof, interested more in matters of policy and institutional well-being than in the individuals or followers in the institution.

Dominant leader. The primary objective of the dominant leader is to secure action in connection with immediate projects or problems. He usually has knowledge of a practical nature of current affairs but is not a thinker, nor is he concerned with details or the background of the problem. He generally works through those under him, controlling patronage, punishing or ousting those who oppose him. By suppressing conflicting ideologies or interests he strives to achieve unification as a need for furthering his objective. By dint of great energy and zeal he may attain considerable power and an entrenched position, but because of ruthlessness and growing opposition may lose his leadership to another more able, and more driving leader.

The persuasive leader. The persuasive leader is most closely in touch with his followers. Whereas the dominant leader is usually cold and aloof, the persuasive leader is warm and approachable, though the more successful ones maintain a measure of dignity and detachment. He observes people's interests and needs, follows newspapers and other media of mass communication, gets from these sources ideas which he then reshapes in his own way to give them expression. This he sometimes does so cleverly that the people give *him* credit for them. He thus appears to be the means whereby the will of the people is attained.

The expert. A fourth type of leader, the expert, does not usually appear in person. He is known through his mastery of some field and by his writings, but is looked up to when an occasion requires his services. In an atomic age the scientist may be sought out for views or counsel. The financier may have considerable insight regarding monetary policy of value to a Congressional committee.

Here again there is no general all-round leader. The expert who is a leader in matters pertaining to fiscal policy, would be a dud if consulted on penal reform. The sociologist who has given a lifetime of study to criminology can hardly be expected to advise on traffic control problems. The experimental psychologist can give advice regarding problems of vision or memory but may be of little help in setting up an accounting system.

In general the leader attains his status as leader by being known to be especially competent in some area of activity or knowledge, or by having qualifications applicable to the situation. There are, however, all manner and kinds of situations demanding impromptu leadership. Many of these are short-lived: the leader appears, performs his function, and resumes his regular status. Sometimes these leaders must be countered by other, better established leaders, in the public interest or to prevent drastic action from taking place.

The Opportunist Leader May Emerge for a Short-lived Occasion

Breaches of decorum, such as the riot or picketing episodes, often call out persons who are not known previously as leaders. There even may be no one leader, but instead a number of actively interested persons who foment trouble and are individually like-minded enough, to push for action. The problem of the law is here to identify the ring-leaders, if possible, and bring the disturbance under control. In some localities where common attitudes are shared by many others in the community, the difficulty is increased by reason of the fact that the ring-leaders may be shielded by the crowd, and if identified, cannot be convicted, even for lynching. The jury, comprised also of like-minded individuals will not return a verdict of guilty. Under conditions such as these public re-education seems to be in order.

The leader of the mob usually has mob membership. In areas where social classes are in conflict, and attitudes toward another race or toward industrial management are antagonistic, overt conflict is readily precipitated. Though a person may take the initiative when conditions become tense, it must be observed that he does not really *cause* the riot or property destruction. The participants commit the act, perhaps under his incitation, but the basic cause lies in the conditions themselves. Bodily injury to others, or damage to property does not usually rectify the conditions immediately, if ever; at most, the violence can only call public attention to prevailing conditions. The leader, being of the mob himself, knows only the conditions as he sees them and in his limited way of thinking, therefore he strikes out at the nearest object presumed to be the cause of frustration. He does not understand problems of production, labor supply, property rights or even his own prejudices against forces that appear to be working against his self-interests. So the recourse to violence occurs.

The problem of the law-enforcement agency in such circumstances is at times a difficult one. Drastic and brutal handling of the participants may not be the best course. Adjudication of disputes or meting out of justice after the event is the function of the Courts. Prevention, where possible, may be a proper function of the police, who can warn, advise as to consequences, and when known in advance, act as a deterrer. The Chief may meet with both sides, suggest avoidance of violence, and acquaint recalcitrants with consequences to be expected. At the initial stages of impending conflict the agitators may be known and singled out for frank, friendly, objective warnings. The danger lies in either or both sides taking an attitude of defiance and disinclination to meet for discussion.

Alien leaders must first become accepted. The mob leader may not be a local person nor even of the same economic or social class as the group. He may be sent to the locale to promote a cause, to unionize unorganized workers, to propagandize for racial or social equality, or for other purposes. In small cities, towns or rural areas, the stranger is usually suspected. The alien leader is unlikely to gain sufficient prestige to become a leader in such areas, until he has been there long enough to have gained the confidence of the more trusted persons in the community and in many communities this is long in coming about. In some inbred communities it is doubtful whether a newcomer can ever become completely accepted for a leadership role.

In urban centers the situation is somewhat different. Many of the people have themselves migrated into the city from other areas. Individuals come and go. Leaders and potential leaders also may come and go. Some types of organizers are even trained in the practice of infiltrating existing groups and organizations. They also are skillful in cultivating association with key persons and in being identified with activities of organizations, knowing that they must be accepted before they can assume leadership functions when the time is opportune.

Where evidence of tension appears in a section of an urban population, and the tension does not seem to be accounted for by known and expected causes, the probability may exist that the conditions so observed are attributable to the activity of agitators or others who have recently come to the area. Should the tension conditions become aggravated by overt disturbances, surveillance of the newcomers, if known, would appear to be in order as a precautionary measure.

Counter-action must be circumspect. Prevention of breaches of public decorum is always desirable, thereby forestalling incidents that may result in loss of life, injury, and property damage; but how counter-action may be planned and executed is usually a difficult matter. Increase of police detail, use of plain clothes investigators, or similar measures may still fail to spot the real sources of tension or to result in identifying the persons back of the agitation. The instigators may, moreover, be working entirely within legitimate bounds. Law enforcement can then confine itself to maintaining order and the suppression of violence, if and when it breaks out.

All forms of potential leadership may be present in the same crowd population. Individuals in a democracy represent a wide variety of attitudes toward the Law, toward sports, toward their fellow men, toward ethical and moral standards. They normally do not suddenly lose these established attitudes when in a crowd situation. There may be *some*, however, not averse even to sadistic practices—cruelty to a fellow man. There are others whose sense of fair play carries over from sports to almost any other situation. There are persons who may be eager to participate in mob action, others who will avoid any such opportunity, and still others who will attempt to deter a mob from taking action.

There is thus within the crowd potential leadership to *commit* violence and potential leadership to *prevent* violence. Knowing the background of the kind of individuals dominating the crowd often offers a clue as to what may happen or not happen. Individuals are impelled by motives. They react to frustrations—a blocking of goals—as failure to have wants satisfied. These conditions may be of recent aggravation and the aggression directed to some person or some group believed responsible. Knowledge of the *motivation* of the individual in a crowd is a first requirement toward understanding what may be done to control the crowd.

Institutional leaders may be used in counter-action. Usually there is little time to learn much about the motivation of the people in a crowd. When a mob breaks there is only concern for containment and control. Summary measures are needed, especially if there are few if any in the crowd who emerge as potential deterrers. One measure is sometimes available: to counter leadership with other leadership having greater appeal and prestige. A trusted labor leader who agrees to appeal to the crowd, if it is a strike incident, or a Catholic priest or other institutional leader who may be prevailed upon, can serve to allay the emotional tension and plead for normal handling of the matter, in a setting wherein the participants are predominantly Catholic. If available, civic leaders who are well known and respected may be induced to intervene.

MINOR ASSEMBLAGES AND THEIR CONTROL

Transient Groups

Pedestrian audiences. When a number of persons going about their business stop to gather in a group it is not to be explained by some simple and facile term as "crowd psychology." The *cause* of each individual's stopping lies within the individual's past experience. Therefore when a person observes others watching a "human fly," he too will pause to look if he is interested in "human flies." If he has only seen pictures of "human flies" in action, and admires acts of skill that have an element of personal danger, he is quite certain to become another *individual* watching the stunt, perhaps quite oblivious of the presence of others about him. However if he has no such interest, he continues on his way. If he does pause to observe the stunt, it is certainly not because of any "irresistible power of crowd psychology," but simply because of interest.

Then again consider the pitchman selling a patented corn remedy on the sidewalk. Some passersby pause only a moment or two and continue on their way; some, who have little else to do, merely stay to hear the "spiel"; still others listen and buy. This type of transient group, known as a pedestrian audience, is of comparatively little interest to law enforcement officers. The officer's chief concern would be with the pitchman whose license he would check, especially if he were selling grossly misrepresented merchandise, as "genuine" diamond rings for $5 each, or products likely to endanger life and health, as "inflammable" sweaters.

Minor street-corner gatherings. The soap-box orator's listeners are usually persons with no immediately pressing business, who are merely curious. Again the interest of law enforcement officers is primarily to see that the usual conditions of orderly assembly are observed. The affable drunk or impromptu "lecturer" may draw a number of curious people, as does an accident or a fist fight. These gatherings, however, usually constitute no special problem. Generally the appearance of a patrol car or an officer on the beat ends the affair. Neighborhood gangs, particularly if they involve "jack-rolling," auto thefts, or gang fighting, create more serious problems.

Closely related to the street-corner gatherings are those incidental to such semi-public assemblages as auctions, that often over-flow onto the sidewalk and into the street. Normally these are orderly groups that require little beyond the need for patrolling traffic. Bargain sales are usually regarded as private events but they too may attain such activity as to cause property destruction along with minor injuries to people. In this case the initiative in invoking police protection and intervention is usually with the proprietor. Stunts, special demonstrations, the appearance of movie characters, and similar outdoor events are usually orderly, and hence create little more than a traffic problem.

The essential characteristic of the pedestrian audience is that chance alone determines who will be drawn into it. Actually it may be anyone who happens to be in that particular spot at that particular time. Certainly there is nothing premeditated about it.

The Audiences

Audiences vary from the quiet passive group watching an animated electric sign, or listening to a pitchman, to groups surcharged with emotions and capable of turbulent reaction. An audience situation implies the presence of a group voluntarily assembled under a leader freely accepted.

The passive audience. When people assemble in a church they participate both in an institutionalized activity (the rituals, singing, etc.) and the exhortation of a leader (the priest, minister, or rabbi) whom they have accepted. They do not come to question or to challenge, but primarily for guidance. The lecture audience likewise comes to hear a designated leader, with or without discussion to follow. They submit to the ascendance of the speaker on the assumption that he has knowledge they do not have, or that he has more complete information on the topic. His task is to create interest in his topic, impress its importance on the audience, lead to conviction and perhaps give direction, if that is the final objective. The theatre audience is a passive audience under the attempted influence of the playwright and the producer, working through the cast, settings and lighting. In this case leadership is not centered in one individual.

The emotionally exhorted audience. In the conversion audience attendance is usually on the basis of interest, but curiosity and fame of the leader may draw many. Billy Sunday, an ex-baseball player, used dramatic actions to arouse interest and to impress the audience and also used a number of spectacular techniques to secure conviction and conversion. Aimee Semple MacPherson utilized many properties borrowed from both formal religion and the stage to impress people. She dramatized biblical episodes and was herself a dramatic personage. She realized the advantage of the packed house; the temple was usually nearly filled with those who already had become followers. In such situations earlier converts may be used as conversion leaders in subsequent audiences.

The political rally follows the same pattern. Most of those in the main section of seats are party workers who lead in the cheering and may turn against hecklers or put down any disturbance. The speaker dwells mostly on the great achievements of his party and the utter inadequacy of the rival party's program. He may warm up (arouse interest) by telling jokes on himself, engage in other pleasantries but in time will drive home his arguments that he expects will lead to conviction and later to action at the polls.

Meetings involving controversial issues. Ordinarily conversion audiences whether religious or political are orderly and peaceful. The political rally may, however, at times have conditions of tension whenever a controversial issue is injected, about which audience members have strong feelings. Some rivalries become so intense that delegations may march into a meeting in progress and attempt to disrupt it. The master of ceremonies may then signal the band to strike up *America*, followed by *The Star-Spangled Banner*, thus immobilizing the intruders. Often this will at least prove a partial counter-action and reduce greatly the impetus of the attempt. If the demonstration continues in force, however, and a repetition of singing or an appeal for fair play fails, there is probably no recourse but to adjourn the meeting. Since the audience came to hear the speakers, such an ending is apt to react more *against* the opposition and hence serve the ends of the party intruded upon. Gallery booing constitutes a like threat to decorum and may be corrected by a threat on the part of the chairman to clear the galleries.

Meetings apt to produce turbulent audience reactions. Under conditions of tension affecting a whole community, an advertised meeting presents a special case of anticipated danger. In the period of mounting feeling against Communists in many urban centers there may be organized resistance toward the holding of a meeting at which a Communist sympathizer is to speak. It may take the form of storming the doors preparatory to rushing in to fill the main seating section so as to be ready to boo and otherwise prevent the speaker from being heard. Or it may take the form of a phalanx of persons organized by the Legion and other groups to prevent anyone entering the hall.

Others, professing to uphold "civil rights" or "free speech" may be just as determined to enter, by force if necessary. The legal aspects cannot be determined on the spot. If the authorities take the position that the Communist Party is a bona fide American party and should be heard, that is one position. If they take, on the other hand, the view that the Communist Party receives orders from a foreign power interested in the overthrow by force of other governments, the matter takes on a different light. In the latter instance, the authorities being fully advised beforehand of the anticipated probable consequences, would be justified in counseling: (a) cancellation of the meeting, or (b) making the owner of the hall accountable for consequences. Preventive measures are normally to be preferred to serious conflict when such appears practically inevitable.

In all audience situations the composition of the audience can be roughly estimated. Church members augmented by a limited number of others will make up the church audience. Interested persons will attend a lecture, a conversion audience or a political rally, mostly drawn from those already inclined to accept or having already accepted the issues or the general philosophy. It is only in the audience with mixed views, as on sharply drawn controversial matters, that breaches of public decorum are apt to erupt and hence require the attention of law enforcement officers.

MAJOR ASSEMBLAGES: PEACEFUL OR TURBULENT
The Passive or Normally Demonstrative Crowd

A crowd may be considered as any sizable assemblage of people with a common interest directed toward a definite person, object or event. The group may have a dynamic leader on whom attention centers, such as Hitler addressing 100,000 persons in a Berlin square; or a common object of interest that may be a famous person to whom the group is paying homage, such as when Eisenhower was greeted in New York City on his return from Europe in 1945, or when he was inaugurated as president. A street parade and other similar events may also become objects of common interest and attention for people who make up a crowd. The fact that there is an object of common interest converts a group of people into a crowd.

Celebrations, parades and special events. It has been estimated that about two million people crowded Times Square in New York City during the evening of VJ Day, the writer being one of them. At times the area from 42nd Street north for five blocks was a solid mass of humanity, mainly engaged in emotional release. Some were cheering, some singing, and others were attempting to kiss girls without escorts. For the most part they were just milling around. Each individual, in the main, was himself. If usually he was inclined to celebrate boisterously, he did just that. If he was a person inclined to be inwardly happy, he just felt happy. If he was a drinking person, he got drunk or he had just a few more drinks than normally. If he was from the Deep South he gave a Rebel yell at intervals until he was hoarse. Considering the number of people involved, the per cent of persons engaged in rowdyism (fist fights, brawls, etc.) was surprisingly small.

Celebrations, parades and special events are usually not selective; they call out just about everyone who has the opportunity to attend. As it is thus a cross-section of the general population, the problem of order is little more or less than the general everyday problem of order. Some will be thoughtless, crowding someone out of a favored spot. Some may be knocked down, and even trampled. Ugly words may be exchanged, dresses may be torn, hats lost, pockets picked. Hoodlums may be present. All these conditions are to be expected in a setting where all kinds of people mingle, where space is limited and good manners are not possessed by all.

The important fact is that each person in the crowd is an individual with a background of family training or lack of it, and with primary group influences that have been good in some and imperfect in others. Each individual's behavior simply reflects that early background. Although the crowd situation may offer an occasion for getting by with some liberties that the person would not ordinarily take, the general pattern of behavior is little different from that expected.

The crowd situation does not in itself make the behavior what it is; that is roughly determined long before.

Aftermath of disaster or major excitement. Major disasters such as earthquakes, large fires, tornadoes, cloudbursts and floods pose problems both for the handling of the victims and the control of the crowds of the curious or would-be helpers. In earthquake regions the population can be inculcated with knowledge of what to do in emergencies. Some cities, such as Portland, Oregon have disaster equipment that can be rushed to areas where major fires or explosions occur. Prompt police action is necessary to keep the curious from obstructing rescue work and away from danger. Usually sympathy for victims is alone sufficient to make most individuals obedient to orders and where needed to render help. Again, these onlookers are individuals who behave much as they do normally, and only the thoughtless are apt to constitute problems.

Radio communication has greatly facilitated control in disaster areas and television has possibilities of being of special additional aid. The authorities find that radio stations make their services immediately available in emergencies. Such appeals to *individuals* further simplify the crowd aspect in that people know what they are expected to do. Usually the reassurance that comes from the civil authorities does much to prevent panic conditions and allay apprehension. Persons with easily aroused fears, however, can magnify them by imagining consequences far beyond those actually existent. Although radio is one means for reaching great numbers quickly for the purpose of allaying panic, the "Invasion from Mars" broadcast on an American network and a similar one in Equador demonstrate that such media can be used for incitation of panic even though unintended.

Civil Defense planning has the objective, among others, of reducing panic, control of the frightened and distraught, orderly and efficient rescue of the injured, and physical care of the homeless. The burden would naturally fall on fire and police personnel, but good organization would permit prompt assistance from volunteer workers. As in all cases of disaster, *pre-planning* is the only way to limit casualties and to bring a demoralized citizenry under control expeditiously.

The Active or Turbulent Crowd: Prelude to Violence

The active crowd may begin as a passive crowd or have its elements simply in a considerable number of unassembled individuals, who are, however, affected by the same general motivation. They may feel aggrieved, resentful, frustrated or just dissatisfied with conditions, either of recent origin or of long standing. If there is improvement in the situation, the state of tension may lessen and eventually may disappear. Should the dissatisfaction or the frustration continue or become aggravated, the whole situation may need watchful concern, for it may be the prelude to violence.

The strike area. In industrial areas not strongly unionized, tension usually increases when an effort is made to break a strike or when the labor force is divided; that is, some are not in sympathy with the strike. The chief concern here is the maintenance of order and the prevention of violence, when possible, by the presence of riot squads or regular details. In isolated mining areas away from metropolitan centers this is usually not possible; law enforcement then becomes the duty of the sheriff and deputies, supplemented by state police if available. As indicated earlier the emphasis may be placed on friendly overtures, or cautioning against violence by warnings as to the consequences. So long as contact can be maintained with known local leaders, with the management kept informed of conditions needing caution, the crowd conditions can be kept within bounds, with perhaps only minor scuffles and little turbulence generally.

Rumor-mongering as productive of tension conditions. Since people believe most readily what they want to believe or that which fits into their biases and prejudices, rumors can reinforce beliefs that may or may not be founded on fact. An eviction of a tenant who has paid no rent in six months may give rise to the story that there is to be a wholesale eviction in an area, regardless of the amount of back rent due. Because of material shortages a mill may be closed temporarily, but the rumor has it that the company is closing down the plant "to break the union." In no time at all an angry crowd may form.

While it is not always clear who should take the initiative in quashing rumors, the police can take cognizance of their existence when the public decorum appears clearly to be threatened. The police reporter can pick up the rumor, check the facts, and quote some official in denying it. Should the tension remain with evidence of agitation, the leaders may be informed of their responsibility and of the law regarding incitation to riot, whenever the situation appears to be heading toward serious action.

Race friction and conflict areas. Economic conflict, while touching upon basic drives, such as, hunger, family, and organic needs, erupts only sporadically. Race friction in some areas is deep-seated and continuous. Many of the poor whites of the Deep South feel a compulsive need to exercise supremacy over the Negro. They resist all recognition of him as an equal, support segregation, and are prone to deal summary punishment upon any Negro suspected or known to molest a white woman. In that situation a condition of tension persists, subject to eruption at any time. The tension may be minor or scarcely existent in some areas and deep-seated in others, but usually it is great where living conditions are hard for both races and economic and cultural advantages are few. Since frustration is common, it frequently leads to sporadic acts of aggression against the minority race.

Improvement of conditions conducive to tension reduction lies largely in the slow process of education and economic betterment. Certainly the law enforcement agencies should tend to support the gradual improvement of attitudes of tolerance toward fellow men, regardless of race or creed or class, rather than connive at or show indifference to acts of intolerance. Support of the law of the land should come before personal attitudes however acquired. Indifferent or weak law enforcement is a sure incentive to undermining the law and as such invites increased tension and is always a potential prelude to violence.

Critical emergencies: pre-riot conditions. On the principle that laws should govern people's behavior and that violence seldom settles anything, the primary concern of law-enforcement agencies should be prevention. Close surveillance of active or turbulent gatherings and contact with leaders is a first precautionary measure. A second precautionary measure is an alerted force with full knowledge of the situation and with instruction to exercise restraint at all times even in spite of great provocation. The calm and cool individual representing the law, who is considerate rather than belligerent, firm and yet not aggressive, can often supply the restraining influence needed to control wrought-up, would-be rioters. It must be remembered that these individuals may have a fancied or real grievance and that they may be victims of circumstances which to them are frustrating. In any case violence is not the answer. Although there may be insults uttered, rocks thrown, or threatening acts of one kind or another, it must be kept in mind that there are *others* in the crowd who do not do these things and that they, in the absence of provocative belligerence on the part of the police, often tend to restrain the more excited crowd members. More often than not the delicate and precarious balance between crowd control and pacification on the one hand and an outbreak of violence on the other turns on the slender thread of which side has the greater calm and forbearance. Suggestion here plays an all-important role.

Violence: Riot and Its Control

All disturbances of public decorum involving crowds are not riots. The charivari or the celebration following the winning of a particularly important football game, for instance, are not true riots even though some people may be hurt and minor property damage occurs. The term *riot* should be reserved for occasions of more serious nature involving high motivation and serious potential consequences.

The "near-riot"; major disturbance of public decorum. In May, 1952, a series of disturbances in the form of raids on girls' dormitories by male students took place on college campuses over the nation. In the press they were characterized variously as "riots," "near-riots" or as "demonstrations." Both college administrations and law enforcement agencies were unprepared to cope with these outbreaks. Some administrators threatened expulsion or suspension, branded the affairs as "childish acts," or tried to single out "ring-leaders." Some law enforcement officers, when called upon, employed nearly everything in the arsenals for riot control: night sticks, tear gas, fire hoses, special details.

These occurrences, classified as a craze, affect youth beset by abnormal conditions. In May, 1952, young people faced uncertainties; they could not plan because of the Korean war. Normally they would be graduating, getting married, getting a job, or raising a family. Many had little if any enthusiasm for the Korean war, regarding it as a job to be done. They were frustrated yet they could not aggress against anything tangible. The raids were thus a token aggression against things in general—a letting off of steam by the less well adjusted and less stable persons. The more stable did not in any great numbers participate. Where police were not called, or called on a stand-by basis, nothing untoward happened. On other campuses a blocking of their "raids" by authorities served to arouse a firm desire to go ahead anyway, resulting in minor injuries and some property damage. These were not "mobs," the episodes were not riots, and there were no leaders. Students were simply motivated alike by common circumstances.

Crowd behavior short of riot. Evictions and sheriff's sales, especially such as were conducted during the depression of the thirties, may produce strong feelings of impending injustice. Sympathizers gather at the sale to hamper and even to halt it. There were the so-called "penny sales" where a friend bought an item for a nominal bid (others refraining) with the purpose of assuming custody of it. In strict legal terms this amounted to conspiracy to circumvent due process of law. To these sympathetic neighbors, however, the law was not taking human rights and real justice into account. The times were abnormal, and since the people were victims of circumstances beyond their control, it was no time to take away a man's means of livelihood and the roof over his head.

In one midwest state an auction sale was broken up by force;

others were threatened. The sheriff telephoned the governor who ordered out the National Guard but with strict instructions to refrain from the use of guns and to avoid manhandling even under extreme provocation. Further evictions were then postponed and not long thereafter the Farm Moratorium Act eased the tension.

These examples of crowd behavior short of riot demonstrate the necessity for calm, prudent action. The governor recognized the fact that these farmers were basically law-abiding citizens very much frustrated by being caught in a web of circumstances blocking their normal drives of hunger, family responsibility and the like. Bloodshed would only aggravate the conditions, and lead perhaps to more bloodshed. The remedy lay in modifying the law and the immediate need was for some emergency act to stall for time. The doctrine of government by law was not abrogated; it was merely adjusted in its enforcement aspect to special emergency conditions not foreseen, by prompt and prudent action.

Crowds and mobs are never *necessarily* irrational, stupid, impulsive or ignorant, as earlier accounts would have us believe. The individual in the mob does not lose his identity, and become as putty in the hands of a leader. Rather the mob is made up of individuals who are driven by a common motivation; the crowd is self-selective, attracting those who are like-minded.

Experimental studies of mob participation, using a faked but extremely realistic kidnapping episode as incitation, showed that individuals exposed to the incitation divide immediately into those who would:

(a) Join the mob to take an active role.
(b) Join but only to play a minor role, as to lend encouragement.
(c) Go to attempt to deter the mob.
(d) Go along as spectators only.
(e) Stay away.

These experiments were directed at separate groups with the incitation the same except for indication of degree of certainty of guilt on the part of the culprits. In the group unsure of certainty of guilt the number of deterrers was larger, the joiners fewer. In the group informed of absolute certainty of guilt, the number of joiners was larger and the number of deterrers fewer. If the general background of the individual is known (primary and secondary group relations, religious training, attitudes toward courts and lawyers), the probable behavior in joining or not joining or deterrence can be roughly predicted.

Riot conditions: desultory violence. Tension conditions do not, as a rule, arise abruptly. They are more commonly accumulative. When more and more "undesirable" migrants move into an already crowded urban section dissatisfaction and resentment on the part of the older residents increase. Minor frictions lead to a feeling that "something ought to be done about it" until some particularly resented happening, such as the moving of an unwelcome family into a neighborhood, occurs. Bricks may be thrown into windows or a raid staged by irate persons bent on ousting the unwanted neighbors, while a crowd of supporters fills the street. If this occurs quickly, the damage is probably done before order can be restored. Under such conditions other raids are apt to be staged unless the conditions are subjected to early study and steps are taken to reeducate the people, or to propose some other solution to the housing problem.

The sporadic, continuing riot. Where migrations continue over a period of years, affecting an expanding urban area, depressing property values, displacing large numbers of families, together with replacing older workers with the newer migrants willing to work for less money, smoldering resentment may break out in a major riot or in a series of continuing riots. The normal increase in production over the years absorbs many of the workers. Yet in the adjustment process many are destined to be hurt, and hence there is widespread frustration, inconvenience, and emotional tension. Usually those affected have their grievances reinforced by talking with others similarly affected. Hence their blocked drives sooner or later find an outlet in aggression against someone near at hand. It takes only one incident, often inconsequential in itself, to touch off a riot. If the riot is promptly suppressed, another may erupt soon, because the basic economic and social conditions remain unchanged, and because the continued presence of the newcomers to the neighborhood continue to stimulate the rioter to action. Until the basic economic and social conditions are changed, trouble is perennial.

Major riot. When a disturbance involves many people, deeply incensed over real or supposed injustice, and bent on vengeance or counter-action, a major riot generally ensues. Of course, leaders may incite people to action, magnify the character of the grievances, and precipitate rather quickly the attack against that which is the object of the people's wrath. Then again, the aggravating conditions may be long-standing and the present attack may be one precipitated by some drastic act, such as a guard firing on strikers, or the arrival of bus loads of strike breakers.

In a major riot, it must be understood, that *underlying causes* are inevitably present. A leader need not always incite men to action, nor does he need to persuade them. They are aware of the conditions that are causing the grievances. Hence their overt action may be due to the fact that they believe that their means of livelihood, their position in the labor force, or their hopes for economic betterment are involved or threatened. The leader may reinforce many of these beliefs but he does not necessarily create them; at best he gives the signal to individuals *already in the mood to act.*

In a midwest coal-mining state miners had been idle since March and no settlement had been reached by late summer. One operator sought and received permission to import itinerants for dirt removal which precedes actual coal mining in the strip mine. When this was done a secret order was given to start loading coal. The miners protested, demanding that the operations cease. After some delay the operator agreed. The miners assembled just outside the mine properties to see that the young men actually vacated the premises. As they were walking in a body toward the railway, some miner opened fire, and was followed by others. Twenty-six men were killed, and others were injured. One needs to place himself in the position of a miner, facing a hard winter, funds gone and children without shoes, to understand the intense feeling and the strong drive affecting basic drives and frustration leading to this tragic event. No leader was in evidence; only irate, angry and vengeful individuals committed this act with motivation tantamount to a survival drive.

Means of riot control. The drastic action of the miners was unforeseen in its intensity, yet the conditions were there. No means were at hand, however, for coping with it. In urban centers means are usually at hand, not ordinarily for preventing, but as in the case of fire, for checking, discouraging, dissipating and controlling. Emergency riot squads can be dispatched with reinforcements aided by radio contact. If the riot involves large numbers the fire hose is an expedient, but the hose itself must be guarded against being cut. The tear-gas bomb also has become a popular item. There is, however, always the need for watching flanks and pressure from the rear. The loud speaker on a mobile unit is at times useful, as is also photography when used as a means of identification of leaders and lieutenants. In both Japan and in France, law enforcement officers have sprayed colored dyes on the skin and clothing of riot participants so that they could be identified as members of the mob at a later time. Smoke bombs have possibilities as a means of distracting attention and dissipating over-active groups. Firing blank cartridges or live ammunition over the heads of rioters sometimes has the desired effect, but it also may result in the fire being returned. Perhaps the most difficult riots to handle are those participated in by burly individuals wielding baseball bats, battering rams, blackjacks, and other similar lethal instruments, especially when these instruments are in the hands of highly motivated, determined men. In these circumstances, discretion is certainly called for and contact with the responsible leaders or organizations involved is possibly the most satisfactory approach. Like the automobile skid, the only sure way to control this type of trouble is to prevent it, if possible, from occurring.

GROUP BEHAVIOR IN EMERGENCY SITUATIONS

Tension Situations: Leadership Unknown

Street corner instigations to riot. When a detective is called in on a murder case, one of his concerns is to find a motive. He asks such questions as: What relations did the victim have with other people? With whom was he last seen? Was he involved in any tension situation? Tension situations may likewise be clues to riot instigation. What individuals harbored ill-will toward whom?

What friction had occurred? Who was involved? Preventive riot control can work on these leads. Small groups gathering on street corners in a known tension area generally presage trouble. Close surveillance can serve to spot potential leaders and to locate centers of incipient riots. On this basis the curfew is used in communities or areas where trouble is expected, but in large urban areas vigilance is the chief precautionary measure.

Secret conclave instigation. The more serious riots generally can not be anticipated because the planning or instigation is secret. Yet there are few possibilities of riot instigation without considerable numbers of people being already conditioned for it. Hence the instigators or would-be instigators are leaders of special interest groups (labor, racial), conspiracy groups (Communism), or vengeance groups, whose tendencies have been disclosed by previous episodes, and expressed views or attitudes.

Gangland operations: goons, "mobs." Gangland operations do not usually affect the public decorum directly, but their hit-and-run tactics cause general apprehension in certain districts, and their operations can include, on occasion, riot instigation. Their control and combatting is usually a special problem requiring inside approaches. In instances wherein the "mobs" are employed to foment trouble in tension areas against economic rivals or racial minorities they become serious threats to public welfare.

Fear, Apprehension and Panic Situations

Anticipatory states of tension are usually aroused by conditions not clearly defined. When the public is kept informed of the facts by radio and the press, the fear or apprehension usually subsides. If the gossip and rumor outrun the corrective measures, panic may ensue.

Tension build-up. A crazed murderer at large keeps about everyone on edge. Reports, true or ill-founded, about his being seen here and there serve to increase tension in proportion to his nearness to them. Publicity about a wave of hold-ups has the same build-up effect, making many people jittery about being on the streets at night. For improvement of the situation *more* publicity should be given to each new arrest or killing of hold-up men by plain-clothes men, than to the increase in the number of hold-ups, once this balance is approached. A good police reporter can do much in this regard. In Chicago in the early 1920's a debonair hold-up man accosted a sixth victim one night. The "victim" happened to be a plain-clothes man, fast on the draw, who dropped his man with a bullet through his neck. In the man's pockets were five "hauls." The newspaper account of this episode was a good tonic for a tense public.

Preludes to panic. Rumors of minor explosions and of dangerous conditions in industrial plants—as escaping gases, or deteriorated storage facilities—are invitations to panic, if they become widely believed. At Red Oak, Iowa, in January 1952, a tank car containing propane gas sprang a leak, allowing the gas to escape in a cloud that overspread much of the community. Panic was averted by the prompt halting of all traffic, the issuing of orders to turn off all heating units and stoves, and by the evacuation of all residences in low places where the gas was densest, and by giving out information that within a reasonably short time the gas would pass the critical air-mixture condition and be dissipated. Prompt and intelligent measures such as these are an urgent necessity, and they ordinarily are sufficient to prevent panics and serious consequences. Since panic thrives on ignorance, full and appropriate information is the normal antidote.

Sudden panic situations. Man has confidence when he is fully prepared to handle an emergency. When he feels at a complete loss as to what he can or should do, panic results, and he may then react in unadaptive or even senseless ways. Thus a hunter suddenly confronted by a wild beast may drop his gun and flee. Soldiers, as in the case of the Italians near Adawa, Ethiopia, having previously heard gory tales about hideous tortures inflicted on captured enemies, fled pell-mell, dropping their guns, completely demoralized, on suddenly meeting a yelling horde in a narrow ravine. In the Iroquois Theater in 1904 in Chicago, a total of 575 persons lost their lives when a spark from an arc light ignited some inflammable stage properties. In serious panic, *leaders* are absent or ineffectual: it is every man for himself, rushing blindly for exits which are soon jammed and blocked. Most of the deaths in the Iroquois

Theater were not caused by physical injury but by asphyxiation from *gases* released in the packed auditorium by the fire. More recently, the fire in the Coconut Grove night club in Boston, with over four hundred dead, was likewise a panic affair. These tragic occurrences can be greatly reduced, if not prevented, by more rigid fire-hazard inspection and enforcement.

On other occasions panic conditions were narrowly averted by quick thinking and intelligent action. In theatres curtains have been rung down, with an explanation given quietly that the leading actor had just had a heart attack, and that refunds would be given out at the box office. Where smoke is detected the explanation is given that there is a small fire in the alley and that some of the smoke is drifting into the building.

Disaster conditions and control. A major disaster, such as an earthquake or a flood, is best handled by prompt publicity that reassures the public and informs them as to recommendations regarding evacuations, when deemed necessary. The Missouri River floods of 1952 saw such orderly and efficient over-all planning and cooperative endeavor that there was an amazingly small amount of apprehension and public loss of the preventable kind.

Crowd Trouble-shooting and Panic-prophylaxis

Fact-finding and public information. As the best way to control a skidding automobile is to prevent the skid from ever starting, the same may be said of panic, riots, mobs, lynchings and other forms of violence. In the past, the concern has been with measures to cope with situations after they have arisen, on the theory that law enforcement can only function when the law is broken. Where law enforcement officers cannot ordinarily undertake peace-making overtures between groups posed for almost certain conflict and violence, there is much to be said for vigilance, preparation for eventualities, or even warnings as to consequences if impending violence is in the offing. Sometimes the mere show of force and a calm attitude of resolute resistance to law-breaking activity is sufficient to give pause to the would-be participants. Within every crowd there are all kinds of persons, including some whose primary group associations have imbued them with respect for law and order. They need only some visible reminder to encourage them to bring pressure on their more hot-headed and irresponsible crowd members. There are deterrents to violence both in the law enforcement officers and in the citizenry, and the latter can often be appealed to effectively.

Spotting of trouble-centers. Human behavior is in large measure understandable from a knowledge of motives present at the time. Often if the motivation is known the behavior can be controlled. Grievances may be real, exaggerated, or fancied; they may become in any form powerful energizers. Men bent on redressing a wrong, with strong emotions as anger or anxiety or rage, do not always seek the real facts in the matter—they are out for action. If violence is to be averted, someone has to learn the facts quickly and make them known; and he has to know those in the group most likely to be receptive to the facts.

Trouble does not emerge from a clear sky—it has a background. It affects human beings who have drives, emotions, goals. They are motivated to realize those goals if not frustrated. Trouble is apt to arise when frustration occurs. It is hence necessary always to know who is affected, who is frustrating whom, and what probable recourse will be taken. Once the pattern is detected the trouble can be at least spotted before it makes serious headway.

REFERENCES

ALLPORT, F. H.: *Social Psychology*. Boston, Houghton Mifflin Company, 1924. A good discussion of crowd behavior is found in Chapter 12.

ALLPORT, G. and POSTMAN, L.: *The Psychology of Rumor*. New York, Henry Holt and Company, 1947. A treatise on the origin, development and spread of rumors.

BIRD, C.: *Social Psychology*. New York, Appleton-Century-Crofts, 1940. Chapters 8, 10 and 11 discuss suggestion, crowd behavior, and leadership.

CANTRIL, H.: *The Psychology of Social Movements*. New York, John Wiley and Sons, 1941. Chapters 1-4, that deal with mental context, motivation in social life and the lynching mob, are especially stimulating.

DOOB, L.: *Social Psychology*. New York, Henry Holt and Company, 1952. Chapters 7-13 that deal with the behavior of groups, and Chapter 17 that deals with strikes and revolutions, are recommended.

KRECH, D. and CRUTCHFIELD, R.: *Theory and Problems of Social Psychology*. New York, McGraw-Hill Book Company, 1948. Chapters 10 and 11 that deal with social groups, group morale, and leadership are excellent, though technical.

LAPIERE, R. and FARNSWORTH, P.: *Social Psychology*, 3rd Ed., New York, McGraw-Hill Book Company, 1949. Part V, on social interaction, treats a wide range of subjects of interest to readers of this chapter.

MEIER, N., MENNENGA, G. and STOLTZ, H.: An Experimental Approach to the Study of Mob Behavior. *Journal of Abnormal and Social Psychology*, 36:506-524, 1941.

Chapter 7

PSYCHOLOGICAL FACTORS IN HIGHWAY TRAFFIC AND TRAFFIC CONTROL

By

A. R. LAUER

THE PSYCHOLOGY OF PUBLIC RELATIONS

Perhaps no one is in greater need of establishing good public relations than the traffic engineer and the highway engineer. The ramifications of these relationships range from placating the landowner through whose property a new right-of-way is being planned, to satisfying the many and various highway users concerning the nature and placement of signs, markers, lane markings and the like. Thus it is very necessary for those in charge of developing, maintaining and regulating traffic on the highway to be adept at public relations. This can be achieved, in part, by a sensible application of the principles of psychology.

Good public relations are predicated on two fundamental premises: (1) that the persons dealt with receive fair consideration in matters concerning them; and (2) that such individuals be educated to realize that the recommendations made are for their benefit. The procedure or technique of accomplishing these two results is primarily an emotional one. People rarely use reason to settle matters pertaining to emotional things such as beliefs and desires. Hence in public relations one must constantly be alert to that which motivates those with whom he is working. Such small details as tone of voice or facial expression may be the key to success or failure. Above all one must keep himself under control.

Of course a great deal of what may be called public relations ability lies in one's personality and personal make-up. These in turn go back to certain of his inherited traits and frequently to habits acquired during early training. A public relations man must be like a bridge or poker player. He must use the cards he holds in his hand and play them to the very best advantage. Sometimes men or women who by ordinary standards would not be expected to possess public relations ability are very adept in this respect. Others who should do a good job of public relations fail utterly. It should help in dealing with people to make a systematic study of the principles of psychology. While the academic psychologist may look askance on the sources suggested here, nevertheless they should help the average man in public work to understand others better and to improve his own technique in public relations.

Morgan and Webb in the book *Strategy in Handling People* have dealt with problems of human relations. Overstreet has also made a valuable contribution in his volume *Influencing Human Behavior*. Any law enforcement officer who is interested in public relations might well look into these two books.

How Highway and Traffic Engineers May Use Psychology

Highway and traffic engineers as well as enforcement officers have numerous problems that involve public relations. Only a few illustrations may be given here. One, for example, might concern the placing of a stop-light. Someone in a community, for one reason or another, may decide a stop-light is needed at an intersection. The problem may not appear serious to the traffic engineer from the standpoint of density of traffic. He may abruptly state that there is no need for the light and assume an obstinate point of view with respect to his stand. This approach is likely to engender antagonism and arouse the interest of others. In this case it may be best to appoint a professional committee to investigate the situation and present the facts. Usually when the facts are presented the person making the request realizes that if a traffic signal is placed at this intersection, one might have to be placed at practically every other intersection in the city. If the tax load resulting from widespread installations is given, the matter usually quiets down immediately.

Also, on the other hand, a careful study of a situation may indicate that the public is right. Napoleon once said that he liked to have experts develop plans for a campaign and let laymen criticize the plans. In such instances a reversal of the engineer's opinion, in view of known facts, will never cost him prestige. Fairness and open-mindedness are the cornerstones of getting along with people. Encouraging a representative local group to study a situation and make recommendations on the basis of needs, costs, and the like, generally is the best solution.

One basic principle is to avoid raising an issue, if possible. In one case highway engineers were very much embarrassed by the problem of removing trees along the right-of-way through a small mid-western city. Apparently the situation was muffed by lack of astuteness in the initial stages and instead of letting it settle down before making any overt moves, an order was given to take the trees out irrespective of the objection of citizens. A bulldozer was put on the ground and started to operate. One woman, very violent in her protest, flung herself before a tree and defied the operator to move. Much time was lost and ill feeling generated for no reason at all because of a slip-up in the public relations procedure. Finally the trees remained and the engineers lost face. It is important to keep issues such as this from arising if at all possible.

A great many problems arise over the location of right-of-ways. In the earlier days of improved highways many of the smaller cities wanted the new roads to pass through or near the business district. At present there is a tendency to take the opposite view. They don't want the highways because of traffic problems.

By the right kind of publicity and with proper discussion of matters in an unemotional way, most such situations can be handled without engendering a great deal of sentiment either way. It is primarily a matter of using the right psychology in dealing with the situation.

How the Enforcement Officer May Use Psychology

A few years ago it was customary for enforcement officers to be very "hard-boiled." The tougher they were, the more successful their work was thought to be. The public had to be pushed around to develop respect for authority. Under certain conditions of mob violence this view may still be correct. In traffic situations, however, such an approach by enforcement personnel does not yield the best results in the long run. If an officer is bullied by a driver, undoubtedly there is a tendency to get a little tough. However, the average driver is not a criminal; he is not even averse to good driving habits. Perhaps he is just negligent, or because of lowered attention or preoccupation he runs through a red light or exceeds the speed limit. Hence the enforcement officer's duty is to remind him of the law and to correct his erroneous ideas or habits in a courteous way. Enforcement is as much a matter of teaching as it is of policing. Education is recognized as the best long-range technique for reducing accidents. Therefore, the traffic officer should consider himself a teacher most of the time and should study the methods of teachers. For the most part the techniques of teaching are quite different from those used by police officers in handling the outlaw group of the population.

In any case, public relations is a very important aspect of traffic-law enforcement. Because of administrative policy most state highway patrols have long stressed the need for courtesy toward the driver on the part of officers. In fact this has become so deeply ingrained that only rarely is the principle violated. The relationship between the public and the highway patrol in general is exceptionally congenial. In Iowa, for example, it is customary for the patrol to be invited to various types of meetings—Parent-Teacher Associations, public school groups, civic organizations, service clubs, etc.—to give talks and advice on various phases of highway safety. This is an excellent way to develop good public relations. Some of the other techniques effective in securing results may be obtained from a study of the sources recommended above.

Public Relations and the Layman

People differ considerably in their attitudes. One person is very cooperative and anxious to conform to all the rules of society; another is a "toughy" who is anxious to violate every rule of the road. This is particularly true of a certain group of delinquent youths who have given the teen-ager a bad name. Such games as "chicken," "spider" and similar misuses of motor vehicles and traffic facilities must not be tolerated. It may be safely said that the layman, as an individual, usually responds to people pretty much as they respond to him. Therefore, if treated reasonably and given proper consideration as a driver, at least 95 per cent of all drivers will try to cooperate with the enforcement body. Herein lies the secret of the effect of public relations. When the lay driver feels that the enforcement officers are trying to help him, and not trap him, he behaves much better and tries to cooperate, and tends to avoid conditions that result in accidents or in violations of a traffic regulation.

If properly handled even the "tough guy" may soften up and show remarkable cooperation. Those who do not, however, should be dealt with in such a manner as to discourage the misuse of the privilege to drive an automobile.

TYPES OF PSYCHOLOGICAL HAZARDS

Psychological hazards may be differentiated from physical hazards in that they are the result of a certain mental state, or attitude of the driver. They often lead to an unnecessary exposure or unwillingness to accept responsibility while at the wheel. From our studies and observations it would seem that psychological hazards, in general, may be classified with respect to the conditions which lead up to taking unnecessary risk, namely: (1) ignorance of the situation, and (2) inattention to danger. Some persons actually drive up to 80 miles an hour without realizing that they are exceeding a safe speed. They are inattentive to danger.

One class of drivers is that in which some motive is so strong that the desire to keep within the law is forgotten or overlooked. For instance, there seem to be persons who are so impetuous that they drive recklessly for no good reason at all except that they are bored by the slow moving state of affairs. Another type may be identified as the malicious nondescripts who take pride in violating all the rules and canons of society. They vary from the irresponsible speed maniac to the malicious type of individual who drives to see how many laws he can violate.

Mental State of the Driver

The mental state of the driver has a great deal to do with his willingness and ability to drive safely. If he is excited or strongly moved to get somewhere because of an emergency, he may exceed the speed limit or fail to notice a STOP sign. If worried and under mental tension because of events transpiring immediately around him, he may be in such a state of mind as to neglect the common courtesies of the road, such as, giving hand signals, staying on the right side of the road, slowing up for the car ahead or otherwise using ordinary care in driving. Again there are other mental conditions which may be better designated as the lack of a "state of mind." Reference is made to the person who is sleepy or otherwise has his mental efficiency lowered through the monotony of highway travel. A man's conduct must be judged in terms of his mental state at a given time.

Unfortunately most accident reports contain little, if anything, relating to the driver's state of mind. Probably this is due in part to the inability to set down objective statements which identify the condition. Again it may be due to the fact that one often tends to disguise his true feelings.

Most mental conditions may be measured best indirectly. Thus indirect consideration of such conditions which may create momentary traffic hazards should be carefully studied by persons qualified to interpret them. This is where the psychological approach fits admirably into accident investigation. It is hoped that in time every city will have an accident squad that will include someone trained to make proper evaluation of the driver's mental state just prior to and at the time of the accident. This would include a routine physical check-up to ascertain whether the person had been drinking, whether he is a diabetic and perhaps suffering from an overdose of insulin, whether he is an epileptic and had a momentary seizure, or whether he is suffering from some other induced condition of a psycho-physiological nature.

An adequately trained psychologist should be on hand to investigate the pattern of behavior just before, during, and after the accident. The consistency with which the various alleged causes are given might be better evaluated. He should also solicit the advice of the medical man on matters pertaining to psychosomatic symptoms and syndromes.

Age and Accidents

Age is an important factor in accident involvement and the relationship is different for men than for women. In general, age is less important in considering the driving records and behavior of women than it is of men. Psychologists have not thoroughly differentiated between the masculine and feminine patterns of behavior between the ages of 15 and 30. This shows up very strongly in the relationships indicated by Figure 12.

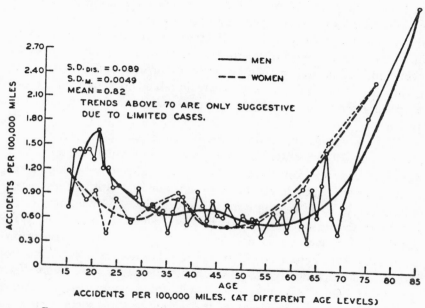

Fig. 12. Frequency of accidents on a mileage basis by age of driver.

This curve was based on a study made of a systematic sampling of nearly 8,000 drivers from the state driver's license files in Iowa. It is in no way unique or sectional since the Center for Safety Education at New York University has obtained results in Connecticut which are very similar in nature to those shown here.

It is a sad commentary on the chivalry and mentality of American manhood that the driving record becomes gradually worse from the time of learning to drive for a period of about six years.

It is particularly significant since women's records are improving constantly during this period. The figures were taken from the 1948-49 records. There is no reason to believe they are exceptional in any way since most of the men had been out of the Army for three or four years and there was no immediate pressure of the draft or other reasons which might abnormally affect mental processes of the individual during that time.

It would be folly to assume that the curve represents the common run-of-the-mill type of behavior characteristic of the male driving population. Actually it is not. A sizeable percentage of individuals of this age manifest such a bad showing that it spoils the good record of all others. In other words, the curve seems to be changed from its normal form, not by the combined effect of every individual being slightly accident-prone, but apparently it is due to a few individuals who are involved in accidents far out of proportion to that which chance would indicate for the age group.

If these curves are studied closely it will be noted that beyond the age of 30 the sexes remain more or less equal except for a slight rise around 35 in the case of women. This may be due partly to the fact that they have family worries or that children are often riding in the car. Certain physiological changes may also be a factor. It should be noted that the upturn in the susceptibility to accidents for women is accelerated after 55. The curve runs on evenly for men until 60 or 65. Such findings are not to be interpreted as being fixed and unchangeable. It is very likely that ten years hence a similar study will yield somewhat different results due to various environmental, economic and social changes. Now, women as a group, may have learned to drive later in life and therefore those who are now 55 or 60 have not had the experience in driving and traffic that men have had. It will be necessary to wait and see exactly how this effect varies with different periods of driving, and with various types of traffic conditions existing over a given period.

How Intelligence Affects Driving

The role of intelligence and judgment in sane driving is very important but the relationships are not all linear. In certain tests used to evaluate driving it seems that judgment particularly is an important factor in the development of good driving habits. Intelligence, as such, above a certain level is less important and may be given as a secondary cause of any apparent association with accident involvement. Baker at the Northwestern Traffic Institute, for instance, has been quoted as saying "morons make the best drivers." It seems certain qualifications need to be given this statement. Our own studies have not confirmed his finding. A moron is a person with an IQ between the limits of 50 and 70. In other words, he is one who is 50 to 70 per cent as intelligent as the average. Our studies have indicated that the safest drivers are persons from slightly below average to slightly above average, particularly among commercial drivers.

These findings have been confirmed to some extent by the experience of some commercial companies. It has been found that C+ drivers, those slightly above average, seem to be the most successful. In their selection they do not choose persons with extremely high intelligence for driving jobs, except for a few who are chosen to be given supervisory jobs later. The applicants are very carefully selected and only persons with a certain type of disposition or temperament are hired at this intelligence level. After a time they are taken into confidence and given a chance of qualifying themselves for supervisory and administrative leadership within the organization.

Judgment, however, while based somewhat upon the intelligence and somewhat dependent upon mental alertness, is a very important factor in driving. Unlike intelligence, it can be highly developed by training. Any person with reasonably good intelligence may develop his specific judgment to a high degree. This may be shown in almost any area where highly trained technicians are used. Because of their training, experience and knowledge concerning certain conditions and phenomena, some individuals become outstanding experts or judges in the field. Note the case of the tea tasters and the wine tasters. They must exercise their judgment as to the value of tea and wines or other drinks and beverages. There is reason to believe that no high correlation between intelligence and judgment exists. Persons above the average in the distribution of mental ability may learn faster but may not persist in mastery of a simpler function.

This is also true of traffic efficiency. Intelligence is an innate ability but judgment is acquired largely through experience. Above a certain minimum level it appears that judgment is much more important than general intellectual ability in so far as highway safety is concerned. However, the general notion that morons are the safest drivers does not fit into the general scheme of scientific facts relating to driving.

Hazards Due to Inadequate Road Marking

This may at first appear to be a non-psychological category. However, there are conditions in which certain mental states are created by inadequate road markings. There are several factors to be considered here. In the first place, there is the condition of inadequate markings which creates an uneasiness in the mind of the driver due to a misunderstanding of signs. Forbes has shown that right-turn signs tend to facilitate the movement of traffic even on such a well-regulated thoroughfare as the Pasadena Freeway. Therefore it follows that where traffic flow is much less well-organized properly designed signs are of even greater importance. In some mid-western states insufficient attention has been given to route marking especially through the cities. In one mid-western city of approximately 100,000 it was extremely difficult for a stranger to pass through without becoming lost and driving several extra blocks before locating the highway again. Such confusion and delay is entirely unnecessary and can be remedied by proper route markings.

At present some highway departments use rather large signs with letters reflectorized and up to 15 inches in height. In Canada and in certain states, pictographic or illustrative markers are used to indicate side roads, main roads, turns, cross-roads, etc. These seem to be very effective in keeping the motorist at ease and properly informed as to the route he is following.

In some instances signs are not properly maintained nor placed most effectively. In Figure 13 an example is given of two railway signs. One of these is very well maintained and set back at a reasonable distance to warn the motorist of the railroad, and the possibility of a train crossing the road. The other sign is very

Fig. 13.   Distance from R.R. track. These two photographs show samples of practices in placing signs and in maintenance.

inadequately maintained, the paint is dull, the letters are rather illegible, and it is placed on the right-of-way, practically next to the tracks. Such inadequate markings as these tend to confuse drivers and to engender disrespect and poor attitudes toward signs in general. Although the uniform code has specifications that remedy such conditions, some states have not taken advantage of the standards for effective signs and markers set up by leading authorities on traffic. When proper psychological principles are applied to the placement, legibility and visibility of road signs and markers, safety is increased.

Psychological Hazards Reduced by Driver Education

The effects of driver education on subsequent accidents and violations have been studied to some extent but it is hardly correct to say that all factors were controlled in some of the studies. Therefore, we can only reason that training in general does reduce personal hazards of driving as has been shown in industry and in other fields. To what extent training may reduce mental hazards depends on a number of factors.

Several organizations are now studying this problem and some rather specific answers may be available within the next two or three years. Various factors in driver evaluation must be very carefully controlled or erroneous conclusions may be drawn (see reference 12).

Studies by the American Automobile Association and others have shown that the accident rate of trained men is about half that of the untrained men. In some of these studies there were so few accidents among women that their records could not be used. It would take a very large sampling of drivers to furnish a sufficient number of accidents to properly evaluate women's records. However, it is conceivable that there are selective factors operating when making comparisons between men and women drivers. Men who are interested enough to seek driver instruction, or whose parents were interested enough to have them trained, may constitute a different psycho-socio-economic group than those who learned to drive by themselves. The results as they stand indicate that training does reduce the possibility of an accident to about one-third or one-half of that expected when the driver is not trained. In a few instances the inferences are that the reduction may be even greater.

Again, the type of instruction may greatly influence this effect. In 14 years of driver education in Iowa, during which time we have trained several thousand drivers, it is quite evident that the effect of training is proportional to the type of instruction given. Teachers who are well trained and adept in this field undoubtedly do a great deal more for the learner than those who are inadequately prepared.

Instructors of driver education must exert their utmost to create the proper attitudes in their trainees. If the sole objective of the course is only to coach the driver so that he may be able to pass the state driver's license examination, it is doubtful whether the accident record will be affected. However, if the objectives are long-range and intended to cultivate good attitudes, as well as to develop an appreciation for the fine points in automobile driving, the results are much better.

Other Psychological Hazards

There are other types of psychological hazards of the highway. These may range from momentary anger through the various emotional states to such abnormal conditions as epilepsy, narcolepsy, amnesia, and the various degrees of insanity. We should, of course, include the mental hazards created by the use of drugs and narcotics of various types. Alcohol is perhaps the most common narcotic used and studies made by the medical profession and psychologists have shown that judgment, one of the most important factors of driving, is only 40 per cent as accurate after drinking seven and a half ounces of gin. Many of the earlier types of coordination tests of drunkenness are not valid. Judgment is affected before the muscular system shows evidence of intoxication (see references 3 and 4).

SELECTION AND TRAINING OF DRIVERS

In 1940 the National Education Association published their Yearbook covering many phases of driver education. The committee reporting changed the name from driver training to driver education. The implications were that driver education is broader in nature and emphasizes attitudes, knowledge of safe driving and similar aspects rather than merely preparing the learner for his state driver's examination.

The Nature of Driver Education

Driver education has been greatly influenced by the methods developed by Amos E. Neyhart of Pennsylvania State College. His method is very practical and has been widely successful and highly popularized. The fact of its workableness and popularity, however, does not necessarily argue for highest efficiency. Some educators have considered the costs per pupil as high. The procedure in general is to start the driver just before the age or period at which he may wish to secure a driver's license. This seems to be the logical time to train a driver. Four students are taken as a group in a car and with varying amounts of classroom instruction are carried through at least 15 or 30 hours of behind-the-wheel practice. Schools usually give the recommended one-semester course for credit. This requires around 50 clock-hours for all types of instruction.

Other schools such as Lane Technical High School in Chicago use "dummy" driving mechanisms in a large classroom or laboratory where the students react to lights mounted on a panel for learning mechanisms and proper movements for operating the controls. Starts and stops are made and the lights indicate wrong movements or maneuvers. At a later stage motion pictures of driving situations are shown which the students are to follow. Finally practice is given in actual driving. In some schools the instruction is limited to classroom work. In Detroit each student is put in a car by himself as early as possible, with an instructor observing from a vantage point on the field. The relative merits of these various methods have not been thoroughly investigated.

In general driver training consists of three phases: (1) practice behind-the-wheel; (2) reading and class discussion on certain phases of safe driving; and (3) evaluation of performance by means of various objective and subjective testing techniques.

How Driver Training Can Be Improved

First and foremost is the matter of properly trained instructors which has not been emphasized sufficiently. In an attempt to get the driver education movement started in the schools, the American Automobile Association and others have offered 40-hour training courses for driving instructors. This has resulted in the development of a sufficient corps of teachers to take care of the demand in most instances. A successful driving instructor needs such traits as: enthusiasm, mechanical knowledge, and a desire to produce results. In some instances instructors are recruited from among poorly prepared teachers. A young man was sent in to take the course at our school who did not have a driver's license. He was expected to learn enough to get his driver's license in a two-week training period. In addition he was to learn enough to teach the youngsters whom he would have in his classes, some of whom may have driven, perhaps illegally, but enough to be quite proficient at the wheel. His lack of enthusiasm and poor personality handicapped him further. He was not accepted.

Some Liaison Needed between Schools and Law Enforcement Groups

For several reasons this is highly desirable and necessary. One is the need for good public relations and mutual understanding of objectives. The problem of safe driving is one of teaching, and whether law enforcement personnel or teachers are involved, close cooperation between the groups is highly essential and mutually beneficial. The teacher must know the problems of the law enforcement officer in order to be able to do an effective job in teaching. The law enforcement officer, on the other hand, must keep in touch with teaching methods and be sympathetic toward driver training. Teachers should emphasize that the law enforcement officer is placed on the highway to assist the driver and to protect the public at large against poor driving habits and irresponsible persons who may not be qualified to drive. The driver-education instructor must appreciate the problems of the traffic engineer and the law enforcement officer in order to teach the essentials of good driving. It might even be a good plan to have every teacher of driving serve for three months or so on the highway patrol as a special project for which he might receive credit.

The Value of the Driver's Examination

The examination for a driver's license may be considered from several points of view. In some states the reasons cited for a driver's license are not in agreement with the fundamental purposes of the examination. It should be given solely to help make the driver safer and to increase the safety of the driving public. In some cases, however, the licensing authorities have been sidetracked by the following narrow, short-range objectives: (1) to obtain a complete registry of all drivers; (2) to conform with practices in other states; (3) to make identification of the driver easier upon arrest; and (4) to raise revenue.

Although the first three reasons are legitimate and need not be questioned, they are secondary and would result from any adequate licensing plan. The fourth reason, however, is entirely unjustified and should be legislated out of existence, especially when the money received does not benefit the driver directly and is not used for purposes of developing a driver-improvement program.

From a psychological point of view the driver's license helps to place responsibility for safe driving upon the driver himself. He is responsible to the state and to the public for safe manipulation of a motor vehicle. Unless a driver's license accomplishes this, its use for other purposes is hardly justified.

In order to be most effective in placing responsibility for safe operation of a motor vehicle there should be different grades of licensing. Thus, a young driver should have some form of probational or junior license for a certain time during his learning period. His privileges would be restricted in certain instances, especially if he becomes involved in an accident or some type of violation. A driver does seem to pass through various stages, such as, apprentice, journeyman, and finally master driver. It is doubtful whether the driver's license will accomplish its best results until every state has some form of graded licensing system which will help tighten the responsibility placed upon the driver.

APPLICATIONS OF PSYCHOLOGY TO ENFORCEMENT EFFICIENCY

Any disciplinary or enforcement policy must be predicated on a fairly sound psychological basis if it is to be effective. To set down specific rules to follow is very difficult as conditions vary from situation to situation. We can only sketch some of the general principles or approaches which may be used to influence the behavior of persons so that a minimum of actual force will be necessary to accomplish the results desired. In any psychological approach one of the fundamental principles is that of using novelty and change in the technique. It is necessary to change constantly the approach in enforcement or the public becomes wary and the method ineffective. Drivers tend to ignore and even try to outguess enforcement agencies.

Results Obtained Through Publicity

By publicity we mean informing the public of the conditions that exist and of certain types of activities that are being carried out to increase safety and accident prevention. Publicity may be secured through talks to civic groups, service clubs, schools, etc. It can be a part of the programs of safety councils, junior chambers of commerce, schools, churches, and the like. Such devices as posters, stickers on cars, accident bulletins and news releases are typical. Radio and television offer excellent facilities for publicity in the way of bringing highway hazards and enforcement objectives to the individual driver. Iowa has recently adopted the policy of displaying on each patrol car the number of persons killed to date. This one factor may be a valuable aspect of publicity.

Strategy as a Psychological Aspect of Enforcement

"Spot enforcement" and other types of strategy have been used to help increase public safety and to make enforcement more effective. Some states have used white vehicles so that the patrol car may be noticed more readily, assuming that the patrol is kept moving about the highway. This, of course, has another side since in some instances drivers may spot the patrol car easier and perhaps try to play "cat and mouse" with the enforcement group. Which is most effective has not been studied experimentally to the writer's knowledge and perhaps some controlled research would be enlightening. It would seem, therefore, that patrol cars should be of two types—marked and unmarked.

The form of strategy known as "spot enforcement" is purely of psychological nature. The patrol concentrates on certain areas and does a rather thorough job, then jumps to some other location, presumably where accidents have been most frequent. The public is uncertain as to where the law will strike next. It should be the function of the accident statistics division of the driver's licensing bureau to locate areas of the state which are having the most accidents at a given period. The patrol can then take these data and lay out their plan of attack to reduce accidents.

Some states use another type of strategy. They do not paint their patrol cars an unusual color, but have only a modest identification or seal on the doors. Then when a football game or other event resulting in a concentration of traffic is anticipated the highway patrol delegates a number of its patrolmen to drive through traffic and mingle with it, or to park at the side of the road so that their patrol cars can be noticed by every passing motorist. Since the patrol cars are in evidence, motorists are more alert to the possibilities of arrest, should they violate traffic regulations or ordinances, and hence they refrain from doing so. Other illustrations of strategy could be given, but these are sufficient to emphasize the need for strategy.

Securing Enforcement Through Good Will

Perhaps no other factor in enforcement is more effective than that of public good will toward the enforcement agencies. And probably no other approach requires the application of psychology more than that of securing such good will. In England it is said that the police have the respect of the public to the extent that when a policeman is taken advantage of by a gang, the public pitches in to help the officer. Unfortunately, in America we can hardly say that this is true. It may even be said, somewhat facetiously, that the public is more likely to take the part of the culprit rather than that of the police. This may stem from undesirable police methods used in the past. Present-day highway patrols are trained in another type of school, and represent a different type of law enforcement. Needless to say, methods have changed. However, without proper respect of the public it is very difficult to secure enforcement.

COMMON MISCONCEPTIONS REGARDING FACTORS OF SAFETY

The traffic officer and safety engineer must constantly be on guard against pseudo-remedies and panaceas for accident control. Anyone having followed the field of safety for a period of time is aware of numerous cranks who have developed "cracked" notions, "fads" and gadgets guaranteed to eliminate accidents. One of the prime indicators of an amateur in safety is emphasis on a single remedy.

Regarding Vision

It is very difficult to show a high correlation between poor vision and accidents as a whole. Perhaps if every accident were traced down, and its precise cause determined along with other existing facts and circumstances, a much higher relationship would be found. What is not generally considered is the fact that the person who has some defect is very likely to compensate for this defect and thus offset the additional hazard. At one time it was thought that a large number of accidents were due to color blindness. This idea has been thoroughly studied and found not true.

A common fallacy of the present day is that the driver's eyes must be fixed on the pavement at all times for safety. Perhaps nothing is farther from the truth. Obviously a person who is leisurely driving and turning his head to examine the landscape without reference to where he is going, is a hazard. It appears from certain observations which have been made that keeping the eyes fixed in a given position will tend to induce fatigue and drowsiness. When one is reading he becomes drowsy unless occasionally he looks off into the distance to rest his eyes. In driving the same is true. It is necessary that a driver look off to the side to some extent and at periodic intervals. From studies conducted in the Iowa State College Driving Research Laboratory, it appears that anything happening within an angle of zero to 30 degrees to each side has little affect when it is of a casual nature. Beyond this range there is practically no effect. If some very unusual occurrence such as a burning house, an automobile rolling down an embankment, or some other unusual condition exists, perhaps this does tend to distract the driver and result in a hazard. However, any ordinary kind of stimulus object which is not moving, and is not likely to interfere with or run across the path of the driver, seems to aid in keeping him awake and at a higher level of efficiency, thus increasing safety.

Another aspect of the problem is that if one's eyes are fixed on the road he will not notice what is going on around him. He may not notice traffic coming from the right or from the left, nor be aware of other hazards which may move across his path. Therefore, it is safe to say that the eyes must be roving and constantly searching for stimuli which will need be evaluated in terms of safety. To restrict normal stimulation in the field of vision, or movement of the eyes, is to impose extra hazards.

The common theory of highway designers now is that all types of interference, visual and otherwise, should be reduced to the minimum on superhighways. This has been carried out to such an extent that it is defeating its own purpose. All are agreed that right angle traffic should be eliminated on superhighways. Certainly this is an excellent principle to follow and has accomplished much to reduce accident hazards. However, the idea that the driver is perfectly safe and in no danger whatever, by virtue of eliminating cross traffic, is far from the truth. He lulls himself to sleep with a false sense of security and therefore frequently gets into trouble. It would appear that some type of exciting stimulation should be introduced along the highway periodically in order that the driver may be kept at his highest level of efficiency.

Noise and Other Types of Sensory Stimulation and Highway Safety

The place of noise in the safe operation of a motor vehicle has been widely discussed and various theories proposed. An outstanding authority in the field of safety was at one time very much opposed to car radios. There is no valid evidence, however, that a radio, per se, has ever influenced a driver so as to cause an accident. Of course, it would not be correct to say that it has never happened since many accidents do occur without a known reason. It is conceivable that under certain conditions a radio does interfere. On the other hand, it may provide the necessary stimulation that is lacking in the environment through the visual sense.

There is a question as to whether the absence of noise, as such, has any deleterious effect upon driving. It has been reported that increased quietness of commercial vehicles has been associated with an increase in accidents. No studies, however, are available that show the effects of smooth pavements and quiet running cars on the efficiency of driving. In general there may be a positive correlation between quietness of operation and accidents, but no one knows to what extent such relationship, if any, holds.

Highway Hypnosis

This subject has received considerable attention recently in various newspapers, periodicals and magazines. Again there is little experimental evidence to support the distraction theory. Some studies from the Iowa State College Laboratory indicate that superimposing stimuli upon a normal driving situation, up to a certain point, tends to stimulate performance, at least no loss in efficiency was noted. In other words, driving efficiency may be increased by introducing certain auxiliary stimuli into the situation.

The term "highway hypnosis" is probably somewhat overworked as a cause of accidents. One should more correctly speak of lowered attention due to the lack of adequate stimulation. However, there is a possibility that fixation of the eyes on the pavement or a tail-light may produce a drowsy condition which does result in the driver momentarily falling asleep. Every driver, especially in his younger days, has experienced this phenomenon. Whether it is hypnosis, lowered attention, drowsiness, or something else, the results are the same, namely, an increased number of accidents on the highway due to insufficient stimulation of the driver.

Psychological Versus Legal Responsibility

Only a few decades ago the insane were whipped for the purpose of driving evil spirits from them, on the theory that they were fully responsible for their acts and that sufficient punishment would restore proper behavior. This theory is no longer held. In fact, we have even begun to recognize a criminal as not entirely responsible for his acts.

In a similar way, we are beginning to recognize that passing through stop-signs or stop-lights is not entirely a deliberate act. In one test situation during the Ford Good-Driver League finals in 1940 and 1941, it was found that approximately 90 per cent of the contestants, when put in a test situation involving a stop-light, missed the signal, even though a $5,000 scholarship was at stake. Since they were instructed to observe all signals, there is no reason to believe that they deliberately missed the lights. It is probably safe to say that a large percentage of other violations are unintentional and not willful. They happen because of poor training, bad habits, lack of understanding of traffic situations and of traffic signals themselves.

Recently when driving in New York City, the writer was faced with the choice, as he was moving up along the West-Side Drive, of going through the Holland Tunnel, the Lincoln Tunnel, or of moving on up further to the George Washington Bridge. The two tunnels were very clearly marked, but directions to the bridge were confusing. Therefore due to inadequate route markings, the driver hesitated, slowed traffic and without a doubt riled some of the drivers behind him. Although the driver's response was somewhat inadequate in that situation, there was nothing intentional about it. Therefore it is a question whether one should be held responsible for acts that are involuntary.

These few instances help to explain to some extent what is meant by psychological responsibility as contrasted with legal responsibility. Quite obviously it is the latter that is most frequently recognized and accepted by law enforcement agencies. When psychological responsibility, however, becomes better accepted and we are able to differentiate it from legal responsibility, law enforcement practices will without a doubt change considerably.

FUTURE OF PSYCHOLOGY IN TRAFFIC ENGINEERING

Psychology is just beginning to be considered an important factor in traffic engineering. Cobb has approached the problem from the standpoint of the driver. Forbes has done research on the effects of location of "right-turn" signs, types of letters, etc. More recently radar speed detectors have been used widely, partly for psychological effect. Following a very effective publicity drive, a radar meter used in Des Moines greatly reduced the speed on city streets. The public is fully alerted to the fact that many new instruments are available and are being used. Signs indicating that a street or road is patrolled by radar speed detection methods puts the public on guard. Knowing that the equipment cannot always be observed, they become cautious and speed is slowed down enormously. In one instance on the New Jersey Turnpike a speed detector hidden from view even slowed traffic coming from the opposite direction, which is rather remarkable.

Use of Basic Principles of Psychology

The application of psychology is best effected when certain basic principles are understood and recognized. Certain simple principles must be kept in mind by the traffic engineer at all times. One of these is that an observer cannot perceive all the things presented in the range of vision. This has been known for decades through tachistoscopic and other studies in the field of psychology. The sooner traffic engineers recognize this fact the better road marking will be.

Another principle that must be recognized is that of the necessity for optimal stimulation. Stimuli must not be presented too rapidly nor too slowly. Neither must it be too sparse, or too concentrated. A certain in-between rate is most suitable for the average person. The principle is almost universal in its application and relates to quantity and quality, as well as to the rate of stimulus presentation.

A third principle that must be recognized is that of individual differences. Not all drivers can drive at 60 miles an hour with safety. Although some may drive 50 miles an hour with safety, at 20 miles an hour they may become unsafe drivers. It is equally true that many who drive 15 or 20 miles an hour safely are unsafe at 50 miles. The principle of *individual differences in abilities* must be recognized and practiced in traffic direction and enforcement.

The Training of Traffic Control Personnel

The effective implementation of any program must be done through properly trained personnel. It would be unfair to expect every traffic enforcement officer to be a college graduate or to have had courses in psychology. It is, however, well within the realm of feasibility to give every traffic officer a short course in the principles of psychology and their application. It is our thought that within the next few years much more of this type of training will be given.

SUMMARY AND RECOMMENDATIONS

In this chapter we have tried to summarize some of the salient features of the psychological approach to traffic engineering. The matter of public relations has been presented as an important phase of traffic control. Certain psychological hazards also have been cited which are associated with the age, the mental state, the judgment and intelligence of the driver, to show how they may be related to accident susceptibility. Psychological hazards that stem from defective road markings and improper training of drivers were also considered, and other miscellaneous mental hazards were pointed out.

Driver education was discussed only to the extent that its function is misunderstood by some persons. Suggestions were given, however, as to how it can be improved through cooperation between the schools and law enforcement groups.

Enforcement practices were considered and it was shown that publicity can be of great help in enforcement. Considerable emphasis was given to strategy, good will, and public relations since all enforcement must be based on a willingness of those policed to follow the dictates of those doing the enforcing.

Certain faulty theories of highway and safety engineering were pointed out, such as those relating to methods of placing signs and other stimuli along the roadsides. It has been assumed that the removal of all stimulating objects from the right-of-way, including cross traffic and pedestrian travel, will reduce accidents to zero or to very near the minimum. This is not entirely true of superhighways. It must be remembered that the roadway is not usually the cause of the accident.

Perhaps some time in the future every driver will be required to secure a special permit, record of safe performance or proficiency certificate, in addition to his license before he will be allowed to enter the superhighway's toll gates. A point system of merit rating might well be used more widely in various states. Then before a driver would be allowed to enter a superhighway, he would be required to show his driver's license showing his point rating. Although some drivers would object to this, others would be willing to cooperate. Some gradation of licensing is needed.

Finally, psychological principles need to be applied in the field of traffic engineering. Traffic personnel trained in such principles have demonstrated that they do a superior job. However, much more needs to be learned about the psychological aspects of traffic engineering before spectacular advances can be made in this area.

REFERENCES

Cobb, P. W.: Selecting the Accident Prone Driver by Means of Tests. Highway Research Board, pp. 24 (mimeographed), 1938.

Forbes, T. W.: Effect of 'Keep Right' Signs on the Arroyo-Seco Parkway. The Institute of Transportation and Traffic Engineering, University of California, Research Report No. 9-3, 1951.

Holcomb, R. L.: Alcohol in Relation to Traffic Accidents. *Journal of the American Medical Association.* 1938, 3:1076-1085.

Lauer, A. R.: The Effects of Alcohol on Driving. *Journal of the Iowa State Medical Society*, July, 1939.

Lauer, A. R.: Psychological Factors in Effective Traffic Control Devices. *Traffic Quarterly*, 1951, 5:186-195.

Lauer, A. R.: Certain Structural Components of Letters for Improving the Efficiency of STOP Signs. *Highway Research Board Proceedings*, 1947, 27:360-371.

Lauer, A. R.: A Study of Driving Efficiency. Driving Research Laboratory, Iowa State College (Unpublished Report), 1951.

Morgan, J. J. B. and Webb, E. T.: *Strategy in Handling People.* Chicago, Bolton, Pierce and Co., 1930.

Overstreet, H. A.: *Influencing Human Behavior.* New York, Norton, 1925.

Pennsylvania State College: *Driver Training Reduces Traffic Accidents One Half*, Washington, D. C.; American Automobile Association, 1945.

Thorndike, Robert L., et al.: *Human Factors in Accidents.* School of Aviation Medicine, Air University, USAF, American Institute of Research, Oct., 1950, pp. 174 (mimeographed).

White, Wendell: *The Psychology of Dealing with People.* New York, Macmillan, 1941.

Young, P. T.: *Motivation of Behavior.* New York, Wiley, 1936.

Chapter 8

PSYCHOLOGY AND THE COURT
By
F. K. Berrien

ONE OF THE most significant developments in criminal law and procedures in the last century is the application of scientific research findings to the law. To those who have grown up in an age of science this statement may be surprising, but it is true that much of our current criminal law, and the procedures used in administering it, are based on folk-lore assumptions about the nature of man—his perceptions, mental operations, motives, capacity for reform and similar characteristics. The courts have evolved a set of rules of evidence that rests, in some instances, on conceptions of human nature that were the common sense views of a century ago, but that are rejected by psychologists today.

The psychological studies relevant to this chapter deal largely with the conditions that affect perceptual experiences and their subsequent reporting. They demonstrate, among other things, that eye-witness accounts—often thought to be the most reliable type of testimony—are open to a number of well-defined errors which can be detected by the law enforcement officer *if he is alert and informed*. Knowing the information presented in this chapter can often lead to a penetrating evaluation of some kinds of eye-witness testimony. Important leads in this direction are often missed at the initial investigation stage simply because the officer does not know which conditions are important.

Before dealing with the psychology of testimony, however, attention will be directed to the psychology of the judge, the counsel and the jury. These constitute the stage on which human tragedy and hopes, acrimonious debate and legal niceties intertwine to form a drama high in interest and rich in psychological implication.

THE COURT ROOM AND JUDGE

The typical courtroom, massive and dignified in furnishings, is purposely designed to impress those who assemble in it with the seriousness and importance of justice. The cumbersome ritual, when executed in what is often a perfunctory fashion, loses its effectiveness even though it is intended to enhance the atmosphere of respect and authority. The fact that the judge is often referred to as *the court* tends to submerge him as a distinct personality and to lift his utterances and decisions to the high level of an impersonal body of law. To assemble before the law is exceeded in solemnity only by the reverence of religious worship and, indeed, many similarities can be drawn between the two types of ritual.

In spite of the restrictions placed by statutes on the freedom of the judge, and the selecting process through which most superior court judges pass before they finally reach the bench, it is not surprising to discover that he has detectable prejudices and unique ways of behaving that find expression in his pronouncements on the law. As Jerome Frank, a noted jurist himself has said, "The Law is what the judges say it is."

Although the laws of a particular state specify the sentences for certain crimes, the judge has considerable discretion in determining the severity of the sentence. Studies of the sentencing behavior of judges show marked variations. In one district court within the Boston area 11 per cent of all those coming before it were convicted, but in two other districts of comparable socioeconomic status about 32 per cent were convicted. If you happened to have been convicted of drunkenness in the first district you had three chances in 100 of being fined. Convicted of the same crime elsewhere in Boston your chances of a fine were about 10 times greater.[1] Less than five per cent of those convicted of larceny or breaking and entering were fined in one district but if the crime had been committed in the adjacent neighborhood—perhaps just a block away—the percentage of fines jumped to 24 per cent.

Similar data could be quoted from all parts of the United States. It has been suggested that the sentencing behavior of the

---

[1] F. E. Haynes: Variations in Sentences. *Classification Exchange*, III, State Penitentiary, 2:41-50, 1940.

judge is a manifestation of his personality. One New Jersey judge was more severe on sex offenders than his colleagues as evidenced by his sentencing to penal institutions 59.4 per cent of such cases coming before him while the average of five other judges was 41.6. On other kinds of cases he showed no similar tendency to be unusually severe.[2] To some psychologists this might mean that the judge was attempting to recitfy some sexual problem in his own life. On the other hand, judges like physicians, develop certain "pet" treatments which in their experience have proven successful. More information about this judge is obviously required before anyone can satisfactorily explain his special severity in dealing with sex cases. Nevertheless, it is important to recognize that the law varies in part with the judge who applies it.

THE JURY

The jury was originally devised to avoid the injustices that arose in the feudal society when the landlord was also judge, jury and sometimes prosecutor. Inevitably because of the circumscribed conditions of travel and living, the jurors were neighbors of the accused and served at first as character witnesses. They were purposely selected at times because they had first-hand knowledge of the issues in litigation. The witness-jurors generally knew how the defendant had acquired his property, or the nature of his relations with other members of the community.

The expansion of population and the rapid flux of living has altered some of the details of the jury system but not its fundamental assumptions. We now take special measures to insure that the jurors do not know the defendant or have any prejudicial knowledge of the issues to be debated. However, we still assume that ordinary laymen—housewives, farmers, businessmen, clerks— are competent to evaluate and coordinate evidence which runs the gamut from highly technical information to highly emotional appeals. The variety of evidence now presented in litigations did not exist in the society which gave birth to the jury system. The basic difficulty in the jury system is not its organizational ineffi-

---

[2]F. J. Gaudet: Individual Differences in the Sentencing Tendencies of Judges. *Archives of Psychology*, 230:24-25, 1938.

ciency—although this should not be ignored—but rather the relative incapacity of the average juror to understand all that he must. To say that the jury's function is to decide the facts at issue is to gloss over an exceedingly difficult task calling for a variety of skills and knowledge.

One further consideration tends to reduce confidence in the wisdom of the jury system. From the psychological standpoint it is curious that the rules of court procedures permit counsel in their opening remarks to declare emphatically that they will prove this or that charge is (true or false) beyond a shadow of doubt. Counsel for the defendant is permitted to emphasize the sterling character of his client, the client's widowed mother or dependent children and a host of distantly related considerations, none of which are in dispute. The prosecution on its side tries to influence jurors' opinions by remarks equally extraneous to the formal charge. However, the moment a witness takes the stand, his testimony is strictly confined to facts as he knows them; his inferences, his hearsay evidence, his opinions are carefully ruled off the record. Upon what psychological assumptions is one kind of inference permitted and another denied? Why should the contending lawyers be permitted to influence jurors' opinions by highly charged emotional appeals while witnesses are constrained even to utter a first order inference?

Those familiar with courtroom tactics, as experienced judges would be, are probably less influenced by the opening and summarizing statements of counsel, than are the ordinary jurors who probably are unacquainted with many of the subtle differences between what is fact and what is inference.

It has been suggested from various quarters that specialized panels of experts be employed as jurors and advisors to the court. Cases, for example, that are likely to involve testimony regarding medical problems would then employ a physician on the panel. Those involving tax evasions or embezzlement might include an accountant or two. Such panels could not only decide the guilt or innocence of the defendant but could advise the court in a more flexible fashion than juries are now permitted. Such a system would meet some of the objections to the present practice of selecting jurors almost on the basis of their ignorance rather than their knowledge. Something approaching this idea has already been adopted in some juvenile courts where the judge has informally sought the advice of a panel sometimes made up of a minister, priest or rabbi, a social service worker, an educator, a physician and a psychologist.

Concentration of the Jury

Most jurors are honest, conscientious and take their responsibilities seriously. However, the conditions of the courtroom sometimes tax human powers of attention and memory to the limit. Some trial sessions are so long that "sitting fatigue" is an important deterrent to alert attention and clear memory for the evidence. Systematic studies of this factor have not been made because the legal profession, and particularly the judges, are not disposed to permit auxiliary activities in a court of law which in any way might suggest an experiment or a survey. There is some merit in the notion that tests of attention or memory applied to jurors would reveal some gross deficiencies and might therefore be employed to gain a retrial. On the other hand, the medical profession has not shrunk from experimentation when proper safeguards for human life can be imposed. Even an error in this field which results in death does not prevent further experimentation.

It would be highly convenient to have some infallible outward sign of the degree of attention. An "alertness meter" has been experimentally demonstrated for use on aircraft pilots. It is conceivable that the device would be useful in the jury box as well.

As one observes a court trial he is impressed with the relatively slow pace with which the evidence is unfolded. On direct examination, counsel may pause for some moments between questions, consulting notes or other members of his "team." He may even refer to law books. Cross examinations are oftentimes interrupted by counsel referring back to records or direct testimony before framing questions. Although it is obvious that deliberations should not be rushed it is equally obvious that consideration should be given to striking a balanced pace in the proceedings, in order to hold the jury's attention.

Factors Affecting Jury Opinions

One of the factors that affects an individual's opinion on controversial issues whether he is a juror or not, is prejudice. No one is entirely free of some strongly held belief for which little if any evidence exists. We may believe that in general Negroes are vicious, or Jews are generally dishonest, or large corporations exploit their employees, or public utilities abuse their franchise. The list could be extended almost without limit. The dynamic character of prejudice—the manner in which it affects behavior, its motive forces and its subtle manifestations—has only recently been clarified. This is not the place to enter into a full discussion of this fascinating topic except to point out that prejudices generally spring from one or more frustrating experiences that blocked the attainment of some goal. The object of prejudice may have had only a remote connection with the blocking conditions, but for a complex of reasons that element was fastened upon as a sort of "scapegoat."

Geographical or regional loyalties sometimes enter in the picture to predispose jury opinions. The lawyers for a large public transportation company report that when sued for damages in rural districts the company, rather than the particular issue of the case, is usually up for trial.

A murder was committed in one of the Relocation Centers established in Arizona for Asiatics shortly after Pearl Harbor. Although the Center was under Federal supervision the area was included in the legal jurisdiction of the county in which the Center was located. Serious difficulties arose because many believed that a fair jury trial in the county would be impossible. No matter who sat in the jury the accused would be convicted almost automatically because of the intense hostility against all Asiatics at that time.

Although law enforcement officers have no official responsibility in selecting jurors or have little occasion to influence jurors' opinions, knowledge of the dynamics of prejudice may be an aid in understanding some courtroom events or actions that would otherwise be mysterious.

Does the order in which evidence is presented have any influ-- ence on the jury's verdict? It most certainly does. This fact was demonstrated by an ingenious series of studies at Cornell University.[3] In one study a detailed report of a criminal case was divided into thirteen sections and read to groups of students who were to consider themselves jurors. At the end of each portion of evidence the "jurors" indicated their belief in the defendant's guilt or innocence on a nine-point scale. One extreme of the scale represented a certainty that the defendant was guilty; the other end of the scale represented certainty that the defendant was innocent. As one would expect, evidence for the prosecution which came first, influenced the jurors toward the "guilty" extreme and evidence for the defendant which followed shifted opinion toward innocence. The interesting comparisons came when the order of presenting the same evidence was changed so that the defense had both the first and last periods with the prosecution sandwiched between. Under these circumstances the defendant had a better chance of being declared innocent.

In other cases using the same technique of requiring "jurors" to indicate their degree of belief in the innocence or guilt of the defendant, the investigators discovered that women were no more gullible nor more stubborn in their opinions than men.[4] This does not mean, however, that women react in the same manner to all evidence as men. The different social roles that men and women in general play in our society may influence their evaluation of evidence particularly in sex cases, divorce proceedings, abandonment cases and the like.

EVIDENCE AND THE WITNESS

Testimony depends upon the accuracy with which the initial observations are made. Much of the early psychological research pertaining to testimony concentrated on this phase of the problem. A long list of studies beginning about 1910 were reported which

------

[3]H. P. Weld and M. Roff: A Study of the Formation of Opinion Based Upon Legal Evidence. *American Journal of Psychology,* 51:609-629, 1938.

H. P. Weld and E. R. Danzig: A Study of the Way in Which a Verdict Is Reached by a Jury. *American Journal of Psychology.* 51:518-536, 1940.

tended to throw doubt on the accuracy of eye-witness testimony, particularly when reports were not required immediately. These studies employed drawings or photographs of street scenes which were exposed to observers for a few seconds or a minute. They were then required to answer a series of factual questions about the pictures. More recently a few experiments have been conducted with motion picture films or staged scenes.

Almost anyone can easily demonstrate the kinds of inaccuracy which creep into testimony by staging a simple short event and then immediately questioning the observers. It is important that the event take place unexpectedly to simulate realistically conditions surrounding an accident, or a series of events related to a crime.

For example, the author arranged on one occasion to have a student walk into a classroom and interrupt the lecture by declaring that some white rats had been lost. The student walked slowly across the room in front of the class, turned around, and went out, all the time carrying on a previously rehearsed conversation with the instructor concerning the loss of and search for the rats. In spite of the fact that the student-actor was well known to many, if not all of the students, estimates of his weight ranged from 145 to 210 pounds (actual weight 190); eight of the 43 students declared he wore a maroon-colored sweater (actually he wore a gray-tan double-breasted coat); a majority declared with certainty that he searched diligently in the corners of the room looking for his rats (he made one furtive glance toward the corner of the room contrary to instructions to keep his eyes on the instructor).

From this and similar experiments it appears the observers tend to get an overall impression of a given scene and then fill in the details in sensible ways to conform to the observer's meaning of the events regardless of whether the details actually did or did not conform. In the above example the student would, if he had actually lost some rats, look in the corners for them. This is the action one would expect in view of the conversation. Moreover, he often wore a sweater and maroon was the dominant color on this campus; hence expectation led to the incorrect testimony on this factor as well.

At times testimony may be in dispute relating to the time order of events. Did the victim of a shooting scream just before or just after the flash of a gun? Did the screech of auto brakes occur just before or after the light turned red? A number of studies agree that accuracy of judgment in these cases depends upon the time interval between the sight and sound; whether the source of sound is also in view; and the position of the observer relative to the events. There is a predisposition to judge light or flashes as preceding sounds when they follow each other in very rapid succession. More errors will occur in judgments when the real order is sound followed by a flash, rather than a flash followed by sound.

Effect of Emotions on Testimony

A doctrine held in high repute in the legal profession declares that "excitement stills the reflective faculties and removes their control." For this reason an exclamation is a "sincere response to the actual sensations during the period when consideration of self-interest could not have been fully brought to bear by reason of reflection."[5] This principle seems to have been the basis for court rulings which accepted as evidence dying exclamations rather than comments uttered in the absence of strong emotion.

The legal doctrine has no scientific foundation. It is merely sagacious speculation which assumes that a factor called self-interest interposes itself somewhere between a sensation and a response—if time permits. It is true, of course, that persons can sometimes be startled into revealing knowledge they have previously denied. A witness may have declared that he has never been acquainted with a certain person who is assumed to be dead or at least not in the vicinity. When suddenly confronted with the person in question the witness may give some sign of recognition which will be accepted by the court rather than the sworn denial of acquaintance. On the other hand, the studies to which we have just made reference show that an existing state of excitement operates to reduce the accuracy of observations and subsequent

---

[5] J. H. Wigmore: *Evidence.* Little Brown and Company, Boston, 1923, Sec. 738.

report. When someone unexpectedly starts a commotion in a classroom, or bursts into a lecture in search of white rats, the excitement not only "stills the reflective faculties" but it also blinds the observers to important events or conditions.

A particularly good illustration of the unreliability of the legal doctrine is found in the murder of Virgil Romine in Jefferson County, Missouri, on January 7, 1929. He was found early that morning in his roadside "hamburger joint" and filling station on the verge of death with serious stomach wounds. The sheriff who found him reported that he had declared his assailants were the same fellows he had had trouble with two weeks previously over the slugging of a slot machine and they were often seen around "old lady Vinyard's place." The sheriff made the usual investigation and found two roughly dressed young fellows asleep in the Vinyard house. They readily admitted having tried to slug the slot machines but insisted they had made good with the owner on that offense and furthermore they had not been near Romine for some days. Romine's exclamation was accepted at the trial as a dying declaration and apparently carried more weight than the boys' alibi because they were convicted and sentenced on a second-degree murder charge.

Before the sentence was carried out, subsequent evidence was uncovered through an informer and confessions were later obtained from the real culprits. The boys who were first convicted bore only the vaguest resemblance to the men who were guilty. In all probability the fight which preceded the shooting had the effect of distorting Romine's observation, or else in the period of agony between the shooting and the sheriff's appearance, Romine rationalized the "Vinyard boys" into the picture because they were the only ones with whom he had recent difficulties, and might therefore be the most probable ones to assault him. In any event the dying declaration was in error even if considerations of self-interest were minimal.

The courts would be better advised to ignore the principle given at the outset of this section and instead remain skeptical of

---

*E. M. Borchard: *Convicting the Innocent*. Yale University Press, New Haven, Connecticut, 1932, 93-98.

all unsupported testimony concerning unexpected events observed when the individual is emotionally disturbed.

Age of the Witness

The witness must be how many years old before reliance can be placed on his testimony? Such a question cannot be answered categorically because much depends upon the particular kind of information and the circumstances surrounding the events. There is some evidence that children are more suggestible than adults and are therefore more easily persuaded to modify their "recollections" of what occurred. The law enforcement officer must be on guard by the manner in which he approaches and questions children at the early investigation stages to make sure that he does not "put words in their mouths." Children in situations that are uncomfortable to them are apt to accept the easiest way out for themselves and their friends, paying little regard to truth. Some hints on methods of questioning that induce inaccuracies will be discussed later. At this point we can merely point out that children are not necessarily less truthful as a whole than adults, but their understanding of responsibility and the consequences of inaccurate reporting have not matured. They are therefore less careful in distinguishing between what they know, what they guessed or fancied, and what someone else told them.

Intelligence

Is a highly intelligent individual more accurate in observing than persons less well endowed? Probably yes, although reported studies do not give this answer. The fact that persons of low intelligence are less competent to express themselves, are less able to make nice discriminations and are more easily led to modify their reports by subtle suggestions, makes them less reliable witnesses. No systematic studies have been reported on the relation between testimony accuracy and intelligence when the full range of intelligence is taken into account.

Manner of Obtaining Evidence

The major effort in research studies relative to the manner of eliciting evidence seems to have assumed that the evidence is first unfolded at the trial from the witness stand. This is wholly unrealistic. *Testimony starts when the investigating officer first comes in contact with some person connected with the offense.* It is the law enforcement officer's responsibility to get the facts as accurately as possible from the start, for if the facts are confused or distorted at this stage, truth will have a tortuous journey and real injustice may result.

Probably the simplest and safest policy to follow in the early stages of an investigation is to listen much and talk little. "Tell me what happened here," is an approach which suggests nothing and gives the respondent complete freedom to tell the story in the most direct or the most circuitous manner.

A study of various methods of obtaining testimony concerning a brief classroom "act" showed that an *uncontrolled recital*, compared to direct examination, was less complete but more accurate. Another report compared a free narrative followed by direct questions pertaining to a one minute movie, with the reverse order —questions first, and then the narrative. The first order—narrative, supplemented by questions—was found to give the most accurate results.[8] These two studies when taken together indicate that whatever incompleteness may characterize the free recital of events can be corrected by later direct questions whose answers are apt to be more accurate than if questions were used at the beginning.

Above all, leading questions should be avoided. "Was the man's coat gray or brown?" assumes that the man was wearing a coat. Unless this fact has been previously established, the question is leading—perhaps misleading. Children and others who are especially open to suggestion are easily induced to answer such questions and thereby mislead others as well as themselves.

Aside from questions having hidden assumptions, other types of questions have been subjected to investigation.[9] Questions begin-

[7]W. M. Marston: Studies in Testimony. *Journal of Criminal Law and Criminology*, 15:5-31, 1924.

[8]T. J. Snee and D. E. Lush: Interaction of the Narrative and Interrogatory Methods of Obtaining Testimony. *Journal of Psychology*, 11:229-236, 1941.

[9]B. Muscio: The Influence of the Form of Question. *British Journal of Psychology* 8:351-386, 1915. H. E. Burtt: *Legal Psychology*. New York, Prentice-Hall, Inc., 1931, pp. 121-129.

ning with a negative verb like, "Didn't you leave the room before six o'clock?" or "Wasn't the light on when you entered?" seem to expect affirmative answers. They almost say, "You did leave the room, didn't you?" or "The light was on, wasn't it?" It would be better to ask, "Did you leave the room?" or "Was the light on?" Avoid using questions with an initial negative verb.

Furthermore, questions that emphasize what the witness himself has observed are more likely to give reliable answers than "objective" questions. "Did *you* hear the bell ring?" is superior to, "Did the bell ring?" In the latter question the respondent may be tempted to report that the bell rang because someone else told him about it. If the question emphasizes his own direct experience fewer errors will creep in.

Manner of Identification

Special aspects of identifying persons in a line-up demand some discussion. It is entirely understandable that public pressures on law enforcement agencies may on occasion induce officers to cut corners in their zeal to solve a case. However, no amount of public pressure can excuse negligence in taking the most rudimentary precautions against false identifications. The case of Bertram M. Campbell, convicted of forgery in 1938 in New York and completely cleared in 1945 illustrates some of the mistakes that can be, and are made. Three witnesses testified against him in his original trial. On the stand they identified him as the man who had passed worthless checks to them as tellers in various banks. Investigation revealed that prior to their being confronted with him in the Attorney General's office the tellers were shown a picture of Campbell on which had been super-imposed a mustache and were given persuasive information that Campbell was the "front" man for a big forgery ring. Furthermore, Campbell had been pointed out to them before they were formally called upon to identify him. Even when the formal identification took place in the attorney's office, he was not placed in a group or line-up. The obvious suggestions in all these conditions plus the rehearsal of the witnesses led them to declare in all sincerity that Campbell was the guilty man.

The minimum precautions in presenting people for identification demand first that the suspect be one of a group similar in dress and appearance. Second, the procedure should be conducted by someone other than the officers responsible for apprehending suspects and "building a case." Finally, the observers should not be permitted to confer with each other during the procedures and should make their identifications isolated from all suggestions which might influence their decisions.

Factors at the Moment of Exposure That Affect Testimony

The conditions influencing identifications lead naturally to a consideration of all sensory impressions. What are the common defects, illusions and limitations of various sensory functions?

Vision. The courts and general public are aware of the common visual defects that may prevent or distort clear observations. Near-sighted persons not wearing corrective lenses could not be expected to give reliable evidence on events taking place some distance away. Conversely, farsighted persons have difficulty in making fine discriminations at distances within arm's length.

An ophthalmologist or oculist can readily determine the kind and degree of defect existing if some question arises concerning the accuracy of testimony which might hinge on the visual acuity of the witness.

Color blindness which occurs in about four per cent of the male population and in only about one per cent of women, may exist for years without the individual knowing about his defect. This is particularly true if the individual is color "weak," rather than color blind. Actually several types of color blindness have been discovered but the most common is the failure to distinguish between reds and greens. Unfortunately, such a defect has great possibilities for producing uncertainties in reading traffic signals and the like. On the other hand, most of the traffic signals are not pure colors and can also be distinguished in part by differences in brightness. A number of standard tests are available which provide a measure of color blindness or color weakness. Among these is the Ishahara test which consists of a number of cards covered with colored dots. Within the dotted field a pattern of similarly colored dots forms a numeral—at least the normal person sees it. The colorblind person may have difficulty seeing it, may not see the numeral at all, or may see a numeral that is different.

The effects of low levels of illumination on color perception is a fascinating topic that if understood thoroughly may be an invaluable aid in investigation work. Typical of the mistakes in this field is the one observed by the author. I had picked up a friend several times after dark in a new car, maroon in color. He had commented on its various features but neither of us happened to mention its color. By chance, my friend had not seen the car in the daylight until some two weeks later when he asked me why I had changed cars so soon—he thought the one he had ridden in before was black. Such a mistake would have been highly improbable if my car had been green—and particularly a light green.

The brightest colors in the spectrum under ordinary daylight are the yellows. As illumination decreases the reds and yellows rapidly decrease in brightness, while the greens and blues become brighter relative to other colors. Of course, all colors decrease in brightness as the illumination decreases but some drop out faster than others. It is, therefore, possible to see greens when the blues or reds are invisible. For this reason it would be wise to check closely on testimony in which the witness reported seeing certain colors when the general illumination was very low.

The color or artificial illumination may upset discriminations that are ordinarily possible. Taxicabs painted white are not easily distinguished from those painted yellow if both are illuminated by the ordinary reddish-orange neon lamps. Sodium vapor and mercury vapor lamps are notorious in producing color confusion.

It is a well-known fact that for an appreciable period of time after you step into a darkened room, it is impossible to see. It takes several minutes before you can see many details that were simply black at first. This change in ability to-see-in-the-dark takes place rapidly in the first three to four minutes but continues at a slower rate for at least half an hour. After a person has been exposed for as much as an hour or so to fluorescent lighting he "dark adapts" less well than if the illumination has been daylight or tungsten. The red end of the spectrum shows the least improvement in visibility under such circumstances and the violet or blue end shows the greatest improvement. This suggests that testimony concerning dim red lights at night or in darkened areas is open to more doubt than testimony concerning equally bright (in physical measurements) blue or violet lights. For example, the investigating officer should check carefully on all aspects of a report from a witness who declares that he had been sitting in a movie theater for about an hour but failed to notice a dim blue flashing light near an exit but did see a red warning lamp. (Care must be taken to establish that the lights were equal in brightness which can be done by a photometer. Wattages of the bulbs would be irrelevant to this question because the light must pass through the glass whose transmissibility affects brightness.)

Illusions of distance, size and shape. Vertical lines or distances are generally over-estimated, such as the height of a flag pole, compared with the same flag-pole lying in a horizontal position. In like manner, people have a tendency to estimate the length of a horizontal line as shorter than it really is, if it is not crossed by other lines. An empty clothes line will seem shorter than the same clothes line with clothes pins hanging on it. "Unfilled" space (an open lot) is judged smaller than "filled" space (the same lot with a house on it). This phenomenon is particularly noticeable when a person with no experience in the Western desert states attempts to estimate distances in that region. The virtual absence of trees, fences, and houses, leaves the observer without the reference cues he is accustomed to, with the result that he underestimates the distance to the mountain, or to the village or to the clump of bushes around the water-hole. Aviators are generally more accurate in their estimations of altitudes above the ground than people without flying experience. In other words, experience and practice in judging distances under particular circumstances helps to dispel some of the common errors in distance judgments.

The estimation of speed is often a matter of controversy in cases involving automobile accidents and elsewhere. Systematic studies of this skill have shown that again experience plays an important part. For all persons, however, excessively noisy cars seem to go faster than they really do; large cars appear to go slower.

Motion directly toward or away from the observer is more diffi-cult to estimate than motion across the field of view.

Distance judgments. Small distances within reach are generally overestimated if they range between one and three inches. Lengths of four to forty inches are more apt to be underestimated. In esti-mating middle distances—10 to 100 feet or greater—judgments de-pend heavily upon numerous cues coming from both eyes. For one thing, the mere fact that the eyes are separated by about two and one-half inches makes it impossible for both eyes to see exactly the same thing. These slight discrepancies in the images are still detectable by special means when viewing objects as far away as a mile. From these slightly different images we are able to estimate distance. Moreover, as objects move from near at hand to greater distances, both eyes turn outward, converging less and less. The convergence of the eyes controlled by the external muscles of the eyes provides signals for distance judgments as well. It is apparent, therefore, that one-eyed persons are less apt to be accurate in judging middle distances than people who can see normally with both eyes.

Auditory sensations. Sounds may seem to come from false direc-tions. This condition is met when several hard reflecting surfaces are in the vicinity of the observer. A man was walking toward a street intersection surrounded by buildings four to six stories high. As he walked south on the right side of the street, he heard a short loud report which seemed to come from the east. When he reached the intersection he was surprised to discover a minor gas explosion had occurred to the west of the corner. The sound had been re-flected off the walls to the man's left while the building beside which he was walking protected him from the direct sound waves.

In an area where reflecting surfaces are absent, the location of sounds is ordinarily accurate except for those that are weak, of short duration, and those which originate at any point in a plane equidistant from each ear. The confusions in such cases are some-times quite baffling because the individual does not know whether they came from in front of, behind, below, or above him.

The range of vibration frequencies which an individual can hear may sometimes be of importance in testimony. It is not rare to find a person who cannot hear the high notes on a piano. He may hear a thud or click somewhat like a typewriter, but no musical tone. As people grow older they tend to grow deaf in the upper range before the lower tones are affected. Hence, these people may not hear high pitched warning sirens or shrill whistles. Fortunately, most sounds which occur "in nature" are complex rather than pure tones of a given frequency. This means that even the high pitched siren has some energy in the low frequencies that can be heard, although faintly. Background noises of low frequencies and low in intensity can "mask" or block out higher frequencies. This situation is often encountered in open air gatherings in which the rumble of a distant train or the low mumbling of a number of people may so blot out enough of the higher speech sounds of a public speaker that he cannot be heard on the edge of the crowd. In marginal situations where some dispute may arise concerning what a speaker may have said in a public address, it would be well to discover whether masking sounds existed. Spaces that are filled with a steady high-pitched noise are difficult for any sort of talking, although some people working steadily in such places learn to speak "under the noise." This means they keep their voice tones low pitched, although strong in intensity. High-pitched noise masks principally the high frequencies, but low-pitched noise has a masking effect on the low and high-pitched tones.

Taste and smell. Occasionally testimony concerning taste is of legal importance, especially in regard to accusations of poisoning. It may come as something of a surprise to learn that not all people agree on what a particular substance tastes like. One group of investigators found, for example, that creatine, a muscle constituent, was as tasteless as chalk to some people and very bitter to others. These men noted that one pound of lean meat may contain close to two grams of creatine, and it is probable that this would cause meats to have a distinctive flavor to some tasters but not to others. The taste differences would be especially pronounced in such things as soups or stews made from lean meats which must contain considerable amounts of creatine. Studies have demonstrated that phenyl-thio-carbamide tastes differently to approximately 40 per cent of the Caucasion American population. One group insists that this material tastes neutral and the other emphatically claims that the compound is extremely bitter, so bitter that it cannot be endured for long.

These studies indicate that some question may legitimately be raised concerning testimony on taste and a test of witnesses might not be impossible to determine whether they agree on the taste of these two substances. If disagreements occurred at this level, such evidence might resolve whatever discrepancies in testimony may have occurred.

Other inaccuracies of this area concern the confusion of taste and smell. In reality, there are, of course, only four primary tastes, sweet, sour, salt, and bitter. Those which seem to be principally fruity or burnt or something other than sweet, sour, salty or bitter are really smelled rather than tasted. Prior taste may also distort gustatory observations. That is to say, if one has been eating something sweet, sour tasts more sour than if the mouth had been neutral prior to tasting the sour. Hence, it is important when assertions are made about a given taste to know what has been eaten or drunk earlier.

Memory Effects on Testimony

Ordinarily there is an interval of varying length between the moment when a crime is committed and when testimony concerning that crime is given. Various factors may operate during that interval to unintentionally distort testimony in addition to those just discussed. Contrary to some legal doctrine, memory is not a unitary faculty of the mind. This assumption seems to underline a common court rule that a witness may be examined as to his memory of events even though they may be unrelated to the events relevant to the case under consideration. If an individual cannot remember where he was on July 14, 1952, it is assumed that he cannot recall clearly the events of July 13, quite disregarding the effect of numerous factors which influence retention other than mere lapse of time. Among the other influences affecting memory is the prejudice existing at the time of the initial impression.

It has been shown that statements contrary to the political preferences of an individual are recognized subsequently less readily than statements which harmonize with those initial preferences. The study which demonstrated this fact showed that a neutral speech on a controversial subject may be interpreted as favorable to the topic of contention by those who are already favorably inclined and interpreted unfavorably by those who are not favorably inclined. A case involving this point concerned the farewell speech made by the manager of an insurance company's branch office. The man had been discharged with a promise of three months' extra pay. The farewell meeting took place at midnight after a day of feverish activity. It was attended by a few representatives of the company and by most of the employees who were deeply moved by the words of their former chief. In the speech, one word analogous to "rascal" or "scoundrel" was probably used, but whether it was used to characterize the trustees of the company or in some other context—this problem divided the listeners. The group favorable to the company believed the word to have been used with offensive meaning. The company accordingly refused to grant the extra pay, but the discharged manager contested the action on the ground that his speech was not offensive to the company, an interpretation with which most of the audience agreed. After consultation with a psychologist who analyzed the situation, the presiding judge induced the company to pay the extra compensation. The judge and the psychologist apparently concluded that the false interpretation placed on the speech was in part due to the attitude of a few listeners.[10]

Eidetic recollections. Eidetic imagery or recollection refers to the ability possessed by a small proportion of the population to describe in exceptionally precise detail, many of their previous experiences. These people are sometimes referred to as having photographic memories. The proportion of these people in the general population is not known, although it is suspected that children are somewhat more skilled in this respect than adults. Their memories appear to be somewhat less selective than older people. The eidetic imager is one who can pass down the street of a strange town and without thinking about it sometime subsequently recall the exact

---

[10]W. Stern: The Psychology of Testimony. *Journal of Abnormal and Social Psychology*, 34:3-20, 1939.

number of stores in a given block. When questioned on how this is done, the eidetic imager generally says something to the effect that "I just recall the picture and just count the number of stores down the street."

One case is reported of a murder suspect whose alibi was too perfect but who was eventually exonerated after it was shown that he possessed very vivid eidetic imagery.

Age. The age of an individual has an influence on the accuracy of his recollection. However, it is not generally known that the decline in memory is not such that all kinds of learned or experienced material suffer equally. It is not uncommon to find old people unable to recall the principal events of yesterday but very clear in their recollections of occurrences of their youth. Memory in these people is less precise generally for recent events than for remote happenings. Moreover, common nouns are generally remembered more accurately than proper names, and verbs are remembered somewhat longer than nouns.

Attempts have been made to set aside a will on the ground that the testator was unable to remember the names of people or their faces. Such evidence, alone, however, would not seem to be sufficient grounds to declare the testator generally incompetent to make a will, since, as mentioned above, proper nouns are forgotten most easily. On the other hand, an elderly person might easily be confused in the names of people to whom he wished to make bequests.

Time interval and activity. The most obvious factor affecting memory is the time interval between the original observation and its recollection. Studies making judicious use of meaningful material such as stories, poems, textbooks, selections, etc., have suggested the conclusion that the essential thought of a selection may be retained with high fidelity over extended periods of time, although the unessentials may be forgotten almost completely within two or three hours.[11] Most of the recollected testimony submitted as evidence in court is of course meaningful to the witness. On the

---

[11]E. B. Newman: Forgetting of Meaningful Material During Sleep and Waking. *American Journal of Psychology*, 52:65-71, 1939.

other hand, sometimes witnesses will give from memory many details concerning financial transactions which have not been recorded, details of conversations used to support claims concerning intentions. Unless such details are intimately related to the main thought or theme of the conversations, some question might be legitimately raised concerning their accuracy, unless it can be shown that the individual had special reasons for remembering the particular conversation and its details.

A factor affecting retention and subsequent recall is the kind of activity engaged in during the interval between the original experience and its recollection. Some evidence suggests that imprisonment is more likely to obscure or distort memory for a crime than freedom on bail. Other studies on this point suggest that violent activity calling for complex mental work following immediately on the heels of an experience is detrimental to its subsequent recall. This process is referred to in psychological literature as *retroactive inhibition,* and may be effective under a number of circumstances. Important in many assault cases is the testimony of the victim concerning his assailants. If the victim has suffered considerable shock or has been knocked unconscious it is unlikely that he can recall clearly many of the events just preceding the actual attack or blow causing unconsciousness. A night watchman, for example, declared that he had been slugged before the property he was guarding had been robbed. Careful questioning elicited from the watchman a wealth of detail about his attackers and their actions right up to the moment when he was struck. The completeness of his testimony aroused suspicions leading to the eventual discovery that the watchman had committed the burglary himself. In some cases, retroactive inhibition may extend backwards for as long as a day or two. That is to say, the individual may be at least hazy or completely unclear on the events which preceded the traumatic experience.

Occasionally one finds that unusual conditions intervening between observation and recall distort rather than merely inhibit or block memory. Quite by accident, an instructor had an opportunity to measure such a distortion when the campus newspaper ran a feature story on the content of one of his lectures. The report of the lecture differed from its actual content in a number of important respects. Several days after the news story appeared the class was examined by means of an objective test on the substance of the lecture. Most of those who had read the newspaper "recognized" it as substantially correct and on examination remembered what they had erroneously recognized. Those who had not read the newspaper account were more accurate on their examinations.[12]

It is entirely likely that rumors or the testimony of other observers may exert unhappy effects upon a given witness. For this reason, there is considerable merit in the practice of separating witnesses not simply to prevent outright collusion but to reduce the unintentional errors. The number of times that a person is called upon to repeat his testimony may affect his feelings of certainty concerning it.

If one repeats a story frequently enough, he becomes convinced himself of its truth, even though originally he may have been quite unsure of the events. This fact has important implications for the law enforcement officer taking statements, since he is oftentimes tempted to force the witness or accused to declare his degree of certainty with respect to alleged facts.

In view of the preceding discussion, there is little reason to accept as valid the legal implication that memory is a unitary function that can be easily tested by a few simple questions devised by counsel on the spur of the moment. Accuracy of recollected testimony depends in varying degrees upon the features just discussed and many more that continue to escape the dragnet of scientific inquiry.

---

[12]C. Bird: The Influence of the Press upon Accuracy of Report. *Journal of Abnormal and Social Psychology*, 22:123-129, 1927.

REFERENCES

Borchard, E. M.: *Convicting the Innocent.* New Haven, Yale University Press, 1932. A series of true cases in which justice miscarried.

Burtt, H. E.: *Legal Psychology.* New York, Prentice-Hall, 1931. A complete discussion of psychological applications to the law.

Inbau, F. E.: *Lie Detection and Criminal Interrogation.* Baltimore, Williams &

Wilkins, 1946. The first part is particularly applicable to this chapter's discussion of interrogating witnesses.

MOLEY, R.: *Our Criminal Courts*. New York, Minton, Balch & Co., 1930. A scholarly, factual account by one who later became famous as a "Brain Truster."

OSBORN, A. S.: *The Mind of the Juror*. Albany, Boyd Printing Co., 1937. An experienced expert witness tells what he believes about juries.

Journal of Criminal Law and Criminology: Sections on Criminal Law Case Notes and Comments. This journal is especially useful in keeping up-to-date on recent psychological aspects of criminal court procedures.

Chapter 9

MENTAL ABNORMALITY AND CRIME

By

DON W. DYSINGER

INTRODUCTION

THE person who must deal with anti-social or asocial behavior from time to time will inevitably have to cope more or less frequently with individuals who have mental abnormalities. The person who violates the law and the person suffering from some form of mental disorder have in common a failure to live in conformity with the rules and regulations of society. Many of these regulations are formalized as laws, while others are included in our customs, conventions, taboos, etc., all of which must be adhered to within reasonable limits if the individual is to continue to enjoy the advantages of social living.

Since both criminals and individuals with mental disorders reflect in their behavior at least a partial disregard for the requirements for social acceptability it has been suggested by some that crime is a product of the latter, that is, the commission of a crime indicates that the offender is suffering from some form of mental abnormality. Actually this is a question which revolves around a definition of terms, and our discussion will not permit a digression into such an area. The position taken for the purposes of this discussion is that not all individuals who violate our laws do so because of a mental disorder, neither do all individuals with mental disorders commit crimes. It may not be possible to draw a sharp line of distinction between these two groups, but our purposes will doubtless be served best by limiting ourselves to those instances in which mentally abnormal people do commit crimes. These are

226

the cases in which the best interests of all concerned will be served most adequately if the condition of the offender is at least suspected by the law enforcement officer, and appropriate measures taken accordingly.

The Meaning of Mental Abnormality

In order to clarify our discussion it is necessary to deal briefly with the meaning of mental abnormality. This term may be misleading in that the mental integrity of an individual is not directly observable, but can be judged only by the characteristics of the person's behavior. A person may have delusions of grandeur or be plotting an attempt on the life of his neighbor, but we have no evidence of these until the person proclaims himself to be, for example, the richest man in the world, or in the second case until a threatening move against the neighbor is made. In other words, the presence of a mental disorder is inferred from behavior, which means that in the absence of abnormal behavior we usually have no way of realizing the presence of mental abnormality. This leads directly to the question as to the basis for differentiating abnormal behavior from normal behavior. Basically there is no sharp line of demarcation between them. Abnormal behavior is usually more extreme than is normal behavior. For example, a person may be so conceited that he has difficulty maintaining a circle of friends, but on this basis alone he is not likely to be considered an abnormal person. On the other hand the man who maintains that he is Napoleon and insists that he be treated with appropriate respect and deference is quite likely to be considered abnormal. Both individuals have inflated opinions of themselves, but in view of the resulting behavior the latter to a much more marked extent than the former.

Another frequent differentiating factor is the appropriateness of the behavior to the conditions or circumstances under which it appears. So-called normal behavior is typically more appropriate to its setting than is abnormal behavior; as a matter of fact certain behavior is considered abnormal not because of its quality or character, but solely because of its inappropriateness. Standing with one's head bowed and hands clasped in an attitude of prayer is not in itself abnormal, but this behavior in the middle of a busy street intersection might well raise some question regarding the individual's mental condition at the moment. Thus we find that abnormal behavior may differ from normal (or socially acceptable) behavior in that it is an exaggerated form of the latter and/or it occurs under circumstances which make it appear inappropriate.

An understanding of behavior, either normal or abnormal, requires an appreciation of the motives which underlie it. In view of the peculiar and frequently bizarre behavior of the mentally abnormal person it is often assumed that his motives are quite different from those of normal individuals, but this is not necessarily the case. An individual who is unsuccessful in satisfying his needs through reasonably normal channels may resort to more extreme behavior in order to attain his goals. For example, a boy who fails to gain desired recognition in his age group in the course of normal activities may try to achieve this goal by daring thefts or defying the authority of the teacher. A man discharged from his job may try to get even with his former boss by circulating rumors about the latter's honesty or incompetence, while another person might conceivably react to his discharge by attempting to set fire to his ex-employer's home or place of business. In other words, the person whose behavior has gone beyond socially acceptable limits may be motivated by the same needs and desires as is the normal person, but repeated failures have led him to resort to extreme measures in order to attain his goals. One might characterize the mentally abnormal as individuals who with some degree of frequence or regularity resort to these extremes of behavior in their efforts to satisfy their own needs and desires. It is the behavior which deviates from standards of social acceptability rather than the unusual nature of the needs and desires.

The Causes of Mental Abnormality

No conclusive statement regarding the causes of mental abnormality can be made at the present time. Doubtless the most popular explanation is heredity, but the evidence available at the present time does not lend much support to the view that this is either the only causal factor or even the most important one. In addition to heredity other possible contributing factors include physiological disturbances, toxic conditions, damage to the central nervous system and many other possible sources of disturbance in the individual's relationships with other people. Perhaps the most widely held point of view today is that the determining factor in the majority of cases lies within the experience of the individual, i.e., the deviant behavior is the way the individual has learned to deal with his own problems of living. The various habits and skills which make it possible for each of us to live comfortably and harmoniously with others are, for the most part, learned. We must learn to control our tempers, to distinguish our own possessions from those of others, and in general to behave in accordance with socially accepted standards. However, habits which are liabilities can be acquired just as readily as socially effective ones. One may learn to use temper tantrums as a means of getting things, or trip a competitor if that appears to be the only way of winning a race. Stealing candy bars and giving them to friends is a way of obtaining recognition in one's age group, just as is being the best passer in football, or flashing the biggest "roll" later on in life. To blame heredity alone for such behavior is to fail to appreciate the urgency of certain needs and the varied avenues through which these needs may be satisfied.

Society protects itself from individuals who persistently resort to unacceptable modes of behavior by providing for their removal from society either temporarily or permanently. Our penal institutions, state hospitals, homes for the mentally deficient, and others are designed to serve a dual purpose—treatment and rehabilitation when possible, and permanent removal from society when indicated. It is to be noted that although the behavior of the mentally disturbed individual may take a great variety of forms, that which is most threatening to other individuals or property, hostile and aggressive actions, are the most likely to be matters of concern to law enforcement officers. From the point of view of behavior pathology the person who is so afraid of other people that he carefully avoids them at all times may be just as pathological as is the hostile and aggressive person, but such behavior is much less threatening to life or property, so he is less likely to be the object of a complaint to the authorities.

In view of the fact that there are no simple and direct ways of distinguishing the individual who commits an offense as an expression of his mental disorder from the person who commits the same offense in the absence of an underlying disorder, some appreciation of the area under discussion is probably to the advantage of all concerned. It is to contribute to this appreciation that the following discussion is designed.

EXAMPLES OF MENTAL DISORDERS

Mental Retardation

Mental retardation is a failure to develop, intellectually and otherwise, at a rate comparable to other individuals within the same age group. All gradations of mental retardation are found, ranging from the almost complete helplessness of idiocy to a level of ability scarcely below that of the average person. Those with extremely limited ability reveal so clearly their lack of development and inability to manage themselves in the simplest aspects of community living that an appropriate disposition of the case can usually be made with little difficulty. Institutional care is indicated, in such instances, if and when the family is unable, for any reason, to provide the care and supervision needed. However, those individuals whose levels of ability more nearly approximate the average or dull within a community are more frequent community problems. Their retardation is not conspicuous so they are expected to handle situations as adequately as others of their own age group, which they are quite unable to do. However, it is to be noted that it is their relative social incompetence which makes them community problems, not merely the presence of mental retardation to an appreciable degree.

In many instances the presence of mental retardation to a significant degree may be suspected on the basis of observations of their daily behavior. Such children are usually retarded in their progress in school, providing promotions are made on the basis of accomplishment rather than on the duration of attendance. It is not unusual to find a 14-year-old retarded child doing work of approximately third grade difficulty. Their interests and play activities are likely to be like those of children much younger than themselves; they are less able to make discriminations and to use good judgment in practical life situations, such as those involving the ownership of toys, etc., or the avoidance of dangers in traffic or play. As adults such persons may be quite successful in work of a simple sort which involves little judgment or planning. Many find useful and satisfying places in our society, managing their own affairs with reasonable success and prudence. For example, a mentally retarded man has for years held a position as janitor and general handy-man in a small office building, paying his taxes, supporting his family and in general behaving in such a manner that he is considered a good citizen of his community.

In view of the above it becomes apparent that mentally retarded individuals are not innately perverse and naturally prone to criminal acts. The explanations for the fact that some become useful citizens and others become chronic delinquents or criminals are doubtless as numerous and varied as for the same differences among those of average or superior intelligence. However, many of the mentally retarded are exposed to unfavorable influences and conditions not ordinarily experienced by normal individuals. Many have mentally retarded parents who are themselves so limited that they are quite incapable of providing even the normal amount of supervision and direction, and less able to give the special attention and care needed by such children. In addition, these parents often serve as extremely poor examples for their children, so that in reality the children whose limitations should be compensated for by carefully planned and thorough training actually receive even less adequate preparation for social living than most of those not so limited.

A second factor of importance is that the retarded child, or adult, may be so suggestible and anxious to please that he is made the "goat" by others. Failing to appreciate fully dangers and consequences, he may be induced to do things which the others would not dare attempt, and if caught the offender is abandoned to his own devices for explaining away his misbehavior. Such a boy may be encouraged to steal candy or money, and when caught his limited ability and the circumstances at the time are not given reasonable consideration. Mentally retarded girls are not infrequently introduced to sexual activities by brighter individuals who feel secure in their own knowledge and her ignorance, knowing full well that their own denials of complicity will far out-weigh the accusations of those so exploited.

A third factor is the irritability developed by many due in no small part to the by-products of their failure to compete successfully either in the schoolroom or playground. Many are given rather heartless nicknames, such as "dummy," "wooden-head" and others equally uncomplimentary, and in addition they have the upsetting experience of being the constant victims of pranks and jokes which are not in the least amusing to them. Such experiences contribute to the development of a degree of irritability which may lead them to strike back, often with a violence appropriate to their lack of judgment and self-restraint.

The problem of dealing with the mentally retarded offender is a difficult one unless the line of least resistance is taken, namely immediate institutional care. As is true with other offenders, however, this step should be the last resort. The fact that retarded persons do have some potential for successful and useful living in our society indicates that initial efforts should be directed toward this goal. In most communities there are public and/or private agencies which can be helpful both in arranging an adequate appraisal of the individual's potentialities which is of primary importance, and also in using the resources of the community for his benefit, if such steps are indicated. In many instances such measures will prevent a recurrence of the same or other offenses, without resorting to the easiest but most drastic measures.

Psychopathic Personality

Another group of individuals who frequently must be dealt with by law enforcement officers are those called Psychopathic Personalities (sometimes known as Constitutional Psychopaths, Psychopathic Deviates, etc.). These individuals exhibit a consistent inability to adapt themselves adequately to society, but at the same time they fail to show the typical characteristics of seriously disturbed mental patients, and are not mentally retarded. Despite the superior ability they often have they are apparently quite unable or unwilling to conform to socially acceptable standards of behavior. Their deviant behavior is usually followed persistently despite the difficulties they encounter and the punishment administered when caught. They are irresponsible, often reacting in a manner which suggests that they feel themselves above any personal obligations to others or to society as a whole. For example, the son of highly regarded parents began to steal at an early age, no one knows just how early. Frequently he stole money, but often the things he took were of no practical value to him, as was evidenced by the fact that he usually destroyed his loot or buried it in an out-of-the-way place. He was caught on several occasions, but he not only expressed no regret or remorse but was quite unresponsive to the efforts of his parents and others to come to some understanding of his behavior. As he grew older he became more clever, and his thefts were detected less often. Because he possessed many attractive personal characteristics he was well liked and able to make friends easily, but he felt no strong attachments to them. He maintained friendly relationships as long as it was to his advantage to do so, following which he ignored his erstwhile friends completely. This behavior persisted through both high school and college. He was a brilliant student and maintained a high scholastic average, but at the same time he expressed more or less openly his contempt for his parents, teachers and acquaintances who lived ordinary and unexciting lives of social respectability. During these years he was arrested several times for larceny, but took a very light-hearted view of his offenses, knowing that his family would make full restitution and thus avoid prosecution. He explained one of his stealing escapades as an effort to demonstrate to the people of the community that the police force was made up of "dumb cops" (although they had caught him in the act, so to speak, on several occasions!). The tears and appeals of his parents, jail sentences, and hospitalization for psychiatric study were laughed off, and he continued on his erratic way, a bright, clever and unscrupulous man who could see no possible advantages in becoming an accepted and respected member of society.

A somewhat different type of behavior was observed in an individual who from childhood on was a misfit in his family. He lived at home until he went to college, but always considered the other members of his family dull and uninteresting. In college he made superior marks in his courses, but also achieved something of a reputation as an excessively critical person who frankly admitted that he was too bright to learn much from his instructors. While a student he experimented with both drugs and alcohol, but abandoned the former in order to concentrate his attention on the latter. After graduation he worked spasmodically at the profession for which he had prepared, but he had three central interests in his life to which he devoted the maximum possible time: drinking, women, and driving at excessive speeds on the highway. He changed positions as frequently as his more important interests and activities required. He married but was divorced within a short time when his wife found that she was sharing him with several other women, each of whom thought herself to be the only woman in his life. He had several serious accidents from each of which he emerged unscathed. He had a long record of arrests for drunkenness, reckless driving, driving while intoxicated, and other similar offenses, but the resulting fines and jail sentences had no noticeable effect on his behavior. For years he ignored his family completely, at one time refusing to provide them with much needed financial assistance, although he could well afford the needed help, offering the explanation that his parents had done nothing for him, so why should he do anything for them! Truth and honesty were characteristics which were admirable in other people, but since they did not serve his own purposes he made little effort to maintain for himself any observable standards in these areas. Despite the impression that might be created by this description he was a poised and polished man, well informed and congenial when he chose to be, but over a period of time completely undependable, unpredictable and irresponsible.

The above examples are cited to illustrate some of the characteristics of psychopathic personalities. The variability of their behavior makes an adequate description practically impossible, but in general it can be said that they are egocentric to the extent that they feel that their own pleasures and satisfactions are of such importance that social acceptability and conformance are of slight consequence. Many are bright, with an ability to be smooth, persuasive and congenial when it is to their advantage to make an impression, but unscrupulous and lacking in any fundamental feeling for family or friends when their own interests and those of others are not in accord. When in a tight spot many will express great remorse, but at the first opportunity will pursue their own desires and inclinations as enthusiastically as before.

These are difficult individuals with whom to deal. As previously mentioned they are not mentally retarded, and do not exhibit the commonly observed symptoms of serious mental disorder, but on the other hand they are not responsive to the customary forms of social regulation. In most states it is difficult to hospitalize such persons, except for diagnosis or observation, as they obviously do not fall within the legal definition of "insane," as this term implies a condition in which the individual is unable to distinguish between right and wrong. Psychopathic personalities readily recognize such distinctions, but do not apply them to their own behavior. The law enforcement officer can probably do little more than obtain psychiatric assistance when such cases are encountered in the hope that a diagnostic study will provide knowledge which will aid him in subsequent cases of a similar nature, or future encounters with the same person.

Compulsive Behavior

Another form of behavior disorder which at times involves the violation of law is compulsive behavior. A compulsion is an irresistible impulse to perform a specific type of act. The reasons for this repeated pattern of behavior may be as baffling to the person as to friends and relatives, i.e., the individual experiences an unaccountable but progressively increasing level of tension until relief is obtained when the activity is carried out. The basis for this kind of behavior lies deep within the personality structure of the person, ordinarily involving factors about which the individual knows little or nothing.

Compulsive behavior takes a great variety of forms, varying from activities which have little significance to the community, such as the compulsive cleanliness of the housewife who rushes for the dust rag at the sight of a particle of dust, to behavior which constitutes a violation of laws. As examples of the latter one might mention kleptomania, or compulsive stealing, and pyromania, the compulsive setting of fires. The person with kleptomania is quite incapable of accounting for his behavior other than by reporting that he becomes increasingly tense and anxious until relief is obtained by engaging in a theft. Often the objects stolen have little value in themselves, but are of symbolic value to the individual. The purchase of the object would not provide the same release of tension indicating that it is not the object which is of primary significance but rather the object plus the fact that it was stolen. They are often contrite and tearful when apprehended, but in the absence of adequate psychiatric treatment they will likely return to the same pattern of behaving when similar tension and anxiety are experienced. Fines and jail sentences are not likely to be effectual in altering this recurring pattern. These are psychiatric problems, and anything short of appropriate treatment will be ineffectual, in that attention is being directed to the act itself rather than the basic cause. The same generalizations will hold for other kinds of compulsive behavior, setting fires, exhibitionism, etc.

In this same connection care must be exercised to avoid providing the apprehended shoplifter with the type of excuse which will aid him in avoiding the penalty for his theft. Knowledge of the kind and value of objects stolen, and the individual's record of previous offenses may prove to be helpful in distinguishing the two, but in the last analysis the basic difference is in the area of motivation, and its exploration requires professional service.

Offenses Involving Heterosexual Behavior

One of the most complex areas of behavior pathology is that related to sexual behavior. In order to gain a better understanding of the setting in which such offenses occur it is important to consider briefly the somewhat unique and ambiguous position of sexual needs and sexual behavior in our society. In the first place, sexual needs have a physiological basis, and although their satisfaction is not required for survival or health they have an urgency which must be recognized. A second consideration is the fact that they reach a high level of intensity at a time when their satisfaction cannot ordinarily be achieved in a socially approved manner, during the years of adolescence. Economic obstacles and lengthening period of education and training required for many vocational and professional careers often necessitate a delay in marriage until well into the third decade of life. In theory at least, this is a period during which the individual is supposed to remain oblivious to the urgency of sexual needs and suppress any indication of them in behavior. This is especially true for girls. At the same time there is no lack of stress on the importance and attractiveness of sex. Mention need be made of only a few of many possible examples—the accent on sexual appeal and allure found in many advertisements, the emphasis on romance and the advantages of sexual appeal implicit in the entertainment world and widely circulated reading matter, the theme of much humor that is circulated more or less openly, and in general a pronounced although at times thinly disguised stress on sex as glamorous, pleasurable, and advantageous in achieving certain goals in life. There are also opportunities to observe the fact that all of the verbally supported conventions and taboos are not adhered to, as evidenced by instances of provocative behavior among adults, and the success of the "beautiful but dumb" secretary. In contrast to this the attraction of the forbidden, the embarrassment of parents when even perfectly legitimate questions about sex are asked, and the absorbing conversations which take place beyond the hearing of parents lend further attractiveness to this area of life.

In the face of such contradictions and inconsistencies adolescents especially are supposed to conform to an ideal of behavior which they do not see reflected in their surroundings. In addition, there is no lack of opportunity for adolescents to explore the possibilities of sex first hand if they so desire. Many sexual offenses within this age group take place in a setting of this kind, which does not excuse the offender, but provides a basis for appreciating the fact that all such offenders are not base and entirely lacking in moral fiber.

An attempt to discuss heterosexual offenses in a reasonably objective manner involves a risk of criticism because of the necessity to view such behavior in a perspective somewhat different from the conventional one. For the purposes of this discussion, however, such an attempt is doubtless warranted. Charges of seduction and rape might well be considered in the light of the individuals involved and the circumstances existing at the time. For example, the seduction of a mentally retarded girl by a normal adult would warrant very different conclusions regarding the offender than if the latter were a mentally retarded adult. Seduction or attempted rape under the influence of soft moonlight, a romantic and sheltered locale, and an even mildly responsive "date" is quite different behavior than the same attempt made toward a strange girl followed down a dark street from a bus stop. In the latter instance we have evidence of malicious intent in flagrant disregard of both the moral and legal restrictions of society, while in the former example, one, or perhaps both individuals were quite unable to exercise their customary self-restraint under the impact of intense emotional stimulation in the absence of the moderating influence of the presence of other people.

Another factor which at times deserves some consideration is the possibility that an accusation of rape may be the result of an active conscience rather than a reflection of the actual course of events at the time of the offense. For example, an adolescent boy was accused of rape by a married woman at least twice his age. It was eventually found that this was not only not rape, but that the initiative in the relationship had been taken by the woman who later became conscience stricken, but not to the point of admitting her share of the responsibility. As is customary, the statements of the accused were dismissed lightly until the truth was finally admitted and the charges withdrawn.

In view of the rigidity of the restrictions, both legal and otherwise, against sexual offenses, especially those involving violence, indications of planning or previous intent are likely to be of special significance. As mentioned previously, an individual may be carried away by the violence of his emotional responses to intense stimulation, resulting in behavior quite inconsistent with his personal standards under normal conditions. However, an individual who deliberately plans a sexual assault or selects as a sex object a child, a mentally retarded or relatively helpless individual is, by the very fact of the premeditation, revealing an indifference to both the moral and legal requirements for social living. Such offenses may be committed by sadistically inclined persons who derive satisfaction from the helplessness and suffering of their victims as well as from the release of sexual tensions.

As mentioned in a previous section, psychopathic personality characteristically provides the background of irresponsibility and indifference to social obligations for repeated sexual offenses. Occasionally elderly men who are showing the characteristic effects of senility may commit such offenses, especially against children, as their moral and ethical standards tend to deteriorate as part of their general decline. During this period their behavior may be quite out of keeping with their previous standards and conduct. Occasionally the mentally retarded may become involved in such behavior because of their lack of judgment and awareness of the consequences of their acts, and their tendency to act on the impulse of the moment under relatively intense stimulation.

From the point of view of the law enforcement officer an important consideration is the relative likelihood that such offenses will be repeated. Although such a prediction cannot be made with complete accuracy a review of previous behavior may reveal valuable information regarding the individual's relative conformance to socially accepted patterns of conduct. Those offenses which seem to be primarily a function of the circumstances of the moment in the course of which the person has apparently deviated from his customary standards of conduct might be viewed in a somewhat different light from those involving offenders with a history of unresponsiveness to the demands of social living. The latter are much more likely to be poorer risks than the former.

There are other forms of sexual behavior which, although less serious in their consequences, doubtless are the basis for many complaints to law enforcement agencies. Examples of such behavior are the activities of the exhibitionist, who exposes himself to members of the opposite sex, and "Peeping Toms" who peer through bedroom or bathroom windows when the opportunity is present. In many instances such activities are forms of compulsive behavior, as previously described, and constitute a satisfying substitute for normal forms of sexual behavior, not preludes to normal sexual responses. Such behavior is of much greater significance if it appears as a recurring pattern in an adult than if it is a casual and more or less accidental act of an adolescent. In the former case it is likely to be evidence of a basic disturbance in the personality structure of the offender, which will likely continue to express itself in similar substitute behavior. In the latter case the attractiveness of the forbidden, keen imagination and curiosity, and an especially inviting opportunity may be sufficient to overcome one's resistance. In the two instances the measures necessary to prevent a recurrence of the offense will obviously be different if both the welfare of the individual and the protection of society are given the consideration they deserve.

Homosexuality

A persistent but infrequently mentioned problem involving sexual behavior is homosexuality. The homosexual is an individual of either sex whose preference for a sex object is a member of the same rather than the opposite sex. A number of such individuals either forego the exercise of their preferred type of sexual activity or are so secretive about it that the existence of the problem is not recognized in many communities.

Nevertheless, homosexuals are to be found in most communities, more or less well organized into their own social groups, usually limited to individuals like themselves. It is found among individuals of both sexes, at all social, economic and occupational levels. As long as they confine their activities to members of their own or similar groups their atypical preferences may escape notice, even by normally oriented friends and acquaintances. It is important to bear in mind the fact that the majority of such individuals do not conform to the popular notions of a depraved person or reveal by their appearance or mannerisms the existence of their abnormal sexual orientation. On the contrary, homosexually inclined persons may marry, attain recognition for competence in their trades, business or professions, and become prominent citizens.

In view of the marked aversion toward homosexuality in our society such individuals customarily exercise caution to avoid revealing their tendencies, so the effeminate man who suggests a homosexual orientation through manner and dress is the exception rather than the rule.

The causes of homosexuality are not definitely known. It has been suggested that it is a condition based on constitutional makeup or aberrations in the structure and/or function of the sexual mechanism, but these do not appear to be adequate as causal factors. Another view is that it develops out of the individual's own background, so that whether one develops a normal or a homosexual orientation is determined by personal experience. It would be comforting to know that the true causes were constitutional or physiological, because under these conditions the number of potential homosexuals would be severely limited. On the other hand, if most homosexuals are as they are because they have learned to satisfy their sexual needs and release sexual tensions in that manner then there is an obligation to eliminate as far as possible the opportunities for such learning.

Not all individuals who engage in homosexual activities are confirmed homosexuals. Some individuals have a few such experiences and then maintain exclusively heterosexual interests from that time on, while some engage in both homosexual and heterosexual relationships over long periods of time. There are other individuals who have homosexual tendencies which they may or may not recognize, who never engage in homosexual activities, and do not show any significant interest in heterosexual behavior, maintaining their contacts with both sexes on a strictly platonic level.

The offenses committed by homosexuals are in many respects similar to those committed by individuals with a normal sexual orientation. Many homosexuals establish relatively permanent relationships with one sexual partner, and feelings of affection and possessiveness develop similar to those which exist in a normal marriage. The parallel can be carried even further in that they experience jealousy, and their reactions to unfaithfulness, occasionally lead to the same kinds of violence that may emerge from heterosexual attachments. Many develop considerable hostility toward other members of society because of the necessity for secrecy and the obvious aversion shown by others once their homosexuality is recognized or admitted. This makes the task of the investigator difficult as those who may be familiar with the circumstances are reluctant to implicate members of the group and thus reveal their own part in its activities.

As long as homosexual activities are confined to groups made up of confirmed homosexuals this type of behavior is not likely to be brought to the attention of the enforcement officer. However, homosexual seductions and the recruitment of sexual partners among adolescents are at least as serious, in terms of social consequences, as similar heterosexual offenses. As is true in the latter cases, those who deliberately and with premeditation seek a sex object among children or others who are less likely to be able to cope with such advances constitute the most urgent problems. Such behavior reflects a basic disregard for social standards so marked that a repetition of the same or similar acts is not unlikely. Once homosexuality is well established as a pattern of sexual preference and behavior it is likely to be a permanent aspect of the person's life, not readily changed either by punishment or treatment.

Amnesia

Amnesia is a type of disorder which may result in behavior of concern to the enforcement officer, but not necessarily involving a crime of any sort. Amnesia is loss of memory, which may be so limited that it escapes notice or so extensive that the person's knowledge of his own identity is lost. The latter cases produce such bewilderment that they are usually brought to the attention of police either on their own initiative or when their condition is noted by others. For example, a man riding on a bus caused no slight commotion among the passengers when he informed the driver that he did not know who he was or where he was going. A subsequent examination revealed that he had lost all knowledge of his past and was completely unaware of who he was, where he had come from, and his destination. Such conditions may follow injury, especially head injuries, or may be the consequence of severe emotional shock. In such cases medical attention should be provided as quickly as possible. In most cases they respond rather promptly to proper treatment, and the greatest service is to provide this immediately. Questioning, especially under pressure, may be harmful and actually delay recovery rather than hasten it.

At this point it should be mentioned that there are malingerers who may try to avoid the responsibility for their actions by claiming a loss of memory. This poses the difficult problem of uncovering the malingering but accomplishing this in such a manner that the well-being of the individual will not be jeopardized if the amnesia is genuine. The difficulties encountered will, of course, be a function of the knowledge and resourcefulness of the malingerer. Doubtless the safest procedure, both to protect the amnesia victim and to detect the malingerer, is to proceed in accordance with competent medical advice and assistance.

MORE EXTREME FORMS OF MENTAL DISORDERS

General Considerations

There are other forms of mental disorder which, in their acute stages, are marked by behavior more readily recognized as evidence that the individual is seriously disturbed. There is the rather popular notion that such persons rush about yelling and screaming, engaging in malicious and/or destructive behavior, and with a strange and wild gleam in their eyes. It would be a great convenience if this were the case as identification would be an easy matter, and the required care could be provided promptly. Unfortunately, there are no such obvious means of identification. As we have pointed out previously, the only dependable clues to the presence of mental disorder are the quality and appropriateness of behavior in life situations, so we might expect the more seriously disturbed to reveal more conspicuous impairments in their ability to meet everyday life situations. Actually this is often the case, but in many other instances the evidences are subtle and inconspicuous.

Another popular notion is that serious mental disturbances develop quite suddenly, that is an individual may be perfectly normal up to the time when "something snaps," following which he is completely abnormal. However, the usual course of development is much slower, perhaps covering a fairly extensive period of time during which increasingly erratic and unusual behavior has been

PSYCHOLOGY FOR LAW ENFORCEMENT OFFICERS

unnoticed or actually ignored. Ideally, care should be provided for such persons before the disorder has progressed to the point that anti-social behavior occurs, but unfortunately the onset of acute symptoms cannot be predicted with any such degree of accuracy. This is a little like saying that if we could only tell which cars would be involved in serious accidents on a given day those drivers could leave their cars at home and thus avoid damage to the cars and perhaps personal injury. Since such foresight is not possible situations must be dealt with as they arise.

Schizophrenia

Probably the most common type of severe mental disorder is schizophrenia (or dementia praecox). The extent of its possible effects on behavior is indicated by the fact that there are approximately one-quarter million such patients in our state hospitals. The variation in behavior from case to case is so marked that it is not possible to give a brief and concise description which is adequate, but in general it is marked by a preference for being alone rather than in the company of others. They lack normal emotional responsiveness to other people and the events in their surroundings, tending to be preoccupied with their own inner world of thoughts, ideas and fantasies. There are disturbances in thinking which are frequently subtle, but may be reflected in odd and peculiar explanations for events, and deriving unusual meanings from their experience. For example, one such patient was positive that he would die when he reached the age of 24 because a friend whose first name was the same as his own died at that age. They may report experiences which are obviously hallucinations, but they accept them as real, as was the case with the young man who reported frequent visits by the angel Gabriel in the course of which the wisdom of the ages was imparted to him.

Schizophrenia occurs in several forms only two of which will be described here. The simple form is marked by a general apathy and indifference toward the world and the events taking place there. The individual shows no zest for life, no animation or desire to achieve in the ordinary sense of the word, is emotionally unresponsive, accepting the ups and downs of life with indifference.

Many become the chronic drifters and ne'er-do-wells in society, taking the line of least resistance at the moment, and often gravitating to begging, petty thefts, prostitution and the like without reluctance or remorse. They may be incarcerated for their offenses or forced to move from one community to another, but in any case they will likely continue in their aimless and shiftless mode of living. From the point of view of social regulation the chief importance of this group is the likelihood that offenses will be repeated and dealt with separately rather than recognizing a pattern of behavior suggesting the presence of a mental disorder. They are infrequently committed to hospitals, but are punished in the customary manner which provides relief to society only during the period of their incarceration.

Paranoid schizophrenia is another form which may produce behavior of serious consequence in the community. Such individuals are similarly dominated by their own ideas and unique meanings derived from experience, but these consist of convictions that they are being persecuted. They become convinced that others are plotting against them and/or attempting to deprive them of their rights, and as a consequence they are chronically suspicious and defensive. They may lodge repeated complaints with the local police about neighbors, placing on the behavior of the latter interpretations appropriate to their own persecutory ideas. As long as this suspiciousness results only in guarded and defensive behavior little real concern may be shown by others. However, such individuals may become aggressive and attempt to retaliate for the alleged persecution by making frequent complaints to the police, filing lawsuits, or through actual personal violence. For example, one such person assaulted a judge who had dismissed a suit in which a series of grievances had been cited which obviously existed only in the delusional system of the assailant. Until the assault he had been a respected member of the community although many acquaintances were aware of the fact that he was extremely suspicious of others and felt that people had grudges against him.

As in this example a sudden and perhaps violent outburst may be the first clear indication of threatening behavior as the significance and potentiality of their consistent suspiciousness has not been appreciated. Even though the complaints are found to be without foundation, a casual or facetious attitude about them may accomplish nothing more than add to future difficulties. In other words, the characteristics of the person who makes the complaints may be as important as the complaints themselves.

The other forms of schizophrenia are not lacking in a potential for violence and crime, but the acute stages are likely to be accompanied by sufficiently bizarre and unsual behavior that an appropriate disposition of the individual can be decided on promptly. Where there are sufficient grounds for suspecting the existence of a mental disturbance medical, and preferably psychiatric, assistance should be obtained as quickly as possible.

Pathological Excitement and Depression

A combination of emotional excitement and excessive activity is found in several disorders, and frequently results in behavior which quite obviously reflects an absence of the customary level of self-control and restraint. Under these conditions the individual is talkative, expanding at length on his own importance, his achievements in the past and grandiose plans for the future. This type of reaction may vary in intensity from a mild form in the course of which the individual appears to be unusually energetic, enthusiastic and optimistic, to a more extreme type of behavior which may well be characterized as frenzied. In view of their boundless energy and excitement they may become destructive and/or combative, but not with the same malicious intent and planning observable in certain other disorders. Their apparent good nature may be quite superficial, hiding a basic irritability which appears when their expansive statements are questioned or efforts are made to restrain their activity. An inappropriately heightened activity level and excitement may be caused by a variety of conditions and their appearance is indicative of a need for immediate care, both for the welfare of the individual and the protection of others. Medical assistance should be obtained promptly so that a suitable course of action can be decided upon in view of the condition of the individual.

A condition somewhat the opposite of the above is a depressive reaction. This is marked by a reduction in activity level and speech production, and feelings of depression and worthlessness. In the more mild stages this may amount only to a general slowing down of the individual with an accompanying feeling of pessimism and personal inadequacy, but in the more extreme forms there is a more marked reduction in activity together with feelings of despair and depression. They may feel so utterly worthless, and the future so completely hopeless that an attempt to end their misery may be made. Self condemnation may lead them to confess crimes which they did not commit. In one such instance a woman sobbingly confessed a long list of legal and moral offenses which careful investigation proved to be complete fabrications. As is characteristic, she ascribed to herself the basest motives which had led to these flagrant violations of social and moral codes.

The most pressing problem presented by these cases is the very real suicide potential. Great caution is needed in this regard, as they are capable of suicide attempts using any possible available means. As is true for excited individuals, the seriously depressed are in need of prompt medical attention so that the indicated treatment may be instituted as quickly as possible.

CONCLUDING DISCUSSION

The above does not constitute an exhaustive discussion of the behavior of mentally disordered persons which may be a matter of concern to a law enforcement officer, neither is it to be considered a guide enabling one to recognize specific forms of behavior pathology. Rather, it is intended to emphasize the fact that such disorders do play a significant and frequently unrecognized part in the difficulties encountered in the enforcement of the legal and social codes of a community. The officer who is aware of these possibilities and sensitive to even gross indications which at times might justifiably lead him to suspect mental abnormality may function more effectively in his capacity than would otherwise be possible.

The mentally retarded boy who is caught peering into a bedroom window might well be handled quite differently than would the adult who shows no evidences of retardation. A realization that the sobbing, forlorn man may be seriously depressed and a potential suicide rather than just thoroughly drunk might conceivably save his life.

In cases of behavior pathology society should and does take into account the condition of the offender, and the law enforcement officer is an important medium through whom this may operate. The chief responsibility for this lies within other professional groups, but in many instances someone other than the abnormal person himself must assume the initiative. A parallel might be drawn between this kind of functioning and that advocated in newspapers and magazines relating to the identification of the early signs of serious organic disorders, such as cancer. The public is encouraged to be sensitive to certain signs which may indicate the presence of cancer, not for the purposes of self diagnosis but as signs of the need for professional medical service. So it is hoped that our discussion and examples will aid the officer in becoming more keenly aware of certain frequently overlooked aspects of behavior which are closely related to his own sphere of activity, and sensitive to certain indications that this behavior warrants appropriate professional attention. This type of functioning requires the exercise of sound judgment, and it is hoped that this discussion will contribute something of value in making this judgment more discriminating.

REFERENCES

Cameron, N. and Magaret, A.: *Behavior Pathology*. New York, Houghton Mifflin Company, 1951. Abnormal psychology presented from a bio-social point of view.

Lindner, R. M. and Seliger, R. V.: *Handbook of Correctional Psychology*. New York, Philosophical Library, 1947. A collection of essays on many topics of interest to law enforcement officers.

Page, J. P.: *Abnormal Psychology*, New York, McGraw-Hill Book Company, 1947. This is an excellent general text.

Thorpe, L. P. and Katz, B.: *The Psychology of Behavior*. New York, The Ronald Press Company, 1948. Chapter 14. This is a good general text.

White, R. W.: *The Abnormal Personality*. New York, The Ronald Press Company, 1948. A discussion of abnormal psychology of interest to the lay reader.

Chapter 10

JUVENILE DELINQUENCY

By

GEORGE J. DUDYCHA

WHAT IS JUVENILE DELINQUENCY?

JUVENILE DELINQUENCY is generally defined in one of two ways, according to the view of the definer. The official view, usually considered narrow in scope, defines juvenile delinquency as any violation of a city ordinance or of a law by a child between the ages of seven and 16 or 18 or 20 or 21 according to the statutory age in the given state. According to this view, a juvenile delinquent is a child who not only violates a law, but one who gets caught doing so, and against whom legal action is taken. By implication, then, a child who is sufficiently clever to avoid detection when he violates a law, or whose parents are sufficiently influential to effect an unofficial disposal of the case, is not a delinquent.

The social view holds that juvenile delinquency is any repeated offense against society, that is punishable as a crime when committed by an adult, and certain non-specific forms of undesirable behavior such as persistent truancy, running away, stubbornness, and the like. This view stresses the fact that the child is persistent in his antisocial behavior, rather than that he is detected or apprehended.

Emphasis on the persistence of the antisocial behavior is important. Many children do antisocial things once which, if continued, are delinquent. Children do steal fruit, take trinkets from store counters, mistreat animals, trample flower gardens, break windows, deflate tires, set fire to buildings, sneak into theaters, indulge in sexual experimentation *once* and yet are not judged delinquent. In one case a small boy even sent a threatening letter through the mail, which is a federal offense. He observed a group of older boys playing minor pranks on an old recluse in the village, and decided to do something on his own. In the Post Office, he wrote a threatening note to the old man (without removing his gloves) dropped it into the slot and awaited developments. Needless to say, the old man demanded protection. His house was watched. The FBI investigated. No clues were found. One small boy, scared half to death, confided in no one. Neither did he repeat the experience. Although he committed a federal offense, he was *never known* as a delinquent child.

It is not isolated offenses that make a child delinquent. Rather it is his attitude towards others, that which motivates him, and the adequacy of his adjustment to social situations and demands that is important. It is the total pattern of his behavior that makes him a delinquent—a pattern of hostility and nonconformity to people and to social institutions that is motivated largely by fear and frustration.

THE NATURE AND RANGE OF JUVENILE DELINQUENCY

Behavior that is classed as delinquent runs the gamut from persistent stubbornness and truancy to rape and murder, from petty stealing to prostitution. Boys, on the whole, commit acts of violence, steal, and commit offenses against property; girls, on the other hand, are more often charged with sex offenses, being ungovernable, running away from home, and the like.

Statistics on the number of delinquents are at best very incomplete and inaccurate. They are an enumeration of the children who were caught or were reported. They are based on the number of arrests recorded, court cases heard, or commitments made, because these are easily counted. Some cases never do become a statistic because they are dealt with on a counseling rather than a legal basis, or because someone desires to protect the child's future, or because of the influence of parents or officials. Extensive as the problem of juvenile delinquency appears to be according to statistical reports, it is only a partial picture. Therefore, to think in strictly legal terms is to close our eyes to the many instances of social maladjustment and personality inadequacy that seldom come to the attention of the authorities. If our interest in children stems from a desire to prevent delinquency, or to decrease the likelihood of its continuance in those in which it is already present, then we must look beyond the strictly legal point of view and consider the child as a *behavior problem.*

This behavior problem is not to be confused with the act that labels the youth a juvenile delinquent. Rather, it must be conceived as the more or less continuous maladjustment that reaches back into the early life of the individual, and that usually becomes increasingly evident as the child grows older. If the final delinquent act of stealing or destruction, or whatever else it may be, is to be avoided, the child's behavior problem must be recognized and treated early. In other words, we must recognize the symptoms of delinquency long before delinquency actually appears. This is not easy. Most people think it incredible that the behavior of a three- or four-year-old may be predisposing him toward delinquency at a later date. They are often reluctant to accept it in the eight- and 10-year-old. Yet each delinquent does tread a path that leads to evident delinquency. Therefore it is imperative that the path the child is following be recognized before he has gone too far, and that he be directed into paths that lead to wholesome social adjustment.

A boy who regularly sneaks into basketball games, and who smokes cigarettes stolen from his father, entered the bold racket of selling parking space on a *public* dead-end street, at a dollar a spot, to people going to a basketball game. He intimidated people into paying by refusing to guarantee that they would have air in their tires on their return. Because of the shortage of parking space and his threat, people paid, never realizing that they were contributing to his delinquency. This youngster is quite certainly on the path to delinquency, yet the seriousness of his behavior goes unrecognized.

SPOTTING THE CAUSE

The layman, like the professional worker, is interested in what lies behind delinquency. Their viewpoints in this regard, however, differ. The layman usually looks for *the* cause. He believes that somehow or somewhere there is *one factor* on which the child's delinquency, yes, all delinquency, can be blamed. The psychologist, the sociologist, and the criminologist, on the other hand, look for a pattern of factors rather than a single cause.

Heredity as a Cause

A generation and more ago heredity was cited as the cause of delinquency. One was a drunkard because his father and his grandfather before him were drunkards. Drunkenness was "in their blood." Not only drunkenness, but other crimes as well were attributed to heredity. One was a *born criminal.* Being a born criminal he could be identified by certain stigmata—peculiar structural characteristics, facial features, or body build. In accord with this view, the hope for improvement was in incarceration and extermination.

The early genetic studies of such families as the Jukes, the Kallikaks, and others, were given in support of the view that heredity is the direct cause of delinquency. Were not most of the members of these families vagrants, ne'er-do-wells, drunkards, prostitutes, and petty criminals? Were they not descended from the same ancestors? The answers to these and similar questions seemed to strengthen the view that heredity is the cause of delinquency even though many valid objections can be raised against this view today.

Intelligence as a Cause

Another favorite explanation of juvenile delinquency is the *lack* of intelligence. Here again the Kallikak family is frequently cited as evidence. Martin Kallikak, in the eighteenth century, had an illicit affair with a (supposedly) feebleminded barmaid whose child and later descendants were not only for the most part drunkards, prostitutes and thieves, but feebleminded as well. This association of mental weakness with delinquency in the Kallikak family led people to infer that the delinquency was *caused* by the barmaid's feeblemindedness. This interpretation leaves out of account all the other many factors that also operated in this family.

More recent studies of the measured intelligence of juvenile delinquents have also been used to support the view that delinquency is caused by the lack of intelligence. Some students of juvenile delinquents report average IQ's as low as 82, where 90 to 110 is average. Others report averages of 85, 87, 92, and 98. All agree that the range of IQ's is broad—some are high (140 and above) others are low (70 and below)—and that there are substantially more delinquents in the feebleminded category than in the gifted group.

Before one draws a hasty conclusion from the above observations, one must remember that these IQ averages are based on children whose brush with the law was of such severity or frequency that their behavior was the subject of court examination and record. These figures obviously do not include the IQ's of those children whose acts are also antisocial but who have not been detected or reported. If the intelligence quotients of these children who are not *statistic delinquents* were included, the average might be changed. Some people think that the average would be raised.

Intelligence is a factor in the daily life and adjustment of everyone—the delinquent is no exception. It is true that some children do get into trouble because they lack intelligence, but others get into equally serious difficulties even though their intelligence is superior. *Actually there is no evidence that delinquency is due to feeblemindedness.*

Poverty as a Cause

When a law enforcement officer deals with a number of delinquents on the same day, each of whom has come from a background of extreme poverty, he is very apt to conclude that *poverty* is the cause of their delinquency. He reasons that poverty strengthens and enhances the drive for the luxuries as well as the necessities of life. Since these strong desires go unsatisfied because of poverty, he presumes that this causes the youth to steal and do other antisocial things. In part, he is correct. However when he generalizes to the extent of thinking "no poverty, no delinquency," he is guilty of oversimplification.

Delinquency is commonly associated with poverty and with slums. Therefore, some people are convinced that the way to decrease delinquency is to replace slum areas with low-cost housing areas. Unfortunately, it is all too often true, that the people who are dispossessed as the result of a slum-clearance project are not the ones who are resettled in the area after the project is completed. The dispossessed are usually forced to invade other deteriorating areas with the almost inevitable result of creating another slum area there. Desirable as slum clearance is, it does not decrease poverty, nor does it change radically the mode of life of people. Let us always remember that it is people who create slums—people whose mode of life is unwholesome.

The common association of poverty with delinquency is far from inevitable as various students of juvenile delinquency have shown. Sheldon and Eleanor Glueck in their monumental study, *Unraveling Juvenile Delinquency*, have shown that for every delinquent boy with a background of poverty, a nondelinquent boy with like background can be found. Likewise, Healy and Bronner in their *New Light on Delinquency and Its Treatment* demonstrated that delinquent children can be paired with nondelinquent children, even in the same family. Poverty can be a factor in juvenile delinquency, but *it is not inevitably so.*

The Single-Cause Fallacy

Man always tries to understand and explain things in simple ways; he looks for magic keys that open all locks. Usually these magic keys turn out to be *magic words.* Falling bodies are explained by *gravity*, mothering behavior in animals by *instinct*, and wars by *human nature.* Magic words! When we consider juvenile delinquency we use such magic words as: *heredity, feeblemindedness, poverty*, and the like.

Perhaps it is unfortunate, but nevertheless true, that most of the problems presented by our society have no simple, easy solutions. Juvenile delinquency is no exception. The delinquent act, or series of such acts, is always the culmination of many interacting and interrelated factors. The meaning and significance of each depends on the presence of others. It is this pattern, this complex of factors, that must be understood. It is this fact that makes "unraveling juvenile delinquency" so difficult.

Finally, this use of magic words diverts our attention. To diagnose juvenile delinquency as due to feeblemindedness seems so satisfying, so sophisticated, so final. Unfortunately when we do so, our attention shifts from THE CHILD to HIS feeblemindedness, concerning which we may be able to do very little. It is on the child that we must rivet our attention—the child who is a dynamic *pattern* of motives, interests, desires, loves, hates, loyalties, skills, habits, and ideas. It is THE CHILD that we must seek to help.

SOCIAL FACTORS IN DELINQUENCY

We have pointed out that juvenile delinquency can not be understood in terms of a single cause. Although heredity, feeblemindedness and poverty may be factors (sometimes rather unimportant factors) in juvenile delinquency, they are only aspects or phases of the total pattern of causation. To these we must add various social factors.

Areas in Transition

Juvenile delinquents are not uniformly distributed in the population; they are far more numerous in some areas than in others. In fact some sections of a city are known as *delinquency areas*. Clifford R. Shaw[1] and others who have studied this problem have found that delinquents are most numerous at the center or near the loop area of a city, and that their numbers, in proportion to the population, decrease in successive concentric circles that extend out to the corporate limits of the city and beyond. The areas in which delinquents particularly abound are also known as areas in transition. These areas, which are of two types, are generally on the fringe of the commercial and industrial sections of the city. It is life in these areas that we want to examine further.

Displacement of residential areas by commerce. One type of area in transition comes as the result of the invasion of business and industry into a residential neighborhood. Stores, warehouses and small factories replace some dwellings and isolate others. These changes bring many others in their wake. Population in the area (especially the daytime population) increases, street traffic is heavier, strangers are everywhere. As a result of the removal of

---

[1]Shaw, Clifford R.: *Delinquency Areas*. Chicago, University of Chicago Press, 1929.

some families from the area, friendships are broken, neighborliness deteriorates, interests and activities become more divergent. Tenancy increases; transients come and go; the future becomes more uncertain; resentment against the encroachment of business develops; friction with the newcomers increases, and conflict prevails within and without.

Although all of these changes are important from the standpoint of delinquency, the most important change and the greatest loss sustained by an area in transition is the loss of a neighborhood of somewhat like-minded and more or less well-acquainted people. The presence of business and industry in an area makes for strangeness, conflict and social deterioration. The very foundations of the neighborhood (a social institution) are undermined. As a result the residents of the area, and particularly the children and adolescents, lose that feeling of belonging, that sense of responsibility, that reciprocity of interest and kindliness that characterize a true neighborhood, and that serve as such effective deterrents to delinquency.

From the standpoint of good living the highly commercialized area is the very antithesis of a true neighborhood. Attitudes in such an area tend to be impersonal, selfish, laissez faire. The youth who lives in this area is among distinterested strangers as soon as he is a short distance from his door. These strangers do little to strengthen his inhibitions; instead they may enhance his temptations. Because the youth is left largely to his own inclinations that may lack social discipline, the opportunity for delinquency is great. With the neighborhood and its social restraints gone, the home is left as the chief bulwark against delinquency. Often it is not strong enough to carry this burden alone!

Population changes. A second reason for areas in transition is the influx into a neighborhood of people whose cultural backgrounds, customs and traditions are substantially different from those of the people originally occupying the area. The coming of large numbers of Sicilians, Mexicans, Orientals, Negroes, Jews, or other minority groups, into a neighborhood of people predominantly of North European descent is very apt to result in neighborhood changes. Because of the existence of prejudices, some of the older families move out of the area, leaving more room for the newcomers. Because of the cultural differences between the original and incoming populations, resentment is followed by resistance, and it in turn by outright hostility. Because the two groups do things differently, have different customs, celebrate different holidays, adhere to different standards of behavior, and sometimes use different languages and believe in different religions, there is a lack of understanding, friendliness and desire to cooperate between them.

This social climate of the neighborhood is quickly sensed and adopted by the children and adolescents of the area. Although much of the conflict between the adults is restrained and restricted to name-calling, among the children the conflict is much less restrained and usually much more violent. Child-adult conflicts are also evident. In fact, the way some people "get it back" on their neighbors is through their children.

It is this type of cultural friction, and the lack of a well-integrated neighborhood, that contributes to juvenile delinquency. It is the psychology of the situation that is important. Juvenile delinquency is the outward expression of feelings of frustration, of hostility, of insecurity, and the lack of a feeling of belonging. In the area undergoing cultural change the stabilizing aspects of the neighborhood are definitely weakened, and the opportunity for delinquency increased.

Culture Conflicts between Generations

Another social factor in juvenile delinquency is the conflict between parents and children that grows out of cultural differences between them. Some conflict between parents and children is inevitable and even natural. Their points of view are somewhat different; so are their loyalties and even their standards of conduct. However it is the children of foreign-born parents who seem to experience the most conflict because their culture is distinctly different from that of their parents.

Immigrants who come to this country as adults, or people who grow to maturity in a section of a large city where the language and culture are definitely foreign, do not cut loose from all they

258 PSYCHOLOGY FOR LAW ENFORCEMENT OFFICERS

have known and done in the past, when they become parents, and adopt completely and wholeheartedly the American culture to which their children are constantly exposed. Instead they continue to think and to speak in the mother tongue. They preserve "old country" customs and traditions. They retain their foreign manner-isms. Sometimes they openly resist our American ways of life.

A girl in our culture who falls in love and wishes to marry believes that it is "right" for her to choose whom she will marry. Her foreign-born father, on the other hand, thinks it is equally "right" for him to make the final choice. The boy who seeks to be an artist or a musician finds himself in conflict with parents whose culture places a great premium on manual skill or on busi-ness. The teen-aged girl whose passion is baseball and whose ambi-tion is to be a movie actress finds that her world clashes with her foreign-born mother's world where a girl's destiny is early mar-riage and a large family.

Statistics show repeatedly that the children of foreign-born parents contribute many more than their proportional share of juvenile delinquents. It certainly seems that one of the chief reasons for this is the fact that the children of foreign-born parents are caught betwixt and between two different cultures each of which demands conformity and loyalty. To satisfy the demands of each is difficult and at times impossible. What is right in the one culture may be wrong in the other. These conflicts in children and adolescents that grow out of irreconcilable cultural differences result in feelings of inferiority, skepticism concerning all standards of behavior, an attitude of futility, and an ever-present feeling of frustration and thwarting. Persistent conflict in youth stimulates action. It stimulates action that is often unreasoned and emotion-ally motivated—action that is not infrequently antisocial and delinquent.

PHYSICAL FACTORS IN DELINQUENCY
Glandular Conditions

The endocrine, or ductless glands, that secrete many powerful substances, in extremely small quantities, directly into the blood-stream are essential to the normal growth and regulation of body functions. Because of the relationship of these glands to body function, and of body function to behavior, the malfunction of endocrine glands does at times contribute indirectly to delinquency. One or several glands may function excessively or insufficiently thus disturbing normal balance. Sex functions may, for example, appear unusually early thus stimulating precocious sex behavior and experience for which the child is unready; or sex development may be delayed long with other equally significant effects on the growing youth. The complexity of the problem of endocrine function and its relationship to behavior is so great that only in the more extreme cases is the relationship somewhat evident.

Physical Defects

All students of juvenile delinquents agree that the physical condition of delinquents, as a group, compared with nondelinquents is definitely poorer. The significance of this has been interpreted variously, but it is quite likely that the important thing is the way in which the defect hinders the child in his social relationships and contacts, and the way in which he evaluates himself because of the defect.

Diseases and Brain Injuries

Injuries to the brain or central nervous system, whether caused by lesions or diseases, have long been associated with abnormal behavior and delinquency. Injury to the brain is permanent since brain cells have no power of regeneration. Hence when the damage or destruction is extensive, or progressive, there is little hope for normalcy. More commonly the deteriorated behavior deteriorates further.

Venereal disease, particularly when it invades the central nervous system, epilepsy, and *encephalitis lethargica*, commonly known as "sleeping sickness," are known to cause behavior difficulties. This is particularly true of encephalitis that in recent years has been found in the medical histories of many delinquents, and particularly in those who do not yield to treatment.

PSYCHOLOGICAL FACTORS IN DELINQUENCY

Conflict between Drives and Society

Drives are strong predispositions to behave in specific or general ways in the presence of certain situations. Some drives are said to be biological (hunger, thirst, and sex) because they are manifestations of *organic* needs; other drives are said to be social (acquisitiveness) because they are *learned* through association.

These biological compulsions that people experience so constantly, and that are so compelling, are not always oriented to the society in which we live. Even our social drives are at times inconsistent with the social demands of the society of which we are a part.

Let us take hunger for food as an example. There is nothing wrong about hunger, but there may be with the manner of satisfying it. Most people learn to satisfy hunger by earning money and purchasing food, or by receiving food from someone who is responsible for them. This implies learning. The child who runs away from home, however, may turn to begging or to stealing food when he is hungry because he has not learned how to secure food in legitimate ways by himself. Unfortunately his method is not sanctioned by society, and hence when he persists, he is labeled a juvenile delinquent.

In the case of the sex drive the situation is similar. The bodily tensions associated with sex are perfectly normal experiences, but society makes satisfaction difficult and in some cases impossible. There are customs, laws, religious precepts and restrictions, and even taboos that regulate sex behavior. True, these restrictions have grown out of social necessity, and they are essential in an orderly society. To recognize this, however, does not lessen the individual's need or demand for satisfaction. Because the drive continues strong, satisfaction may be sought by any readily available or immediate means even though it is illegal and may be injurious to another.

This incompatibility between man's biological drives and social necessity often places a severe strain on the individual. Sex delinquency is found in those adolescents, therefore, who fail to adapt their biological urges to the demands of society.

The Importance of Learning

Practically everything that man does is learned. Social responses —those activities that are essential for meeting and getting along with other people in a society—are definitely learned. Not everything that one learns, however, is desirable and good—some people learn to live in ways that are inconsistent with the public good and detrimental to their own welfare. In fact much of what we call mental abnormality is the result of inadequate learning in *right living*. When it is children and adolescents who fail to live in accord with the demands of society, we call them juvenile delinquents.

Learning the social pattern. There are some types of behavior, such as *fighting and acquisitiveness,* that are so characteristic of people in our society that they are often called instincts. And because they are called instincts they are thought to be characteristic of mankind the world over. This, however, is not the case. People in some parts of the world have no desire to accumulate goods, and people in other parts have no tendency to fight. Since acquisitiveness and fighting are characteristic of our society, we too learn to be acquisitive and to fight. Both of these traits are enhanced further by another characteristic of our American society, namely, *individualism*—sometimes called "rugged individualism." This too we learn.

There are yet other traits that are also characteristic of our culture, such as: cooperation, justice, fair play, and majority rule. These are quite the opposite of the tendencies toward individualism, fighting and acquisitiveness. Our society is full of these contradictions. Therefore what the child must learn is to temper individualism with cooperation, fighting with justice and fair play. This is not at all easy. A child may learn well the habit of fighting and of acquiring things; but he may learn not at all the habit of cooperation or of fair play. Therefore learning some of the habits of our society and neglecting others results in juvenile delinquency.

Learning from adult example. We learn to do that which others around us do. Therefore when children live in areas in which the delinquency rate is high, and where violation of the law is common, they too learn to be delinquent. In not a few cases their own parents, grandparents and other relatives contribute heavily to this learning.

CONFLICT WITH THE HOME

Psychologists are coming to realize more and more that the kind of person one is depends to a large extent on one's early life. Infancy and early childhood are periods during which fundamental habits of living are learned, attitudes are formed, and meanings to things and life situations are given. It is the period that sets the pace and gives direction to life. Each act, each experience contributes much or little to the life one is building, whether it is a life of respectability and honor or one of delinquency and crime. Life is a path that we tread but once. The nature of its course and its destination rest by and large on the home in which it originates and with which it is associated during the early life of the individual.

Stability of the Home

The homes from which many delinquents come show various signs of instability. In not a few cases the very inception of the delinquent's family is an attempt to preserve the form of respectability because conception has taken place out of wedlock. The Gluecks report that this was true in nearly two in every 10 of their 500 delinquents. Certainly such a beginning is less likely to make for family stability.

Lack of stability is also evident in the irregular employment of the delinquent's father. Either he shifts from job to job, separated by periods of unemployment and relief, or he engages in illegal ventures separated by jail terms. Since steady employment is rather uncommon, the family lives from day to day. The future is unpredictable. The stabilizing effects of routine are absent. Life lacks direction. Therefore the delinquent fails to see the value of direction in his own life—direction that is socially consistent.

Shiftlessness results in low income, low income necessitates frequent moving from place to place, a frequent change of residence uproots the family. Associations and friendships are as a result frequently broken. The feeling of belonging, of being a part of a neighborhood, is not given a chance to develop, and hence whatever restraining influences the neighborhood may offer are ineffectual. In this soil delinquency flourishes.

A further indication of the instability in the delinquent's home is found in the number of such homes that are broken. Some are broken by death, by disease, or because of occupational necessity. Others are broken by separation, divorce, or incarceration of one parent in a reformatory or prison. The latter types of broken homes particularly indicate the earlier presence of instability in the family. Quoting the Gluecks again, six in ten of the delinquent boys they studied came from broken homes, and only a half of them had the experience of living continuously with *one* or *both* parents. Other investigators report like observations. Figures such as these poignantly indicate the role of the deteriorated home in the life of the juvenile delinquent.

Parent-Child Relationships

Parent-child relationships in the homes of delinquents are often poor. Either the parents are excessively permissive or excessively dominant rather than wholesomely firm and yet kind. Supervision of the child by the mother is much more lax in the case of delinquents than nondelinquents, and there is less concern about misbehavior. The fathers of delinquent boys generally tend toward excessive strictness and inconsistency in the administration of discipline. Both parents use physical punishment more than any other type of punishment. As a result there is less than one chance in five, according to the Gluecks, that a delinquent boy regards his father as an ideal to pattern after.

Parental affection in the homes of delinquents is definitely less than in the case of nondelinquents. The Gluecks report that only four fathers of delinquents in every 10 show affection, sympathy or a warm feeling toward their sons, and that only seven in 10 mothers display similar attitudes. Consequently only three in every 10 sons feel a close affectional tie with their father, and less than seven in 10 with their mother. Is it any wonder that only a small proportion of delinquent boys believe that their parents are interested in their welfare?

Because parental affection for delinquent children is somewhat uncommon and interest in their welfare often lacking, little constructive attention is given to developing standards of behavior, cultivating family pride, and protecting the family name. Responsibility in the home is not encouraged, and group recreation in the family is the exception. Because the delinquent learns that he has little in common with his parents, and that they have little or no interest in him, he turns elsewhere—outside the home—in his quest for affection, entertainment, and security.

Activities Outside of the Home

The activities of delinquents outside of the home seem to indicate a desire to achieve three things: (1) to escape from restraint; (2) to experience adventure; and (3) to find oblivion in the group.

The desire to escape from restraint and regulation is evident in delinquents' dislike for organized recreation, poor adjustment to school routine, frequent truancy, lack of interest in competitive activities, and irregularity in church attendance. Even in their employment they tend to enter the street trades where supervision is less. This dislike of routine, rules of action, and domination by adults, may stem from the excessively dominant or *laissez faire* attitudes of the home.

Delinquents' desire for excitement and adventure stands out prominently in their leisure-time activities. They do things and go places where the risk is great. They hop trucks, steal rides, sneak into movies, frequent the waterfront and the railroad yards, stay out late nights, and roam the streets after dark. They run away from home, "bunk out" nights, set fires, destroy property, and indulge in petty stealing. They are precocious in smoking, in drinking, and in having sexual experiences. About a half of them attend the movies excessively. Even in their employment they enter the various street trades where the chances for excitement are definitely greater.

This craving for adventure probably also stems from the home —the home that is dull, uninteresting, emotionally cold, and full of conflict. In contrast to the home, the delinquent's outside activities offer excitement and adventure—release from tensions and pent-up emotions.

The third characteristic of delinquents is their desire for group membership. They gang together. Younger boys seek the companionship of older boys probably because of identification and the feeling of greater security. They also participate in delinquent acts with others because of the anonymity that the gang offers. Numbers also give a sense of strength and invincibility. Hence the gang satisfies fundamental desires, and gives a feeling of belonging, not found in the home.

THE PSYCHOLOGY OF FRUSTRATION

The Importance of Motivation

To understand the behavior of people one must have insight into that which motivates them. By motivation we do not mean that which the layman has in mind when he uses the word "motive." A motive, in this sense, is a reason for action. Sometimes it is scarcely more than a verbalization. Psychologically conceived, motivation is all those factors, activities and experiences that *predispose one to act* in a certain way rather than in other ways.

Should a person address us in an insulting way, we may hit him, be insulting in return, walk away quietly, or be kind to him. What we do depends on our training, "gang" experiences, Boy Scout background, Sunday School and religious training, past insults, present associates, past fights or social successes, contacts with a favorite teacher, and a host of other things. All these things condition us—predispose us—to behave in the way we do behave at the moment.

Although much of this predisposition to behave in particular ways is *individual*, there are some broad similarities that we find in most people. W. I. Thomas[2] has stressed four such broad motivating factors that he calls desires. These are the desires for *new experience*, for *security*, for *response*, and for *recognition*. True these four desires may not exhaust the list, but all are fundamental and all are important to an understanding of delinquency because the delinquent satisfies these desires in abnormal ways.

The delinquent's desire for new experience expresses itself in his roaming the streets at night, running away from home, hopping trucks, frequenting waterfront areas and scores of other things that are a part of his eagerness for adventure. His desire for

---

[2]Thomas, W. I.: *The Unadjusted Girl*. Boston, Little, Brown and Company, 1923.

security, quite the opposite of that for new experience, is very often not satisfied in the home. Therefore he seeks security elsewhere, as in the gang. The desire for response is the most social of the desires. Since the delinquent finds the home not very satisfying, he again turns elsewhere for the satisfaction of this desire. The desire for recognition is a desire to enhance the self. It is quite likely that this desire accounts, in part, for the extremities to which a delinquent sometimes goes in his delinquent acts.

That the delinquent experiences the same desires found in other boys and girls is abundantly evident. The difference is that his desires are much less likely to be satisfied by the home and by the neighborhood in which he lives. His drab, uninteresting home environment gives him little in the way of new experience. The loose organization of his family and the don't-care attitude of his parents afford little security. His disinterested parents who are self-seeking or continually away from home give him little opportunity for social response. Neither do such parents place much of a premium on his individuality or satisfy his desire for recognition. Since the delinquent lacks opportunity to satisfy strong, normal desires in lawful ways, he satisfies them in unlawful ways. This is not because he is perverse, but because he has not been given an opportunity to do otherwise, nor to learn to use socially acceptable ways of satisfying strong desires.

Reactions to Frustation

The home is the first and the major source of need-satisfaction throughout childhood. Early in life this is a biological necessity; later it becomes a social necessity. If the child's home does not satisfy his biological and psychological needs, and if the child feels that he is rebuffed, ignored or rejected by his parents, frustration and conflict are almost inevitable results. Unless his frustration tolerance is high, the child is very apt to react intensely and emotionally to continuous thwarting, and the greater the thwarting the more intense is his reaction apt to be. It is this very *intensity* of his responses that often makes of the child a delinquent. When the delinquent teases another, he does not merely annoy, he also *injures* his victim. Whereas a normal child runs through a neighbor's garden and kicks a keep-off-the-grass sign, the delinquent *tramples* the garden and *breaks* the sign. Tasting liquor, for the delinquent, is too tame; he must get drunk. Necking is not satisfying enough; he must rape the girl. It is this intensity of the delinquent's behavior—this drive to go to the limit—that distinguishes him as a juvenile delinquent.

Another characteristic reaction to frustration generated by the home is to attack someone or something outside of the home. It is like a man kicking his dog after having a fight with his wife. One might think that the juvenile delinquent would fight back against his parents whose attitudes toward him are poor, and sometimes he does, but in many cases this is impossible. He can not fight with a father who is physically stronger than he, nor resist a mother who scolds continually or who calls the police. Therefore the delinquent's resistance is redirected. Sometimes he "takes it out" on his brothers or sisters, or on the neighbors' children, or on the teacher, or on his school books. These are vicarious ways of "getting it back" on his parents. Sometimes his frustration reaction takes an even more general turn. He overturns monuments in a cemetery that belong to families he does not know; or he breaks windows; or sets fires; or derails trains; or steals merchandise for which he has no need. All this is a kind of blind retaliation, that even he does not understand, to perpetual thwarting. This principle may be called *generalization*.

There is yet another aspect of the psychology of frustration to consider, namely, *redintegration*. Sometimes a youngster's delinquent acts seem to be out of all proportion to the stimulus or the situation that arouses them. Unprovoked, the delinquent beats a well-dressed child much younger than he. He sees his teacher pass in a car and immediately destroys the textbook he is carrying. His mother reprimands him mildly and he goes out and commits an act of violence. Although his behavior certainly seems uncalled for, we can understand his behavior better if we note that the stimulus that "sets him off," redintegrates, or reinstates, or stands for a whole complex of experiences in his past. He beats the child because the child *stands for* wealth of which he is deprived and discipline that he resents. He destroys his textbook because the teacher stands for authority—authority in the home that has been cruel and inconsistent. His mother's mild reprimand results in violence because it *stands for* the insecurity and the hostility that characterize his home. When we recognize that this is the psychology of the delinquent's behavior, and accept the principle of redintegration, we have more insight into that which lies behind his delinquency.

THE PREVENTION OF DELINQUENCY

The Sociological Approach

The use of restraint. Many people honestly believe that the way to stop juvenile delinquency is by the use of force. Therefore they cast the problem into the laps of the police and other law enforcement officers. "Better law enforcement" is their demand. What these people do not appreciate is that penal procedures have been used for centuries and crime still flourishes. The reason for this is that arrests and penalties, necessary as they are, do not reach the *disease* that juvenile delinquency is; they merely strike at its symptoms.

The improvement of physical conditions. In this category belong such suggestions as: slum clearance, establishment of playgrounds, and campaigns against unwholesome entertainment, such as crime movies, lewd burlesque shows, pornographic literature, and establishments that sponsor gambling and prostitution. The object of this approach is to *remove the opportunity* to commit delinquent acts. There is no doubt about the desirability and the necessity of this approach, but like restraint, it does not strike at the heart of the problem—it does not get at that which motivates the delinquent. It is like denying candy to a child who craves sweets, and failing to recognize his diabetic condition.

Organized recreation. This approach to juvenile delinquency stresses the importance of youth centers, playground programs, and clubs and organizations, such as: Boys' Clubs, Boy and Girl Scouts, Teenagers' Clubs, and a host of others. Each of these activities is very worthwhile, and all need to be maintained and extended, but let us not suppose that the way to wipe out delinquency is to have more and more organized recreation. As for delinquents, who may need organized activities most, they generally avoid them because they dislike rules and regulations. Even predelinquents may not be kept from later delinquency, except in some cases, because their delinquency comes from thwarting, frustration and conflict that centers largely around the home, and organized recreation does not remove this motivation.

In this connection I wish to suggest two things. First, that there is a need for more *small* playgrounds with opportunity for spontaneous rather than organized play, where the crowding and the friction would be less. I also suggest that youth organizations be made much less expensive, and thus more available to the delinquent, by the elimination of uniforms and expensive trappings. I would like to see *activity*, *resourcefulness* and *attitudes* stressed more, and emphasis on physical equipment lessened. These two things, I believe, would help us reach delinquents more than present procedures do.

The Psychological Approach

Counseling and guidance. Everyone has problems but not everyone is able to meet them adequately. The parents of delinquents are certainly no exception to this—in fact they are apt to have more problems and less competence in meeting them than the average family. Therefore they are particularly in need of assistance from someone who can help them understand their problems better and point the way to a solution. Many communities these days do offer their citizens such services in the child guidance centers, family consultation bureaus, mental hygiene clinics, and the like. These centers are usually staffed by a psychiatrist, one or more psychologists, and several social case workers, each of whom is a well-trained specialist who is able to assist people with their personal, home, and child problems. To make counseling services more effective, many more centers are needed, particularly in the small communities; greater cooperation between all social agencies must be achieved, and the public must be "sold" on their value. Law enforcement officers can do a good job of selling these services by calling delinquents to the attention of agency workers, and by selling the parents of delinquents on the idea of seeking aid at guidance centers.

Another attack on the problem of delinquency by the use of psychological services and guidance is found in the school. School psychologists are doing a fine piece of work, but too few school systems have the services of a competent school psychologist. This approach to delinquency needs to be extended greatly.

Parent education. For every type of occupation and profession, with the exception of parenthood, some type of education or training is required, yet we have more people engaged in the "business" of rearing children than in any other type of endeavor. People somehow think that by virtue of the fact that one is a parent he has the knowledge and the skill needed for success. Nothing is farther from the truth. Although every untrained parent is not necessarily a poor parent, because some people are better suited temperamentally to parenthood than others, most parents are better able to accept the responsibilities of parenthood with training. Greater knowledge and skill in child rearing would certainly prevent some and possibly much delinquency. Unfortunately those who need it most usually have it least. Therefore the need for training for parenthood must be brought home with vigor to all parents and prospective parents. This can be done by courses in courtship, marriage, parenthood and child training given in the high schools and the colleges, in seminars for parents, by neighborhood councils, and by welfare agencies and guidance centers. A concerted effort to raise parenthood to the status of a profession is certain to bring results.

The great advantage of the psychological approaches to the problem of juvenile delinquency is in their emphasis on the individual. *His* unique problems are studied, and courses of action are tailored to *his* needs. Whereas the sociological approaches aim to improve conditions in general so as to make for better living, the psychological approaches seek to get at the heart of *the child's* problem and to make of him a better person.

REFERENCES

GLUECK, SHELDON and ELEANOR: *Unraveling Juvenile Delinquency*. New York, The Commonwealth Fund, 1950. A thorough and provocative study of 500 delinquent and 500 nondelinquent boys.

GLUECK, SHELDON and ELEANOR: *Delinquents in the Making.* New York, Harper and Brothers, 1952. A popular account of the above study that is of exceptional interest to the lay reader.

HEALY, WILLIAM and BRONNER, AUGUSTA F.: *New Light on Delinquency and Its Treatment.* New Haven, Yale University Press, 1936. A report on a very interesting study of juvenile delinquents.

MERRILL, MAUD A.: *Problems of Child Delinquency.* Boston, Houghton Mifflin Company, 1947. An interesting book that stresses the multi-factor view of juvenile delinquency.

TAPPAN, PAUL W.: *Juvenile Delinquency.* New York, McGraw-Hill Book Company, 1949. A comprehensive text on juvenile delinquency.

Chapter 11

THE PSYCHOLOGY OF THE ADULT CRIMINAL*

By

HAROLD LINDNER

INTRODUCTION

Wнo is a criminal? How shall we define the term so that it shall be applied correctly? To the unsophisticated person, a definition of so popular a word and so convenient a label may seem irrelevant. To those who are concerned with this problem, however, the need for definition is great. Unfortunately much of the difficulty in coming to grips with the study of crime and criminals lies in the fact that too little attention has been devoted to the specification of exactly what is meant by this term. A review of the popular and scientific literature will show that the task of definition has received too little attention, and that students are prone to accept definitions which, on closer and more objective inspection, prove quite unrealistic or downright ridiculous.

Let us, at the start, be realistic: the law is the final arbiter of what is or is not criminal. Any transgression against existing law, any behavior which contravenes statutes relating to such behavior, makes one liable to "criminal prosecution"; and, on conviction, one automatically becomes a "criminal." In terms of legal realism, then, the mere commission of an act which breaks established legal codes of behavior may be sufficient to label one a "criminal."[1]

---

*This work was completed while the author was Consulting Clinical Psychologist for the State Industrial Farm for Women at Goochland, Virginia, Virginia Division of Corrections.

---

[1]Naturally, the law does provide certain safeguards which serve to protect the citizenry from undue process of the law, e.g., the *mens rea* (guilty mind), the minimum age of legal responsibility, the ability to "know" right from wrong, the voluntary commission of the act.

272

The first problem to confront the student of human behavior, then, is whether it is justifiable to accept all who are legally labeled criminal as truly criminal; should we, in other words, accept the jurist as the authority for our operational frame of reference? Obviously, the legal definition is not sufficient for the operations of the social sciences. An acceptance of the legal definition eventually must lead to the proverbial blind alley. In this alley one then finds himself indiscriminately labeling various and sundry acts as "criminal." As proof of this we should, momentarily, reflect on the so-called "Thought Police" systems of fascistic and communistic countries. The law, in such alien societies, applies the label "criminal" to all those who either think or act in ways opposed to the existing political ideology. Are we, in unbiased truthfulness, as serious students of human behavior, willing to conform to such a "legal" definition? Or, to take a contemporary example from our own culture, according to Kinsey perhaps two-thirds of the unmarried male population in the U. S. engage in homosexual practices of one variety or another. The law, in most sections of the country, considers homosexual practice a violation of the criminal code; the convicted homosexual, in these communities, is a "criminal" and is often remanded to the prison. Can the scientist, the student of human behavior, continue to condone such "legal" jurisdiction over a psychosexually deviant condition? Obviously not.

Examples of such legal transgressions against scientifically validated findings are too numerous to explore any further; they are within the experience of all, especially the law enforcement officer to whom this work is being directed. He, perhaps, is in the most ideal situation to note the hypocricy of legality in its attempts at moral and judgmental substantiation of the unrealistic legal definition of "criminal." Certainly, he is the one who is confronted with the serious task of handling those whom society has, through its legal maneuvers, labeled "criminal." This chapter is designed to provide the law enforcement officer with a psychological frame of reference within which he might be able to function to better advantage.

TYPES OF CRIME

Law Breaking

The simplest form of legal transgression is involved in that behavior, which, because of unintentional action, circumstance, or situations to which the person cannot make rapid changes in established response patterns, is properly defined as *simple law-breaking*. In essence, those illegal acts which the psychologist considers as law-breaking behavior rather than criminal behavior results from the fact that a law exists in regard to this behavior. R. M. Lindner referred to this phenomenon by saying that law-breaking behavior possesses the quality of criminality "only by courtesy of the law." The essential point in this definition is that the *personality* of the offender is not involved in the offense; and the offender gets no tension-relief from his anxieties through the commission of the act. Or, more directly, the behavior satisfies no psychological needs the offender may possess. But when an offense *does* satisfy psychic needs, *does* become symptomatic behavior, then—and only then—does it become criminal and not simple law-breaking.

M. J. G. had taken his automobile to the garage for repairs and, following these repairs, was driving his car homeward when a wheel came off the car and, at some speed, crashed into a baby carriage on the sidewalk of the street. The baby was instantly crushed. Investigation determined that, through mechanical failure, the repairs had not been sufficiently completed. However, M.J.G., obviously, had no personal knowledge of this fault or neglect and, consequently, could not be accused of negligence or criminal behavior. There was no human element involved here; the accident was of a purely impersonal kind and a direct result of a mechanical or instrumental failure.

Habitual Practices

Along the continuum of illegal activities which commence with simple law-breaking and extend in severity until it reaches real criminality, the *habitual* type offense is the intermediary category. This too is not *real* criminality. Rather, habitual offenses are those actions which transgress against the law because the transgressor is unable to adopt a new mode of response, in conformance with the law, when his old mode of response is no longer legally permissible. In this group, then, are those people whose habitual modes of response—although they may not have been illegal when adopted—conflict, at the time of offense, with established regulations relating to such behavior.

Much of the "crime" that results from cross-cultural differences may be included in this category of habitual offending. Specifically, the nomadic tribes of India present such a picture. The established cultural pattern of theft among these tribesmen is not illegal within their sub-cultural group. However, once they leave their native communities and venture into other cultural areas, such habitual practices are considered illegal and the tribesman finds himself accused of common theft. Sociologists have reported numerous situations in which habitual modes of response in one sub-culture are at variance with the condoned modes of response in other sub-cultures. The social statisticians report the high "crime" rate among the first generation Americans within the immigrant populations of the larger cities. More analytic studies of such immigrant "criminality" reveal that the behavior, usually of a law-breaking variety, is a product of cross-cultural differences which have arisen through differences in training and customary response patterns to various circumstances from the old culture to the new. Thus the immigrant's son, who learned from his father that street peddling was an honorable vocation, on engaging in street peddling without knowledge of the licensing regulation pertaining to such pursuit, finds himself accused of "breaking the law"; and, to his chagrin and the falsification of statistical inference, he becomes a statistic in the local "crime rate."

E.H.W. was committed to prison for moral delinquency. Interview revealed that he had but recently arrived in this country and was still a citizen of a foreign country. His offense, for which he was committed and faced deportation, was violating the Mann Act. He told the interviewer that he had "picked up" a neighborhood child of 16 years of age (although he didn't know her age at the time the experience occurred), took her to a hotel room where they registered as man and wife and had intercourse with her. He stated that he had no knowledge that this was illegal in America and that it was quite common an occurrence in his native city.

B.H.K. was examined at a local jail. She was of limited intelligence and originated from an extremely rural farm community. Her "crime" was delinquency and neglect of children. She had been an habitual drunkard—as had most others in her native community—and had neglected her children (of which she had eight, five through marriage and three illegitimately) to the extent that they were found suffering from various serious illnesses and physical starvation. Study of the case revealed that B.H.K. had no realization of the seriousness of her offense. She considered the whole episode a farce and stated that her behavior was no different from that of her parents towards her and her siblings and no different from the accepted behavior in her native community. Significantly, she was reported by federal agents—persons of different acculturation—who happened upon the situation during a routine inspection of this backward community for purposes of locating illegal liquor stills. She insisted that no one in her community had accused her of this offense, even though her neglect was quite obvious and that this was not an unusual way for parents to act in that community. (To note that it was "criminal neglect" is, probably, quite justified. To condemn B.H.K. as a "criminal" appears absurd.)

No brief is held here for those who engage in law-breaking activities, or for those whose habitual practices lead them to transgress established law. This survey is not an attempt at apology. The essential point in this, however, is that if we, the students of criminology and law enforcement, are ever to define and study *crime*, we must learn what *is* and what *is not* criminal. Only after we make such distinctions can we make those necessary conceptualizations which will lead toward our understanding of the criminal and enable us to apply our professional tools towards the treatment of criminals and the prevention of crime.

Criminosis

Now that we have seen what crime is not, let us examine what crime is. As already indicated, one basic criterion of crime is that the activity is symptomatic of a personality need which, to some extent, satisfies this personal need. In essence, *true crime* implies that the person himself is involved in the activity; that the accidental or circumstantial factors involved in the behavior are secondary to the primary need the person has for engaging in such action. In crime one finds, as Theodore Reik has said, "the criminal's calling card." That is, the crime is an expression of the perpetrator's personality—distorted and complicated through being expressed in anti-social ways, but personal and identifiable upon analysis of the psychological condition of the offender.

It is only crime, as here defined, which should be the concern of those who choose the profession of criminology. The law-breaker and the habitual practices offender, because their personalities do not fundamentally contribute to the pattern of the crime, are not the concern of the criminologist. The criminal—he who commits crime out of personality distortions and is so motivated by unconscious psychological needs—is the individual with whom we should concern ourselves. For he is the real criminal, he whose behavior is an expression of his personal qualities and not the result of some circumstantial, accidental quirk of society or mechanical failure.

M.F. had been a rejected child, his parents having been business people who had little time for family life. He matured in an environment lacking in emotional warmth, an environment typi-fied, perhaps, by his comments to the therapist: "My mother gave me her milk with one breast while she concentrated on the day's receipts." He had an early career as a juvenile delinquent and was considered by neighborhood people as incorrigible. He culminated his delinquent career by an attempted robbery that, through his emotional lability, evolved into manslaughter. He told his prison therapist that when the storekeeper he had robbed showed resistance to his crime, he felt an uncontrollable desire to shoot the man. Psychological analysis revealed that M.F. shot the store-keeper because, unconsciously, this man represented his own rejecting father, who, although he had emotionally rejected M.F., had, nevertheless, been an oppressive authoritarian in his daily demands on the boy. M.F.'s criminal behavior is understandable when we learn of the psychopathology underlying it: the parental rejections; the authoritarian, unloving, father-image; the personal feelings of inadequacy and insecurity; the need to "prove" his masculinity through the use of guns and by engaging in criminal behavior against established law and society.

The case of M. F. is typical of many juvenile delinquents whose criminal behavior is based on their psychopathological need to "prove their masculinity." This leads one, therefore, to a study of the *causes* of criminality. The next question we must ask ourselves is what motivates the criminal.

MOTIVATION OF CRIME[*]

Mental Mechanisms

We have asked ourselves what is real crime and have concluded that it is the purposive acting out in unlawful behavior of those facets of personality that are symptomatic of internal stress and pathological distortion in order that the perpetrator may satisfy those needs which make such behavioral demands on him. If we accept this definition of crime, we must concomitantly recognize that criminality is a product of psycho-social development—for how else could one acquire such symptoms and have such need-reduction requirements? To understand how these psycho-social developments occur, we have to study the psychological development of the person; and to do this, we must take as our point of origin the infant, since, other than for those phenomena which occur during the intra-uterine stage, birth is the beginning of life and, thus, of experience.

Contrary to the maudlin notions possessed by most people, the infant is not a sweet little bubble of pleasantry and joy. Rather he is a demanding, autistic and non-compromising little imp who strives only to appease his own appetites and seeks continual need-reduction through crying, eating, soiling and babbling for affection. His world is himself and he is omnipotent in that world—to paraphrase another writer: he is the King of the Cradle (any mother, hastening to accommodate her bleary-eyes to a 3 A.M. feeding, will testify to this!). His energies are directed toward the sole goal of satisfying his appetite, and his entire psycho-biological being strives toward this happy state of unequivocal comfort, avoidance of pain and search for pleasure. This state has been

---

[*]The presentation in this section is from the point of view of Psychoanalysis, which is one of several ways in which the nature and development of personality can be viewed. *The Editor.*

identified as being governed by the *pleasure principle*.

Unhappily for the infant his dictatorial reign over the cradle and household is not long-lived. Soon he comes in conflict with social and cultural factors; he must meet and make his peace with the world and those who inhabit it. Thus he finds, to his eternal frustration, that he cannot continue along the merry pathway of demanding all and receiving all; he must compromise and meet the realities of life. He learns to compromise through parental pressures (i.e., the parents soon limit his pleasure by making demands on him, such as toilet training, eating habits, social habits, "right from wrong," etc.) which serve to make him conform with the accepted norms of behavior in the particular culture. Thus he abdicates his cradle throne of omnipotence and commences upon the future course of his life; the *reality principle*, which entails dispensing with immediate pleasure and adjusting to the society of others. This, we may parenthetically mention, is, perhaps, the most difficult adjustment he will ever have to make, because to make it he must learn to cease engaging in activities which serve to bring immediate pleasure or relief from pain in order to (perhaps) ensure pleasure at some future time.

The amoral and asocial energies which the infant possesses at birth are known as the *id;* it is charged with energy (libido), and is in continual, unbridled struggle toward gaining for him satisfactions of his physical, emotional, sexual and affectional appetites, it knows no limitations to pleasure and is not concerned with compromise. The strata of personality that offers the infant a concept of himself is known as the *ego*. The ego is a composite of attitudes and wishes relating to the self. It is the "I," "me" and "mine" quality that we possess. While, as Freud said, the id is "a chaos, a cauldron of seething excitement," the ego is that part of the id which has been modified through direct contact with the external world through the senses and whose function is the conscious testing of reality. The other member of this personality triad is the *super-ego*, that compendium of social forces which is the representative of the culture, folkways, mores and habits of the social group into which the person is born. This pattern of acculturation, the process of selection and incorporation of the culture, serves to complete the ego growth and to form the super-ego. It is the super-ego which is the crucial mechanism for determining whether the child will develop into the adjustable adult—for it is the super-ego which contains that storehouse of social codes, folkways, mores and habit patterns so essential to group belongingness. It is the super-ego, then, which is that part of the mental apparatus which controls the ego by limiting the ego's undifferentiated acceptance of impulses emanating from the id. It acts as an inner censor (analagous to "conscience") which, unconsciously, transmits the predilections of the social group to the person's "self" (ego) so that the person can conform to the socialization processes required by that group for adjustment and acceptance by the group authorities.

To develop this theoretical outline of the adult criminal, we must spend a bit more energy on the processes of personality formation; for, it is our thesis, only through this particular personality genesis (i.e., the psychological) can one ever define crime and criminality in such a way that avenues of eliminating its cancerous growth may be found. Therefore it is now necessary to delve one step deeper into the developmental genesis of the personality, so that, later, we may make use of these dynamics in our understanding of criminal development and the psychology of the adult criminal.

Psychosexual Stages

The oral stage. The period from birth to approximately eighteen months is the *oral stage* of psychosexual development. This is customarily divided into two sub-stages, the *oral sucking* and the *oral biting* stages, so designated to represent the actual behavior of the infant during this early developmental period. The oral sucking stage, which lasts from birth to approximately the ninth month, is characterized by the fact that motivation, here, is chiefly directed upon feeding (sucking) and the mouth is the specially charged erotic (libidinal) zone. Here the infant is autonomous and autistic and makes no distinctions between himself and others in his environment. The mother (or the mothering-one) is also not distinguishable from the self, at this early period in development. Through the trauma of frustrations (e.g., feeding delays, weaning processes, episodes of social and physical trauma) and with the natural development of the teeth, however, those destructive drives (id) find outlet in biting and aggression—and the ego begins to form. Essentially, then, through this period the infant can best be characterized as a retentive, incorporative, narcissistic being who expresses some limited aggressions.

The anal stage. The anal stage extends from about the age of six months through three years and is commonly divided into two sub-stages: *anal expulsive* and *anal retentive*. Obviously, since these stages emphasize natural functions and parental-cultural attitudes, we find they include the further strengthening of the ego and the first signs of super-ego development. Since, in western culture, fecal production is considered so obnoxious, the child obtains his first sense of power through the use of his natural functions. During the early anal stage (expulsive), when his sphincter control is not fully developed, he obtains relief and satisfaction through the release of feces and urine. During the later anal stage (retentive) he gets similar delight in aggressive and egoistic control over his functions by expending them in times and places inconvenient to his parents, or by conforming to parental standards and thus obtaining parental rewards.

It is obvious, then, that this crucial stage in developmental history is one in which there is much psychological conflict. The child must decide whether feces and urine should or should not be expelled; at what times and places; and under what circumstances. Here too there is much *reality testing*. The child must "test" to see just how far he can go before he reaches the point where his activities are limited by the culture. The anal retentive stage, then, is characterized by the child's becoming endowed with a super-ego: he learns to conform to reality and submerge his id urgings to ego and super-ego demands. In essence, then, the character traits, which will prove of concern to us later when we discuss characterological and psychopathic behavior problems in crime, find their developmental origins in this psychosexual stage and are reality-bound in accordance with parental, social, cultural, economic and personal interpretations.

The phallic stage. As its name implies, the phallic stage finds the child concerned with genital equipment. He becomes interested in his genitals, manipulates them and thus becomes anxious because of parental condemnation of masturbation. He compares his immature genitals with those of his parents and siblings and observes the large genitals of his father and brothers and the lack of visible genitals in his mother and sisters. During this period in his development notions of sexuality emerge and become confused in the typical anxiety which, in western culture, surrounds sexuality. It is here that the oft-quoted *Oedipus situation* occurs. The child becomes infatuated with the opposite-sex parent but this sexual interest is an anxiety-arousing one because this parent is already claimed by the powerful same-sex parent, and thus the child fears retaliation; the situation being resolved through the healthy identification with the same-sex parent through introjection. Here, too, the origins of *castration anxiety* are to be found. The child feels threatened because of his masturbatory indulgences and because of his Oedipal romances. Because of his undefined and confused notions of sexuality, he suspects that the absence of visible genitalia in his mother and sisters is due to a punitive deprivation. Thus he has anxieties that he, too, will be punished for his Oedipal strivings and his sexual aggressions.

The latency stage. By approximately the seventh year of life the child enters upon the *latency stage* that lasts until about the time of puberty. This period of psychosexual development is noted for the absence of overt libidinal striving and the presence of excessive moralistic and social concerns. This is not to say that there is no sexuality during the latency period. Rather, what sexuality there is is relegated to the unconscious while the conscious is concerned with further super-ego development. By the time latency has arrived, infantile sexuality (the libidinal strivings of the oral, anal and phallic stages) has been successfully repressed and the ego and super-ego have been fully developed. The behavioral pattern in latency is of the "moral" type in which the child effuses with "milk and honey kindness," makes strong identifications with that which is "right" as opposed to that which is "wrong," attends Sunday School with much interest, joins boy and girl scout groups and is terribly conscious of social mores and folkways. In a word, during latency, the libidinal urges are sublimated (a social value is substituted for a frustrated, denied libidinal urge or wish) through reaction formations (behavior directed at denying a libidinal urge by performing in a manner opposite to the libidinal dictate) which serve to remove them from consciousness. Essentially, then, latency serves to broaden the scope of the super-ego. It is the stage of socialization and acculturation.

The genital stage. This stage, in the present theoretical framework, is a description of the mature, well-adjusted adult who has achieved an harmonious balance between his libidinous, aggressive urges and the cultural demands. It describes one who is without irrational anxiety in interpersonal relationships. Genitality comes in with puberty and is the psychosexual stage of adolescence. In the genital stage there is apparent a crystallization of all that came before only now to be expressed in different behavioral modes and to be dealt with in other, more "social" ways. It is as though the person were revivifying the previously lived-through psychosexual stages. In behavior, therefore, we find the expressions of infantile sexuality—only now the mode of expression is different and in accord with higher socialization and cultural dictates (mores and folkways). Thus the revival of oral and anal behavior (e.g., cigarette and pipe smoking, kissing games, exhibitions of oral and anal flatus). Phallic interests are noted in renewed masturbation and, because castration is still an active anxiety, homoerotic interests and aggressions toward the opposite sex are also noted (e.g., emphasis on athletic games, often noted for expressions of "masculinity" and rough body-contact displays; disdain for sharing athletics with opposite-sex members; excessive concerns with proper dress and grooming). The pinnacle of genital success, finally, is achieved in maturity and adaptability when libido is invested in a member of the opposite sex and when the person's concern is dominated less with receiving satisfaction than with sharing and giving love to his chosen mate. At this stage in psychosexual development, true genitality has been achieved; and the person is now considered as truly mature and "adult."

Psychological Development

Although this verbal portrait of psychosexual development and growth has been, of necessity, drawn here in a continuous and, seemingly, progressive manner, this is not necessarily the way in which it is lived. Progress from stage to stage involves the renouncing of certain adjustment mechanisms because their retention has become painful and frustrating. However, the rewards for progress along this continuum lie in the further psycho-social development of the individual and in his greater individualization. First he is dependent upon the mothering-one. Then, with ego development, he learns to maintain himself and compromise with reality. Following this comes his socialization and acculturation based on adaptation to family constellations and those security feelings it provides. With adolescence comes a more complete attempt at social responsibility and, as he matures, increasing liberation from these familial dependencies until the time of adulthood (in the "genital" sense) when he is finally liberated from familial ties and he is able to accomplish the difficult feat of "cutting the umbilicus."

As a consequence of all this, it should be realized, this growth process is decidedly difficult—and, unfortunately not as many reach the goal of "genitality" (maturity) as we might wish. Too often infantile sexuality is not sufficiently repressed to allow for socialization; too often the trauma of childhood makes for the growth of a weak rather than a strong ego, and thus the person has a difficult time adjusting to reality; too often the super-ego becomes too tyrannical or too under-developed and thus socialization is impossible. Too rarely do we find that beautiful combination of a sufficiently repressed infantile sexuality and a strong ego and capable super-ego which makes for psychological adulthood (genitality). Instead we more often find that the child is exposed to objects or events which have so traumatic an effect on him that they tend to fixate his behavior at a particular stage or place in psychosexual development. These fixation points are the factors which add to interpersonal differences. They are also the factors which deny maturity to the individual and give society its mass of persons who either defeat their personal growth processes in fruitless attempts at sublimation and reaction formation—or who, as in criminotics, act out their personal frustrations in unlawful, criminotic behavior, such behavior symptomatically expressing the precise fixation point in their infantile sexuality.

Sublimations and reaction formations are, however, often capable of bringing about socialization and sufficient harmony to allow for adjustment. A person fixated at the oral sucking stage may sublimate by excessive eating indulgences or by smoking; while his reaction formations may be of the variety indicated by vegetarianism, teetotaling or smoking and kissing inhibitions. If he is fixated at the oral aggressive stage his sublimation may be through fingernail biting, chewing tobacco or through verbal language; and his reaction formations may lead him to be precise in grammatical use in speech and written documents or, perhaps, an exaggeration of the importance of table manners. In essence, those who are fixated in the oral sucking stage will show a characterological bias for passivity, optimism and psycho-social dependency. The character of those who are fixated in the oral aggressive stage will be aggressive, pessimistic and independent.

Fixations at the anal expulsive stage show such sublimations as philanthrophy and interest in the arts; while their reaction formations involve sensitivity to odors and a compulsive emphasis on cleanliness. The anally retentive fixations are sublimated in parsimony and interests in zealous collecting and hoarding of desired goods; while their reaction formations are demonstrated in behavior opposed to the basic drive for retaining. The anal character may be identified as one who is devoted to details, petulant and parsimonious, and showing pronounced superiority ideas (resulting from his capacity to manipulate his natural productions). Fixations to the phallic stage are sublimated in exhibitionism, artistic compositions of erotic qualities; and his reaction formations cover the range from extreme purity and modesty to puritanism.

The phallic character is typified by literalness, constriction, moral aggressiveness and exhibitionism. Finally, the genital character is he who works for social betterment in a true interest in the welfare of others. His characterological bias, because he is mature and well-balanced in adulthood, is typified by an achievement of personal adaptation, without libidinal and aggressive frustrations, to cultural demands. He is able to regulate his behavior and emotions and to establish appropriate interpersonal relationships without these being stymied by personally wasteful, aggressive skirmishes with anxiety-arousing authority figures. Essentially, he has achieved a healthy balance—a homeostasis—between the components of his personality and those of his society, which perpetuates adjustment and adaptation.

THE PSYCHOLOGY OF CRIMINOSIS

The perceptive reader now knows that crime is not circumstantial. Crime is determined. Crime involves the deepest layers of personality sub-strata. Crime is behavior which is motivated by interpersonal and social conflict and frustration, expressed in ways which run counter to the law. Whether crime results from a failure to achieve psychological harmony between the person and the environment, or whether it is due to the environment's inability to provide adequately for the person's satisfactions, it is behavior symptomatic of internal conflict, specifically motivated and, under certain conditions, in contravention of established law.

In essence, then, the understanding and treatment of criminosis —real crime—lies in the proper evaluation of those *predisposing motivants* which predispose one toward criminal behavior, as well as those *precipitating (environmental) factors* which kindle the crime and offer the external media in which it is enacted. Criminosis results when the predisposing motivants are ignited by the precipitating factors. Criminotic behavior is an attempt to alleviate the internal crisis and restore internal balance. Albeit, it is a nefarious and anti-social means of restoring personal harmony. This, therefore, is precisely why the analysis and treatment of criminosis (the disease) and the criminotic (the perpetrator) requires psychological insight and methodology.

Much of the answer to "why criminals?" lies in the motivation of crime—and that is why it was necessary to explain the psychological development of the individual. We noted that a healthy, law-abiding, mature person is one whose id, ego and super-ego develop in proper proportion to each other and combine in a united effort to continue the person's internal harmony. Such a psychic development typifies the so-called normal adult and guarantees him a maturity and emotional life replete with satisfactions antees him a maturity and emotional life replete with satisfactions and undaunted by irrational anxieties. The most essential element in this "psychic compound" is the ego. If the ego is a healthy one the person can deal with life situations without becoming overwhelmed by anxiety. If, as in the psychoses, the ego is weak and damaged, the id takes prominence, infantile sexuality rules, the person loses "contact with reality" and lives, as it were, by the pleasure principle. If, as in the psychoneuroses, the ego is uncompromising and unyielding, the battle is joined with the id and super-ego forces and, although the person remains in contact with reality, infantile sexuality rules at whatever fixation point is involved.

In the criminotic, however, the problem is not one of an obdurate ego nor one of a destroyed ego. In the criminal the ego is permeable and, even, malleable. Therefore, crime entails the complicity and the cooperation of the ego-structure. In the neuroses, the conflict is between the ego and the id. In the psychoses, the ego retires and the id reigns mighty. In criminosis, the ego compromises and cooperates with the id. Thus we find, in actual practice, criminals choose—quite consciously—the most adventitious means of carrying out their criminal behavior; that is, the ego, in its collusion with the id-forces, acts as a moderator on the id-strivings. Thus, most crime is not of the very vicious sort, which would prevail if it were not for the helpful fact that the ego modifies the destructive, hateful energy of the extremist id.

This distinction, which separates crime from other psychopathology, is crucial to a proper understanding of the genesis of criminality. To quote from R. M. Lindner: "Ego is the ally of criminosis, the resistor of psychoneurosis, the abject and pitiful slave of psychosis." In crime, the ego shares in the act; in psychoneurosis, it assists in the protection of the neurotic symptom; in psychosis, it is vanquished. These differentiations illustrate why criminal behavior differs so much from other, non-criminal, psychopathology. In psychosis, the id-urgings freely influence the person and his behavior. In neurosis, the person *suffers out* his internal conflicts. In criminosis, the person *acts out* his internal conflicts.

Crime is often involved in the psychoneuroses, in the psychoses, and in conditions of organicity and mental deficiency. Since this is dealt with elsewhere in this book,[3] it would seem more valuable if—now that we have studied the definition of crime, the motivation of crime, the developmental factors in normality and crime, and the psychopathology of crime—we turn our attention to those less psychologic and more sociologic factors which play so large a role in perpetuating criminality and juvenile delinquency,[4] and survey the criminal in custody.

THE CRIMINAL IN CUSTODY

I have dealt with the functions of the prison psychologist in Chapter 14 of this book. I should like to conclude this chapter with an analysis of the institutional problem from another perspective: that of the offender. I consider this important because it offers further insight into those attitudinal biases, frames of reference and the psychology of the adult criminal, all of which are crucial to an understanding of the law enforcement officer's problem.

One type of criminal has, elsewhere, been referred to as a "rebel without a cause." The criminal psychopath has been so designated because research in psychoanalytic theory has shown that this type of criminotic commits crime out of unbridled hate and is a rebel against socialization processes. I believe that we will be aided in our analysis of the adult criminal if we, too, consider the criminotic a "rebel"—a rebel against authority. If we assume that the criminotic, in most instances, is a social violator, a rebel against all authority, then we may appreciate the difficulties encountered by those who engage in abortive attempts to treat criminosis in the penal environment. The criminotic—this rebel—confined in a community of social violators is given "therapeutic" dosages of *authority*. A typical prescription of institutional "treatment" includes liberal doses of discipline, suppression of individualism, emphasis on irrational authority and frequent punishment. The criminotic, instead of being treated as a socio-psycho-

---

[3]See Chapter 9. [4]See Chapter 10.

logically debilitated person, is given precisely that authoritarian razzle-dazzle which *originally caused* the social disease and which can serve no other purpose than to perpetuate it.

Dear Doc,

You asked me to write you about my feelings about "The Hole." O.K., you asked for it . . . I'll give it, do whatever you want with it . . . here goes. The place is a stinking hell-hole. The judge told me I'd be sent there for "a cure for your criminal behavior and addiction." I got there one night, sick as a dog and retching with pain because they cut off my "junk." What did they do for me? (Remember, the judge said I would get "the cure" there.) They shoved me into a cell, on the floor, cold and damp, and let me spend the night in a condition of "living death," laying in my own puke and crap. O.K., I was at fault for being a "junky." A month later one day they pulled me out of line, made me strip bare in front of all the guys in the cell block (the bastards wouldn't even give me the benefit of doing it in a cell where no one could watch), and frisked me all over—and I mean *all over*. I've never been so bitter about anything in my life; and I'm telling you again, as I told them then, if it takes me the rest of my life I'll get even with that low-down S.O.B. who did that to me. I was sick with rage for that whole week. I still wake up dreaming at night of that screw's hands searching up my ass for a "needle" with all the guys jeering him on and laughing at my embarrassment. Yes, they sent me there for "the cure"—ha! For a carton of cigs, any screw would kill his own mother to get you some junk. Well I'm out now and I'm back on it again. The only "cure" I got there was just like a Virginia Ham is cured to keep the juices in it—I got a veneer on me: outside I'm "cured," but inside I'm worse than ever; I hate everyone and everything. You and Doc T. tried hard, Doc, but you couldn't overcome the brutality and stupidity of those Hacks. Sorry I couldn't learn much from you Docs.

R.W.C.

I quoted from this very informative testimony because, I believe, it emphasizes the thesis that criminotics (and all others who are, for one reason or another, inmates of any type institution) require the type of institutionalization which will *strengthen their own concepts of themselves as individuals* and as men. The prison community fails to accomplish this because it *suppresses* individuality and human dignity. Thus, the inmate who was incarcerated because of an inability to function rationally and socially—soon learns, if he is to exist in this community, to perpetuate those neurotic, infantile and anti-social behavioral patterns that originally caused him to become socially inadequate.

The adult criminal is one who has not developed these essentials for social adaptability: strong ego, sufficient super-ego. The child who is given sufficient love and affection will feel secure in social relationships and will never become criminotic. If his parents do not give him this security, he will be threatened by social circumstances and become anxious in interpersonal relationships. Thus the ingredients which make for social adjustment (normal, adult adaptability) come to the individual through that properly compounded mixture of affectional and secure psychological development in combination with advantageous sociological and cultural rationality. The criminotic suffers from an inability to assuage social and personal relationships without recasting them into the images of his childhood frustrations at the hands of injudicious parents. To the criminotic, who operates on an unconsciously motivated system of social rebelliousness, all authorities are hateful and demanding since, psychologically speaking, that is his impression of his parent. In other words, this predisposing motivant (resentment and apprehension towards authority figures) is basic to the criminal's psychology. Before the criminal behavior is indulged in, the precipitating motivants must also be present to trigger-off the act. In essence, then, the adult criminal is one who acts irrationally (because of the predisposing motivants) to irrational situations (precipitating motivants).

This is one of the problems which society must solve. The manner in which it has attempted to solve it has, indeed, been frustrating and taxing. We now know, however, that the prison is not the place in which criminals will be "cured" or criminality eradicated. *The place to stop crime is in the cradle.* Since criminal behavior is but an expression of improper psycho-social development, a most necessary prophylactic task is one which invades familial privacy and the parent's authority over the child. We must exert an opposing influence—so strong that it cannot be undermined—over the parent's "inherent" privilege to make his (or her) child a future criminal. This can only be done by reaching into the home and apprizing all within of those psychological and social factors which make for criminality. It is not enough to teach proper psychological and social living. We must *live* it. This means that society itself must forego its privilege of catering to irrational institutions, such as, false modesty, hypocritical morality, unfair economic distribution, the inequities of racial and religious discrimination, etc.

A step that is within the scope of immediate action, lies in a re-orientation and re-implementation of the penal system. Crime can be radically reduced *if* prisons become more rehabilitative through the incorporation of those psychological and sociological factors which have been shown to affect the genesis of crime. The major task in "curing" criminosis lies in the strengthening and reorienting of the criminotic's ego-structure. The adult criminal must be relieved of his burden of infantile anxieties and aggressions against authority. This can only be done by placing him in an environment in which irrational and arbitrarily punitive and hostile authority figures are not present. The present penal system promotes antagonism to authority and aggression against authority-figures because it is operated on the unpsychologic foundation of punitive reprisal for those who commit social transgressions. Instead of recognizing that the criminotic is as responsible for his behavior as the tubercular patient is responsible for his contaminating cough, those who manage our penal system allow their representatives (custodial personnel) to behave toward the criminal as though he were the original Brutus.

It is not the criminotic who is responsible for criminosis. Society—with all its hypocricy and pseudo-moralistic irrationality—is the responsible agent for crime. As such, then, the incarcerated criminotic should be treated with all the armamentarium that the psychological, psychiatric, sociological and educational practitioners can conjure up—in an environment that is oriented to develop individuality and self-respect rather than to destroy it.

We have much, in prisons today, by way of professional

competence. What we do have, however, is defeated by the psychological climate of the institution. One cannot treat criminality or any other social disease in a climate which serves to vitalize those "bacteria" which infect and re-infect the patient. Prison treatment, to this writing, is defeated (except in those rare instances where, for specific reasons, such interferences are nullified) by the poor psychological atmosphere of the institution and the psychosociologically poor orientation of the personnel who staff these institutions. A remedy, therefore, lies in removing this negative psychological atmosphere and in reorienting those custodians who become society's representatives in the institutions. Unless this is effected, there is no hope for the prison to rehabilitate criminotics. Without such sweeping attitudinal and conceptual changes in prison management, the penal system is doomed to remain that which it has always been: the outstanding perpetrator of crime and moral degradation. With such psychologic and social changes, it may, yet, become a truly rehabilitative social instrument.

SUMMARY

We have examined the psychology of the adult criminal and found that much of what we have, mistakenly, considered to be criminal behavior was only law-breaking by virtue of habitual practices or circumstantial and situational incidents. For the criminologist and the law enforcement officer, therefore, the *true* adult criminal (the criminotic) is one who purposefully acts out his internal conflicts in unlawful behavior that is symptomatic of his personality disorder.

In order that we might understand the genesis of crime (criminosis) we studied the psychological development of the "normal" person and, thus, analyzed the motivation of criminosis as a variation (illness) of normal psychological development. We discovered that the criminotic has a malleable ego which, without the resistance of a sufficient super-ego, compromises with id strivings. We learned that this warped ego development occurred because the criminotic's psychological development was nurtured by parental and social images which compelled fixations to immature stages of psychosexual development and thus interfered with a proper growth to psychological and social maturity (adulthood). The criminotic, then, stands as one who is fixated to a pre-genital psychosexual stage in development and, therefore, abreacts on a level of infantile sexuality in accordance with the pleasure principle rather than the reality principle.

Essentially, then, criminosis is the behavior of criminotics who combine their predisposing developmental motivants with the precipitating environmental motivants which a society that worships irrational hypocritical institutions provides in order that they may act-out in behavior that which is symptomatic of their internal conflicts.

Finally, we glanced, but briefly, at the criminal-in-custody and saw that the penal environment was perpetuating criminal attitudes instead of eradicating them. Because the prison constitutes a repressive, irrational and punitive authority-situation, it defeats rehabilitation and serves to cement those aggressive and anxiety-ridden confusions which the criminotic presents to all authoritarian circumstances and in all interpersonal relationships.

Our recommendations for the eventual reduction in crime and criminals calls for three fundamental social changes: First, a reassessment of the prerequisites for parenthood based on the conclusion that criminotics often come from biologically and psycho-socially deficient parents who cannot provide them with the psychological, sociological or educational foundations for strengthening their ego-structures through which they can mature into adaptable, "normal," adults. Second, a program of social invasion into what is now sacrosanct, namely, the home and the family, based on the assumption that criminogenesis commences in the cradle and that the prophylactic approach requires that parents be trained in the proper psychological and sociological care of their children so that these children will not become maladjusted, neurotic, psychotic or criminotic. Third, a reorientation of the unpsychologic attitudes of those who staff our institutions (those law enforcement personnel who care for the criminotic), and a change in the penal philosophy to one based on the fact that the criminotic is one who suffers from a psycho-social disease which makes him anxiety-ridden and aggressive towards all authority.

and hence unable to establish proper interpersonal relationships on a rational basis. The criminal requires not punishment but helpful guidance in order that he may strengthen his weak and warped ego and develop a sense of individuality and personal-moral strength to permit him to develop into a non-anxious, self-respecting, law-abiding person who will not become overwhelmed with anxiety in interpersonal relationships or by contacts with persons in authority.

While no panacea is yet known for the social disease of crime, our social scientists do have a sufficient knowledge of the psychological, sociological and educational artifacts which make for criminality. They are also able to define the ingredients which make for the growth of crime. A little intellectual courage and much more implementation of the known techniques for the prevention of those facets of our culture which nurture criminal psychopathology, may, yet, reveal the actual remedy.

REFERENCES

ALEXANDER, F. and STAUB, H.: *The Criminal, the Judge and the Public*. New York, Macmillan Co., 1931. An historically important publication of the psychoanalytic theory of crime and criminals.

CLECKLEY, H.: *The Mask of Sanity*. St. Louis; C. V. Mosby, 1950 edition. A clear and brilliant study of the psychopathic state personality.

FENICHEL, O.: *The Psychoanalytic Theory of Neurosis*. New York, Norton, 1945. An authoritative exposition of psychoanalytic theory.

LINDNER, R. M.: *Rebel Without A Cause*. New York, Grune & Stratton, 1944. A description of the criminal psychopath and a theoretical statement of the diagnostic and therapeutic problems inherent in the penal care of psychopathic state personalities.

LINDNER, R. M.: *Stone Walls and Men*. New York, Odyssey Press, 1946. A basic textbook in criminal psychology.

REIK, T.: *The Unknown Murderer*. New York, Prentice-Hall, 1945. An ingenious analysis of the psychodynamics in criminal behavior emphasizing the psychological determinants in crime.

Chapter 12

THE PSYCHOLOGY OF THE ALCOHOLIC
By

Peter Jan Hampton

THE MAGNITUDE OF THE PROBLEM

The "alcohol problem" has become one of the great issues of the twentieth century. From every standpoint—social, economic, legal, medical, psychiatric, and psychological—it presents a tremendous challenge to the scientist, the law enforcement officer, and the layman. There are approximately 40,000,000 users of alcoholic beverages in the United States. Of these, some 37,600,000 are moderate drinkers. The remaining 2,400,000 are intemperate drinkers. They harm themselves and they cause trouble for others; they are the creators of the "alcohol problem."

The campaign to get the American public to look upon alcoholism as a medico-psychological problem is young; it found its formal beginning in 1940 with the formation of the Research Council on the Problems of Alcohol. This does not mean, of course, that nothing was done about the problem of the alcoholic prior to 1940. In recent years an almost incredible number of books and articles have appeared on some phase of the "alcohol problem"— all attesting to the vigorous attempt on the part of individual investigators to learn more about the alcoholic, with the aim of helping both him and the community in which he lives. These attempts, prior to the formation of such organized bodies as the Research Council on the Problems of Alcohol, and the Yale School of Alcohol Studies, however, were individual and fragmentary. The community as such did little constructive work to help the alcoholic.

Recently it has become increasingly clear that a scientific approach to the "alcohol problem" requires an understanding of the fact that all drinkers are not alike. Drinkers must be classified according to kind; and each kind must be studied and treated in accordance with the symptoms, the causes, and the effects which characterize it. Thus the moderate drinker differs from the habitual drinker. The habitual drinker in turn differs from the symptomatic, the psychotic, the stupid and the compulsive drinkers; while each of these differs from all of the other kinds. The differences, of course, are not exclusive. There is a good deal of overlapping in the symptoms, causes, effects, and treatment of the different kinds of drinking; and there is in many cases a surprising continuity beginning with moderate drinking and ending in chronic alcoholism. But for all these similarities, drinkers differ in kind. By and large all are alcoholics—actual or potential, pure or secondary. Individually, however, they are moderate, habitual, symptomatic, psychotic, stupid, or compulsive drinkers.

THE MODERATE DRINKER

In view of the fact that moderation is a relative term, it is difficult to define the moderate drinker. One way of doing this would be to apply the chemical test for determining alcohol content in the blood, commonly used to establish the sobriety of motorists. By legal acceptance it is assumed that a person with less than .05 per cent alcohol in his blood at any one time is sober. Allowing some variation in quantity for the size of the person, this would mean that the moderate drinker consumes no more than about two highballs, two cocktails, or one quart of beer at a sitting on an empty stomach, and no more than double these quantities on a full stomach.

Whether a definition of the moderate drinker, based on actual standards set for amounts drunk, is altogether satisfactory is questionable. It excludes the subjective factor of motivation on the part of the drinker, as well as a consideration of the possible consequences of behavior in terms of physiological, mental, and social effects. It would seem then that the effects desired and produced, rather than the amount drunk, determine whether a person is a moderate drinker.

Viewed thus, the moderate drinker may be defined as a person who does not want to become intoxicated, and does his best not to put himself into a situation where he might become drunk. The moderate drinker uses alcoholic beverages as a food and at times as a mild sedative. Alcohol does not constitute a necessity in his life. This definition allows for an occasional slight intoxication without depriving a person of the status of moderate drinker. If, for example, a person, through faulty judgment becomes slightly intoxicated on such special occasions as Christmas or New Year's Eve, he may still be classified as a moderate drinker.

Reasons for Moderate Use of Alcohol

The reasons for the moderate use of alcohol are of course not all exhausted by stating that the moderate drinker uses alcoholic beverages because he likes their taste and enjoys their soothing effects. Occasionally he uses them also as a means of allaying irritation and assuaging minor pains. Then, too, alcohol serves the moderate drinker as a social lubricant, easing frictions and promoting conviviality.

The tired and worried business man who is unable to forget the vicissitudes of an active competitive existence, or the exhausted housewife who is troubled by her daily grind, and the little rubs and irritants of family life, gets a lift from a scotch and soda, a cocktail, or a glass of beer. Both are moderate drinkers. Drink serves them as a temporary escape from the responsibility and burden of mature emotional life and its decisions.

Effects of Moderate Use of Alcohol

There are difficulties confronting the scientist who is interested in teasing out the effects on body and mind of small amounts of alcohol. The first difficulty is to distinguish between the problem of moderate drinking and that of excessive drinking. The second difficulty is to determine the extent to which total behavior is affected by variation of increase or decrease of behavioral components such as vision, hearing, association of ideas, memory, judgment, and muscular dexterity, resulting from small amounts of alcohol. The third difficulty is to find valid and reliable methods of measuring the mental and physiological effects of small amounts of alcohol.

The general, more subjective effects of small amounts of alcohol, may be listed as relaxation, comfort, pleasure, reduced tension, change in mood, and sensation of warmth. The overall effect consists in a feeling of well-being and a self-complimentary state of mind. Fatigue is less noticeable, and the mind is diverted from worries and annoyances. The individual appears more carefree and not so bowed-down by his problems. These and other subjective effects and the changes in total behavior which result from them, have not been studied to any extent by the experimental psychologist because most of them are beyond quantitative investigation. They rest on assumptions based sometimes on clinical experience, but more often on nothing more than unverified hypotheses.

The experimental psychologist, however, has succeeded in measuring the influence of moderate amounts of alcohol on a number of psycho-physiological functions. The most direct determination of the influence of small doses of alcohol on these functions is that on the senses of hearing, sight, and touch. An analysis of psychological experiments on the effects of alcohol reveals that sensitivity to sound is increased by moderate doses of alcohol, but the ability to distinguish between the loudness of two sounds is diminished. Much the same holds true for vision. Sensitivity to light is increased, but discrimination is impaired. Sensitivity to touch is neither increased nor decreased; while sensitivity to pain and ability to localize points of stimulation on the skin are diminished.

Since much of human behavior is based on the impressions that come from the senses, loss of discrimination between such impressions, resulting from small doses of alcohol, inevitably leads to an impairment of judgment with accompanying loss in degree of reflection, observation, attention, association of ideas, and memory. The highest centers of the brain are first affected, manifested in a blunting of the finer grades of judgment, reflection, observation, and attention, together with slight changes in mood and disposition, usually resulting in a feeling of euphoria and good fellowship, along with an increased confidence in one's mental and physical powers. Actually, however, there is a decrease in reflex irritability and sensory sensitivity, with slowing in reaction time, slower muscular movements, less adequate and less accurate muscular control, and less agile mental operations.

Therapy for the Moderate Drinker

Moderate use of alcoholic beverages presents a real problem only in so far as it may lead to excessive drinking. Small non-intoxicating doses are without any appreciable harmful effect, notwithstanding measured effects on single functions. In other words, demonstrated change in single psychophysiological functions resulting from moderate intake of alcohol, does not necessarily result in a corresponding change in total behavior. Hence the therapy for moderate drinking revolves about the criterion of "control." If a person can take alcohol or leave it alone, and thus has complete control over his drinking, no therapy is prescribed. By definition the moderate drinker does not suffer from alcoholic sickness and therefore needs no therapy. However, when looking at the problem from a preventative point of view, treatment is necessary. Treatment here would consist in total abstinence attained by unlearning or a process of relearning.

Preventative therapy for the moderate drinker is advanced on the ground that the ill effects associated with excessive drinking may also develop in the moderate drinker by sheer process of accumulation. Many substances which, while beneficial when taken at first, become harmful when taken over a long period—even in small doses. This is equally true of small amounts of alcohol. The moral standpoint is that the intake of small amounts of alcohol inevitably leads to larger amounts and eventually to excessive drinking. The pleasurable effects obtained at first from small doses of alcohol require more and more alcohol over a period of time to provide the same results.

THE HABITUAL DRINKER

The habitual drinker uses alcohol almost every day, but in view of his health and tolerance for alcoholic beverages, he does not as a rule become intoxicated nor does he develop any alcoholic disease. He indulges in alcohol for the lift he gets from it. Alcohol breaks down his inhibitions, and thus gives him a chance to work up enthusiasm for social activities and self-expression. Alcohol aids him also in covering up any neurotic faults he may have.

A credit manager for a retail store claims that drinking makes him a better social companion and at the same time gives him a feeling of importance. "When drinking," he says, "I feel like a 'big shot' and have no worries." An inspector of machine parts puts it this way: "Because of my backward and timid nature, especially when I have to meet people, I take a few drinks to bolster me up. I feel as though the only time I can assert myself is when I am half drunk. I honestly believe that my being shy, timid, and having an inferiority complex is the main reason for my drinking."

Habitual Drinking Contrasted with Moderate Drinking

Basically the need for alcohol is the same for both the moderate and the habitual drinker. Both look for temporary psychological escape from the ills and discomforts of everyday life. But here the similarity ends. The moderate drinker needs only an occasional escape; the habitual drinker needs constant escape. As a result, the latter uses more alcohol more often than the former.

For the well-integrated individual habitual drinking may still be controlled drinking, with the only serious and real damage that of substituting effortless escape for the learning and use of strategy and skill in meeting life's difficulties.

The habitual drinker limits his use of alcohol to occasions when he wants a self-acting substitute for mental adjustment. He carries on without noticeable interference from alcohol in his working day accomplishment. However, if tension becomes too great and he is hard pressed, he will drink more heavily. With frequent repetition of such tension catastrophes the habitual drinker turns into a normal excessive drinker.

For the weaker, neurotic individual who is frustrated and ill at ease, alcohol becomes a constant means for personal relief. With psychological escape so accessible the discouraged and the baffled find more and more difficulties and annoyances from which they feel justified in seeking refuge. Very often the habitual neurotic drinker loses control altogether. When this happens the habitual neurotic drinker becomes a symptomatic drinker.

Effects of Habitual Use of Alcohol

The effects of habitual use of alcohol are more extensive and more pronounced than those found as a result of moderate drinking. Alcohol, used in quantities resulting in blood concentration of more than .05 per cent, acts as a depressant. This is shown in poorer coordinative thinking, diminished acuteness of sensory perception, delayed and weaker motor response, and in depression of respiration, heart beat, blood pressure, and appetite.

Effects on motor functions and control. Toettermann found that the remote alcohol effect on voluntary motor functions from consumption of 25 cc. of absolute alcohol in a 25 per cent solution amounts to a decrease of 6 per cent. Miles, using a concentration of 47 cc. of alcohol in 500 cc. of total fluid, found a decrease in speed of voluntary motor control amounting to about 4 per cent.

Experiments on the influence of an alcoholic beverage with 40 gm. absolute alcohol concentration on marksmanship have been reported by Kraepelin. He writes that in spite of high skill and strong motivation, practically every subject participating in the experiments did poorer shooting at the height of the alcohol effect. Vernon, investigating the effect of alcohol on speed and accuracy of typewriting, found that 30 cc. of alcohol diluted to 150 cc. taken with food had little effect on speed but increased the errors by 67 per cent. When the same dose was taken without food the average typing speed was increased by 5.6 sec. and the errors were increased 105 per cent. At the height of its influence, alcohol is about twice as active in upsetting neuromuscular coordination when taken on an empty stomach as when taken with food. Similar results were obtained by Miles in a series of experiments on trained male typists who were moderate habitual drinkers. Miles reports that errors in typing all grades of copy were increased about 40 per cent in the first two hours after taking 21 gm. of alcohol in a 22 per cent solution, and 70 per cent in the first two hours after taking 42 gm. of alcohol also in a 22 per cent solution. Speed of typing was decreased only 3 per cent.

Results of the experiments described are representative of the literature on the effects of moderately large doses of alcohol on motor functions and control. They agree in general that the various movements of the body are not only somewhat slowed by alcohol but are also made more random in character and therefore less well adapted to the voluntary accomplishment of specific ends.

Effects on learning and memory. Vogt studied the influence of alcohol on his own ability to learn poetry. He gave himself doses of from 15 to 50 cc. of alcohol in diluted form and then proceeded to memorize equal portions of the Odyssey. Fifteen cc. of alcohol taken with food required 10 per cent more learning time than was required on a passage without alcohol; 50 cc. of alcohol taken without food required 50 per cent more learning time than was required without drink. When, after a lapse of several weeks, Vogt tried to relearn the passages he had previously learned, he found that more time was required to relearn passages which formerly had been learned under the influence of alcohol than those learned without alcohol. Vogt concludes that learning is somewhat slowed by alcohol, while memory becomes more transient.

Cattell, using the method of writing answers to general information questions, found that the average memory loss after 12.5 cc. of absolute alcohol was a little lower than normal, while the dose of 25 cc. of absolute alcohol produced about twice as large a loss. Results of the alcohol experiments on learning and memory show that alcohol when taken in doses of from 30 to 50 cc. tends to diminish effectiveness of both learning and memory.

Effects on mental association. Joss, studying the influence of alcohol on the mental association involved in arithmetical adding, reports that 10 to 40 gm. of absolute alcohol in solution results in a 5 to 12 per cent poorer performance than normal. A similar experiment on addition conducted by Hollingworth on subjects given 39 cc. of absolute alcohol in solution, resulted in a 15 per cent loss in time.

These and other alcohol experiments on mental association show on the psychological side how the physiological changes brought about by moderate doses of alcohol result in the obstruction of mental processes.

Effects on sensory thresholds. It has been found that the ability to hear faint sounds and see dim lights increases slightly after ingestion of alcohol. However, the ability to distinguish differences in pitch between two sounds, and differences in intensity between two lights is poorer after ingestion of alcohol. Dodge and Benedict, in a study of the effect of moderate doses of alcohol (30 cc. of absolute alcohol in 20 per cent dilution) on sensitivity of the skin and muscles, found a slight loss of sensitivity. Finally, Mullen and Luckhardt, studying the effect of alcohol on cutaneous tactile and pain sensitivity, found a decrease in pain sensitivity but no appreciable loss in sensitivity to touch.

The results of these and similar investigations lead to the conclusion that the eye and the ear show slightly greater sensitivity after moderate doses of alcohol, while the skin and muscles are slightly less sensitive. Investigators also are unanimous in agreeing that alcohol decreases the ability to discriminate between similar sensory stimuli such as two sounds or two lights.

Effects on attention and concentration. It has been found that a subject who takes alcohol is less than normally sensitive to extraneous stimuli, and is also less likely to reorganize and integrate mentally the materials to which he is directing his attention. The alcohol produces a kind of narrowing and prolongation of attention, the opposite of spontaneity of mental manipulation. The drinker is fairly contented, wrapped up in his own doings, and to this extent is fulfilling the outward gesture of attention but actually the condition is one of brain and nerve depression with consequent psychological lethargy.

Effects on thinking and reasoning. The alcohol experiments on thinking and reasoning conducted by Cattell and by Hollingworth are typical of those found in the literature. Cattell compared the intelligence scores of 25 men and 25 women without alcohol with their performances on equivalent tests after doses of 10 and 20 gm. of absolute alcohol in solution had been consumed. He reports that the 20 gm. alcohol dose lowered the intelligence quotient by 1 per cent; the 10 gm. dose produced no measurable change. Hollingworth, in a similar study, using doses of 39 and 79 cc. of absolute alcohol in solution, reports a loss of mental efficiency of 15 per cent for the smaller dose and 25 per cent for the larger dose.

Therapy for the Habitual Drinker

Most of the habitual drinkers are not problem drinkers. They have acquired a secondary addiction to alcohol partly because of tolerance for the drug and partly because of the tension reducing effects which alcohol, taken in moderate doses, seems to have. They are not running away from reality, but are merely trying to make reality somewhat more acceptable. For these people treatment is a matter of self control when the habit of moderate alcohol addiction is still permeable, and a matter of external control through conditioned response, substitutive, and psychological re-educational methods of treatment when the habit has become fixed.

Conditioned response method. The conditioned response method of treatment is an outgrowth of the old method of creating disgust for alcoholic beverages. During the seventeenth century, for instance, a standard "disgust treatment" for alcoholic addicts was to have them drink wine in which several eels or green frogs had been suffocated. This treatment was supposed to make the drinker loathe wine ever after and abstain from it.

While twentieth-century lay therapists are less naive than their seventeenth century predecessors, they have continud to use the method of creating disgust, and with considerable success, by pouring admixed alcoholic beverages on every bit of food consumed by the habitual drinker. Of late the method of creating disgust for alcohol has taken on the name of "conditioned response method" and as such is widely used to control or abolish the desire for alcohol expressed by the habitual moderate drinker.

In essence the treatment consists of administering a nauseating drug at the time a person drinks various alcoholic beverages; none is given when he drinks non-alcoholic beverages. Thus the unpleasant sensation of vomiting is in time associated with alcoholic beverages but with no other beverage. Success is claimed for about 60 per cent of all habitual drinkers treated with this technique.

Substitutive method. Substitutive treatment is used with success with those habitual drinkers who, while they are not problem drinkers, do have certain emotional and intellectual difficulties for which alcohol serves as an antidote. The treatment is psychological in nature and consists mainly in finding acceptable substitutes for alcohol. New interests are created and old ones are revived.

Psychological-reeducational method. A few of the habitual drinkers are neurotic and as such are regarded by the psychologist as problem drinkers. They are neurotic introverts who, because they are unable or unwilling to assume the emotional responsibilities of adult life, seek to hide under the cloak of alcohol. The neurotic drinker has to overcome his fear of people and things before he can regain control over alcohol. The pleadings and prayers of others have no effect on him. It is only when he shakes off his juvenile thinking and begins to realize that peace, contentment, relaxation and happiness come from within himself, and not from the inside of a beer glass, that he is on his way to recovery from the bondage of liquor.

To help him in making this readjustment, a psychological re-educational treatment which is reinforced by correction of physical damage—if any—and by a careful nutritional program has met with great success. The treatment consists essentially in having the drinker, with the assistance of the therapist, retrace his life course, and re-make, or make anew, an emotional adjustment that will fit into reality that demands such adjustment. To accomplish this, the drinker and the therapist together explore higher and higher emotional levels, and finding them satisfactory, the desire to live permanently on those levels is born in the drinker. Proper attention to health and nutrition does the rest.

THE COMPULSIVE DRINKER

The habitual drinker stands at the cross-roads. He may become a symptomatic, a psychotic, a stupid or a compulsive drinker. *Symptomatic* drinkers are those individuals whose excessive drinking is a symptom of a disturbed mental state. They are classified into acute alcoholic hallucinotic, alcoholic paranoid, and dipsomanic drinkers. *Psychotic drinkers* are those individuals whose excessive drinking leads to alcoholic psychoses. They are classified into delirium tremens patients, Korsakoff psychotics, and chronic alcoholics. *Stupid drinkers* are those individuals whose excessive drinking is the result of mental deficiency. They are classified into spineless, moderately anti-social, and criminal drinkers. Finally, *compulsive drinkers* are those individuals who have developed an abnormal craving for alcohol and an inability to resist it. They are classified into degenerate, impassioned, and self-aggrandizing drinkers.

The most direct line from habitual drinking is to compulsive drinking. The compulsive drinker is best known of all the different alcoholics. Degenerate compulsive drinkers are indifferent to the emotional and intellectual stimuli of life. They are unsociable and lack the vivacity required for living. They drink not to forget but to make life tolerable.

The impassioned compulsive drinker is a very confused individual. He lacks emotional stability and in many respects acts the part of an immature child. Unable to reduce or resolve his conflicts, he experiences many emotional flareups. He drinks to forget his troubles.

Finally the self-aggrandizing compulsive drinker is a person with great ambition but little energy. He craves to dominate others but does not have the willpower to effect such domination. Failing in real life, he finds an outlet for his boastings and aggressive tendencies through the "bottle."

CAUSES OF ALCOHOL ADDICTION

The causes which lie behind alcohol addiction are many and varied. They include personality, heredity, constitution, psychotic and psychopathic tendencies, the emotional situation, environmental factors, tolerance, and the physiological processes. The superficial motives for compulsive drinking are reflected in the benefits or effects the addict expects to get from drink. Alcohol provides him with release of inhibitions, compensations, and a means of escape from conflict and anxiety.

Physiological Factors in Alcohol Addiction

The physiological theories on the causes of alcohol addiction are limited to a discussion of factors responsible for secondary addiction. They do not deal with the initial factors which start the process of addiction. Ladrague believes that in the course of excessive drinking an accumulation of toxins occurs which then leads to a pathological drive for drink. Williams mentions metabolic poisoning as the cause for dependence upon alcohol. Several investigators stress the allergic state, resulting from an increasing sensitization to alcohol over a more or less extended period of time. Others hold that secondary addiction to alcohol rests on a predisposing physiological constitution.

Hereditary Factors in Alcohol Addiction

A few investigators concede that while the hereditary factor is of importance as an etiological factor in most alcoholic addicts, in some it plays no part. Other investigators hold that hereditary constitution does play a role as a cause of alcohol addiction, but not out of proportion to numerous other factors which enter into the situation.

Taking exception to the all-inclusive generalizations on causes of alcohol addiction made by writers who base their claims on hereditary predisposition or psychopathic constitution, Bowman and Jellinek point out that recent investigations have shown that only some 35 to 40 per cent of alcoholic addicts have a hereditary liability or a psychopathic disposition. Psychopathic disposition and hereditary liability may be expected in the symptomatic drinker and the true addict. The large group of drinkers which furnishes the secondary addict is generally free from hereditary liability as well as from psychopathic disposition.

Tolerance as a Causal Factor

According to Bowman and Jellinek, gastric alcohol intolerance is practically always preventive of the development of addiction, while psychological alcohol tolerance fosters addiction. High psychological tolerance, i.e., the facility for managing the stress set up by alcohol may lead to heavy drinking and ultimately to secondary addiction.

Social Factors in Alcohol Addiction

The following is a partial list of social factors which supposedly foster alcohol addiction: child labor, unemployment, long hours of work, low wages, unsanitary living conditions, uncertain opportunities of recreation and leisure, poverty, easy accessibility and cheapness of alcoholic beverages, high pressure advertising, certain occupations (brewery worker, distillery worker, bar attendant, waiter), social customs, social mores, and social ambivalence. Most of the social factors advanced as causal explanations of alcohol addiction, however, do not go beyond the stage of mere suggestion.

Personality as a Factor in Alcohol Addiction

Most important of the causal factors responsible for alcohol addiction is personality. There are few students of alcoholism who fail to recognize that personality plays the decisive role in alcohol addiction. The majority of investigators of the alcoholic personality are interested in its structural aspects. Others, especially the psychoanalysts, have concentrated on the developmental aspects of personality. A third group of investigators, mostly those interested in the constitutional background of the drinker, have emphasized the genetically determined personality factors. Finally, a fourth group of investigators has been looking for unitary personality types among drinkers. The personality studies encountered in the literature, whether they are concerned with the structural, developmental, constitutional or the typological aspects of the drinker's personality, are best understood when we approach them by way of the four methodological orientations most commonly used, viz., naturalistic, clinical, psychometric, and psychoanalytic.

PERSONALITY STUDIES

Naturalistic Studies

The naturalistic personality studies of alcoholics consist of generalizations framed by observers who have had considerable experience with both normal and abnormal drinkers. The generalizations are based on personality types encountered by medical and psychological practitioners, and as such rest mostly on subjective impressions. However, the consistency with which certain personality types have come up gives them the verity and congruence required for serious consideration.

The constitutional psychopathic inferior drinker. This type is seen as an individual who, though he is often engaging and charming in manner and not at all intellectually defective is, nevertheless, grossly defective in practically all other functions of the mind and and personality. He is unstable in his emotions, defective in his judgments, deficient in his ethics, and totally inadequate and unreliable in his personal and social reactions and behavior. He fights drink but does not have sufficient will power to stop drinking.

The aggressive drinker. The aggressive drinker is choleric in disposition. He is inconsiderate and anti-social. Alcohol often leads him into serious aggressive behavior and sometimes turns him into a vicious maniac.

The unstable drinker. This type is restless, impulsive, impatient, and impetuous. Alcohol, while it removes some of his conflicts and inhibitions, leaves him in an extremely nervous and depressed state of mind.

The adynamic drinker. This drinker is characterized by lack of drive. He has little or no ambition, flits from one job to another, and usually belongs to a comparatively low socio-economic level.

The primitive drinker. Like the adynamic dull drinker, the primitive drinker belongs to a low socio-economic level. His behavior is generally based on primitive impulse. He lives for the moment, does little rational planning, and is too absorbed in sensual pleasures to care much about the consequences of his drinking.

The psychoneurotic drinker. This type has an overwhelming desire to escape from the burdensome facts of everyday life. He is emotionally immature. Unhappy childhood experiences, together with lack of training in responsibilities have shaped for him a personality that lacks integration. Every new experience of life, tinged as it is with the possibilities of conflict, has hastened in him the development of an ingrown or introverted personality. Alcohol helps the psychoneurotic drinker to shut out reality. In alcohol he finds an agent which quickly and effectively does away with reality.

Clinical Studies

Many of the clinical personality studies of drinkers rest on observations made by clinicians during repeated interviews with alcoholic patients. Other studies are based on detailed analyses of the case histories of addicts. Quite often the clinician lacks confidence in his own generalizations, and rather than open himself to criticism, he makes epigrammatic statements about the personality of drinkers which he culls from reasons given by alcoholics for their drinking. While such remarks do not give us as sound a picture of the personality of the drinker as those coming from clinical observations or case history analysis, they nevertheless postulate personalities which show the needs expressed in reasons for drinking. Hence these remarks have to be considered in any clinical evaluation of the drinker's personality.

The clinical approach to alcohol and personality is best illustrated by Tiebout's description of the personality syndrome of alcoholic addiction. Tiebout's observations rest on an exhaustive study of more than 200 alcoholics over a period of nine years. Tiebout crystallized his observations into a uniform picture of the alcoholic personality only after they were checked and re-checked by clinical experience.

The nuclear pattern of the personality of alcohol addicts, according to Tiebout, consists of the following six traits: (1) an unconscious drive or need to dominate; (2) a prevailing negative, hostile feeling tone; (3) a capacity for ecstatic peaks, in which all hostile emotions become temporarily submerged in an overflow of affirmative feeling; (4) a sense of loneliness and isolation; (5) feelings of inferiority and superiority which exist simultaneously in the individual; and (6) a striving for perfection.

Psychometric Studies

Psychometric studies of the personality of alcohol addicts may be divided into two main groups, viz.: (1) studies which make use of questionnaires and inventories such as the Humm-Wadsworth Temperament Scale, Strong Vocational Interest Blank, Bernreuter Personality Inventory, Minnesota Multiphasic Personality Inventory, personal history questionnaires, rating scales, and similar personality techniques; and (2) studies which make use of projective psychometric techniques such as the Rorschach Psychodiagnostic Test and the Murray Thematic Apperception Test.

Inventory and questionnaire approach. The inventory and questionnaire approach to alcohol and personality is well illustrated by

Hampton's study. Hampton studied 100 compulsive alcoholics without psychoses, culled by random sampling from the population of Alcoholics Anonymous, and compared them with 100 equated normal controls. In a study of the personality characteristics and configurations of these groups, Hampton used the Minnesota Multiphasic Personality Inventory, the Strong Vocational Interest Blank, the Bernreuter Personality Inventory, the Otis Self-Administering Tests of Mental Ability, and a twelve-page Personal History Questionnaire prepared especially for alcoholics.

Hampton found that compulsive alcoholics are not a definitely homogeneous group as far as personality is concerned; they differ significantly from normal controls with respect to a number of characteristics and they exhibit several personality constellations, but there are also many exceptions.

In general alcoholics do not drive themselves as hard at work or play as do non-alcoholics. They are more decisive in their opinions, judgments and actions; they are quick, exceedingly nervous, quick-tempered, and easily aroused emotionally. They are also more original and more witty than non-alcoholics. While they are good-natured and uninhibited, they are not as easy-going as they appear to be. Although resourceful, they apparently are unable to apply this resourcefulness to further their own adjustment. They often feel lonely, are easily discouraged, and feel criticism too much. In spite of their sensitivity, however, alcoholics are not as cynical as they have often been thought to be and they are more active, more intelligent, more energetic, and more ambitious than non-alcoholics. They show greater initiative and are more versatile, but they also procrastinate more freely than do non-alcoholics.

Personality constellation of alcoholics. The clinically defined "psychopathic" and "neurotic" personality syndromes are encountered more frequently among alcoholics than any other constellations. Psychopathic alcoholics are more assertive and show a higher degree of extroversion and dominance in face-to-face relationships than do non-alcoholics; they are somewhat less stable emotionally but more self-confident and more gregarious than non-alcoholics. As a group they lack deep emotional response, are unable to profit from their experience, and show disregard for social mores, leading to such digressions in conduct as lying, stealing, and sexual immorality. They show a marked overproductivity in thought and action, are over-ambitious, extremely vigorous and enthusiastic, and full of grandiose plans, many of which are half-formed and few of which are carried to completion. They undertake too many things, are almost always on-the-go, but never seem to get anywhere in particular.

Neurotic alcoholics are less assertive and show a higher degree of introversion and submission in face-to-face relationships than do non-alcoholics. They are considerably less stable emotionally, less self-confident and less gregarious than non-alcoholics. As a group they are too much concerned over their health; they frequently complain of pains and aches which are obviously hypochondriac defenses; immature in their approach to adult problems, regressive in their behavior, pessimistic in their outlook, they show poor emotional morale, and invariably react to the stresses and strains of life with deep avoidant depression.

Projective approach. The over-all picture of the personality of the alcoholic based on projective studies, is one of self-centered wish-fulfillment, weak emotional control, anxiety and concern about the body, and rather high ambition with limited actual achievement. A few alcoholics show good understanding of everyday reality. By and large, however, the alcoholic tries to withdraw from his usual environment. A few try to extravert their introversion, but with little success.

Psychoanalytic Studies

Since the motivational level of personality structure is basic to other levels, as perceptual and behavioral, psychoanalytic studies furnish us not only with the deepest insight into the personality of the alcoholic, but also with the most thorough developmental approach to it. Unfortunately, however, psychoanalytic studies are based on small samples and deal almost exclusively with the true neurotic drinker and the primary addict. There is little—except in inferred statements—in psychoanalytic studies of the personality of drinkers which gives us insight into the abnormal drinker whose addiction is primarily externally rather than internally determined.

While psychoanalysts are agreed on the basic personality elements involved in alcohol addiction, e.g., regression to oral phase, mother fixation, perverted sexual activity, repressed homosexuality, suicide, castration anxiety, and primary narcissism, there is disagreement about which element or elements are of true causal significance.

In comparing male and female alcoholics, Wall found significant sex differences. Men alcoholics present a fairly composite personality picture. They exhibit a systematized Oedipus complex (mother attachment); they lack ambition; they are irresponsible; they tend to solitary drinking, indicative of introversion; and they show a gradual deterioration of personality. In women alcoholics the personality picture is much more individual and thus more varied. Alcohol addiction in women is usually traceable to some definite life situation which has resulted in catastrophic emotional involvements.

This cleavage in the personality pictures of men and women alcoholics is only peripheral, however. Underneath, both men and women alcoholics suffer from an all-enveloping narcissism which increasingly incapacitates them for adequate adjustment to reality and the responsibilities that it engenders. Alcohol, according to Wall, serves as an escape to the infantile level of behavior; it is a regression to the happy (in retrospect) state of infantile oral omnipotence.

The family background of most alcoholics, Knight claims, consists of an oversolicitous mother opposed by a stern, harsh and cold father. The inconsistency of discipline and training resulting, made the child (the potential alcoholic) too dependent upon the mother and afraid of the father. Never gaining real integration of personality, the child grown into an adult is incapable of adjusting adequately to the vagaries of a competitive life. Rather than acknowledge failure, he begins to think of the world about him as hostile, and he identifies it with his father. Alcohol provides him with an opportunity to escape from this hostile world (father) and return to the infant stage of mother dependence, where harm is warded off by a solicitous mother and gratifications are easy and simple and oral.

Robbins, on the other hand, sees the regression as a sham drama staged by the alcoholic. The alcoholic does not really want to go back to his real mother; he drowns her in alcohol, so to speak. The mother he wants to go to and encompass is a fantasy production, a figment of his own imagination. He has built up in his own distorted mind a delusional picture of a mother who is loving, kind, great and ever-satisfying. The picture is a delusion, but the alcoholic needs it to sustain his illusion of self-sufficiency.

Alcohol then, in a sense, becomes a substitute for mother deprivation. In the state of inebriety the delusional picture of a mother takes on flesh and bone; in the state of sobriety the delusional picture gives way to rational orientation and the alcoholic is back with his mother deprivation complex. Alcohol, according to Robbins, serves the inebriate in three ways: (1) it gratifies oral, bodily and cellular cravings; (2) it maintains a personality economy in which narcissism is vital; and (3) it sustains the existence of a manufactured delusional mother on whose shoulder the alcoholic may (which is quite often) cry out his troubles and feed his self-pity.

TREATMENT OF ALCOHOL ADDICTION

Psychological Treatments

Punitive methods. The therapeutic effectiveness of abrupt withdrawal of alcohol, punishment and legal confinement in an asylum, penal, or similar institution has been favorably reported on by various writers who claim cures ranging from five to 50 per cent. However, since the criterion of cure is not stated and the length of abstinence following discharge is at best for only two to three years, these statistics on cure must be accepted with caution. Voluntary commitment may result in an appreciable percentage of probable cures, but prohibition, punishment, or enforced hospitalization is not likely to be of much use in the treatment of alcohol addiction.

Psycho-social therapy. Psycho-social therapy consists of proper medical care during the acute stage followed by advice and help in securing employment, the correction of faulty home environment, associates, etc., and aid in smoothing out domestic and other incompatibilities. Results obtained with this method are so disappointing that most medical-social workers avoid it.

Religious conversion. A survey of reports on various forms of spiritual appeal as a method of treating alcoholic addicts points to a cure in from 30 to 70 per cent of the cases treated. The religious therapy is best exemplified by Alcoholics Anonymous. The successes claimed by this body of ex-alcoholics—from 50 to 70 per cent —are largely due to an effective mobilization of affective relationships. Other religious treatments such as those sponsored by the Salvation Army, the Alcoholic Committee of the Greater New York Federation of Churches, and the many homes and farms for inebriates in this country and abroad, have had successes ranging from 30 to 50 per cent. While spiritual conversion is the motivating power behind the religious cures, other therapeutic measures are used to support the beneficial work of a religious reawakening.

Conventional psychotherapy in controlled environment. This method practiced in a controlled environment—farm, hospital, or sanitarium—has resulted in from 15 to 75 per cent of cures. This type of treatment is usually limited to selected cases and extends over a considerable period of time, from six months to two or more years. Treatment is on a strictly voluntary basis. Hence only the sincere and persevering alcoholic can benefit from it.

Conventional psychotherapy in normal environment. Treatment in a normal environment—outpatient treatment—is apparently favorable for the neurotic addict but unfavorable for the psychopathic addict. The method is thus of limited application. Results are said to be good, but no percentages of cure are given. The primary objective of this method is to establish a mentally conditioned aversion to drinking. But practically every therapist who has tried the method has his own ideas on just how the aversion is to be established. The procedures advocated under psychotherapy in the normal environment run the gamut of every therapy tried.

Psychoanalysis. This method is by far the most representative of the psychotherapeutic methods, but its application to alcohol addicts has failed to produce very encouraging results. The procedure is cumbersome, lengthy, and too costly for most alcoholics to afford. The number treated by this method is small and the reports are barren of statistical data that might indicate percentages of cures.

Hypnosis. Use of hypnosis by itself as a method of treating alcoholic addicts has been discarded by most therapists. In connection with other therapies, however, the method is still widely used. Cures by hypnosis in conjunction with conditioned response therapy range from 50 to 75 per cent.

Physiological Treatments

Conditioned response therapy. Of the physiological methods for treating alcoholic addicts, conditioned response therapy seems to hold out the greatest hope. This method is widely applicable, consumes little time, and results in a large percentage of cures. The basic method of operation of the conditioned response method involves the establishment of an aversion or distaste for alcoholic beverages by virtue of their association during treatment with some sort of noxious stimulus. The latter stimulus is usually concerned with the elicitation of nausea or vomiting and is called the unconditioned stimulus. The conditioned (or conditioning) stimulus is represented by various alcoholic beverages. The repeated association of these two stimuli, under appropriate circumstances, will result finally in the ability of the conditioned stimulus (liquor) to elicit the (noxious) response formerly elicited by the unconditioned stimulus. Among the unconditioning stimuli used are apomorphine, piecac, and painful shock.

Elevation of blood sugar level. Students of alcoholism who stress the hypoglycemic causation of alcohol addiction feel that therapy should consist of raising the blood sugar levels of alcoholics. This is affected by administering glucose, insulin, or sucrose. Spinal puncture, hydrotherapy, and psychotherapy apparently can be used to advantage as adjunctive methods of therapy for the hypoglycemic alcoholic. Since hypoglycemia is found only in a relatively small percentage of alcoholics, this method of treatment has obvious limitations for application. In the treatment of the average alcoholic the elevation of blood sugar levels has not been very successful.

Spinal drainage. The use of spinal drainage over a prolonged period, with concomitant reduction of intracranial pressure and relief of cerebral edema, apparently has beneficial effects on alcoholic addicts, especially those suffering from alcoholic psychosis. A number of therapists have reported using this type of treatment with varied success. The cases treated, however, are too few in number, and the results too inconclusive to warrant making any definite conclusions with respect to the efficacy of spinal drainage as a therapeutic measure for the alcoholic addict.

Convulsive therapy. Insulin or metrazol, used in convulsive or subconvulsive doses, has also been tried by a number of investigators as a curative measure for alcoholic addicts. A survey of the literature on convulsive therapy reveals two definite schools of thought. The first emphasizes the personality change following shock; the second, an unexplained effect following sub-shock doses of insulin or metrazol.

Pharmacological Treatments

Pharmacological methods of treatment for alcohol addiction have fallen into disfavor in recent years, probably because psychologists and psychiatrists feel that these methods cannot possibly combat a problem which is largely psychological in nature. Results obtained from the use of pharmacological methods corroborate the pessimistic attitudes expressed by the psychotherapists.

Results reported with benzedrine sulphate are conflicting. With respect to one thing, however, there is agreement. Benzedrine therapy does alleviate the acute depression which follows an alcoholic debauch. The very nature of this relief, however, presents difficulties which in many instances lead, not to cure, but to even greater addiction. When the patient discovers that the distressing after-effects of a spree can be quickly dissipated by benzedrine, he becomes habituated to the drug and goes about drinking with greater abandon.

Much interest has recently been aroused in vitamin therapy for the alcoholic addict. Thus far this interest has not sufficiently crystallized into experimental investigations to warrant a definite statement on the curative possibilities involved.

Atropine and strychnine therapy furnishes results which are too insignificant to warrant acceptance. The therapy has some value in the treatment of acute alcoholic episodes, but since these drugs act only as sedatives, they have no lasting curative properties.

REFERENCES

ANONYMOUS: *Alcoholics Anonymous*. New York, Works Publishing, Inc. 1948. The story of how many thousands of men and women have recovered from alcohol.

EARLE, C. J.: *How to Help an Alcoholic*. Philadelphia, The Westminster Press, 1952. A brief account of some approaches to alcoholism.

KANT, FRITZ: *Treatment of the Alcoholic*. Springfield, Illinois, Thomas, 1954.

HIRSH, J.: *The Problem Drinker*. New York, Duell, Sloan & Pearce, 1949. A general discussion on the problem.

JELLINEK, E. M.: *Alcoholic Addiction and Chronic Alcoholism*. New Haven, Yale University Press, 1942. A report on an extensive study of the problem.

FORRESTER, GLEN C.: *Use of Chemical Tests for Alcohol in Traffic Law Enforcement*. Springfield, Illinois, Thomas, 1950.

KING, A. R.: *The Psychology of Drunkenness*. Mt. Vernon, Iowa, Cornell College, 1943. A brief psychological approach to the problem.

McCARTHY, R. G. and DOUGLASS, E. M.: *Alcohol and Social Responsibility*. New York, Thomas Y. Crowell, 1949. Much emphasis on the educational approach.

MANN, M.: *Primer on Alcoholism*. New York, Rinehart, 1950. A general discussion of the problem.

NATIONAL FORUM: *The Alcohol Problem*. Chicago, National Forum Inc., 1948. Facts concerning alcoholism presented largely in pictographs.

STRECKER, E. A. and CHAMBERS, F. T., JR.: *Alcohol: One Man's Meat*. New York, Macmillan, 1938. An older account of the problem that has received much attention.

Chapter 13

THE PSYCHOLOGY OF THE DRUG ADDICT[1]

By

ALFRED R. LINDESMITH

INTRODUCTION

Drug addiction is an old problem, found in many areas of the world. Many different attempts to control or eliminate it have been tried but it has shown a remarkable resistance to all attempts to suppress it or to prevent its spread. Our discussion will be concerned mainly with the problem of drug addiction as it exists in the United States today. To understand the psychology of the drug addict it is first necessary to understand the unique properties of the drugs used by addicts and the physiological reactions which they produce.

Types of Drugs

The drugs that are most important in the problem of addiction are those substances generally classified as "depressants." They have a narcotic or sedative effect on the organism, induce sleep, and reduce anxiety. The raw material for most of these drugs is a gum obtained from the seed pod of the opium poppy. Heroin, the drug most widely used today by addicts in the United States, and morphine are both derived from opium. Other derivatives occasionally used are codeine, dilaudid, and metopon. Synthetic substitutes for the opiates, with similar addicting properties, have recently been developed, but these are seldom used by addicts. The barbiturate drugs, commonly known as "sleeping pills," are chemically manufactured sedatives which are not legally defined as addicting drugs,

---

[1]The author acknowledges, with thanks, the contribution of James W. Hughes, Instructor in Sociology, University of Kentucky, to the preparation of this chapter.

319

although current research indicates that they have many of the characteristics of the opiates. Marijuana, derived from Indian hemp, and cocaine, derived from coca leaves, are both controlled under federal narcotics legislation, but these drugs induce a reaction quite different from that produced by the opiates. Neither produces illness when its use is discontinued, a distinguishing characteristic of the opiates and barbiturates. The significance of marijuana is that it introduces the user to dependence on a drug for satisfactory adjustment to life and may lead him later to turn to a stronger drug such as heroin. Cocaine, unlike the opiates, is a "stimulant," inducing sleeplessness and excitability, and is sometimes used in combination with one of the opiates in what addicts call a "speedball." The addiction problem in the United States consists primarily of the use of the opiates, particularly heroin, and the following discussion will be concerned primarily with opiate addiction.

THE ADDICT AND THE LAW

Historical Development of Narcotics Legislation

Little effort was made in the United States to limit the distribution or use of narcotics until after the first decade of the twentieth century. They generally were dispensed rather freely by the medical profession; drug stores sold supplies cheaply and openly, and many patent medicines containing opiates were advertised widely. The distribution of drugs was not linked with crime and those who became addicted, although not socially approved, were not regarded as criminals. Knowledge that many persons had become addicted to narcotics came to general public attention early in the present century and this growing concern led to a series of attempts to regulate the use of narcotics. In 1909 a federal law was passed which aimed at the suppression of opium smoking and in 1914 the Harrison Act was enacted, providing the legal basis for the present program of narcotics control.

Legal Status of the Addict

Prior to 1914, most addicts were not criminals. They were usually medical patients who had become addicted in the course of treatment or persons addicted through the practice of self-medication with legally purchased drugs. The effect of the Harrison Act, as it was interpreted by the Treasury Department and the courts, and later as supported by additional legislation, was to make it impossible for drug users to obtain supplies legally as they had done before. Dealers were prohibited from dispensing drugs except on medical prescription, and physicians were no longer permitted to prescribe drugs for the addicted person. Addiction itself, in the technical sense, was not a violation of federal criminal statutes, but since all legal sources of drugs were suddenly cut off, the addict now almost inevitably and automatically became a criminal. The law made it an offense to buy, sell, transport, or have any illicit drugs in one's possession. This means that although addiction itself is not criminal, the drug user today, with rare exceptions, must constantly violate federal law to maintain his habit. Before 1914 the morphine or heroin addict of the criminal type so common today was rarely found in federal or state prisons. The only exceptions were a few violators of an earlier law designed to suppress opium smoking. It was not until the Harrison Act was passed that narcotic addiction, and the illicit traffic on which the addict then became dependent, assumed their present dimensions. Some states and communities made attempts before 1914 to regulate narcotics, and since then they generally have passed legislation patterned after the Harrison Act. In 1932, in cooperation with the Federal Bureau of Narcotics, the National Conference of Commissioners on Uniform State Laws proposed a Uniform Narcotic Drug Act. This act or similar legislation, modeled after the Harrison Act, has now been enacted by all but three states. Some states and cities have laws which make addiction itself a punishable offense.

THE EXTENT OF ADDICTION

The Number of Addicts in the United States

After 1914, when their legal status became that of criminals, it became necessary for the drug addicts to keep their drug use concealed. It must frankly be admitted, therefore, that the secret nature of addiction makes it impossible to estimate accurately the number of addicts in the United States today. The estimates made, usually on the basis of federal arrest and conviction rates, frequently have been influenced by the vested interests of agencies or individuals, leading to minimizing the number at one time and to exaggerating at another. All that accurately can be said is that the number is unknown but that all evidence indicates a substantial recent increase.

After the addiction problem became a police concern, the main source of data concerning the extent of the illicit traffic became police statistics on narcotics cases. These are of two types: federal and non-federal. Unfortunately, complete national figures of both types are not available from 1915 to the present, and therefore it is hazardous or impossible to use such data alone to estimate the extent of addiction.

Federal Narcotics Violations

During the early years of the Harrison Act, not only was there confusion among physicians, police, and the general public concerning the precise meaning of the law but also a lack of adequate law enforcement machinery. The Act was not finally given its present interpretation until about 1920. Enforcement first was the responsibility of the Bureau of Internal Revenue and relevant data were published in the annual Report of the Commissioner of Internal Revenue. When the Volstead Act went into effect in 1920, both drug and liquor laws were enforced by a prohibition unit created within this bureau. From 1927 to 1930, enforcement was directed by a Commissioner of Prohibition, who published statistics in his annual reports. After 1930 a separate Federal Bureau of Narcotics was organized and became responsible for control of the narcotics traffic. It since has reported annually on its enforcement activities.[2] Table II indicates the total number of violations and convictions under the federal narcotic drug laws from 1915 to 1951.

---

[2]United States Treasury Department, Bureau of Narcotics: *Traffic in Opium and Other Dangerous Drugs*. Washington, D. C.

Sources: 1915-1926 Reports of the Commissioner of Internal Revenue; 1927-1929. Reports of the Commissioner of Prohibition; 1930-1943 Federal Bureau of Narcotics, annual reports; 1945, 1950, 1951 Press release, Federal Bureau of Narcotics.
   xNo data available.
   *Beginning in 1931, "violations reported" is changed to "persons reported for criminal violations."

TABLE II
Federal Narcotics Laws: Violations and Convictions
1915-1951

Year	Violations	Convictions	Marijuana Violations
1951	3442	3042	1177
1950	4494	3247	1490
1949	3779	x	1643
1948	2814	x	1278
1947	2340	x	911
1946	2339	x	953
1945	1774	1120	603
1944	2169	x***	901
1943	2402	1301	912
1942	2520	1447	962
1941	2467	1471	1198
1940	3009	2084	..950
1939	4300	2697	951
1938	3783	2531	1191
1937	4071	2577	250**
1936	5531	2880	
1935	6221	3118	
1934	5698	2674	
1933	4392	2590	
1932	5169	2888	
1931*	5035	3128	
1930	7004	4962	
1929	6732	5193	
1928	6119	4738	
1927	6129	4469	
1926	6602	5120	
1925	7232	5600	
1924	5685	4242	
1923	5629	4194	
1922	5168	3104	
1921	2707	1583	
1920	2425	908	
1919	1008	582	
1918	888	392	
1917	803	445	
1916	1910	663	
1915	4886	115	

**Federal Marijuana Tax Act became effective in 1937; violations and convictions totals do not include marijuana violations or convictions.

***From 1944 to the present, total convictions were not reported; totals for 1945, 1950, and 1951 were included in a press release from the Federal Bureau of Narcotics, March 23, 1952.

In the first five years of the Harrison Act, the number of convictions remained under 1000. Beginning in 1918, when the present interpretation of the law was being established, convictions under federal law increased sharply to a total of 5600 in 1925, the highest level ever reached. From then through 1930, convictions averaged about 5000 annually. Then, in 1931, a change in federal policy transferred a large portion of the responsibility for narcotics law enforcement to non-federal agencies, and a sharp drop occurred in convictions reported by the newly established Federal Bureau of Narcotics. From 1931 to 1939, the total number of convictions averaged less than 2800 annually. A further decrease occurred during the war years of 1940 to 1945, when the international drug traffic was disrupted and many young men were mobilized into the armed forces. The total of 1120 convictions in 1945 was the smallest number since 1920. An increase followed World War II until 3247 convictions were reported for 1950, the largest number since 1930, and only a slight decrease to 3042 was reported for 1951. These statistics on federal convictions show a sharp increase after passage of the Harrison Act and World War I, followed by a progressive decline for twenty years, and then a second post-war increase to slightly over half the previous maximum. However, since non-federal agencies have taken increased responsibility for enforcement of the narcotics laws, attempts to estimate the extent of addiction should be based increasingly on the reports of non-federal agencies.

Non-Federal Narcotics Violations

Until 1930 violations of the narcotics laws had been regarded as an exclusive concern of the federal government, but then the Federal Bureau of Narcotics was organized as a separate agency within the Treasury Department and began to urge the states and their political subdivisions to enact and enforce anti-narcotics laws of their own. From 1948 until the present there has again been an increase in non-federal enforcement activities. Many states have set up special state narcotic law enforcement squads, and some of the larger cities such as New York, Chicago, Philadelphia, and Los Angeles have both special police squads and special narcotics courts.

This increased state and local responsibility means that consideration of federal law violations alone does not give a complete picture of the extent of narcotics law violations.

The best source of national data on anti-narcotics activities of non-federal agencies is provided by the Federal Bureau of Investigation. The annual reports of narcotics law violations are based upon the analysis of fingerprint records sent in by local and state police jurisdictions throughout the country. They exclude federal offenses and do not provide a completely reliable basis for estimating the extent of addiction. They were not available until 1932, not all cases are fingerprinted, and many jurisdictions do not utilize the fingerprint services of the FBI.

The following table gives the annual totals of narcotics cases reported to the FBI and the rates per 100,000 of the population. They include violations of the anti-marijuana laws, whereas the

TABLE III

Non-Federal Arrests for Narcotics Drug Law Violations
1932-1951

Year	Total Arrests	Rate per 100,000
1951	13030	12.8
1950	8539	10.2
1949	6546	9.5
1948	4846	6.3
1947	3388	5.3
1946	2807	4.7
1945	1935	3.9
1944	1731	4.5
1943	1361	4.6
1942	1123	4.1
1941	2593	3.8
1940	5014	4.7
1939	4599	5.9
1938	4164	6.7
1937	3996	7.2
1936	3896	7.7
1935	3679	7.9
1934	3918	x
1933	3370	x
1932	2648	x

Source: *Uniform Crime Reports*, Federal Bureau of Investigation, Department of Justice, Washington, D. C. Based on fingerprint reports only; excluding federal violations.

federal conviction totals given above do not. These figures summarize police reports from communities which, in 1951, covered only about one-third of the population of the United States, and even the coverage for that area is probably incomplete.

The FBI figures are generally consistent with those on federal activities, especially when rates are used, eliminating some discrepancies resulting from variations in the size of areas reporting. Like the federal statistics, they indicate that the smallest number of narcotics law violations occurred in the early 1940's, the total remained low during the war years, but beginning in 1946 rose sharply to the present all time high of 13,030 arrests or a rate of 12.8 per 100,000 of the population. These arrest rates also reflect the increasing responsibility of state and local agencies in enforcing the anti-narcotics laws. Therefore, they also indicate that the recent increase in narcotics law violations has been greater than that shown by the federal figures alone. This confirms, to some extent, claims in the press that narcotics law violations are increasing each year and are now more prevalent than at any previous time in our national history. While the federal data alone indicate that a crest had been reached by 1950, with a subsequent decline, the non-federal data indicate that the increase continued through 1951, and as yet shows no sign of a decline. Consideration of the social characteristics of recent violators makes the present increase seem even more significant.

SOCIAL CHARACTERISTICS OF DRUG ADDICTS

Sex

The law enforcement officer today finds that drug addicts known to him are predominantly males. Before 1914, however, the reverse was true. When drug use was unrestricted and most addiction began with self-medication, at least two-thirds of the addicts were women. After 1914, as addiction and criminality became associated, the number and percentage of female addicts gradually dropped, and as with criminals in general, males became predominant. By 1935 the Bureau of Narcotics estimated that only 20 per cent of the addicts were women, and the Uniform Crime Reports consistently indicated after 1942 that women constituted less than 15 per cent of the violators, with a low of 10 per cent from 1947 to 1949. The trend was arrested in 1950, however, women constituting 12 per cent of the narcotics law violators in 1950, 15 per cent in 1951, and 20 per cent in the first six months of 1952.

Race

Before the Harrison Act, most drug addicts were white. Of the non-whites, the largest group was composed of Asiatics, particularly Chinese immigrants who had brought with them the practice of opium smoking. In 1933, the first year in which the FBI reported information on the race of drug law violators, 15.8 per cent were Chinese, but by 1951 this proportion had decreased to an insignificant 1.7 per cent. On the other hand, as shown in Table IV, the proportion of Negroes has consistently increased from 10.7

TABLE IV

Non-Federal Narcotics Violators: Arrests by Race

1933-1951

Year	All Races	Total Arrests by Race			Percentage of Total		
		White	Negro	Chinese	White	Negro	Chinese
1951	13030	5873	6697	227	45.1	51.4	1.7
1950	8539	3939	4262	175	47.3	49.9	2.0
1949	6546	3620	2677	135	55.3	40.9	2.1
1948	4846	2876	1776	107	59.3	36.6	2.2
1947	3388	2167	1120	62	64.0	33.1	1.8
1946	2807	1773	903	96	63.2	32.2	3.4
1945	1935	1205	567	130	62.3	29.3	6.7
1944	1731	1009	517	186	58.3	29.8	10.7
1943	1361	806	347	169	59.2	25.4	12.4
1942	1123	694	244	165	61.8	21.7	14.7
1941	2593	1540	543	267	59.4	20.9	10.3
1940	5014	3118	968	527	62.2	19.3	10.5
1939	4599	2940	856	457	63.9	18.6	9.9
1938	4164	2553	779	444	61.3	18.7	10.7
1937	3996	2193	797	609	54.9	19.9	15.2
1936	3896	2224	593	698	57.1	15.2	18.0
1935	3679	2178	496	581	59.2	13.5	15.7
1934	3918	2327	511	621	59.4	13.4	15.8
1933	3370	2251	362	x	66.8	10.7	x

Source: *Uniform Crime Reports*, Federal Bureau of Investigation, Department of Justice, Washington, D. C.

Note: Percentages do not total 100% because miscellaneous groups are omitted.

per cent in 1933 to an all time high of 51.4 per cent in 1951. This increase has been particularly sharp since World War II, and is one of the most significant trends in drug addiction today.

Age

The most widely publicized aspect of narcotic addiction since World War II has been the increasing involvement of young people. Most studies of addicts before 1930 found that the majority had not begun the use of drugs until 25 to 30 years of age and the addict known to law enforcement officers was invariably an adult. The present situation is the culmination of a long term trend, related to the need of the illicit drug distributors for new customers as the number of persons addicted before the Harrison Act slowly decreased. The Bureau of Narcotics first reported in 1949 that for several years there had been an increase in the number of young

TABLE V

Involvement of Youth in Narcotics Violations

Percentage of Arrests by Age

	Percentage of Narcotics Violators		
Year	*Under 25*	*Under 21*	*Under 18*
1951	45.5	18.7	3.7
1950	44.6	18.1	2.9
1949	41.1	16.5	1.6
1948	40.7	18.6	1,4
1947	37.0	16.9	1.5
1946	31.0	12.4	1.6
1945	26.7	11.3	1.4
1944	24.0	9.0	
1943	20.7	8.6	
1942	17.2	6.7	
1941	27.1	10.1	
1940	26.8	7.3	
1939	22.8	7.0	
1938	23.9	7.9	
1937	22.3	7.8	
1936	19.2	5.8	
1935	17.1	4.5	
1934	16.4	4.7	
1933	15.5	4.1	
1932	15.1	3.3	

Source: *Uniform Crime Reports,* Federal Bureau of Investigation, Department of Justice, Washington, D. C.

people arrested. During 1950, over 400 teen-age addicts were treated at the Lexington Hospital. Many large cities became especially concerned and established police squads, courts, and treatment centers to deal especially with these young addicts.

Inspection of the FBI figures reveals a trend toward increased youthfulness of drug law violators ever since the first report. In 1932, only 15.1 per cent were under 25 and 3.3 per cent under 21. There was a progressive increase until in 1951, 45.5 per cent were under 25 and 18.8 per cent were under 21. In 1951, 5935 persons arrested were under 25, 2440 under 21, and 481 under 18. If these figures are valid, they show that large numbers of a new generation are making early contact with illicit drugs. Unless treatment is more successful with them than it has been with other groups, they will be of concern to law enforcement agencies for many years.

Place of Residence

When drugs were legally available, addicts were evenly distributed throughout the country, but after 1914 a trend began toward concentration of addicts nearer the illegal sources of supply in the large cities. The Uniform Crime Reports indicate that, during the last 20 years, cities of over 250,000 population always have had the highest rate of narcotic law violations. During the last 10 years these largest cities have had a rate of violations 10 times that of cities under 10,000, and in 1951 it was 23 times as high. Of the 7119 violations reported for 1951, 5174, or 73 per cent, occurred in cities of 250,000 or more. Even more significant, the sharp increases in violations since 1945 have been almost entirely the result of increases in these largest cities. Information on the geographic distribution of violations indicates that they are concentrated in the large urban centers on the coasts and borders of the United States.

Trends in Addiction

The above information on the changing characteristics of the drug addict population indicates some trends that are significant to the present and future problems of the law enforcement officer. With the change in the legal status of the addict and the development of the illicit traffic since 1914, addiction increasingly has been concentrated among urban males, particularly in the coastal and

TABLE VI

Non-Federal Narcotics Violations by Size of Community
Rate per 100,000 persons charged
1932-1951

		Size of Community					
Year	Total	Over 250,000	100,000- 250,000	50,000- 100,000	25,000- 50,000	10,000- 25,000	10,000 Under
1951	12.8	23.1	12.5	6.5	4.2	3.4	1.0
1950	10.2	18.8	8.5	5.7	2.7	3.0	1.5
1949	9.5	16.8	6.8	7.2	4.0	3.0	2.6
1948	6.3	9.9	6.2	5.9	2.9	2.0	2.6
1947	5.3	7.5	4.2	5.2	4.9	2.1	2.4
1946	4.7	7.1	4.7	4.7	2.2	1.8	1.5
1945	4.0	5.7	4.3	4.2	1.8	1.7	1.7
1944	4.5	7.4	3.5	4.5	1.8	1.3	1.2
1943	4.6	7.5	3.0	4.9	2.1	0.9	1.0
1942	4.1	7.7	3.5	3.7	1.1	1.6	2.2
1941	3.8	5.8	2.9	4.9	1.5	0.9	1.7
1940	4.7	7.7	3.7	4.9	1.2	1.0	1.1
1939	6.3	10.7	4.8	2.7	1.8	2.3	2.3
1938	6.7	10.0	7.6	4.0	2.4	1.8	2.6
1937	7.2	11.4	6.0	5.2	2.0	1.4	2.0
1936	7.7	11.9	6.8	4.4	3.2	1.1	1.7
1935	7.9	12.0	10.5	3.9	3.4	1.6	2.0
1934	7.6	11.4	9.0	4.0	3.0	2.3	1.0
1933	7.9	9.7	21.0	3.2	2.7	1.8	1.9
1932	5.9	8.5	8.2	3.1	2.3	2.5	3.6

Source: *Uniform Crime Reports*, Federal Bureau of Investigation, Department of Justice, Washington, D. C.

border regions where illicit drugs enter the country. As those addicted before 1914 decreased in number, the extent of addiction apparently declined, but in recent years a new group established contact with the illicit drug supply. The new addict is typically a young male, living in a large metropolitan area, and a member of a non-white minority group. There is some slight evidence that young females also are becoming involved. With the involvement of this new group, the extent of addiction has again increased and now may be greater than ever before in the history of American narcotics law enforcement.

NATURE OF THE DRUG HABIT

Initial Use

The non-addict finds it difficult to comprehend why anyone

uses narcotics, except for medical purposes. Obviously, at the time the drug is first used, the purpose is not to become addicted, and no one can be forced to purchase a supply of drugs or to use them continuously. As with alcohol, although excessive amounts of the opiate-like drugs may have a severe toxic and even fatal effect, reduced amounts produce a state of contentment, relaxation, and decreased emotional tension. Worries are forgotten, the individual feels more comfortable in social situations, conversation becomes easier, and an illusion of more efficient functioning is created. Although the first experience with the drug may temporarily produce nausea, this usually accompanies only the first few administrations, is temporary and of brief duration, and is followed by the feeling of well-being. This feeling, sometimes called "euphoria," is frequently exaggerated in the popular literature on addiction. The use of the opiates does not produce exotic mental imagery, abnormally aggressive behavior, or extreme pleasurable sensations, and it does not stimulate the user to engage in strange and unusual crimes. Pharmacologically, the drugs are depressants, not stimulants. In fact, the effects vary with different personalities, and the feeling of well-being is much more pronounced when the person is fatigued, depressed, or under emotional stress.

The motivations of the drug user are not unlike those of the user of alcohol and other intoxicating substances. There may be a desire to escape from the humdrum monotony and vexing problems of life, and someone recommends the use of drugs. Particularly with the young addict, the use of narcotics may have been recommended and approved as an exciting experience, a good way to get "high." Many of the young people in his neighborhood may be "playing around" with heroin or other drugs, and a desire to display bravado, to avoid being labeled "chicken" may motivate him to experiment for himself. Perhaps he has already been using marijuana and proceeds to the use of more powerful drugs with the erroneous assumption that they are similar except that they produce a stronger "kick." Frequently the members of a loosely knit neighborhood or street corner group dare him to try it. He may not be aware of the potential addicting properties of the drug, or he assumes that addiction only occurs in "weak-willed" individuals and will never happen to him. The pleasurable effects of the initial shots and the absence of any "hangover" lead him to try a few more until he becomes a regular user and eventually realizes that he is physically dependent on the drug and joins the ranks of full-fledged addicts.

In addition to the drug user and his associates, other persons are involved and their motivations also are important. The primary requirement in the recruitment of potential addicts is that a supply of the drug must be available so that they can use it long enough to establish addiction. Since the dispensing of narcotics by physicians and pharmacists is severely restricted by law, exposure to drugs therefore must take place through exposure to the illegal underworld traffic. The motives of the drug distributors are quite simple but important. They are interested in the best possible price and the assurance that a future customer has been gained. The direct contact is usually with an established addict whose continued supply of the drug is dependent on his success in selling the drugs which he has obtained from the next higher link in the distribution chain. If necessary, he may use all the techniques of the skilled salesman in encouraging the purchase and use of his wares.

Establishing the Habit

The motivation for the initial use is not nearly so significant, in understanding addiction, as the motivation for continuous use of the drug. After the user becomes aware of the nature of certain essential physiological reactions inherent in the chemical nature of the narcotic, the process of motivation is self-contained. Although addicts originally use the drug to induce its pleasurable effects, as use is repeated they find that they require increased amounts at shorter intervals to produce the desired results. This condition, called "tolerance," is similar to the reaction of the human organism to other toxic substances. Eventually the accommodation of the body to the drug reaches the point where the initial effects can no longer be obtained and the amount of drugs which can be used is limited only by the availability of the supply and the practical difficulties of preparation. Eventually, after drugs have been used regularly several times a day for two or three weeks, "physical dependence" is established. This means that if the body does not continue to receive the amount of the drug to which tolerance has developed, the person becomes ill. This disturbance of the physiological balance resulting from withdrawal of the drug is termed "withdrawal distress" or the "abstinence syndrome." At about the time for what would have been his next regular administration of the drug, the physically dependent person becomes restless and moves aimlessly about, is covered with "gooseflesh" and yawns violently. About eight to 16 hours later, he becomes drowsy and falls into a restless sleep, the "yen sleep," which lasts for several hours. Restlessness and nervousness then become pronounced and progressively worse, sneezing and chills appear, his eyes and nose run, he perspires profusely, and muscle cramps develop. Muscular spasm and twitching from side to side are common, sleep is impossible, and nausea and diarrhea develop. He refuses all food and water and may lose from five to 15 pounds in one day. These symptoms increase in intensity until about 48 to 72 hours have elapsed and then begin to disappear slowly. All acute symptoms usually disappear from five to seven days after the last intake of drugs. However, insomnia, restlessness, and general physical weakness may not completely disappear for three or four months.

Even when these abstinence symptoms are most acute, a new administration of the drug brings about a radical change, and in an hour or less, the addict becomes well. When the addict reaches the stage of physical dependence on the drug and is aware that only continued use of the drug will prevent withdrawal illness, a new motive for use of narcotics is introduced. After this, the addict's chief concern is to avoid the acute suffering of withdrawal distress. As he uses drugs to prevent this abstinence illness, the habit becomes more and more firmly established. After several months it may become virtually impossible for the addict to endure voluntarily the severe suffering involved in discontinuing his habit. His body becomes increasingly tolerant to the opiates and every ache and pain is interpreted as a sign of encroaching abstinence illness, so that he gradually uses larger quantities in more frequent doses. There has occurred what is sometimes called the "reversal of effects." The original feeling of well-being can no longer be attained, and when he is using drugs the addict merely feels normal.

Only without drugs does he feel abnormal. They have become an indispensable element in his body equilibrium and their absence produces illness. At this stage, only a rare individual can maintain this powerful habit, costing from five to sixty dollars daily at black market prices, on his legitimate income, and most are forced to resort to theft or other illegal means.

The Nature of Addiction

Each year hundreds of people have an opiate administered therapeutically in regular doses over long periods of time without becoming addicted. Not everyone in whom tolerance and physical dependence are established is an addict, even when the extreme discomfort of withdrawal distress is experienced, although these physiological reactions are conditions necessary to addiction. The person who is addicted must also experience psychological dependence upon the drug. Experiencing withdrawal distress, he must also recognize that further administration of the drug will immediately relieve this condition, and then use the drug to alleviate his abstinence symptoms. The patient who unknowingly is receiving an opiate, who is unaware that the source of his discomfort when the drug is withdrawn is the absence of the opiate, or who has not learned from experience that further administration will relieve his discomfort is not an addict. He must know what he needs and develop a specific and self-conscious desire or "craving" before he can continue using the drug as an opiate addict. It is for this reason that physicians administering opiates take such careful precautions to prevent the patient from knowing what he is receiving, and whenever possible use oral administration rather than the hypodermic needle in order to better disguise the identity of the drug.

The case of the young user also illustrates the necessity of this specific knowledge before addiction can exist. Frequently he experiences nasal discharge, cramps, nausea, and other symptoms of abstinence, but he interprets them as symptoms of a cold or an upset stomach. He is not "hooked" until a more experienced user informs him that he is sick because he needs another shot. Further use of the drug proves this to be true and he then develops the self-conscious desire for continuous use of the drug which distinguishes the addict.

Once this craving is established, it motivates virtually all the subsequent behavior of the addict. It persists long after the original physiological reactions have disappeared, even when no drugs are being used. The addict thus becomes like the alcoholic who dares not taste liquor if he wishes to remain sober. In comparison to the passive recipient of opiates, such as the hospital patient, the addict has an intense and continuous desire for the drug. He knows that he is addicted to opiates and accepts himself as an addict, looking upon the drug as a twenty-four hour necessity and tending to increase the amount of his intake progressively far beyond his actual bodily needs. Even when he is not using drugs, following a "cure," the susceptibility to relapse seems to be permanent and there are recorded cases of relapse following more than ten years of abstinence.

Effects of Addiction

The law enforcement officer should remember that there are no sure signs of addiction. The physical effects are much less noticeable than is commonly believed and vary considerably with the amount and the frequency of intake, the duration of addiction, the method used, and the individual personality. Even the abstinence symptoms are difficult to distinguish by observation from other pathological conditions. No specific pathological tissue changes are produced by opiate use. Sometimes large amounts produce contraction or unresponsiveness of the pupil of the eye, pallor, and drowsiness. Regular use greatly reduces sexual desire, frequently produces an unusual desire for sweets, and occasionally causes digestive and eliminative disturbances. Use of unsterile needles or drugs may cause abscesses at the injection sites, and frequent "mainline" or intravenous shots bring about discoloration of the veins, usually in the left arm of most addicts.

Not only is it very difficult to identify an addict by symptoms, but most of the symptoms that are observed are not direct products of drug use. They are results of malnutrition, poverty, and other indirect effects associated with the social situation of most addicts.

If the addict can afford both an adequate supply of drugs and an adequate diet, while maintaining good personal hygiene, these symptoms are less noticeable. The degenerate "dope fiend" described in much of our popular literature does not represent all addicts. Many addicts have reached positions of prominence and have been successful vocationally. Some die of old age after years of regular use of narcotics. When physical deterioration occurs, it results from the use of all available funds to maintain the expensive illicit drug supply.

The addict is forced to lead a life of deceit, shame, secrecy, and lying, unless he has a very substantial legitimate income. However, these personality traits are not the direct results of drug use in itself. They are indirect results produced by the social situation which frequently is the concomitant of addiction. These traits, frequently termed "character deterioration" and attributed directly to the drug, are really products of the punitive attitude toward the addict in America. He must maintain a continuous effort to avoid detection and the stigma of arrest. Failure in this effort results in loss of social prestige, family conflict, unemployment, and the necessity for resorting to criminal activity in order to support his habit.

THEORIES OF ADDICTION

The Addict Is an Abnormal Personality

The conventional explanation of addiction is that it is caused by human weakness, and only abnormal persons become addicts. Addiction is looked upon as a symptom of personality maladjustment. The basis for this theory is that many types of abnormal personality are found among addicts. Many are classified as emotionally immature neurotics to whom drugs provide a satisfactory solution to problems which they otherwise cannot face squarely. Narcotics help them to feel equal or superior to their situations. Other addicts are classified as psychopaths, extremely disturbed and antisocial individuals who are self-centered and have no respect for law and order or for standards of right and wrong. Frequently this behavior is called a "character disorder."

These types of personality are assumed to be so constituted that they are "addiction-prone." They need only to have some contact with the narcotic to become addicted. On the other hand, it is believed that emotionally normal and mature persons practically never become addicted, except perhaps as an accident in the process of medical treatment. Such individuals are termed "accidental addicts" and are suspected of being abnormal unless they are easily cured. Most of the clinical studies of addicts have found a proportion of normal individuals among them, but the adherents of the "weakness" theory question these diagnoses as products of insufficient knowledge about the addicted individuals. This theory is acceptable to many individuals who find it difficult to understand why any normal individual would use drugs for non-medical purposes or engage in any other type of unconventional behavior. It also is accepted as the best explanation of addiction by many psychiatrists, including some who have had frequent clinical contacts with addict patients. This theory has been advocated by the Federal Bureau of Narcotics in its publications and by the staff members of the United States Public Health Service, the agency in charge of the federal hospitals for addicts.

Addiction Is a Socio-psychological Process

An alternative to the foregoing theory is the theory that anyone can become an addict, whether he is normal or abnormal, if he experiences the sequence of events which is characteristic of all cases of addiction. It is not denied that many addicts are emotionally disturbed, their behavior motivated by inferiority feelings, frustration, and the desire to escape disturbing situations. However, these motivations are found among large numbers of the non-addict population also, and are not specifically characteristic of drug addicts. Furthermore, even those who accept the weak personality pattern as the cause of addiction have admitted that in the groups they have studied, a substantial number of addicts were normal before they were addicted. The evidence of personality defects was not found until after addiction had occurred, and many individuals were diagnosed as normal even after they had become addicted.

The conclusion that addicts are abnormal personalities usually has been based on contacts with addicts who have been arrested and imprisoned, or who have been hospitalized under some degree of compulsion. They are a selected group perhaps unrepresentative of all addicts. Some of the traits observed may have been effects rather than causes of addiction, since there is no evidence that they existed before addiction.

Personality traits such as secrecy, shame, deception, lying, and law violation frequently are characteristic of drug addicts. However, they are not so much mechanisms of escape from inner weakness as they are attempts to escape detection and to maintain a habit which is considered a crime in the United States. The magnitude of our addiction problem should not be attributed to a greater degree of psychological abnormality in the United States. The addict's personality is a response to our punitive attitude toward him and to the criminal status into which we force him when he is discovered. Many undiscovered addicts in the more well-to-do segments of our population regularly pursue normal vocational activities, live satisfactory married lives, and show no signs of psychological disturbances. Personality abnormality did not cause their addiction.

Individuals who are addicted in the course of medical treatment raise another question regarding the abnormality theory. Motivations to use drugs in these cases came from the physicians rather than from the patients. Most of them did not know what they were receiving at the time they became habituated to drugs, and even may have been unconscious. It is questionable scientific procedure to exclude such cases from consideration with the statement that they are accidental addicts. An adequate theory should explain all cases of drug addiction and exclude no accidental cases.

A second theory of addiction attempts to explain the addiction of all types of personalities in terms of the sequence of behavior which leads to addiction in all cases. It explains the narcotic addiction of both normal and abnormal, accidental and non-accidental, impoverished and well-to-do, arrested and unarrested, American and non-American addicts on the basis of a common socio-psychological process. This theory is that addiction results only when a person who has used drugs experiences the abstinence symptoms, understands the meaning of these symptoms, and then uses the narcotic to alleviate and to prevent the recurrence of these symptoms. He then has a conscious and continuous desire for drugs, accepts himself as a drug addict, and organizes his life around these characteristics.

TREATMENT OF ADDICTION

The Desire for Cure

Contrary to prevalent beliefs, most drug addicts demonstrate some desire to escape from their habit. This is especially true when they have reached the stage in addiction when, in spite of the use of progressively larger quantities, they can no longer experience the original effectiveness of the drug. The author never has met a person addicted for a year or more who has not tried to "kick the habit." Most addicts have a history of numerous attempts at voluntary cure, although some others may have "cures" forced upon them by arrest and imprisonment. This desire for cure reflects the addict's realization that he is engaged in behavior disapproved by the larger society, which classifies him as a "dope fiend." It also develops from a realization that he has become involved in behavior which eventually absorbs all his energy and resources, disrupts his personal and social life, and forces him into closer and closer contact with the criminal underworld. The relapse which invariably seems to follow these attempted cures can be attributed to individual weakness only by ignoring the excruciating withdrawal illness which accompanies abstinence from drugs and motivates the resumption of drug use.

Methods of Treatment

The prevailing method of treating addiction is based on the assumption that the first steps should be to place the addict in a drug free environment and completely withdraw the drug. For most addicts in the United States, treatment actually consists in arrest and confinement, taking them off drugs "cold turkey," and release after a sentence is served. Private treatment by a physician is almost completely prohibited under our present law. The federal government, through the United States Public Health Service, operates two hospitals for the treatment of the drug addict. One at

Lexington, Kentucky is exclusively for addicts and has a capacity of about 1400 patients. Another hospital at Fort Worth, Texas has space for a few hundred addicts. Patients are admitted as federal prisoners sentenced for narcotics or other law violations, probationers, and volunteers. With the recent increase in juvenile addiction, a few localities have established hospitals especially for young addicts. In July, 1952, New York City began admitting juvenile addicts to a newly established treatment center, Riverside Hospital. A few addicts also are admitted to state mental institutions or other types of hospitals.

Hospital treatment is usually patterned after the methods developed at the Lexington hospital on the basis of the findings of their Addiction Research Center. Usually methadon, one of the newer synthetic drugs, is first substituted for the drug which the patient has been using. This opiate-like drug is capable of preventing the appearance of the abstinence symptoms. When it is withdrawn, the suffering from withdrawal distress is less pronounced. After the addiction has been transferred to methadon, the amount of the drug administered is rapidly reduced and complete withdrawal is accomplished within about ten days. The patient is then treated for any other organic pathology and is assigned to programs of occupational and recreational therapy, completing the total treatment process in about 135 days. A psychiatric staff provides individual psychotherapy for a few patients and group psychotherapy for others. An outstanding deficiency in this program is the absence of adequate assistance and supervision after discharge from the hospital. The discharged patient usually has to work out his own arrangements for a job, a place to live, and for becoming established in a drug free environment. A few larger cities now have groups called Addicts Anonymous, patterned after Alcoholics Anonymous, which attempt to assist him.

Tendency to Relapse

Even after complete withdrawal of the drug has been achieved and has persisted for several months, the outlook for a permanent cure is not too hopeful. In fact, the term "cure" is rarely used by those engaged in the medical treatment of addiction. The desire for the drug persists even after the apparent physiological basis for this desire has been removed. The incentive to relapse is continuously present. The addict may be tempted to "play around" with a few shots, in the company of his addict friends, just for old times' sake. He may resort to drugs to relieve a hangover after excessive drinking. One addict is even known to have taken a shot to celebrate achieving abstinence after a 13 month struggle, only to become re-addicted as a result. Every addict is well acquainted, from personal experience, with the efficiency of the opiates and has developed a natural tendency to think of them as possible alleviation for any physical discomfort or the vicissitudes of life. A desire to remain abstinent is particularly difficult to maintain if the addict has returned to the same environment in which he became addicted, surrounded with acquaintances who are on drugs, with a source of supply known and readily available. Although relapse sometimes may not occur for several years, the rate for all cases is close to 100 per cent. Most studies of addicts who have been hospitalized have found less than 15 per cent claim to have remained abstinent following treatment. This percentage decreases as the period of time covered by the survey is lengthend. In many cases the only effect of treatment has been to enable the addict to "taper off" and thus temporarily reduce the cost of his habit. He resumes drug use immediately after treatment ends, but requires lesser quantities of drugs to maintain his habit. The punitive attitude toward the addict, forcing him to accept the status of a criminal and providing treatment only under various degrees of compulsion, is not conducive to successful treatment. Abstinence achieved under compulsion usually results in relapse as soon as the compulsion is removed.

CONTROL OF NARCOTIC ADDICTION

The Role of the Illicit Traffic

The spread of addiction in the United States is intimately connected with an illicit traffic in narcotics, brought into existence as a consequence of legislation aimed at suppressing addiction by means of police action. This lucrative underworld racket centers in the large port and border cities, being dependent on drugs smuggled from abroad, but it reaches out to provide addicts every-where with their sole source of supply. It is controlled by criminals of the racketeer or gangster type, operating internationally, and brings them enormous profits. Heroin purchased in such places as Iran, India, or Turkey is smuggled in, adulterated, and sold for over one hundred times its original cost. The principal profiteers are usually well concealed and actually may never handle the drugs directly. The majority of arrests, consequently, are made in the lower echelons of the trade, composed mainly of drug users who are "pushing" drugs in order to support or maintain a supply for their own habit. Such arrests do not seem to suppress the traffic, although they probably cause the price to increase.

The American System of Control

Since the Harrison Act of 1914, technically a revenue measure but later interpreted as a police measure, the system of narcotics control used in America has been essentially the attempted sup-pression of narcotic addiction through prohibitive police action. The police interpretation was strengthened by the Jones-Miller Act of 1922. This Act also established the Narcotics Control Board to determine the amount of opiates legally permitted to enter the country in order to meet legitimate needs. The Marijuana Tax Act of 1937 used the taxing power of the federal government to prohibit importation and internal trade in marijuana. The United States has also cooperated in multi-lateral international agreements, including those sponsored by the League of Nations and the United Nations, aimed at restricting production and international trade in narcotics.

The responsibility for enforcing federal narcotics laws is in the hands of the Federal Bureau of Narcotics, aided in the control of smuggling by the Coast Guard and the Customs Bureau. The federal government now spends $3,000,000 annually for the opera-tion of this agency, and a similar amount to support the hospital program. Each year recently has seen the state and local agencies take increasing responsibility for the enforcement of the narcotics laws, with many large cities having special police squads. Insofar as estimates can be made, this police method of control has been rather unsuccessful in suppressing the narcotics traffic. The principal results have been numerous and repeated arrests of addicts and addict peddlers, while the racketeers who control the traffic remain relatively untouched. When their activities increased following World War II, Congress responded with an increased appropriation to the Federal Narcotics Bureau which enabled them to add 87 additional agents, making their total force 270. As addiction increased there also was a demand for stiffer penalties for narcotics violators, resulting in the passage of the Boggs Act in late 1951. This provided for a fine up to $2000 for narcotics offenders, and mandatory imprisonment of two to five years for a first offense, five to 10 years for a second offense, and 10 to 20 years for subsequent offenses. These measures certainly will increase the price of drugs on the black market and increase the difficulty of supporting a habit by legal means, but a generation of experience with this method of control raises some doubt about its effectiveness in reducing addiction and suppressing the drug traffic.

The European System of Control

The American police-prohibition system of narcotics control, like similar efforts to control alcoholic beverages and gambling, has produced a lucrative underworld racket. In sharp contrast, most European nations consider addiction a medical problem. The addict is permitted to obtain narcotics legitimately but in limited amounts from medical sources, and underworld sources of supply do not exist. In contrast to the estimated 60,000 or more addicts in the United States, a figure which violation reports suggest may be too low, the estimated number of addicts in Europe and other nations using the European system is amazingly low.[3] Great Britain, with one-third the population of the United States, reported 326 known addicts to the United Nations, plus a few non-European opium smokers. Of the 168 prosecutions for drug violations in 1949, 91 involved non-Europeans. In the same year the United States had 3779 federal and 6546 non-federal violations, with a subsequent increase in later years. The most startling devel-

---

[3]United Nations: *Summary of Annual Reports of Governments, 1949,* May, 1951. All quotations in this section are from this publication.

opment in the United States since the war has been the increase in the addiction of young people. Other Western nations, with populations and social institutions not fundamentally different from ours, report neither a juvenile problem nor a postwar boom in addiction. Great Britain reported "the large majority of addicts are over 30 years of age." In France, out of a total of 426 addicts discovered in four years, one was under 20. In Norway, "the registered drug addicts are all adults," and in the Netherlands, "addicts are generally of middle age and in most cases women." New Zealand had a total of 45, with none under 20, 2 under 30, and 6 under 40. In Austria they were "mostly of the higher age groups." All these nations allow the addict to obtain drugs legally from his physician.

Most Americans are astonished that in these countries the addict does not lose social status, human dignity, nor legal rights. He is not referred to as a "dope fiend" or a "young hoodlum," and has neither the reputation nor the record of a criminal. Knowledge of his condition is a confidential matter between the addict and his physician. Persuasion to discontinue or medical treatment may be attempted, but they are not compulsory. Once the patient is registered as an addict, the physician may supply him with sufficient drugs to maintain his habit and enable him to live an otherwise normal life. The incomparably greater success of this system in controlling addiction and preventing the development of an illicit traffic has led to suggestions by many outstanding individuals in the fields of law enforcement, social welfare, medicine, and social science that it be used as the pattern for improvements in the American system of narcotics control.

Possible Modifications

The addiction problem in the United States can be dealt with in two ways. One is to expand and to strengthen the present system by spending more money for law enforcement, passing more laws with stiffer penalties, making hospital treatment compulsory, further restricting private medical treatment of addicts, and generally treating them more like hardened criminals. We have used this method for over a generation and have seen addiction spread to new and younger groups, the police become burdened with an impossible problem, the failure of treatment attempts, the forcing of distressed individuals into crime, and the development of a lucrative underworld racket whose victims are prosecuted but whose leaders cannot be touched.

Another way of dealing with addiction would begin with a reinterpretation of the Harrison and Jones-Miller Acts so that the treatment of narcotic addicts by physicians would be considered legitimate medical practice. Both addicts and physicians would be registered, and the dispensing of narcotics would be transferred from racketeers to doctors. Modern methods of identification would be used to prevent cheating. Once physical examination had established the amount of drugs needed by the patient to prevent abstinence illness, a controlled supply dispensed only by physicians to registered addicts at a nominal cost would eliminate the lucrative illicit profits obtained today by the underworld. To avoid the disorganization caused by a sudden complete change, a transitional plan would be to use a series of clinics supervised by the United States Public Health Service in cities where addicts are now concentrated, later transferring the functions to private physicians.

Such a program would enable us to determine for the first time, through registration, how many addicts there are in the United States and factual data about them could be accumulated. New cases of addiction could be detected rapidly and preventive measures also could be taken. Like addiction to alcohol, drug addiction would be regarded as a private vice rather than as a crime and the addict would be considered a patient under the care of a physician rather than a dope fiend to be arrested by police and imprisoned. The addict would no longer need to resort to deceit, lying, and secrecy, and many addicts now living as criminal victims of the present narcotics racket could be treated and restored to useful lives.

CONCLUSION

The sensationalism and hysteria which frequently characterize any discussion of the drug addict limit the possibility of a rational understanding of the psychology of the drug addict. Drugs have been charged with producing both exotic behavior and stimulating aggressive criminal impulses in weak and abnormal individuals. Some claim that the addiction problem is an illusion, ignoring the thousands of addicts arrested by law enforcement officers each year. Others ridiculously exaggerate the number of addicts, making no distinction between addicting and non-addicting drugs. In the face of the continued persistence of addiction, many people claim that the problem will disappear if only we strengthen our present controls. Meanwhile, addiction increases, the addict has his life disrupted and his reputation destroyed, and is forced to become a criminal. Racketeers continue to reap tremendous profits from selling the essential drugs at black market prices. An attempt has been made to describe drug addiction, in its historical perspective, as an integral but not inevitable aspect of the American social structure. Within this framework, the psychology of the drug addict can be understood. The addict is a patient needing treatment, but we have treated him as a criminal. Addiction has been considered a police problem and enforcement activities have been directed primarily against the victims of an organized criminal racket while the important criminals remain relatively immune. Treating the addict as a criminal does not help the addict but it gives considerable help to the racketeer. We need to eliminate the hysteria from our thinking and look upon the addict as a human being in distress. Only then can we understand the psychology of the drug addict and use the full resources of our society to assist him in leading a useful and productive life.

REFERENCES

LINDESMITH, ALFRED R.: *Opiate Addiction*. Bloomington, Indiana, Principia Press, 1947. A more extended treatment of the psychology and sociology of drug addiction.

MAURER, DAVID W. and VOGEL, VICTOR H.: *Narcotics and Narcotic Addiction*. Springfield, Illinois, Charles C Thomas, Publisher, 1954.

MEYER, ALAN S.: *Social and Psychological Factors in Opiate Addiction*. New York: Bureau of Applied Social Research, Columbia University, 1952. A review of research findings and an annotated bibliography of psychological and sociological studies of addiction published in the United States since 1928.

TERRY, CHARLES E., and PELLENS, MILDRED: *The Opium Problem.* New York: Bureau of Social Hygiene, 1928. An extensive summary of world literature on addiction.

VOGEL, VICTOR H. and VIRGINIA E.: *Facts About Narcotics.* Chicago, Science Research Associates, 1951. A brief, simplified account of the theory that drug addicts are abnormal and the implications of this theory for treatment and control of addiction.

Chapter 14

THE WORK OF COURT AND PRISON PSYCHOLOGISTS*

By

HAROLD LINDNER

THE COURT PSYCHOLOGIST

BEFORE THERE was any knowledge of the psycho-social determinants of crime there was little need for court psychology. The courtroom was commanded by cold legalism with little or no concern for the human variable. If a crime was committed and the offender met the criteria of law (legally-responsible age, intentional act, knew difference between right and wrong, performed the act voluntarily) there was no deterrent to the absolute power of the law.

As psychological research and the social sciences amassed information about human motivation it became evident that beyond the legalistic "guilty mind" lay a veritable fund of data relative to crime and criminals. It was only when this study had been admitted to the courtroom that court psychology, in any real sense, was born.

It is the function of the court psychologist to apprize the court on the social and psychological factors in crime and how these affect the subject of the court—the criminal. Thus, with the acceptance of court psychology, a relatively unheralded revolution in courtroom procedure occurred; the legal formula was made to share prominence with the human variable! No longer was testimony restricted to the legal "facts" of the case. It now is recognized that a proper judicial procedure requires knowledge about

---

*This work was completed while the author was Consulting Clinical Psychologist for the State Industrial Farm for Women at Goochland, Virginia, Virginia Division of Corrections.

the "person." Instead of merely asking the question, "What did he do?"; the court in many cases now wants to know, "Why did he do it?" Obviously, to obtain answers to this latter query, social scientists have to be admitted to the court. The court psychologist —along with the psychiatrist, the social worker, the sociologist, the anthropologist and the educator—has been asked to contribute his services toward this end.

Thus we now find various consultants from the social sciences, social agencies and clinical services attached to most court systems. The jurist, when the situation is relevant, may call upon any or all of these for assistance in determining the character and disposition of the case over which he is presiding.

> E.B. was accused of attempted robbery. The trial judge noted that the defendant had a history of many robberies. Further examination revealed that E.B. gained entry into the home only to steal a woman's shoe; and had never taken anything else from the premises. He was remanded to the local hospital where psychological and psychiatric evaluation revealed that a compulsive character disturbance and a psychosexual deviation were the causative factors in his crime. E.B. was a fetishist and was only able to obtain the gratification of his needs by stealing shoes and obtaining erotic pleasures from fondling them.

The Operation of Court Psychology

Since it is impossible for any *one* discipline to amass all the information, or for any single person to master all the various techniques for studying personality, the team concept of clinical functioning has been found to be advantageous in studying mental illness. The "team" consists, usually, of a psychiatrist, a psychologist and a psychiatric social worker. These students of behavior combine their respective efforts to obtain an over-all understanding of the patient's problems. Each clinician brings his own frame of reference to the problem and the end result is a definitive analysis of the whole problem in which every facet of the situation has been surveyed.

> H.F. and his wife petitioned the court for permission to adopt an 11-month-old male child. H.F. had a history of homosexualism. The court referred the case to its clinical team. Psychiatric exam-

ination revealed that H.F. was not a true homosexual and that the history of such behavior should not now prejudice the court. Psychological testing and examination showed that the petitioner was a homoerotic (inverted Oedipus situation) and that H.F.'s relationship with his wife was a tenuous one. Testing indicated the presence of much internal emotional strife; and that H.F. had strong unconscious destructive feelings toward women. On these grounds the psychologist recommended against adoption. The psychiatric social worker felt that H.F.'s family and marital history did not favor adoption. The members of the clinical team combined their respective opinions into a joint recommendation to the court. They recommended against adoption because of H.F.'s immaturity and his latent hostility toward his wife. They were chiefly concerned that the marriage might disintegrate and thus cause the child more psychological trauma. This factor, rather than the homosexual history, therefore, was the basis for the recommendation to the court.

The Functions of the Court Clinical Psychologist

As illustrated above, it requires a "team" effort to properly integrate case findings into a definitive, objective analysis. The court psychologist—whether he be attached to the court as a full time employee or as a consultant—is an integral member of this clinical team. He functions, as does each other member, as a specialist in his discipline's techniques. He brings the unique contributions of psychology to bear on the legal problem. Thus, it is important to recognize that there is no intrinsic difference between the court psychologist and any other clinical psychologist.

The "court psychologist" practices in the courtroom situation and, beyond his training in clinical psychology, has experience in, and knowledge of, the legal, criminological and penal literature and practice. He has to be aware of the various facets of the court-room situation and of the institutional and agency liaisons the court maintains. To do so he should be in close touch with the problems and personnel of local social agencies, probation and parole departments, jail and prison groups, hospitals and schools. Essential to the proper functioning of this clinician is his active participation in correction and penal programs, and in identification with those social services and psychiatric-psychological groups which serve the court. In essence, then, the court psychologist is a clinical psychologist whose interests and occupation make him a specialist in correctional psychology.

As a clinical psychologist, the court psychologist takes with him into the courtroom one of his unique contributions—the psychological test. There was a period in the history of psychology when a clinical psychologist was a mental tester only. It is not enough to consider him a "tester" today. He is a trained diagnostician and psychotherapist who utilizes his battery of psychological tests to assist him in making a valid and reliable analysis of the problem he is studying. Like any technique, the test is a means to an end and not an end in itself; therefore, the psychologist uses the test—his unique contribution—as a basis for independent clinical practice. The test is his framework, his guide and his guarantee that his analyses are objective, valid and reliable.

Intelligence testing. The basic member of any psychological test battery is the intelligence test. As has been pointed out in the first chapter of this book, intelligence tests indicate mental ability in terms of scores or intelligence quotients.

K.L. was referred to the court psychologist for examination. This 22 year old male was accused of vagrancy. Psychological testing revealed an IQ of 54 on the Wechsler-Bellevue Test, with the performance scale being higher than the verbal scale and interest variability being limited. The diagnosis was of mental deficiency, moronity status. A recommendation was made for commitment to the state institution for defective delinquents rather than to a prison.

The IQ is often the least important result of an intelligence test. As a clinician, the court psychologist is concerned with the character and personality of his subject and with the dynamics and motivants which have led to their formation. Thus he seeks to glean from the traditional intelligence test and from all other data, information relative to behavior which may give him insight into personality dynamics. He accomplishes this by subjecting the various parts of the whole test to clinical inspection—a procedure known as *scatter analysis*. The following case illustrates this.

On the Wechsler-Bellevue, E.C.P. obtained an IQ of 62. Scatter analysis revealed large interest discrepancies. Verbal sub-test totals were higher than the performance test totals. On the information sub-test he did well, but in response to the questions: "What does the heart do?" he replied, "Spits blood"; "Who invented the airplane?" he replied, "I never been in one." He was very poor in arithmetic, and in digits backwards, but good in digits forward. Comprehension was good but inconsistent. To the question: "Why stay away from bad company?" he answered, "Get you in trouble . . . like my mother told me never to go with strange men." The court psychologist reported to the judge that E.C.P. was not a mental defective but rather was suffering from schizophrenia, the simple type; and that rather than be committed to prison for habitual vagrancy, he be sent to the state hospital.

Aptitude and interest testing. The court psychologist is often called upon by the presiding jurist to make vocational recommendations. In those cases he has to make reference to the large inventory of aptitude and interest tests which are also a part of his stock-in-trade. Often such findings make the difference between an offender being sentenced to a penal institution or his being released on probation.

A former marine corporal was convicted of drunkenness. The judge wanted to suspend sentence contingent on the offender's promise to seek educational and vocational training under the GI Bill of Rights. The court psychologist was requested to make a recommendation. A battery of aptitude and interest tests was administered and the subject showed an aptitude for sales work, which, combined with his interest-pattern for dealing with people, indicated that educational training in commercial subjects and a vocational plan of sales work might combine to stimulate the subject toward social adjustment. Because this key had been found, the judge was able to suspend the sentence, and the waste and possible harm of a few months in prison was averted.

Concept formation testing. One of the striking complications to juristic routine is found in those cases where organic mental impairment affects socialization. While the organic problems are primarily of medical concern, clinical psychology has developed a number of fairly reliable tests of mental impairment and concept formation which assist one in making diagnoses.

W.Z.A. was found guilty of armed robbery. During the trial W.Z.A. exhibited confusion, poor judgment and was subject to losses of memory. He was referred to the court psychologist for examination and it was noted that his conceptual quotient was very poor. His ability to comprehend was limited. He could not form abstractions even on some simple test levels. He showed a stereotypy and perseveration of ideas on the tests. Based on his responses to the tests of mental impairment and to the concept formation tests, the psychologist's impression was that W.Z.A. showed evidence of organic impairment and the recommendation to the judge was that he be committed to the state hospital where thorough medical and neurological examinations could be conducted. This was done and sometime afterwards the court received a report from the hospital: W.Z.A. had been suffering from a brain tumor.

Projective testing. Of all the psychologist's techniques the projective tests provide him with what are probably his most useful tools. These tests are designed to allow the testee the greatest latitude in expressing his inner conflicts through his responses to the ambiguously designed and relatively unstructured test material. Because it is difficult for a person to reveal his innermost feelings to either himself or to others, and because the structure of our society makes for inhibition and constriction rather than for a freedom to express our feelings, it had long been known that "objective" personality tests were not too reliable indices of a person's own feelings about himself or others. The projective test was designed to permit a person to express his personal feelings without realizing that he is doing so, by inducing him to give definite interpretations to ambiguous or innocuous stimuli. Thus he reveals his real feelings through symbols and fantasies. For example, he may be given a picture of a flower or some other object and asked to tell the examiner everything he sees in the picture. The interpretations he gives to the picture describe quite thoroughly, to the trained clinician, his thoughts and feelings about himself and about others in his environment. The Rorschach or "ink-blot test" is well known. This series of 10 cards, of chromatic and achromatic symmetrical designs, is shown to the subject, one at a time in proper sequence. The subject tells the examiner what he sees on these cards, whatever comes to his mind, no matter how important or unimportant. The subject takes these indefinite test stimuli and projects his own thoughts and feelings into them and thus his responses are as much a part of him as is his own name. By analyzing these responses, both quantitatively and qualitatively, the psychologist can make personality diagnoses, understand something of the dynamics of motivation and behavior, recommend necessary treatment possibilities, and make adjustment prognoses.

The Thematic Apperception Test is another well known projective technique. This consists of forty pictures representing various life situations. The subject is asked to make up a story about each picture, telling what leads up to the depicted situation and what will happen in the future. Thus, here too, the subject projects his feelings and attitudes into the pictures; and analysis reveals the character of the internal needs of the person and the external presses of the environment on him. This test is especially important in understanding the person's concern about interpersonal relationships, and, as such, is often invaluable in planning for psychotherapy.

There are numerous other projective and expressive tests. Their essential characteristic, as with the Rorschach and TAT, is their relatively unstructured nature and the freedom they offer for varying interpretations to identical stimuli.

M.T.L., 26 years of age, was convicted of burglary. Because of the offender's bizarre behavior the judge requested pre-sentencing examination by the court psychiatric and psychological consultants. Psychiatric examination revealed that M.T.L. was suffering from a manic-depressive psychosis in remission. Psychological examination yielded the following results: IQ 106. Rorschach test showed contamination and confusions of thinking as evidenced by variations in form level of responses; relative lack of color use; evidence of sexual conflicts with incomplete psychosexual development indicated; and a dysphoric reaction to the black aspects of some test cards, indicating a depressive element. Sentence Completion test responses showed extensive use of symbolism, such as "eyes," "steam," "smoke," etc., some of which appeared to have paranoid qualities. General immaturity throughout examination was noted in behavior and in test responses. At beginning of examination M.T.L. asked for a pencil and paper and drew a picture of a shield which he then put in his pocket. This was probably symbolic of his need to protect himself from the clinician's scrutiny. It was also noted that he drew enveloping circles around his Bender-Gestalt drawings and his Draw-A-Person test figures. Psychologist's impression was that the subject was psychotic; that while manic-depressive elements were present the basic personality structure was a schizophrenic one, and that the maniacal behavior was probably a reaction formation. The psychiatric and psychological consultants submitted a joint report to the judge who, on this authority, committed M.T.L. to an indefinite sentence in the state hospital where he was given a combined treatment course of electro-convulsive shock therapy and psychotherapy.

Recommendations based on psychological examinations. As a member of the court's clinical staff, the court psychologist assists the legal authorities in their attempt to secure justice for both the accused and for society. Although false, it is often believed that the clinical staff interferes with justice by making so many referrals to hospitals and institutions. Actually, on reflection, one should remember that those cases that are referred to the psychiatrist or psychologist are those in which, *prior to the referral*, a suspicion about the subject's mental stability has already been aroused. Thus when a person is sent for clinical evaluation, it is likely that he *is* mentally sick—so much so, in fact, that the judges, custodians and social service workers (people with limited or no clinical training) have chosen him as a possible candidate for the clinic or hospital. Without any doubt, a certain percentage of those who do claim to have emotional disturbances are malingering. However, justice is better served if we allow one malingerer to escape the retribution of the law in preference to having a truly sick or defective person destroyed by it. Further, to the extent that one will volitionally malinger, one is actually mentally ill. In reality, the malingerer's illness is so subtle that his "malingering" is a defense against admitting to himself the extent of his illness.

A study of court records will show that, contrary to popular opinion, the clinician does not always recommend dismissal of charge or commitment to a hospital. Often it is only the clinician who can discern the key subtleties which establish the guilt.

Three 14 year old girls accused W.H.E. of having given them

lewd literature and he was arrested for contributing to their delinquency. The accused was adamant in his denial of the charges. He was married (had no children), came from a respectable family, was a home owner and a promising young architect. Because of the differing opinions on either side of the bench the judge referred the accused to the court psychologist for evaluation. Psychological testing and examination revealed that the subject was psychosexually inadequate and that he was psychically impotent. On the Rorschach test he gave many responses indicative of one who gets erotic pleasure from observing sexual activity and from "seeing things." Psychological impression was of scopophilia (sexual pleasure obtained from the use of the eye). The psychologist reported this to the judge and pointed out that, although there was nothing in the examination to *prove* that the subject had committed the offense, that this type offense is almost precisely what one would expect a scopophiliac *might* commit. Further, that, in response to one of the Rorschach details, he had associated: "a cliff on either side with three little creatures pulling something or each other or tugging at something or pulling at something or lifting something . . . both fall on their heads." Symbolically, the psychologist reported, this association might be considered a recapitulation of the crime: "One may hypothesize that the subject might have, here, symbolically referred to his presumed offense in which he is alleged to have given the children something lewd or sensual ("three little creatures pulling at something or each other") in expectation that they would be so aroused as to engage in sexual (masturbatory) behavior ("pulling at each other or tugging at something or lifting something") which he could observe and thus gain erotic satisfactions from, without himself engaging them in overt sexual practices." With this information at hand the judge was able to continue the trial and eventually the defendant admitted his guilt and was, accordingly, sentenced.

Recommendations for treatment procedures. Integral to his function as a diagnostician, the court psychologist must assist the judge by making treatment recommendations where these are indicated. In the case of W.H.E. the psychologist recommended that the patient be referred to a psychiatrist for electro-convulsive shock treatment. This was suggested because W.H.E. had a tremendous amount of underlying guilt. Before any psychotherapy could be initiated, it was believed that W.H.E. should be relieved of his guilt by being "punished" (i.e., shock treatment, from at least one theoretical standpoint, serves in this manner).

Not only must the court psychologist recommend treatment procedures but he oftentimes must carry out palliative psychotherapy and practice counseling and guidance. While offenders are awaiting trial or are in the midst of courtroom procedures, they are often in need of supportive treatment to allay their anxieties. Here both the psychiatrist and the psychologist are active. It is their task to offer clinical assistance to the offender during this interim. Once the officer has been convicted and remanded to the penal authorities, it is they who must assume this responsibility.

In order to carry out this therapeutic function the psychologist must know the possible dispositions of the case. If he plans to offer the offender clinical assistance, he must recognize the limitations imposed upon his program. One common limitation is the dictum of not starting a therapeutic course that cannot be continued when the subject leaves the court's jurisdiction. If the clinician feels that a program of insight psychotherapy is indicated but knows that before he can make sufficient progress the patient will be sent to a penal institution where there is no one to continue this treatment, it should be obvious that he cannot even begin such treatment. However, if the subject will be sent to an institution where treatment is obtainable, then preliminary treatment can, and should, be inaugurated. Obviously, then, the psychologist must be familiar with all the possible dispositions. Moreover, he is often called upon to recommend a disposition. Thus his contacts with psychiatric services, social agencies, hospitals, penal institutions, out-patient treatment facilities and probation resources must be very close.

Research. The final function of the court psychologist, to be but briefly mentioned, is that of research. As a clinician and a student of behavior he is interested in scientific advancement. Because of his location—close association with the inhabitants of the social hinterland—he is in an ideal situation to collect data and to study various types of behaviorisms and attitudes. It is axiomatic that only a relatively small proportion—and not necessarily a representative one—of offenders are actually imprisoned. However, almost all offenders will, at one time or another, reach the courts. Thus the court psychologist is in an enviable research situation; he can obtain data on those whom most other clinicians never see.

THE PRISON PSYCHOLOGIST

Social theory and sociological technique have historical precedence in criminology. Psychological research, practice and methodology have more recently contributed to the scientific wealth in this area. The study of crime and the criminal, by virtue of its dependency on motivation theory and personality study, is peculiarly appropriate to the techniques of psychological analysis.

European penology can boast a long history of prison psychology. The first recorded instance of psychological services being employed in a prison in the United States was in 1913, in a women's reformatory in New York State. Since that time the employment of clinical psychologists in prisons, reformatories, correctional institutions and penitentiaries has been increasing at an unbelievably slow rate.

This relatively slow progress in the extension of psychological services in correctional institutions appears to defy justification. Psychiatry and psychology have become two of the most widely accepted disciplines among the social sciences. The public increasingly looks to these for solutions to its welfare, moral and ethical problems. The demand for psychologists in the nation's schools, institutions and industries is so great that they will not be met for many years to come. Yet, in the correctional domain, there is probably not more than one psychologist for every three thousand inmates.

While the reasons for the failure to utilize psychological services are many, not a small reason is the unattractiveness of some of the conditions of penal work. At a period when the demand for professional services is great, few first-rate psychologists care to serve in a system so rigid and inflexible that the "psychological climate" is opposed to personal and professional growth.

In this section of the chapter we will have an opportunity to study the functions of the prison psychologist. This should provide

a realistic appraisal of the value of institutional psychological services. When those who administer the prison community become
more familiar with the potentials of psychological services, the
reasons which have precluded the growth of prison psychology
will begin to fade-away. However, until objective evaluations—
based on a knowledge of function and potential—can be made,
there is little hope of extending the role of prison psychology.
In view of the contemporary theory of the psychological causation of crime, it must also be expected that without a growth of
psychological services in the prison community, this community—
like Pinocchio's nose—will continue to grow and grow and grow.

Intra-professional Relationships

Crucial to the argument on the expansion of prison psychology
is the relationship the psychologist must maintain with other members of the prison's administration. In too many penal institutions
the psychologist functions in a literal vacuum; he performs his
mental testing duties quite apart from the pulsating, breathing
community. This atmosphere breeds the bacteria of professional
impotence. By virtue of his interest and training, the prison psychologist maintains his most functional relationship with the institution's medical department and, principally, its psychiatrist. These
two, brethren disciplines, share in the operational responsibility of
maintaining and constructing mental health within the institution.

H.R. was a prison "politician," a trouble-maker, and a ring-leader;
hence his activities brought him into constant difficulty with the
prison administration. A youngster of but 23 years of age, he was
serving his fourth commitment and had already spent 14 of his
23 years behind bars. Having recently knifed a fellow prisoner,
the warden had him put in solitary confinement where he developed an hysterical amnesia and was referred to the professional
staff for examination and recommendations. Psychiatric diagnosis:
character disturbance, inadequate personality. Psychological impression concurred with psychiatric conclusions. Rorschach test
indicated the presence of some therapeutic possibilities. Psychologist suggested psychotherapy and inaugurated a course of insight
psychotherapy with H.R. After 15 months of such treatment, H.R. was in sufficient command of his anxieties that his

behavior was perceptibly altered and his attitude toward authority was more realistic and less belligerent. Treatment not completed because patient was discharged at end of sentence. He returned to civilian life, obtained a job as a clothing salesman, and recently married. He is now quite happy with life, working regularly, and has had no trouble with the law for over two years.

Since administrative personnel often refer inmates to the prison psychologist, the avenues of liaison between these two departments must always be open. The psychologist must have a close relationship with the head of the institution because the attitudes and thinking of the top prison administration are reflected in the management of the institution and in the behavior of the custodians and inmates.

A member of a state legislature was interested in penal affairs. One of his recommendations was to have the psychiatrist and psychologist of the state juvenile institution sit on its disciplinary board. The superintendent of the institution carried out this recommendation and appointed the board. The two professional workers concerned appealed to the superintendent to reverse his decision. They pointed out to him that one could not be a "therapist and a policeman" at the same time. Because the superintendent was under pressure to follow the legislator's recommendation he was not receptive to the plea of the two staff members. These clinicians invited the superintendent to visit their clinic. They apprized him of some material from their respective treatment notes in which inmate-patients had verbalized feelings about institutional personnel; and showed how these feelings were being modified by psychotherapy. They also showed him direct data which proved that inmates accepted treatment *only* because they knew that the doctors were not associated with the disciplinary or custodial regime. On this confidential and personal basis the importance of this matter was made clear to the superintendent, who then acceded to their contention and reversed his decision. In this manner a whole rehabilitative-therapeutic program was saved. If it hadn't been for the good rapport that had been established between the superintendent and these two clinicians, the institution, the inmates and society might have suffered irreparable harm from a well-meaning, but psychologically-naive legislator.

The custodial officer because of his position of "low man on the totem pole" is the much maligned member of the institutional staff. Psychologically speaking, however, his is the singularly most important job; he is the one person who can do the most good or the most harm for the inmate. He holds *the one* prison job that has the greatest potential for erasing crime. The guard, the only person to live with the inmate on a very personal, 24-hour-a-day basis, is society's representative to the prisoner. If, as dynamic theory teaches, the criminal is a violator of "father-images," a rebel against authority, it would seem appropriate to give him as his "father-surrogate" during incarceration, as mature and emotionally stable a person as society can provide. Instead, as is well known, the typical guard is one who, because of his own personal dissatisfactions and psycho-social problems, accepts an unrewarding job during the performance of which his behavior reflects these frustrations. Certainly this is not true of all prison custodians. Unfortunately, however, because of the procedures for appointing and rewarding this custodial position, it is far too commonly true. It would not seem too presumptive to predict that until the position of prison guard is raised to one which will attract properly trained, educated and socialized persons with an understanding of their own emotional problems and ability to counsel those who have not established mature interpersonal relationships, there is little hope for the prison to become a rehabilitating environment.

R.D. had been a tier-guard for eight years and was known for his "strong-arm" methods and his ability to over-work a crew. He took pleasure in reporting "skaters" and in catching "kites"; and was one of the most hated and disrespected employees in the prison. One day R.D. asked to see the psychologist and told him that he had recently become insomniac, easily fatigued and had had periods of uncontrollable sobbing. R.D. said that he knew what the inmates thought of him and added: "I hate those lying bastards; just no-good, the whole bunch of 'em." He told the psychologist that he had had a number of terrible nightmares of being chased and then knifed by inmates, and that he recently had dreamed that he was disemboweled by a group of them. During the interview it became quite apparent that in his present condition he could no longer be trusted to perform his prison job. The psychologist immediately conferred with the warden and plans were made to have the guard transferred to the state hospital for observation. While waiting for this transfer, the psychologist attempted to give R.D. supportive-palliative counseling and administered a Rorschach test. The Rorschach showed extensive psychopathology and revealed a psychotic personality structure of a paranoid schizophrenic type. This diagnosis was confirmed by extensive psychological and psychiatric examinations at the state hospital. In this case it was fortunate that the prison psychologist had established the necessarily good relationship with the custodial personnel so that R.D. had sufficient confidence to seek his counsel. If this relationship had not been in effect, it is not improbable that R.D. would have broken-down while on the job and might have done irrevocable harm to himself, prisoners and other employees.

Functions of the Prison Psychologist

The prison psychologist is, or should be, a member of the prison medical department. In the better penal situations his office and his clinic are in the hospital or dispensary. In lesser institutions, the psychology clinic may be associated with the social service personnel, the parole people, or be maintained as an independent office. The preference for a medical liaison is obvious: the psychologist's major function is integrated with the hospital function – locating, observing and treating sick people.

Intake-diagnosis. When a prisoner arrives at an institution he is usually placed in quarantine for a period of ten days to a month. During this period the initial administrative, medical and psychological studies are made. The primary function of the "intake," consisting of a battery of mental tests and psychological interviews, is to obtain a gross impression of the new prisoner. That is, through these early procedures, serious mental illnesses, significant deviations in behavior, attitude or thought processes, or mental deficiency can be spotted and noted for further study.

The most common technique for conducting the intake-examination is to have all those in the quarantine section who have not previously been examined, congregate in a large testing room for a series of group intelligence and mental abilities tests. Following this, during the remainder of their quarantine period, prisoners are individually summoned to the psychology clinic for more intensive evaluation. The latter includes individual intelligence testing, aptitude and interest testing for occupational and vocational use, and a thorough personality testing program (i.e., Rorschach, TAT, DAP, Szondi, Bender-Gestalt, Word Association, Sentence Completion, tests of organicity and concept formation).

Following the testing program the prisoner is interviewed. In this interview, the psychologist makes an independent clinical appraisal of the prisoner's mental capacity, attitude, character and personality structure and adeptness at conforming to and adjusting in the prison community. He also seeks to correlate his clinical judgment with the test results which have by this time been analyzed and charted. The intake-diagnostic is a major responsibility and, in many institutions, the primary justification for the employment of psychological services. This survey is designed to assist the prison administration in deciding whether the prisoner should be assigned to a cell, dormitory or special treatment center; whether he should be continued in prison confinement or referred to an institution for mentally defective delinquents; and whether he should be offered further educational or vocational training or be assigned to "inside" or "outside" work-duty. It also shows whether there is any need for counseling and guidance or psycho therapy.

Since the war, however, the trend has been away from having each institution conduct its own intake-diagnostic services. More recently, the various penal systems have delegated one institution—or a portion of an institution—as its "diagnostic center." Here the prisoner is received from the courts (usually sentenced to the "prison system" rather than to a specific institution within that system) and, based on the various evaluations and impressions made during his sojourn in the diagnostic center, he is transferred to a specific institution to serve his sentence. This trend appears to be a progressive movement and allows those administrators and professional personnel in the penal system to assign a prisoner to that institution where the physical and psychological climates are most suited to his needs. This serves to make for better classification and placement within the penal system. It obviates many difficulties often placed upon an institution by a sentencing justice who, indiscriminately or prejudicially, confines an offender to an institution where he is not fit to remain or one which lacks the physical and social outlets which might be required for his rehabilitation.[1]

Cell assignments. Once the inmate has been assigned to a regular prison life, the prison psychologist has a number of functions to perform beyond his initial intake-diagnostic duties. His recommendations are often valuable when it comes to deciding how to house the inmate. This problem of cell or dormitory assignment has, since time immemorial, been a prison administrator's headache. The bogeyman of "sex" rears its ugly head at this juncture in prison routine and is a source of concern to all law enforcement officers.

Only the naive or blind would deny that sex is rampant within the prison. All the moral and judgmental protestations to the contrary, there is no prison that does not have a "sexual problem." Sex is a biological drive and, although our moralistic friends would perhaps deny this, a quite natural one. What is a natural drive in a mixed male and female situation, will, obviously, in an all-male (or all-female) situation, also be a natural drive—and will also require energy release. Thus the prison has a sex problem. More correctly, it would seem, the prison system by its denial of the "facts of life," by its habit of erecting artificial barriers to the natural release of a basic biological sex urge, by its hypocritical moralistic and pseudo-religious diatribes against sex perpetrates its own problem. If the effort and expenditure that have gone into these protestations and reprisals were directed at sensible means of redirecting this biological energy, it is likely that the problem could be minimized. A social-psychologic approach to the problem of sexual perversion is desirable because sexual aberrations fall in that area of behavior which has been shown to be based on psychopathology. The so-called "strong-arm" methods of segregation

---

[1]Needless to add, this situation does not apply to the sentencing of female offenders. They are sentenced directly to institutions for women.

and punitive reprisal for sexually deviant behavior can only result in the subjugation of sex; they cannot stop sex practice.

S.S. arrived at the prison and was assigned to quarantine. Psychiatric and psychological examinations revealed that S.S. was a youthful, sensitive lad of 21 years of age who showed minor neurotic anxieties, but who gave evidence of no significant psychopathology. He was assigned to a work detail in the prison dining room and apparently adjusted to prison life. Approximately six months after his arrival he was seen on sick call and clinical examination indicated severe anxieties and psychosexual disturbance which were manifested by insomnia, general fatigue and lethargy. Psychological testing confirmed the clinical evidence and pointed to the basic sexual disturbance. Careful study of the case showed that S.S. had been under incessant surveillance by a couple of the known prison "wolves" and that, on a few occasions, physical advances had been made against his person. That none of these had been successfully consummated was due to his luck in escaping these sexual assaults. He now feared, however, that the pressure was so great that he might be unable to continue to protect himself. The psychologist discussed the matter with the deputy warden who promised to look into the situation. A short while afterwards S.S. and a known sexual pervert were discovered while engaged in mutual fellatio. They were locked in the prison's segregation cells. After approximately three weeks in segregation, S.S. attempted suicide and was sent to the prison hospital. Psychological examination indicated that psychotherapy might be of value and a course of interpretive-insight therapy was begun. After eight months of this treatment S.S. was no longer symptomatic (i.e., insomnia, fatigue, lethargy, nightmares, sexual confusions) and was returned to the general prison community where he was able to live out the rest of his "time" without incidence.

This case illustrates the importance of proper cell assignment and the value of approaching sexual deviations from the psychosocial, therapeutic standpoint.

Classification. Classification procedures vary in the different institutional systems. The point of least variability, however, lies in the negative psychological climate which pervades the classification atmosphere. For the most part, the members of these classification boards take their cues from the chairman who often is the deputy warden, his deputy or one with similar status in the institution's administrative hierarchy. A later development has been the so-called "chief of classification"—one who has been sociologically trained and often has some casework experience to his credit. No matter who presides, however, the inmate is likely to be treated as a "prisoner in the docket" made to grovel before the mighty; or, on the other extreme, given a performance of nauseatingly unrealistic kindness which has the avowed purpose of making him feel that the board members are "his friends" and that each board member is "the nicest guy in the world." The former approach has been humorously entitled the "strong-arm" or "fix-the-bastard" technique; while the later the "Rotary Club" technique. No matter what variation of these extremes may be utilized, the essential point is that neither one, nor any variation of either one, is realistic or honest. Both are pretentious. Therefore, both are doomed to failure. The only way to effect a sincere classificatory approach is to deal with the inmate on an impartial and realistic basis. This means that the members of the board should have but one primary objective: to attempt to survey the individual's case from all possible angles before making any decision and to treat the inmate on an objective but sympathetic basis. Unfortunately, as the unwritten history of classification proves, "objectivity" and "sympathy" are closeted in an anteroom—while the board goes merrily along its way either perpetrating a punitive atmosphere or indulging in the needless luxury of inept milk-and-honey kindness.

There is no *one* proper classification technique. Neither the psychologist nor the psychiatrist—nor anyone else—knows the panacea for insuring proper classificatory procedures. The teachings of the social sciences do offer certain principles, adoption of which might improve classification. The primary qualification for each member of a classification board should be that *he likes people*. He should also have a fundamental conviction of the basic dignity and value of an individual. Combine these two qualities with personal integrity and an inquisitive curiosity into those factors which influence human behavior and a good classification program is assured. Without these human qualities, all the technical skill and training which one may have cannot solve the dilemma. With these qualities one may acquire some skill in communicating with others and, by identifying with the humanity in the inmate, proper classification is guaranteed.

Work, training and educational assignments. The prison psychologist is also concerned with the inmate's education and vocational training. He assists the education department through the mental testing program by ferreting out those with defective intelligence and those who are illiterate. He also assists the prison school teachers with their textbook, library and curriculum problems. His relationship with the education department is a reciprocal one. Often, when treating a patient, he requires the assistance of a teacher or librarian. Growth through psychotherapy may require further educational achievement so that the patient can utilize those newly-recognized resources which had, prior to treatment, been dormant. Bibliotherapy (i.e., treatment obtained through selective readings) is often best dispensed by the librarian and the psychotherapist, cooperating in the proper selection of reading matter.

Psychotherapy, counseling, and guidance. The prison psychologist operates the psychology clinic. As a clinician, his duties range from those which are purely diagnostic to those which are therapeutic. He practices (with the psychiatrist) whatever psychotherapy and counseling is conducted in the institution. A definitive treatment program requires that the patient live in as normal an environment as possible. The prison community, because it limits all freedom of expression and is rigid, authoritarian and disciplinary, is probably one of the least desirable environments for psychological treatment. These factors are sufficient to defeat most therapeutic attempts. Beyond these are those intangibles which hamper treatment procedures. The prison psychologists and psychiatrists are responsible for the mental health of the entire inmate population. Because of the overwhelming patient load, the clinician is fortunate if he can offer treatment to a few inmates each year. Thus, in the average prison, the population of which may total twelve to sixteen hundred, perhaps six inmates can obtain psychotherapy each year.

Withal, however, psychotherapy is a primary function of the prison psychologist. Rarely is he able to attempt depth therapy of the analytic or interpretative types. Parenthetically, few prison psychologists are trained in the one type of treatment procedure (i.e., psychoanalytic) which appears to be the most capable of dealing with the crime problem. Until such time as the prison community will attract clinicians who are analytically trained, there is little expectation that prison treatment will significantly alleviate criminal behavior.

In view of this, we find that the prison clinician attempts to obtain palliative and supportive therapeutic goals. He tries, except in those rare research or experimental problems which might attract his attention, to help the patient achieve a more realistic insight into his social and emotional problems. He may do this by utilizing one of the suggestive therapeutic techniques (e.g., hypnotherapy); one of the persuasive treatment techniques (e.g., directive counseling and guidance); or one of the less directive and more dynamic treatment techniques (e.g., analytically oriented psychotherapy or non-directive counseling).

H.H. was referred to the psychology clinic because of symptoms of depression and feelings of worthlessness. Rorschach testing indicated a basic neurosis with psychosexual disturbances. H.H. told the psychologist that he was convicted of rape and that he was proud of his ability to "get any girl I want". Treatment was indicated and H.H. agreed to cooperate. Treatment of choice was analytically-oriented interpretive therapy. H.H. revealed that he was the middle son of three boys and said that his mother didn't like him but that she had always favored his oldest brother and had always preferred his younger brother to himself. He told how his mother had rejected him. During his army years he married a camp-follower and, upon learning of her pregnancy through intercourse with another man, divorced her. When he returned home after the war he became an idler and spendthrift—earning his money through gambling and petty burglary. He remarried, found his second wife sexually frigid and soon realized that, although she was "a beauty," he didn't love her. He began to carouse about with other women and boasted of his sexual exploits to his mother and his wife. A legal separation followed and, two days later, he was arrested for raping a 16-year-old neighborhood child. Through continued treatment the dynamics of the case became obvious: H.H. felt rejected by his mother and, because of her preferences for his brothers and father, he felt inadequate and unloved. His psychosexual disturbances were based on the unresolved Oedipal situation; his inadequacy and inferiority feelings involved the sibling rivalry situation; and his aggressive sexual behavior was his manner of "proving his masculinity" and obtaining the love of a mother-image ("I like to make women crawl"). In treatment H.H. learned to understand his behavior and recognize the unrealistic basis of his feelings of inadequacy and inferiority. With the helpful guidance of his therapist he was able to experiment in proper interpersonal relationships without overwhelming anxiety. His depression, which was of a reactive variety, soon disappeared and he was able to adjust to life situations. Following his release from prison he became an airplane mechanic and is still successfully performing these duties. He recognizes that he is not "cured" and that further psychotherapy is required. As soon as it is financially possible for him to do so he plans to seek definitive treatment.

Research. Perhaps the most rewarding function of prison psychology is that of research. The prison is a researcher's heaven because it provides him with a sample that is readily available for experimental manipulation and which contains almost the whole range of behavioral and attitudinal variations. Only through research—into the criminal, the crime and the prison—will an understanding of crime and criminal causation be achieved. The psychologist, by virtue of his training and interest, is a specialist in research methodology and experimental design. Whatever progress has been made in the study of those psychological and social factors which are causative to crime and criminal behavior, has come through painstaking research.

REFERENCES

CORSINI, R. J.: Non-directive Vocational Counseling of Prison Inmates. *Journal of Clinical Psychology*, 3:96-100, 1947. A discussion of the value of non-directive vocational counseling in prisons.

GIARDINI, G. I.: The Place of Psychology in Penal and Correctional Institutions. *Federal Probation*, 8:29-33, 1944. An interesting analysis of the potentials for psychological services in penal and correctional institutions.

JACKSON, J. D.: The Work of the Psychologist in a Penal Institution. *Psychological Exchange*, 3:53-55, 1934. A description of the practical uses of psychological services within penal institutions.

LINDNER, R. M.: *Rebel Without a Cause*. New York. Grune and Stratton, 1944. A dynamic description of a case of criminal psychopathy with a theoretical analysis of the pathology of psychopathic states.

LINDNER, R. M.: *Stone Walls and Men*. New York, Odyssey Press, 1946. A textbook in criminology in which crime is dynamically defined and the criminal is examined from the psychological point of view with recommendations for the care and cure of criminality.

Chapter 15

PSYCHOLOGY APPLIED TO PAROLE

By

Wilson L. Newman[1]

INTRODUCTION

A MAN STARTS his journey to prison long before the gate clangs shut behind him. The trip may start in his infancy even though no one notices that beginning. The attitudes of his parents and of the neighborhood may give him a push along the road. As he grows older, his friends may add their push. And there may be pushes from other sources. There are pushes inside the prison, too, and pushes after he leaves.

What are the results of these pushes? Millions of people go through life without conflict with the law. Why do *some* people break it many times? What is to be done about them? How should they be treated in prison? How long should they stay in confinement? What should be the basis for release? Should they serve their sentences and go out without supervision? Or should they be paroled and serve part of their sentences under supervision outside the walls? If they are paroled, what kind of supervision is desirable?

The purpose here is not to attempt an exhaustive treatise on the problems of parole but to raise still another question: How can parole boards and parole agents make use of psychologists to help with inmates and parolees? Many of the questions not treated here are discussed in the references at the end of the chapter.

Though the masculine gender is used in all the examples, much

[1]Appreciation is expressed to Harvey L. Long, to Ben S. Meeker, Hugh P. Reed, and Eugene S. Zemans for their assistance. However, the opinions of this chapter are not necessarily theirs. In no instance has a confidence been violated.

of what is said would of course apply to women. In any case, adult offenders are in mind. The psychological factors affecting juveniles require another chapter.

The persons mentioned (parolees, parole board members, parole agents, and psychologists) are not necessarily typical. Identification cannot be made of any individuals, events, institutions, localities, and states.

To provide a basis for discussion, only some of the highlights of the stories of Tom, Jim, Joe, and Bob are sketched.

The word "psychologist" refers to a person who carries on psychological work—work that may be diagnostic or therapeutic. In the sketches the term "psychologist" does not imply that only one person is performing all the activities mentioned.

TOM ADJUSTS SUCCESSFULLY

Before Tom, an inmate in the prison, sat down before the parole board, the members of the board read some details of his history.

Tom grew up in an average sort of family and graduated from high school. He married at 20. After his two children were born, his wife urged him to get more money. He took extra jobs in the evening; but she thought more money was needed. He finally resorted to robbery to surprise her with a fur coat. When he went to prison, his wife divorced him; and he has never seen her or his children since then.

He was in and out of prison over a period of 16 years and then finally received a discharge. He lived with an older brother, got a job, settled down, and seemed to be going straight. He was picked up occasionally on suspicion but each time was dismissed.

When he was 44, he was identified in a robbery and sent to prison. Although he was vehement in asserting his innocence, he could not prove his alibi. Shortly after he arrived in prison, his brother—his only relative—died. Tom had already been turned down twice by the parole board.

In the minds of the parole board ran such questions as these: What does this man have to go to? Will he be back as a parole violator? Has he such well-entrenched habits of dependency that he cannot make decisions for himself? Are there any agencies that can help this man? What is this man's attitude toward authority? Has he served long enough to pay his debt to society? What will the newspapers say? Are there people who want this man to stay in prison? What are the factors in his favor? Was he guilty of this crime in the first place?

The parole board requested that a psychologist from the prison be present at the meeting. As Tom entered the room, he was apparently agitated as he glanced at the various faces. He managed a smile when he saw the psychologist, whose face was the only one he recognized.

When a board member asked what Tom intended to do if he were paroled, Tom became nervous and blurted out that he did not know. The psychologist reminded Tom of a recent conversation in which he had expressed some definite ideas concerning work. Tom smiled again and falteringly pointed out that he had learned tailoring while in prison and that he hoped to get a job with a manufacturer of men's clothing. He had known of other parolees who had obtained jobs there. Other questions followed; and Tom was more assured in his replies.

After Tom left the room, the psychologist mentioned that Tom has been worried over such questions as: Am I too old to keep a job for long? Since I know no one, what shall I do for recreation? Should I seek out companions who are easily met in taverns? Will people avoid me because of my record? What am I to do if I am sick? Should I tell a prospective employer about my record? How can I get along with the police? Will they pick me up whenever they have the least suspicion of me?

A board member asked whether Tom was intelligent enough to get along. The psychologist replied that tests indicated ability that ranked with the average adult. Whether Tom would always use his native endowment to the best advantage might be another question.

Another board member wanted to know whether Tom's nervousness would keep him from adjusting. The psychologist pointed out that tests and extensive interviewing had revealed no deep conflicts. There was a tendency to pity himself. Otherwise, he appeared to accept the fact that he would be alone on the outside and that he would have to rely on his own efforts and decisions. After some additional discussion the board voted to grant Tom a parole.

Before Tom left the prison, he attended several conferences of prospective parolees and met his future parole agent. Tom learned the parole rules and discussed some points with his agent. The prison psychologist discussed with the men some of the problems they might face beyond the walls.

Tom left the prison, got a job as a sewing machine operator for a manufacturer of men's clothing, and settled at a nearby YMCA. The parole agent made several visits and seemed pleased that Tom was doing so well. On one visit Tom remarked that he wanted permission to leave the clothing manufacturer. When the parole agent pressed him for reasons, he related that the workers at adjoining sewing machines had found out about his prison record and were continually making taunting jibes. Tom found himself more and more irritated. The parole agent suggested that Tom make an appointment with the psychologist attached to the parole office.

The parole psychologist saw Tom several times; and Tom came to realize that he had been rather sensitive. He also realized that he should go out of his way to be pleasant and helpful. Later Tom reported to the psychologist that his fellow workers rarely referred, if at all, to his past. In due course the parole agent stated that Tom had completed his parole satisfactorily.

JIM THE CABINETMAKER

The parole board asked the psychologist for data about Jim before his hearing began.

Jim was reared in a small town along with one brother and one sister. His parents were respected members of the community, owned their home, and attended church regularly. His father ran a small furniture repair shop. All three children in the family finished high school.

While Jim was in school, he worked some afternoons and on Saturdays in Mr. Smith's grocery. After he graduated, Mr. Smith offered him a full-time job.

When Jim was twenty-two, he married his high school sweet-heart. They had two children. When he was twenty-seven, he was offered a job in a small factory in the town. Jim did not want to leave Mr. Smith; but the factory job did pay more. A year later the factory closed.

Jim could not find work immediately; but he did not worry because he had some savings. Then his wife had an emergency operation. Soon his savings were almost gone. He did not want to ask his family or any one else for help. He began to feel uneasy.

Now and then it was Jim's custom to go to a tavern. There seemed to be nothing much else to do. One Saturday night a stranger became friendly and bought several rounds of drinks. Jim protested that he should not drink so much; but the stranger urged him on. Sunday afternoon Jim awoke with a headache. He looked around to find that he was in a jail cell. He called out. The sheriff came in response and explained that Jim had been caught in Mr. Smith's grocery. In Jim's hand had been a cigar box in which Mr. Smith had put the Saturday receipts to wait for Monday bank-ing. Mr. Smith had put the box in its usual hiding place. The money was gone; but Jim could not explain its disappearance.

When Jim came to prison, he worried about his wife and children. She wrote him that her money was not sufficient to keep them going.

After Jim settled himself on a chair in the board room, the chairman asked him what problems he would face when he left prison. Jim slowly spoke and mentioned such questions as these: When he goes home, what will be the attitude of his children? Though they are small, will they respect him? Will their play-mates call him an ex-con? How will his friends receive him? Can he keep away from liquor? Does his wife still care for him? Can he hold a job?

When the question was raised regarding the work that he would do, he nodded toward the psychologist. Since Jim seemed to be having difficulty in speaking, the psychologist explained that, when Jim entered, he appeared to be at a loss as to the kind of work he might do when he was released. There was no basis to recommend a program of training. However, test results indicated that Jim had interest in furniture-making and aptitude for that occupation. He himself had not been aware of any interest or ability although his father followed that line of work. Jim had learned a great deal in the prison furniture shop. Jim interrupted: "Dad wants me to work in his shop." After other discussion, Jim was excused from the room.

A board member raised a question about Jim's relationship to his wife. The psychologist stated that testing and interviewing had revealed a strong affection on his part. A letter from his wife to the parole board was read, saying that she wanted Jim back. The board voted to parole Jim; and he met his parole agent during the pre-release conference at the prison.

Jim had a long bus ride to his old home town and hence had a lot of time to think. He wondered whether the passenger beside him recognized his suit as prison-made. Now and then along the highway there were taverns that he was tempted to enter and have a short one. He remembered what he hated most about prison— the nights. Sometimes the cell seemed so small; and he felt that he was smothering. As Jim lived again these torments, he wondered whether anyone on the bus noticed the shudder that ran through his body. As the bus neared the home town and he gazed at familiar scenes, he felt happy. Presently his mood changed because he was curious as to how he would be received.

Jim went from the bus to a telephone. The parole agent had given him his number in the town ten miles away where he lived. Jim requested the agent to come over and go with him to his home. Although the agent protested that a man ought to be able to go home by himself, he finally agreed to come. As Jim waited in the combination store and bus station, he thought two or three people glanced too frequently in his direction. He was not sure that he had seen them before, but he was curious about their thoughts. Jim shook the agent's hand long and hard and murmured thanks for coming. They started walking down the street and soon Jim was walking across the small porch of a small house. The agent saw a woman throw her arms around Jim and two small children try to climb his legs. Jim's parents made a visit that evening; and the father reminded Jim that he was to come to the furniture shop the next morning.

Three days later the parole agent came to the shop while Jim's father was gone out to deliver a chair. Jim indicated to the parole agent that he thought he would like furniture repairing. The agent asked about things at home. Jim said that the house appeared to be so small—the bedroom especially seemed tiny. As a result he had felt a smothering sensation even though he knew that there was plenty of fresh air. One night his wife awoke to find him pacing the floor and opening the screens on the windows, and she could not understand.

The parole agent agreed to make an appointment with the parole psychologist for Jim. Jim was glad to go because he felt that he needed help. In fact, he went five times, took tests, and talked freely. As a result he came to see that there were some carry-overs from his prison experience and that he should explain them to his wife, for whom his affection was genuine.

As time went on, Jim remarked to the agent how surprised he was that so many people had dropped in the shop to say "hello." Even Mr. Smith, the grocer, had wished him well.

JOE MAKES GOOD

Before the parole board saw Joe, they learned something about him from the prison psychologist.

Joe was born in a slum area of a city. He had three brothers and five sisters. His father never earned enough to give the family more than the necessities . . . sometimes not all of those. Joe learned before he was nine that, if he got some things, he would have to get them by himself.

Joe was indifferent to school although he was passed along to the sixth grade. No one seemed to care except when the truant officer came around.

When Joe was ten, he wanted a bicycle more than anything else. He and two other boys saw their chance in the park and stole three bikes. Though they had no psychological examination, they were declared feebleminded and sent to an institution. Joe got out when he was thirteen. At fourteen Joe was apprehended for stealing a car. He spent two years in a state school for boys, where he was considered too dumb for more education although no psychological examination was given.

Joe tried many jobs, but he never found one that he liked. He was fired by four employers. At eighteen his principal interest was in girls and joy riding. He never possessed a car, but he told the girls that he was the owner of the cars he drove. He was just nineteen when he was admitted to the prison.

The psychologist found that Joe had a third grade level of school achievement but an ability to learn that compared with the average American adult. Joe resisted the idea of school because his memories of it were painful; however, after a month in the prison school, he found it different from the school he had known as a child. When Joe was in the sixth grade, he went before the parole board for consideration; but the board had decided that he should remain in prison to complete the eighth grade and to learn a trade.

Joe told the psychologist, when he completed the eighth grade, that he was happy to read magazines and newspapers for himself . . . and not depend on someone else. Joe was in a quandary as to which trade he should take up. The tests which the prison psychologist gave revealed high interest and aptitude for automobile mechanics. After two years in the course, Joe was believed to be one of the best students; in fact, the instructor thought that Joe was probably good enough to take a job.

As Joe approached a possible parole, the psychologist thought that his concern might be summed up in such questions as the following: How can he get along at home? What will his old crowd expect of him? How can he meet people who are law-abiding?

After the psychologist spoke, the parole board members expressed their concern about Joe in the form of questions: Why was he ever considered feebleminded? How likely is he to fall in with his old crowd? Can he settle down?

As Joe came in the board room, one of the members remarked that he looked better than he had before . . . he had a more businesslike air. A member inquired as to whether working with cars made him want to steal more cars. Joe admitted that, when he first started working in the auto repair shop, that thought had crossed his mind.

He had become somewhat alarmed because he knew that stealing cars or anything else would put him back in prison . . . and he did not want to have another sentence. Yet there were occasions when he imagined himself speeding along at the wheel of a beautiful late-model car—the envy of all the neighborhood. He was concerned that the tendency to steal was still present.

The board voted that Joe should appear again in a month or two after he had a chance to have interviews with the psychologist. When he appeared again, Joe related that he had seen the prison psychologist a number of times. "There were some tests and stuff; and the psychologist talked about what they meant." Joe had done considerable thinking about himself. Often he had lain awake for an hour or so after the lights went out in his cell. He had come to the conclusion that he had always wanted to be a big shot and to have things that his friends did not have. The fellows talked about cars a lot and which ones they wanted. Furthermore, the girls he knew seemed to prefer fellows with fine cars. Nobody could afford such cars, so the only thing to do was steal them. Joe was of the opinion that his passion for cars could be satisfied by working on them. There was some more talking back and forth; and then Joe was dismissed from the room. The board voted to parole Joe.

Joe was introduced to his parole agent at the pre-release conference, and shortly afterward Joe left the prison. Joe and the agent decided that the best bet was to live with his folks, at first. There were only one brother and two sisters at home now; and so there was room for Joe. Moreover, the agent found a job at a nearby garage.

After Joe had been away from prison for three weeks, he told the agent of his difficulties in getting along. Some of the old joy riding crowd had come around. Joe wanted to move; and, if he moved to another part of the city, he might have to change his employer. The agent reminded Joe of the parole rule that changes in living arrangements and in jobs have to be approved. It was up to Joe, rather than the agent, to make the new arrangements.

Whenever Joe had the chance, he investigated jobs in garages in the outlying sections of the city. When garage owners asked where he got his training in auto repairing, he would be flustered —he always hesitated to say that he had learned his trade in prison. At that point some owners would make a pretext to terminate the interview. Joe was strongly tempted not to tell the truth the next time but to invent a good work history. Finally an owner said: "If you are a good auto mechanic, I don't care where you learned." Though Joe had been with his first employer only a short time, he was able to get a good reference for the second one. Joe liked his new job, and his employer gave him a raise after he had been there a month.

Joe found a room in a private home near the garage. The owners of the home were a couple whose children had married and left home, and they had decided to rent two rooms. The occupant of the other room was a young engineer. There was a struggle in Joe's mind about telling his new acquaintances of his parole status. He was afraid that the parole agent would give the secret away on his first visit. However, when the agent came to the front door, he told the landlady that he wished to see Joe about some insurance. In Joe's room the agent and Joe discussed the matter of secrecy. Joe wondered how the others in the household would receive the announcement that he was a parolee. Anyway, he later felt that he had done right to tell them.

One evening the young engineer told Joe about a party which the young people in the church were having and invited Joe to go with him. Joe was surprised and pleased at the invitation; and he finally managed to say that he would go. After the party Joe lay awake in his room. He had felt rather embarrassed, but the engineer and some others had urged him to join in the games and fun. He did have a good time; there was no doubt about it. Yet here he was without a hangover, and he would be able to work tomorrow. The parties that he remembered were affairs that knocked one out for a couple of days. The young people at the parties he remembered were different from those at the church. The difference was particularly noticeable in the girls. Joe was not sure that he liked the church girls, but there was that girl in the blue dress that matched her eyes. Yeah! That was Mary Something-or-Other.

There were other church parties. For one feature Joe drew

Mary as a partner. While they were talking, he managed to ask her for a date; and she accepted. Joe was in hot water. He took his perplexity to the engineer and the parole agent. His question was: What do you do on a date with a *good* girl?

There were more parties and dates—and more dates than parties. Joe told the agent that he was beginning to like Mary. He had even thought about marriage. The agent reminded him of the rule that a parolee must obtain permission to marry. Had Joe considered the matter carefully? Perhaps a talk with the parole psychologist would be helpful.

Joe and the psychologist found that they had to take several sessions for their talks. Joe even reported on some books which the psychologist suggested that he read. Then he asked to bring Mary to their last meeting.

Joe's employer told the parole agent that Joe had been a good worker for two years. One evening the agent handed Joe a piece of paper, which was his discharge from parole. The agent shook his hand and said: "I suppose I won't be seeing you again." Joe smiled, exclaimed: "I'm not so sure," and handed the agent a piece of paper. The agent glanced at it and saw that it was an invitation to a wedding.

BOB FAILED

Before Bob entered the room where the parole board was meeting. the psychologist was asked to give a summary of Bob's history.

Bob's parents were divorced when he was an infant; and he has never had any contact with his father since then. His mother struggled to make a living for both of them for she wanted Bob to have things that other children had. For instance, there was the period when she did not buy lunches in the company cafeteria in order to save the money to buy Bob a bicycle.

Many times Bob was left alone in the two-room apartment. He liked school sometimes; but there were other times when he preferred to spend the day at a movie. When the truant officer came around, the mother would cry.

When Bob was nine years old, he was picked up by the police for pilfering from a store. When he was eleven, he was caught in a burglary with some older boys; all were sent to the state reform school. Before Bob was 20, he was arrested on several occasions for speeding and for drunken driving. He was treated for a venereal disease and he had experimented with narcotics. There were two jail sentences.

Bob was 21 when he entered the prison. He had repeatedly said: "I just want to do my time and get out." Now he was 23.

The psychologist was asked to present the results of any psychological examinations made on Bob. Tests revealed that Bob had underneath his smooth exterior a mass of conflicts. He loved his mother but he resented her authority. He was volatilely emotional and capable of viciousness. He liked to picture himself as a hero.

The psychologist also reported that Bob had been concerned with such questions as these: How would he look in the clothes given him when he leaves prison? Will he be spotted as an ex-con? Will his pals in prison look him up? What should be his attitude toward them? Will his fiancee be waiting for him? How can he have a social good time while he is on parole? How can he live from the time he leaves the prison till he gets his first pay check?

The recital of Bob's history brought forth some questions from the parole board: Has this man learned anything useful in prison? Will he drift back to his old crowd of friends? Does he still want to make easy money? Can his mother give him an adequate home? Will he be responsive to supervision?

As Bob entered the room, the parole board members noticed that he was tall, well-built, neat, and good-looking. He seated himself with poise and looked straight at each person in the room. He had a nod and a smile for each one; and some members smiled back.

When Bob was asked about his plans for the future, he said that he wanted more than anything else to help his mother. He realized, he said, that she had worked hard and that he owed her much. He thought that she could obtain a job for him in the factory where she worked. He would make his home in her apartment. He just wanted to work and make good.

One member asked what was the possibility that Bob would get into trouble again. Bob smiled and stated his determination to keep out of trouble, that he would never "do time" again.

There were a few more questions; and then Bob was told that he might leave the room. He glanced at each member of the board, smiled, arose slowly, turned, walked erectly to the door, and slowly closed the door behind him. There was silence in the board room.

Finally one member said: "I was expecting a brash youth—just as the psychologist depicted. But now I see a quiet, sincere man—he ought to have a chance on parole." The board members listened attentively while a letter from Bob's mother was read, in which she told how she needed her boy. The psychologist started to speak; but the chairman of the board stated that there was no more time.

Bob met his parole agent at the pre-release conference in the prison. The agent told him that he thought plans would work out for a job at the factory where Bob's mother worked, but Bob did not appear to be particularly pleased.

The agent made a visit to the little apartment the next evening after Bob arrived home. Bob was not there; but his mother assured the agent that he would be home soon. She insisted that he sit down and wait. She chatted on—mostly about Bob. Bob was a good boy and would do well when people recognized his talents. She glanced at the clock. She then suggested making coffee. As she sipped, she glanced again at the clock. The agent realized that it was time for Bob to be home, according to the parole rules. Finally, as the agent was starting to leave, Bob opened the door. He seemed startled to see the agent there and explained that he had been trying to find his fiancee.

The agent dropped in the next Sunday. Bob remarked that his mother had begged him to accompany her to church but that she had gone on alone. Bob explained that his mother meant well but that she would not let him live his own life. She had nagged because he did not arise early enough. "Heck, what was the sense of getting to work 10 minutes ahead of time?" She did not approve of his fiancee and pleaded with him not to try to find her. Bob honestly could not understand why the girl had disappeared so completely.

A few weeks later Bob's parole agent told the parole psychologist of his concern about Bob, who had stayed out late at least several times, had given some indication of too much drinking, and had missed two days at work. The psychologist agreed to see Bob.

When Bob arrived at the parole office one evening, the psychologist was waiting. Bob was apologetic for being late. He assured the psychologist that he had no problems. Yes, he had stayed out a few times later than the parole rules allowed and without permission from his agent; but, after all, a fellow had to have some fun. "When you are out with a dame, you can't stop and phone a parole agent for permission. You never know how it will be. You stroll in a tavern and sit down. A 'broad' squats on the stool beside you. Naturally you start talking and buy her a drink. After a while she suggests you go somewhere with her. So what? So you don't feel like getting up at 5:30 the next morning; and you miss a day at work. So what! They don't pay you for days you miss; why should they care? Oh, it's all the fault of that skirt I thought was my fiancee. She writes to me in prison and pretends she's waiting— pure as the driven snow. But how she drifted!" Bob laughed at his own joke.

The parole psychologist reported to the parole agent that Bob did not seemingly respond to any attempts to encourage his insight. Perhaps another effort should be made.

A week later the agent told the psychologist of a telephone call from the personnel department of the factory where Bob worked. Bob's efficiency had grown worse; furthermore, he did not work every day.

The agent and the psychologist resolved on a conference with Bob and his mother. As they entered the apartment, they noticed that Bob was apparently about to leave. When all were seated, the agent remarked that it was probably time to have an understanding about some things. Bob stood up and shouted that no one would tell him what to do. Then he darted out the door. His mother was in tears. Two days later the agent telephoned Bob's mother and learned that he had not been home and had not been at work. She was worried.

A few hours afterward the police called the parole agent to say that Bob was under arrest. At a busy street corner he had run up to a woman and stabbed her once. A nearby policeman kept him from stabbing her again. Bob muttered something about his fiancee. So Bob went back to prison.

DISCUSSION

The sketches of Tom, Jim, Joe, and Bob illustrate, to some degree, how psychologists and psychological findings can be useful to members of parole boards and to parole agents who supervise parolees. To be sure, not all parole boards and not all parole systems are using psychologists in the ways indicated in these cases. And these ways are not necessarily the best ways or the only ways; but let us consider some of them under the categories of areas of information, counseling, and interpretation of behavior:

Areas of Information

From a diagnostic standpoint, a psychologist can be helpful in providing objective information in such areas as the following:

Intelligence. Often an evaluation of general ability is desirable. An example may be taken from the story of Tom when a board member asked about Tom's capacity. In Joe's case, information about his intelligence proved that he was not feebleminded.

School achievement. Joe was found to be at a third grade level; however, he had gone to the sixth grade in school. This fact points out that schools differ widely in their standards of thoroughness and in their policies regarding failures. Some men who go to prison can barely write their names, but they have eighth-grade diplomas. There are also men who have had only three years of formal schooling but who can score at a seventh grade level on a school achievement test because they have learned much from their experiences.

Vocational interest. Both Jim and Joe did not know what they really wanted to do. The vocational interest test was useful in helping them make wise vocational choices. There are many men in prison who have drifted about from job to job and have never found anything that challenged their full attention. Some men have turned to crime because they could not stand the boredom of their jobs. On the other hand, interesting jobs usually prove to be rehabilitative—in prison or outside.

Aptitude. Both Jim and Joe were benefitted by getting jobs that they could do. Interest in work must be supplemented by ability to do it—or the ability to learn to do it.

Evaluation of personality. There is often a need for objective information about a man's attitudes, feelings, emotions, motives, affections, hates, prejudices, conflicts, etc. Too often information about these important matters is gained from trivial impressions, and so it is not surprising that gross errors can occur. In the case of Bob the psychologist found deep, underlying hostilities which Bob could ordinarily cover up in prison but which sprang into action on the outside. In Tom's case the psychologist was able to give objective data that were reassuring in spite of Tom's nervous manner. Joe was told some things about himself that helped him to understand himself better. An alert psychologist had anticipated questions concerning Jim's marriage.

Counseling

Often there is little point in trying to make a distinction between diagnosis and therapy. Usually both are involved in whatever contacts a psychologist has with inmates and parolees. In the case of Tom, the prison psychologist helped him to think realistically of his situation while the parole psychologist helped him clarify and improve his relationships to his fellow workers. The prison psychologist helped Jim to make a vocational choice and to settle some doubts in his mind about his wife. The parole psychologist aided Jim also in quieting his fears. It was a psychologist who helped Joe to choose a vocation and to realize what it was that motivated his stealing. Moreover, Joe was influenced by the parole psychologist to think soberly about marriage. Bob did not seek the services of a psychologist in prison; neither did he want any help from the parole psychologist. He needed counseling, but he was not inspired to seek it.

Interpretation of Behavior

A psychologist can be helpful to a parole board by interpreting the behavior of inmates as they appear before the board. For instance, a psychologist helped Tom express himself; after Tom left the room, the psychologist was able to point out that his agitated manner was probably superficial. The psychologist also aided Jim to speak out. Joe's anxieties were explained by the psychologist. The good impression that Bob made on the board needed some interpretation, but the psychologist was not permitted to give it.

A psychologist can be helpful to a parole agent by interpreting the behavior of parolees. Jim's fears after he arrived home were explained to the agent so that he understood why Jim was upset. Some insight into Bob's character was also given the agent by the psychologist.

SOME SUGGESTIONS

Perhaps the most practical summary of this chapter can be in the form of suggestions which parole boards and parole agents might ponder in order to utilize psychologists for effective outcomes in dealing with inmates and parolees.

Considerations for Parole Boards

If a parole board saw an inmate shortly after he entered prison, the board could evaluate his needs and formulate goals for achievement. Then psychologists and other prison personnel could carry out a program designed to achieve the desired results. When the board saw the man again, it could note whatever progress had been made. Such a plan might provide a greater incentive than is now the case for the inmate to work for his own rehabilitation.

A psychologist can render a service to the members of a parole board because of their concern with the problem of prediction. They want to know which inmates that they see will be successful in completing parole and how their characteristics differ from parolees who fail. They want to know the attitudes of the men appearing before them. If the psychologist has made use of the various diagnostic devices at his command, he can say with some assurance what the inmate's assets and liabilities are and whether they predict success on parole. For example, Joe showed that he had gained some education and a trade while in prison. He had also gained some knowledge of himself and had discovered a goal in life. His motivation was to make good. These characteristics predicted parole success. On the other hand, Bob's characteristics predicted parole failure. He had not used his time to improve himself or to work out his essential problems; he was content with himself and thought that he could do as he pleased. His worries were about trivial matters.

If the possibility of parole is an incentive for inmates to work toward their own rehabilitation, it may be desirable that laws and practices be changed so that *all* inmates leave prison as parolees. Such a procedure would, of course, place a greater responsibility on both parole boards and psychologists to do a thorough job.

If parole boards and psychologists are to obtain more beneficial results from their efforts, it may also be necessary that parole boards see each inmate at least once a year.

Considerations for Parole Agents

Psychologists can be helpful to parole agents in interpreting past reports on parolees and in ascertaining additional objective information when the need arises. Psychologists can also aid parole agents by offering counseling to parolees. The solution of psychological problems will lead to more intelligent cooperation with agents as well as to greater stability.

REFERENCES

DRESSLER, DAVID: *Parole Chief*. New York, Viking Press, 1951. The story of the author's experiences as chief of the parole service in New York.

DRESSLER, DAVID: *Probation and Parole Practice*. New York, Columbia University Press, 1951. A more technical work than *Parole Chief*.

GIARDINI, G. I.: *Manual of Parole Procedures and Supervision*. Harrisburg, Pa., Commonwealth of Pennsylvania, 1951. Presents many suggestions for the handling of indivdual parolees in various situations.

HILLER, FRANCIS H. and REED, HUGH P.: *The Probation and Parole Service of the Wisconsin Department of Public Welfare*. New York, National Probation and Parole Association, 1948. A survey of conditions in a state parole system, with recommendatons for improvement.

LONG, HARVEY L.: Pre-release Preparation of Parolees. *Focus*, September, 1952, pages 1-4. (Published by National Probation and Parole Association.) An account of pre-release conferences in Illinois.

OHLIN, LLOYD E.: *Selection for Parole*. New York, Russell Sage Foundation, 1951. A description of the application of actuarial methods to the selection of parolees for the guidance of parole boards.

SCUDDER, KENYON J.: *Prisoners Are People*. Garden City, New York, Doubleday and Company, 1952. Here is a description of a prison without walls and without guns at Chino, California.

APPENDIX

List of Psychological Tests and Publishers

INTELLIGENCE TESTS

Army General Classification Test. Science Research Associates.

Henmon-Nelson Tests of Mental Ability. Houghton Mifflin Co., or Psychological Corporation.

New California Short-Form Test of Mental Maturity, Advanced Form. California Test Bureau.

Ohio State University Psychological Examination, Form 21. Science Research Associates.

Otis Employment Tests. World Book Co., or Psychological Corporation.

Otis General Intelligence Examination. World Book Co., or Psychological Corporation.

Otis Quick-Scoring Mental Ability Tests, Gamma Test. World Book Co., or Psychological Corporation.

Otis Self-Administering Tests of Mental Ability. World Book Co., or Psychological Corporation.

Personnel Test. By Wonderlic. Psychological Corporation.

Revision of Army Alpha Examination, Forms A and B. Psychological Corporation.

Revised Army Alpha Examination, Forms 5 and 7. Psychological Corporation.

Revised Alpha Examination, Form 6, Short Form. Psychological Corporation.

PERSONALITY TESTS

Cornell Index. Psychological Corporation.

Social Intelligence Test. Center for Psychological Service, or Psychological Corporation.

The Adjustment Inventory, Adult Form, by Bell. Stanford University Press, or Psychological Corporation.

The Personality Inventory, by Bernreuter. Stanford University Press, or Psychological Corporation.

Thurstone Temperament Schedule. Science Research Associates.

390

ARITHMETIC TESTS

Moore Test of Arithmetic Reasoning. Psychological Corporation.

Otis Arithmetic Reasoning Test. World Book Co., or Psychological Corporation.

Rogers Achievement Test in Mathematics. Psychological Corporation.

Schorling-Clark-Potter Hundred Problem Arithmetic Test. World Book Co., or Psychological Corporation.

Stanford Achievement Arithmetic Test, Advanced Form. World Book Co.

PRACTICAL JUDGMENT

Test of Practical Judgment, Form AH, by Cardall. Science Research Associates.

VOCABULARY AND READING TESTS

Columbia Vocabulary Test. Psychological Corporation.

Cooperative Vocabulary Test. Educational Testing Service.

Iowa Silent Reading Test, Advanced Form. World Book Co., or Psychological Corporation.

Minnesota Speed of Reading Test for College Students. Psychological Corporation.

Minnesota Reading Examination for College Students. Psychological Corporation.

Nelson-Denny Reading Test. Psychological Corporation.

O'Rourke Survey Test for Vocabulary. Psychological Corporation.

Wide Range Vocabulary Test. Psychological Corporation.

PERCEPTION OF RELATIONS

Minnesota Clerical Test. Psychological Corporation.

Revised Minnesota Paper Form Board. Psychological Corporation.

ADAPTABILITY

Policeman Examination General Adaptability Test. International Association of Chiefs of Police.

INTEREST TEST

Strong Vocational Interest Blank for Men. Stanford University Press, or Psychological Corporation.

ADDRESSES OF PUBLISHERS

California Test Bureau. 5916 Hollywood Blvd., Los Angeles 28, California.

Center for Psychological Service. George Washington University, Washington, D. C.

Educational Testing Service. Cooperative Test Division, 20 Nassau Street, Princeton, N. J.

Houghton Mifflin Co. 2500 Prairie Ave., Chicago 16, Illinois.

International Association of Chiefs of Police. 1424 K Street, N. W., Washington 5, D. C.

The Psychological Corporation. 522 Fifth Avenue, New York 36, New York.

Stanford University Press. Stanford, California.

Science Research Associates. 57 West Grand Avenue, Chicago 10, Illinois.

World Book Company. Yonkers-on-Hudson 5, New York.

AUTHOR INDEX

393

SUBJECT INDEX

A

Accidents and age, 183-184
Acquisitiveness, 142-143
Adaptability, test for, 65
Addiction,
  alcohol. *See* alcohol addiction
  drug. *See* drug addiction
Addicts, drug, 319-347
  abnormal personality of, 336-337
  age of, 328-329
  and the law, 320-321
  desire for cure, 339
  legal status of, 320-321
  number of, in U. S., 321-322
  place of residence of, 329
  psychology of, 319-347
  race of, 327-328
  sex of, 326-327
  social characteristics of, 326-330
  tendency to relapse of, 340-341
  treatment of, 339-340
Adjustment, 37-40, 135-137, 265-268
  adequacy of, 135-137
  and conflict, 37-39
  and frustration, 37-39, 265-268
  types of, 39-40
Adult criminal, psychology of, 272-294
Alcohol addiction, 306-318
  causes of, 306-308
  hereditary factors in, 307
  personality factors in, 308
  pharmacological treatment of, 317-318
  physiological factors in, 306-307
  physiological treatment of, 316-317
  psychological treatment of, 314-316
  social factors in, 307-308
  tolerance for, 307
  treatment of, 314-318
Alcohol,
  effects of use on, 301-303
    attention, 303

learning and memory, 302
mental association, 302
motor functions, 301-302
sensory thresholds, 302
thinking and reasoning, 303
  moderate use of, 297-299
    effects of, 297-299
    reasons for, 297
Alcohol problem, 295-296
Alcoholic personality, 295-318
  clinical studies of, 309-310
  psychoanalytic studies of, 312-314
  psychology of, 295-318
  psychometric studies of, 310-312
Alien leaders, 155-156
Amnesia, 242-243
Anger and aggression, 139-140
Appeals, 147
Aptitude, 386
  testing, 352
Aptitudes, tests for, 63-65
Arithmetic, tests for reasoning
  and skill, 64
Army Alpha intelligence test, 31
Army Beta intelligence test, 31
Army General Classification Test
  (AGCT), 33-34
Ascendance-submission, 145
Assemblages, 158-171
  major, 161-171
  minor, 158-161
Attention, 63-64, 206, 303
  effects of alcohol on, 303
  of jurors, 206
  tests for, 63-64
Audience, 158-161
  emotionally exhorted, 159-160
  passive, 159
  pedestrian, 158
  turbulent, 161
Auditory sensations, 218-219

397